Beacons
of The Light

One hundred people who have shaped
the spiritual history of humankind

Dear Eric,

Thank you for your friendship
and encouragement
With our love
Mary and Moven

8 June 2009

First published by O Books, 2009
O Books is an imprint of John Hunt Publishing Ltd., The Bothy, Deershot Lodge, Park Lane, Ropley,
Hants, SO24 0BE, UK
office1@o-books.net
www.o-books.net

Distribution in:	South Africa
	Alternative Books
UK and Europe	altbook@peterhyde.co.za
Orca Book Services	Tel: 021 555 4027 Fax: 021 447 1430
orders@orcabookservices.co.uk	
Tel: 01202 665432 Fax: 01202 666219	Text copyright Marcus Braybrooke 2008
Int. code (44)	
	Design: Stuart Davies
USA and Canada	
NBN	ISBN: 978 1 84694 185 6
custserv@nbnbooks.com	
Tel: 1 800 462 6420 Fax: 1 800 338 4550	All rights reserved. Except for brief quotations
	in critical articles or reviews, no part of this
Australia and New Zealand	book may be reproduced in any manner without
Brumby Books	prior written permission from the publishers.
sales@brumbybooks.com.au	
Tel: 61 3 9761 5535 Fax: 61 3 9761 7095	The rights of Marcus Braybrooke as author have
	been asserted in accordance with the
Far East (offices in Singapore, Thailand,	Copyright, Designs and Patents Act 1988.
Hong Kong, Taiwan)	
Pansing Distribution Pte Ltd	
kemal@pansing.com	A CIP catalogue record for this book is available
Tel: 65 6319 9939 Fax: 65 6462 5761	from the British Library.

Printed by Digital Book Print

Beacons of The Light

One hundred people who have shaped
the spiritual history of humankind

Marcus Braybrooke

BOOKS

Winchester, UK
Washington, USA

CONTENTS

Introduction	3
Adam and Eve	6
Abraham	11
Zoroaster	18
Vyasa	26
Akhenaten	32
Krishna	37
Rama and Sita	43
Moses	46
David	51
Isaiah	57
Jeremiah	65
Lao-tzu	71
Confucius	76
Mahavira	83
Buddha	88
Plato	93
Aristotle	100
Asoka	105
Mary	109
Jesus	115
Peter	125
John	130
Paul	135
Johannan ben Zakkai and Rabban Gamaliel II	143
Origen	149
Constantine and Helen	156
Augustine of Hippo	162
John Climacus and Gregory of Sinai	169
Benedict	177
Brigid	183
Nagarjuna	189
Muhammad	194
A'isha	201

Sankara	208
Rabia	214
Manikkavacacar	220
Saicho and Kukai	224
Ramanuja	228
Al-Ghazali	233
Abelard	239
Maimonides	247
Avicenna and Averroes	255
Hildegard of Bingen	262
Honen, Shinran and Nichiren	268
Eisai and Dogen	276
Ibn 'Arabi	282
Francis of Assisi and Clare	286
Aquinas	292
Mother Julian of Norwich	299
Tsong Khapa Losang Drakpa	306
Kabir	310
Eckhart	316
Jalal-ad-Din ar-Rumi	321
Sergius of Radonezh	327
Guru Nanak	332
Martin Luther	338
Thomas Cranmer	345
Ignatius Loyola	350
Mirabai and Tulsidas	356
John Calvin	364
Servetus	370
Teresa of Avila and John of the Cross	378
Akbar	387
Guru Arjan Dev and Guru Gobind Singh	392
George Fox	401
Ba'al Shem Tov and Elijah ben Solomon	408
Mendelssohn	414
John and Charles Wesley	421
Seraphim of Sarov	427
William Wilberforce	432

William Blake 440
Sri Ramakrishna and Vivekananda 449
Sayyid Iqbal Khan and Muhammed Iqbal 454
Nakayama Miki 460
Baha' Allah 465
Te Whiti-O-Rongomai 472
Rudolf Steiner 478
Freud and Jung 484
Tagore 489
Black Elk 497
Gandhi 503
Albert Schweitzer 510
Aurobindo 518
Teilhard de Chardin 524
Francis Younghusband 531
Pope John XXIII 537
Bede Griffiths 544
Khalil Gibran 552
Martin Buber 559
Mother Teresa 565
Yukitaka Yamamoto 571
Elie Wiesel 579
Martin Luther King 585
Haile Selassie I 593
Thich Nhat Hahn 601
Patrick Dodson 609
The Dalai Lama 619
Desmond Tutu 626
Seyyed Hossein Nasr 635
Rosemary Ruether 642

Which Beacon Shines Most Brightly? 651
Bibliography 662
Index 664

To my family with love and gratitude

Mary,
Rachel and Peter
Jeremy and Amanda,
Kathryn, Helen,
Sarah, Anna,
Elizabeth, Christina

One may read for years and for years
And spend every month of the year in reading only;
And thus read all one's life,
Right up to one's last breath.
Of all things, a contemplative life
Is what really matters;
All else is the fret and fever of egoistic minds
Guru Granth Sahib

Anyone who loves God must love his brothers and sisters also
James 4, 21

Preface

I would like once again to thank my publisher John Hunt for his patience and encouragement and his suggestion for this book and express my thanks to all at O books for their help.

I am deeply grateful also to Mary for her continued love and support - even to the extent of allowing me on holiday to spend more time with my laptop finishing this book rather than with her!

I am conscious how much my life has been enriched by the wisdom and friendship of people of many faiths across the world and especially by my many colleagues in the interfaith movement. I treasure too all the kindness I have received from congregations where I have ministered. Having worked on this book I believe even more strongly in the debt we all owe to the 'communion of saints,' who still inspire us by how they lived and what they taught.

I am also grateful to many librarians in Oxford who have helped me find the books on which I have relied for my research.

Marcus Braybrooke

16 November 2008 (my seventieth birthday)
Clifton Hampden, Oxfordshire.

Introduction

We are today heirs to the spiritual wisdom of every age and every religion. Yet so often our knowledge is still parochial. I recognised this was true in my case when, some years ago, I watched a Son et Lumière at the Red Fort in Delhi. I had a degree in history, but I knew nothing of the Great Moghul Emperors of India. In the same way, although we live in a world, at least for some people, of global communications and travel, we know too little about the cultures and religions of each other. Yet if we are to live together in our global village we need to become aware of this rich and varied cultural and spiritual inheritance. I hope this book will contribute to this by helping a wider public learn about some of the people of different religious traditions and from many countries and centuries who have shaped the spiritual life of humankind.

The last century and especially the last two decades have seen a very significant, although often unrecognised, development in the religious life of humankind. This is thanks to the devoted work of scholars and translators. Not only the scriptures of most religions but also the writings of innumerable holy people are now available in English and other modern languages and often easily accessible on the World Wide Web. I realise, with little talent for learning languages, that fifty years ago I could not have studied the world religions in the way that is now possible.

I was asked by my publisher to list the one hundred people who have had the greatest influence on the spiritual life of the world. Many of those I have chosen were very holy people, but the key word is influence not holiness. I do not presume to anticipate the work of the recording angel. As the Bible says there are those who have left a name behind them so that there praises are still sung, while others were the glory of their day but are no longer remembered and other good people have left no memory.[1]

How do you determine influence? Maybe it is by founding a religion or a significant movement within a religion. Maybe it is by the influence of writing, whether by devotional works, theological studies or poetry. Others have been influential by their practical work for peace and in care for the suffering and by setting an example for others to copy.

Most people are influenced by those who have gone before them. The book, therefore, is arranged historically. If you want to know the order in which I have listed the people whom I have included in this book, you will have to wait till the end. I hope you are not one of those people who cheat when reading a detective story and begin by looking at the last pages! I also hope that you will want to make your own list, as an exercise that encourages you to reflect more deeply on the significance of the people whom I have included.

The book is intended to be read as a whole and not just used as a reference book or dictionary to look up particular people – although of course it can be used in this way. What I have found fascinating is the interaction between spiritual movements through the ages. Interfaith dialogue in the way we think of it today may only date from the end of the nineteenth century, but different religions over the centuries, have in many places interacted sometimes by disputation, sometimes by borrowing and learning from each other. I have found it helpful to picture the spiritual history of humankind as a great river with various springs, sources and tributaries, always changing, sometimes dividing, maybe with backwaters, but moving forwards and enriching the present with what is carried forward from the past and opening up new vistas for the future. Diana Eck, a renowned scholar of religions, I have discovered since writing this, uses the same image. 'Religious traditions are far more like rivers than stones' in that 'they flow and change, sometimes drying up in arid land, sometimes dramatically changing course in new territories. All of us contribute to the rivers of our traditions. We do not know how we will change the river or be changed as we experience its currents.'[2]

The book centres on people, but it becomes a history of the world's religions, because as Ralph Waldo Emerson (1803-1882), an American mystical thinker, said 'There is properly no history, only biography.' Biographies hold our attention because we are interested in people, but if we are to learn history through them, the life of the person has to be set in context and illuminate major themes of his or her times – as I have tried to do.

Religion of course includes doctrines, rituals and much more. Yet essentially, I believe it is a meeting with the Divine. The people about whom I have written speak of the wonders of this meeting and how it transformed their lives. They are an example to us. To adapt what St Augustine said of his *City of God*, I have, therefore, not written for the sake of writing, but that 'readers may be moved to enter into the City of God without delay... and continue in righteousness. For, if those by whom these books are read do not actually take action, of what good are books?'[3] My hope is that as we all become more aware of the varied spiritual heritage which we now share we shall discover the spiritual resources to enable us to live together in peace, to relieve the suffering of the hungry and marginalized and to treasure the planet that has been entrusted to us.

CHAPTER NOTES

1. See Ecclesiasticus 44, 1-14.
2. Peter Brown, *Augustine of Hippo: a Biography* London, Faber 2000 (Revised edition), p. 472.
3. Diana Eck, *Encountering God: A Spiritual Journey from Bozeman to Banares*, Boston, Beacon Press, 1993, p. 2

1

Adam and Eve

Humanity's awareness of the Divine, growing over four millennia, may, I have suggested, be pictured as a mighty, ever changing life-giving River with many sources, diverse tributaries and even some backwaters. It is appropriate, therefore, that the story begins in Paradise, which was bounded by four great rivers perhaps to be identified with the Indus, the Upper Nile, the Tigris and the Euphrates.[1] It is there according to the Bible that the first human beings, Adam and Eve, had their home – and even if they are only mythological, it seems good to start with them, as this book deals with named people rather than the many anonymous people who have helped to shape human history. Certainly it is in the fertile valleys of these rivers that we have the earliest evidence of the human response to the Divine. This is not surprising, as 'one must remember that in the Orient water is absolutely the basis of all civilized life.'[2]

It was in the idyllic garden of Paradise that Adam and Eve 'heard the voice of the Lord God.'[3] Hearing it, Adam was afraid and ashamed. This over the centuries has been the reaction of those who have had an authentic encounter with the Holy One.

Such a life-changing encounter with a Spiritual Reality, which cannot adequately be described, determined the pattern of their life for most of those included in this book. Various terms have been used of this ineffable 'presence that disturbs'[4]: God (by many names), the Absolute, the Truth, the Real. Yet human language always falls short. 'Eyes cannot see him, nor words reveal him.'[5] 'The thing that is called Tao is eluding and vague.'[6] 'That which is Selfless, hard it is to see; not easy is it to perceive the Truth.'[7] 'By what name, shall we call You, You who are Beyond all name?'[8] 'God comprehended is no God.'[9]

The Romantic poet William Wordsworth (1770-1850) expressed this sense of the numinous in these well known words:

> 'A presence that disturbs me with the joy
> Of elevated thoughts; a sense sublime
> of something far more deeply interfused,

Whose dwelling is the light of setting suns,
And the round ocean and the living air,
And the blue sky, and in the mind of man'[10]

Who first experienced the Holy? We do not know. The first stirrings of the Spirit are lost in pre-history and myth. It is right that this book should begin by paying tribute to those animists or aboriginals who first acknowledged the Divine Mystery. Archaeological evidence suggests that from the dawn of human history people have been aware of another dimension to life. Many theories on the subject have been much debated and there are those who regard this awareness as an illusion.

An attempt to analyse this experience was made in a famous book called *Das Heilige*, 'The Idea of the Holy,' by Rudolf Otto (1869-1937), a German philosophical theologian. He spoke of what he called the 'numinous,' as an experience of a *'mysterium tremendum fascinans et augustum'* (a fearful, fascinating, awe-inspiring mystery). Otto wrote,

'The feeling of it may at times come sweeping like a gentle tide, pervading the mind with a tranquil mood of the deepest worship. It may pass over into a more set and lasting attitude of the soul, continuing, as it were, thrillingly vibrant and resonant, until at last it dies away and the soul resumes its 'profane', non-religious mood of everyday experience. It may burst in sudden convulsion, or lead to the strangest excitements, to intoxicating fury, to transport, and to ecstasy.'[11]

By the Latin word 'tremendum', Otto means a sense of awe and fear arising from how small we feel amid the vastness of the universe. There is a feeling too of being over-powered, but also of excitement and attraction or fascination. With this comes a sense of forgiveness, peace, joy and exaltation. The experience has been described as 'like the effect of some great orchestra, when all the separate notes have melted into one swelling harmony, that leaves the listener conscious of nothing save that his soul is being wafted upwards and almost bursting with its own emotion.'[12] Such moments are more common than is usually recognised. [13]

In the Bible, the first human beings, Adam and Eve, are portrayed as having had such an experience. So it seems right to begin this book with them, although many other religions and civilizations have different myths about the origins of human life and of spiritual experience.

The Bible begins with God's creation of the world, which culminates with God saying, 'Let us make human beings in our image, in our likeness.' So, says the narrator,

> 'God created human beings
> In God's own image.
> In the image of God
> God created them;
> Male and female
> God created them.'[14]

Image does not imply physical likeness – 'no one has ever seen God'[15]. It speaks of a human being's unique intellectual capacity, moral responsibility and potential for a relationship with the Divine. Moreover, humans are called to share in God's work of creation. God told them to be fruitful and to 'rule over the fish of the sea and the birds of the air and over every living creature that moves on the ground.'[16] This was not a licence to exploit the Natural and Animal world but to act as stewards, reflecting God's care for the creation.

Although human beings are, according to the Book of Genesis, created in God's image, they are all different. There is a Rabbinic saying that 'A king of flesh and blood stamps his image on a coin, hence all coins look and are alike; but the King of Kings puts the stamp of the first man on humanity, yet no man is like any other.' This means, in the words of the Jewish spiritual teacher, Baal Shem Tov, that 'Every man should know that since creation no other man ever was like him. Had there been such another, there would be no need for him to be. Each is called on to perfect his unique qualities. And it is his failure to heed this call which delays the Messiah.'[17]

Yet although each person is different no one can say 'My parents were greater than yours', because all people are descended, according to the Bible, from the same forebears. Indeed when in the second century CE, there was a debate about which principle in Jewish teaching was the most important, the famous Rabbi Akiba (c.50-135 CE) said,

'Love your neighbour as yourself', but another Rabbi said that a more important verse was Genesis chapter 5, verse 1: 'This is the record of Adam's line – When God created human beings, God made them in the likeness of God; male and female God created them.'[18] Thus in the opening chapters the Bible insists on the oneness of all humanity and the sacredness of every human life. The Qur'an also teaches that because all things are derived from God, all people should constitute a single community (*umma*), obedient to God.

Yet, the Bible recognised the inherent ambiguity of all human experience, even if it only tells the story of the first human beings. According to the story, God told Adam and Eve that there was one tree in the Garden of Eden of which they were not to eat the fruit. Yet, persuaded by the serpent (identified with the devil), Eve ate some of its fruit and gave some to her husband. In punishment God expelled them from Paradise and inflicted the pain of childbirth on women and hard toil on men. At the same time, Adam and Eve became sexually aware and conscious of their mortality.

Christianity has, traditionally, held that the disobedience of Adam and Eve has had consequences for all people, making necessary a Saviour to restore the relationship. 'As in Adam all die,' wrote St Paul, 'So in Christ will all be made alive.'[19] Judaism, which recognises that there is a tendency both to evil and to good in each person, holds that godly deeds are the way to salvation. The Qur'an says that although Adam violated the Lord's will and went astray, the Lord subsequently showed him favour, relented and guided him, saying '… Guidance on my part will avail you and whoever follows My guidance will not go astray nor come to grief.'[20] The Qur'an also speaks of Adam as a prophet.[21] In Jewish tradition God made a covenant with the first human beings.[22]

There are numerous other myths of the origin of human life. The Hindu Vedas speak of the Lord as 'the giver of life' and on occasion speak of the spiritual identity of *atman*, the human soul, with *Brahman* the Divine.

These various myths reflect different ways of seeing humankind's relationship to the Divine. This variety is mirrored in the teaching of the spiritual luminaries that we shall ponder, but in the kaleidoscope of religious belief and practice, there is an age-old and worldwide yearning for communion or oneness with the Real. The awe-inspiring fascination of the Holy is evident in every generation and is still real today.

CHAPTER NOTES

1. The Biblical Book of Genesis, 2 10-14, calls the rivers Pishon, Gihon, Tigris, and the Euphrates. The suggested identification is that of Gerhard von Rad in his commentary on Genesis, SCM Press, 1956, p. 77.
2. Gerhard von Rad, p. 78.
3. Genesis 3,8.
4. William Wordsworth, 'Lines composed a few miles above Tintern Abbey', 1798.
5. From the Hindu Mundaka Upanishad 3.1.8 in *World Scriptures*, p. 47.
6. From the Tao *Tao Te Ching*, 21, in *World Scriptures*, p. 47.
7. From the Buddhist *Udana*, 80 in *World Scriptures*, p. 48.
8. From the Early Church Father Gregory of Nazianzen (329-89). The translation is by Mary Rogers in *World Faiths*, No 99, Summer 1976.
9. Gerhard Tersteegen (1697-1769), a German Protestant mystic, quoted by Rudolf Otto in *The Idea of the Holy*, translated by John W Harvey, Oxford, Oxford University Press, 1923.
10. William Wordsworth, 'Lines Composed Above Tintern Abbey,' 1798.
11. *The Idea of the Holy*, p. 13.
12. Otto in *The Idea of the Holy*, p. 37, quoting from an anonymous account in William James, *Varieties of Religious Experience*, p.6.
13. See, for example, Timothy Beardsworth, *A Sense of Presence*, Oxford, Religious Experience Research Unit, 1977.
14. Genesis, 1,27.
15. John 1,18.
16. Genesis 1,28.
17. The Rabbinic material is taken from *The Torah: A Modern Commentary*, Ed. W.G.Plaut, p. 24.
18. Plaut, p. 55.
19. I Corinthians, 15,22.
20. Surah 20,123.
21. Surah 3.33-4.
22. Ecclesiasticus, 17.

2

Abraham

Abraham was perhaps the first monotheist. The Bible says that he was to be a blessing to all people[1] and calls him 'the friend of God.'[2] He is a symbol of hope that Jews, Christians and Muslims, all of whom revere him, can at last put behind them long centuries of misunderstanding and bitterness and recognise each other as 'children of Abraham.' His influence on these three religions has been and still is enormous.

With Abraham, the Bible moves from myth to history. Abraham, who may have lived in the first part of the Second Millennium BCE, is the first historical person mentioned in the Bible, although there are those who hold Abraham is a fictitious or mythical character.

Our growing knowledge of the Ancient Near East, including the excavation of the city of Ur, provides an authentic backdrop to the drama. Ur is situated on the great river Euphrates, not far from the Persian Gulf. This was the city, in southern Mesopotamia, in which the sons of Noah had settled after the Flood. Ur was a centre of civilization, dominated by a great towered building, known as a ziggurat, which was probably a place of worship used by the semi-divine Sumerian rulers. This tower may have inspired the Biblical story of the Tower of Babel, which its builders - at a time when there was only one language - hoped would reach up to heaven. The Lord frustrated this, however, by confusing their language so they no longer understood each other. Palaces, a royal cemetery and more ordinary dwellings, have also been excavated. The city of Ur was protected by walls, built of brick, with a moat filled with water from the River Euphrates.

Abram, as Abraham was at first called, was born near the city of Ur. His parents were probably nomads, tending sheep and cattle in the vicinity. When Abram was a young man, recently married to Sarai - better known as Sarah - his father Terah decided to leave Ur and to set out for the land of Canaan (now Palestine). They travelled along the river Euphrates as far as the city of Haran, in Mesopotamia, where Terah and the family settled, instead of continuing the journey to Canaan. After his father Terah's death, God told Abram to leave his

11

country and his people and 'go to the land I will show you.'[3] Abram obeyed, took his wife and his nephew Lot and all their possessions, and set out for an unknown destination. This proved to be the land of Canaan, which God promised to give to his offspring.

Then, however, there was a famine in the land. Abram moved on to Egypt. There Pharaoh took Sarah, who was very beautiful and said by Abram to be his sister, as a wife. But, when Pharaoh was afflicted by disease, he discovered the truth and he expelled Abram and Lot. Lot then settled near Sodom, close to the Dead Sea while Abraham pitched his tents near Hebron, where God appeared to him and again promised that he would give him and his descendents the land of Canaan. Abram and Sarai, however, had no children. Sarai, therefore told Abram to sleep with her maid Hagar, who bore him a son, called Ishmael.

Sometime later, God appeared again to Abram and changed his name to Abraham, because, God said, 'I have made you a father of many nations.'[4] God told Abraham that he and his son Ishmael were to be circumcised. God also promised that his wife, now to be called Sarah, would have a son. She laughed at the idea because she was too old to bear a child, but in due course she had a son who was called Isaac.

Meanwhile God, who had determined to destroy the people of Sodom and Gomorrah in punishment for their wickedness, warned Abraham what was to happen. But Abraham protested. 'What, if there were fifty righteous people in the city? How could the Judge of all the Earth kill the righteous with the wicked?' – the unanswered question of 'why do bad things happen to good people?' Abraham persisted and went on haggling until he got the number down to ten. 'For the sake of ten', the Lord said, 'I will not destroy it.' But destroy the cities he did – only Abraham's nephew Lot escaped with his family, although Lot's wife looked back and was turned into a pillar of salt.[5]

Soon Abraham's trust in God's justice was to be even more severely tested. God told him to take his son Isaac to Mount Moriah, traditionally thought to be the Temple Mount in Jerusalem, where the Dome of the Rock now stands. When they got there, Abraham built an altar, arranged the wood, bound Isaac, laid him on the altar and took the knife to kill him. At that point an angel called to Abraham, 'Do not lay a hand on the boy.' Abraham then saw a ram caught in the thicket, which he sacrificed instead. The angel applauded Abraham's obedience and God promised to make his descendants 'as numerous as the stars in the sky.' It is noteworthy that Isaac does not accompany his father home.[6]

Is Abraham to be admired for being willing to kill his son in obedience to God? The question has been discussed through the centuries and has a chilling relevance today when parents send their children, supposedly in obedience to God, to be suicide bombers. In the New Testament, Abraham's trust and obedience is held up as an example because he continued to believe God's promise that he would have numerous descendants even though he was told to sacrifice his son.[7] The Church Fathers saw in the story a foreshadowing of Christ's actual sacrifice of himself on the Cross. The rabbis usually thought of Isaac as a grown man, who willingly offered himself as a sacrifice to God and referred to the event as the *Akeda* – the Hebrew word for 'the Binding of Isaac'. In the Qur'an, Abraham's obedience, even under such severe testing is commended. Moreover the son – usually taken by Muslims to be Ishmael – when he is told of what Abraham is about to do, replies, 'O my father! Do as thou art bidden: thou wilt find me, if God so wills, among those who are patient in adversity.'[8] Both father and son submit unconditionally. God has to be obeyed.

By contrast, the philosopher Immanuel Kant (1724-1804), said that the command was opposed to the moral law and that Abraham should have known it was not the true voice of God. The twentieth century Jewish scholar Eliezer Berkovits (1908-1992) saw Abraham's trust mirrored in those Jews who retained their faith in God's covenant, even during their sufferings in the concentration camps. Feminists have wondered what Isaac's mother, Sarah thought. As one poet puts it 'the mother's weeping lives forever.'[9]

A modern Jewish commentary says that the story may be read as a 'paradigm of a father-and-son relationship. Every parent', it says, 'seeks to dominate his child and is in danger of seeking to sacrifice him to his parental plans or hopes. In the Biblical story, God is present and can therefore stay the father's hand. In all too many repetitions of the scene God is absent and the knife falls.'[10]

Soon after this dramatic event on Mount Moriah, Abraham's wife Sarah died. Abraham then bought the cave of Machpelah, near Mamre at Hebron and buried her there. Abraham subsequently took other wives, but although he gave gifts to their children, he left all his possessions to his son Isaac, whom he had seen married to Rebecca, a relation who had been fetched from Haran. When he died, Isaac and Ishmael joined together to bury Abraham in the cave of Macpelah, at Hebron – a place holy to Jews and Muslims.

Isaac and Rebecca had two sons, but again it was the younger son Jacob, who tricked Esau out of his birthright and his father's blessing, who was chosen by God to be the father of the people of Israel. Jacob had twelve sons by his two wives Leah and Rachel. Joseph was Jacob's favourite to whom he gave a 'coat of many colours.'[11] The other brothers were jealous and sold him into slavery in Egypt. Joseph, however, rose to be Pharaoh's right hand man. Joseph as a result was able to provide for his father Jacob and for his brothers and their families when they fled to Egypt from Canaan, where there was a severe famine. By the time of Moses, Joseph had been forgotten by the Egyptians and the Israelites had become slaves.

Abraham was the perhaps the first person to acknowledge and obey the One God who is the 'Judge of all the earth.' Some scholars say that he only recognised one god for *his* people ('henotheism') rather than that there is only One God for *all* people ('monotheism'). To Abraham, God promised that his descendants would be as numerous as the stars in number – and Jews, Christians and Muslims all count themselves among his descendants.

For Judaism, the patriarch Abraham, with whom God made a covenant to give to his descendants the land of Canaan, is the first Jew. When God called to Moses from the burning bush, God identified himself as the 'God of Abraham, Isaac and of Jacob.' It is to Moses that God gave the Law, but at circumcision a Jewish male enters into 'the Covenant of Father Abraham' and the convert to Judaism takes the patronym *Avraham Avinu* (the child of 'Abraham our Father.'). In the liturgy Jews pray to 'our God and the God of our ancestors: God of Abraham, God of Isaac, God of Jacob.'

Abraham is mentioned several times in the Hebrew Bible.[12] For the philosopher Philo, Abraham's study of astrology led him to faith in the One God. Philo, therefore, saw him as an example of how reason and faith go together. The Rabbis held that Abraham observed the Torah (Law), even though it had not yet been revealed to Moses. There are many Rabbinic references to him. The Babylonian Talmud, for example, says that when Abraham passed away, all the great ones of the nations stood in line and said, 'Woe to the world that has lost its leader and woe to the ship that has lost its pilot.'[13] The Jewish philosopher Maimonides (1135-1204 CE) said that Abraham was the first to accept that the world came into being from nothingness and to recognise the existence of God on the basis of reason. There are also many traditions about Abraham in the Midrash or non-Biblical commentaries, including one that says that Abraham's father was a manufacturer of idols. One day, when he left his son in charge, Abraham broke many of them and mocked the worship of an object that had just been made. This got him into trouble with the ruler, Nimrod, who threw him into a fire from which he escaped unhurt. Was this why his father had to leave the city?

The New Testament also often speaks of Abraham. Jesus is said to be a descendent of Abraham.[14] Mary sees in the birth of Jesus the fulfilment of God's promise to Abraham.[15] Jesus describes his mission as reclaiming the lost sons of Abraham[16] and promises that 'many will come from east and west and sit at table with Abraham, Isaac and Jacob.'[17]

In St Paul's writings the question of who are the true children of Abraham is raised more sharply. Paul insisted it was not a matter of physical descent or keeping the Law, but of sharing Abraham's faith. Abraham, he said, received God's promise four hundred and thirty years before the Law was given to Moses.[18] Gentiles who believed in Jesus should, therefore, have an equal place in the Church with Jewish believers. The Letter to the Hebrews holds Abraham up as a model of faith in God.[19]

The Qur'an regards Ibrahim, as it calls him, as a monotheist and as the 'original Muslim.' He rejected his father's idolatry[20] and, with his son Ishmael, restored the original monotheism of the Kaba at Mecca.[21] The promise that Ibrahim's wife would have a son in her old age and the rescue of Lot from the city whose indecency he had denounced are both recounted.

Muslim tradition has a high opinion of Ibrahim, who is sometimes spoken of as sinless and inerrant. It is said that Muhammad had a physical resemblance to Ibrahim. Arabs claim descent from Ibrahim through his first son Ishmael. The Bible too, although it concentrates on

Isaac, lists Ishmael's sons and makes clear that Abraham was distressed to send Hagar and her son away and that he gave them some food and drink to take with them to the desert. The Bible itself says that 'God was with the boy' (Ibrahim).[22]

The relationship of Jews, Christians and Muslims has often reflected the worst features of sibling rivalry. Followers of each religion have claimed to be the only true children of Abraham. Indeed, the only beloved children of God. Can they begin to see that like a good parent God loves each child equally but differently?

In the words of the Israeli poet Shin Shalom, Isaac appeals to Ishmael,

Ishmael my brother,
How long shall we fight each other...
Ishmael my brother, hear my plea:
It was the angel who tied thee to me...
Time is running out, put hatred to sleep,
Shoulder to shoulder, let's water our sheep.[23]

After the Crusades and the Holocaust, Christians should make a similar appeal to both Muslims and Jews,

Time is running out, put hatred to sleep.

CHAPTER NOTES
1. Genesis 12,3.
2. 2 Chronicles 20, 7; Isaiah 41, 8.
3. Genesis 12,1.
4. Genesis 17,5.
5. Genesis 18,16 ff and chapter 19.
6. Genesis 22.
7. Hebrews 11,17-20.
8. Surah 37,102.
9. Hayyim Robinson, quoted by W. Gunther Plaut, *The Torah: a Modern Commentary*, p. 154.
10. Plaut, p. 151.
11. This is the perhaps rather inaccurate but well known translation in the Authorised Version of the Bible.
12. For example, Psalm 47, 9; 105, 9; Isaiah 29, 22.
13. 'bBaba Bathra 91a/91b.

14. Matthew 1,1.
15. Luke 1,55.
16. Luke 19,9.
17. Luke 13,28.
18. Galatians 3,17.
19. Hebrews, 11, 8, 11 and 17.
20. Surahs 6,74 and 19,41ff.
21. Surah, 2,124-7.
22. Genesis 21,20.
23. From www.liberaljudaism.org, accessed, 2.12.08

3

Zoroaster

Zoroaster or Zarathustra was the founder of one of the most ancient surviving monotheistic religions. The number of Zoroastrians alive in the world today is small – perhaps about 150,000. Yet the teachings of Zoroaster have had a deep influence on Judaism, Christianity and Islam. Zoroaster is mentioned by several ancient Greek authors and by the early church father St John Chrysostom (c.347-407).[1] William Temple (1881-1944), an outstanding Archbishop of Canterbury, included Zoroaster with Plato and the Buddha as one through whom the Divine Word was revealed.[2] Zoroaster's 'clarion call to "resist evil"' is as relevant today as it was more than three thousand years ago.'[3]

Because Zoroastrianism is such an ancient religion, our knowledge of its history is incomplete. The oldest parts of the *Avesta* or holy book of the Zoroastrians are the liturgical texts or *yasna*, which bear a close relationship to the earliest Hindu scripture, the *Rig-Veda*. This suggests that the peoples from the Asian steppes who invaded both India and also Iran, in the middle of the Second Millennium BCE, were related. It implies also that these texts date to a slightly earlier time in the first part of the Second Millennium. The *yasna* texts were recited during the daily offering of fire and water. The most important scriptures are the seventeen hymns or *Gāthās*, which were written by Zoroaster himself. There are also later scriptures, often known as the 'Younger Avesta,' and ancient lives of the prophet. Although the latter are no longer extant, material from them is found in later writings. For centuries, the scriptures were memorised and passed on orally. They were not written down until hundreds of years later, when, during Sasanian times (224-651 CE), an alphabet was specially invented for this purpose. By that time, only the priests understood the language in which the scriptures had been composed. The most ancient copies of the texts were destroyed under Muslim rule. The oldest extant Avestan manuscripts is dated 1323 CE.

Yet despite the antiquity of the sources and the need to distinguish fact from legend, we have a surprisingly clear outline picture of the life of Zoroaster and a good knowledge of his teachings.

Zoroaster, according to the Roman writer Pliny the Elder (23-79 CE), was the only human being that laughed as he was being born.[4] Zarathustra, or Zoroaster to give him the Greek name by which he is usually known in the West, was a member of an ancient family. He had two older and two younger brothers. His father was called Pourusaspa, which means 'possessor of grey horses' and his mother Dughdhova, or 'milkmaid.' These names reflected typical occupations of a nomadic people. Zarathustra, the prophet's own name in the ancient Iranian language of Avestan, probably means 'one who can manage camels.' This was a skill which would have earned respect, although the name given to a child often reflects the parents' hopes rather than the reality!

Zoroaster speaks of himself as a fully qualified priest. His training would probably have started at the age of seven, when, with others, he would have been put in the care of a religious teacher. The training was demanding. He would have had to acquire knowledge of the rituals and their significance, of the art of composing hymns and prayers, and an understanding of a complex mythology. This was followed by deeper theological study at a *zaotar* or priest school. In ancient Iranian society, a boy reached manhood at the age of fifteen, when he was invested with a sacred girdle. It is probably at this stage that Zoroaster was initiated as a priest. Five years later, Zoroaster, against his parents' wishes, left home and embarked on a wandering and questioning life. He seems to have sought ought teachers revered for their secret wisdom, becoming himself 'one who knows.' Eventually, in his thirtieth year, Zoroaster had a spiritual experience that was to be decisive for him. He was attending a spring festival celebration. At dawn he went to fetch water from a nearby river to be used in the ceremony. He waded deep into the current to draw the purest water. As he returned to the bank – now himself in a state of ritual purity – he had a vision. He saw on the bank a being, clad in a garment like light itself, who revealed himself as Vohu Manah, Good Intention. Vohu Manah brought Zoroaster into the presence of the Lord Ahura Mazda and the other five Immortals, before whom, 'he did not see his own shadow on the ground, because of the brilliance of their light.'[5] 'Then', he said, 'did I recognize Thee in mind to be the first and the last, O Lord.'[6]

This was the first of a number of times in his life when Zoroaster saw the Lord, or felt conscious of his presence or heard his voice.

Zoroaster felt called by God to a special mission. 'For this I was set apart as yours from the beginning,' he wrote in one of his hymns.[7] In another, he said, 'while I have power and strength, I shall teach people to seek after the right.'[8]

Inspired by this vision, Zoroaster tried to teach a new understanding of God, but his message was 'unheeded.'[9] One tradition says that it was ten years before he gained his first convert, who was a cousin. Eventually, feeling rejected by his fellow countrymen and complaining like Jesus that 'a prophet was without honour in his own country'[10] Zoroaster left his homeland and settled in a new country, where he was better received. He won the favour of Queen Hutaosa. Thanks to her help, the king, Kavi Vistaspa, was converted and the new religion 'was set in the place of honour.'[11]

Zoroaster married three times – indeed in Zoroastrianism a priest is required to be married. Two of his wives, whose names are not recorded, bore him children, but Hvovi, whose name we do know, did not.[12]

Zoroaster lived to an old age, traditionally 77 years and 40 days. By the time of his death, his religion was securely established, partly because the king did battle with some neighbouring princes in its defence.

But when did Zoroaster live? This has been a matter of much debate. Some ancient writers said that Zoroaster lived 6,000 years before Plato or even 5,000 years before the Trojan War.[13] Other writes said that he lived a mere 258 years before Alexander the Great, so around 600 BCE. Until quite recently Western scholars dated Zoroaster to the sixth century, but the more recent work of Mary Boyce and others suggests a date towards the end of the Second Millennium BCE or a little earlier. The seventeen hymns or *Gathas* of Zoroaster himself reflect a nomadic society and may have been written before Zoroaster's kinsmen moved into Iran. Some neighbouring people may by that time have started to use chariots and so threatened other more traditional groups. Certainly Zoroaster lived at a time of unrest and social change.

One of the great innovations that Zoroaster made in the religious thought of his people was to acknowledge Ahura Mazda, who was probably already recognised as a deity, as the One God, the Lord Wisdom or the Wise Lord. Ahura Mazda, Zoroaster proclaimed, was the only eternal Being, self-existing, wholly wise and good. Central to Zoroaster's teaching was this belief in a primal unity. It is important to emphasise this as sometimes Zoroastrianism is misunderstood as dualistic with two equal powers: one, good and the other evil.

In the beginning, Zoroaster said, there was only one good God, who was the focus of worship. But Ahura Mazda fathered twin spirits, Spenta Mainyu, the Beneficent Spirit and Angra Mainyu, the Hostile Spirit. 'There are two primal spirits, twins renowned to be in conflict. In thought and word and act they are two: the better and the bad. And those who act well have chosen wisely between these two, not so evil doers.'[14]

Angra Mainyu, like God, was self-existing and therefore wholly independent of God, but he was utterly malign. It was in order to destroy this evil Sprit and cleanse the universe that Ahura Mazda created this world to be a battle ground where good and evil could meet and evil be overcome. Ahura Mazda created the world and all that is in it, including human beings, to be good, but in his omniscience he had seen that Angra Mainyu would invade the world and corrupt it, filling it with misery and vice.

Angra Maniyu is to be unflinchingly resisted – consciously by man, instinctively by the rest of creation. Zoroaster, therefore, saw the whole world, animate and inanimate, as striving for salvation from evil in all its aspects.

To help in this great task the prophet believed that Ahura Mazda recruited the help of the beneficent gods of the Old Iranian pantheon and other lesser divinities. In the *Gathas*, Zoroaster speaks of seven Bounteous Immortals as well as Ahura Mazda. Perhaps this was a concession to the polytheism that was prevalent before Zoroaster. Angra Mainyu also had his cohorts of evil agents, including the war-gods of the old pantheon and a host of minor demons.

Zoroaster had a deep belief in the justice of God and was vocal in condemning the injustices in the society of his day. But he realized that goodness often does not get its desserts in this world. True justice was only to be realised in the next world. Already his contemporaries had a vague belief that the spirits of the dead had a shadowy existence in the underworld and that at least some of the most virtuous would rise to join the gods in a bright kingdom above the sky. This belief is echoed in the Biblical book of Daniel, which says, 'Those who are wise shall shine like the brightness of the heavens and those who lead many to right-eousness like the stars for ever and ever.'[15]

There was also an early belief that the bodies of the righteous would be resurrected so that they might enjoy all the delights of the heavenly kingdom. Zoroaster linked these two ideas with his profound ethical belief in justice. Everyone, he said, who accepted his teaching and lived a moral life could attain to heaven. But first they had to be judged on the third day when the soul ascended to the peak of Mount Hara, the mythical mountain at the centre of the earth. There a person's good words and actions were weighed in a balance against the bad. If the bad were heavier, the spirit would plunge through a chasm into the under-world, which Zoroaster pictured as a place of punishment, presided over by the Evil Spirit, Anga Manyu. The good spirits ascended to heaven. Zoroaster believed that eventually when the earthly struggle against evil was triumphant, a general resurrection of all bodies would take place on the Last Day, followed by the Last Judgment.

Following the ancient practice of ordeal by fire – in which a person demonstrated his or her innocence by surviving torture or walking though a fire - Zoroaster saw the Last Judgment as also a cosmic ordeal by fire. Molten metal would flow out of the mountains to form a burning river. Souls reunited to their resurrected bodies would be required to pass through the fiery torrent. The good would be saved by divine intervention, but the wicked would be utterly destroyed – hell, in this scenario would not be eternal. Indeed, the fiery river would flow down into hell and cleanse it and Angra Mainyu and his legions would be destroyed. Thus Ahura Mazda's great goal would be accomplished. With the extinction of evil, time and history would come to an end and there would be no more birth or death. The blessed would receive the gift of immortality and live happily for ever on earth in the kingdom of Ahura Mazda.

At a later period, some time after 600 BCE, a further major belief developed that in the last battle the forces of good would be led by a World Saviour, the *Saoshyant*, who would be miraculously conceived by Zoroaster's own seed. The scriptures say:

'He shall be the victorious Benefactor (*Saoshyant*) by name and World-renovator (*Astavat-ereta*) by name. He is Benefactor because he will benefit the entire physical world; he is World-renovator because he will establish the physical living existence indestructible. He will oppose the evil of the progeny of the biped and withstand the enmity produced by the faithful.'[16]

Zoroastrians, especially in times of persecution, have eagerly awaited the coming of the Saoshyant, with wise men or *magi* looking for signs in the stars of his coming. The wise men who, according to St Matthew's Gospel, were led by a star to worship the infant Jesus, may have been Zoroastrians.[17]

Zoroastrianism was slow to gain wide acceptance. This was partly because it was opposed by the established religious authorities, who felt threatened by Zoroaster's teachings. By the seventh century BCE, however, Zoroastrianism had spread across the Iranian plateau. It was adopted by Cyrus the Great, who was King of Persia from 559-529, as the official religion of the Persian Empire, which spread from Northern India to Greece and Egypt. Cyrus encouraged also the practice of traditional religions and, for example, allowed the Jews who were in exile in Babylon to return to Judea and to rebuild the temple. In the book of Isaiah, Cyrus is hailed as 'the Lord's anointed.'[18] The Persian Empire, under the Achaemenid dynasty, was well ruled. Authority was delegated to local rulers, effective communications established, with improved roads and a rudimentary postal service. Subject people, on the whole, regarded Persian rule as benevolent and there were few revolts. The Greeks were the main enemies. They repelled a threatened Persian invasion at the battle of Marathon in 490 BCE. Subsequently the Greeks conquered Iran, under Alexander the Great (356-323 BCE), who in Zoroastrian texts is referred to as 'the accursed', but whom Greeks called 'the great' –the title by which he is known in the West. Alexander destroyed Persepolis, the great royal and cultural centre, and killed some of the priests. Under Alexander's successors, Hellenistic culture became dominant in the area. Under the Parthians, Zoroastrianism regained some ground. The Parthians, who ruled parts of Asia Minor, Syria and even, in 40 BCE Jerusalem - although they were expelled by King Herod after only two years - were a major rival to the Romans.

In the third century CE, the Sasanians overthrew the Parthians and sought to legitimize their rule by reasserting Persia's Zoroastrian legacy. There is some question how far the Zoroastrianism of the

Sasanids was true to the teaching of Zoroaster himself. It is sometime suggested that it was influenced by Zurvanism, which Zoroastrians regarded as a heresy because it questioned free will and the essential goodness of the material world.

This revival of Zoroastrianism was quickly reversed by Muslim conquests. The Sasanian army was defeated at the battle of Nihavend. The last Zoroastrian king, Yazdegird III, fled and was killed by one of his own people. At first the taxes exacted by the Muslims were less than those demanded by the Sasanians and the clarity of the new religion appealed to some people. Many people embraced Islam under the influence of Abu Muslim in the eighth century. Arabic was soon imposed as the national language and the ancient religion oppressed, as, unlike Judaism and Christianity, it was usually not regarded by Muslims as a religion of the book - even though the Avesta had by then been written down and was revered as a holy text. To escape persecution, in the tenth century some Zoroastrians left their home country and settled in India, where they became known as Parsis – people from Pars or Persia. Mumbai or Bombay is still today an important centre of the Zoroastrian religion. In Persia, some Zoroastrians courageously remained faithful to their religion. In the late nineteenth century, there was some improvement in the conditions in which Zoroastrians lived, thanks to the efforts of a Parsi, Mankeji Limji Hataria. Under the Shah, a Zoroastrian even became deputy prime minister.

Many Zoroastrians were apprehensive when the Islamic Republic, under Ayatollah Khumayni, was established in 1979. Some returned to their desert homes, but many others left the country to find a new life in the USA and, to a lesser extent, in Britain, Canada and Australia. This has helped to make Zoroastrianism better known. In fact those who remained did not suffer the persecution they feared, but their rights in law are limited and their educational and employment opportunities are restricted.

Although the total number of Zoroastrians today is small, the teachings of Zoroaster have had a lasting influence on Judaism, Christianity and Islam, especially in their teachings about the end of the world. Traditional Christian pictures of heaven and hell – with its unquenchable fire – are borrowed from Zoroastrianism. So is the traditional belief in the resurrection of the body on the Last Day, which has been held uneasily together with teaching about the immortality of the soul. Some of the imagery applied by Christians to Jesus as the Saviour also comes from Zoroastrianism.

Most important, of course, is Zoroaster's clear message that there is One God, who is all good, who calls human beings to share in the struggle against evil. Zoroaster urged his followers to 'keep your feet, hands and intellect ready, in order to practice lawful, timely, well-done deeds...so as to make the needy prosperous.'[19] His message that all that we do should be righteous and for the praise of the Wise Lord is at the heart of the teaching of many great religions and is still relevant today.

CHAPTER NOTES

1. See references in A V Williams Jackson, *The Prophet of Ancient Iran*, New York, Macmillan Company, 1899, Appendix V, pp. 226-273.
2. William Temple, *Readings in St John's Gospel*, London, Macmillan, 1939, St Martin's Library edtn, 1961, p. 9.
3. Quoted by M.N Dhalla in his *History of Zoroastrianism*, Bombay, The K.R.CAMA ORIENTAL INSTITUTE, 1963, P. 84.
4. Quoted by M.N Dhalla p.143.
5. *Zadspram*, XXI, 9, quoted by Mary Boyce, *A History of Zoroastrianism*, Leiden, E J Brill, 1975, Vol 1, p.185.
6. *Yasna*, 31,8. quoted in *World Scripture*, p. 76.
7. *Yasna*, 44,11, quoted by Boyce, p. 185.
8. *Yasna*, 28.4, quoted by Boyce, p.185.
9. *Yasna*, 31,1, quoted by Boyce, p. 186.
10. Luke, 4,24.
11. *Yt*, 13.99-100, quoted by Boyce, p. 187.
12. Boyce, p.188.
13. See Dhalla, p.143 and also Boyce, p. 190 and p. 286.
14. Boyce, p.193 Ys 30,3.
15. Daniel, 12,3.
16. Farvardin Yasht, 13,129, in *World Scripture*, p. 785.
17. Matthew, 2,1.
18. Isaiah 45,1.
19. *Avesta, Visparad* 15,1, quoted in *World Scripture*, p. 713.

4

Vyasa

The Vedas, which are the authoritative Hindus scriptures and of which Vyasa is the legendary complier, date back to about 1500 BCE or slightly later. They are usually thought to belong to the Aryans or Indo-European people who overran the ancient Indus Valley civilization in the second half of the second millennium BCE.

The Indus valley civilization itself dates back to the middle of the third millennium BCE.[1] It flourished in the Indus and Ghaggar-Hakra river valleys, in what is now Pakistan and north western and western India. The mature phase of this civilization is technically known as the Harappan Civilization (2600–1900 BCE), named after Harappa, which was the first of the cities to be excavated.

Archaeological evidence shows that the Indus Valley civilization was a sophisticated and technologically advanced urban civilization. There seem to have been efficient municipal governments, which placed a high priority on hygiene. The streets of major cities such as Mohenjo-daro or Harappa were laid out in perfect grid patterns. Within the city, individual homes or groups of homes obtained water from wells. Houses opened only to inner courtyards and smaller lanes. The advanced architecture of the Harappans is shown by their impressive dockyards, granaries, warehouses, brick platforms and protective walls. Massive citadels protected the Harappans from floods and attackers.

There is no conclusive evidence of palaces or temples - or of kings, armies, or priests. Most city dwellers appear to have been traders or artisans, who lived with others pursuing the same occupation in well-defined neighborhoods. Materials from distant regions were used in the cities for constructing seals, beads and other objects. Among the artifacts discovered were beautiful beads of glazed stone called faïence. The seals have images of animals, gods and other types of inscriptions. Some of the seals were used to stamp clay on trade goods. In view of the large number of figurines found in the Indus valley, it has been suggested that the Harappan people worshipped a Mother goddess symbolizing fertility, although this interpretation is disputed. In the earlier phases of their culture, the Harappans buried their dead. Later, however, they also cremated their dead and buried the ashes in burial urns. Many Indus valley seals show animals and one seal shows a figure seated in what has been compared to yoga postures. There may also be evidence of phallic symbols. It has been suggested that some features of Dravidian culture and religion date back to this early civilization.

Vyasa is a legendary figure but mention of him allows for an introduction to the Hindu scriptures. He is also known as the author of the Mahabharata, which is one of the two great Hindu epic poems.[2] Some Hindus regard him as an *avatar* of the God Vishnu.

One tradition is that at an early age Vyasa told his parents that he wanted to withdraw to the forests and live an ascetic and religious life. His mother eventually agreed on condition that he should appear before her whenever she wanted his presence. He is said to have studied under various great teachers. The vast amount of writing attributed to him may suggest that the word Vyasa refers to a class of scholars rather than to an individual. The *Vishnu-Purana* says that

'in every third world age, Vishnu, in the person of Vyasa, in order to promote the good of mankind, divides the Veda, which is properly but one, into many portions. Observing the limited perseverance, energy and application of mortals, he makes the Veda fourfold, to adapt it to their capacities; and the bodily form which he assumes, in order to effect that classification, is known by the name of Veda-vyasa.'[3]

The dating of the Vedas is disputed. Tilak (1856-1920), a scholar and early advocate of Indian independence, argued that the oldest Hindu scripture, the Rig Veda was composed – although not written down – no later than 4,000 BCE. Some orthodox Hindus would even put the date much earlier. Critical scholars, as already mentioned, suggest a date around 1500 BCE or slightly later - perhaps three centuries after Abraham set out from Haran.

The word 'Veda' means knowledge or wisdom. Orthodox Hindus believe that the Vedas are divine and eternal truth and that they had no human author. 'They are the breath of God, eternal truths revealed to the *rishis* of yore.'[4] The *rishis* are seers, who see the eternal truth – or perhaps more correctly those who heard the silent truth in the depths of their heart. The Vedas were transmitted orally before they were written down.

There are four Vedas: the *Rig Veda*, the *Yajur Veda*, the *Sāma Veda* and the *Atharva Veda*. Each Veda consists of hymns, rules for performing sacrifices, and allegorical interpretations of the rituals. There are also a large number of writings of philosophical speculation, known as the Upanishads. They, together with the Vedas and the Bhagavad-Gita, are the best known of the Hindu scriptures.

There are over one thousand hymns or *mantra* in the oldest collection, the Rig Veda, which in Sanskrit - the language in which the scriptures are written - means 'wisdom in verse.' Most of the hymns are addressed to gods. The first hymn, for example, addressed to Agni, the god of fire begins:

I magnify God, the Divine Fire,
The Priest, Minister of the sacrifice,
The Offerer of oblation, supreme Giver of treasure.[5]

Some of the most beautiful hymns are addressed to Dawn. For example,
Dawn comes shining
Like a Lady of Light,
stirring to life all creatures.
Now it is time
To kindle the Fire.
The light of Dawn scatters the shadows.

Her face turned toward
This far-flung world,
She rises, enwrapped in bright garments.
Shining with gold,
With rays of light bedecked,
she sends forth the world on its course...

Beam forth your light
To guide and sustain us,
Prolonging, O Goddess, our days.
Give us food,
Grant to us joy,

Chariots and cattle and horses.[6]

The famous Hymn of Origins gives a profound sense of the mystery of reality, which is lost in the subsequent dogmatism of much religion. It deserves to be quoted in full:

At first was neither Being nor Non-being.
There was not air nor yet sky beyond.
What was its wrapping? Where? In whose protection?
Was Water there, unfathomable and deep?

There was no death then, nor yet deathlessness;
Of night or day there was not any sign.
The One breathed without breath, by its own impulse.
Other than that was nothing else at all.

Darkness was there, all wrapped around by darkness,
and all was Water indiscriminate. Then
that which was hidden by the Void, that One, emerging,
stirring, through power of Ardor, came to be.

In the beginning Love arose,
which was the primal germ cell of the mind.
The Seers, searching in their hearts with wisdom,
discovered the connection of Being in Nonbeing.

A crosswise line cut Being from Nonbeing.
What was described above it, what below?
Bearers of seed there were and mighty forces,
thrust from below and forward move above.

Who really knows? What can presume to tell it?
Whence was it born? Whence issued this creation?
Even the Gods came after its emergence.
Then who can tell from whence it came to be?

That out of which creation has arisen,

Whether it held firm or it did not,
He who surveys it in the highest heaven,
He surely knows – or maybe He does not![7]

Over two hundred works have been called Upanishads, but perhaps as few as nine date from the later Vedic period, which modern scholarship dates to somewhere between 600 and 400 BCE – years which saw Socrates teach in ancient Greece and the great prophets of Israel proclaim God's message. The word Upanishad is usually thought to mean 'to sit close by to a guru or teacher who imparted secret mysteries.' The philosopher Sankara interpreted the word to mean teaching that 'destroys' ignorance.

The central teaching of the Upanishads is that the Self or *atman* is one with the ultimate ground of Reality or *Brahman*. The person who realises this finds liberation or *moksha*, and is freed from the circle of rebirth or *samsara*. This teaching provided the basis for the philosophical speculation of Sankara and Ramanuja, whom we shall consider later.

Vyasa not only classified and edited the Vedas. He is also said to be the author of the great epic poem called the Mahābhārata, which includes the much-loved Bhagavad-Gita, in which the Lord Krishna reveals the deepest truths to Arjuna. The Mahābhārata centres around the great battle for kingship fought at Kuruksetra between the Pandavas and Kauravas. It is very lengthy, with over 100,000 verses. It is said that Vyasa asked the god Ganesha to help him write the text. Ganesha agreed on condition that Vyasa narrated the story without pause. In response, Vyasa insisted that Ganesha must understand the verse before he transcribed it, but Ganesha could not always keep up, which explains the complications in the text. Vyasa also appears in the epic as the father of Dhritarshtra and Pandu.

If 100,000 verses were not enough, Vyasa is also credited with having written eighteen of the major Puranas, secondary scriptures, which contain mythological accounts of ancient days.

Sri Swami Sivananda has written that 'Vyasa's life is a unique example of one born for the dissemination of spiritual knowledge. His writings inspire us and the whole world even to this day.'[8] It is certainly remarkable how very ancient texts still provide spiritual sustenance and can continue to be a resource to all who seek the meaning of Life.

CHAPTER NOTES
1. The first Mesopotamian civilization is dated to the middle of the preceding millennium.
2. The other is the *Ramayana.*
3. *Vishnu-Purana*, Book 3, chapter 3.
4. T M P Mahadevan, *Outlines of Hinduism*, Bombay, Chetana, 1956, p. 29.
5. *Rig Veda*, 1,1,1. From Raimundo Panikkar, *The Vedic Experience*, 6 p. 36.
6. *Rig Veda*, 7,77. From *The Vedic Experience*, p. 169.
7. *Rig Veda*, 10,29 from, *The Vedic Experience*, p. 58.
8. From Sri Swami Sivananda, *Lives of the Saints*. Shivanandanagar, The Divine Life Society, 1941. Also available at www.dlshq.org/books.

5

Akhenaten

Akhenaten was one of the world's great religious reformers, who abandoned the gods of Ancient Egypt and proclaimed that there is only one absolute God, named Aten. His reforms were quickly abandoned and subsequent generations of Egyptians regarded him as a heretic. He was, certainly, Egypt's most controversial ruler and opinion about him is still divided today.

The amazing civilization of ancient Egypt has long been buried under the sand, although much of it has been excavated during the last century. Its fascination, however, can still draw many visitors to the pyramids and tombs of the kings and attract great crowds to Tutankhamen exhibitions. The civilization of Egypt was already ancient when Abraham journeyed there early in the Second Millennium BCE. The first Dynasty of Pharaohs is dated to about 3,000 BCE and Egypt's pre-history goes back for several more millennia. The 'Step Pyramid' of Djoser, the world's first big stone building, was built under the Third Dynasty in about 2770. Akhenaten belonged to the Eighteenth Dynasty, which ruled from 1580 to 1314 BCE.

Akhenaten, sometimes spelt (Ikhnaton), was the son of Amenhotep III and Tiye, and was originally known as Amenhotep IV. When his elder brother died, he became heir to the throne and possibly for a time co-regent with his father.

At the beginning of his reign he started to build a great temple at Karnak, for which smaller blocks than usual, which could be carried by one man, were used. The main temples were dedicated to the sun disc Aten, rather than as would have been expected, to the god Amun. The carved relief also, unusually, gives a prominent place to his queen Nefertiti. Her beautifully moulded and painted bust is world famous. During the early days of the rule of Akhenaten, he and Nefertiti were inseparable. Contemporary artists depict them in tender domestic scenes enjoying dinner, paying homage to the Aten and relaxing with their daughters. Akhenaten's great love for Nefertiti is reflected in this stone love-letter that he apparently wrote to his wife:

The heiress, great in favour, lady of grace, sweet love,
Mistress of the South and North,
Fair of face, gay, with the two plumes
Beloved of the living Aten [the King],
The Chief Wife of the King, whom he loves,
Lady of the Two Lands, great of love,
Nefertiti, living for ever and ever.

The way in which Akhenaten and his wife were depicted was also unusual. They have long narrow faces, elongated skulls, sagging bellies, narrow shoulders and in the case of the king pronounced breasts. Was this a way of emphasising the supernatural otherness of the royal family? Did it reflect the Pharaoh's actual appearance – caused perhaps by some genetic disorder? Some scholars have suggested that the features of Akhenaton and the other members of his family were unquestionably African. We do not know.

After Akhenaten had been on the throne for about six years major changes took place. He altered his name from Amenhotep to Akhenaten, which means 'transfigured spirit of Aten.' He left Thebes and built a new capital known as Akhenaten – now Amarna – in Middle Egypt. Excavations suggest that it would have been an attractive place to live. Officials lived in spacious villas, with trees, pools and gardens. The walls were painted with scenes from nature and daily life. There is a gradual variation in the size of houses but the difference between rich and poor is not excessive. The difference, however, between the royal family and the rest of the population is emphasised. The discovery of the Amarna letters, a cache of diplomatic correspondence, gives us a vivid account of relations with foreign rulers and subject princes.

The major change that Akhenaten introduced was to the religion of Egypt. As the Pyramids and their excavations suggest, much attention was paid to the Next Life, but religion permeated every day life and the Pharaohs' claimed to be the embodiment of the deities.

According to tradition, before creation the Absolute Spirit Ra was diffused in primordial Chaos. At the beginning of time Ra became aware of himself, 'seeing' his own image (Amon). Then in the Great Silence, he called his double, 'Come to me.' This was the beginning of the creative process, carried forward by the fertilizing force of Osiris, the water of life, and the generating force of Isis. Over time, the god Amon-Ra, like Pharaoh, acquired a court of gods and as Egypt's empire extended, local gods were incorporated into the pantheon. Even so, Alberto Carlo Carpiceci claims that 'All Egyptian cosmogonies are deeply permeated by the feeling of a one and only absolute God, beginning and end of all visible and invisible things and of an eternal creation where the gods have a thousand faces and are the thousand manifestations of the same god, as are all his creatures and all of humankind.'[1] Of central importance is the myth of Osiris, (the Greek name for the Egyptian Ousir) who became human and taught his subjects how to grow food and to build homes. He was the enemy of all violence and travelled widely, spreading civilization by gentleness and charming people everywhere with his songs and music. In his absence, Isis governed Egypt well, but soon after his return his brother Set plotted against him and killed him. Isis, however, found the body of Osiris and restored him to life. Instead of resuming his earthly reign, however, Osiris retired to the 'Elysian Fields' where he welcomes the souls of the just.

All this was swept away by Akhenaten, although his religion is not completely understood. Aten was for him the sole God. He changed his name to avoid reference to the god Amon, whose name was hacked out of inscriptions across Egypt. The funerary religion dropped Osiris and Akhenaten became the source of blessings for people after death. The figure of Queen Nefertiti replaced the figures of protecting goddesses at the corners of stone sarcophagi or coffins. People were expected to be grateful to the sun for life and warmth. Presumably the existing moral code of Egypt's Wisdom literature was upheld, but the threatening warnings of the old gods seem to have disappeared.

Akhenaten's religion is best summed up in this hymn:

When thou settest in the western
horizon of heaven
The world is in darkness like the dead...
Every lion cometh forth from his den,
The serpents they sting. Darkness reigns...
Bright is the earth when thou riseth in the horizon...

The Two Lands are in daily festival,
Awake and standing upon their feet...
Then in all the world they do their work.
How manifold are thy works!
They are hidden from before us.
O thou sole God, whose power no other possesses.
Thou didst create the earth according to thy desire, being alone:
Man, all cattle, large and small;
All that are upon the earth.[2]

Akhenaten's hymn is often compared to the Biblical Psalm 104

Thou makest darkness and it is night,
Wherein all the beasts of the forest do creep forth;
The young lions roar after their prey;
they seek their meat from God...
The sun ariseth, they get them away
And lay them down in their dens.
Man goeth forth unto his work
And to his labour until the evening...
O Lord, how manifold are thy works!
In wisdom hast thou made them all.

Akhenaten insisted that all men were equal. 'God created every man equal to his brother.' He saw the universe as a single act of love uniting the Creator and the Creature. In his words,

'You are the flow of life itself and no one can live without you... You nourish the child from when he is in his mother's womb, you calm him so that he will not cry, you open his mouth and you bring him what he needs... You are the lord of all, who takes care of all. You create the life of all people, you have placed the Nile in the Heavens so that it may descend over us and bathe our fields with its floods and fertilize the fields of our countryside.'[3]

The reforms were not popular. As time passed, the Egyptians showed signs of discontent with their Pharaoh of love. Foreign tribute fell off as the empire diminished in size. There was a serious epidemic, perhaps the first recorded outbreak of influenza. The priesthood grew weary of its narrow role in the new theology and the people longed to return to the traditional gods. His religion survived until his death in

1362 B.C, but was quickly reversed by his son Tutankhamen (c.1358-1340 BCE).

The mystery of Akhenaten remains. Was he the first monotheist who preached a religion of love or a megalomaniac who thought of himself and his wife as the only gods? Did his reforms vanish, like his capital, without trace or leave a lasting legacy? Freud suggested that Moses had been a priest of Aten, who was forced to leave Egypt with other believers, after the death of Akhenaten. Most scholars, however, question whether there was a link with Moses and the beginnings of Biblical monotheism. The novelist Thomas Mann in his fictional *Joseph and his Brothers* (1933-43) made Akhenaten the 'dreaming Pharaoh' of Joseph's story – *Akhnaton* (*sic*) was also the title of a play by Agatha Christie. After his reign the god Amon-Ra returned, but was now conceived of as one who 'cannot be represented in that He is pure Spirit.' In the words of one Egyptologist, 'Akhenaten's religious experiences and his pantheism, throbbing with love, penetrated everywhere, even in such completely different systems of thought as the Greek and the Hebrew.'[4]

CHAPTER NOTES
1. Alberto Carlo Carpiceci, *Art and History of Egypt*, Florence, Casa Editrice Bonechi, 1997, translated by Erika Pauli p. 14.
2. A different translation is included in Mircea Eliade, *From Primitives to Zen*, London, Collins, 1967 p. 28.
3. Quoted by Carpiceci, p. 16.
4. Carpiceci, p.16.

6

Krishna

Should Krishna be included in this book? When I asked some Hindu scholars, I got different answers. The question is whether he was a historical character. But that is a 'Western' question and to many Indians it is irrelevant. Gandhi, for example, said of the crucifixion of Jesus that he did not care whether it was historical, it was truer than history. As we shall see there is much uncertainty about historical details of many of the people included in this book, whose lives have been elaborated by myth and legend. Several also have come to be seen as divine.

As I have visited the birthplace of Krishna (also spelt Krsna) at Mathura in Uttar Pradesh, and also Vrindaban, where he is said to have danced with the cow-maids, I think there was such a historical person, although dates for him are elusive. The name Krishna appears in the Rig Veda (c.1300 BCE) and the Chandogya Upanishad (c. 600 BCE) mentions a Krishna, son of Devaki, who was a scholar. The main sources for the story of Krishna, here woven together, are the epic poem the *Mahabharata* (5th century CE), the *Vishnu Purana* (end of the 3rd Century CE) and the *Bhagavata Purana* (9th century CE).

Krishna, the name means 'black', was born into the Yadava clan, the son of Vasudeva and Devaki – sometimes Krishna is also referred to as Vasudeva. Devaki's brother was Kamsa, the evil king of Mathura, who had been warned that he would be killed by one of Devaki's sons. He, therefore, slaughtered his nephews, except Krishna and his elder brother Balaram, who were smuggled across the river Yamuna to Gokula, where they were brought up by the leader of the cowherds, Nanada and his wife Yasoda. There are several stories of his childish pranks, such as stealing butter. Krishna is often worshipped as a child. More significant was his association with the cow-maids (*gopis*), who were persuaded by the sound of his flute to follow him into the forests. Krishna reproached them for leaving their husbands, saying that love for him came more through singing and dancing than through physical proximity. They replied that they had come out of devotion to the Primal Spirit (*adi-purusha*). Krishna laughed and in compassion danced ecstatically with them. Krishna, then, disappeared with his favourite, the beautiful Radha. The gopis prayed, 'You are not the son of a cowherd, you are the inner soul of all beings.' When, Krishna returned, with their eyes glowing with love, they welcomed him as their most 'beloved Lord.' Similar passion is shown in the relationship of Krishna with his first wife Rukmini and with his other wives.

These erotic stories were frequently retold by India's poets in several languages and illustrated by many artists. Sexual passion as a symbol for the devotee's intense love for God is not uncommon – as for example in the Song of Solomon in the Bible. On one occasion, when Krishna saw the cow-maids bathing in a river he stole their clothes and climbed into a tree, the story is interpreted as teaching that the soul has to come naked to God.

At length, Krishna and his brother returned to Mathura and killed the evil Kamsa. Later, finding the kingdom to be unsafe, Krishna led the Yadava tribe to the western coast and established his court at Dvarka, probably the modern Dwarka in Gujarat.

During the great war between the Kauravas and Pandavas, Krishna refused to take sides. He offered them the choice of his personal assistance or the loan of his army. The Kauravas chose the army, so Krishna joined the Pandavas as Arjuna's charioteer. On the eve of the battle, Arjuna voiced his sadness at having to kill his own relations.

O Krishna, when I see my relatives here
Who have come together and want to fight,
I feel paralysed,
My mouth becomes dry,
I tremble within,
My hair stands on end.[1]

To this Krishna replied - as will be described in a moment - in the words recorded in the Bhagavad-Gita. After the battle, he returned to Dvarka, where one day a brawl broke out between the Yadava chiefs, in which Krishna's brother and son were killed. As Krishna sat mourning in the forest a huntsman, called Jaras (old age), mistaking him for a deer, shot him in his foot, his one vulnerable spot, and killed him. After his cremation by Arjuna, the dark Kali age descended on the earth.

In the Bhagavad Gita, often known for short as the Gita, Krishna offers a number of answers to Arjuna's despondency at the thought of killing his cousins in the looming battle. First, Krishna shows that the soul is indestructible:

Who thinks this one a slayer,
Or who thinks of him as slain,
Both lack understanding.
He neither slays nor is slain.
He is never born.
He never dies.[2]

He then emphasises the importance of disciplined and detached action.

Considering also the duty of your own class,
You should not waver.[3]

Arjuna should fulfil his caste duties but without concern for the fruit of his actions. For with detachment, actions do not entail Karma, which is the cause of rebirth.

The man who has given up all desire
And moves without wanting anything,
Who says neither mine *nor* I,
Wins peace.[4]

Later, Arjuna is told to offer all his works in devotion to God – as that will ensure complete salvation.

Cast all works on Me, directing
Your thought to the reality of your self.
Become free from desires, from selfishness,
And fight without anxiety.[5]

Gradually Arjuna becomes aware that Krishna is more than a charioteer. Krishna explains that although unborn, whenever righteousness declines and ill-behaviour increases, by his own mysterious power, he comes to earth.

For whenever
Right languishes
And unright ascends,
I manifest myself.
Age after age I appear
To establish the right and true.[6]

As the book progresses, Krishna reveals deeper divine truths. His lower nature is seen in the elements of the visible world, but his higher nature is the Life by which the universe is sustained. He explains the cyclical nature of creation and dissolution and re-creation. Krishna emphasises experience of the divine and eventually in response to Arjuna's entreaties, reveals his supreme form.

With these words, Vishnu
The great Lord of mystic power,
Gave Arjuna the vision
Of his highest, absolute form –

His form with many mouths and eyes,
appearing in many miraculous ways,
With many divine ornaments
And divine, unsheathed weapons...

If the light of a thousand suns,
Should effulge all at once,
It would resemble the radiance
Of that God of overpowering reality.[7]

Arjuna, amazed, chants his astonished description of the vision and bows his head to God.

I bow before you, supreme God.
Be gracious.
You who are so awesome to see,
Tell me, who are you?
I want to know you, the very first Lord,

For I do not understand what it is you are doing.[8]

Exhilarated and overwhelmed by the vision, Arjuna shows some relief when Krishna resumes his usual form, with his crown and with his club and discus in his hand. Krishna explains that the vision that Arjuna has been granted is not achieved by study of texts or by austerity or by sacrifices, but only given to the devotee. After further teaching, the Gita ends by repeating the 'highest of mysteries' that has been revealed:

I truly love you,
Therefore I shall tell you what is best for you
Turn your mind to me, devoted to me.
Doing your rituals for me, bow to me.
You will come to me.
I promise it to you surely. I love you.[9]

Finally, Krishna affirms that whoever loves and worships him will certainly come to him.

You may have noticed that the Gita speaks of Vishnu revealing himself in the vision. Vishnu, Brahma and Siva constitute the *Trimurti*, or three forms of the Godhead. At moments of great distress in the world, Vishnu has descended to earth as an *avatara*, most notably as Krishna and Rama. The word *avatara* or avatar means literally a 'coming down' or 'manifestation.' *Avatara* is quite often translated as 'incarnation' and some Indian Christians speak of Jesus as an avatar. Other Christians say that the word obscures their claim that Jesus is 'the only Son of God' and that Krishna was a mythological and not a historical figure - the question with which we began. Transposing terms from one faith tradition to another may make for a quick explanation, but also leads to confusion, which is why I avoided the translation 'Trinity' for *Trimurti*.

Be that as it may, there can be no doubt about the enormous influence of Krishna on the spiritual life of millions of Hindus as well as on the artistic life of India. Thanks especially to the International Society for Krishna Consciousness, founded in the USA by Bhaktivedanta Swami Prabhupada (1896-1977) in 1965, Lord Krishna now has many devotees in the West. The *Bhagavad-Gita* is certainly one of the world's best known sacred texts.

CHAPTER NOTES

1. *The Bhagavad-Gita* 1,28-29 Translation by Kees W. Bolle in *Universal Wisdom*, ed Bede Griffiths, Fount, 1994.
2. 2,19-20.
3. 2,31.
4. 2,71.
5. 3,30.
6. 4,7-8.
7. 11,9-10 and 12.
8. 11,31.
9. 18,64-5.

7

Rama and Sita

Rama, like Krishna, is an avatar of Vishnu. He is widely worshipped and powerfully embodies the traditional Indian notions of *dharma* or righteousness. Sita is the model wife, who is worshipped as Lakshmi.

Rama was perhaps a tribal hero of ancient India. The story of the defeat of Ravana may also reflect the colonization of Sri Lanka by Indians of Aryan speech. His story is told briefly in the 'Forest Chapter' of the Mahabharata and at great length in India's other famous epic, the *Ramayana*, which the poet Valmiki composed in about 300 BCE, although additional material may have been added. There are some 24,000 couplets divided into seven books.

The poem tells of Rama's royal birth in the kingdom of Ayodhya (Oudh) and of his childhood during which he was tutored by Visvamitra. By managing to bend Shiva's mighty bow, he was successful in the bridegroom tournament of Sita, the daughter of King Janaka and thereby won her as his wife. As the result of a court intrigue he was deprived of his position as heir and was banished for fourteen years to a forest, accompanied there by his faithful wife Sita and his favourite half brother, Lakshmana.

One day, when her guards were busy chasing a deer, Sita was abducted by Ravana, the demon king of Lanka. Sita resolutely resisted Ravana's advances. Eventually with the help of his monkey friends and especially of the monkey general Hanuman, (later a god) Rama defeated and killed Ravana and rescued Sita. In some versions of the story, Rama did not believe Sita's protestations that she had remained faithful to him whilst a prisoner of Ravana. Sita therefore asked Lakshmana to build her a funeral pyre, on which she threw herself but was rescued by the gods. Even when Rama and Sita returned to Ayodhya, false rumours persisted that Sita had been unfaithful. So, although she was pregnant, Sita was again banished to the forest, where she met Valmiki, the reputed author of the *Ramayana*. It was at his hermitage that she gave birth to Rama's two sons.

When they were fifteen, Rama ordered a horse sacrifice, but the boys captured the horse when it reached their forest home. Rama attacked them, but his army was defeated by the boys. In the conflict, they came face to face. Rama was astonished at the boys' likeness to himself. Valmiki then told him that he was their father. Eventually the family was reunited and Sita was restored to favour, but by this time her heart was broken. She called upon her mother-earth, from which she had been born, to receive her and so to prove beyond doubt her devotion to her husband and her chastity.

O Lord of my being, I realize you in me and me in you. Our relationship is eternal. Through this body assumed by me, my service to you and your progeny is complete now. I dissolve this body to its original state.

Mother Earth you gave form to me. I have made use of it as I ought to. In recognition of its purity may you kindly absorb me in your womb.

As she fell to the ground, which opened to receive her, she left Ayodhya for ever.

In the epic's first and last parts, which may be later, Rama is identified as an avatar of the god Vishnu. In the rest of the work, he is regarded as the perfect man and king. Sita is the ideal wife and came to be worshipped as Lakshmi, the embodiment of beauty and the goddess of good fortune - not that Sita had much of that. And. Lakshmana is the true brother.

The Ramayana, which was written in Sanskrit, was translated into many of the languages of India - most notably into Tamil and Bengali. The story was retold in Hindi by the poet Tulsidas (1532-1623), in a work known as the *Ramcaritamanasa*, which has been called 'the Bible of North India.'

The events of the story are annually re-enacted in the Ram-Lila and Ravana's defeat is remembered during the North Indian festival by the burning of effigies of Ravana and the demons. The *Ramayana* has also inspired many artists and a serialised version on television was watched by millions.

The epic illustrates the eternal struggle of good and evil, symbolised by the battles involving the avatar of Vishnu. We can also see all the characters as part of ourself. Rama, for example, is the innate principle of goodness, Ravana is our dark side. Sita represents our devotion to the Supreme. If we lose 'our Sita', like Rama we see evil demons all around. To restore our union with the Divine, we have to kill our ego.

It is said that 'whoever reads and recites the holy, life-giving

Ramayana is freed from sin and attains heaven'. The same result is achieved by anyone who, like Gandhi, repeats the name of Rama as he or she is dying, or for a dying person by someone repeating the name of Rama in his or her ear.

CHAPTER NOTES
Tulsidas is referred to again in chapter 59

8

Moses

Moses had a unique relationship with God, who revealed to him the Ten Commandments and the Torah. He is the central figure in story of the origins of the Jewish people, whom he led from slavery in Egypt through the wilderness towards the Promised Land of Canaan. Moses has also deeply influenced Christianity, Islam and world history.

By the time Moses was born, Joseph, whom we met in chapter 2, had been forgotten and the Israelites had become slaves in Egypt, labouring on the building projects of the Pharaohs. Because the Israelite population was growing too rapidly and might pose a threat to the Egyptians, Pharaoh ordered that every Hebrew baby boy was to be thrown into the river Nile. Moses' mother hid her child for three months. She then made a basket, put him in it and placed him in the reeds along the bank of the Nile. There, the baby was discovered by Pharaoh's daughter. Moses' sister, Miriam, who was keeping watch, then suggested to the Princess that she could find a Hebrew woman to nurse the infant. The nurse, of course, turned out to be Moses' mother.

Later, when Moses was a child, the Princess came for him and adopted him as her son. Moses, therefore, was brought up at the court of Pharaoh, the ruler of Egypt. It is usually thought that the Pharaoh in question was Rameses II (1304-1237). The Bible says that the Hebrew slaves built Pithom and Rameses as store cities. Rameses II came to the throne less than sixty years after the death of Akhenaten (Amenhotep IV). But in that period Akhenaten's religious revolution had been reversed and a new dynasty had come to power. Yet one wonders whether some memory of Akhenaten's worship of Aten may have helped prepare Moses for the revelation he was to receive.

As a grown man, Moses was troubled to watch the oppressive labour required of his fellow Israelites. When he saw an Egyptian beating a Hebrew, he killed the Egyptian and hid his body in the sand. But when the next day he tried to stop two Hebrews from fighting each other, one of them said, 'Are you thinking of killing me as you killed the Egyptian?'[1] Realising that what he had done was known and that Pharaoh wanted to kill him, Moses fled from Egypt and went to live in

Midian, which may be the area to the east of the Gulf of Aqaba. Midian was the son of Abraham by Keturah, one of the women he married after the death of Sarah.[2] So Jethro the priest, whose daughter Moses married, was perhaps a distant relation and perhaps worshipped Abraham's God.

One day, while Moses was looking after his father-in-law's sheep, he saw a bush on fire, but that the fire did not burn it up. St Catherine's monastery in Sinai is said to have been built at the place where this happened. Moses went to have a closer look. He then heard the Lord calling him and saying, 'I am the God of your father, and the God of Abraham, the God of Isaac and the God of Jacob.'[3] God commanded a reluctant Moses to go back to Egypt, to liberate the Jews (the children of Israel), and to lead them to the Promised Land of Canaan.

Pharaoh refused to let the Israelites go, despite plagues of increasing severity. Only after ten plagues had befallen the Egyptians, was Pharaoh at last willing to let the Jews leave – their departure is known as the Exodus. Even after they had left, Pharaoh with his chariots chased after them. Miraculously – or perhaps there was a strong wind - Moses led his people across the Red (or Reed) Sea on dry land, but the waters engulfed and drowned the pursuing army.

There is considerable questioning about the route that the fleeing Israelites followed. The traditional, although disputed view, is that they at first followed the coast of the Gulf of Suez and then made their way to the foot of Mt Sinai, although sometimes the mountain is called Horeb. Moses climbed this imposing mountain more than once and received from God the Ten Commandments and the Law (*Torah*). It was on this mountain, too, that God spoke to Moses 'face to face.'

The Israelites soon wearied of the desert and dreamed of the flesh-pots of Egypt. Even though God fed them with manna from heaven and quails, they grumbled and were rebellious. God therefore decided that the generation, which came out of Egypt, would not enter the Promised Land. Instead the children of Israel spent forty years in the wilderness. Moses himself was only allowed to see Canaan from afar from the top of Mount Nebo, which is now in Jordan. It was Joshua who was to lead the people across the Jordan to start occupying the land of Canaan.

Moses is important in many ways. He was one of the first people to describe an overwhelming awe-inspiring or 'numinous' experience of the reality of God, who transcends any image or language. When Moses asked God his Name, God replied, in words of which the meaning is still debated, 'I am who I am' or 'I will be what I will be.' The Divine is not an object to be described but known only in a living relationship. Suggested translations include 'I will be what tomorrow demands' – that is to say 'God is capable of responding to human need', or 'I will be what I want to be' – emphasizing God's freedom. Moses, in the Christian tradition is sometimes seen as a mystic who guides the believer to the mountaintop on which God is to be encountered, as for example in the *Life of Moses* by the Cappadocian theologian Gregory of Nyssa (c.335-95).

It was to Moses that God gave the Torah, which is often translated 'Law', but 'Teaching' is more accurate – the meaning is similar to the Hindu word *dharma*. It included instructions for how the individual should behave and how the life of a community should be regulated. It also prescribed the worship God required.

The Torah – the word is used in several rather different senses - consists of the first five books of the Bible – often known as 'the Five Books of Moses' or the Pentateuch. Jews do not use the term 'Old Testament' as it implies a new testament. Quite often people today speak of the Hebrew Scriptures. Orthodox Jews believe that the Torah is the word of God, given by direct inspiration. Some rabbis taught that the Torah was in existence before the creation of the world. Indeed Rabbi Akiva (c.50-135 CE) said the Torah was 'the precious instrument by which the world was created.' Reform Jews assume that 'the Torah is a book which had its origin in the hearts and minds of the Jewish people.'[4] 'It is ancient Israel's distinctive record of its search for God.' [5] Critical scholars argue about what, if anything, in the Pentateuch actually comes from the time of Moses.

In addition to the written Torah, Orthodox Jews also ascribe to Moses the oral law, which is the traditional rabbinic teaching of how the written law was to be interpreted. Their view is that God made known to Moses all that what was required of the chosen people, who were to express their thankfulness to God for rescuing them from slavery by joyfully obeying his teaching. Critical scholars hold that the oral law is the repository of various traditions from different times.

Despite their differences, the Torah is still central to Jewish life, although Orthodox and Reform Jews interpret it in rather different ways. It has also profoundly influenced the legal systems of the West. Churches often used to have large copies of the Ten Commandments beside the altar and many Christians were expected to know them by heart.

The festival of Passover, according to the Bible, was instituted by Moses on God's command. Most Jewish families still come together for Passover, which is a celebration of freedom and a reaffirmation of Jewish identity. A special meal recalls the night before the Israelites fled from Egypt, during which the first born of the Egyptians were struck down, but the Israelites were spared. In their hurry to depart, the Israelites were told to eat roasted lamb and unleavened bread, the 'bread of affliction', which is still eaten at a Passover meal today. Christians, in the Easter Vigil, see the deliverance of the Israelites from Egypt as foreshadowing the release 'from the tyranny of sin and death' achieved by the death and resurrection of Jesus Christ.

Passover is often called the festival of freedom. The phrase 'Let my people go' has been emphasised by Liberation theologians, who stress that God is on the side of the poor and downtrodden. There is a Jewish mystical saying that 'We should also pray for the wicked peoples of the world; we should love them too. As long as we do not pray in this way, as long as we do not love in this way, the Messiah, who will bring an era of peace and justice, will not come.'

The rabbis usually spoke of Moses as 'Mosheh Rabbenu' or 'Moses, our Master.' They did not disguise his faults, such as his quick temper. This was to discourage the development of a personality cult. Moses, it was said, did go up to meet God, but he stopped when he was ten hand breadths from heaven – thus maintaining the distinction between the human and the divine. Several traditions extolled Moses' learning, but there is a well-known passage in which Moses listens to one of the greatest rabbis, Rabbi Akiva, teaching the Torah, but is unable to understand the rabbi's creative interpretations. When asked, Rabbi Akiva replied 'this is a teaching that was given to Moses on Mount Sinai.' The story is usually taken as underlining the massive development of the oral tradition, which is nonetheless seen only as drawing out what is implied in the written Torah, which was given to Moses.

In the New Testament, Moses appears to Jesus on the Mount of

Transfiguration. Jesus' miracle of the 'Feeding of the Five Thousand' is compared to the manna or 'bread from heaven' which God gave to the Israelites in the desert. Matthew, in his account of the 'Sermon on the Mount' may intend to present Jesus, like Moses, as a Law-giver, and he quotes Jesus as saying, 'Do not think that I have come to abolish the Law or the Prophets; I have not come to abolish them but to fulfil them.'

In Islam, Moses is known as Musa, because he was rescued from water in a basket made from a tree. He is called both a prophet and a messenger, who brought a scripture to his people. Sometimes he is seen as foreshadowing the career of Muhammad who was a messenger from God, a lawgiver and the leader of a community. The Qur'anic account of Moses' life and work is in some details different from that in the Bible. The few references to the Exodus are more concerned with the punishment of Pharaoh for his refusal to listen to God's message than with the escape of the Israelites.

The Bible says that there has never been a prophet like Moses, 'whom the Lord knew face to face' and that no one has ever performed such miraculous signs and wonders.[6] It also says that 'Moses was a very humble man, more humble than anyone else on earth.'[7] Moses, however, who was known for his humility, would not have wanted such praise for himself. As he sang after the rescue from the Red Sea,

'The Lord is my strength and my song;
He has become my salvation.
He is My God and I will praise Him,
My Father's God and I will exalt him.'[8]

CHAPTER NOTES

1. Exodus 2,11ff.
2. Genesis 25,1-4.
3. Genesis 3,6.
4. W. Gunther Plaut, *The Torah: A Modern Commentary*, p. xviii.
5. Plaut, p. xix.
6. Deuteronomy, 34,10-12.
7. Numbers, 12,3.
8. Exodus 15,2.

9

David

King David, the second ruler of Israel, came to be regarded, despite his faults, as 'the shepherd of his people.'[1] Jews through the centuries have traditionally hoped that the Messiah would restore the kingdom of David. Christians claim that Jesus was of the lineage of David and was born in 'David's city' – Bethlehem. Muslims also hold David in high esteem. The Psalms, attributed to David, have nourished the spiritual life of innumerable Jews and Christians through the centuries.

David was the second king of Israel, succeeding King Saul. God, as we have seen, rescued the Israelites from Egypt. They were guided by Moses, through the wilderness, towards the 'Promised Land' of Canaan. It was, however, his successor Joshua who led the people across the river Jordan. The first city that they captured was Jericho, one of the most ancient cities in the world. Gradually the Israelites extended the territory under their control. They came into frequent conflict with people who already inhabited the land and, a little later, with the Philistines who, from about 1200 BCE, settled along the costal plain of Canaan. From time to time, charismatic leaders, such as Gideon or Samson, known as 'judges' or 'seers,' enabled the Israelites to get the upper hand. The last of the judges was Samuel, who reluctantly gave into the people's demand that he should appoint a king, so that 'we shall be like all the other nations, with a king to lead us and to go out before us and to fight our battles.'[2]

The first king Saul initially was successful, but, because he disobeyed God's instruction, Samuel warned him that his sons would not inherit the kingdom. Secretly, Samuel then went to Bethlehem and invited Jesse to meet him and present his sons to him. Not one of them, however, was 'the chosen of the Lord.' Samuel asked Jesse if he had any more sons. 'Yes,' he replied, 'the youngest one is looking after the sheep.' This was David, who was the one chosen by God to be the king.

David soon came to the notice of King Saul when he offered to challenge in single combat the gigantic Philistine champion Goliath. David killed Goliath with a stone from his sling, which sank into the Philistine's forehead. David was brought to court and married to the king's daughter, Michal. It was with the king's son, Jonathan, however that David formed a deeper relationship. King Saul, however, who could easily fly into a rage, became jealous of David's military successes and saw him as a threat to his rule. He tried to kill David. Thanks to Jonathan's help, David escaped and fled for his life, but he was pursued by Saul. Although David had the chance to kill Saul, he refused to touch 'the Lord's anointed.' Saul was to die at his own hand after a massive defeat by the Philistines on Mount Gilboa, in which Jonathan was also killed. 'How are the mighty fallen,' David lamented when he heard the news.[3]

After Saul's death, the people of Judah soon acclaimed David as king. This took place in the city of Hebron where the patriarchs were buried. After a period of conflict with one of Saul's sons, David was also recognised as king by the tribes of Israel. Soon afterwards, David captured Jerusalem from the Jebusites, leading his men in through the water shaft. He brought the Ark of the Covenant to Jerusalem, which became the capital and the centre of both the nation's religious and its political life. Yet, although David built a royal palace, he was told by the prophet Nathan to leave the building of the temple to his son Solomon. Nonetheless, David, to whom God had promised that he would 'establish the throne of his kingdom for ever,'[4] embodied in himself both spiritual and political power, but was sensitive to the democratic traditions of the people and unlike other Near Eastern rulers did not claim himself to be divine.

Thanks to King David, Jerusalem became and has remained a 'holy city' – holy now to Jews, Christians and Muslims, whose claims, sadly, often compete. Jerusalem is a symbol of God's presence with his people now and in the age to come. For centuries Jews have ended their Passover observance with the words, 'Next year in Jerusalem.' Christian hymns often sing of Jerusalem as an image for the heavenly city. For Muslims, Jerusalem is the city from which the Prophet Muhammad set out on his mystical night journey.

Although David protected the Israelites from the Philistines and ruled for forty years, his reign was not without its troubles, as much from his own family as from external enemies. This was partly God's punishment for his adultery with Bathsheba and for then engineering the death of her husband, Uriah. The most serious trouble was from his son Absalom, who forced David to flee across the Jordan. Absalom, however, was eventually defeated and killed in battle, but instead of rejoicing in the victory and praising his loyal followers, David lamented the death of his rebel son:

'O my son Absalom! My son, my son Absalom!
If only I had died instead of you –
O Absalom, my son, my son.'[5]

Clearly David was a person of deep feeling, shown also when he heard of the death of Jonathan, of whom he said,

'I grieve for you, Jonathan my brother,
You were very dear to me.
Your love was wonderful
More wonderful than that of women.'[6]

The same deep feeling is shown in the Psalms, which have traditionally been referred to as the Psalms of David. The Hebrew probably means that the Psalms were written 'by David,' although it has been suggested that they were written by others for David.

It is clear that not all the Psalms were written by David. The headings were added later but many of them are found in ancient Hebrew manuscripts - although not always in modern English translations. They indicate the occasion on which a psalm was written and they link a number of psalms with King David. Other psalms are attributed in the headings to The Sons of Korah, who were members of a priestly family, to Asaph, who was one of the people whom David put in charge of the music, and to David's son King Solomon. At the end of Psalm 72 there is a note that 'The Psalms of David are ended', although a number of later Psalms are said to be by him. Probably the order in which the Psalms have reached us has changed over the centuries.

Critical scholars in the early twentieth century denied that David had any hand in the writing of the Psalms, but this view is now regarded as not proven. Archaeologists have provided us with a rich treasure store of religious songs from many parts of the Ancient Near East. C. S Rodd's conclusion that 'as nothing is known about David outside the Hebrew Bible, there is no way of determining whether he wrote any of the Psalms' is judicious.[7] Yet David was known as a musician and in one account it was his skill with the lyre that first brought him to King Saul's attention. The sudden changes of mood seem to fit his volatile personality. Some psalms express a deep longing for God's mercy:

> O Lord, do not rebuke me in your anger,
> Or discipline me in your wrath.
> Be merciful to me, Lord, for I am faint;
> O Lord, heal me, for my bones are in agony...
> I am worn out from my groaning,
> All night long I flood my bed with weeping
> And drench my couch with tears.[8]

In other Psalms he expresses his fear of the enemy and often he voices his praise of God for his deliverance.

> I will praise you, O Lord, with all my heart;
> I will tell of all your wonders,
> I will be glad and rejoice in you,
> I will sing praise to your name, O Most High.
> My enemies turn back,
> For they stumble and perish before you
> For you have upheld my right and my cause,
> You have sat on your throne
> Judging righteously. [9]

The Psalms have had a deep influence on Judaism and Christianity. The Rabbinic Midrash to the Psalms states that David composed them in five books just as Moses wrote the Pentateuch – the first five books of the Bible. Many psalms have been incorporated into the liturgy of the synagogue. The Daily Prayer Book provides a psalm for each day of the week.

The authors of the New Testament often refer to the Psalms and Jesus died with the opening words of Psalm 22 on his lips, 'My God, my God, why have you forsaken me?'[10] They also traditionally have had a central place in the worship of the Church and especially in the daily offices of monastic communities. Many well-known hymns, such as 'The Lord's my Shepherd' or 'All people that on earth do dwell', are based on a Psalm.[11]

Ambrose (c.339-97), Bishop of Milan and one of the four original doctors of the Church, wrote,

'A psalm is the prayer of praise of the people of God, the exaltation of the Lord, the joyful song of the congregation, the cry of all humanity, the applause of the universe, the voice of the Church, the sweet sounding confession of faith, entire surrender to divine power, blessed freedom, a cry of happiness, an echo of joy. A psalm softens wrath, relieves care and lightens sorrow. It is a weapon at night, teaching in the day, a shield in fear, a festival celebration in holiness, an image of quietness, the pledge of peace and harmony. The psalm arises at day's beginning and is still sounding at day's end.'[12]

Whoever wrote the Psalms certainly provided us with beacons of light. But a Rabbinic Midrash warns against conceit.

'When King David had completed the Book of Psalms he felt very proud and said, "Lord of the universe, have You a creature that proclaims more praises of You than I?" So God sent him a frog which said, "David don't be so proud of yourself. I chant the praises of my Creator more than you do. Moreover, I perform a great virtue that when my time comes to die, I go down to the sea and allow myself to be swallowed up by one of its creatures. So, even my death is an act of kindness.' [13]

A verse in the Qur'an, more positively, says, in David 'We recruited to our praise the very mountains at the fall of day and at the sun-rising, and the birds also mustering in flight, each echoing his song.'[14]

David was very old when he died. He was succeeded by King Solomon, who was famous for his wisdom and his many wives. Under Solomon's son, the Kingdom split into two – Israel in the North and Judah in the South. Increasingly both countries became pawns in the struggles of the great powers. The capital of the Northern Kingdom, Samaria, was captured and destroyed in 722 BCE by the Assyrians.

Many of the people were deported – one Assyrian record gives the number as 27,290 people. People from other parts of the Empire settled in the North.

Judah, as we shall see, struggled on until early in the fifth century, when in 597 the city, as the prophet Jeremiah had foreseen, surrendered to the Babylonians. A puppet king was appointed, but when he rebelled, the city was again attacked and the temple destroyed. All but the poorest people were taken into exile in Babylon.

Amidst all their troubles, the Jewish people hoped and prayed that one day they would have another king like David, who 'shepherded his people with integrity of heart and led them with skilful hands.' [15]

CHAPTER NOTES

1. Psalm 78,69.
2. I Samuel 8,20.
3. II Samuel 1,27.
4. II Samuel 7, 14.
5. II Samuel 18, 33.
6. II Samuel 1, 26.
7. C.S Rodd in *The Oxford Bible Commentary*, p. 359.
8. Psalm 6,1-2 and 6.
9. Psalm 9,1-2.
10. Psalm 22,1.
11. Psalm 23 and Psalm 100.
12. Ambrose, *Explanatio Psalmi* 1, quoted in *The International Bible Commentary*, Collegeville, Minnesota, The Liturgical Press, 1998, p. 779.
13. Quoted by Jonathan Magonet, *A Rabbi Reads the Psalms*, London, SCM Press, 1994, p. 1.
14. Surah 38,17.
15. Psalm 78,72.

10

Isaiah

Isaiah was one of the four great prophets of Israel. The collection of prophecies runs to over sixty chapters, but probably includes the oracles of several people. The prophecies of Isaiah are regularly read in Synagogues. Many passages from the book of Isaiah are also well known to Christians, who sometimes see in them predictions of the coming of Christ.

Isaiah vividly described his call to be a prophet. He was in the Temple in Jerusalem when he had this vision:

'I saw the Lord, seated on a throne, high and exalted, and the train of his robe filled the temple. Above him were seraphs, each with six wings: With two wings, they covered their faces, with two they covered their feet, and with two they were flying. And they were calling to one another:
Holy, holy, holy, is the Lord Almighty;
The whole earth is full of his glory.

Isaiah was overwhelmed with a sense of his sinfulness. 'Woe to me! I am ruined. For I am a man of unclean lips and I live among a people of unclean lips and my eyes have seen the King, the Lord Almighty.' Then one of the seraphs touched his lips with a burning coal and told him, 'Your guilt is taken away and your sin atoned for.' He then heard the Lord tell him to go and convey his message to the people.[1]

Isaiah said that his vision occurred in the year that King Uzziah died. This was in about 742 BCE, when Uzziah, who suffered from leprosy, was succeeded by his son Jotham. We know little about Isaiah's life prior to the decisive vision. His father's name was Amoz, who should not be confused with the Biblical prophet Amos. Isaiah had two sons, who were given names, which reinforced Isaiah's prophetic message. It has been suggested that he had connections with the royal family or that he was of a priestly family, but there is no real evidence for either conjecture. His prophecies show a wide experience of people of different classes and occupations.

We know rather more about the historical background. The seventh century BCE was dominated by the expansion of the Assyrian empire into Palestine, especially after Tiglath-pileser came to power in 745 BCE. The kingdom of Aram, with Damascus as its capital, and Israel, the Northern Kingdom, with its capital at Samaria, with some backing from Egypt entered into a coalition to resist the invader. They tried to coerce the southern kingdom of Judah, which was now ruled by Ahaz (735-726), into supporting them. Isaiah encouraged Ahaz to refuse, telling him, 'keep calm and don't be afraid. Do not lose heart because of these two smouldering stubs of firewood.'[2] The armies of Aram and Israel proved unable to overpower Jerusalem. Before long, as Isaiah warned, Samaria was captured and destroyed and its people taken into captivity. Ahaz managed to buy off the Assyrians by paying tribute and by setting up an altar to Assyrian gods in the Temple – much to Isaiah's disgust.

Hezekiah, when he became king in 716, took note of the prophet's protests and tried to brake away from Assyria. He also introduced a number of reforms aimed at restoring the purity of the Jewish religion. In 705 BCE, when Sennacherib, who had just become the Assyrian ruler, was faced by a major rebellion. Hezekiah stopped the payments of tribute. Aware that this was a risky policy, Hezekiah strengthened the country's defences, extended the walls of Jerusalem and ensured that Jerusalem's water supply would be protected in the event of a siege by building a tunnel known as 'Hezekiah's tunnel.' During this work Hezekiah fell ill and was warned by Isaiah that he was about to die. Hezekiah wept bitterly and prayed to God, who then told the prophet to reassure Hezekiah that he would live for another fifteen years and that God would defend Jerusalem from the Assyrian attack.

In 701, Sennacherib attacked. His armies swept through Phoenicia and seized the Philistine cities of Ashkelon and Ekron. He then attacked Lachish, which was a key stronghold. We have a good picture of the siege of Lachish from a large wall relief, which has been excavated from Sennacherib's palace in Nineveh. It shows defenders shooting arrows and hurling stones and flaming torches at the attackers. It also shows the battering rams used by the Assyrians to break down the walls. The fate of the defeated is also shown. Many were led away into captivity and others were impaled on stakes.

Sennacherib then turned his full fury on Jerusalem. He demanded enormous tribute, which could only be provided by stripping the gold from the temple. As the situation became more desperate, Hezekiah put on sackcloth, and went to the Temple to pray for God's help:

'O Lord Almighty, God of Israel... You have made heaven and earth. Give ear, O Lord, and hear... Listen to all the words Sennacherib has sent to insult the living God. It is true, O Lord, that the Assyrian kings have laid waste all these peoples and their lands. They have thrown their gods into the fire. Now, O Lord our God, deliver us from his hand, so that all kingdoms on earth may know that you alone, O Lord, are God.'[3]

Isaiah was sent to reassure the king.
'Therefore this is what the Lord says concerning the king of Assyria:

"He will not enter this city
Or shoot the arrow here.
He will not come before it with shield
Or build a siege ramp against it.
By the way he came he will return;
He will not enter this city" declares the Lord.
"I will defend this city and save it,
for my sake and for the sake of
David my servant."'[4]

We are then told, that 'the angel of the Lord went out and put to death a hundred and eighty-five thousand men in the Assyrian camp. When the people got up the next morning – they were all dead bodies. So Sennacherib king of Assyria broke camp and withdrew.'[5] Why, we do not know for sure. Was it a plague? Possibly, or maybe Sennacherib faced a further serious revolt in Babylon.

Hezekiah's final years were peaceful, but Isaiah warned him that the destruction of Jerusalem was inevitable, but not in his lifetime. 'The time will surely come when everything in your palace, and all that your fathers have stored up until this day will be carried off to Babylon. Nothing will be left, says the Lord. And some of your descendants, your own flesh and blood who will be born to you, will be taken away, and they will become eunuchs in the palace of the king of Babylon.' Hezekiah was relieved, however, that there was to be peace and security in his lifetime.[6]

The destruction of Jerusalem was not to take place for another century. The Jews were then taken into exile in Babylon, but soon after the Persian king Cyrus came to power in 539 BCE, the Jews were allowed to return to Jerusalem and Judah. Isaiah chapter 45 refers to this, but obviously the Isaiah, whose call to be a prophet was in 742 BCE, could not have been alive then. In the past, people often thought of prophets as being able to foresee the future, even centuries ahead. Today, it is usually assumed that their message was for their own day.

The dominant view of critical Biblical scholarship, therefore, has been that the book of Isaiah contains the work of at least two prophets. Partly this is because of the historical references, partly because of different styles of writing and vocabulary. Moreover there are significant differences in the prophetic messages. Chapter 40 begins with a message of hope for Jerusalem:

'Comfort, comfort, my people,
says your God.
Speak tenderly to Jerusalem
And proclaim to her,
That her hard service has been completed.'

Chapter 52 speaks of a restored Jerusalem, saying, 'Rise up, sit enthroned, O Jerusalem.'

The book, therefore, is often divided into two or three parts. Chapters 1 to 39 are considered to be mainly the work of First Isaiah, who lived in the eighth century. These chapters warn of judgment on Israel and on the nations, but there is also a message of hope that one day, 'A king will reign in righteousness and rulers will rule with justice.'[7] Chapters 40 to 55 are ascribed to an anonymous Deutero-Isaiah or Second Isaiah. They speak of the imminent deliverance of the Jews from exile and include the famous passages about the 'Servant of the Lord.' The final chapters, 56-66, seem to have a Palestinian background. They are sometimes said to be the work of Third Isaiah, but there is too little unity of theme or style to suggest that these final oracles were proclaimed by a single person.

Yet despite the arguments of Biblical critics, the most ancient sources witness to the unity of the book. For example, the Apocryphal Book of Ecclesiasticus, which dates from the second century BCE, refers to Isaiah in an eighth century context,[8] but also speaks of him foreseeing 'what should come to pass at the last' and comforting 'them that mourned in Sion.'[9] The earliest scrolls of Isaiah found among the Qumran Dead Sea Scrolls show no sign of division between chapters 39 and 40.

More recently, many scholars have emphasised that the book should be read as a whole. Some scholars picture an Isaiah tradition or school of prophets. They refer to a verse in which the Lord told Isaiah to

'Bind up the testimony
and seal up the law among my disciples.'[10]

Other scholars who take what may be called a literary approach suggest that the book, like other pieces of literature, should be read as a whole. It is more important to appreciate the message of the book than to speculate about who wrote particular passages.

Certainly, the book has been much read and treasured over the centuries. There are nineteen copies of it among the Dead Sea Scrolls – one of which has pride of place at the Shrine of the Book in Jerusalem. It is also often quoted in the writings of the Essenes. Many Jewish commentaries were written over the centuries. Christians also soon wrote commentaries. One by the early Church father St Hippolytus (c.170-c.236) survives.

For Christians, the Book of Isaiah had a vital role in helping to prove their claim that Jesus was the Messiah or Christ foretold by the prophets. Particular attention was given to Isaiah's message to King Ahaz that 'The Lord Himself shall give you a sign. Behold, a virgin shall conceive and bear a son, and shall call his name Immanuel. Butter and honey shall he eat, that he may know to refuse evil, and choose good.'[11] Matthew, in his account of the birth Jesus, makes specific reference to this verse.[12] In the Greek Septuagint translation of the Hebrew Scriptures, the word for the mother is *parthenos*, which means 'virgin.' In the Hebrew original the word is '*almāh*', which means young woman. Christians still often read other passages from Isaiah at Carol Services, as pointing forward to the coming of Christ. For example:

'The people that walked in darkness have seen a great light... For unto us a child is born, unto us a son is given: and the government shall be upon his shoulder: and his name shall be called Wonderful, Counsellor, The mighty God, The everlasting Father, the Prince of Peace. Of the increase of his government and peace there shall be no end, upon the throne of David, and upon his kingdom, to order it and establish it with judgment and justice from henceforth even for ever. The zeal of the Lord of hosts will perform this.'[13]

Incidentally, the tradition that there was an ox and a donkey in the stable where Jesus was born is based on the verse in Isaiah, which says:

'The ox knows his master,
the donkey his owner's manger.'[14]

Christians have also often interpreted the ministry and death of Jesus in the light of the passages in Isaiah about the Servant of the Lord and it may be that these verses shaped Jesus' own self-understanding of his vocation.

'Before I was born the Lord called me' the Servant declares, 'from my birth he has made mention of my name.'[15] The Servant of the Lord was called to 'be a covenant for the people and a light for the Gentiles.'[16] But the Servant also had to endure terrible suffering:

'He was despised and rejected by men,
a man of sorrows and familiar with suffering.
Like one from whom men hide their faces
He was despised and we esteemed him not.
Surely he took our infirmities
      And carried our sorrows...
He was pierced for our transgressions
He was crushed for our iniquities.'

Yet all this was the Lord's will, although in the end the Servant would be vindicated:

'It was the Lord's will to crush him and cause him to suffer...
But I will give him a portion among the great
And he will divide the spoils with the strong.'[17]

'Who is the prophet talking about, himself or someone else?' asked an Ethiopian eunuch, who was a high treasury official of the Candace, the Queen of Ethiopia. The Ethiopian had gone to Jerusalem to worship. On his way home as he sat in his chariot, he was reading the scriptures. The Ethiopian was joined by Philip, who was a deacon of the Early Jerusalem Church. Philip explained that the Servant, whom the prophet had predicted, was Jesus. This has been the usual Christian interpretation. Jews, however, usually see the Servant as a collective figure, who is a symbol for Israel, which has been exposed to persecution and suffering through the centuries and which is called to be a 'light to the Gentiles.'

Incidentally, there is an apocryphal book, called the *Ascension of Isaiah*, which says that Isaiah was martyred, by being sawn into pieces on the orders of King Manasseh, and then ascended to heaven. The complete work only survives in Ethiopic – an ancient Semitic language, which is still used in the liturgy by Ethiopian Christians - and probably dates from the end of the first century CE. The book is not considered to have any historical value.

Despite these disagreements, Jews and Christians, as well as other people of good will, can take hope from Isaiah's vision that the day will come when the peoples

'will beat their swords into ploughshares
and their spears into pruning hooks.
Nation will not take up sword against nation,
Nor will they train for war any more.'[18]
And his confidence that one day
'The wolf will live with the lamb,
the leopard will lie down with goat,
the calf and the lion and the yearling together

and a little child with lead them...

They will neither harm nor destroy
On all my holy mountain,
For the earth will be full
of the knowledge of the Lord
as the waters cover the sea.'[19]

CHAPTER NOTES
1. Isaiah, 6,1-9.
2. Isaiah 7,4.
3. Isaiah, 37,15-20.
4. Isaiah, 37,33-35.
5. Isaiah, 37,36-7. See also II Kings, 19,35.
6. Isaiah, 38,6.
7. Isaiah, 32,1.
8. Isaiah, 48,20.
9. Ecclesiasticus 48,24.
10. Isaiah, 8,16. The meaning of the verse is disputed.
11. Isaiah 7,14-15.
12. Matthew 1,22-3.
13. Isaiah 9,2 and 6-7.
14. Isaiah 1,3.
15. Isaiah, 49,1.
16. Isaiah, 42,6.
17. Isaiah, 53.
18. Isaiah 2,4.
19. Isaiah, 11,6 and 9.

11

Jeremiah

Jeremiah has been called 'the father of personal religion,' who spoke of a time when God's law would be written on peoples' hearts. He was one of the four major Biblical prophets. The others were Isaiah, Ezekiel and Daniel. There is much biographical information about Jeremiah in the book that bears his name. Its accuracy is sometimes questioned and it has been argued that Jeremiah is a literary figure created to link the diverse material rather than a historical character.[1] Be that as it may, the story of Jeremiah's suffering and courageous witness is full of drama and inspiration.

Jeremiah lived at a time of great change in the Ancient Near East. The kingdom of Israel, as we have seen, had been at its height under David and his son Solomon, who built the first temple. After Solomon's death, the kingdom split into two states: Israel in the north and Judah, centred on the city of Jerusalem, in the south. The Northern State succumbed to the Assyrians in 722 BCE.

The Assyrians also threatened the southern state, but Judah survived and when Assyrian power waned in the middle of the seventh century, Judah, under King Josiah (640-609) reasserted its independence. Towards the end of the century, the Babylonians and Medes, led by Nebuchadnezzar (c.630-562) captured and destroyed the Assyrian capital city of Nineveh in 612. Judah was now caught up in a power struggle between the Babylonians and the Egyptians, who during the 26th Dynasty, had a short-lived resurgence of power.

This was the context for Jeremiah's prophetic ministry. Jeremiah was born in a small village just North-east of Jerusalem, called Anathoth. His father was a hereditary village priest. Throughout his life, Jeremiah recalled the images and experiences of his childhood. He had a love for the natural world and spoke of the migration of birds and the nesting habits of the partridge. He used images of the almond tree putting forth its blossom and the farmer clearing his ground to illustrate God's actions.

Jeremiah's call to be a prophet is often dated to 627 – the thirteenth year of King Josiah's reign. The word of the Lord came to him, saying,

'Before I formed you in the womb I knew you,
before you were born I set you apart;
I appointed you as a prophet to the nations.'

Jeremiah was horrified at the call, protesting, 'I do not know how to speak; I am only a child.' Then the Lord touched his mouth saying, 'I put my words in your mouth.'[2]

Jeremiah's early message was a condemnation of false worship and social injustice and a call to repentance. Quite soon in 621, during building work to repair the temple, a book was discovered - possibly parts of Deuteronomy. On reading this, King Josiah instituted far-reaching religious reforms. These seem to have found some favour with Jeremiah who was told by God to urge the people to obey the covenant. Even so, Jeremiah complained that the reforms dealt too much with the externals of religion and not enough with the inner spirit and the need for upright behaviour.

When Josiah died in 609, he was succeeded by his son Jehoiakim, whose selfish policies, which were denounced by Jeremiah, encouraged materialism and social injustice. The political situation was also becoming more perilous. King Jehoiakim hoped Egyptian power would deter the Babylonians from attacking his kingdom. But at the battle of Carchemish in 605, the Babylonians decisively defeated the Egyptians. Jeremiah delivered oracles against Egypt. He also dictated to his scribe Baruch prophecies of the impending disaster that would fall upon Judah. After Baruch had read the scroll in the Temple, officials warned him and Jeremiah to go into hiding. The scroll was then read to the king, 'who was sitting in the winter apartment with a fire burning in the brazier in front of him. Whenever Jehudi had read three or four columns from the scroll the king cut them off with a scribe's knife and threw them into the brazier until the entire scroll was burned in the fire. The king and all his attendants who heard these words showed no fear.'[3]

When in 601, Jehoiakim withheld tribute from Babylon, Jeremiah again warned the Judeans of the destruction that would follow. Nebuchadnezzar did indeed send an army to lay siege to the city, although by that time Jehoiakim had died and been succeeded by his son Jehoiachin. The city fell on March 16th, 597. The king and the leading citizens were deported to Babylon.

The Babylonians now made Zedekiah (597-586) king. He was a weak ruler, who could not decide between the pro-Babylonian and pro-Egyptian factions at court. At one point, when the Babylonian armies had temporarily withdrawn for besieging Jerusalem because of a nearby Egyptian army, Jeremiah set out from the city to see to some property nearby, but was arrested and accused of deserting to the Babylonians. 'That's not true!' Jeremiah protested, but in vain.[4] He was beaten, imprisoned and put in a dungeon.

After a long time, King Zedekiah sent for him and asked him, privately, if there was any word from the Lord. 'Yes, you will be handed over to the king of Babylon', Jeremiah replied.[5] Jeremiah was now placed in a guard-room and given bread each day, until the city ran out of food. Even so, Jeremiah continued to warn people of the fate that lay ahead. The officials were so angry, that they took him and flung him into a cistern, where Jeremiah sank into the mud. An Ethiopian eunuch at the court told the King what had happened. The King then sent thirty men to pull Jeremiah up from the muddy cistern and return him to the guard-room. Twice Zedekiah sent secretly for Jeremiah, whose message was that if the King surrendered, his life and the city would be spared. His advice was ignored and the city fell to Nebuchadnezzar in August 586. Its destruction is still remembered each year by Jews at the fast of Tish'ah B'-Av. Zedekiah tried to escape but was captured by the Babylonians. His sons were killed in front of him and his eyes put out. He was then taken in chains to Babylon. The city of Jerusalem was destroyed.

A recent archaeological find has made these events seem more immediate. An Assyrian cuneiform has been found which mentions Nebuchadnezzar's chief eunuch, Nebu-sharrussu-ukin, who is also mentioned by Jeremiah as Nebo-Sarasekim, 'the chief officer', who took part in the siege of Jerusalem in 587.[6]

Jeremiah was released from prison and offered safe conduct to Babylon. He refused and preferred to stay in the land, being put under the protection of Gedaliah, a prominent Judaean, who had been appointed governor by the Babylonians. Jeremiah continued to oppose those Jews who wanted to rebel against the Babylonians. Some of them assassinated Gedaliah and then forced Jeremiah to come with them to

Egypt. Even there he warned his fellow exiles. There is an extra-biblical tradition that Jeremiah was eventually stoned by his exasperated fellow citizens. Whether or not this is true, it is probable that he died in Egypt in about 570 BCE.

Although Jeremiah called for repentance and warned of impending doom, he prophesied that after seventy years the exiles would return to Jerusalem. Meanwhile, he advised them to make themselves at home in their new country. 'Build houses', he wrote, 'and settle down: plant gardens and eat what they produce. Marry and have sons and daughters... Also seek the peace and prosperity of the city to which I have carried you into exile. Pray to the Lord for it, because if it prospers, you too will prosper.' This advice has been heeded through the centuries by Jewish people, who have settled in so many different parts of the world. Babylon itself did become for many generations an important centre of Jewish life.

Jeremiah recognised that although God was a God of judgment, he was also a God of mercy.

'For I will forgive their wickedness
and will remember their sins no more.'[7]

He also held out the hope that in due course the Lord would bring them back to the Land of Promise.

'Do not fear, O Jacob, my servant
Do not be dismayed, O Israel.
I will surely save you out of a distant place,
and your descendants from the land of their exile.'[8]

This prophecy came true when the Persian king Cyrus, who defeated the Babylonians and captured the great city of Babylon in 539 BCE, allowed the exiles to return home. The people of Israel, God promised, 'will never cease to be a nation before me.'[9]

The Book of Jeremiah tells not only of the prophet's physical sufferings but also of his doubts and inner conflicts. Isolated and aware of the plots against him, he asked, 'Why does the way of the wicked prosper?'[10] He wished he had never been born.[11] He prayed to the Lord,

Heal me, O Lord, and I shall be healed,
Save me and I shall be saved,
For you are the one I praise.[12]

Later, he acknowledged that God had heard him,

Sing to the Lord!
Give praise to the Lord!
He rescues the life of the needy
From the hands of the wicked.[13]

Jeremiah longed for people to share his intimate relationship with God. This is why he was critical of external religious observance and called people to a life of holiness. He looked forward to the day when God would make an inner covenant with his people.

'"This is the covenant that I will make with the house of Israel after that time," declares the Lord, "I will put their law in my minds and I will write it on their hearts. I will be their God and they will be my people. No longer will a man teach his neighbour, or a man his brother saying, 'Know the Lord', because they will all know me, from the least of them to the greatest," declares the Lord.'[14]

The early Church believed that this promise was fulfilled in the death and resurrection of Jesus. Paul, in what is probably the earliest account of the Last Supper, writes, 'For I received from the Lord what I also passed on to you: The Lord Jesus on the night he was betrayed, took bread, and when he had given thanks, he broke it and said, "This is my body, which is for you, do this in remembrance of me". In the same way, after supper he took the cup, saying, "This cup is the new covenant in my blood; do this, whenever you drink it, in remembrance of me.'[15] In his Second Letter to the Corinthians, Paul speaks of the new covenant in Christ as a covenant of the Spirit.[16] In the Letter to the Hebrews, Jeremiah's words about a new covenant are quoted in full.[17]

There are other references to Jeremiah in the New Testament and several of the Church Fathers refer to him. The great Alexandrian theologian Origen (c.185 -254) saw Jeremiah's life as a foreshadowing of the life of Jesus. Christians, however, in claiming that the promise of a new covenant of which Jeremiah spoke was fulfilled by Jesus need to remember that the prophet also spoke of God's unfailing care for the people of Israel, who 'will never cease to be a nation before me.'[18]

The story of Jeremiah' suffering and courageous witness as well as his prophecies continue to influence both Church and Synagogue even today.

CHAPTER NOTES

1. See the Commentary on Jeremiah by Kathleen M. O'Connor in *The Oxford Bible Commentary*, pp. 448-9.
2. Jeremiah 1,4-9. (New International Version).
3. Jeremiah 36,22-24.
4. Jeremiah 37,14.
5. Jeremiah 37,17.
6. Jeremiah 39,3.
7. Jeremiah, 31,34.
8. Jeremiah, 46,27.
9. Jeremiah, 31,36.
10. Jeremiah, 12,1.
11. Jeremiah, 15,10.
12. Jeremiah, 17,14.
13. Jeremiah 20,13.
14. Jeremiah 31,34.
15. I Corinthians 11,23-25.
16. II Corinthians 3,6.
17. Hebrews, 8,8-12.
18. Jeremiah 31,36.

12

Lao-tzu

Two figures have exercised a pervasive influence on China's religious, cultural and political life for nearly two and a half millennia. They are Confucius and Lao-tzu. It is difficult to know which to put first. My choice is for Lao-tzu, because of the respect that Confucius, then a young man, showed to Lao-tzu when they met and because of the continuing spiritual influence both in China and neighbouring countries and now across the world of the *Tao-te Ching*, which after the Bible, has been more often translated into Western languages than any other book. Confucianism teaches the way to a harmonious society, Taoism encourages the individual to live in harmony with Ultimate Reality (the *Tao*).

Lao-tzu is an honorific title that means 'the Old Master'. His original name was Li Erh and his appellation was Tan. According to the Chinese historian, Si-ma Qien who wrote an account of the sage's life in about 100 BCE, Lao-tzu was born in 604 BCE at a town now called Luyi in the Honan province. He was appointed to take charge of the sacred books at court.

In his old age, he is said to have met Confucius, whom Lao-tzu criticized for his pride and ambition. Confucius was so impressed by Lao-tzu that he compared him to a dragon that rises to the sky, riding on winds and clouds.

Recognising that the Chou dynasty was declining, Lao-tzu journeyed to the West. As he came to the pass which lead away from China, the guardian of the pass begged Lao-tzu to write a book for him. Lao-tzu obliged by writing quite a short book (*Tao-te Ching*) - in two sections – of five thousand characters, about the *Tao* (the Way) and *Te* (Virtue). Lao-tzu then left and, according to Si-ma Qien, 'nobody knows what has become of him.' Another story, however, says that on his death, one disciple went to console Lao-tzu's son, but was upset by the wailing of young and old men, which was so out of character with the Master's teaching. 'When the Master came', said the disciple, 'it was at the proper time: when he went away it was the simple sequence of his coming. Quiet acquiescence in what happens at its proper time and quietly submitting (to its ceasing) afford no occasion for grief or for joy.' It has been suggested that 'journeying to the West' may have been a euphemism for dying.

The accuracy of Si-ma Qien's account of the life of Lao-tzu has, of course, been disputed and some scholars have suggested that there was never such an actual person. Probably not all that is in the *Tao-te Ching* was actually written by Lao-tzu - the book as a whole dates to about 300 BCE – but this is not sufficient reason to doubt that there was a creative thinker to whose work others have added. Even so, a number of subsequent stories about him were mythological. Accounts of his miraculous birth are similar to those told about the Buddha's. It was also said that the family name was Li because the baby came to the light at the foot of a plum (*li*) tree. Mythological or not, the stories became part of the popular cult of those who revered Lao-tzu as a divine figure.

It is the remarkable and inspiring book known as the *Tao-te Ching* that ensures Lao-tzu's continuing influence. The book begins with these words:

The Tao that can be told is not the eternal Tao.
The name that can be named is not the eternal name.
The nameless is the beginning of heaven and earth.
The named is the mother of ten thousand things.
Ever desireless, one can see the mystery.
Ever desiring, one can see the manifestations.
These two spring from the same source but differ in name;
this appears as darkness.
Darkness within darkness.
The gate to all mystery.[1]

These words imply that the underlying but ineffable principle, which pervades the universe and is the origin of the cosmos, is the Tao, the Way. Human lives should conform to the rhythm of Nature. Just as Nature acts with complete spontaneity, so also human beings should behave with spontaneity and naturalness. This is not a matter of teaching, or a path in which one can be instructed, but a mystical discovery or realization of the pre-existent Reality upon which all else depends that, because it is prior to everything, cannot be named. The twelfth-century female sage Sun Bu-er described the ultimate realization in these words:

> All things finished.
> You sit still in a little niche.
> The light body rides on a violet energy,
> The tranquil nature washes in a pure pond.
> Original energy is unified, yin and yang are one;
> The spirit is the same as the universe.[2]

The disciple Chuang-tzu (c.370-286 BCE) makes this clearer in a book which bears the author's name. The Tao is the quiet spirit that pervades everything. The dualities to which we are accustomed – health and sickness, life and death, pleasure and pain, darkness and light – are our artificial creations. We should cultivate serenity or in the popular saying 'go with the flow.' The sense of balance is illustrated in the ancient symbol of *yin* and *yang*. These words, which originally referred to the dark and light side of a hill, indicate the dark, receptive 'female' aspect of life (*yin*) and the bright, assertive 'male' aspect (*yan*). Wisdom lies in recognising the ever-changing but regular and balanced patterns of life and moving in harmony with them. This wisdom is discovered through meditation and a contemplative awareness of nature. T'ai-chi, which is popular in China and increasingly also in the West, is a way of using the body to experience harmony with the rhythm of Nature.

The Taoist takes a low profile. Flowing water is a Taoist model for behaviour. Water bypasses or gently wears away obstacles rather than fruitlessly attacking them.

> Water is the softest thing on earth,
> Yet its silken gentleness
> Will easily wear away the hardest stone.
> Everyone knows this;
> Few use it in their daily lives.
> Those of Tao yield and overcome.[3]

'Wu-wei', doing nothing, is a spontaneous way of life which lacks assertion of the ego. 'Love the world as your own self, then you can truly care for all things.'[4] Such love was not confined to human beings. The disciple Lieh-zu (c.300 BCE), told the story of a man who gave a feast with a thousand dishes of meat, fish and fowl. As a sort of grace, he said, 'How kind Heaven is to the human race. It provides the five grain crops and nourishes the fish and birds for us to enjoy and use.' A twelve-year old son of one of the guests stood up and replied, 'My lord is wrong. All life is born in the same way that we are and we are all the same kind. One species is not nobler than another... Things eat each other and are then eaten, but they were not brought into being for this... After all, mosquitoes and gnats bite our skin, tigers and wolves eat our flesh. Does this mean Heaven originally created us for the sake of the mosquitoes, gnats, tigers and wolves?'[5]

It has been claimed that Taoist sympathy for nature encouraged the study of chemistry, botany, zoology and other natural sciences. The emphasis was on direct observation and experience, unlike the Confucian reliance on the authority of tradition.

Taoism is very much more than the teaching of Lao-tzu. It has served as an umbrella term for a variety of religious groups - sometimes known as *Hsien* ('Immortals').Taoism - which developed from the second century CE. Whereas the disciple Chung-tzu taught people to accept death as natural, Ko Hung (c.280-340 CE), who is best known as the author of *Pao-p'u tzu* (Book of 'the Master who Embraces Simplicity') reaffirmed belief in immortality, which could be achieved by various techniques such as breathing exercises, dietary restrictions, sexual practices and alchemy. Another movement is linked to Chang Tao-ling, who in a vision in 142 CE, was instructed by the deified Lao-tzu to introduce a new pattern of worship, in which blood sacrifices were abolished and the old gods abandoned. Another movement, inspired by the Classic of the Great Peace, *T'ai P'ing Ching*, offered the individual heavenly peace, through a shamanistic type of meditation.

Taoism, thus, came to combine ancient quietism, fervent devotion to a heavenly Lord - embodied in Lao-tzu himself and to a lesser extent in other immortals – and a belief that the essence of divinity is in each individual and can be cultivated by meditation, breathing, diet and alchemy. What Lao-tzu would have thought of this religious amalgam is another question.

Besides the Taoist contribution to Chinese science, already

mentioned, Taoism had a deep influence on Chinese art and literature. The painter and critic Hsieh Ho (c.500 CE) puts as the first principle of painting 'consonance with the vital breath.' The artist and craftsman, in whom spontaneous creativity and close attention to Nature was encouraged, needed to see his subject with the eyes of the spirit so as to grasp its vital breath.

Although Taoism has suffered some eclipse in Communist China, it continues to be influential in Taiwan. It is also attracting increasing attention in the West, with its emphasis on contemplation, harmony with nature, the interdependence of male and female and its encouragement 'to go with the flow.'

Mao Tse-tung, who held absolute power over the lives of one-quarter of the world's population, as Jung Chang (the author of *Wild Swans*) says at the beginning of her biography of the Chinese leader, 'was responsible for well over seventy million deaths in peacetime.'[6] Would that he and other twentieth century leaders had remembered the words of China's ancient sage Lao-tzu, who said 'He who has killed multitudes of men should weep for them with the bitterest grief; and the victor in battle has his place with the mourners.'[7]

CHAPTER NOTES

1. Translation by Gia-Feng and Jane English in *Universal Wisdom*, p. 255. Verse 1.
2. Sun Bu-er in *Immortal Sisters: Secrets of Taoist Women*, translated by Thomas Cleary, Shambala Publications, Boston, 1989, p. 50.
3. *Universal Wisdom*, verse 78.
4. *Universal Wisdom*, verse 13.
5. Quoted by Martin Palmer, *The Elements of Taoism*, Element Book, 1991, p. 60.
6. Jung Chang and Jon Halliday, *Mao, the Unknown Story*, Jonathan Cape, 2005, p. 3.
7. *Universal Wisdom*, verse 31.

13

Confucius

'Was not Heaven's Way embodied in Confucius?' asked the Chinese scholar Yang Xiong (53 BCE – 18 CE) many centuries ago. In due course, in the seventh century, temples to honour Confucius were established. But his primary interest was in ethics and politics. His lasting influence was in shaping Chinese society and the way it was governed. Confucianism permeated Chinese life for two and a half millennia and deeply influenced China's neighbours. Everything changed with the victory of Communism. During Chairman Mao's Cultural Revolution, Confucius was bitterly attacked in the 'Criticize Lin (Biao) and Criticize Confucius Campaign', but now in China there is renewed interest in 'the Master.'

Confucius is the Latinized version of K'ung-fu-tzu. His father's name was K'ung and his personal name was Qiu, which means 'hill' - said to have been given to him because his forehead looked like a hill. *Fuzi* is an honorific title usually translated as 'Master.' There is uncertainty about the details of his life, to which mythological stories were later added. It is generally agreed that Confucius was born in 551 BCE in the city of Tsou in the state of Lu, now Qufu in Shandong Province. His Grandfather came from the state of Song in the south west and his ancestors may have been descended from the ruling clan of the Shang dynasty. His father was known for his physical strength and courage. At the age of seventy, after his wife, who had born him nine daughters, died, he married again to a young woman who bore him a son who was to become world famous. His father, not surprisingly, died when Confucius was young. The family, it seems, had fallen on hard times. Confucius himself said, 'When I was young I was poor, so I am capable in many menial things.' Even so, largely self-educated, he became the most learned person of his day.' 'At fifteen,' he said, 'I set my heart on learning.'[1]

At the age of nineteen, Confucius married a lady from the state of Sung. They had a son in 531 who was called K'ung Li, but who in the *Analects* is known as Po Yü, which means the Carp, because at his birth, the Duke of Lu, for who Confucius was working, sent a carp as a present. Confucius was a sportsman, who liked fishing and archery, although he never aimed at a resting bird.[2] As we shall see, he was very particular about his behaviour. Confucius was a lover of music, which he saw as an attempt to interpret the harmony of the universe.

On one occasion he is said to have met with Lao-Tzu, of whom he said, 'I can only compare him to a dragon.'[3] It may be that Lao-Tzu encouraged him to meditate, but Confucius said, 'I spent a whole day without food and a whole night without sleep in order to meditate. It was of no use. It is better to learn.'[4]

Under China's first two dynasties, the Shang (trad.1523-1027) and the Chou (1027-221), China was much less economically centralized and culturally united than under later dynasties. This was increasingly the case during the so called Eastern Chou period (771-221), when China was being attacked on its Western frontier and the semi-independent feudal states, themselves divided by competing nobles, struggled for power. It was how to cure this chaotic, warlike situation, in which the people often suffered from starvation and oppression that became Confucius' over-riding concern. He looked back to an ideal past 'when the age of the Great *Tao* prevailed and the world was a community of all people. Men of virtue and talent were upheld and mutual confidence and goodwill were cultivated.' Such an ideal might now be unattainable. Order and prosperity, however, could be recovered if the rulers upheld benevolence (*jen*) 'as an ideal and exalted courtesy, so that the common people were led to the cardinal virtues.'

Confucius believed that radical reform of government was essential. The priority for rulers should be the welfare of their subjects, not their own pleasure. As he said to one ruler, 'To govern means to guide aright. If you, Sir, will lead the way aright, who will dare to deviate from the right?'[5] He advocated the reduction of taxes, mitigation of severe punishments and avoidance of unnecessary wars. On one occasion he was asked what the essentials of government were. Confucius replied, 'Sufficient food, sufficient forces, and the confidence of the people.' When asked if one had to dispense with one of these which should it be, he replied, 'Forgo the forces.' When asked again if one had to dispense with a second, he answered, 'Food, for from of old death has been the lot of all men, but a people without faith cannot stand.'[6]

His unfulfilled lifelong hope was to obtain a senior government position in which he could put these ideas into practice. He held some minor positions but never had the authority for which he longed. Instead, he educated a younger generation, many of whom did come to occupy influential positions. They collected his teachings in the *Analects* (*Lun yu*), which subsequently, during the Han dynasty (206 BCE – 220 CE) and subsequent dynasties, became required reading for the governing class in China. Twelve other officially approved texts - the Confucian Classics - which treat of many subjects, including ritual practices, ancient poetry and history, are also attributed to Confucius. He may have edited or written a commentary on the ancient *I-Ching* (Scripture of Changes) and may have used some other texts, but it is unlikely that he was their author.

Even without an active role in government, Confucius held that one can transform society by acting virtuously and serving as an example for others. This is why he emphasised education. 'The "superior person" is not one of noble birth but of noble character. Capacity to govern has no necessary connection with birth, wealth or position; it depends solely on character and knowledge.' He, therefore, accepted the poorest and humblest individuals as students, provided that they had the ability and motivation to learn. His teaching methods seem to have been informal and conversational. He encouraged students to think for themselves. 'If when I point out the corner of a subject, the student cannot work out the other three for himself, I do not go on.'

The most important characteristic of the superior person is benevolence (*jen*) or a feeling of shared humanity, which enables one to feel what the other person is feeling. A King asked Confucius, 'Is there one saying that can serve as a principle for the conduct of life?' Confucius replied, 'Do not do to others what you would not want others to do to you.' A person shows benevolence by treating people on the street as if they were important guests, by being reticent in speaking, being respectful where one dwells, reverent where one works, and loyal where one mixes with other people. Together with benevolence, Confucius emphasised wisdom and moral courage.

These qualities need to be learned and practised in the home. He quoted from 'The Book of Songs:'

When wives and children and their sires are one,

'Tis like the harp and lute in unison.
When brothers live in concord and at peace
The strain of harmony shall never cease.
The lamp of happy union lights the home,
And bright days follow when the children come.[7]

A son should honour and respect his father, who should show kindness to his child. What is learned in the home needs to be practised in society. 'From Emperor down to the common people, all, without exception, must consider cultivation of the individual character as the root.' When a ruler asked him, 'What should I do to have my people follow me?' the Master answered, 'If you promote the upright and place them ahead of the corrupt, then your people will follow you.' The ruler was to be like a good father.

By cultivating noble behaviour, a person becomes attuned to Heaven (*T'ien*) or the Mandate of Heaven. Mencius (c.391-308), an early Confucian thinker said, 'He who has exhaustively searched his mind knows his nature. Knowing his nature, he knows Heaven.' The concept of Heaven as the supreme deity and the son of Heaven as the supreme ruler date back at least to the Chou dynasty. Heaven, which has a moral quality, is the final and absolute principle, underlying the universe. The individual cultivates himself to achieve this. Heaven gives each person a vocation or destiny to fulfil and Confucius clearly believed that the attempt to reform society was his calling.

Confucius emphasized the importance of ceremonial or ritual (*li*), which, he held, helps to shape a person's character. For example, funeral rites provided a way for the proper expression of the mourners' emotions, avoiding apathy in the presence of death or excessive grief. The person who is punctilious in the performance of their ritual duties will also be punctilious in observing their social obligations. Confucius himself was very particular in performing ritual ceremonies. It was said that 'if a mat was not correctly laid, he would not sit on it.' The correct gift for his services was meat, which he acknowledged with a ritual bow. Yet even if the gift was of greater monetary value, for example a carriage and horses, he would not receive it with a ritual bow.[8] He was careful about his dress and particular about his food. 'He did not speak when eating and once in bed he did not talk. Though his food was only coarse rice and vegetable broth, he invariably offered a little in sacrifice, and always with solemnity.'[9]

Confucius was not interested in speculative questions of belief. According to *The Analects*, 'the topics the Master did not speak of were prodigies, forces and gods.' The disciple Chi-lu asked him how the spirits of the dead and the gods should be served. 'You are not able even to serve men,' the Master replied. 'How can you serve the spirits?' But Chi-lu persisted, 'May I ask about death?' 'You do not understand even life,' Confucius answered. 'How can you understand death?'

When Confucius himself died, he was mourned for three years by his disciples, said to be seventy in number, who carried on his teaching. *The Analects* or *Conversations of Confucius with His Disciples and Certain Others* - to give the book its full title – was probably compiled after his death by two disciples, Tseng and Yu. It is, however, remarkable that the book survived. In 213 BCE, the Emperor Ch'in Shih Huang, who wanted to found a new dynasty, ordered that all books should be burnt and all scholars buried alive. His was only a short reign, so a few precious relics and books, including *The Analects* survived. One copy of *The Analects* was found in about 150 BCE in a cranny of a wall in a house in which Confucius had lived for a time. Another copy was found in a neighbouring state. By that time, however, the style of writing had changed and only a few scholars were able to decipher ancient books.

Not much is known about them. The most important of his followers were Mencius (Meng Tu), already mentioned above, and Hsun Tzu (b.c. 300 BCE). Mencius held that people were naturally good. 'The tendency of human nature to do good', he said, 'is like that of water to flow downward.' Hsun Tzu, however, thought human nature was naturally evil and had to be restrained by proper education and by the law. He regarded Heaven as impersonal and that it did not over-ride natural law to support good government or in response to human wishes. 'Heaven does not suspend the winter because men dislike cold', he said. Hsun Tzu's careful reasoning provided a basis for the new legalistic structure of government, whereas the idealism of Mencius, who stressed the moral duty of rulers to seek the good of the people, was revived later in response to Buddhism and from the thirteenth century became a requirement of the civil service examinations. Despite their differences, Confucian teachers all stressed the importance of virtuous living, which can be attained through self-cultivation, and the need for harmony in the individual, the family, the state and the world.

From early days, rulers in China were regarded as the link between Earth and Heaven. This idea was elaborated by Confucius and his followers and under the Han Dynasty, Confucianism soon became the imperial ideology and the state cult. Temples were built in his honour, eventually in every one of the two thousand counties of China.The so-called Confucian Classics became the basics of the state educational system.

At a later date it was claimed that Confucius had given secret religious teaching and he came to be regarded as a prophet. The role of the Master was further developed in response to the growing influence of, first, Buddhism and later of Christianity. During the Tang (618-907 CE) and Son (960-1280) dynasties, for example, artists often depicted Confucius in a style similar to that which they used for the Buddha. Some Christian missionaries saw Confucius as a teacher of a Natural rather than a revealed religion, whereas others Westerners spoke of him as a philosopher and a moralist.

With the coming of the Communist Revolution, Confucianism was under attack for its allegedly elitist culture, which was designed to ensure the continued subordination of the common people. Mao saw his *Little Red Book* as a replacement for Confucius' *Analects*, which, he said, was also a collection of quotations. The orders to desecrate Confucius' home came from Mao's office. The building in Shandong was a rich museum, to which emperors and artists had come to pay homage and to offer gifts. The locals had been ordered to wreck it, but had played for time. So Red Guards were dispatched from Peking, pledging to destroy 'to death the enemy rival of Mao Tse-tung's thought.' Jun Chang in her biography of Mao comments 'Mao did, indeed, hate Confucius, because Confucianism enjoined that a ruler must care for his subjects.'[10]

Clearly Confucius has had an unparalleled influence on Chinese society in the past. If the renewed Chinese interest in him continues, so as China with its growing economic power exercises a greater role in world affairs, Confucius' influence is likely to spread even more widely. His teaching remains a challenging criticism both of all who exercise power for their own benefit and the emphasis of global capitalism on unfettered profit, which can even damage basic human relationships. Two thousand five hundred years ago the Master commented that 'to be considered filially pious today requires nothing more than being able to provide nourishment for one's parents. Yet providing nourishment is something that one might even do for dogs and horses. Without reverence, what is the difference between the two?'[11] He insisted that 'Filial piety is the root of all virtue, and the stem out of which grows all moral teaching... It commences with the service of parents; it proceeds to the service of the ruler; it is completed by the establishment of [good] character.'[12] Many of society's social evils today relate to the break down of family life.

CHAPTER NOTES

1. *The Analects of Confucius,* translated by William Edward Soothill, edited by Lady Hosie, London, Humphrey Milford, Oxford University Press, 1910, 1945 edtn, 2, 4, p. 9.
2. *The Analects,* p. xii. Much of the biographical information is taken from the Introduction.
3. *The Analects,* p. xxiii. See chapter 12.
4. *The Analects,* p. xxv.
5. *The Analects,* p. 123. See also p. xvi.
6. *The Analects,* p. 119.
7. *World Scripture,* p. 167.
8. *The Analects,* 10, 15, p. 99.
9. *The Analects,* 10, 8 p, 97.
10. Juan Chang and Jon Halliday, *Mao, the Unknown Story,* Jonathan Cape, 2005, p. 542.
11. Quoted in Mary Pat Fisher, *An Anthology of Living Religions,* p. 144
12. *World Scripture,* p. 172.

14

Mahavira

Mahavira was the last of the Jain's omniscient spiritual teachers or Tirthankaras. Jainism is one of India's most ancient religions, which may date back as far as the Indus Valley civilization, and is certainly pre-Vedic. Jainism has never attracted large numbers, but its contribution to Indian life over the centuries has been out of all proportion to its size. The Jain emphasis on non-violence, *ahimsa*, especially through its espousal by Mahatma Gandhi, now has a worldwide influence.

Jains venerate twenty-four Tirthankaras or 'Ford-Makers' – holy teachers who show the way to liberation from earth's bondage. The first Tirthankara was called Rsabha (which means bull) or Adinatha. The nineteenth was a princess called Mallinatha. The names of others are lost in the mist of time. Mahavira's immediate predecessor, on whose teaching he based his own, was Parsvanatha, the twenty third Tirthankara, who was a ninth century teacher in the holy city of Varanasi (Benares) and was said to have been a contemporary of Krishna.

Mahavira's original name was Vardhamana – Mahavira is a title meaning the 'Great Hero.' He was born in about 599 BCE in what is now Bihar and was an older contemporary of Gotama Buddha. His father was a petty prince who, like his mother belonged to the warrior (*Kshatriya*) caste, which at the time were challenging the demands of the priestly or Brahmin caste. Vardhamana was brought up in luxury, married and had a daughter. At the age of thirty, he renounced the world and became a monk. He joined the order of Parsvanatha, to which his parents belonged. They are said to have died by voluntary starvation. Mahavira was, therefore, no stranger to asceticism.

As a member of the order of Parsvanatha, Mahavira used one garment for over a year. Later he went about naked. He had no possessions – not even a bowl for begging his food or for drinking water. He allowed insects to crawl on his body and bite him and bore pain and abuse from villagers with patience. 'Once when he sat in meditation, his body unmoving, villagers cut his flesh, tore his hair and covered him with dirt. They picked him up and dropped him, disturbing his meditational postures. Abandoning concern for his body, free from desire, the Venerable One humbled himself and bore the pain.'[1] He meditated day and night and slept under the trees and even in places for cremation. He went to great pains to avoid injuring any other living being and also refused food specially prepared for him.

After twelve years of wandering and of austerity, in 557 he attained the highest knowledge, *kevala-jnana*. He then set about reviving Jain teaching and re-establishing the Jain community of monks, known as the *sangha*. This is why, somewhat inaccurately, Mahavira is often described as the 'founder of Jainism.' For thirty years he travelled throughout North East India, teaching by word and example the path of purification. 'Whoever conquers mind and passion, and acts with true austerity, shines like a fire into which the oblation has been poured.'[2] He attracted a large following, said, by the time of his death and liberation (*moksa*), to number 14,000 monks, 36,000 nuns and over 500,000 lay followers.

Jainism teaches that the world is infinite – so there is no need for a Creator God. The universe is pictured like a human body, with the region of mobile souls at the centre. Jainism is dualistic. Reality is constituted by two separate eternal entities: soul or living substance and non-soul or inanimate matter. The soul or *jiva*, in its pure state, has limitless knowledge and infinite bliss and power, but it is polluted by contact with the material. The soul can only be freed by extreme austerity or yoga. In Jainism, this consists of the 'three jewels' of knowledge of reality, faith in the teachings of the Tirthankaras, and cessation from doing evil.

Jains accept the widespread Indian belief in *karma*, that all phenomena are linked together in a universal chain of cause and effect. Every thought and action has a consequence. Purification of the mind is essential, but other austerities are pointless. Only if the mind is free from violence will a person refrain from physical violence. Special emphasis is placed on non-violence to all living beings and this helped to reduce animal sacrifice in India. Many Jains have gone to great extremes to avoid harming any form of life. Some monks – the Digambaras or 'Sky-clad' – wear no clothes. Many monks have a mask over their faces to ensure that they do not swallow any insects and will sweep the path in front of them to avoid accidentally treading on an insect. 'All breathing, existing, living, sentient creatures should not be slain, nor treated with violence, nor abused, nor tormented, nor driven away. This is the pure, unchangeable, eternal law.'[3]

These rules are strictly enforced. When I joined pilgrims to the beautiful and peaceful holy hill of Shatrunjaya in Gujarat, I was told not to wear anything made of leather and to take no food. In that part of Gujarat, near to where Gandhi was brought up, most people are strictly vegetarian and teetotal. Jains have usually avoided agricultural work and, besides much welfare work, they have in several places set up sanctuaries for sick animals. Jainism rejected the caste system and insisted that all people were to be treated equally. In the words of a modern Jain leader, Acharya Tulsi (1914-97), the founder of the Anuvrat movement, 'A non-violent man is he who does not in the least discriminate between rich and poor or between friend and foe... A truly non-violent man is ever awake and is incapable of harbouring any ill will.'[4]

Mental non-violence is also encouraged by the principle of 'many-sidedness' or *anekanta*. We should recognise that our knowledge is always only partial. A comparison is often made to the attempt of blind men to describe an elephant. The one who feels the trunk says the elephant is like a tree branch; the one who touches the ear says the animal is like a fan; the one who grasps the tail says the creature is like a rope. What each says is true but each person only has a partial grasp of reality. Clearly this is an outlook suitable for a small minority community, but it resonates with some post-modernist teaching and with the outlook of some advocates of interfaith understanding.

After Mahavira's death, his teachings were memorised by his followers and not written down for some time. The first attempt to systematise his teaching was at a Council held in Patna towards the end of the fourth century BCE and there is now an extensive canon of Jain texts. Over time Mahavira's followers divided into Digambaras, who, as mentioned above, wear no clothes and the Svetambaras, or 'white-clad', who wear a white piece of cloth. Other differences are that the Digambaras do not use a bowl for begging, whereas the Svetambaras do. The Svetambaras believe that a woman can obtain deliverance whereas Digambaras hold she must first be reborn as a man. There are differences too about ritual and which texts are accepted as authoritative, but general agreement on the main teachings and way of life.

Although the number of Jains has always been quite small, some became wealthy and achieved – and still do achieve - positions of influence. Several kings showed them favour and temples were built in different parts of India – those on Mount Abu and in Rajasthan are amongst India's most beautiful buildings. Jains have made a notable contribution to Indian art, sculpture and literature. Mahavira himself had a great interest in mathematics and the movement of celestial beings. Jain communities are to be found in many parts of India and now also in America and in Europe. In the nineteen seventies, the Jain monk Shri Chitrabhanu (b 1920), who had walked barefoot for more than 30,000 miles across India teaching Jain principles, made history by travelling to the West to address a meeting of the Temple of Understanding, which is an international interfaith organisation founded by Juliet Hollister (1916-2000) and based in New York.

Chitrabhanu, whom I have had the honour to meet, has said that he personally became disenchanted with business life as a child, when he lost his mother, sister and later a friend. No wealth could have saved them from death, so he started searching for the meaning of life. After consulting many gurus, he found one who told him to rely on his own experience rather than solely on the words of others. So at the age of twenty, he became a Jain monk, and spent the next five years almost entirely in silence to determine the meaning of life.

He said subsequently,

'And then after five years, I experienced life! I realized that death is nothing but a transformation, it is dropping old clothes and wearing new clothes. Something like Einstein's saying that energy is indestructible. I realized this conscious energy is in me. Because of fear, we are afraid of death, but it is like a mother who is feeding her baby on one breast. When she realizes that on the left breast there is no milk, she takes it and is about to put it on the right, but meanwhile the baby cries for it feels lost. But no sooner does it cry than the mother puts it on the right one. So the human mind is like the baby: it cries when it has to leave the old body. But leaving the empty body it is put into a bright, beautiful body. So then I realized—it was a dawning, Joyful experience - an ecstasy.'[5]

There can be little doubt that the emphasis on non-violence or *ahimsa* is the most significant Jain contribution to the evolving spiritual life of humankind. Gandhi, who gave the term worldwide currency, spoke of Shrimad Rajachandra (1867-1900), one of the best-known Jain laymen of recent times, as among his *gurus* or teachers. Rajachandra preached *ahimsa*, but one of his letters shows that he attached supreme value to truth. Truth and non-violence were likewise to be the keynotes of Gandhi's life and teaching. To quote the Jain leader Acharya Tulsi, once again, 'Non-violence is the best guarantee of humanity's survival and progress'

CHAPTER NOTES
1. From the *Akaranga Sutra*.
2. *Isibhasiyaim* 29, 17.
3. *Akaranga Sutra*, 4,1.
4. Quoted by Mary Pat Fisher, *Living Religions*, p. 128.
5. http://www.thecrimson.com/article.aspx?ref=179636.

15

Buddha

The wisdom and compassion of Gautama Buddha have, for centuries, inspired millions of people in East Asia and are now increasingly appreciated in the West.

The birth name of the historical founder of Buddhism is Siddhartha Gotama. Gotama, a Pali word, is also known in Sanskrit as Gautama.The term 'Buddha' is a title which means an enlightened person or one who has awakened to the truth.' Gotama is also known, especially in Japan, as 'Sakyamuni' – the wise one of the Sakya tribe– or as 'Tathagata' – the 'Truth finder' or the one who shows the way – which was the title that Gotama preferred for himself. Those who belong to the Theravada tradition of Buddhism usually just call him 'Buddha.' Followers of the Mahayana tradition believe there have been many Buddhas.

There are uncertainties about Gotama's dates and mythology surrounds accounts of his life. His teachings were not written down until several centuries after his death. The usual dates given are about 566-486 BCE or maybe rather later, perhaps about 448-368 BCE. He was born in what is now Nepal. His father was a raja or chieftain and Gotama had a very sheltered life in the royal palace. He married Yasodhara and they had a son. Despite his father's best efforts to shelter his son from the stark realities of life, on four occasions, Gotama ordered the royal carriage to take him for a ride. On the first outing he saw a very sick man and in answer to his questions was told that everyone suffers illness. Next, he saw a decrepit old man and was told that everyone grows old. On the third occasion, he saw a dead man being carried away and discovered that everyone must die. On his fourth journey, Gotama, disturbed by thoughts of what lay ahead of him and how to avoid suffering saw a monk who had abandoned the world. Gotama resolved to do the same. Leaving his wife and his new born son, he escaped from the palace, while everyone else was celebrating his child's birth. He soon exchanged his princely robes for the clothes of a wandering holy man and embarked on a life of extreme asceticism.

After some years, he realised that all his austerities had not set him free from suffering. 'I thought', he said, "Suppose I practice entirely cutting off food." Then the deities came to me and said, "Good sir, do not practice entirely cutting off food. If you do so, we shall infuse heavenly food into the pores of your skin and you will live on that."'[1] Gotama, therefore, once again started to beg his food – to the disgust of those who had been his companions - and reverted to 'the middle way' - a term often used as a name for Buddhism. He made his way to a place in Bihar, now known as Bodhgaya, where he seated himself beneath a Bo or Bodhi tree. He made a solemn vow that he would not move from the spot until he had solved the riddle of suffering. The events of that night, during which Mara, the Evil One, tried, in vain, every device to divert Gotama from his intention, are described in dramatic mythology. After recalling his previous births, Gotama, concentrating on 'seeing things as they really are,' passed through four stages of progressive insight, until he reached enlightenment.

At first he stayed where he was, but eventually was persuaded to share his discovery with others. His teaching is summed up in the Four Noble Truths:

1. *All life involves both physical and mental suffering (dukkha) and is transient.* Buddhists do not deny that life has its pleasures and times of happiness – but these fade. We do not achieve our ambitions, we get ill and old, our loved ones die. 'Birth is ill, decay is ill, sickness is ill, death is ill.'

2. *The reason why we suffer is our desire or thirst (tanha).* We crave for sensuous enjoyment, for money, for fame, for self-perpetuation – but craving is never satisfied. It is like a fire, which always requires more fuel.

3. *But there is a cure for suffering. We can eradicate desire.* The cessation of desire leads to *nirvana*, which is usually described in negative terms.

4. *The way to end desire is to follow the Eightfold Path,* which involves right understanding and the right way of living. This includes meditation which can lead to the realization of no self. Even those

who do not follow all his teaching can find concentration on the present moment or 'one-pointedness', as it is sometimes called, helpful.

Perhaps the most startling part of the Buddha's teaching is the doctrine of 'no self' (*anatman*). Buddhists reject the concept of the soul or of a permanent self which is the subject of experience. The sense of self is essentially an illusion. Rather like watching a film, people on the screen have a certain reality and we can feel deep emotion as we watch, but, in fact, we know that the characters are only constantly changing images created by celluloid. Just as the body is constantly changing, so is the mind. One thought gives rise to another and so on like a flowing river, but in Buddhist teaching there is no permanent self which is the subject of all these thoughts. Indeed, the deep-rooted feeling of 'I-ness' is the cause of suffering and has to be rooted out. There is no 'I', but our belief that there is, is the cause of rebirth.

In a famous conversation with King Milinda, the Buddhist monk Nagasena (second century BCE) asks the king, 'What is a chariot?' 'is it the wheels?' and the king answers no, or 'is it the shaft?' or 'is it the seat?' and so on and the king keeps having to answer 'no' until he comes to see that the chariot is only its constituent parts, aggregated in that way and not another. So with human beings, we are aggregates, identifiable by particular names, 'but in the absolute sense, there is no ego here to be found.'

Within that philosophical world view, as the Dalai Lama says, 'it is almost impossible to have any room for a temporal, eternal, absolute truth. Nor is it possible to accommodate the conception of a divine Creation.[2] The lack of reference to God has often puzzled people who have asked whether Buddhism can be called a religion – but that depends on how you define 'religion.'

What then is 'Nirvana'? In one sense, there is no answer, as it cannot be described. It is a Sanskrit term which means 'extinction' or 'blowing out', although some people suggest the negative is used because no language can describe the reality.

Although at first reluctant to do so, the Buddha spent most of the rest of his life walking and teaching in the area of the larger Ganges basin. He attracted a growing number of disciples, who became the nucleus of the Sangha or monastic community. They too became itinerant teachers, begging their food, except in the rainy season when they gathered together in community. He told them, 'Teach the dharma which is lovely at the beginning, lovely in the middle, lovely at the end. Explain with the spirit and the letter in the fashion of Brahma. In this way you will be completely fulfilled and wholly pure.'[3]

The Buddha insisted that his task was to point the path to self-discovery or enlightenment. 'I only show the way.' His followers were urged to work out their own salvation. There is a story of a Hindu Brahmin student called Dhotaka who implored the Buddha, 'Please, Master, free me from confusion.' The Buddha replied, 'It is not my practice to free from confusion. When you yourself have understood the Dharma, the Truth, then you will find freedom.' This explains the Zen Buddhist saying, 'If you meet the Buddha on the way – kill him.' One should not rely upon another's teaching or merit, but realise enlightenment for one's self.

It is said, that a distraught mother came to the Buddha carrying her dead baby son. She asked for medicine to cure the child. The Buddha asked her to bring him a handful of mustard seed from a house where no child, or husband, or parent or friend had died. The woman went from house to house, but at every home someone had lost a relative or friend. At length the woman realised that death and sorrow are the common lot of all and she came back to the Buddha at peace. 'Decay is inherent in all compounded things.'

The Buddha embodied the spirit of non-violence, which was central to his teaching. 'Hatreds do not ever cease in this world by hating, but by love; this is the essential truth... Overcome anger by love, overcome evil by good. Overcome the miser by giving, overcome the liar by truth.'[4] He stressed the need for empathy. 'If you do not tend another, then who is there to tend you? Whoever would tend me, he should tend the sick.'[5]

Mahayana Buddhism, which is prominent in East Asia, emphasizes the value of compassion and sets before people the ideal of the bodhisattva, who is a person who has achieved realization, but, who instead of liberation, dedicates himself to relieve the sufferings of others. Mahayana Buddhists also believe that there have been many Buddhas and indeed that every person has the potential to realise his or her Buddha-nature.

Although Gotama lived and taught in India, by the fifth century C.E., Buddhism was in decline and by the twelfth century had largely disappeared from the land of its birth. Instead it took root in Sri Lanka, Burma, Thailand, Korea, Tibet, Vietnam and China and Japan. In the nineteenth century Buddhism began to better known in the West. Buddhist texts were translated into English by Mr and Mrs Rhys Davids and other members of the Pali Text Society. Then, in 1893 the Singalese Buddhist Anagrika Dharmapala, who two years before had founded the Mahabodhi Society in Colombo, came to the World Parliament of Religions in Chicago and gave two long addresses. 'Buddhism', he said, is a scientific religion, inasmuch as it earnestly enjoins that nothing whatsoever be accepted on faith.' During the twentieth century, the number of Buddhist adherents and centres in the West has grown steadily.

Although the majority of Buddhists still live in Asia, the example and teaching of the Buddha now have a universal appeal. The characteristic Buddhist emphasis on 'right mindfulness' can be of value to people of every religion and of none: The Buddha said,

Check your mind
Be on your guard.

CHAPTER NOTES
1. *Majjhima Nikaya* 36,27.
2. Dalai Lama, *The Good Heart*, London, Rider, 1996, p. 39. See further chapter 97 below.
3. *Vinaya, Mahavagga* 1,11,1.
4. *Dhammapada*, 1,5 and 17,3
5. *Vinya, Mahavagga*, 8.26.3

16

Plato

'Plato was, with Socrates and Aristotle, one of three philosophers of ancient Greece who between them laid the philosophical foundations of Western culture.'[1] They have exercised a lasting influence on Jewish, Christian and Muslim thought. Indeed the Hebrew Bible, Roman law, and the Greek love of wisdom and beauty are the bedrocks of European civilization.

To understand Plato, we have first to know a little about his teacher Socrates, who was born in about 470 BCE. It is thought that Socrates' father was a sculptor and his mother was a midwife. He served for a time in the army, but took no part in politics. He himself left no writings, so we know of him mainly through the writings of his disciple Plato and from Xenophon's *Memorabilia*, although, with his 'grotesque' appearance and unusual way of life, he was also the subject of two comedies written at the time. He was said to live in extreme poverty in his old age.

Socrates lived in the chaos of the Peloponnesian War, with its erosion of moral values. He felt called to shore up the ethical dimensions of life by the admonition to "know thyself." He challenged his disciples to question the prejudices of popular opinion. Socrates was a man of deep piety with the temperament of a mystic. He regarded mythology, with its foolish and often immoral tales about the gods, as a mere invention of the poets. He held that God's existence was evident both by the order of nature, the universality of belief in a Divine Being, and by dreams and oracles. He was clearly aware of the religious ideas about the divine origin and destiny of the soul of the philosopher and mathematician Pythagoras (c.500-c.500).

Plato says that from childhood Socrates often heard a 'voice' and he tells of his curious spiritual trances, during one of which Socrates stood spellbound for twenty-four hours.

The oracle of Apollo at Delphi pronounced Socrates to be the wisest of men, although this, he said, was because he was prepared to admit his ignorance. He believed himself charged with a mission from God to make his fellow citizens aware of their ignorance and to recognise what was important for the good of the soul. His criticisms were not welcome, but Socrates was willing to sacrifice his life to fulfil his task. His attacks on some of the leaders of the Athenian democracy made him very unpopular and he was accused of encouraging disloyalty to the democracy among his young associates or in the words of the charge laid against him of 'perverting the young.'

Socrates treated the trial with contempt and rejected the opportunity to escape punishment by withdrawing anything he said or by paying a bribe. Instead, as Plato, movingly describes in the *Phaedo*, Socrates was willing to die as a martyr for his beliefs. The death of Socrates had a decisive effect on Plato.

Plato was born in 428-7 BCE,[2] a year after the death of Pericles, Athens' great ruling statesman. Already Athenian power and culture, at its height under the leadership of Pericles (c.495-429 BCE), had begun to decline. The Peloponnesian War had started three years before Plato was born and it was to last for another twenty-seven years, ending in starvation and surrender. Cleon who succeeded Pericles, was an able man but totally focussed on victory and envious of the old, well-to-do, educated families, of which Plato's was one. Plato's father, Ariston, claimed descent from the god Poseidon. His mother, Perictione, was related to the early Greek law-maker, Solon (c.630-560), who was one of the Seven Wise Men of Greece. Her second husband, in whose house Plato was mainly brought up, was a prominent supporter of Pericles. Although Plato grew up during the long years of war, his writings are set at an earlier time when Athens was at its zenith and the philosopher Socrates was alive.

Socrates is the central character in Plato's *Dialogues*. Socrates seems to have been a friend of the family. It is likely that Plato met him when he was a boy. Socrates was not someone that a person forgot. He was a short, stiff-legged, stocky figure topped by a head of fascinating ugliness. Socrates was bald, with a bulging forehead, a snub nose and protruding eyes. But there was magic in his eyes, which looked out from beneath his eyebrows in a humorous and quizzical manner.[3] Socrates was highly intelligent, an effective debater with a sense of irony. His relentless questioning left an indelible impression on his students, of whom Plato was one.

After Socrates' death, Plato left Athens and for a time took refuge at

Megara with his younger contemporary, Euclid, a philosopher and geometrician. He then spent time travelling in Greece, Egypt and Italy, where he was disgusted by the gross sensuality, although he found a kindred spirit in Dion, brother-in-law of Dionysius I, the tyrant of Sicily. Later in life, on the death of Dionysius I, Plato was persuaded by Dion to return to Syracuse to tutor Dionysius II. This was not a success and Plato's later attempts, after the murder of Dion, to mediate between the hostile Sicilian factions also failed.[4]

On his return from his earlier travels, in about 387, Plato founded the famous Academy in Athens, which continued to educate young men for nearly nine hundred years. Plato concentrated his energies on education and writing. He died in 348/347 'at a marriage feast' or, others say, 'while he was writing.' He was buried at the Academy. Although Plato is known for his writings – thirty-six works are attributed to him - he himself regarded the foundation and organization of the Academy as his chief accomplishment. The contact of living minds as a 'vehicle' of philosophy was, in his estimation, more important than written works.

Plato had originally planned to enter politics, but he was disillusioned by Socrates' execution. He did, however, draft a complete constitution, indeed a whole political, social and educational system in the *Laws*. In the *Republic* he described the ideal state, which would be ruled by philosophers.

Plato's chosen way of writing was in the form of Dialogues, which are dramatic conversations, or as Aristotle said, akin to Mime, which was meant to be both humorous and realistic. No doubt, this was a method that Plato used in his educational work. The difficulty is that it is not always clear what Plato himself thought. Plato's thought was wide-ranging, strongly ethical, at time mystical, but always rational. He hoped that that his teaching about eternal Ideas or Forms, which are changeless abstract or universal concepts, would dispel the moral confusion of his day.

In Plato's earlier dialogues, the main features are his theories of Forms or of Ideas and of the 'tripartite soul' and also that knowledge is 'recollection.' Greek philosophy began with the question, 'What is the world made of?' Water, fire and air were identified as the basic components. The question, however, was asked, 'Can we trust our senses?'

What we perceive at one moment is quickly replaced by a new perception. Plato argued that beside the appearances known to our senses, we can by the use of our reason attain true conclusions about the realities of which the phenomena are appearances. The underlying realities are what Plato meant by Ideas or Forms. In part, this may have been suggested by his knowledge of geometry and, for example, the mental concept or Idea of a circle.

Plato, therefore, held that behind the world which we perceive there is another world, more real and true and beautiful, which we dimly perceive by reason but which we shall only know fully in another life. In the *Meno*, Plato, who held that the soul is immortal, argued that in the world where the soul had previously lived, it had contemplated all truth and reality. In the dim prison of the body, however, the soul forgets what it knew and has to be reminded. The process of being reminded is what we call learning. In the *Republic*, in which the concept of Ideas is taken for granted, Plato speaks of the Idea of the Good as the supreme Idea.

In a famous simile, Plato suggested that men are like prisoners in a cave, fastened so that they sit facing the back of the cave. The sole light of the cave comes from its mouth, which is behind them. Outside, quite close to the cave is a road flanked on the near side by a wall. Along the road people keep passing up and down, and occasionally stop to talk. Some are carrying things in their hands or on their heads. Beyond the road a great fire is burning, which shines into the cave and casts its light on the wall at which the prisoners are gazing. The prisoners can see the shadows of those moving folks, or at least shadows of what is above the wall. At the same time, the prisoners can also hear sound of the talk, which, from outside, echoes from the cave wall. The prisoners, who have never been out of the cave, Plato suggests, are bound to imagine that the shadows are real flesh and blood. But suppose one of the prisoners is allowed out of the cave and sees the world in its true colours? At first he is dazzled by the light, but gradually he becomes accustomed to it. Out of pity for his fellow prisoners, the man goes back and tells them what he has seen, but he is treated as an impostor. The philosopher is like the man who leaves the cave and discovers the reality, but who is shunned by his contemporaries.

The great task of the philosopher is to contemplate the Idea of the

Good, for which, as he makes clear in the *Republic*, a person has to prepare by hard intellectual effort. The Form of the Good, which is like the sun in relation to visible things, is the source at once of the reality of all things and of the light by which they are apprehended, as well as of their value. The Good is the supreme beauty, which dawns suddenly upon the pilgrim of Love as he draws near to his goal.

In later writings, Plato allows a greater reality to the world of the senses. He also, especially in the *Timaeus*, speaks of God as the intelligent, efficient cause of all order and structure in the world of becoming. The book is a myth about the creation of the world by a divine Craftsman, who had its Forms before him as an eternal model. The world that God moulded was based on that model. The real world, Plato holds, is not the world around us that our senses report to us and that we uncritically think to be real. Rather, the real world is what we grasp in thought when exercising our minds in abstract philosophical arguments.

Plato's picture of a Divine Craftsman who made the best possible world because he is good and who wanted it to be as good as possible contrasted with the popular belief of Ancient Greece in many gods, who could be jealous and destructive. Although Plato never rejected the forms and practices of the religion he knew, his theology made a sharp break with most peoples' understanding of that religion. Indeed in the *Republic*, Plato said that censorship of popular stories about the gods would be necessary. In the *Laws*, he says that people should have no private shrines of their own and they should only take part in public ceremonies. Moreover citizens would be required to be re-educated to believe that there really are gods who care for human beings and who cannot be bribed to overlook wrong-doing. Those who refused to be re-educated would be executed - a dangerous precedent for the Inquisition and other religious witch-hunts.

For many centuries Plato's *Timaeus* was the work that attracted most attention. Compared to the story of the creation of the world in the book of Genesis at the beginning of the Bible, Plato's God is a workman who does the best he can with the materials he has. Plato does not blame the Creator for the evil in the world, which are the effects of 'Necessity' and the unavoidable defects of the materials he had to use. He creates order out of chaos – but he does not create the original materials. Greek philosophers thought that the idea of creation out of nothing was an incoherent idea. Although some passages in the Bible suggest that God made the world from a primeval chaos, the Bible has usually been understood to teach that God created the world *ex nihilo*, from nothing.[5] This means that God cannot escape ultimate responsibility for the existence of evil,[6] even if it is blamed on the rebellion of Satan, the Eternal Serpent. As the poet Milton (1608 – 1674) wrote,

Th' infernal Serpent; he it was, whose guile
Stir'd up with Envy and Revenge, deceiv'd
The mother of Mankind, what time his Pride
Had cast him out from Heav'n.[7]

Plato put great emphasis on the mathematically calculable nature of the heavenly bodies' motions. Indeed, in the Middle Ages, God is sometimes pictured with a compass in his hands as he created the world.

Plato held that the soul is immortal. In Greek thought at the time, it was generally agreed that the soul, *psyche*, is what causes living things to be alive. Plato said that the soul is immortal because it is always in motion or changing and that its motion never fails because it moves itself, while everything else is moved by it.[8] It is not clear whether Plato is thinking of individual souls or that the world as a whole has a soul, of which individual souls are portions.[9] The soul is akin to the unchanging Forms or Ideas, which are the objects of pure thought which are unaffected by any of the sources of change in the world of our sensory experience.

There was debate at the time about the relation of the soul to the body. Plato was clear that the soul was a different kind of thing than the body and the soul was the real person. Thus, Socrates, on his deathbed jokingly reminded his friends that they would not be burying him, but only his body. In the *Phaedo*, Plato speaks about the body as an evil which drags the soul down. Death is indeed a welcome release for the soul from its infection by the body. Philosophy, properly understood, was, Plato said, a preparation for death, when the soul finally escapes from the prison of the body. This dualism of soul and body has had a lasting influence on Christianity, especially to be seen in the asceticism of the monastic tradition. Only quite recently has Christian theology recovered the Hebrew emphasis on the human being as a psycho-somatic whole. Indeed, some scientists see the mind and indeed the 'soul' as totally dependent on the physical body.

Plato had a profound influence on Christian thought. The second century apologist Justin Martyr hoped to see Plato in heaven. William Temple, a twentieth century Archbishop of Canterbury, wrote that 'With regard to the two fundamental problems, the character of God and the destiny of Man, Plato comes curiously near the Christian position. The same can be said of his conception of moral excellence.'[10] In addition, the Medieval idea of Christendom was related to the Ideal State, which Plato imagined.

It is hard to over estimate the influence of Plato. Professor A N Whitehead (1861-1947), an eminent twentieth century metaphysician wrote, that 'The safest general characterisation of the European philosophical tradition is that it consists of a series of footnotes to Plato.[11]'

CHAPTER NOTES

1. *Encyclopaedia Britannica*, 1977, 14, p. 531.
2. The Athenian year began in different months to the calendar used today.
3. This description is based on J A K Thomson's account in his *Plato and Aristotle*, London, Ernest Benn, 1928, p. 7.
4. See *Epistles* vii and viii.
5. For an interesting discussion of this see Jon D Levenson, *Creation and the Persistence of Evil*, New York, Harper and Row 1987, and Princeton, Princeton University Press, 1988.
6. So Isaiah, 45,7.
7. John Milton, *Paradise Lost*, 1.
8. *Phaedrus*, 245c-246a.
9. See *Laws*, 893b-899d and also in the *Timaeus*.
10. William Temple, *Plato and Christianity*, London, Macmillan, 1916, p. 87.
11. Encyclopedia Britannica, 14, p. 538.

17

Aristotle

Aristotle, with Socrates and Plato, was the third pre-eminent philosopher of Ancient Greece. Aristotle was born in 384 BCE at Stagirus, a little Ionian colony of considerable antiquity close to the sea in Northern Greece. His father Nicomachus was for a time physician at the Macedonian court, which was in Aristotle's memory a den of intrigue, murder and drunkenness. The town was also increasingly threatened by invading 'barbarians.'.

At an early age, Aristotle was introduced to Greek medicine and biology by his father. After his father's death, Aristotle, when he was seventeen, was sent to Athens to study at Plato's Academy, which was already a major centre for scientific research. Aristotle was a brilliant student of science but less interested in mathematics. This may be why he was passed over when the time came to appoint a successor to Plato. Aristotle remained faithful to Plato while he was still alive, but after his death in 348-7, Aristotle left Athens and after a time of travelling settled at Assus, on the Asiatic coast of the Sea of Marmar. There he founded an Academy. There also he fell in love with and married Pythia, who was a niece of the ruler of the city. After her death, he married Herpyllis. Later, Aristotle moved to the island of Lesbos, where he gave particular attention to the marine fauna – his work on them is still highly regarded by zoologists. Then in 343-2, he was summoned by King Philip of Macedonia to share in the education of the king's son, Alexander. Aristotle, who held that civilization at its finest was to be found in democratic city states, can hardly have been enthusiastic about the enormous empire that his pupil won by conquest.

After King Philip's death in 335-4, Aristotle returned to Athens and set up his own school, known as the Lyceum, which was the name of a pleasant grove where he walked and discoursed with his pupils – hence the nickname 'Peripatetic.' Twelve years later, however, following the death of Alexander the Great, anti-Macedonian feeling swept through Athens. Aristotle thought it wise to withdraw to his mother's home town of Chalcis, north of Athens, where he died in 323. His will has survived and it shows his concern for others. He is said to have been something of a dandy – bald, with little eyes, good features and a lisp.

Aristotle's learning was prodigious. Of his many writings, forty seven survive. He wrote about Logic, Rhetoric (the art of speaking and writing), Physics, Metaphysics, Biology, Psychology, Ethics and Politics and other subjects. Into each of them, often for the first time, he introduced system and order.

Although Aristotle began by accepting Plato's Theory of Ideas, which exist independently of things, Aristotle eventually came to doubt the existence of any reality independent of what we call things. He accepted, however, that although things are real, they are also in part appearance. He, therefore, distinguished between form and matter – a distinction that was to have a lasting influence on Western philosophy. Whereas for Plato there was an ideal form of a horse, for Aristotle, the form lies *within* the species of horse, not outside it.

Aristotle also held that the end or goal explained the process. If there is no grand Designer to give things form, how then do material things acquire form? Aristotle held that there are four causes for the existence of things. One was the material cause. A tree, for example, must have bark or leaves and so on. It needs also to have the formal cause, which, say, makes it an oak or a cedar. The efficient cause is what makes it become a tree in its particular environment: for example, the soil, and the sun and the rain. Fourthly, things have a purpose or *telos*. A sapling, for example, aims to become a fully grown tree. All things strive toward their final condition. They have both potentiality and actuality. For example, a man is the actuality of the boy who has the potentiality to become a man. Nature, for Aristotle, is a battleground between chaotic, formless matter and the shaping force that moulds material into specific figures and purposes.

Aristotle asked himself 'how did this whole process start?' Although it was possible that matter might have no beginning – motion (the search for actuality) must have had an origin or a Prime Mover. Aristotle's Prime Mover, or Unmoved Mover, is incorporeal, indivisible, sexless, changeless, perfect and eternal. Such language has been taken over into Christian philosophical reflection. For example, the *Thirty Nine Articles of Religion*, printed at the end of the Church of England's *Book of Common Prayer* begins by saying God is 'everlasting, without body, parts or passions...' Yet such a picture of an impassable

God seems to conflict with a God whose Son took upon himself the suffering of humanity and it has been rejected by some twentieth century Christian theologians who speak of a 'Suffering God.'

Aristotle's Prime Mover has self-consciousness, but, other than setting the universe in motion, has no further role. The Prime Mover is the detached God of eighteenth century Deism. Such a Divine Being seems far away from the Biblical God, who acts in history and enters into relationships with human beings. Nonetheless, Aristotle's views had an enormous influence on some Christian theologians such as St Thomas Aquinas. Aquinas borrowed Aristotle's argument that motion must have a beginning. He also used Aristotle's teaching that all things have a potential and argued that human beings' potential is to reflect God's nature and goodness.

Moreover, Aristotle said that every living thing has its own soul. Each soul has three faculties: the nutritive concerns itself with food and procreation; the sensitive is concerned with perception and only possessed by animals; and the rational or use of reason is confined to human beings. You cannot, he held, separate soul from the body. He, therefore, appears not to have believed in personal immortality, although the soul is immortal.

God is the only entirely reasonable soul and possesses knowledge in the highest degree. The human desire to know is the highest truth of our being and is potentially a sharing in God's knowledge of Himself. This aspiration was in part handed down in myth, but through reason, Aristotle held, humans can attain to knowledge of God. Indeed, it has been claimed that Aristotle's philosophy is 'deeply religious'[1], although this is a view of Aristotle that is not often expressed.

Both Plato and Aristotle have had a lasting influence on European thought. Plotinus (205-270 CE) and his pupil Porphyry (c. 234-c. 305), who developed Neo-Platonism, which was itself to be very influential, were influenced by both Plato and Aristotle. Indeed Porphyry was the first great harmonizer of Plato and Aristotle. Plato also influenced the Jewish philosopher Philo of Alexandria (c.15 BCE to after 40 CE), who expressed his philosophical religion in the form of lengthy allegorical commentaries on the Hebrew Scriptures. Some early Christian writers, such as St Justin, who was martyred in about 162-168, and Clement of Alexandria (c.150 – c. 215), suggested that the teachings of Plato were essentially in harmony with Christian belief. Origen (c.184 – c.215), the greatest of the Alexandrian Christian thinkers, was more critical of Plato, but also deeply influenced by him. Plato's writing also influenced the theologians of Cappadocia, such as St Gregory of Nazianzus (329-89) and St Gregory of Nyssa (c.330-c.395). St Augustine was another Platonist, insisting on the soul's superiority to and independence of the body. His theology about God was also much influenced by Platonism.

In the Middle Ages, Plato's influence was primarily mediated by a book, erroneously, attributed to Dionysius the Areopagite, one of the few Athenians who was converted to Christianity by St Paul.[2] Aristotle's influence, partly mediated by the writings of the Roman scholar and statesman Boethius (c.480 - c.524), was confined to his writings on logic, which Boethius translated from Greek into Latin. Plato's thought continued to influence Christian thinkers throughout the Middle Ages.

Aristotle's influence on the thought of the early Middle Ages was limited, because up till 1115 the only works of Aristotle which were known in Christendom were his short *Categories* and *On Interpretation* – both in Latin translations. His works, however, were known to Syrian Christians, who in the ninth century translated them into Arabic. Aristotle's writings, therefore, came to influence some of the great Muslim thinkers, such as Avicenna and Averroës, well before they became widely known in Christendom. By 1278, however, almost all his works existed in Latin translations from the Greek. This caused great excitement amongst Christian scholars, although at first attempts were made in Paris to ban any lectures on his philosophy and metaphysics. Albertus, who was the teacher of St Thomas Aquinas, said, to avoid criticism, 'I only expound Aristotle, I do not endorse him.' St Thomas Aquinas, however, as we shall see, made great use of the writings of Aristotle, even if he did not always agree with him. There were heated debates between so-called 'Christian Platonists' and 'Christian Aristotelians,' but the rivalry is often exaggerated.

Both writers continued to be much studied during the Renaissance and they have had a lasting influence on Western thought. Raphael's famous painting, the *School of Athens*, which is in the Vatican, is dominated by the enormous figures of Plato, holding the *Timaeus*, who points upward and Aristotle, holding his *Ethics*, who gestures outwards. Their contrasting gestures suggest that Aristotle was more concerned to understand the world around us in terms of philosophical principles, while Plato was more austerely focussed on the abstract and theoretical principles themselves. European thinkers through the ages have been indebted to both masters of the School of Athens.

Chapter Notes
1. See the entry on Aristotle in *The Oxford Dictionary of World Religions*, p. 88.
2. *The Acts of the Apostles*, 17, 34.

18

Asoka

Asoka, who has been credited with making Buddhism a world religion, is one of the few people in the ancient world about whom we have rock hard evidence. That is because his edicts, which include some biographical information, were inscribed on polished pillars of stone or on rocks.

Asoka's grandfather, Chandragupta, who ruled from about 322 – 298 BCE, seized the opportunity created by the power vacuum after the death of Alexander the Great - whose Empire included India's north western provinces - to establish a vast empire. Bindusara, Chandragupta's son and successor, was a peace-loving ruler, who is said to have had sixteen wives and over one hundred sons. Not surprisingly there were disputes about the succession. Eventually Asoka, whose mother's name was Subhadrangi, who was born in about 304 BCE, established himself as emperor in about 274 or maybe eight years later. Asoka, like his father, had several wives and at least four sons and two daughters. He was concerned for his family and in Kalinga Edict I, he said, 'I desire for my children that they may enjoy every kind of prosperity and happiness both in this world and the next.'[1]

Asoka was probably educated by members of the Hindu Brahmin priestly caste and was taught behaviour appropriate to a king. As a prince, he served as Viceroy of a rather remote province in Western India. When Asoka, came to the throne, he at first imitated his grandfather's expansionist policy. Among his many bloody wars, the one against the neighbouring kingdom of Kalinga (modern Orissa), in about 262, was the most cruel. 'One hundred and fifty thousand persons were carried away captive, one hundred thousand were slain, and many times that number died.'[2] The Edict acknowledged that the losses in war were not confined to the combatants, but that terrible suffering – in modern parlance "collateral damage" - fell also on the family and friends of those who had been killed.

Asoka's life was changed by the horrors of this campaign. 'Directly after the conquest of the Kalingas, the Beloved of the gods became keen in pursuit of *Dharma*', which is a Sanskrit word for the practice of the truth as taught by the Buddha – the Pali term is *Dhamma.* 'The chiefest conquest,' Asoka declared 'is not that by arms but by *Dharma.*'Asoka, who had already become a nominal Buddhist, now became a very committed follower of the Buddha. After the slaughter in Kalinga, he never again fought an aggressive war, although he kept an army to deter invasion.

'All men are my children. Just as I seek the welfare and happiness of my own children in this world and the next, I seek the same things for all men.

Unconquered peoples along the borders of my dominions may wonder what is my disposition towards them. My only wish with respect to them is that they should not fear me, but trust me; that they should expect only happiness from me.'[3]

He did all he could to improve the life of his subjects. He provided wells and rest-houses for travellers, supported medical aid for humans and for animals. *Dharma*-officials were appointed to encourage virtue and to look after old people and orphans and to ensure that justice was upheld throughout the empire. Asoka abolished the use of torture and perhaps the death penalty, although judicial beatings were still allowed. Prisoners, on their release, were given some short-term financial help and encouraged to earn 'merit' for their future lives.

Besides seeking the uplift of the people by legislation, Asoka also sought to encourage them to live a moral life, especially by his emphasis on *ahimsa* (non-violence), which is often mentioned in the edicts. Respect for parents was encouraged, as well as good behaviour towards friends and families. Good treatment of servants was praised. Truthfulness, sexual purity, gentleness and contentment were encouraged. The aim was to create a harmonious society and to encourage people to seek a heavenly rebirth. Asoka himself set an example at his court. Hunting was abandoned. Instead he went on pilgrimage to Buddhist holy sites. The court became entirely vegetarian. Animal sacrifices were stopped.

Asoka gave Buddhism a central place in his empire, but he supported Brahmins and Jain ascetics as well as Buddhist monks and nuns. He urged respect for other people's beliefs and practices. As Rock Edict XII says,

'The faiths of others all deserve to be honoured for one reason or another. By honouring them one exalts one's own faith and at the same time performs a service to the faith of others... If a man extols his own faith and disparages another because of devotion to his own and because he wants to glorify it, he seriously injures his own faith.

Therefore concord alone is commendable, for through concord men may learn and respect the conception of Dharma accepted by others.

King Priyadarshi (The Beloved of the Gods – Asoka's way of referring to himself) desires men of all faiths to know each other's doctrines and to acquire sound doctrines... he does not value gifts or honours as much as growth in the qualities essential to religion in men of all faiths.'[4]

On his pilgrimages to Buddhist sites, Asoka erected shrines and memorial pillars. He is said to have opened up the ten original *stupas*, which contained relics of the Buddha and holy monks, and distributed some of the relics to other places in India. This helped to popularise the *stupa*, as a focus of devotion. Asoka was keen to spread the message of Buddhism and sent out parties of monks to 'border areas.' His edicts also say that he sent out embassies to several other countries. His son the monk Mahinda was sent to Sri Lanka and established Buddhism there.

According to tradition, questioned by some scholars, Asoka played a leading role in the Council of Pataliputra, held in 250. This Council resulted in the Great Schism between the 'Teaching of the Elders' (Theravada), which rejected innovation and claimed to uphold the original tradition and the 'Great Assembly', from which Mahayayana ('Great Vehicle') Buddhism derives.[5]

Asoka's influence on Buddhism and thereby his continuing influence on the world is enormous. Asoka is seen as the model Buddhist ruler and certainly from his own account his policies would appear more enlightened than those of many modern governments. He insisted that morality should be the basis of political action. For the Beloved of the Gods moral conquest was the only conquest that counted. Yet even the satisfaction that this could give was, he said, of no value compared to the consequences of action in the other world.[6]

CHAPTER NOTES
1. Kalinga Edict I, quoted by Radha Kumud Mookerji, *Asoka*, Delhi,

Motilal Banarsidass, 1962, p. 6.

2. Rock edict XIII in *The Edicts of Asoka*, edited and translated by N A Vicam and Richard Mckeon, Chicago, University of Chicago Press, 1959, pp. 27-30, quoted in Mircea Eliade, *From Primitives to Zen, A Thematic Sourcebook on the History of Religions*, p. 562.

3. Kalinga edict II, Nikam and McKeon, pp.53-4, Eliade, p. 566.

4. Rock edict XII, Nickam and McKeon , pp.51-2, quoted in Mircea Eliade, p. 254.

5. The differences between Theravada Buddhism and Mahayana Buddhism are explained more fully in the chapter on Nagarjuna.

6. Rock edict XIII, Nikam and McKeon, pp. 27-30, Eliade, p.563.

19

Mary

St Mary the Virgin, the mother of Jesus, is herself a focus of devotion for Christians. Her cousin Elizabeth called her 'the most blessed of all women.'[1] She was soon spoken of as 'Mother of God' and as *Theotokos* or 'God-bearer.' Images of her are to be seen in many churches. She has been the subject of great works of art and appears on numerous Christmas cards. 'The tradition about Mary forms a vast and multi-layered aspect of Western history, culture and spirituality.'[2] Yet, whereas she is venerated by Roman Catholic and Orthodox Christians, Protestants have paid little attention to her, some suspecting that excessive devotion to her can divert attention from the saving work of Jesus Christ.

The story of the birth of Jesus and Mary's role in it has been retold countless times through the centuries, sung about in Christmas carols, painted by famous and unknown artists and re-enacted by innumerable young children.

The Bible tells us nothing about Mary's birth or childhood. According to the second century *Gospel of James*, which the Church regards as apocryphal or unauthentic, Mary's parents were called Joachim and Anne. At Marsh Baldon where I was vicar there was a mediaeval stained glass window of Anne teaching the young Mary how to read, which, in the thirteenth century was quite a popular subject in England for paintings and stained glass work. In Jerusalem, a beautiful Crusader Church of St Anne, built over earlier Christian buildings, which may date back to the third century, is said to be on the site of the home where Mary grew up. Maybe Joachim had some position at the Temple. Certainly Mary's uncle Zechariah was a priest at the Temple.

In St Luke's Gospel, the story begins with the message of the Angel Gabriel to a young woman in Nazareth, telling her that she would give birth to a son to be called Jesus. Puzzled, she replied, 'I am a virgin. How, then, can this be?'[3] The Angel explained that God's power would rest upon her, and that, therefore, the child would be called 'the Son of God.' The great majority of Christians believe in Mary's miraculous virginal conception of her son Jesus. She is usually known as the Virgin Mary. Sometimes she is spoken of as 'ever Virgin', although the New Testament refers to brothers and sisters of Jesus.[4] The Virgin birth, as it is often, if inaccurately called, 'is an eloquent sign of the divine sonship of Christ...and points to the new birth of every Christian.'[5] Some Christians, however, feel that a Virgin Birth 'tends to mar the completeness' of Jesus' identification with humanity if he was not like us in all ways.[6]

Mary was already promised in marriage to a carpenter called Joseph, who, thanks to a message received in a dream, did not disown her.[7] Shortly before the baby's expected arrival, Joseph with Mary had to set out on a four or five days' journey from Nazareth in Galilee, to Bethlehem - a town a few miles south of Jerusalem. This was because the Roman rulers were taking a census for taxation purposes. They required people to register at their family's hometown. Bethlehem was the birthplace of King David and Joseph was a descendant of David. The town was so crowded that when Mary and Joseph arrived, no accommodation was available, so they took shelter in a stable, probably a cave used for animals. It was there, in poverty, that Jesus, whom Christians worship as the Son of God, was born. Luke tells of the visit of the shepherds[8] and St Matthew recounts the arrival of wise men, who had seen a star in the East.[9]

Jesus was brought up in a devout Jewish home. His parents arranged for his circumcision eight days after his birth and a few weeks later presented him in the Temple in Jerusalem. Every year Mary and Joseph, with their child, went up to Jerusalem for the Passover. Once, when he was twelve, they set off with the other pilgrims to return home, only to discover in the evening that Jesus was nowhere to be seen. After three days of anxious searching, they found he was in the Temple, listening to the rabbis and asking them questions. When Mary reprovingly said, 'My son, why have you treated us like this? Your father and I have been searching for you in great anxiety.' Jesus answered, 'Did you not know that I was bound to be in my Father's house.'[10]

According to John's Gospel, at the start of Jesus' ministry, he accompanied his mother to a wedding at nearby Cana. To their embarrassment, the hosts ran out of wine, but at Mary's prompting, Jesus turned the water into wine. Otherwise, little is heard of Mary during his ministry. On one occasion when she and his brothers and sisters wanted to contact him while he was teaching, he seems to have rebuffed them, pointing to the crowd and saying, 'Here are my mother and brothers! Whoever does God's will is my brother, my sister, my mother.'[11]

Mary, in her grief, watched her son die an agonizing death on the cross. As he was dying, Jesus commended her to the care of the disciple John. After his Ascension to heaven, Mary was with the disciples as they spent their time in prayer waiting for the gift of the Holy Spirit. Nothing more is known for certain about her. There is one tradition that she died in Jerusalem, on Mount Zion, where the Church of the Dormition now stands. Another tradition says that Mary went with John to live in Ephesus and that in her old age she moved to a small house in the nearby countryside, where she died.

The story of how the site was rediscovered is itself fascinating. In the early nineteenth century, Catherine Emmerich (1774-1824), a Bavarian visionary, had a dream in which she saw where the house had been built. In 1892 two Catholic priests came to try to find it. On their last day they discovered a place which fitted Catherine's description, where there were some ruins of a building, now said to have been a ninth century church dedicated to St Mary. The house has been restored and in 1967 Pope Paul VI visited it and verified the site. With its nearby spring of healing water, the house has become a place of pilgrimage for Christians and Muslims, both of whom reverence the Virgin Mary. They come to pray for healing or the gift of a child. Our own prayers for a granddaughter were answered.

It is often a surprise to Christians that Mary is mentioned thirty four times by name in the Qur'an and only nineteen times in the New Testament – although this is partly because in the Qur'an Jesus is often called 'Son of Mary'. The Qur'an emphasises Mary's virginity. When she carried home her baby, which was born beneath a palm tree, she was accused of improper conduct. She replied 'I am the servant of God.'[12] The Sufi mystic Rabi'a was called 'a second spotless Mary.' The Qur'an rejects the heretical idea that holy people do not need food and says of Mary and Jesus (Isa) that 'both of them ate food.'[13] The Prophet Muhammad had a deep respect for Mary. It is said that when he gave orders to his followers on their triumphant return to Mecca to obliterate the idols and pictures at the holy Ka'ba, he put his hands on the picture of Jesus and Mary and said, 'Wash out all except what is below my hands.'[14]

In the early Church, Mary was seen as a model of holiness. At a time when celibacy was highly honoured, her virginity was thought to reflect a single-hearted devotion to God. Her obedience to God was contrasted with Eve's disobedience. Theologians in stressing the real humanity of Jesus emphasised that he was born of Mary and was 'man, of the substance of his mother.'[15] His virginal conception, however, was evidence that Jesus was also truly divine. Mary soon became known as 'God-bearer', *Theotokos*, although Nestorius (d. c.451), patriarch of Constantinople, who gave his name to the ancient Nestorian Church of Persia, rejected this. By the fifth century, Churches began to be dedicated to her and major events in her life were celebrated as festivals.

The first Christians had a strong sense of their communion with the saints, who, in time, they asked to intercede for them to Christ. Mary, of course, was pre-eminent. In the Later Middle Ages, as the role of Christ as Judge at the end of the world was emphasised, so increasingly Christians, conscious of their sin, prayed to Mary to ask her Son to show them mercy. Mary came to be seen not just as representing the faithful Church, but as a dispenser of Christ's graces to the faithful. In popular religion, Mary came to be seen as an intermediary between God and humanity and even to be the worker of miracles. Scholars, meanwhile, speculated on whether Mary, like her son, was free from both original sin and actual sin.

In the sixteenth century, such 'exaggerated devotions' were criticised by the humanist scholars Erasmus (c.1466-1536) and Thomas More (1478-1535) and rejected by the Protestant Reformers.[16] By contrast 'to be Roman Catholic came to be identified by an emphasis on devotion to Mary.'[17] This emphasis on Mary reached its fullest expression in the nineteenth and early twentieth centuries with the definition of the dogmas of the Immaculate Conception (1854) – that Mary herself was conceived with out sin – and of the Assumption (1950) – that at her death her body was taken up into heaven. Mary has often been spoken of as 'Co-Redemptress', although this title has not been officially approved. The Second Vatican Council spoke, more modestly, of Mary as a sign of hope and comfort for God's pilgrim people.[18] Although the great Protestant theologian Karl Barth (1886-1968) said of Mary, 'she is simply man [sic!] to whom the miracle of revelation happens,'[19] some Anglicans and Protestants are today showing a more sympathetic attitude to Mary. Recently, with the founding in 1967 of the Ecumenical Society of the Blessed Virgin Mary, there has been a growing consensus among Christians about the reverence that should be paid to her.

One example of this is the shrine at Walsingham, which is now a place of pilgrimage for both Roman Catholics and Anglicans. In 1061, a Lady Richeld had a vision, in which she was told to build a replica of the house at Nazareth, where the angel Gabriel had told Mary that she was to have a child. It soon became a place of pilgrimage, especially as few people could make the long and arduous journey to Nazareth itself. Devout pilgrims would remove their shoes at the 'Slipper Chapel' and walk the last mile barefoot. The shrine and nearby priory were destroyed at the Reformation, but a new shrine was built in the twentieth century and attracts many visitors. Other main centres of pilgrimage and healing, usually where appearances or apparitions of Mary have been reported, are at Lourdes in France, known as a centre of healing, Fatima in Portugal, Loreto in Italy, Czestochowa in Poland, Knock in Ireland, Betania in Venezuela and Guadalupe in Mexico, where an Indian peasant had a vision of a dark-skinned Mary. Appearances continue to be reported, some of which gain the support of the Church, whereas others have been met by Episcopal disapproval.

Some theologians and feminists, influenced by Carl Jung (1875-1961) see Mary as a valued way of expressing a feminine dimension in the Godhead. Other feminists see Mary as a model of harmless feminine passivity created by a male-dominated Church.[20] Yet her great hymn of praise, the Magnificat, which has been repeatedly set to music and is treasured by Christians of all traditions, not only celebrates the fulfilment of God's promises to Abraham but looks forward to the coming of God's kingdom, which, as Liberation theologians have emphasised, overturns the accepted values of the world.

My soul glorifies the Lord
and my spirit rejoices in God my Saviour,
For he has been mindful

of the humble state of his servant.
From now on all generations will call me blessed,
for the Mighty One has done great things for me –
holy is his name.
His mercy extends to those who fear him,
from generation to generation.
He has performed mighty deeds with his arm;
he has scattered those who are proud in their inmost thoughts.
He has brought down rulers from their thrones
but has lifted up the humble.
He has filled the hungry with good things
but has sent the rich away empty.
He has helped his servant Israel,
remembering to be merciful
To Abraham and his descendants for ever,
even as he said to our fathers. [21]

CHAPTER NOTES

1. Luke, 1,42. Good News Bible.
2. Tina Beattie, 'Mary' in *Christianity the Complete Guide,* pp. 728-33.
3. Luke 1,34.
4. Mark, 3,31-5.
5. ARCIC Report, Para 18. See also *Studying Mary: Reflection on the Virgin Mary in Anglican and Roman Catholic Theology and Devotion: the ARCIC Working Papers,* ed. *Adelbert Denaux and Nicholas Sagovsky,* Edinburgh, T and T Clark, 2007, *passim.*
6. *Doctrine in the Church of England,* 1937, London, SPCK, 1957 edition, p 82.
7. Matthew, 2,18-25
8. Luke, 2,8-18. The historical accuracy of the infancy narratives has been the subject of much scholarly debate.
9. Matthew 2,1-12.
10. Luke 2,48-50.
11. Mark 3,34 (NIV).
12. Qur'an 19,28ff.
13. Qur'an 5,79.

14. This is according to Azraqi (d. 858 CE), quoted by Geoffrey Parrinder, *Jesus in the Qur'an*, London, Sheldon, 1965, p. 66.

15. From the Athanasian Creed.

16. Agreed Statement of the Anglican-Roman Catholic International Commission (ARCIC), Report Para, 2004, 44.

17. ARCIC Report, Para 47.

18. ARCIC Report, Para 47.

19. Karl Barth, *Church Dogmatics* I/2, 140).

20. See further my chapter on 'Gender from a Christian Perspective' in *Abraham's Children*, pp. 224-235.

21. Luke 1,46-55 (NIV).

20

Jesus

The influence of Jesus of Nazareth, whom Christians worship as the Son of God, has been incalculable. Traditionally, Western society has dated historical happenings by whether they occurred before or after his birth – B.C. and A.D. Events from his life have inspired Europe's greatest artists and musicians. John, at the end of his Gospel, said that if everything Jesus had done had been written down, 'even the whole world would not have room for the books that would be written.'[1] Certainly, the books written subsequently about him have more than filled great libraries.

Yet his story, as known from the gospels to many millions of Christians in many centuries and many countries, is quite short. He was born in Bethlehem in Palestine a city made famous by King David, Israel's most honoured king. His human parents were Joseph, a carpenter, and Mary, a virgin who conceived him when the Holy Spirit came upon her. Because the imperial government had ordered a census, Joseph with his heavily pregnant wife, had to travel from Nazareth in Galilee, where they were living, to Bethlehem. The crowds there, however, were so great that the only shelter they could find was a stable and 'for his bed a cattle stall.'[2] An ancient church, built over the cave, marks the site where tradition holds that Jesus was born. It has through the centuries been a place of pilgrimage where like the shepherds pilgrims have come to worship 'Christ the Lord.'[3]

Jewish by birth, Jesus was circumcised and presented in the Temple. He was born before the death of King Herod, who died in 4BCE. We are told that to escape King Herod's massacre of the baby boys of Bethlehem, the family fled for a time to Egypt. When it was safe to do so, they returned to Nazareth, where Jesus spent his childhood. We know little about this, but he must have been taught to read and write, as we know that he could read the scriptures. He would have worshipped at the synagogue - although the one which pilgrims to Nazareth are shown is of a later date – and joined in the Jewish festivals. Each year, his parents took him up to Jerusalem for the Passover and once, when he was twelve, as they set off back to Nazareth, they realised the boy was not with them. After three days of anxious searching, they found him in the Temple.

It was probably not until he was about 30 years old, that Jesus began his ministry. His cousin John the Baptist had just started a preaching mission, calling on the people to repent and be baptised in the river Jordan. When Jesus himself went to be baptised, 'he saw the heavens torn open and the Spirit, like a dove, descending upon him. A voice spoke from heaven, "Thou art my Son, my Beloved, on thee my favour rests."'[4] Jesus immediately withdrew to the desert wilderness, where he was tempted by the Devil.

On his return, Jesus began his ministry of teaching, healing and casting out devils. People at once commented, 'He speaks with authority.'[5] He spoke and acted as one who was directly in tune with God. His ministry, as the Gospels show, was based on prayer. His disciples asked him to show them how to pray. His response was to teach them what is known as the Lord's Prayer:

Our Father in heaven,
Thy name be hallowed,
Thy kingdom come,
Thy will be done,
On earth as in heaven.
Give us our daily bread.
Forgive us the wrong we have done,
as we have forgiven those who have wronged us.
And do not bring us to the test, but save us from the evil one.[6]

The Gospels record several of Jesus' miracles of healing. He assured sinners of God's forgiveness and his stories or parables told of God's pardoning love and challenged people to acknowledge the sovereignty of God in their lives by repentance and loving care for other people. One well known story was of the 'Prodigal Father,' who had two sons. The younger asked for his share of the inheritance, then left home and squandered the money during his travels. When he had spent all that he had and was starving, he decided to go to home, apologise and ask to be treated as a servant. Instead, the elderly father, when he saw his son in the distance, ran to meet him and arranged a great party to welcome him home. The elder son, who had stayed at home, working hard, resented this.[7]

In another parable about a Good Neighbour, Jesus told how a man, on the lonely road down from Jerusalem to Jericho, was attacked by robbers and left half-dead. A priest and a temple official went by without stopping, but a man who was a Samaritan – a people Jews looked down upon – went over to the man, treated his wounds and took him to an inn and paid for the inn-keeper to look after him. 'Which of the three,' Jesus asked, 'acted as a neighbour to the man who had been attacked?'[8]

Jesus' best known words, apart from the Lord's Prayer, are in his 'Sermon on the Mount', which begins with the Beatitudes:

Blessed are the poor in spirit: for theirs is the kingdom of heaven.
Blessed are they that mourn: for they shall be comforted.
Blessed are the meek: for they shall inherit the earth.
Blessed are they which do hunger and thirst after righteousness: for they shall be filled.
Blessed are the merciful: for they shall obtain mercy.
Blessed are the pure in heart: for they shall see God
Blessed are the peacemakers: for they shall be called the children of God.
Blessed are they which are persecuted for righteousness' sake: for theirs is the kingdom of heaven.'[9]

Jesus' teaching and actions aroused controversy. Although his approach was close to that of the Pharisees, one school of Jewish teachers, some found his radical attitudes provocative. The priestly party – the Sadducees – were alarmed that Jesus might cause popular unrest, which the Romans would use as an excuse to suppress the worship of the Temple. When Jesus with a number of followers from Galilee came up to Jerusalem and was welcomed by a cheering crowd, waving palm branches, they prepared to take action.

Aware of the growing danger, Jesus at his last meal, perhaps a Passover meal, warned the disciples of what lay ahead. At the supper he broke bread and gave it to them and shared with them a cup of wine. Ever since, his actions on that night have been re-enacted in the central act of Christian worship, known as the Mass, Holy Communion, the Eucharist or the Lord's Supper. After the meal, Jesus went with some disciples to pray in the Garden of Gethsemane. One of the disciples, however, Judas, told the authorities where they could find Jesus and they sent soldiers to arrest him. Jesus was tried by the high priests who brought him before Pilate, who eventually agreed that he should be crucified. The Gospels tend to put the blame for Jesus' death on the Jewish authorities – and this, tragically, has been a cause of anti-Semitism through the centuries. Today scholars emphasise the responsibility of Pilate, who was known for his cruelty. The Romans were quick to suppress any challenge to their authority.

Crucifixion was a particularly horrible form of death. On the Cross, Jesus prayed for those who had inflicted this on him. 'Father, forgive them, for they know not what they do.'[10] The day of his death, paradoxically, is known by Christians as 'Good Friday', as it is the day on which they believe God's limitless love was revealed and atonement made for the sins of the world.

After his death, Jesus' body was taken down from the cross and placed in a new tomb, which was a cave, with a stone rolled over the opening. Two days afterwards, some women who were his devotees, went there to prepare his body for burial. They found the stone had been rolled away and the tomb was empty. The Risen Lord then appeared to one of the women, Mary Magdalene, and later that first Easter day, to other disciples. Forty days later the Risen Jesus ascended into heaven 'to the right hand of God.' The disciples seem to have expected Jesus' early return to earth in glory, but Christians are still waiting for the Second Coming.

Questions are asked about both the historical accuracy and the mythological elements of the tradition. It was some time after Jesus' ministry that the four Gospels in the Bible were written. Mark's gospel is the earliest and probably dates to the sixties. The Evangelists used stories, which in the context of preaching, had been told and retold and applied to the concerns of those who listened to them. Some scholars accept the overall accuracy of the Gospel accounts, others are much more sceptical. There are several other so-called apocryphal gospels but it is questioned whether, apart from the Gospel of Thomas, they add much that is authentic.[11] Questions are also asked about the 'miraculous,' especially by those with a scientific outlook. It may be that explanations of the healing miracles can be found, but the Ascension is alien to a modern world-view. Some Christians interpret the Virgin birth literally, others theologically. In the same way, some think of the Resurrection as a physical event, others speak of a spiritual occurrence.

Christians, however, agree in speaking of Jesus as Son of God. Even here, however, there will be differences. Does the term 'Son' imply a moral obedience to God's will or is Jesus of the same substance as the Father? The emphasis of the Creeds is on God who becomes man – but sometimes at the expense of the full humanity of Jesus. If he was sinless, was he really human? Others start with the historical Jesus and see in his self-giving love a reflection of the character of God. They may prefer to say 'God was in Christ,' rather than 'Jesus is God.'[12] Yet, the differences should not be exaggerated. As the great twentieth century theologian Karl Barth (1886-1968) wrote, the theology of Christ has to be simultaneously 'from above' and 'from below,' or as the Orthodox Christian theologian Kallistos Ware has said, both the nearness of Jesus and the otherness of Jesus are to be affirmed.[13] Poets have perhaps expressed this better than theologians. Ephrem the Syrian (c.306-373) voiced the paradoxes in these words:

Whom have we, Lord, like you:
The Great One who became small,
The Wakeful who slept,
The Pure One who was baptized,
The Living one who died,
The King who abased himself to ensure honour for all,
Blessed is your honour.[14]

St Germanus (634-734) wrote a hymn 'A Great and Mighty Wonder,' which is still sung today and a hymn by T Pestel (1584-1659) echoes these paradoxes:

Behold the great Creator makes
Himself a house of clay.[15]

Jesus' relationship to God is not only a matter of debate among

Christians. Jews and Muslims part company with Christians over the latter's claim that Jesus is the Son of God. Both hold that this claim and therefore the doctrine of the Trinity jeopardises the Oneness of God – monotheism. Muslims, however, have great respect for Jesus. The Qur'an makes a number of references to *Isa* (Jesus). Geoffrey Parrinder was right when he said that 'the Qur'an gives a greater number of honourable titles to Jesus than to any other figure of the past.'[16] Jesus is always regarded with reverence by Muslims, who add, 'May God bless him', whenever they mention his name. He is called a 'sign', a 'mercy', a 'witness' and an 'example'. 'What good fortune, Jesus, you are for the Christian,'[17] wrote the Sufi Muslim mystic Rumi (1207-73) long ago.

Talmudic and Mediaeval Jewish references to Jesus were derogatory, which was natural at a time when Jews were oppressed by Christians. In the nineteenth century, some Jews, such as Abraham Geiger (1810-74) began to write historical studies, which emphasised the Jewishness of Jesus. Early in the twentieth century, Claude Montefiore (1858-1938), a Liberal Jew, who wrote a commentary on the Synoptic Gospels, said that Jesus should be considered as part of Judaism. Martin Buber (1878-1965), a Jewish philosopher, said, 'I have found in Jesus my great brother.'[18]

Members of other faiths may also revere Jesus. Some Hindus, such as the early nineteenth century reformer Raja Ram Mohan Roy (1772-1833), emphasised the moral teaching of Jesus. 'I found the doctrine of Christ more conducive to inculcate moral principles and better adapted to rational beings than any other that has come to my knowledge.'[19] Sri Ramakrishna (1836-1886) had a vision of 'Jesus, Love Incarnate.'[20] Mahatma Gandhi (1869-1948), who often spoke of Jesus, wrote 'the gentle figure of Christ, so patient, so kind, so loving, so full of forgiveness that he taught his followers not to retaliate when abused or struck but to turn the other cheek - it was a beautiful example, I thought, of the perfect man.'[21] Jesus, he said, 'was non-violence *par excellence.*'[22]

The Dalai Lama and the Venerable Thich Nhat Hahn, both Buddhists, concentrate on the Sermon on the Mount. The Dalai Lama compares Jesus' saying 'Love your neighbour and hate your enemy' with the Mahayana Buddhist text, 'If you do not practice compassion toward your enemy then towards whom can you practice it?'[23] Thich Nhat Hahn, who came close to Christian peace-workers during the Vietnam war, emphasises the example of Jesus. 'The life of Jesus is his most basic teaching; more important even than faith in the resurrection or faith in eternity.'[24] 'The teachings must be practiced as they were lived by Jesus.'[25]

In the outskirts of Delhi, there is a Sikh ashram, with a 'Jesus place,' which marks the spot where Jesus appeared to the founder, His Holiness Baba Virsa Singh (b. 1934). Liberation theologians have seen in Jesus a champion of the poor and Feminists see him as one who ignored the taboos of his day and was prepared to speak freely with women, such as the Samaritan woman, whom he asked for a drink of water.[26]

Jesus, furthermore, is admired by many who have no faith commitment. He has been the subject of several films. Not everyone, however, has been his admirer. The philosopher Nietzsche (1844-1900) condemned Christianity as 'the one great curse, the one intrinsic depravity, the one immoral blemish upon humankind.'[27] He argued that Christian values are anti-human and hostile to life, being fit only for slaves or the weak and inadequate.

The various ways in which Jesus has been pictured are innumerable. Ephrem, the Syrian monk, said in the fourth century, 'This Jesus has made so many symbols that I have fallen into the sea of them.'[28] In the centuries since then, the symbols have multiplied. Albert Schweitzer (1875-1965), a Christian theologian and mission doctor, argued that the pictures of Jesus constructed by modern scholars tell us more about the scholars than about Jesus. Looking into the deep well of history, the scholars see a reflection of themselves.[29] Yet the test of great art and music is that it can speak to individuals across generations and cultures. The same is true of the holy people, the 'beacons of the light,' who continue to influence and inspire us. Jesus speaks to people in many ways. Christians, like the disciple Thomas, hail him as 'My Lord and my God.'[30]

CHAPTER NOTES

1. John 21,25.
2. From the carol, 'Infant holy, infant lowly.'
3. Luke 2,11.
4. Mark 1,10-11. (New English Bible).
5. Mark 1,27.
6. Matthew, 6,9-13 (NEB) The version in Luke is slightly different.
7. Luke 15,11-32.
8. Luke 10,25-37.
9. Matthew 5,2-10 (Authorised or King James Version).
10. Luke 23,34.
11. See *The Complete Gospels,* ed Robert J Miller, San Francisco, HarperSanFrancisco, Pbk edtn, 1994.
12. See D M Baillie, *God Was in Christ,* London, Faber, 1961.
13. Kallistos Ware, quoting Karl Barth in *Abraham's Children* p 84.
14. Quoted by Kallistos Ware from Hymns of the Resurrection, 1, 22 in *Abraham's Children,* Eds. N.Solomon, R. Harries, T. Winter, London, T and T Clark, 2005, p. 86.
15. *English Hymnal,* Nos 19 and 20.
16. E.G. Parrinder, *Jesus in the Qur'an,* Sheldon 1965, p. 16.
17. Quoted in *Jesus in the World's Faiths,* Ed. Gregory A Barker, Orbis, 2005, p.125.
18. W. Jacob, *Christianity Through Jewish Eyes,* Cincinatti, OH, Hebrew Union College Press, 1974, p. 17.
19. Quoted in M M Thomas *The Acknowledged Christ of the Indian Renaissance,* London, SCM Press, 1969, p.9.
20. *The Gospel of Ramakrishna,* New York, 1942, p. 34.
21. Mahatma Gandhi, *The Message of Jesus,* Bombay, 1940, Preface.
22. Gandhi, *What Jesus Means to Me,* 1959, p.18.
23. Dalai Lama reflects on the Sermon on the Mount in Dalai Lama, *The Good Heart,* London, Rider, 1996. See also *Jesus and the Buddha: The Parallel Sayings,* Ed Marcus Borg, Duncan Baird, 2002.
24. Thich Nhat Hahn, *Living Buddha, Living Christ,* New York, Riverhead Books, 1995, p. 36.
25. Thich Nhat Hahn p. 70.
26. John, chapter 4.
27. Quoted in *The Dictionary of the World Religions,* no reference given.

28. Quoted by Kallistos Ware, *Abraham's Children*, p. 73.
29. From the concluding paragraph of Albert Schweitzer's *The Mystery of the Kingdom of God*, published in German in 1901 and published in an English translation in 1925. See further in the chapter on Albert Schweitzer, No 82.
30. John 20,29.

21

Peter

Simon Peter was the most colourful character among the disciples of Jesus. He was the first to acknowledge Jesus as 'the Christ, the Son of the Living God.' To him, despite his denial of his Master, Jesus gave 'the keys of the kingdom of Heaven.'[1] Through the centuries, Popes have claimed to inherit Peter's primacy and authority.

Simon and his brother Andrew, who grew up in Bethsaida in Galilee, were fishermen on the Lake of Galilee. According to Mark's Gospel, as Jesus was beginning his public ministry he walked along the seashore near Capernaum and saw Simon and Andrew casting their nets. He called to them, 'Come after me and I will make you into fishers of people.'[2] According to John's Gospel, Andrew was already a disciple of John the Baptist and it was the Baptist who had pointed out Jesus to him and said, 'Look, there is the Lamb of God.'[3] Subsequently, Andrew took his brother Simon to meet Jesus, who told Simon he was now to be called Peter or Cephas, which means Rock. Other Gospels give slightly different accounts of when Simon was given the name 'Peter.'[4]

Peter and Andrew, with James and John whom Jesus had also called, then followed Jesus to Capernaum. There, Jesus preached in the synagogue and healed a man with an evil spirit. Afterwards they went to the home of Simon, where his mother-in-law, who was ill, was healed by Jesus. Without this reference we would not have known that Peter was married! The probable site of Simon Peter's home, very near to the ruins of the synagogue in Capernaum, has been excavated.[5] It soon became a place where the early Christians met together.

The human failings of Peter, who was an impetuous character, are not disguised in the Gospels. Once after a night's fishing, when the disciples had caught nothing, Jesus told him to put out again into deep water and to let down the nets.[6] Peter was reluctant to do so, but Jesus was proved right. The catch was so big that the nets began to tear. Again, on the Mount of Transfiguration and in the Garden of Gethsemane, Peter, instead of praying, was overcome by sleep.[7] When Jesus predicted that he would be tried and put to death, Peter protested and earned the sharp rebuke from Jesus, 'Get behind me, Satan.'[8] To

Peter's lasting shame, on the night that Jesus was arrested, three times, as had been predicted, he denied that he knew Jesus.[9] Yet it was Peter who first confessed that Jesus was 'the Christ, the Son of the Living God.'[10] Later after Peter, who was one of the first to see the empty tomb, had affirmed his love for the Risen Jesus, the Lord told him to 'Take care of my sheep.'[11]

In the Acts of the Apostles, Peter is shown to have a leadership role in the early Christian community, although James, the brother of Jesus, also seems to have had considerable authority. Peter threw his weight behind Paul in the heated debate on whether Gentiles could join the early Christian community, without first converting to Judaism and being circumcised. (At the time, devout Jews, because of Biblical dietary rules would not eat with Gentiles and avoided social contacts with them). Peter had been convinced that the Gospel was intended for Gentiles as well as Jews by his own miraculous experience. This happened when Peter was staying at the ancient port of Jaffa or Joppa. There on the rooftop Peter, who was hungry, had a dream. He saw a big sheet full of animals of every kind being let down from heaven. A voice told him, 'Now Peter, kill and eat.' 'Certainly not, Lord', Peter replied, 'I have never eaten anything unclean.' The voice answered, 'What God has made clean, you have no right to call profane.' Almost at once there were messengers at the house from the Roman centurion Cornelius - a Gentile – who had also had a vision. When Peter arrived, Cornelius invited him in. Peter told the assembled company about Jesus. When these Gentiles, like the first Jewish disciples, suddenly received the gift of the Holy Spirit, Peter asked, 'Could anyone refuse the water of baptism to these people, now they have received the Holy Spirit just as we have?'[12]

Little is known about Peter's latter years. There is a strong and early tradition, mentioned for example by Clement of Rome (died c.100 CE) and Ignatius of Antioch (martyred c.107) that he eventually went to Rome. According to the second century *Acts of Peter*, he fled from the Emperor Nero's persecution of Christians, but as he left the city, he saw Jesus who asked him '*Quo vadis*? 'Where are you going?' Jesus replied 'I am going to be crucified in your place.' A beautiful simple church now marks the spot. Peter turned back and was crucified, perhaps head-down. Excavations have suggested that his tomb beneath the great basilica of St Peter's, in Rome, may be authentic. It is thought that St Mark' Gospel was written soon after Peter's death and that it preserves some of his memories of Jesus' ministry.

The question of the authority that Peter received from Jesus and which Roman Catholics claim was transmitted to the Pope has been much debated over the centuries. In St Matthew's Gospel, after Peter confessed that Jesus was the Son of God, Jesus said, 'Blessed are you, Simon son of Jonah, for this was not revealed to you by man, but by my Father in heaven. And I tell you that you are Peter and on this rock I will build my church, and the gates of Hades will not overcome it. I will give you the keys of the kingdom of heaven; whatever you bind on earth will be bound in heaven, and whatever you loose on earth, will be loosed in heaven.'[13] As we have seen, the Risen Jesus told Peter to 'Take care of my sheep.' Roman Catholics claim that the primacy of Peter has been transmitted to the Pope, who is infallible in defining matters of faith and morals. These claims are rejected by Orthodox, Anglican and Protestant churches. Even so, no one can doubt the enormous influence on Christian and world history of the Papacy, which looks for its authority, under God, from St Peter. Peter urged the disciples to live in harmony with each other, to be sympathetic, compassionate and humble. 'Do not repay evil with evil,' he said, 'or insult with insult.' It is sad that Christians have so often failed to heed his words.[14]

Two letters in the New Testament are attributed to Peter, although there are some scholarly doubts especially about his authorship of the second letter. In a moving passage written to Christians who were suffering persecution, Peter recalled the patience of Jesus in his Passion:

'Christ suffered for you and left you an example for you to follow in his steps. He had done nothing wrong and had spoken no deceit. He was insulted and did not retaliate with insults; when he was suffering he made no threats but put his trust in the upright judge. He was bearing our sins in his own body on the cross, so that we might die to our sins and live for uprightness; through his bruises you have been healed. You had gone astray like sheep but now you have returned to the shepherd and guardian of your souls.'[15]

Numerous apocryphal works have also been attributed to Peter. One of these, the Coptic *Apocalypse of Peter* was found among the Nag Hammadi papyri, which were discovered in 1945 buried near the Nile in Egypt. In it Peter has a vision of Jesus being seized and crucified, but laughing, because as Jesus explains a fleshly substitute had actually been fixed to the cross. Such a denial of the actual crucifixion was, of course, regarded as a Gnostic heresy by most Christians. There is another *Apocalypse of Peter*, with a vivid description of the punishments in hell that awaited any Christian who might repudiate the faith. There is also a second century *Gospel of Peter*, which said that the 'brothers' of Jesus were sons of Joseph by a former marriage.

The *Act of Peter*[16] has a story about his daughter, who suffered from paralysis. People asked Peter why, if he could heal others, he did not heal his own daughter. He, thereupon, commanded his daughter to get up, which she did, but then told her to relapse into her paralytic state. Peter then explained that the girl was of great beauty and, when she was only ten, she attracted a rich man called Ptolemy. When Ptolemy's advances were rejected, he abducted the girl. The onset of paralysis, however, prevented him having intercourse with the girl. Ptolemy was so upset that he was about to commit suicide when thanks to a divine intervention, he converted to Christianity and gave his money to the poor. The *Act of Peter*, mentioned by Tertullian in about 190 was probably written towards the end of the second century, not by Gnostics, but by an extremely ascetical sect known as Encratites, who extolled chastity.

There are other apocryphal works attributed to Peter, but none of them give us additional reliable information about him. It is worth mentioning them, however, because occasional, often uncritical, television programmes or press articles about them imply there is a lot of secret knowledge about Jesus, which has been suppressed. Such speculation, which may be disturbing for traditional Christians, remains no more than conjecture, because there seems no way of establishing if any of the recently discovered texts contain any authentic new information about Jesus and the disciples. It does show, however, that there were in the early centuries of Christianity wide differences in the way that people understood the significance of story of Jesus. [17]

Peter, however, insisted that he was not slavishly repeating 'cleverly invented myths' but what he had seen with his own eyes and that, with his own ears, he had heard the voice from the mountain which said of Jesus, 'This is my Son, the Beloved, he enjoys my favour.'[18]

CHAPTER NOTES

1. Matthew 16,16-20.
2. Mark 1,16-17.
3. John 1,35-6.
4. See Matthew 16,18 and Luke 5,1-11.
5. The ruined synagogue probably dates to the third century CE but is built over an older synagogue.
6. Luke 5,4.
7. Luke 9,32 and Luke 22,46.
8. Mark 8,33.
9. Mark 14,6-72.
10. Matthew 16,6.
11. John 21,17.
12. Acts chapters 10 and 11 and 15,7-14.
13. Matthew, 16,17-20.
14. I Peter 3,8-9.
15. I Peter 3,21-25 (Jerusalem Bible).
16. The *Act of Peter* is a Coptic translation of an orginal Greek text. It was perhaps intended as an introduction to the *Acts of Peter*, which was also originally written in Greek, but only survives in a sixth or seventh century Latin translation
16. There is a good summary of the various apocryphal works in *The Lutterworth Dictionary of the Bible*, pp. 672-6.
17. II Peter 1,16-18.

22

John

John, the 'beloved disciple' was the first to believe in the resurrection of Jesus.[1] His Gospel explains the deeper meaning of the life of Jesus.

John and his brother James, the sons of Zebedee, like Peter and Andrew, were fishermen on the Sea of Galilee, whom Jesus called to follow him. The fact that there were hired men in the boat suggests that Zebedee was quite prosperous. John and his brother James were nicknamed 'Boanerges' or 'sons of thunder' by Jesus, because of their fiery temperament. When a Samaritan village refused to let Jesus enter because he was on his way to Jerusalem, they asked him to call down fire upon it.[2] Jesus, however, rebuked them. Jesus also told them that they would indeed by their martyrdom drink the cup that he was to drink.[3] It may be that John's family were of priestly descent.

It is usually thought that the follower described as the 'disciple whom Jesus loved', who reclined next to him at the Last Supper, was John. John like Peter was present at the Transfiguration and at the tomb on the first Easter morning. He was also at the foot of the cross, as Jesus died. Before his death, Jesus commended his mother Mary to her care, saying to Mary, 'Woman, this is your son' and to John, 'This is your mother.'[4]

Soon after the death and resurrection of Jesus, James, John's brother, was put to death with the sword by King Herod. At some stage, John may have settled at Ephesus. According to tradition, John, by then an old man, himself suffered persecution under the Emperor Domitian and was banished to the beautiful island of Patmos. Both Ephesus and Patmos claim to be the place where John was buried.

There are various traditional stories about John. It was said that when John was too old to preach, he simply repeated, to the tedium of his hearers, 'Love one another. That is the Lord's command: and if you keep it, that by itself is enough.' This certainly seems to echo the message of John's letters. As he put it in his second letter, 'I am asking you...not as though I were writing you a new commandment, but only the one which we have had from the beginning – that we should love one another.'[5] John insisted that the love, which united the believer with

Christ, was also to bind believers together in fellowship. He quoted Jesus' words 'Love each other as I have loved you;'[6] and again, 'A new command I give you: Love one another. As I have loved you, so you must love one another.'[7] That mutual love, John emphasised in his letters, should find practical expression. 'If anyone has material posses-sions and sees his brother in need but has no pity on him, how can the love of God be in him?' he asked. 'Let us not love with words of with tongue but with actions and in truth.'[8]

Other traditions about John are reflected in the work of artists. He is sometimes pictured holding a cup with a viper, in memory of the challenge made to him by a high priest at the temple of Diana at Ephesus to drink a poisoned cup. He is also portrayed holding a book and his emblem as an evangelist is an eagle.

All ancient sources agree that the author of the Fourth Gospel was John, the son of Zebedee, although a number of modern scholars have disputed this. Tradition suggests that John wrote the Gospel in his old age, possibly as late as 95 CE. A papyrus fragment of the Gospel has been found which is dated to about 130.[9] It may be that several people had a hand in writing or editing the Gospel. Some early Fathers of the Church spoke of John's Gospel as the collective memory of the apostles and that John recorded his 'witness' with the help of a scribe. There is more uncertainty whether the same John wrote the mysterious *Book of Revelation*, with which the Bible ends.

The 'feel' of the Fourth Gospel is, certainly, very different to that of the other three Gospels, which are often called the Synoptic Gospels because, despite differences of emphasis, they see Jesus with same eye or from the same perspective. The Synoptic gospels consist of short stories and sayings. In John's gospel there are long discourses and philosophical discussions. The Synoptic gospels focus on the kingdom of God or of Heaven, but John speaks of eternal life. John's Gospel is more meditative and the divinity of Jesus more clearly asserted. There is a sharp contrast between light and darkness.

Yet John's Gospel has vivid historical touches, which may suggest that it is, at least in part, by an eyewitness. For example in recounting the miraculous feeding of the crowd, it is noted that 'there was plenty of grass in that place.'[10] John describes the washing of the disciples' feet by Jesus. Yet, although John records a long discourse given by Jesus at his last meal with his disciples, there is no mention of the institution of Holy Communion or of the words, 'Do this in remembrance of me.' There is, however, a long discourse about the 'Bread of Heaven' earlier in the gospel, following the account of the Feeding of the Multitude.

It is still a matter of debate whether John knew the other Gospels. There are some marked discrepancies. For example, the Cleansing of the Temple of traders and sacrificial animals comes in the second chapter of John's Gospel, at the beginning of Jesus' ministry. In the other Gospels it takes place early in the week that culminates with the death of Jesus. Only John mentions Jesus' conversation with the woman of Samaria. Again, there is disagreement whether the Last Supper was on the evening of Passover. Only John's Gospel tells of the raising of Lazarus from the dead. John also emphasises the mutual indwelling of the believer and Christ. He tells of Jesus saying:

'I am the true vine and my Father is the gardener... I am the vine you are the branches. If a person remains in me, and I in him, he will bear much fruit... As the Father has loved me, so I have loved you. If you obey my commands, you will remain in my love... Greater love has no-one that this, that he lay down his life for his friends. You are my friends if you do what I command.'[11]

Arguments about authorship also relate to disputes about milieu in which the Fourth Gospel was written and especially the philosophical background to the term 'Logos' or 'Word' that John uses in the Prologue to his Gospel. It was commonly thought in the first part of the twentieth century that the Gospel came from a Gentile setting and reflected Hellenistic ways of thinking. This made it unlikely that a Jewish fisherman would have written it. It is now, however, quite widely held that the background was a Jewish one, because we now know that the Judaism of the first century CE was very varied. Some scholars suggest that the high claims John made for Jesus were, in his eyes, compatible with Jewish monotheism.[12]

The opening sentence of John's Gospel is, 'In the beginning was the Word, and the Word was with God and the Word was God. He was with God in the beginning.' John goes on to say 'The Word became flesh and made his dwelling among us.'[13] John may be adapting Rabbinic Judaism's way of speaking of the Law (Torah) or Wisdom as being with God before creation.[14] John may, alternatively, draw on Hellenistic ideas, whether from Stoic philosophy or Gnostic speculation. In that case Logos would be the rational principle underlying the universe or the intermediary between God and the world. Maybe, like a poet, John deliberately uses a word with wide resonance. This is why perhaps the Gospel continues to have such wide appeal and I remember a Hindu teacher saying to me that it is the most beautiful book in the world.

The Book of Revelation begins with three chapters, which describe the call of a seer named John, who was in exile on the island of Patmos and records letters to the seven churches in Asia Minor. The larger part of the book describes a series of visions, which encourage the faithful to stand firm. Other visions proclaim judgement on the world and predict the downfall of the Whore of Babylon (namely the city of Rome). There is also the promise of a New Jerusalem, in which those whose names are written in the Lamb's book of life live in the presence of One seated on the Throne and of the Lamb.

The Book of Revelation was probably written at a time of great persecution. We do not know who the John was to whom it is attributed. Luther and some others question whether the book should have been included in the New Testament as, in his view, it did not sufficiently proclaim the message of Jesus. The book, partly because of its obscurity has provided a mine for those who have wished to speculate on the future. Yet the image of Christ as the Light of the World knocking on the door of the heart, made famous by the painting by Holman Hunt (1827-1910), and the vision of the ultimate completion of God's purposes have continued to inspire many of the faithful.

CHAPTER NOTES
1. John 20,8.
2. Luke 9,54.
3. Mark 10,35-45.
4. John, 19,26-7.
5. 2 John verse 5.
6. John, 15,12.
7. John 13,34.
8. I John 3,18.
9. Mark Edwards, *John*, Oxford, Blackwell, 2004, p.2.
10. John, 6,10.

11. John, chapter 15, *passim*.
12. See James Dunne, *The Partings of the Ways*, London, SCM Press, 1991.
13. John, 1, verse 1-2, and 14.
14. John Marsh, *St John*, London, Penguin, 1968, p.97. See also Ecclesiasticus 1,4.

23

Paul

St Paul, dramatically converted on the Damascus road from a perse-
cutor to a believer in Jesus, has been called 'the real founder of
Christianity.' This is an exaggeration and suggests a false distinction
between the gospel of Jesus and the preaching of Paul. Nonetheless,
'Paul's influence on the development of Christian faith has been greater
than that of any other man, for without his conviction that the gospel
was intended for Gentiles *qua* Gentiles, Christianity would have
remained a Jewish sect.'[1] His writings have profoundly influenced
Christian life in every generation and times of renewal have all been
nurtured by fresh interest in his teaching.

Our knowledge of Paul is based on his letters and the story of the
early Christian community told in the *Acts of the Apostles*, half of which
is devoted to Paul's activities. Traditionally *Acts* is thought to have been
written by St Luke, who was the author of the third Gospel. It suggests
that, for at least for some of the time, Luke was a companion of Paul.
There are, however, discrepancies between what *Acts* says and what
Paul himself wrote.

Paul had a dual identity. He was a Roman citizen and a devout Jew.
He was born in Tarsus, which he described as 'no mean city.'[2] Tarsus
was in the Roman province of Cilicia, situated on the Mediterranean
coast in what is now South Eastern Turkey. Oriental in the background
of its life and traditions, Tarsus was markedly Greek in its culture. It
had a school of philosophy, where the emphasis was on the teachings
of the Stoics. Tarsus was also an important commercial centre. The
lingua franca of intellectual life in the Eastern Empire was Greek and
Paul wrote his letters in Greek. He would also have understood Latin
and indeed he preferred to be known by his Latin name of Paul. As a
Jew, however, he would have spoken Aramaic at home and would have
studied the scriptures in Hebrew. As a Jew, he was named Saul, after
the first King of Israel, who like Paul was of the tribe of Benjamin. Saul's
family were Pharisees, members of a renewal movement, which
emphasised God's care for the individual and encouraged personal
holiness. At a young age he was sent to Jerusalem, where he studied

under the famous Rabbi Gamaliel (early first century) and probably trained as a rabbi.

Paul said of himself that he was zealous for God. He persecuted the followers of Jesus and was present and gave his approval when St Stephen, the first Christian martyr, was stoned to death. It was to continue his heresy hunting that Paul set out for Damascus. On the way an event happened that changed his life and, arguably, the history of the world. Paul, as reported in the *Acts of the Apostles*, described what happened.

'About noon as I came near Damascus, suddenly a bright light from heaven flashed around me. I fell to the ground and heard a voice say to me, "Saul! Saul! Why do you persecute me?" "Who are you Lord?" I asked. "I am Jesus of Nazareth, whom you are persecuting," he replied. My companions saw the light, but they did not understand the voice of him who was speaking to me.'[3]

Paul, blinded by the brilliance of the light, was led into Damascus, where a follower of Jesus called Ananias was sent by God to visit him. Paul's sight was restored. Ananias told Paul that he had been chosen by God 'to be his witness to all people of what he had seen and heard.'[4]

This was to become the great task of his life - to spread the good news of Jesus throughout the Mediterranean world. He travelled vast distances, as I have discovered in pilgrim journeys in the footsteps of Paul. He certainly went as far as Italy and just possibly may have reached Spain.

The *Acts of the Apostles* records three missionary journeys and also Paul's final voyage to Rome.[5] Soon after the visit of Ananias, Paul started preaching in Damascus that 'Jesus was the Son of God.' Because of a threat to his life, he escaped from the city, lowered over its walls by his followers. He then went up to Jerusalem where he was introduced to the other disciples by Barnabas - whose name means 'son of consolation'. After that he travelled down to Caesarea and from there sailed back to his hometown of Tarsus. Then, some while later Barnabas went to Tarsus to find Paul and brought him to Antioch.

It was from Antioch that Paul and Barnabas set out on the first missionary journey, accompanied by John, surnamed Mark, who is usually identified as the author of the second gospel. They went first to Cyprus: landing at Salamis, they made their way across the island to

Paphos in the West. They then sailed to Asia Minor (now Turkey), but Mark left them when they landed at Perga. Why Mark 'deserted', we do not know, but he may have been unhappy at a mission to the Gentiles, whereas in Cyprus Paul and Barnabas had preached in the synagogues.

Without Mark, Paul and Barnabas travelled from Perga 80 miles through rugged, bandit-infested countryside, to Antioch in Pisidia. There, they began by preaching in the synagogue. Although they had some supporters, they also met with fierce opposition, which included physical stoning. As a result, Paul told them, 'We had to speak the word of God to you first. Since you reject it and do not consider yourselves worthy of eternal life, we now turn to the Gentiles.'[6] The Gentiles were more enthusiastic and at Lystra, to the apostles' horror, the crowd cried out, 'the gods have come down to us in human form.'[7] When Paul and Barnabas got back to Antioch, they discovered that not all the disciples in Jerusalem shared their joy that some Gentiles had come to believe in Jesus. A gathering of the leadership in Jerusalem, at which Paul explained what had happened, agreed with him, that on certain conditions, Gentile believers did not have to be circumcised nor obey all the commands of the Jewish law.

After a time Paul wanted to go back to Asia Minor to see how the Christians there were faring. Paul, after an argument with Barnabas, refused to take Mark on the second missionary journey, because he had left them on their first journey. Paul, therefore, took Timothy with him, while Barnabas went back to Cyprus with Mark. On this journey, Paul had a vision of a man from Macedonia who begged him, 'Come over to Macedonia and help us.'[8] This they did, so bringing the Gospel message to Europe. They landed at Neapolis and made their way to the major Roman city of Philippi, where today much of the ancient city has been excavated, including the prison from which Paul and Timothy were miraculously set free. On this journey, Paul went on to Thessalonica and then made his way down the coast to Athens and Corinth. From there he journeyed back to Antioch, with a brief call at Ephesus.

On his third journey, Paul kept his promise to return to the vast city of Ephesus, where his preaching provoked a riot from the silver-smiths, who shouted out, 'Great is Diana of the Ephesians.' They feared that their trade in images of the goddess Artemis (Diana) would be ruined if people deserted their worship of her. Paul also revisited Christian communities in Asia Minor and Greece.

On his return, a visit to the Temple in Jerusalem got him into trouble with the Jewish leaders. A Roman commander intervened and Paul was eventually taken to Caesarea, the Romans' regional capital. There, as the Acts of the Apostles records, various high officials questioned him. Paul was afraid, however, that the Romans might hand him over to his enemies. Exercising his right as a Roman citizen, Paul addressed the court saying, 'If I am guilty of doing anything deserving death, I do not refuse to die. But if the charges brought against me are not true, no one has the right to hand me over to my enemies. I appeal to Caesar.' The governor Festus replied in the famous words: 'You have appealed to Caesar. To Caesar you will go.'[9]

Festus, baffled by Jewish arguments, did not know on what charge to send him to Rome and so asked for the help of King Agrippa. After considerable delay, Paul was despatched on the perilous journey to Caesar's court in Rome. Luke graphically describes the terrible storm, which overtook their ship and their shipwreck on the island of Malta. Eventually Paul got to Rome where he was held under house arrest. There, tantalisingly, the *Acts of the Apostles* ends. According to tradition, Paul was martyred at Rome during the persecution of the Emperor Nero in about 65 CE. As a Roman citizen he was beheaded, unlike Peter who endured (head-down) the agony of crucifixion. It is believed that they died on the same day, which is why Peter and Paul share June 29th as their feast day.

Paul's letters or epistles, which make up over a third of the New Testament, are thought to have been written in the fifties. There is dispute whether all of them are genuine. The letters as printed in the Bible are not in date order. The longest, the letter to the Romans, which is the most theologically complex, comes first and the shortest to Philemon, whose slave Onesimus was with Paul in prison, comes last. It is now generally agreed that the Letter to the Hebrews is not by Paul. The earliest letters were probably the two to the Thessalonians, whom he visited on his second missionary journey. There are two surviving letters to the church in Corinth and one each to the Galatians, the Ephesians, the Philippians and the Colossians, as well as two letters to his junior colleague, Timothy, and one to Titus. The letters have a number of personal greetings and it is important to remember that, despite the theological significance of the letters, they were dictated by Paul to deal with problems arising in the newly formed churches he had founded. His thought, therefore, develops and is not always consistent.

The decisive experience of Paul's life occurred on the road to Damascus. This event is often called Paul's 'conversion', 'yet Paul's new faith was in many ways the fulfilment of his earlier beliefs, not their denial. Moreover, Paul's own references to the event view it primarily as his commission to be an apostle especially to the Gentiles.'[10] This sense of his mission is often today seen as the key to understanding the thought of Paul, who was convinced that in Jesus God had reached out in love to Gentiles just as much as to Jews.

There was at the time considerable Jewish speculation about the new age that God would bring in. Some Jews seem to have expected that in the last days Gentiles or at least some of them would turn to the One God, whom Israel worshipped.[11] Indeed a number of Gentiles were 'God-fearers', who regularly attended synagogue services. If Paul had come to believe that the death and Resurrection of Jesus Christ marked the crucial turning point in human history and that the new age had dawned, then the mission to the Gentiles was a necessary consequence. Paul, however, had to stand firm against those Jewish followers of Jesus who insisted that would-be Gentile disciples had first to convert to Judaism, which for men required circumcision, before they could become members of the Church. Paul insisted that in Christ 'there is no Greek or Jew, circumcised or uncircumcised, barbarian, Scythian, slave or free, but Christ is all and is in all.'[12] Paul in his letters, therefore, criticises so-called 'Judaisers' who wanted to make Gentile converts observe all the requirements of the Jewish Law or *Torah*. Paul does not criticise Jews or the Torah as such. For Paul, it was enough for Christians to imitate Christ, who had fully obeyed the Law. Sadly, for too long this was not recognised and Paul's writings were used to fuel the anti-Judaism, which for centuries characterised much of the teaching of the Church.

Even now, this is a matter of dispute, as is the question whether Paul expected Christianity to replace Judaism. In his letter to the Romans, Paul asked 'Did God reject His people? By no means.'[13] Are, as some contemporary Christian scholars suggest, Jews and Christians both 'People of God?' If so, they argue, Christian missionary efforts to convert Jews are inappropriate. Other Christians, especially Messianic Jews, pray that all Jews will recognise Jesus as the true Messiah.

At the time of the Reformation, emphasis fell on Paul's teaching about 'justification by faith'. Martin Luther claimed that Paul insisted that a person could not by his or her own efforts gain the approval of God. What was required was complete trust or faith in God's mercy, revealed in the death of Christ. 'God demonstrates his own love for us in this: While we were still sinners, Christ died for us.'[14] Confident in God's love, the believer should then allow the Spirit of Christ to transform his or her life – a process known as 'sanctification' or the growth in holiness – until he could say, with Paul, 'I have been crucified with Christ and I no longer live, but Christ lives in me. The life I live in the body, I live by faith in the Son of God, who loved me, and gave himself for me.'[15]

Paul spoke in the highest terms of Jesus Christ as 'Son of God,' 'Image of God,' and 'Wisdom of God' but he seems to have stopped short of identifying Jesus with God – a step that the Church was later to make in formulating the doctrine of the Trinity.[16] Paul affirmed that just as Jesus had died and rose again so the believer would share in the resurrection. Paul confidently looked forward to the return of Jesus Christ in glory.

According to the apocryphal *Acts of Paul and Thecla*, Paul was small in stature, bald and bandy-legged, with a long nose. In his letters, he mentioned he had some physical affliction. When he asked God to heal it, he was told, 'My grace is sufficient for you, for my power is made perfect in weakness.'[17] Paul is often depicted as holding a sword in one hand and a book in the other, because in the Letter to the Ephesians, he urged Christians to arm themselves with 'the sword of the Spirit, which is the word of God.'[18]

At times Paul could be argumentative and opinionated, but at other times he could wax lyrical in his praise of God, and the beauty of Christ's divine love. He wrote in his Letter to the Romans:

'Oh, the depth of the riches of the wisdom and knowledge of God!
How unsearchable his judgments
And his paths beyond tracing out!

Who has known the mind of the Lord?

Or who has been his counsellor?..

For from him and through him and to him are all things.

To him be the glory for ever.'[19]

Again to the Romans he wrote,

'Who shall separate us from the love of Christ? Shall trouble or hardship or persecution or famine or nakedness or danger or sword? ... No, in all these things we are more than conquerors through him who loved us. For I am convinced that neither death nor life, neither the present nor the future, nor any powers, neither height nor depth, nor anything else in all creation, will be able to separate us from the love of God that is in Christ Jesus our Lord.'[20]

Perhaps most famous of all is Paul's hymn of love in his First Letter to the Corinthians.

If I speak with the tongues of men and of angels, but have not love, I am only a resounding gong or a clanging cymbal... Love is patient, love is kind. It does not envy, it does not boast, it is not proud, it is not self-seeking, it is not easily angered, it keeps no record of wrongs. Love does not delight in evil but rejoices with the truth. It always protects, always trusts, always perseveres. Love never fails... These three remain: faith, hope and love. But the greatest of these is love.'[21]

CHAPTER NOTES

1. Morna D Hooker, 'Paul' in *The Oxford Companion to Christian Thought*, p. 524.
2. Acts of the Apostles, 21,39.
3. Acts 22,6-9. There are other accounts in Acts, 9 and 26.
4. Acts 22,15.
5. For details see James Harpur and Marcus Braybrooke, *The Journeys of St Paul*, London, Marshall editions, 1997.
6. Acts 13,46.
7. Acts 14,11.
8. Acts 16, 9.
9. Acts 25,11-12.

10. Morna Hooker, p. 521. Paul spoke in this way in I Corinthians,9,1-2; 15,8-9; Galatians, 1, 16 and 2,7.
11. See Zechariah 8, verses 8, and 20-21.
12. Colossians 3,11.
13. Romans 11,1.
14. Romans 5,8.
15. Galatians 2,20.
16. See further James D G Dunn, *The Partings of the Ways,* London SCM Press, 1991, Chapter 10, see especially, p. 206, but for a different view see L W Hurtado, *One God, One Lord: Early Christian Devotion and Ancient Jewish Monotheism,* London, SCM Press, 1988, *passim.*
17. 2 Corinthians 12,2-9.
18. Ephesians 6,17.
19. Romans 11,33,34,36.
20. Romans 8,35-39.
21. From I Corinthians chapter 13.

24

Johannan ben Zakkai
and Rabban Gamaliel II

The city of Jerusalem with its holy Temple, which had been destroyed by the Babylonians in 587 BCE, was again razed to the ground in 70 CE by the Romans. That Judaism and the Jewish people survived the onslaught of the Romans is due, under God, primarily to Johannan ben Zakkai and Rabban Gamaliel II and their fellow rabbis.

After Cyrus the Great, who was a Zoroastrian, had defeated the Babylonians with his alliance of the Medes and Persians, he allowed the Jewish exiles to return from Babylon to Jerusalem. Gradually the city and religious life were restored, under the leadership of Nehemiah and Ezra and the temple was rebuilt, although it lacked the splendour of Solomon's building.

Tiny Judah was a pawn in the conflicts between the super-powers of Persia, Greece and Egypt. The conquests of Alexander the Great (356-323) destroyed the Persian Empire. From 322 to 200 BCE the Jews were ruled by the Egyptian Ptolemies. They then came under the control of Seleucids. These developments also opened Jews and Judaism to the influence of the Greek language, literature and civilization. This, of course, was a threat to traditional Jewish values and practices. Matters came to a head when in the middle of the second century, Antiochus IV (215-164), known as Antiochus Epiphanes, prohibited the practice of Judaism, on pain of death. Temple worship was abolished and the building defiled, with swine's flesh being offered on the altar to the Greek god Zeus. This provoked a rebellion led by the Maccabees, who secured a measure of independence for the Jewish people.

Internal arguments among the Jewish leaders gave the Roman general Pompey the pretext to interfere. Pompey (106-48) captured Jerusalem in 63 BCE and Judea was reduced to the status of a Roman vassal state. Some of the puppet rulers, especially Herod the Great (37 - 4 BCE) – whom the Wise Men visited on their way to Bethlehem – had considerable autonomy. In the early years of the first century CE, Judaism, it has been said, 'was at a high point both in numbers and in influence, in Palestine as well as in the Diaspora.'[1] Religious and cultural life was vigorous and varied. The main religious groups were the Sadducees, an establishment group led by the high priest, which controlled the Temple; the Pharisees who were leaders of a religious revival that emphasised a personal relationship with God; and the Essenes who, to ensure their purity, had withdrawn to a life of extreme austerity close to the Dead Sea. There were also various political groupings. Some Jews worked closely with the Romans, others avoided them and others, known as the Zealots, wanted to drive the Romans out by force.

In 66 CE some Jews revolted against the Romans, who eventually inflicted a devastating defeat on the rebels. In 70 CE Jerusalem was totally destroyed. The Temple was razed to the ground and the population massacred or exiled. The Sadducees lost their political and religious authority; the Essene retreat at Qumran was destroyed; the surviving Zealots either died at the Dead Sea fortress of Massada when it was captured by the Romans, or they escaped to North Africa or went underground. Some groups, including the Jewish Christian community and some Pharisees opposed the rebellion.

Rabbi Johannan ben Zakkai, a leading Pharisee, was one of those who opposed the rebellion. It is said that Johannan (sometimes spelt Yohanan) had been a student of the famous Rabbi Hillel (late first century BCE to early first century CE) and that he had spent eighteen years in the Lower Galilee. When he moved to Jerusalem, his school became so famous that students would go to great lengths to be admitted to it. Later generations would speak of his prodigious knowledge. He seems to have been a humane and moderate figure. For example, he stopped the practice of a woman suspected of adultery being made to drink 'bitter water.' It is not know whether Johannan was a pacifist or whether he realized that rebellion could only end in disaster. It is said that he was smuggled out of the city, before its capture, in a coffin. Johannan said to the chief of the Zealots, who was his nephew, 'Find some sort of remedy for me to get out of here, maybe there will be a possibility of saving something.' His nephew replied, 'Pretend to be sick and have everybody come and ask about you; have something bad smelling and put it by you, so people will think you're dead. Then let your disciples carry you but nobody else – so that no one will feel that you're still light, since people know that a living being is lighter than a corpse.'[2]

Having escaped, he went to the Roman camp and apparently obtained permission to set up an academy in Jamnia (Jabneh), near the Mediterranean coast between Jaffa and Ashdod. Here, building on Pharisaic learning, he laid the foundations for Rabbinic Judaism. He saw nothing was gained by antagonizing the Romans. 'Do not rush to destroy the altars of the Gentiles, lest you will have to rebuild them yourselves.' He was sceptical of Messianic groups, saying, 'If you have a plant in your hand and someone says "The Messiah has come", go and complete the planting and afterwards go out and receive [the Messiah].'

Johannan was realistic in his reaction to the destruction of the Temple. This tragedy had left some people in deep gloom, as these verses from the Syriac apocalypse of 2 Baruch indicate.

Blessed is he who was not born,
or who was born or died.
But we, the living, woe to us,
because we have seen those afflictions of Zion,
and that which has befallen Jerusalem.

Others indulged in vain apocalyptic speculation that God would act to revenge his people. Johannan acknowledged the distress but encouraged people to make what life they could. One of his disciples expressed his Master's views, saying

'My sons, mourning too much is undesirable and not to mourn at all is undesirable. Rather, our sages have said, "A person should plaster his house and leave a small portion [unplastered] as a memory of Jerusalem. A person should make all preparations for a meal and leave a little bit [unfinished] in memory of Jerusalem. A woman should make jewellery for herself and leave a little [of herself unornamented] as a memory of Jerusalem."'[3]

Johannan, therefore, set about restoring what he could of Jewish life. Clearly the sacrificial system of the Temple was at an end, but some of the practices could be transferred to the worship of the synagogue. For example, before 70, the *shofar* or ram's horn could only be blown at the New Year, (Rosh Hashanah) in the Temple. He said it could be blown anywhere. When Yohanan was asked, 'Now that there are no sacrifices, how can we seek atonement?' he replied that good deeds (literally acts of loving kindness) will atone as sacrifices once did.[4]

Johannan ben Zakkai's work was continued by his successor, Rabban Gamaliel II (c.90-115). He received recognition not only from the Jewish community but also from Gentile authorities.

Gamaliel II belonged to a well known Pharisaic family. His great grandfather was Hillel, who when asked to recite the whole of Torah while standing on one leg, replied, 'What is hateful to you, do not do to others. That is the whole of Torah; the rest is commentary on it.' His grandfather, Gamaliel the Elder (early first century CE), was also a much respected scholar. When some of his colleagues wanted to persecute members of the early church, he advised them to leave the followers of Jesus alone, saying 'If this enterprise... is of human origin, it will break up of its own accord, but if it does in fact come from God you will be unable to destroy them. Take care not to find yourselves fighting against God.'[5]

Gamaliel II's leadership was acknowledged by other rabbis despite his youth. In the court of law, he sat in the middle, with elders to his right and left. On one occasion, however, he had to apologise for embarrassing an opponent in front of his colleagues.

Nearly 100 rabbis congregated at Yavneh. Legal questions were brought there from all parts of the country and the rabbis themselves travelled to neighbouring towns and cities.

Under Gamaliel II, Rabbinic Judaism was a given a shape that has influenced it ever since. It became an obligation for all Jews to offer daily prayer, either privately or in a synagogue. Decisions were made which helped to decide which books should be included in the canon of the Hebrew Bible. Much time was devoted to clarifying and codifying the Law. It was recognised that both the schools of Shammai (c.50 BCE-30 CE) and Hillel, which existed before the destruction of the Temple in 70 were legitimate but priority was given to Hillel's more liberal interpretations. New liturgies were created for the observance of the High Holy Days. Observance of Passover was now to be at home - it was impossible at the Temple – and an order of service, known as *haggadah*, was developed, although it has continued to evolve during the centuries.

The Rabbis at Yavneh sought rapprochement with the Roman authorities and Gamaliel II received recognition from them as the spokesperson for the Jewish community. It is said that he went to Syria 'to be granted authority by the Roman governor.'[6] Other Jews, however, still harboured hopes of revenge and a second rebellion, led by Bar-Kokhba, broke out in 132 CE, but was eventually crushed by the Romans. Afterwards, the name of the province was changed to Syria-Palestinia – instead of Judea - and a new pagan city, Aelia Capitolina, was built on the site of Jerusalem.

Nonetheless Judaism survived, largely thanks to the foresight and work of Johanan ben Zakkai and Gamaliel II. Their importance, however, is not confined to the Jewish world. After centuries of antagonism and persecution at the hands of Christians, it is increasingly recognised that Christianity did not replace Judaism. Rather, in the second century two new religious movements emerged. One was Rabbinic Judaism: the other was the Christian Church, most of whose members were by then Gentiles. But both grew from the same Hebrew and Biblical roots. Moreover, the 'Parting of the Ways', as it is often called, was as much caused by historical events - not least the destruction of Jerusalem – as by theological disagreement. This offers the hope that the misunderstanding and bitterness of the past need not determine Christian-Jewish relations in the future. Study of the origins of Rabbinic Judaism has helped many Christians in the last fifty years to gain a new appreciation of Judaism and to recognise that Jesus was a faithful Jew.

Even more important, the early Rabbis preserved the best traditions of first century Judaism and handed them on to future generations. Despite many vicissitudes, Judaism has helped to shape European civilization. Still today, although one of the smaller world religions, Judaism continues to make a significant contribution to the growing consensus on the moral values necessary for the health of our emerging global civilization.

CHAPTER NOTES

1. Louis H Feldman in *Christianity and Rabbinic Judaism*, Ed Hershel Shanks, Washington, Biblical Archaeological Society, 1992, London, SPCK, 1993, p.9.

2. Quoted in *The Blackwell Reader in Judaism*, Ed Jacob Neusner and Alan J Avery-Peck, Oxford, Blackwell, 2001, pp. 60-61.

3. Passages are quoted by Lee I A Levine in *Christianity and Rabbinic Judaism*, p. 135.

4. Quoted by Levine, p.136.

5. Acts of the Apostles, 5, 38-9 (Jerusalem Bible).

6. Quoted by Levine, p. 138.

25

Origen

Origen was the most creative and original thinker of the early church. His ideas have had a lasting influence, although some, after his death, were condemned as heretical. He lived under the shadow persecution and at a time of theological speculation, when Gnosticism was a strong rival to Christianity.

The accounts of Origen's life by the Christian historian Eusebius (c.260-c.340) and by the Neoplatonist and anti-Christian philosopher Porphyry (c.232-c.303) differ. Origen was born in about 185 CE, probably in Alexandria, which was a major centre of intellectual life in the Ancient world. According to Eusebius, Origen's parents were devout Christians. His father was highly educated and ensured that Origen had the usual Hellenistic education, as well as being schooled in biblical studies. It is said that his father died in 202, during the persecution of Christians launched by Septimius Severus (146-211), who was Emperor from 193-211. Origen was only seventeen at the time and now had to help support his mother and his six younger brothers. The persecution also forced Clement of Alexandria (d.215), who was a distinguished theologian, under whom Origen had studied, to flee from Alexandria. As a result, at the early age of eighteen, Origen became head of the Christian Catechetical School in the city.

Eusebius says that Origen as a young man castrated himself, so as to be free to teach female catechumens. Years later, Origen was to denounce the fanaticism of those who took literally the words of Jesus that 'there are those who have made themselves eunuchs for the sake of the kingdom of heaven.'[1]

Porphyry says that Origen attended lectures given by Ammonius Saccas, who is sometimes called the founder of Neoplatonism, which is an influential school of philosophy made famous by Porphyry, who himself studied under Ammonius Saccas. At the classes, Origen met Heraclas, who, later, as bishop of Alexandria, was to refuse to have communion with Origen. At this stage, however, Origen asked Heraclas to help teach at the Catechetical School. This allowed Origen time for study, during which he learned Hebrew. He then in about 212 began to compile the *Hexapla*. This is a remarkable piece of work, which brings together different versions of the Hebrew Scriptures, known to Christians as the Old Testament. The *Hexapla* (from the Greek for 'sixfold'), prints in six parallel columns the Hebrew text, then that Hebrew text transliterated into Greek letters, and then four Greek translations of the scriptures, including the Septuagint, which was the Greek translation usually used by the Church. For the Psalms there were two further translations, including one Origen found in a jar in the Jordan Valley - perhaps an early discovery of one of the Dead Sea scrolls.

Thanks to a wealthy convert, who provided him with shorthand writers, Origen wrote extensively. Many of his works have only survived in fragments or in translations. His commentary on St John's Gospel, which was written to refute one written by the Gnostic Valentius (2nd century CE), was so long – it extended to thirty-two books - that it is perhaps not surprising that few copies were made. The best surviving codex preserved in Munich has only a few of the books. Origen also at this time wrote his very important *On First Principles (De Principiis)*.

Origen was soon increasingly in demand as a lecturer and preacher. In about 229, he went to Greece to dispute with a leading Gnostic. On the way he was ordained at Caesarea. This infuriated the Bishop of Alexandria, whose permission had not been asked and who was already annoyed by some of the views of a lay teacher, whom he was not able to control. Origen, therefore, decided to settle in Caesarea, although he continued to travel widely. He was, however, late in life to suffer as a victim of persecution by the Emperor Decius in 250. He was imprisoned and tortured, but survived, although he died soon afterwards in Tyre in about 254. His tomb was honoured for many centuries and is mentioned during the time of the Crusades.

Origen in his commentaries made use of and defended the allegorical interpretation of scripture. He complained that 'Fundamentalists' or 'Literalists', as he called them, 'believe such things about [God] as would not be believed of the most savage and unjust men.'[2] True interpretation must uphold the goodness of God. Literalists, he said, misunderstood the meaning of poetry, metaphors, parables and figures of speech. They also had no interest in trying to discover what the original author of a text was trying to say.

Origen believed that the Bible has three levels of meaning, which correspond to the threefold division of a person into body, soul and spirit. The bodily level or straightforward meaning was helpful for the simple Christian. The level of the soul was to encourage progress in the spiritual life and the spiritual allowed the believer to be 'a partaker of all the doctrines of the Spirit's counsel.'

Origen distinguished different levels of discipleship. Christianity for him was a ladder of divine ascent – a theme which was to become common in Orthodox spirituality. This approach was consistent with Origen's overall theological framework.

Origen began his *On First Principles* like a typical Platonist by establishing a divine triad, but he uses Christian terms: Father, Son or Christ, and Holy Spirit. The Father is a perfect unity and pure spiritual mind. The Son is an emanation from the Father, who is superior to all rational creatures. The Spirit dwells only with Christians. His view suggests that the Son is inferior to the Father, for which later Arius (c.250-c.336) was to be condemned as a heretic, but Origen wrote before the Creeds of the Church were determined.

According to Origen, God's first creation (although not in time) was a collectivity of rational beings in close proximity to God. These souls are eternal, but they grew weary of the intense contemplation expected of them and they fell away from God. They misused the supreme gift of freedom that God had bestowed upon them. The only rational creature who escaped this fall was Christ. As souls moved away from God, they fell away from their original ethereal and invisible bodies and entered the more solid bodies with which we are now familiar. As a result no rational spirit can now exist without a body.

Origen held together complete faith in the unfailing goodness of God and the freedom of the human soul to choose the good. God, he believed, would eventually reconcile all souls, even the devil, to Himself, although this may take many ages. Origen could not conceive of a God who would punish souls for all eternity or of a God who would allow souls to dissolve into non-being. Indeed, in his view, all punishment should be remedial and for the good of the offender. Retributive punishment, he held, was useless. It leads to deeper ignorance and sin, because the soul grows resentful and does not understand why it is being punished. Origen was convinced that God's love is so powerful that it would eventually soften the hardest heart. He also thought that the human intellect – being in the image of God – would never freely choose oblivion instead of proximity to God. He recognised that this process of reconciliation could not, for most people, be completed in one life-time. This is why he spoke of multiple ages and of the soul being reborn. Origen clearly believed in reincarnation or the transmigration of souls, but he rejected the teaching of the Greek philosopher and mathematician, Pythagoras (c.580-c.500 BCE) and others who held that the basest of souls would take on the bodies of animals. After his death, Origen's denial of the eternity of hell was condemned at a church council, but a growing number of Christian thinkers today find the doctrine of eternal punishment is incompatible with their belief in the unfailing love of God.

Some of Origen's writings were motivated by the desire to defend Christianity against its opponents – especially Gnostics and pagans. Gnosticism was an amorphous religious movement, as difficult to define as 'New Age Spirituality' today. Until the discovery of a library of Coptic Gnostic texts – translated from the Greek - at Nag Hammadi, near the Nile in Egypt, in 1945-6, knowledge of Gnosticism was based on the criticisms of its opponents. Indeed the Nag Hammadi texts, most of which are now in the Coptic Museum in Cairo, may have been buried by Christian monks afraid of a heresy hunt.

It is probable that Gnosticism was originally a pre-Christian movement with its roots in speculative Judaism. It seems to have borrowed ideas from paganism and maybe Eastern religions. Some writings were philosophical; others were more interested in mythology and magic. The Bible was used and expounded and Jesus was highly regarded. Although Gnosticism was suppressed by the Church, it continued to have an underground influence on so-called heretical groups such as the Manichaeans, to whom St Augustine belonged for a time, the Mandeans, a Gnostic religious group which still survives in Southern Iraq and Iran and the Cathars or Albigensians, who were a serious threat to the Church in North Italy and southern France in the thirteenth and fourteenth centuries. More recently, the analytical psychologist Carl Gustav Jung (1875-1961), in his autobiography, admits that he was influenced by Gnostic ideas, especially in his writing about Archetypes. One of the Nag Hammadi papyri was presented to him and is known as the Jung Codex.

The key differences of Gnosticism from orthodox Christianity were that Gnostics distinguished a remote Supreme Divine Being from the Demiurge or Creator God, who created this imperfect material world in which souls are now imprisoned. The term 'Demiurge' is taken from an account of the formation of the visible world by the Greek philosopher Plato (c.428-347BCE) in his *Timaeus*.[3] In contrast, orthodox Christianity affirms that the world was made by God and that the creation is good. Gnostics emphasised esoteric or secret knowledge as essential to ensure the deliverance of the soul from its material body. Gnosticism was, therefore, a religion for the spiritually elite, who were sometimes called *pneumatikoi*. Christianity is 'catholic' in the sense of being 'all-inclusive.' It proclaims redemption of body and soul by repentance and forgiveness. Whereas Gnosticism sees humanity's problem as ignorance, Christianity sees the root cause of evil to be sin and rebellion against God. Jesus was regarded by Gnostics as an emissary of the supreme God – sometimes in opposition to the Demiurge. He was a divine being, who appeared in human form, rather than an incarnate person who was both human and divine. In effect Gnostics denied the actuality of the incarnation.

One of the most important Gnostic leaders of the second century CE was Valentinus. He was Egyptian by birth and, like Origen after him, he studied philosophy at Alexandria. He moved to Rome in about 136 and taught there for some twenty-five years. It seems he hoped to be chosen as Pope and that when he was passed over, he left the Catholic Church. He moved from Rome to Cyprus in about 160. Some of his writings are amongst those found at Nag Hammadi. He is said to be the author of the *Gospel of Truth*, which was a mixture of Pauline theology and Gnostic principles.

Origen's lengthy commentary on St John's gospel was written to refute a commentary written by Heracleon, who was a follower of Valentinus. Origen, with his emphasis on human freedom, was particularly opposed to the Valentinan determinism, which held that people were predestined to salvation or damnation.

Origen also defended Christianity in his *Contra Celsum* from the strong attack made on it by the pagan Celsus. This was written in about 248. It was an answer, paragraph by paragraph, to the *True Discourse*, which was written by Celsus in about 178 and which had provided the pagan intelligentsia with arguments against Christianity. Origen and Celsus share the presuppositions of Platonic thought, but Origen insisted that it was possible to hold together philosophy and Christian faith. He rejected Celsus' mockery of miracles and defended the refusal of Christians to take a full part in public life – Christians at the time refused to participate in the worship of the emperor or to serve in the army.

Origen's whole-hearted commitment to the defence of orthodox Christianity cannot be doubted. He was, however, after his death to suffer attack on several counts. Rufinus (c.345-410), a monk who founded a monastery on the Mount of Olives, translated Origen's *De Principiis* into Latin. This led to a bitter attack from St Jerome (c.342-420), who was largely responsible for the Vulgate Latin version of the Bible, and whose views were very influential in the West. Origen's writings were also attacked in the East by Epiphanius (c.315–414), bishop of Salmis in Cyprus, who was a strong supporter of the Nicean settlement. Even so, his writings had a lasting influence on Eastern Orthodox monasticism. The Cappadocian father, Gregory of Nyssa (c.330-c.395), adopted Origen's doctrine of the 'restoration of all things.' More recently, Origen influenced the Russian theologian Nicolas Berdyaev (1874-1948), who emphasised human freedom. Berdyaev also said that no soul will be saved in isolation: all must be saved together or none will be saved.

Above all, Origen was motivated by an over-whelming sense of God's love revealed in Jesus Christ. He even dared to suggest, like some modern writers who speak about the Suffering God, that God himself shares human suffering. He wrote:

'If he (Jesus) came down to earth, it was out of compassion for the human race. Yes, he suffered our sufferings even before suffering the cross, even before taking our flesh. Indeed, if he had not suffered, he would not have come down to share our life with us. First he suffered, then he came down. But what is this passion that he felt for us? It was the passion of love. And does not the Father himself, the God of the universe, "slow to anger and abounding in steadfast love"[4] also in some way suffer with us? Are you not aware that whilst governing human affairs he has compassion on our sufferings? Look how, "the Lord your

God bore you, as a man bears his son."[5] In the same way as the Son of God 'bore our griefs,' God bears with our behaviour. The Father is not impassable either... "He has pity, he knows something of the passion of love, he has merciful impulses which it might seem his sovereign majesty would have forbidden him."[6]

CHAPTER NOTES

1. Matthew 19,12.
2. Origen, *On First Principles*, 4.1.8.
3. See chapter 16
4. Psalm 103,8.
5. Deuteronomy 1,31.
6. Origen, 'Sixth Homily on Ezekiel 6,6, in Olivier Clément, *The Roots of Mysticism*, tr. Theodore Berkeley and Jeremy Hummerstone, Hyde Park NY, New City Press, 1993, pp. 45-46.

26

Constantine and Helen

After three hundred years of persecution, Constantine's 'conversion' led to Christianity becoming the official religion of the Roman Empire. This enormously increased the influence of Christianity, but some critics have suggested that this was at the expense of its spirituality. Helen, his mother, however, was known for her piety and was a pioneer of Christian pilgrimage.

Constantine was born on February 27th, around 285 CE, although the exact year is not known. His father was Flavius Valerius Constantius, who in 293 was raised to the rank of Caesar or Deputy Emperor. His mother was Helen, but when Constantius became a Caesar, he had to separate from Helen, so that he could marry the step-daughter of the Emperor Maximinian. Constantine was brought up in the Eastern Empire, where Latin was the predominant language of government. He was never entirely at home speaking Greek and later in life when he liked to deliver edifying sermons, he composed them in Latin and then read them in Greek from texts prepared by professional translators.

No doubt as a youth Constantine would have heard discussions about Christianity, which was a major issue for the ruling classes. In 303, on orders of the Emperor Diocletian, Christians were subject to fierce persecution, especially in the Eastern Empire. It is possible, however, that some members of Constantine's family were already Christian - his half-sister's name was Anastasia (Greek for Resurrection) and his mother Helen became a devout Christian about the time of Constantine's vision.

As a young officer, Constantine took part in a successful campaign on the lower Danube. In 305, Diocletian and Maximinian resigned, but Constantius, who was now in the West, was passed over as a successor. He asked his son, who was still in the East, to join him and went to meet him at Boulogne. Father and son then crossed over to Britain and fought a campaign, during which Constantius died at York in 306. Constantine was immediately acclaimed as Emperor by his army.

Constantine now embarked on military campaigns and political intrigue until by 324 he had become sole Emperor. The decisive battle in the West was at Milvian Bridge, near Rome. Constantine ascribed his victory to the Christian God. A statue of him made at the time, showed Constantine holding up a cross, with these words on the memorial, 'by this saving sign I have delivered your city from the tyrant and restored liberty to the Senate and people of Rome.' Later after his victory over Licinius, the Emperor in the East, in 324, he wrote to the Persian king Shapur II that he had come from the farthest shores of Britain as God's chosen instrument for the suppression of impiety and that, aided by the divine power of God, he had come from the borders of the ocean to bring peace and prosperity to all lands.

But in the opening sentence of this chapter I put 'conversion' in inverted commas because there is continuing debate about whether Constantine became a believing Christian or merely used Christianity to further his political ambitions. Tradition holds that he saw a vision before the battle at Milvian Bridge. Eusebius (c.260-340), the historian of the Early Church, who wrote a *Life of Constantine*, said that before setting out to march to Italy, Constantine prayed to the god whom his father honoured. He was rewarded by a vision in the sky of a cross-shaped trophy accompanied by the words, 'by this conquer.' Lactantius in his *On the Death of the Persecutors* said that, the night before the battle, Constantine had a dream, in which he saw the *chi-rho* (χρ) symbol, which was a monogram made from the first two Greek letters of Christ. Eusebius' *History*, however, does not mention this vision. A speech made two years before the battle speaks of a vision of Apollo. Constantine also continued to mint coins with the symbol of the sun on them. The seven days of the week were named after the seven planets. It may well be, however, that while Constantine did believe he was divinely commissioned and wanted to enlist the support of Christians, it was politically unwise to alienate unnecessarily those who were still pagan. Every side in the complex power struggles of the time wanted to claim divine backing.

After his victory, Constantine met with Licinius to confirm political and dynastic arrangements. One outcome was the so-called Edict of Milan, drafted by Licinius, which promised toleration to Christians and the restoration of property confiscated during times of persecution. Constantine himself went further. He donated the imperial property of the Lateran to the Bishop of Rome, where a new Cathedral, Basilica Constantiniana (now S. Giovanni in Laterano) was soon built. The church of St Sebastian was probably started at the same time. Constantine also issued laws giving fiscal and legal privileges to the clergy and freeing them from civic burdens, 'for when they are free to render supreme service to the Divinity, it is evident that they confer great benefit upon the affairs of the state.'

Constantine was also greatly concerned to ensure the unity of the Church because schism was, in his words, 'insane, futile madness.' The first dispute he was concerned about was the Donatist movement in North Africa, in which St Augustine was later to be embroiled. The Donatists held that priests and bishops who had renounced their Christian faith under persecution could not be readmitted to the church. Constantine, in his letters, said that the Donatists were denying the clemency of Christ, and he urged other Christians to show patience and long-suffering.

Following the defeat of Licinius in 324, Constantine was confronted by the bitter dispute about Arianism. Arius (c. 250-336) was a popular preacher at one of the churches in Alexandria – a city in Egypt, which housed the most famous library in the ancient world and was a major centre of scholarly research. Arius was respected for his asceticism. He held that the Son was subordinate to the Father, which his opponents said made the Son a 'creature' rather than fully divine. His best-known opponent was Athanasius (c.296-373), who became bishop of Alexandria. Constantine quickly convened a Council that met in Nicaea in May 325. It opened with an address by the Emperor himself, who, unversed in the intricacies of Greek philosophy and theology, regarded the matter as trivial, fostered by too much leisure and academic niceties. The Council, backed by Constantine, condemned Arius, and produced the first version of a creed, known at the Nicene Creed - although the Nicene Creed often recited in churches today is an expanded version produced at the Council of Constantinople in 381. The Council affirmed that the Word made flesh in Jesus was God in exactly the same sense as God the Father is God. Despite Constantine's best efforts the dispute continued until well after his death.

Soon after the Council of Nicaea, Constantine celebrated the twentieth anniversary of his reign at Constantinople, which was the new name he had given to Byzantium. In 326, he went to Rome to repeat the celebrations in the West – but he offended many of the leading citizens there by refusing to take part in a pagan procession. It was a short visit and he was never to return to Rome. While he was away Constantine, for reasons which are still obscure, had his eldest son and deputy Emperor Crispus killed as well as his wife Fausta, who was Crispus' step-mother.

On his return from Rome, Constantine set about rebuilding Constantinople, which now became the political centre of the Empire. In his last years he was engaged in conflict with the Persian Empire and as he was preparing for a campaign against it, he fell ill at Helenopolis. He tried to return to Constantinople but had to retire to bed at Nicomedia, where he received baptism, putting off the imperial purple for the white robes of a neophyte[1]. He died on May 22nd, 337. He was buried in the Church of the Apostles, whose memorials, six on each side, flank his tomb, reflecting his belief that he had completed their work.

Why did Constantine delay his baptism till the last moment? Was he influenced by the fear that sins committed by those who were baptised were more grievous and perhaps unforgivable? Did he hope to be baptised in the River Jordan and waited in vain for an opportunity for this to happen? We do not know.

What is clear is that he was much interested in religion. He spent hours in discussion with bishops. He built churches in many major cities, including the original church of the Holy Wisdom (Hagia Sophia) in Constantinople and of the great church of St Peter in Rome. He wrote to Eusebius for new copies of the Bible for the growing congregations in Constantinople. He composed a special prayer for his troops and had a mobile chapel when he went on campaign. He also abolished crucifixion and the branding of some criminals 'so as not to disfigure the human face, which is formed in the image of divine beauty.'

Just as there is still debate about Constantine's motivation and many of his actions, so there are still mixed feelings whether becoming the official religion of the Roman Empire was a blessing or a curse for Christianity. 'For some modern observers this was the moment when the simple Christianity of the apostles and the early church was overwhelmed by secular power, while for others it was the point of the final triumph of the faith.'[2] Whatever view one takes, no one can doubt the conversion was a turning point in history.

In the discussion of Constantine's own faith, no mention has yet been made of the influence of his mother. Helen (sometimes Helena) was almost certainly born in Asia Minor about 250 CE and was the daughter of an inn-keeper. Geoffrey of Monmouth (d. 1154), however claimed she was of British origin and the daughter of Coel, the legendary king of Colchester. This was widely believed in England, where a number of churches were dedicated to her and the towns of St Helen's in Lancashire and in the Isle of Wight were named after her. The Atlantic island of St Helena, which was discovered by Spanish sailors on her feast day, was also named after her.

Helen, as we have seen, married Constantius but was divorced by him for political reasons. Their son Constantine always had a deep respect for her. There can be no doubt that her conversion, which occurred about the time of Constantine's vision was genuine. Thereafter she dressed modestly, gave generously to churches, to the poor and to prisoners. Helen was later to become famous as the first Christian pilgrim. Eusebius said that by visiting the land where Jesus lived, she had 'venerated the saving places', thereby fulfilling the words of the prophet, 'Let us worship at the place where his feet have stood.' She made her pilgrimage to Jerusalem in 329 when Constantine was starting his building programme there. Many of the traditional sites were identified at that period. Her most famous discovery was said to be the true cross, which was unearthed when the foundations for the Church of the Holy Sepulchre were being made. This find, in the words of the historian Stephen Runciman, made her 'the most successful of the world's great archaeologists.'[3] It was also the theme of the poem *Elene* by the Anglo Saxon poet Cynewulf (ninth century), who describes Constantine's dream and conversion, Helen's voyage to Jerusalem and her discovery of the cross and the nails used in the crucifixion of Jesus.

Eusebius also credits Helen with finding the cave at Bethlehem 'where (the Saviour) had undergone birth in human flesh' and the cave on the Mount of Olives, which is a 'memorial of his ascension into heaven.'[4] She also sent money at the request of some of the hermits who had settled in the desert near Mount Horeb, so that a small chapel could be built for them at the site of the Burning Bush, where God spoke to Moses.[5] A small fortified enclosure was also built where the hermits could find protection from the attacks of nomadic tribes.[6]

Helen died in about 330 and was buried at Rome. Eastern churches celebrate Constantine and Helen with a joint feast day on May 21st. Constantine's legacy certainly had more impact on the worldly life of Christians, although Helen's encouragement of piety and pilgrimage may be the greater spiritual legacy.

CHAPTER NOTES

1. Neophyte is the technical term for a convert about to be initiated into membership of the Church.
2. Hugh Bowden in *Christianity: the Complete Guide*, p.280.
3. Stephen Runciman, *A History of the Crusades*, Cambridge, 1951, 1.39. Eusebius does not mention this.
4. The quotations from Eusebius are taken from Robert L Wilken, *The Land Called Holy: Palestine in Christian History and Thought*, New Haven, Yale University Press, 1992.
5. Exodus 3,2 *et seq.*
6. Athanasios Paliouras, *St Catherine's Monastery*, Sinai, St Catherine's Monastery, 1985, p. 10.

27

Augustine of Hippo

St Augustine of Hippo was the most profound Christian thinker of the early church. He has had a lasting influence – not always beneficial - on Christian theology in the West. His very personal *Confessions* still resonate so well with readers today that he has been called the 'first modern man.'

Aurelius Augustinus, who was to become Bishop of Hippo in North Africa, which was then part of the Roman Empire, is not to be confused with St Augustine, the first Archbishop of Canterbury (d.604), who was sent by Pope Gregory (c.540-604) the Great to re-establish the Christian Church in England.

Augustine was born on 13th November 354 CE to parents of modest means who owned a few acres of farmland at the small town of Thagaste. This is now Souk-Ahras in the hills of Eastern Algeria about 45 miles inland from the coast. In Augustine's day the area was in the thriving province of Numidia in the Roman Empire. Augustine's mother Monica, coming from a Christian family, was a devout believer. Augustine, who was not baptised as an infant, learnt from her at an early age to reverence the 'name of Christ.' His father Patrick, however, was not baptised until his deathbed in 372. Augustine was such a bright child that at the age of fifteen he was sent for further education to the nearby town of Madauros. After a year there he had to return home, because his father, who 'had more enthusiasm than cash',[1] had run out of money. When he was seventeen, however, the modest family savings were spent on sending him for higher education at Carthage. His father, who died soon after Augustine left for Carthage, hoped to equip his son for a career in government service.

Augustine was an unruly youth – his words, 'unbridled dissoluteness' may be an exaggeration.[2] At Carthage, 'all around me hissed a cauldron of illicit loves.'[3] At the age of seventeen he began a long lasting relationship with a girl, whom his mother thought was entirely unsuitable, who, he said, was 'the only girl for me and I was faithful to her.'[4] They had a son, who died, as a youth, at the age of 17.

Augustine's studies were designed to lead him to being an advocate in the law courts, 'where one's reputation is high in proportion to one's success in deceiving people.'[5] But a philosophical book by the Roman author Cicero (106-43 BCE), which he was required to read, changed the direction of his life. Augustine started to take an interest in religion and philosophy. He tried reading the Bible, but was offended by the polygamy of the Old Testament patriarchs and the poor literary style of the Old Latin Bible - which was soon to be replaced by the Vulgate, which was a translation into Latin from the Greek by St Jerome (c.342-420), which became the standard version of the Catholic Church. Augustine was attracted instead to Manichaeism, a religion, popular at the time, which was founded in Iran by Mani, who was put to death by the Persian government in 276 CE.

Manichees were dualists. They made a sharp division between the spiritual and the material. God, they believed is good, but not all powerful and therefore not to be blamed for the evil in the world. Souls, sparks of light, were imprisoned in the flesh by procreation. Full members – the 'Elect' – were required to be strictly celibate and vegetarian. 'Hearers', of whom Augustine became one for a time, were allowed wives, provided they avoided having children. Manichees, who denied the historical reality of the crucifixion of Jesus, saw the cross as a symbol of the suffering of humanity.

Augustine was in sympathy with the Manichees' criticisms of the Church and found their books were written 'in good Latin,' but the more he learned about astronomy, the more he questioned their elaborate mythology. Manichees, however, helped Augustine, who had founded his own school in North Africa, to move to Rome and then to Milan, where he gained an entrée into the homes of rich and powerful senators. Augustine now needed a rich wife so that he could pay the bribes necessary to get a good appointment. So his long-standing concubine was sent back to Carthage. 'The woman with whom I habitually slept was torn away from my side because she was a hindrance to my marriage. My heart, which was deeply attached, was cut and wounded and left a trail of blood. She had returned to Africa vowing that she would never go with another man.' His mother found a suitable bride, but the marriage had to wait until the girl was twelve - the minimum age for marriage in Roman law. In the interim, Augustine says, 'I procured another woman... but the wound, inflicted by the earlier parting, was not healed.' [6]

At the same time as his domestic life was in turmoil and he was vainly seeking for a good job, Augustine finally abandoned his belief in the teaching of Mani and became sceptical about the possibility of any certainty. He came in contact, however, with some Christian thinkers who had been influenced by the philosophers Plato (428-347 BCE) and Plotinus (c.205-270 CE). Pre-eminent among these Christian thinkers was Ambrose (c.339-97), the bishop of Milan, whose sermons had an intellectual content that attracted Augustine. This was a period of intense inner struggle for Augustine. One day, in his distress, when he was in a garden, he heard, as he says, the voice of a child saying repeatedly, '*Tolle lege, tolle lege*, Pick up and read, pick up and read.' 'I hurried back to the place where ... I had put down the book of the apostle [St Paul]... I seized it, opened it and in silence read the first passage on which my eyes lit: "Not in riots and drunken parties, not in eroticism and indecencies, not in strife and rivalry, but put on the Lord Jesus Christ and make no provision for the flesh in its lusts." I neither wished nor needed to read further. At once, with the last words of this sentence, it was as if a light of relief from all anxiety flooded into my heart... All the shadows of doubt were dispelled.' [7]

Augustine was baptised by Ambrose in the spring of 387. Soon afterwards he and his mother returned to North Africa, where Augustine was ordained in 391. He quickly became an assistant bishop and in about 396 bishop of Hippo (now Bone in Algeria). Besides his episcopal and pastoral responsibilities, Augustine, despite suffering from agonizing haemorrhoids, was a prolific writer, especially in arguing against the Donatist and Pelagian heresies, of which more in a moment. The initial agreement when he became a bishop, although it was never honoured, was that he should devote five days to the study of the Scriptures, without being importuned by members of his flock.

This was a turbulent time not only in the Church, but also in the Roman Empire which was shaken by the capture of Rome itself by the Visigoths in 410. Augustine wrote his *City of God* (*De Civitate Dei*), which with the *Confessions*, are his best known works, to argue against pagan claims that this disaster was a result of abandoning the ancient gods. By the time Augustine died in August 430, Vandal armies were surrounding Hippo. In the midst of these trials, Augustine found comfort in the words of Plotinus that 'He is no great man who thinks it a great thing that sticks and stones should fall and that men, who must die, should die.' The Roman Empire was disintegrating, but Augustine had left a lasting legacy to the Catholic Church, which was now, in the growing political vacuum, to occupy centre stage in Western Europe.

Augustine was a prolific author. His first biographer Posidius, Bishop of Calama, wrote of him 'So numerous are the works that he has dictated and published... that a studious man could scarcely read them in their entirety.'[8] In the library at Hippo, where Augustine spent much of his last three years editing and cataloguing his writings, there were 93 works, comprising 232 books and codices. When the Vandals sacked the city, the library escaped and most of Augustine's writings reached Italy in safety. Even now, new unread manuscripts are being discovered hidden away in libraries, including a number of letters and some sermons preached towards the end of his life. He did not write for the sake of writing, but, as he said of his *City of God*, that 'readers may be moved to enter into the City of God without delay... and continue in righteousness. If those by whom these books are read and praised do not actually take action and do these things, of what good are books?'[9]

Although we depend on the *Confessions* for much of what we know about Augustine, the book is not an autobiography in the modern sense and Augustine did not get paid for writing it! It was written some thirteen years after his conversion at Milan. Some people, aware of Augustine's past life and opposition to the Church, were uneasy when he was made a bishop. The book is an attempt to allay their suspicions. At much the same time a wealthy aristocrat called Paulinus, who had converted to Christianity, had asked Augustine's friend Alypius for an account of his life. Alypius, whose reply does not survive, certainly shared the request with Augustine, who perhaps answered the request instead. Towards the end of his life, Augustine, in a review of his writings, said of the *Confessions* that they serve to excite the human mind and affection towards God; and the act of writing the book had done that for himself at the time, and 'that is the effect when it is read now.' Aware that not everyone admired the work, he added that it had 'given great pleasure to many brethren and still does.'[10]

The book is a confession in two senses: it is a statement or confession of praise and faith, but also an acknowledgement, or confession of his faults and failings. It is, in Henry Chadwick's words, 'a prose-poem addressed to God, intended to be overheard by anxious and critical fellow Christians.'[11] Not everyone appreciates the elaborate rhetorical style of Augustine's writing and he was aware that some people 'are suspicious and refuse to accept the truth if it is presented in polished and rich language.'[12] What is perhaps most remarkable is the self-knowledge and his almost modern awareness of the complexity of human motivation.

The City of God contrasts the earthly city built on principles of self-love and the city of God based on love of God. This is not a contrast between good and evil. The two cities are also not to be identified with the state and the church. Augustine recognised that the church includes sinners as well as saints and he acknowledged that secular society has a proper function within the purposes of God. In his *Retractions* he explains that the twenty-two books fall into two parts. The first part is a refutation of those who blamed the fall of Rome on the prohibition of the worship of pagan gods and those, more moderately who believed that such worship should still be tolerated. But, as Augustine said, 'I did not wish to be accused of having merely controverted the doctrines of others, without stating my own.'[13] In the second part, therefore, he wrote of the origins, progress and 'appointed ends' of the two cities.

Augustine was caught up in two major controversies. During the great persecution under the Emperor Diocletian, which lasted for ten years early in the fourth century, a number of Christians renounced their faith but subsequently returned to the Church. As we have seen, the Donatists, who had not denied the faith, broke away in protest, claiming that they alone were members of the true church. Augustine after long reflection insisted that the defining characteristic of the church was love not holiness and that therefore there had to be a place in the church for those who had failed and were penitent. Moreover the validity of the sacraments was not dependent upon the purity of the priest who celebrated them. Augustine tried hard for reconciliation, but without success, and eventually agreed that legal penalties should be imposed on the schismatics.

The other controversy was with Pelagius, a British theologian who was a contemporary of Augustine. Known for his own holiness, Pelagius was also concerned about moral laxity in the church. He held that sin was a willing act of disobedience to God's will, but for Augustine this glossed over the radical nature of human sin and our need for divine grace. Why otherwise was it necessary to baptise infants 'for the remission of sin?' In Augustine's view, every new-born baby inherited the guilt of Adam's disobedience, which was transmitted in the act of procreation. By linking original sin and sexuality, Augustine contributed to the suspicion of human sexuality that has at times been prevalent among Christians. Yet, in other writings, at a time when celibacy was highly regarded and couples sometimes were urged on the first night of their honeymoon to take a vow of celibacy, Augustine affirmed the proper place of intercourse in marriage.

Because of inherited guilt, no one, Augustine claimed, could win salvation by his or her own good conduct, as Pelagius seemed to suggest. Only God's grace, through the death of Christ, could set a person free. This indeed reflected Augustine's own experience and that of many believers. But why did God choose some and not others, especially if it was nothing to do with how they behaved? Augustine's answer was predestination – God had pre-ordained that some people would be saved. Later some Christians also taught, what was logical enough but morally repellent, that God destined others for damnation – the so-called doctrine of 'double predestination.'

Augustine's many other writings, especially his work 'On the Trinity', *De Trinitate*, have continued to influence Christian thought. Indeed, no theologian, whether or not he or she agrees with Augustine, can afford to ignore him. Yet, despite his willingness to use his brilliant intellect in the exposition and defence of Catholic Christianity, Augustine was aware that it is only by devotion that we come to know God and are remade in the divine likeness. As he wrote at the beginning of the *Confessions*, 'You have made us for yourself, and our heart is restless until it rests in you.'[14] The depth of his personal devotion is shown in his many beautiful prayers, some of which, like this evening prayer, are still used today:

Watch, dear Lord, with those who wake, or watch, or weep tonight,
And give your angels charge over those who sleep;
Tend your sick ones, O Lord Christ, rest your weary ones,
Bless your dying ones, soothe your suffering ones,

Pity your afflicted ones, shield your joyous ones,
And all for your love's sake.[14]

CHAPTER NOTES

1. References are to the translation of the *Confessions* by Henry Chadwick, Oxford, Oxford University Press, 1991, II.iii.5.

2. II.iii.8.

3. III.i.1.

4. IV.ii.2.

5. III.iii.6.

6. VI.xv.25.

7. VIII.xii.29. The passage which Augustine read was Romans, 13, 13-14.

8. Serge Lancel, *Saint Augustine*, London, SCM Press, 2002, p. 458.

9. Peter Brown, *Augustine of Hippo: a Biography*, London, Faber 2000 (Revised edition), p. 472 .

10. Chadwick, p. xiii.

11. Chadwick, p. ix.

12. V.vi.10.

13. Quoted by Sir Ernest Barker in the Introduction to the Everyman translation of *The City of God*, London, Dent 1945, p.xii.

14. Quoted in *The Lion Prayer Collection*, Ed. Mary Batchelor, Oxford, Lion Publishing 1992, p. 274

28

John Climacus and Gregory of Sinai

If the conversion of the Emperor Constantine to Christianity enormously extended the influence of the religion, it also resulted in a greater worldliness among some of its followers. Many of the more devout Christians, who wanted a life of simplicity and silence, left the cities to live in the wilderness. The Sinai desert quite early became a place of retreat and two monks, John Climacus and Gregory of Sinai, who both had a deep influence on Eastern Orthodox spirituality, lived for a time at the ancient monastery at the foot of Mount Sinai. They represent the spiritual tradition of Hesychasm, known especially for the 'Jesus Prayer,' which has for centuries been widely influential among Orthodox Christians and is now being adopted by some Christians of other traditions.

It was near Mount Sinai that the Bible says God revealed Himself to Moses. In 330 CE, Helena, the mother of the Emperor Constantine, as we have seen, had a small chapel built on what was believed to be the site of the Burning Bush, where God appeared to Moses.[1] The bush is now in the grounds of the monastery, with its great, fortified walls, which was founded by the Byzantine Emperor Justinian between 527 and 547 CE. On a pilgrimage to the monastery, as a priest, I was allowed to see the bush. Muslim rulers and Napoleon protected the lonely monastery when they ruled the area. The Basilica is bejewelled with lamps and icons and the library contains a great collection of spiritual writings. The monks, headed by an archbishop, are autonomous.

Presumably, the building of the monastery was nearly complete by the time John Climacus arrived there. St John Climacus (also Klimakos) or John of the Ladder, also surnamed Scholasticus and the Sinaita, was born in Syria in about 525 CE. He seems to have had a good education, but at a young age opted for a life of solitude. He made his way to the Sinai, which was already known for the holiness of the monks who lived in its lonely desert at the foot of the mountain, which is also known as Gebel Musa, 'the Mountain of Moses.' It was on this mountain, often also called Mount Horeb as well as Mt Sinai, (although the identification is disputed) that Moses received the Commandments from God.

John Climacus was trained by a monk, who was called Martyrius John. After his teacher died, John withdrew to a hermitage – perhaps to get away from the builders! He spent the next twenty years there by himself, studying the lives of the saints. He became one of the most learned Christians of his day.

In the year 600, the monks of Sinai persuaded him to become their abbot. He showed such wisdom that his reputation spread widely. Even Pope Gregory the Great (c.540-604), his contemporary, wrote to ask for his prayers and sent him some money to help provide lodgings for pilgrims. As he felt death approaching, he resigned as abbot and retired to his hermitage. He is revered as a saint by the Roman Catholic, Oriental Orthodox, Eastern Orthodox and Eastern Catholic churches.

He wrote two important books. The *Ladder of Divine Ascent*, from which he gets his name, and the *Book to a Pastor*. The *Ladder of Divine Ascent* has been very influential and has been translated into most classical and modern European languages. The contemporary English-born Greek Orthodox Bishop Kallistos Ware has written that 'with the exception of the Bible and service books, there is no work in Eastern Christianity that has been studied, copied and translated more often than *The Ladder of Divine Ascent* by St John Climacus. Every Lent in Orthodox monasteries it is appointed to be read aloud in church or in the refectory, so that some monks will have listened to it as much as 50 or 60 times in the course of their life.'[2]

The book is addressed to those who choose a solitary life. The First three steps deal with the break from the world, which involves renunciation, detachment and exile. This approach is very different from that of those modern Christians, who emphasize Jesus' words, 'I came that they might have life in all its fullness'[3] and who stress the value of the individual. The Second Section is the longest with various sub-divisions. It deals with the practice of virtue, the struggle against the passions, physical temptations and failings such as insensitivity as well as the higher virtues of the active life. The body and the soul are in continuing opposition, which again is alien to the modern world. Even John asks, 'How can I hate him (the body) when my nature disposes me to love him?'[4] Yet John does not reject the body altogether like some extreme ascetics who inflicted injury on themselves. For John, it is misuse of the body that is the problem. Eating is not sinful, but gluttony is. Sex for procreation is allowed, but not for fornication. The final section is about union with God and the transition to the contemplative life.

St John stresses at the beginning that the essence of the spiritual life is 'a Christian as an imitator of Christ.'[5] He recognised that people become monks for various reasons 'either for the sake of the coming kingdom, or because of the number of their sins or on account of their love of God.' He was not interested in the outer trappings of religious life. He stressed personal experience of God. 'The true teacher is one who has received directly from heaven the tablet of spiritual knowledge, inscribed by God's own finger, that is by the active working of illumination.'[6] He shows the path a person should follow to grow in holiness. 'Such a man', he added, 'has no need of books.'[7] Besides providing a traditional guide to asceticism for beginners, the *Ladder* is original in giving systematic guidance in the paths of higher psychic and spiritual awareness.

The idea of a ladder was suggested by the dream of the Old Testament patriarch Jacob, in which he saw an angel connecting heaven and earth with angels going up and down. There is a sculpture of this on the West End of Bath Abbey in England. John's thirty steps correspond to the thirty hidden years of the life of Jesus prior to his public ministry. There are many stories and parables as well as historical references. The style is very concise. For example, he wrote:

'If war demonstrates the soldier's loyalty to the emperor, then prayer demonstrates the monk's love for his God.

Your prayer demonstrates exactly what condition you are in. Theologians say that prayer is the mirror of a monk.'[8]

The links in the argument are not always clear. As a result numerous commentaries have been written on the book. There is also an ancient icon, showing Jesus at the top receiving the climbers into heaven.

John Climacus' *Ladder of Divine Ascent* belongs to a form of spirituality known as Hesychasm, which is derived from the Greek word for quietness. The word, 'Hesychasm,' in the early Byzantine period from the sixth to the eleventh century refers quite generally to the ascetic training by which a monk sought to gain inner quietness by fasting, prayer and recollection, although all the time he was liable to attack by demons. Once quietness of the soul was achieved, according to this tradition, the soul, in stillness, was ready to hear the word of God and to receive the grace of special communion with God. St John of Damascus (c.675-749), who as a monk spent much of his life at the Mar Saba monastery near Jerusalem and who was a well known theologian, summed up the teaching like this: 'Hesychia gives birth to prayer and prayer is the mother of the vision of glory.'[9]

This emphasis on stillness practised by the desert monks was later enriched by the Syrian monastic tradition according to which the heart of the disciple was trained to focus on the inner presence of the Spirit of God. As these traditions came together, monks of the Sinai region and of Mount Athos in Greece began to emphasise the Jesus prayer. It is to this development that people usually refer when they speak of Hesychast tradition.

The Jesus prayer – which is not to be confused with 'The Lord's Prayer' - is a short invocation, of which the most common version is 'Lord Jesus Christ, Son of God, have mercy on me.' There is a longer version, which is commonly used by members of the Russian Orthodox Church, 'Lord Jesus Christ, Son of the Living God, have mercy on me, a sinner.' The saying derives from Jesus' parable of the Pharisee and the Tax-collector. The Pharisee thanked God that he lived a life obedient to the Law, whereas the tax-collector merely cried out, 'God, have mercy on me, a sinner.'[10] Jesus commented that it was the tax-collector rather than the Pharisee who went home at peace with God. The monks, following St Paul's instruction 'to pray continually,[11] believed that, by frequent repetition, this prayer would help them to attain the spiritual stillness for which they sought. The words were to be repeated slowly in tune with breathing – the first part as one breathes in, the second as the breath is exhaled. Gradually the heart itself would absorb the rhythm of the prayer.

St John Climacus himself commended the Jesus prayer. 'Let the remembrance of Jesus be present with your every breath.' 'Let the remembrance of death and the concise Jesus prayer go to sleep with you and get up with you.'[12] The word concise literally means a single phrase, so there is some question whether John just meant the repetition of the name 'Jesus' or the standard form of the prayer mentioned above. The first specific reference to the words, 'Lord Jesus Christ, have mercy on me' is in an Egyptian text called *the Life of Abba Philemon*, which dates to the sixth century and was, therefore, contemporary with the *Ladder of Ascent*.

Gregory of Sinai, (also known as Gregory Koukoulos) our second representative of Hesychasm, was a keen advocate of the Jesus prayer. He was born in the latter part of the twelfth century in Smyrna in what is now Turkey. He belonged to a wealthy family, but as a young man he was captured and enslaved by the Turks. After eventually being ransomed, Gregory left his family and went to Cyprus, where he joined a monastery. Then he spent a time at St Catherine's monastery in Sinai and became a convinced practitioner of the disciplined mental prayer taught by St John Climacus and by Symeon the New Theologian (949-1022), who stressed felt devotion. Whether he learned the Jesus prayer at Sinai or as some sources say in Crete from a monk named Arsenios, he certainly was an advocate of it by the time he reached Mount Athos and he was to make Mount Athos a centre of Hesychast influence.

Mount Athos, also known as the Holy Mountain, like the Sinai desert, was a lonely place that attracted ascetics. It is a mountainous area of great beauty that juts out into the Aegean Sea from Macedonia. It is claimed that some of the monasteries go back to the third or fourth century. Certainly the monastery of Megisti Lavra was there by the middle of the tenth century. Today, there are twenty monasteries and about 1,500 monks. During the Greek War of Independence in the early nineteenth century, several valuable libraries were destroyed, but some ancient manuscripts survived. Many of the churches still contain precious icons. No women or animals are allowed on Mount Athos.

Gregory spent twenty-five years at Mount Athos, from 1310 to 1335. He lived in a small hermitage close to the Pilotheou monastery. Increasing Turkish raids, however, destroyed the necessary stillness so Gregory left, first for the Black Sea and then to Mount Paroria in Bulgaria, where he founded a monastery that became the intellectual and spiritual centre of the Balkans. With the patronage of the Bulgarian Tsar John Alexander, Gregory was able to edit and publish his collected works.

Gregory taught a moderate form of the practice. His best-known book is the *137 Chapters* or *Spiritual Meditations*, in which he taught how the gulf between the human and the Divine could be overcome. The highest form of communion is a vision of the 'divine light' or 'uncreated energy', similar to the Transfiguration of Jesus described in the Gospels.[13] 'When you have renewed the Spirit and kept the gift of grace', Gregory wrote, 'you will be transfigured and embodied in Christ; and you will then experience the state of deification that transcends nature and all our attempts to describe it.'[14] Hesychast literature tells of similar transforming experiences in periods of intense concentration, controlled breathing and repetitive prayer. Gregory compared disciples at prayer to pregnant mothers. 'Whoever has received grace is like a woman impregnated, conceiving a child by the Holy Spirit.'[15]

Gregory suggested that the best posture for Hesychast payer was to sit on a low stool, about nine inches high. This would have been surprising at the time as it was then customary to stand for all types of prayer. The shoulders were to be bowed, the back bent over, with head tucked into the chest – rather like the brace position to be adopted in an aircraft in the event of a crash. This position was intended to synchronise the breathing and the prayer, as it would be easy to hear the breathing. It also restricted the inflow of breath and so aided attention. For Gregory the 'Prayer of the Heart' or 'Jesus prayer' was 'not only for beginners, but the quintessence of advanced prayer.'[16]

A theological justification of this approach was given by Gregory of Sinai's contemporary at Mount Athos, St Gregory Palamas (c.1296-1359), who was involved in a dispute whether the Uncreated Divine Light of God could be seen directly with created human eyes.

The Hesychast teaching was given wider circulation in the eighteenth century by a collection of texts known as the *Philokalia*, a Greek term, which means love of the good and the beautiful. The *Philokalia* has become a major secondary spiritual written resource of the Orthodox Church along with St John Climacus' *Ladder of the Divine Ascent*. Holy Scripture is, of course, the primary resource.

One of the compliers, Nikodimos (1749-1809), was well educated, highly intelligent and with a photographic memory. At an early age, he met three monks from Mount Athos, who introduced him to their spiritual practices. They also introduced him to the Bishop of Mount Makarios (Notaras) of Corinth (1731-1805). Nikodimos and Makarios met on Mount Athos in 1777. They collected many of the great spiritual writings of Orthodox monks in the *Philokalia*. The aim of the collection, as Nikodimos said, was to be a 'mystical school of inward prayer.'[17] He stressed that 'unceasing prayer' should be practised by all, not just monks.[18] True to this tradition, the ultimate goal of the spiritual life, taught in these writings, is to share in the divine nature, sometimes referred to as 'theosis,' 'deification,' or 'divinization' – a teaching summed up in the words, 'Christ became human so that humans could become divine.' The way to the goal is prayer and in particular the Jesus prayer, with its constant repetition of the name of Jesus. A companion volume, which stressed practical action, was published in the following year. It is named *Evergetinos* because it is based on a collection of texts made by Paulos Evergetinos, the eleventh century founder of an important monastery in Constantinople.

The *Philokalia*, which includes five works by Gregory of Sinai, has been translated into many languages. A Slavonic translation by St Paisii in 1793, was published in Moscow and later reprinted in 1822. St Seraphim, the most important Russian Orthodox spiritual teacher of the nineteenth century, learned of the *Philokalia* from a *staret* (holy man), who had helped to edit it. The Slavonic translation would also have been the version carried by an unnamed central character in *The Way of a Pilgrim* and was largely responsible for a spiritual revival in Russia in the nineteenth century, which influenced many people, including the great novelist Fyodor Dostoevsky (1821-81).

In its turn the *Way of the Pilgrim* has been translated into several languages and continues to spread the practice of the Jesus prayer among an ever-growing number of spiritual seekers. Some practitioners use a rosary, counting off the knots with each recitation of the prayer.

Bishop Kallistos Ware has said of the *Philokalia* and more widely of the writings of the monks of Sinai, Mount Athos and other centres of Orthodox piety and, of course, of the writings of St John Climacus and St Gregory of Sinai, that

'It is surely astonishing that a collection of spiritual texts, originally intended for Greeks living under Ottoman rule should have achieved its main impact two centuries later in the secularized and post-Christian West, among the children of that very 'Enlightenment' which St Makarios and St Nikodimos viewed with such misgiving.'[19]

CHAPTER NOTES

1. Exodus chapter 3.
2. Kallistos Ware, in *The Ladder of the Divine Ascent*, translated by Colm Luibheid and Norman Russsell, London, SPCK, 1982, p. 1.
3. John 10,10.
4. Quoted from *The Ladder*, p. xx.
5. Quoted from *The Ladder*, p. 17.
6. Quoted from *The Ladder*, p. xxi.
7. Quoted from *The Ladder*, pp. 7-8.
8. St John Climacus, *The Ladder of Divine Ascent*, translated by L. Moore, 2nd edtn Boston, Mass, 1991, 28,33-4.
9. Quoted from the article on 'Hesychasm' by John Anthony McGuckin in *The New SCM Dictionary of Christian Spirituality*.
10. Luke 18,9-14.
11. I Thessalonians 5,17.
12. Quoted in *The Ladder*, pp. 47-8.
13. Mark 9,2-13.
14. Quoted by J A McGuckin, *Standing in the Holy Fire: the Byzantine Tradition*, London, Darton, Longman and Todd, 2001, p. 122.
15. *Standing in the Holy Fire:* p. 121.
16. *Standing in the Holy Fire* p. 123.
17. *The Philokalia*, p. 12.
18. *The Philokalia*, p. 13.
19. Kallistos Ware in his Introduction to *The Ladder*.

29

Benedict

St Benedict of Nursia, who founded the great monastery at Monte Cassino, was the guiding spirit of the monastic movement in Western Christianity, which preserved at least some Roman and Greek civilization during the Dark Ages and helped to spread Christianity in Western Europe. Benedict's influence on European civilization was so great that in 1964, Pope Paul VI proclaimed him to be the patron saint of all Europe.

Benedict did not start the Christian monastic movement, but his rule became the basis for community life in most monasteries in the West. The word 'monasticism' is derived from the Greek word, which means 'to live alone.' Through the centuries, there have been some Christians who have chosen a life of solitude as the way to a closer relationship with God. They are called recluses or anchorites, who were walled up in a self–chosen prison - as for example Julian of Norwich (c.1342 – after 1413), who had a series of visions of the Passion of Christ, which she described in her *Shewings*.[1] Other people chose to live in solitude in forests or lonely countryside, far away from disturbance by other human beings, as for example St Giles, a seventh century hermit, who became a very popular saint in the Middle Ages and whose name is still remembered in Oxford at the famous St Giles Fair, which dates back to the Mediaval period.

Monks, despite the origin of the name, mostly live in a community. The proper word for this is 'coenebite', derived from the Greek for having things in common.

The origins of Christian monasticism, which date back to the late Roman period, are to be found in the Eastern Mediterranean. When Christianity became the official religion of the Roman Empire, it also, in the eyes of some devout believers, became more worldly. In protest, Desert Fathers, such as St Anthony (251-356) withdrew to the wilderness to live a life of extreme austerity. St Simeon the Stylite (390-439), for example, known for the severity of his fasts and self-inflicted bodily punishments, lived on top of a pillar, initially for four years on a pillar nine feet high and for the last twenty years of his life on a pillar sixty feet high. Often, however, monks settled quite near to each other and might come together for Mass or for a weekly meeting. Some of the monks, who were specially known for their holiness, attracted disciples. Gradually, the development of a sense of community required some rules. The rules drawn up by St Basil the Great (c.330-379) still provide the basis for monastic life in the Orthodox Churches.

The 'Rule of St Benedict' was to have a similar importance in the Western Church. Benedict, according to Pope Gregory the Great (c. 540-604), was born in about 480 of a high class family in Nursia in Umbria, Italy. He was sent to good Roman schools, although Roman civilization was crumbling under the weight of attacks from the North - Rome was sacked in 546 by the Gothic King Totila. As a young man, Benedict, shocked by the permissive society in Rome, withdrew to a cave near what is now Affile. There he lived alone, with his food supplied from a nearby monastery. As fame of his holiness spread, he was persuaded to become abbot of a local monastery. His enthusiasm for reform, however, was so great that an attempt was made to poison him. He, therefore, withdrew to his cave. But now disciples flocked to him. He, therefore, established twelve monasteries, each with twelve monks, with himself in overall control.

After a time, disturbed by the intrigues of a neighbouring priest, Benedict, leaving the twelve monasteries to continue without him, travelled south with a few disciples to Monte Cassino, which is on a hill half-way between Naples and Rome. There, on the abandoned citadel, Benedict established a monastery, which was to become the parent house of Western monasticism and a centre of learning – the great theologian St Thomas Aquinas, as we shall see, received his early education there. Because of the strategic importance of its situation, the monastery was several times attacked and re-founded. It was stormed by the Lombards in 589, by the Saracens in 884, and by the Normans in 1030. In the Second World War, Monte Cassino was a key point in the German defensive line set up to block the Allied advance on Rome. The monastery and town were almost completely destroyed, although both have now been rebuilt. The Abbey was reconstructed much on the lines of it predecessor. The archives, library and some paintings survived, but most of artefacts were destroyed, except for bronze gates, which had been cast in Constantinople in 1066 for the then abbot Desiderius.

The area around Cassino was still largely pagan when Benedict arrived there, but people were soon converted by his preaching. His sister Scholastica joined him and established a nunnery nearby. She died shortly before her brother, whose death is thought to have been in about 547.

Benedict's lasting influence rests upon the Rule named after him, which Pope Gregory I described as clear in language and outstanding in its discretion. How far it was original or based on existing sources is a matter of debate. The Rule of St Benedict provides a succinct and complete directory for the government of a monastery and for the spiritual and material wellbeing of its members.

Benedict said that his intention 'was to establish a school for the Lord's service' and continued, 'we hope to impose nothing harsh or burdensome.'[2] His approach has been described as sensible and humane. Benedict discouraged extreme austerities. He allowed the monks adequate sleep – seven and a half to eight hours, clothes fitted to the climate and enough food. 'Two cooked dishes on every table should be enough to allow for differences of taste.' Monks were allowed a full pound of bread every day, but if the workload was especially heavy, the abbot could authorise extra food.[3]

The monks' time was divided roughly into three. Of central importance was the time spent in prayer, much of it in the shared liturgical services of the community, which was the work or 'office' of the monk. A good amount of time was spent in manual work: in the kitchen, on the land, engaged in a craft, copying manuscripts or teaching the boys who were sent to the monastery for their education. Monasteries aimed to be self-supporting. Benedict emphasised work because it was a great equaliser. This was a shock to members of the higher class, who joined the community. There is a story of one monk who declined an invitation to give a prestigious lecture 'because it is my day for the laundry.' Thirdly, time was spent in study of the Scriptures and other spiritual writings.

All monks were expected to commit themselves to a life of poverty, chastity and obedience. Benedict also required a lifelong commitment to a particular community. At the time, many religious people wandered from place to place, depending on the charity of others. Benedict believed that community life was a powerful path to self-awareness and spiritual growth. In community, one becomes aware of one's own and other peoples' strengths and weaknesses. The key to spiritual progress, Benedict believed, is to see Christ in every person. Moreover, by their promise of obedience and fidelity, monks committed themselves to the routine of the community. They would pray when the bell sounded, not when they were so inclined. 'The first step to humility', the Rule says, 'is to obey an order without delaying for a moment.'[4]

The abbot, who has the place of Christ in the community, is a powerful figure, who is appointed for life. He should take advice, but he makes the final decision and makes all appointments. He is bound by the Rule and should constantly remember that he would have to answer at the Judgment Seat of God for himself and for his monks. The rule covers matters of discipline. It also gives detailed instructions about the responsibilities of the cooks, the servers and the porters. Provision is made for the care of novices and of the sick.

St Benedict's Rule has certainly stood the test of time. Some 25,000 Benedictines and 10,000 members of other Orders still live by it. It also shapes the way of life of many lay people, known as oblates or associates.

In the Middle Ages, many monasteries and convents or priories for women were founded. They became centres of learning as well as providing care for the sick and education for the young. They also became the base for missionary efforts. Pope Gregory I sent monks to evangelize England and the Celtic or Irish monks spread the Gospel in German lands. Over the centuries, the need for reformation and renewal prompted the founding of new Monastic orders, such as the Carthusians and the Cistercians. Franciscans and Dominicans, the so-called mendicant or begging orders, unlike monks journeyed from place to place, although in time they established settled houses. The para-military orders, such as the Knights Templars, founded during the Crusades, and the Knights Hospitallars or Order of St John, dedicated to providing medical care, adopted constitutions, which drew heavily on St Benedict's Rule.

Monastic life has remained a significant feature of the Roman Catholic Church. Although recruitment in Western Europe and North America is now difficult, there are a good number of people in Latin

America, Africa and some parts of Eastern Europe who seek to join monastic orders. In England King Henry VIII dissolved the monasteries in the 1530s, although there has been some revival of monasticism in the Anglican Church since the middle of the nineteenth century. In Protestant countries monasticism died out because the Reformers were unsympathetic to it. Monasticism has continued from early days in the Eastern Churches. The most famous centre, as already mentioned, is Mount Athos, a self-governed part of Greece.

Monasticism, of course, is not peculiar to Christianity. The *Sangha*, a Sanskrit word for 'community' or 'gathering' is one of the Three Jewels of Buddhism. In Hinduism, there are monasteries founded, amongst others, by the great teachers Sankara and Ramanuja, and in the nineteenth century, by Swami Vivekananda, the disciple of Sri Ramakrishna. Today there is growing and significant dialogue between monks and nuns of different faiths.

The question, however, remains whether God is to be found by withdrawing from the world or in its midst? Mahatma Gandhi said that if he could have found God in a Himalayan cave, he would have gone there at once, but he could only find God in the service of the poor. The American spiritual writer Wayne Teasdale (1945-2004) describing himself as 'a monk in the world' said, 'I wish to be near the least, the forgotten and ignored, so I can be a sign of hope and love for them.'[5] In Buddhism, there is a growing movement of 'Socially Engaged Buddhists.' The question, perhaps, suggests a false dichotomy. In the twentieth century, it could be claimed that it is people of deep spirituality who have been most aware of social injustice. The Trappist monk and writer, Thomas Merton (1915-68), who was politically active, said that 'True solitude is deeply aware of the world's needs It does not hold the world at arms length.'[6] The solitary 'dwells in the solitude, the poverty, the indigence of every man.'[7] Moreover, as the contemporary Buddhist writer Judith Simmer-Brown has said, 'The Rule speaks of disciplines and practices and can be instructive to anyone who wonders how to establish a domestic environment that nurtures the contemplative development of everyone in the family.'[8]

Recent television programmes about monastic life have shown that it has an attraction in the modern world where many people are stressed by constant movement and noise. There are also numerous experimental communities, which might perhaps still learn something from the wisdom of St Benedict. On a lighter note, a brandy-based liqueur, known as Benedictine, was also named after him and I remember once being given some to drink on his feast day by Benedictine monks in Jerusalem.

The profound influence of St Benedict is not confined to the past but is still growing today as people of many spiritual traditions and different ways of life find in the Rule 'a beginning of their eager search to reach the Father's home in heaven'[9]

CHAPTER NOTES

1. See further chapter 49
2. *St Benedict's Rule*, printed in *Benedict's Dharma*, Ed. Patrick Henry, Continuum, 2001. The translation of the rule is by Patrick Barry, OSB. Prologue, 8. p. 145.
3. *St Benedict's Rule*, 39, 1-2.
4. *Benedict's Rule*, 5.1, p. 155.
5. Wayne Teasdale, *A Monk in the World*, Novato, California, New World Library, 2002, p.xxxi.
6. Thomas Merton, *Thoughts in Solitude*, London, Burns and Oates, 1958, p. 86
7. Thomas Merton, *Conjectures of a Guilty Bystander*, London, Sheldon press, 1977, p.58
8. *Benedict's Dharma*, p. 2.
9. Based on the concluding words of St Benedict's rule, 73.2: 'Whoever you may be, then, in your eagerness to reach your Father's home in heaven, be faithful with Christ's help to this small Rule, which is only a beginning.'

30

Brigid

During the so-called Dark Ages, Christian civilization was at its brightest on the Celtic 'fringe', especially in Ireland, where St Brigid, played a formative role in the growth of Christianity in her native land. Brigid, with St Patrick and St Columba, is one of the patron saints of Ireland.

Brigid's influence was not confined to Ireland. The Abbey, which she founded at Kildare, became one of the most prestigious in Ireland and was famous throughout Christian Europe. Moreover, in due course, Irish missionaries were to spread the Gospel to other lands. Her fame spread throughout Christendom and she is recognised as a saint by the Orthodox as well the Catholic Church.

In the Eastern Mediterranean, the Byzantine Empire survived until the fifteenth century. In Western Europe, invaders gradually eroded Roman civilization, especially north of the Alps. In due course, the monasteries, thanks to St Benedict, became centres of Christian life and learning, and the Papacy increasingly asserted its authority. For a brief while, however, there was a rich flowering of Celtic Christianity.

In recent years there has been an enormous growth of interest in Celtic Christianity. Celts are first mentioned by Greek writers in the fifth century BCE as living in the upper Danube region. As the Roman Empire expanded, the Celts moved westwards, from France and the Low Countries into Britain. Celtic civilization is pre-Roman in origin and flourished for over one thousand years.

Celtic society was tribal, with elected chiefs, who were also judges. Druids were priests and teachers, trained in tribal law and administration. Bards were story-tellers, poets and minstrels. With the spread of Christianity, the druids and bards became priests and monks.

In that part of Britain, which was incorporated into the Roman Empire, Christianity had been brought there by traders and travellers, and by those members of the Roman army and administration and their slaves, who belonged to this 'illegal' sect. Beyond the boundaries of Roman Britain, some Celts, who escaped from Gaul and came to Scotland and Ireland, may have been Christians. The spread of

Christianity in Ireland, however, is primarily associated with St Patrick (c.390-c.460), who was abducted from his home in Britain and brought as a teenager to be a slave in Ireland. He escaped and made his way back to his home in Britain, but later returned as a missionary to Ireland, where Celts, who already believed in immortality and the sacredness of nature, were responsive to the Christian message. Later, Ireland, in turn, was to send missionaries, such as Columba (521-97), who made Iona the base for his work, and Columbanus (543 – 615) of Leinster, to Scotland, Gaul and the German lands. Several of these Irish saints could have been included in this book, so I hope Brigid can be a representative for them, although she deserves to be included in her own right.

There are several variants of Brigid's name - Brigit, Bridget, Brigida, and Bride. In Wales she is known as Ffraid Santes. (She should not be confused with St Bridget of Sweden). There are numerous mediaeval biographies of Brigid, of which the earliest are those written by Cogitosus and by the anonymous author of *Vita Prima*, both of which date to the middle of the seventh century. According to tradition, Brigid was born in County Louth at Faughart, where pilgrims still visit the old well near the ruined church. Her father was a pagan chieftain of Leinster and her mother, Brocca, a slave, may have conceived her out of wedlock. Brocca had perhaps been kidnapped in Portugal and brought to Ireland by pirates. She was a Christian and had been baptised by Saint Patrick and was inspired by his preaching. On one occasion, however, onlookers saw she had fallen asleep during a sermon, although Patrick said she must have seen a vision.

Brigid, from an early age, wanted to join a religious community, although her father strongly objected. As a girl, she used to give his milk, butter and flour generously to any poor person who came to the house. When eventually she gave his jewel-encrusted sword to a man with leprosy, she got her way and her father let her become a nun. Some accounts say that she also had to resist being married to an aristocratic suitor. On entering a convent, she received her veil from St Mel (d. 488), a disciple of Patrick, who became Bishop of Ardagh.

Brigid founded several monasteries, of which by far the most famous was at Kildare or Cill-Dara, 'the church of the oak.' Her own cell was under a large oak tree. This was in fact a double monastery – one for monks and one for nuns. The abbess was superior to the abbot. There is a story that at a ceremony of blessing, the elderly bishop Mel, inadvertently, read the rite for the consecration of a bishop. This was not something that could be rescinded. Perhaps there is a mediaeval precedent for the contemporary consecration of women as bishops in North America! Certainly the administrative authority of the abbesses of Kildare was for several centuries akin to that of a bishop.

The abbey at Kildare became a great centre of spiritual life, learning and crafts, including the production of illuminated manuscripts. Brigid was credited with a beautiful singing voice and is sometimes depicted holding a harp. She also could whistle sweetly and is said to have invented the art of whistling as a way by which she and her companions could communicate with each other in the dark or the mists of Ireland. In the Canary Islands, I have listened to some shepherds displaying the whistling language by which they communicate across the hills and valleys – so perhaps there is something in the tradition. Brigid died around 525 and was buried before the high altar of her abbey church. Subsequently her body was moved to Downpatrick to be placed alongside the body of St Patrick and St Columba of Iona.

Besides being a patron saint of Ireland, Brigid is listed as a patron saint, to name only a few, of blacksmiths, poultry farmers, sailors, scholars and of babies and midwives - sometimes Brigid is said to have been midwife to the Virgin Mary. Her cult was brought to Britain and mainland Europe by Irish missionaries. Many churches are dedicated to her, including the well-known St Bride's church in Fleet Street in London.

St Brigid's feast day is on February 1st. It is surely no coincidence that the feast day of the Celtic goddess Brigit or Briganta (Celtic for 'High One') was also on February 1st, the date of the festival of Imbolc, at which time the ewes come into milk. The Church celebrates Candlemas on February 2nd and seems to have incorporated some pre-Christian ceremonies. Traditionally at Candlemas, candles were blessed for use during the coming year. Indeed, it is sometimes suggested that much that is said of St Brigid was a Christian 'take-over' of the Celtic cult. There was in some places in Ireland a tradition that before a birth the midwife would open the door and ask St Brigid to come in – just as the Celtic goddess Brigit had been invited in to help a woman in her labour. The abbey at Kildare may have been built on the site where a sacred fire, guarded by 'a community of virgin priestesses', burned continually in honour of the goddess.[1]

Today there is renewed interest in St Brigid as part of the rediscovery of Celtic Christianity. 'An enthusiastic following,' writes Mark Atherton, 'now seeks to adapt and reuse the texts of the older tradition to the spiritual needs of the present-day world...The "popular" camp can speak of "environmentally friendly" Celts, who were "non-hierarchical and non-sexist."'[2] Mark Atherton contrasts this with the concerns of the scholars. They see the texts as products of different historical situations, whereas the enthusiasts do not distinguish between the contexts from which the surviving texts emerged. Some scholars also question whether the Christian cultures of the Celtic nations had any particular connection with nature.

Be that as it may, Brigid was certainly not the only woman of that time to have exercised leadership. St Hilda (c. 614) became abbess of Hartlepool and later founded a famous monastery at Whitby. During her time as abbess (657-80), the Synod of Whitby, at which the English church was brought into line with Roman practices, took place there. Radegund (520-87) was another influential woman. She was a princess who became Queen of the Franks when, against her will, she was married to King Clothair of the Franks in 532. Eventually, she left her husband, became a nun and founded a monastery dedicated to the Holy Cross at Poitiers. Both Hildegard and Radegund were patrons of the arts. For example, the old English poet Caedmon was encouraged by Hilda and Radegund was a patron of Venantius Fortunatus (530-609), some of whose hymns are still sung today.[3]

It is also evident that Celtic literature has a deep feel for nature. This prayer is but one example:

'As the rain hides the stars, as the autumn mist hides the hills, as the clouds veil the blue of the sky, so the dark happenings of my lot hide the shining of your face from me. Yet if I may hold your hand in the darkness it is enough. Since I know that, though I may stumble in my going, you do not fail.'[4]

This Celtic outlook is sometimes contrasted with the emphasis on human domination over nature, which is found in later periods of

Christianity. It is claimed, moreover, that, to the Celtic Christian, in the incarnation God became one 'not just with human flesh, but with the wind and air, the sun and the stars, salt, bitterness, stones, the earth and flowers.' Likewise, 'every material and every element and very nature which is seen in the world were all combined in the body in which Christ arose, that is in the body of every human person... All the world arose with him, for the nature of all the elements was in the body which Jesus assumed.'[5]

That the Celtic spiritual tradition survives to inspire us today is in no small measure thanks to St Brigid. Her prayers, of which these are two examples, can still today enrich our spiritual journey. The first makes a good start to the day:

I arise today
Through a mighty strength:
God's power to guide me,
God's might to uphold me,
God's eyes to watch over me;
God's ear to hear me,
God's word to give me speech,
God's hand to guard me,
God's way to lie before me,
God's shield to shelter me,
God's host to secure me.[6]

The second makes a suitable grace.

God bless the poor,
God bless the sick,
And bless the human race.
God bless our food,
God bless our drink,
All homes, O God, embrace.[7]

CHAPTER NOTES

1. Janet E McCrickard, *Brighed: Her Folklore and Mythology*, Glastonbury, Fiedlfare Arts and Design, 1987, p.3.
2. Mark Atherton in *Celts and Christians*, edited by Mark Atherton, Cardiff, University of Wales Press, 2002, p. 1.

3. For example, the Passiontide hymns, 'Sing, my tongue, the glorious battle' or 'Faithful Cross! Above all other...' *English Hymnal*, 95 and 96.
4. In *1,000 World Prayers*, p. 220.
5. *Celts and Christians*, p. 15. See also chapter 8 by Mary Low.
6. *1,000 World Prayers*, p. 126.
7. *1,000 World Prayers*, p. 145.

31

Nagarjuna

Nagarjuna was an outstanding and original philosopher who founded the Madhyamaka ('Middle Way') school of Buddhism. He has had a lasting influence on Buddhism in South East Asia and has been called a 'second Buddha.' He is known particularly for his philosophy of 'emptiness' or sunyata, which challenges all conventional ways of thinking.

There are two major branches of Buddhism, although there are many more schools and sub-divisions.

Theravada Buddhism or 'The Way of the Elders' is prevalent in Sri Lanka, Burma (Myanmar), Thailand, Cambodia (Kampuchea) and Laos. It follows the traditional pattern of monastic renunciation. Basing its teaching on the early Pali scriptures, it encourages forms of meditation which promote mindfulness and awareness of the present moment.

Mahayana Buddhism is dominant in Nepal, China, Korea, Mongolia and Japan. The word 'Mahayana' means 'Greater Vehicle', because its adherents believe that theirs is a bigger raft to carry more people across the ocean of life (*samsara* or 'rebirth') than Theravadin teaching, which they call 'Hinayana' or the 'Lesser Vehicle.' Zen Buddhism is a development of this tradition. Vajrayana ('thunderbolt' or 'diamond vehicle') Buddhism, which emphasises the feminine aspect of reality, is closely related to Mahayana and is especially prevalent in Tibet.

There is considerable uncertainty about Nagarjuna's life. Indeed Max Walleser begins his study of the Tibetan and Chinese sources by saying that Nagarjuna is 'the name of a man of whom we cannot even positively say that he has really existed, still less that he is the author of works ascribed to him.'[1] Some modern scholars think there were at least two Nagarjunas: a philosopher who lived in the second century CE in the Andhra region of southern India and a later Tantric yogin and alchemist who perhaps had links with Tibet. If so, it is the philosopher with whom we are concerned.

The earliest biography was written in about by 405 CE, by Kumarajiva, who translated many Buddhist texts into Chinese. It is thought that Nagarjuna, who was a brilliant child, was born in South

India. His name may indicate a connection with the Naga people, who lived in South India. (The word 'naga' literally means serpent and perhaps the tribe worshipped snakes. Some mythological accounts suggest the Nagas were under-water serpents). His parents belonged to a Brahmin or Hindu priestly family. Buddhism, however, was widely practised at the time and it seems that Nagarjuna was placed in a monastic order at an early age. There he learned some basic Mahayana Buddhist teachings, but it was the 'Perfection of Wisdom' texts (*Prajnaparamita-sutras*), that had the greatest influence upon him.

The scholar of Buddhism Edward Conze (b.1904) wrote that the thousands of lines of the 'Perfection of Wisdom' literature, which includes the *Diamond* and the *Heart Sutras* (c.300-500) can be summed up in the following two sentences:

'One should become a bodhisattva (or Buddha to be) i.e. one who is content with nothing less than all-knowledge attained through the perfection of wisdom for the sake of all beings.

There is no such thing as a Bodhisattva, or as all-knowledge, or as 'being' or as the perfection of wisdom or as an attainment. To accept these contradictory facts is to be perfect.'[2]

We shall reflect later on this contradiction.

Nagarjuna was befriended by a ruler who belonged to the Satavahana dynasty, which, in the period after the Emperor Asoka, ruled in the North-Western Deccan of India.

Nagarjuna's 'Friendly Epistle' was probably written to the King, who built a monastery for him. In return, Nagarjuna is said to have kept the king alive by his medical knowledge and by magic. This upset the Crown prince, who, impatient to succeed to the throne, persuaded Nagarjuna, as an act of charity, to commit suicide. The Prince, according to tradition, wanted Nagarjuna to demonstrate his perfect generosity by donating his head, but the only weapon that could be used for this was a blade of sacred grass. This was because at one time Nagarjuna had accidentally killed some insects when gathering grass for his meditation cushion. At some future date it is believed that his head will be reunited with his body and he will again work for the benefit of sentient beings. Nagarjuna, it is said, was reborn in the Pure Land of Amitabha Buddha.

There are numerous writings ascribed to Nagarjuna, which survive in Sanskrit, Chinese or Tibetan. His most important philosophical works were 'Fundamentals of the Middle Way' (*Madhyamakakarika*) and 'Averting the Arguments' (*Vigrahavyavartani*). The Tibetan tradition also attributes to him a number of Tantric and medical works. He also wrote a number of hymns.

Nagarjuna's philosophical works criticise false views about how existence arises, the means of knowledge, and the nature of reality. Nagarjuna did not believe that anything is self-existent. 'The broad approach, therefore, … is to take a claim made by an opponent that something really exists and to show to the opponent, through reasoning, using principles acceptable to the opponent, that such cannot be the case.'[3] He did not put forward an alternative. 'I do not myself have any thesis. I negate nothing.'[4] No person or object has substantial independent reality. They depend on each other and have no more reality than their interdependence. Developing the Buddha's teaching of 'no-self' Nagarjuna held that the true nature of phenomena was to be empty of a self or a self-essence. This teaching of 'Emptiness' (*Sunyata* in Sanskrit or *Sunnatta* in Pali) has had a profound influence on Buddhism. It is difficult to describe it in a way that does not cause misunderstanding. 'Emptiness' is not another existent. Rather any entity when considered is seen not to have its own substantive reality, but, rather like a river, every thing is in constant flux. All things are empty of an absolute reality and exist only in relation to other transitory realities. Max Walleser says that 'Sunyata means neither "nothing" nor "an empty void" nor a "negative abyss", but it is charac-terised by them as indescribable.'[5] If that is the case, then there are similarities to other mystical traditions, which say that the Ultimate transcends all human language.

If all is emptiness, then there is nothing to cling to. Nagarjuna's philosophy reinforces the Buddha's emphasis on detachment. What people cling to is seen, when analysed, to have no real existence. Even the worlds of change and the ultimate hope of Nirvana have the same nature of emptiness.

Some opponents at the time accused Nagarjuna of destroying Buddhism, but he replied that Buddhism has two truths – conventional truth and ultimate truth. You need a completely new mind set to recognise, as a seventh century follower called Candrakirti put it, that 'everyday practice does not exist from the point of view of ultimate truth.' Another follower, Atisa (982-1054), who had a deep influence on Tsong Khapa Losang Drakpa[6] - one of the most influential Tibetan thinkers - said, 'If one examines with reasoning the conventional as it appears, nothing is found. That non-findingness is the ultimate. It is the primeval way of things.'[7] Few of us, however, can so transcend our conventional ways of thinking to be in a position to judge such a claim. Indeed, as the Japanese Buddhist Dogen (1200-1253) said, 'To say you understand universal emptiness is to defile the truth – universal emptiness falls to the earth... You must be careful not to cling to such a discovery of universal emptiness... Universal emptiness cannot be grasped with our hands.'[8]

For Nagarjuna, his teaching freed a person from all attachment. The search for perfection is unnecessary, since the pursuit of perfection is itself illusory because perfection itself has no reality. The bodhisattva does not, therefore, give up any reward by returning to help those who are caught up in the world of change and rebirth. In his hymns, Nagarjuna celebrated the freedom from illusion and pain that was inherent in his teaching. The bodhisattva is both totally disinterested and truly compassionate. Wisdom and Compassion are inseparable.

In verses addressed to a king, he asked him not to be offended by his candour:

But because of my affection for you,
And through my compassion for all beings,
I tell you without hesitation
That which is useful but unpleasant...

O steadfast one, if true words
Are spoken without anger,
One should take them as fit to be
Heard, like water fit for bathing.[9]

In another verse, he wrote:

Even three times a day to offer

Three hundred cooking pots of food
Does not match a portion of the merit
Acquired in one instant of love.[10]

CHAPTER NOTES

1. Max Walleser, *The Life of Nagarjuna from Tibetan and Chinese Sources*, New Delhi, Asian Educational Services, 1990, p.1.
2. E. Conze, *Prajnaparamita-sutras*, 1978, pp. 7-8 . See also *The Oxford Dictionary of World Religions*, p. 745.
3. Paul Williams, *Mahayana Buddhism*, London, Routledge, 1989, p. 63.
4. *Vigrahavyavartani*, vv. 29/36, quoted by Williams, p. 63.
5. Walleser, p.xxvii.
6. See chapter 50.
7. *Dharmata*, 21, quoted by Williams, p. 70.
8. Dogen Zenji, *Shobogenzo (The Eye and Treasury of the True Law)* quoted by Mary Pat Fisher, *An Anthology of Living Religions*, Upper Saddle River, N.J., Prentice Hall, 2000, p. 123.
9. Nagarjuna *The Precious Garland and the Song of the Four Mindfulnesses*, trans J. Hopkins and L. Rimpoche, London, George Allen and Unwin, 1975, 303-4.
10. *Precious Garland*, 283.

32

Muhammad

The Prophet Muhammad proclaimed that there Is One God and that he was the messenger of God. Those who accept this are known as Muslims, members of the house of Islam. The word *Islam* is derived from the same root as the Hebrew word *shalom*, which means peace.

There is now considerable scholarly agreement about the main events in Muhammad's life, based both on what can be learned from the Qur'an and from the *Hadith*, or narratives about 'the words, deeds or silent approval' of Muhammad. He was born in the 'Year of the Elephant' (570 CE) at Mecca, which was a busy commercial centre in Arabia with a near monopoly of the trade between the Indian Ocean and the Mediterranean. In the year he was born, the city was attacked by an Abyssinian army - although the Ka'bah, the central shrine, was miraculously saved.

Muhammad was of the family Banu Hashim of the leading tribe of the Quraysh. He was born after the death of his father and became ward of his grandfather, Abd al-Muttalib. At an early age he had an experience of a visitation by two figures - later identified as angels - who 'opened his chest and stirred their hands inside'. It was the first of several unusual experiences that led Muhammad increasingly to search for the truth of God and religion on his own. This quest was strengthened when a widow, called Khadijah, employed him to take trading caravans north to Syria. There he met Christians and Jews, especially the monk Bahira who recognised in him the signs of the promised Messiah. By now Muhammad was under the protection of his uncle Abu Talib. At the age of 25, he married Khadijah. They had two sons, who died young, and four daughters. Muhammad was increasingly influenced by the Hanifs, who sought to preserve a monotheism which they traced back to Ibrahim (Abraham). The people of Mecca, however, were polytheistic and worshipped idols. Often Muhammad went by himself to a cave on Mount Hira. It was there that he had the strong sense of a presence, later identified as Gabriel, who three times insisted 'Recite.' The third time, the angel overwhelmed him and said,

'Recite in the name of your Lord who created!
He creates man from a clot of blood.
Recite; and your Lord is Most Bountiful,
He who taught by the pen,
Taught man what he did not know.[1]

At first Muhammad thought he was possessed, but as he fled the cave and was half way down the mountain, he heard a voice saying to him, 'O Muhammad, thou art the messenger of God and I am Gabriel.' On his return home, with a still quaking heart, he said to Khadija 'Cover me, cover me.' Khadijah went to tell her old and blind cousin Waraqah, who was a Christian. He exclaimed that the angel of Revelation who had come to Moses had now come to Muhammad. A further divine revelation reassured Muhammad. After further revelations, he began preaching, but met strong opposition. He was clear that if God is One, then there cannot be a Christian God and a Jewish God and certainly not the many deities of Mecca. He was also convinced that the idolatry of Mecca had to be swept away. For Muhammad there was only One God from whom all creation derived. Therefore all human beings should live in a corresponding unity (*umma*). Islam is the attempt to realise this unity under God.

The first believer, after his wife Khadijah and his cousin Ali and his slave Zayd (whom the Prophet set free), was Abu Bakr. They were called *al-muslimun* or Muslims, those who enter into a condition of safety because of their commitment to God.

Opposition and persecution increased. But then, Muhammad was invited to Yathrib - soon to be known as Madina - to make his way of unity a practical reality by reconciling the town's two rival ruling families. He made this move, known as the *Hijra*, which means emigration and breaking the bonds of kinship, in 622, a date which was to become the first year of the Muslim calendar. There under the guidance of fresh revelations from God he began to establish a community. All the revelations, preserved in the Qur'an, were clearly distinct from the words that Muhammad spoke as an ordinary human being. It is said that his appearance changed and the style of utterance, which was rhythmic and with a loose pattern of rhyme, was different to his normal speech.

At Madina Muhammad was joined by some seventy other emigrants, known as the Muhajirun. Opposition from Mecca continued, partly because Muhammad raided some of their caravans. In 624 the Muslims defeated a much larger Meccan army at the battle of Badr, but in the following year the battle of Uhud, in which the Prophet was injured, was inconclusive, largely because the archers disobeyed their orders because they were too eager for booty. In 627 the Quraysh failed in their attempt to besiege Madina. Then in 630, Muhammad captured Mecca and purified it from idols. Besides these military engagements, Muhammad both organised the pattern of life in Madina and built up relations with neighbouring tribes.

Muhammad died two years after his return to Mecca. Almost immediately after Muhammad's death, Abu Bakr (d.634) who was to become the first Caliph, declared, 'If any of you have been worshipping Muhammad, let him know that Muhammad is dead. But if you have been worshipping God, then know that God is eternal and never dies.' He quoted the verse: 'Muhammad is no more than a Messenger.'[3] Muhammad is not regarded as superhuman nor divine or without sin. This is why pictures or statues of Muhammad are forbidden in case he was to be turned into an idol. There is also disagreement among Muslims about whether his birthday should be celebrated.

Muhammad was the messenger of God. The message is recorded in the Qur'an. For Muslims, the Qur'an is God's final word to humankind, vouchsafed to the Prophet Muhammad in pure Arabic. Strictly speaking, the Qur'an cannot be translated. The whole of the Qur'an is in rhymed or assonance prose and this is usually lost in translation. The generally accepted view among Muslims is that some portions of the Qur'an were written down during the Prophet's life time and that the first collection of revelations was made during the caliphate of Abu Bakr (632-4 CE).[4]

The Qur'an is divided into 114 *surahs*, which for the most part are arranged according to length. The longest comes at the beginning and the shortest at the end. They are not in the order in which they were revealed. Commentators often distinguish the earlier Meccan *surahs*, which date from the time when the Prophet faced much opposition, and the *surahs* from the time when the Prophet was at Madina and had the responsibilities of ruling and leading a community.

Most Muslims first experience the Qur'an aurally rather than visually. Listening and learning to recite from memory are prior to understanding and reading. According to tradition, the first part of the Qur'an to be revealed was the beginning of Surah 96, of which the very first word is 'Recite.' During Ramadan – the month of fasting – all 114 surahs are recited in canonical order. During the five daily prayers a Muslim recites some verses of the Qur'an, including very regularly the *Al-Fatihah*, or opening *surah*:

In the name of Allah, Most Gracious, Most Merciful.
Praise be to Allah,
The Cherisher and Sustainer of the Worlds:
Most gracious, Most merciful;
Master of the Day of Judgment.
Thee do we worship,
And Thine aid we seek.
Show us the straight way,
The way of those on whom
Thou hast bestowed Thy grace
Those whose (portion)
Is not wrath,
And who go not astray.[5]

Muhammad died without making clear provision for the future, although in his last illness he asked Abu Bakr to lead the prayers in his place. Despite his various marriages, Muhammad had no surviving son. His nearest relation was his cousin Ali, who had married one of his daughters, but the majority of the community chose as his successor Abu Bakr, who was one of his first followers, and who was known as caliph. There were those, however, who thought that Ali should have been his successor and within a generation of Muhammad's death, this lead to the division of Islam between Sunni and Shi'a, which persists to this day. The expansion of Islam after Muhammad's death was amazingly rapid.

The teaching of Islam is often summed up in what are called the Five Pillars of Islam. They are witness to the Oneness of God and that Muhammad is his prophet (*ash-Shahhāda*); regular times of prayer (*salat*); tithe for the poor (*zakat*); pilgrimage to Mecca, *hajj*; and fasting during daylight throughout the month of Ramadan (*sawm*).

Muhammad was a man of deep prayer, who besides the five required times of prayer would spend much other time in prayer. He had a particularly intense communion with God. His followers regard him as special and he is sometimes called *insan al-kamil*, the Perfect man. Countless stories, *hadith*, were told about him, the authenticty of which was carefully checked. Various collections were made – mainly for use as legal precedents. The best known is the collection made by al-Bukhari (810-70), which contains over 7,000 narratives. The sayings and actions of the Prophet, therefore, inform the mind of the Muslim.

He is regarded as the Exemplar and first living commentary on the meaning of the Qur'an and how to apply it to daily life. Muslims' love of the Prophet is perhaps the strongest binding force in a religion, which has such a sense of community. al-Ghazali (d.1111), an outstanding Muslim leader, said of him,

'The Messenger of God (upon him be peace) was the mildest of men, but also the bravest and most just of men. ... He would take only the simplest and easiest of foods: dates and barley, giving anything else away for God's sake... He would become angered for his Lord, never for himself... He never despised any pauper for his poverty or illness; neither did he hold any king in awe simply because he was a king. He would call rich and poor to God, without distinction.'[6]

This love for Muhammad explains why Muslims are so offended by any criticism of the Prophet.

Initially Muhammad put up courageously with the abuse and perse-cution heaped upon him. Even when odiously reviled he did not answer back. Once when he was in prostration in the courtyard of the Ka'aba, some one placed the entrails of a camel over his shoulders, but he continued in his prayers until his daughter came and removed them so that he could get up. He remained constant in his faith during long years of frustration.

Although the Prophet stressed the importance of fasting, he equally insisted on the need to break the fast. Islam is not an ascetic religion. The Qur'an stresses the importance of giving thanks to God for the rich provision of nature and for the blessings of life, such as hearing and sight and sleep, and for the joy of marriage. Muhammad who had four wives - which was not unusual at the time - insisted that they had to be treated equally and with affection.

Muhammad was also a person of great compassion. There are many stories of his kindness to animals. I like the one of the occasion when he came into a house and put down his cloak. Whilst he was talking, a mother cat and her kittens settled on the cloak. Rather than disturb the cats, Muhammad took a knife and cut round them leaving the cats part of his cloak.

His compassion was shown even more clearly in his treatment of his enemies. After the capture of Mecca, Muhammad sent for the leaders of the Quraish. They appealed for mercy. The Prophet forgave all the scorn and hatred and hardship and suffering, which he had endured. In the moment of victory Muhammad granted a general amnesty and chose the way of reconciliation. The Prophet showed great skill in diplomacy and his truthfulness was recognised.

Muslims over the centuries have regarded Muhammad in many ways. Some look to him to intercede for them. As a Persian poet wrote, 'We, encircled by our sins, look on as you bend your head in prayer, calling out: "Forgive my people, God, forgive them."' Others tell of the Prophet appearing to them, when they were praying, to console and guide them. Mystics have looked to him as their model. Jalal al-Din Rumi (1207-73), a mystic and poet, spoke of him as 'the astolabe of God,'[7] who is 'my beloved, my physician, my tutor and my cure.' Some modern writers have seen him - perhaps in their own image - as an anti-colonial hero, an Arab nationalist, a pacifist and a feminist.

Non-Muslims have been more critical, even scurrilous. The great Christian poet Dante (1265-13210) placed Muhammad in the inferno and Luther regarded Muhammad and the Pope as the two arch-enemies of Christ.

One of the first British writers to attempt a more sympathetic portrait was Thomas Carlyle (1795-1881), who saw Muhammad as a genuine hero among the prophets. The twentieth century saw many more scholarly accounts of Muhammad's life and times, although the application of historical criticism by so-called Orientalists to the Qur'an was unacceptable to Muslims. For Muslims, the Qur'an is the message of God, of which the Prophet was the mouthpiece. To talk of what Muhammad borrowed from Judaism and Christianity, as if he were an author composing a book, is for Muslims a total misunderstanding.

It is equally mistaken to depict him as a man of violence. He was willing to use force in the defence of his community and to protect the weak, but in fact he only spent a few days in battle. Muslims, like many Christians, have accepted that there are circumstances when the use of force may be justified. Even so, *jihad* is primarily a personal struggle to purify the self.

Gradually some Christians are recognising that the message of Muhammad has universal significance and that it is appropriate to speak of him as *a* Prophet but not, for Christians, as the seal of the Prophets. One mediaeval Yemenite Jewish philosopher Netanel ibn Fayyumi asserted the authenticity of the prophecy of Muhammad, but this was an individual opinion. Others, such as Moses Maimonides and Judah Halevi, both of whom were highly respected, saw Islam as helping to prepare for the Messianic kingdom with its message of the Oneness of God. All who share that belief and the conviction that society should be based on moral principles, which have Divine sanction, will recognise that the message Muhammad proclaimed belongs not just to Islam, but to the world. The Qur'an says that God did not choose to make a single people, so that people of faith would compete with each other in virtue and good works.

Non-Muslims need to learn more about Islam to prevent a 'clash of civilizations.' In so doing their admiration for the Prophet is likely to increase and they may discover how much Judaism and Christianity and indeed other world religions have in common with Islam.

CHAPTER NOTES
1. Qur'an 96,1-5.
2. Qur'an, 4,69.
3. Qur'an, 3,144.
4. The definitive text was determined during the Caliphate of Uthman, see chapter 33.
5. From the Holy Qur'an, English translation and commentary revised by The Presidency of the Islamic Researches, IFTA, Call and Guidance, Saudi Arabi
6. Quoted by Tim Winter in *Abraham's Children*, pp. 115-6.
7. An astrolabe was a medieval instrument used by astronomers to determine the altitude of the sun.

33

A'isha

A'isha was the third and favourite wife of the Prophet Muhammad. She provided much of the personal information that we have about the Prophet, which is an invaluable supplement to the revelation recorded in the Qur'an. She also shows the importance and dignified status that the Prophet accorded to women.

A'isha Bint Abi Bakr was born in Mecca in about 614 CE. She was the daughter of Um Ruman and Abu Bakr, who was of the same tribe as Muhammad and who was the first male convert to Islam. Abu Bakr was a close friend of Muhammad and his faithfulness earned him the title *al-Siddiq* or 'the truthful one.' A'isha is said to have accepted Islam as a child and to have been taken with him by her father when he went to Abyssinia (Ethiopia) to avoid persecution in Mecca.

Muhammad's first wife, who was also the first person to believe in his message, was Khadija. She was a rich widow who employed Muhammad in her trading business. She was about forty when she married the twenty five year old Muhammad. Khadija bore him several children. The most important was Fatima, who was to marry Muhammad's nephew Ali – the fourth Caliph. Fatima was mother to Hasan and Husain. It was the death of Husain at the battle of Karbala in 680, which led to the division between Shi'ites and Sunni Muslims– to which we shall return.

After Khadija's death in 619, Muhammad was leading a lonely life and asked for God's guidance. Two people were suggested to him as suitable wives: one was the widow Sudah bint Zamma and the other was the young girl A'isha - polygamy was allowed, provided the wives were treated equally. The *nika* or marriage contract was agreed, but as A'isha was only a child, the wedding was postponed until after the Migration to Medina in 622. A'isha was not actually present at the *nika* and the main difference it made to her was that she was no longer allowed to play outside the house but had to play with her friends in the courtyard.[1] Even when she came to be married, she recalled, 'I was playing on a see-saw and my long streaming hair was dishevelled. They came and took me from my play and made me ready.'[2] Even when she moved to the Prophet's home, she continued to play with her dolls with the girls who were her friends. The Prophet would sometimes join in the games.

A'isha had known the Prophet from her earliest childhood, as he visited her parents' home almost every day. A'isha seems to have been very attractive and with a lively mind. Revelations often came to the prophet while he was in her company.

In 627, A'isha accompanied Muhammad on one of his expeditions. At one of the places where the army halted, A'isha's onyx necklace, which had been given to her by her mother on the day of her wedding, came undone and fell to the ground. A'isha went to look for it. By the time she came back her howdah - or covered seat - had been strapped to the camels and she was left behind. She found the necklace where one of the camels had been lying on it. She then waited, expecting someone to come back and look for her. Instead, a young man called Sawfan, who had fallen behind for some reason, saw her and escorted her to the camp. This set the rumour-mongers talking, but her reputation was saved when the Prophet received a revelation confirming her innocence.[3]

Islam is not an ascetic religion. Human sexuality, rightly used, is accepted as a gift of God to be enjoyed. Muhammad said to Uthman, who wanted to make himself a eunuch and spend the rest of his life as a wandering beggar, 'Am I not a fair example? I go into women, and I eat meat, and I fast and I break fast…the body has its rights.'[4]

'Although Muhammad tried to treat his wives equally, there was bound to be some jealousy between them and they were rebuked for their unruliness.[5] 'A'isha's feelings' as Martin Lings says, 'were always clear from her face and usually from her tongue.'[6] She admitted, later in life, that it was Khadija of whom she was most jealous, because Muhammad kept recalling her virtues. She knew, however, that jealousy was only for this life, because a revelation said that in Paradise 'we remove whatever there may be of rancour in their breasts.'[7] One day, A'isha asked the Prophet, 'O Messenger of God, who are thy wives in Paradise?' 'You are of them', he replied and A'isha treasured those words for the rest of her life, as she also treasured the message that 'Gabriel is here and he gives you his greetings of Peace.'[8]

A'isha was only about eighteen when Muhammad died. During his last illness it is said that Muhammad went to her apartment and died with his head upon her lap. The Sunnis take this as evidence of his fondness for her, although in the Shi'ite tradition he is said to have died with his head on Ali's lap. Before the Prophet died he had a vision of Paradise and A'isha heard him murmur 'With the supreme communion in Paradise, with those upon whom God hath showered His favour, the prophets and the saints and the martyrs and the righteous, most excellent for communion are they.'[9] After his death, Abu Bakr remembered a saying of Muhammad's that 'No Prophet dies but is buried where he died.' Accordingly, the Prophet was buried where he died under the floor of A'isha's room.[10]

A'isha was now a young widow and childless. As a widow of the Prophet she was not allowed to marry again.[11] Nonetheless she was an influential figure and some years after the Prophet's death she made an unsuccessful attempt to determine who should be the caliph. To understand her intervention, it is necessary to recount the rather complex history of the early caliphs and the disputes about who should be caliph, which led to the division between Sunni and Shi'ite Muslims.

A'isha's father Abu Bakr (d. 634) became the first caliph or leader of the Muslims. It is not clear whether she played any part in his election. As we have seen, Abu Bakr was one of the first Meccans to believe in Muhammad. Moreover the Prophet had appointed him to lead the farewell pilgrimage and to lead the prayers when Muhammad himself was too ill to do so. A'isha had, in fact, objected when Muhammad told the wives to ask Abu Bakr to lead the prayers, saying 'Abu Bakr is a very sensitive man, not strong of voice and much given to weeping when he recites the Qur'an.' However, Muhammad was insistent, despite further objections from A'isha. Abu Bakr, therefore, led the prayers during Muhammad's final illness.[12]

Almost immediately after Muhammad's death the military expansion of the Muslims began in Arabia and then in Syria. The Byzantines were defeated at the battle of Aghnadayan in 634. The same year saw the death of Abu Bakr who appointed Umar (d. 644) to be his successor. Umar had been one of the early Meccan companions of the Prophet and was also a father-in-law to Muhammad. At his inauguration, Umar declared, 'The Arabians are truly an unruly camel, and, by God, I am he who can keep them on the right path.' He proved to be a good leader and organiser and further extended the Muslim empire.

His relations with A'isha were good. He provided well for her and her 'sisters.' 'He sent us our share of everything, even to the heads and shanks of 'slaughtered beasts.'[13] In 644 Umar was assassinated by a frustrated slave. He was succeeded by Uthman ibn 'Affan, who ruled until 656. A'isha seems to have been reasonably pleased with his election, but she soon became aware of his weakness and favouritism. Moreover, Uthman seems to have reduced her pension to the same amount as the other wives, whereas she had previously had a privileged position.

During Uthman's Caliphate, the text of the Qur'an was finalised. A complaint had been made to the Caliph 'Uthman (ruled 644-56) that divergences had appeared in Qur'anic recitations. Caliph Uthman, therefore, asked A'isha and others to send him the leaves in their possession. He then appointed a group of five to copy these into a single volume, monitoring the text as they did so. They also collected some additional material. Once the work was complete, Uthman sent copies of the new text to the provinces and ordered all other versions to be destroyed.[14] As a result the Qur'an always and everywhere has the same verses, of which there are over six thousand, and in the same order.

The collection and editing of the Qur'an annoyed the Qur'an reciters – people who had memorised the *surahs* – because they were now redundant and their importance diminished. In any case, from the time of Muhammad's death there had been tensions between the Meccan and Medinan parties. Uthman's centralizing polices and favouritism to his family also made him unpopular in some quarters. In 656 the discontented gathered in Medina and there were protracted negotiations. A'isha was among the critics of Uthman but made it clear that she was opposed to those who were plotting his murder, although, subsequently not everyone believed her protestations and suspected that she was involved in Uthman's death. At least A'isha, by persisting in going on her annual pilgrimage to Mecca, despite Uthman's pleas, may have weakened his position. In her absence, a group, from Egypt, stormed Uthman's house and murdered him.

Following Uthman's death, there were three main rivals for the caliphate: Ali, Talhah and Zubair. Many Muslims now wanted 'Ali ibn Abu Talib (d. 661) to be the caliph. Ali was the cousin and son-in-law of Muhammad and had distinguished himself in the early battles. He had, however, been too young to be considered as caliph when Abu Bakr and Umar were appointed and he had been a supporter of Uthman. There is general agreement that Ali was a pious man who lived an austere life and that he was a powerful speaker. He was not, however, welcomed by the Meccan aristocrats. There were rumours – probably unfounded - that Ali had been involved in the murder of Uthman. It was at this point that A'isha comes back into the story as she was one of those who opposed Ali, which is why some Shi'ite Muslims are sometimes critical of her. Ali was proclaimed as caliph by the Medinans, while A'isha was still on pilgrimage in Mecca. A'isha soon sided with Ali's opponents and raised an army, which confronted Ali's army outside Basra. A'isha directed her forces from a howdah on the back of a camel, which is why the engagement is known as the Battle of the Camel. Her army was defeated and she was captured. Ali, however, had no wish to harm her and sent her back to Medina under military escort. She subsequently led a retired life until she died in about 678.

Ali was also opposed by Mu'awiyya, who was governor of Syria and a relation of the murdered Uthman. Civil war broke out and Ali was assassinated in 661 in the mosque of Kufa. At least publicly A'isha seems to have expressed her grief and praised Ali's good qualities, although privately she may have felt some relief at the news. Mu'awiyya (ruled from 661-680) now persuaded the Prophet's eldest grandson, Hasan, with the grant of a large sum, to stand aside and let him become caliph. Mu'awiyya probably also sent gifts to A'isha, who on one occasion gave him one of the Prophet's tunics. There seems also to have been quite frequent correspondence between them, although its content is not known. Nonetheless A'isha's political influence declined during Mu'awiyya's caliphate. On the other hand, she was increasingly consulted for advice and for her memories of what the Prophet had said and done - A'isha had an excellent memory. She also had a good knowledge of Arab poetry.

Another grandson Husain (626-80), the son of Ali and Fatima, who was much loved by Muhammad, kept in the background during Mu'awiyya's rule, but refused to recognise Yazid (ruled 680-688) as his successor. Husain's supporters were annihilated at the battle of Karbala and his male descendants massacred. Shi'ite Muslims regard Husain as a martyr and commemorate his death each year.

The cause of A'isha's last illness is not known. It was her wish to be buried with the sisters. She died during Ramadan on July 13th, 678 or in Year 58 of the Muslim calendar. Her burial, at night, was attended by a very large crowd. Her dying wish was for oblivion, but this has been ignored and her importance is evidence of the esteemed status granted to women at the time of the Prophet.

A'isha's military intervention may have been unsuccessful, but it may surprise some readers to think of a woman at that time leading an army. Yet Muhammad's first wife was a successful business-woman. Moreover, the wives of the Prophet were clearly not afraid to express their opinions. Indeed, as already mentioned, the Qur'an reproves the wives for their behaviour and tells them that 'if you connive together with each other against him (Muhammad), God is His great custodian... and the angels will come to his aid.' It then adds the warning: 'Were he to divorce you, his Lord would give him other wives instead better than you.'[15]

In time, however, the wives came to be seen as role models for Muslim women. Saadia Khawar Khan Chisti, who has been a Professor at the College of Education for Women in Lahore and a member of the Council of Islamic ideology of Pakistan, has written,

'The exemplary lives of the noble women of the Prophet's household echo the message contained in many verses of the Qur'an ... to the effect that a Muslim woman's religious duties lie in keeping an orderly home which breathes tranquillity amid both the plenty and the scarcity of the necessities of life.'[16]

The Prophet conferred on women a dignified status and made clear that it is possible for women to attain the knowledge of God amid their social and family responsibilities. 'The vistas of spiritual growth and development were fully opened to the female sex.'[17]

Khadijah – the first wife – was also a model of motherhood. 'A'isha', writes Saadia Khawar Khan Chisti, 'was particularly important; it was in her arms that the Prophet died and in her company that he received revelations... A'isha, the learned mother of believers, lived through the rules of the four rightly guided caliphs of Islam and wove the sapiential dimension into the fabric of their reigns. Her most intimate closeness with the Prophet as his wife makes her an inseparable part of him. She survived her prophet-husband for nearly half a century and guided the faithful with her Divine knowledge.'[18]

Over two thousand of the stories or *hadiths* of what the Prophet said or did derive from A'isha. It is from her memories, for example, that we know of the importance the Prophet put upon night vigils and the constant remembrance of God. Her narrations have given us a vivid picture of the man who for so many millions of people has shown us the pattern of human behaviour at its best. When A'isha was asked about the character of Muhammad, she replied, 'Have you not read the Qur'an? ... Truly the character of the Prophet was the Qur'an.'[19] The Prophet said of her 'Learn two thirds of religion from A'isha.'[20]

CHAPTER NOTES

1. Martin Lings, *Muhammad: His Life based on the Earliest Sources*, London, George Allen and Unwin, 1983, p.106.
2. Quoted by Lings, p. 133.
3. Qur'an 24,4.
4. Lings, p. 165.
5. Qur'an 66,1.
6. Lings, p. 271.
7. Qur'an 7,42; 15,47.
8. Lings, pp. 271-2.
9. Quoted by Lings, p. 341.
10. Lings, p. 344.
11. Qur'an 33,53.
12. Lings, p. 339.
13. Quoted by Nabia Abbott, *Aishah, the Beloved of Mohammed*, Chicago, University of Chicago Press, 1942, p. 94.
14. Some scholars question the accuracy of this tradition.
15. Surah 66,4-5 in the translation of Kenneth Cragg in *Readings in the Qur'an*, London, Collins, 1998, p. 243.
16. Saadia Khawar Khan Chisti in *Islamic Spirituality*, 1, London, SCM press, 1989, p. 203.
17. Saadia Khawar Khan Chisti, p. 203.
18. Saadia Khawar Khan Chisti, p. 206.
19. Quoted by Marcus Braybrooke, *What Can We learn from Islam*, Alresford, John Hunt, 2002, p. 53.
20. Quoted by Saadia Khawar Khan Chisti, p. 206.

34

Sankara

Sankara was the most influential Indian theologian and philosopher. His work led to the lasting revival of Hinduism in India. His teaching, known as Advaita, has been central to the thinking of Indian philosophers whether they agreed or disagreed with him. Dr Radhakrishnan (1888-1975), a distinguished philosopher and a President of India said, 'Sankara stands out as a heroic figure of the first rank in the somewhat motley crowd of religious thinkers of mediaeval India. His philosophy stands out complete, needing neither a before nor an after.'[1]

Some words of explanation may be helpful. The Hindu scriptures, as we have seen, are known as the Vedas, the revelation of the sacred and eternal truth.[2] The earliest text is the Rig Veda which consists of hymns dating, at least in their oral from, to the fifteenth century BCE. The latest Vedic scriptures from about 600-400 BCE are the Upanishads. The philosophy based on the Upanishads is known as Vedanta, because it is based on the final scriptures – the word Vedanta means the end or culmination of the Vedas. In addition, there is the Bhagavad Gita, often known just as the Gita, which is part of one of the epics.

The dominant schools of Vedanta philosophy are Advaita, Vishistadvaita and Dvaita. The word Advaita means 'non-dual' because it is claimed there is ultimately only one Reality, Brahman, who is spoken of in impersonal terms. The soul is ultimately one with the Real, just as a river flows into the ocean. The word Dvaita means dual. This tradition holds that even in the final union the worshipper is distinct from the Divine. Ramanuja, whom we shall consider after Sankara taught a mediating position, called Vishistadvaita. The main age-old debate in Hindu philosophy has been between adherents of these three rival positions. The question also relates to continuing discussion of the nature of mystical experience.

Besides the three main schools of Vedanta philosophy, there is a theological difference between the worshippers of the god Siva, who are known as Saivites, and those who worship the god Vishnu, who are called Vaishnavites. Vishnu, as we have seen, has from time to time taken bodily form as an avatar, most notably as Krishna and Rama.

Brahmā, the third god of the Hindu Trinity or *Trimurti*, is seldom worshipped. (The god Brahmā should be distinguished from Brahman or Brahma, the Absolute all-pervading Spirit. The word Brahmin refers to members of the priestly caste).

Sankara is the outstanding exponent of Advaita philosophy, although he did not invent it. Before discussing his teaching, however, I shall outline the main events of his short life. There is, of course, the usual difficulty of discovering what is historical. There are a dozen or so biographies of Sankara, but they were all written several centuries after he died and are full of legends and miraculous happenings, partly because Sankara came to be regarded as an *avatar* or embodiment of the God Shiva.

There is considerable debate about when Sankara lived. The traditional monastic chronology places him in the sixth or fifth centuries BCE, but this 'contradicts the entire chronology of ancient India as determined by scientific history.'[3] The generally accepted outline of his life is that he was born in 788 CE and that he died at the early age of 32 – although some scholars put his dates a century or more earlier. He grew up in a village in Kerala in South West India.

The settled age of the great and stable empires of the Guptas (319 CE – 606 CE), of whom Asoka was one, and of the Vakatakas, who ruled in the Deccan from the mid-third century to the end of the fifth century had ended. It was a period of political instability and upheaval. Culturally, however, it was an age of vigorous creativity and some fine temples were built at that time. The traditional Vedic religion of the Brahmins was still commonly practised, but devotional worship of a personal god (*bhakti*) was widespread, especially in the South of India. There was also lively debate between the different philosophical schools of Hinduism. Buddhism was strong especially in the cities and Jainism attracted a number of followers. Some Arab traders came to the coast of Kerala, but it is not known whether this led to any local familiarity with Islam. The Syriac Christian church had long been established in South India, dating back perhaps to the missionary efforts of St Thomas. There were a few Jews and even today there is a rather charming old synagogue in Cochin, which dates back to 1568 and is the oldest synagogue in the British Commonwealth. In the synagogue there are copper plates granting the Jews certain privileges which date back to the tenth century. Certainly Sankara lived at a time of interfaith disputation, if not of dialogue.

Sankara's family were pious Brahmins, probably worshippers of Siva and his consort Sakti. He is said to have been a precocious child with an exceptionally retentive memory so that he knew many of the scriptures by heart at a very early age. His Tonsure was formally performed in his third year. When he was five his father, at a ceremony in which the boy was given the sacred thread, initiated him into study of the Vedas. His father, however, died before Sankara had reached the home of his teacher. When he was eight, Sankara wanted to renounce the world and become a wandering holy man or *sannyasin*, but his mother objected. Some month's later, when he was bathing in a river, he was seized by a crocodile. He cried out to his mother to let him make his act of renunciation, as his death seemed imminent. His mother agreed and miraculously the crocodile released his grip on Sankara. He then left home for the itinerant life, but fulfilled his promise to return to perform the funeral rites for his mother on her death, although this was in defiance of accepted behaviour for a *sannyasin*.

When Sankara reached the Narmada river, which flows into the Arabian Sea south of Baroda, he came upon a revered teacher called Govindapada in a cave on the river-bank. He became his pupil and settled there for a time. Nothing is known about Govindapada other than that he was himself a disciple of Gaudapada, who had written an important work on the Mandukya Upanishad – one of the Hindu scriptures – in which he gave a systematic outline of Advaita Vedanta.

When Sankara resumed his wandering life, he made his way to the holy city of Varanasi (Benares), where he began to teach and to write and to attract disciples of his own. A Chinese traveller, Hsuan Chwang, who visited the city in the seventh century, said there were more than a hundred temples with some ten thousand holy men. 'Some cut their hair off, others tie their hair in a knot, and go naked, without clothes, they cover their bodies with ashes, and by the practice of all sorts of austerities they seek to escape from birth and death.'[4] There were also a number of Buddhists in the area.

It was in Varanasi or perhaps in Badarinatha - in the foothills of the Himalayas, near to the source of the river Ganges - to which he travelled next that Sankara composed his famous commentary on the

Brahmasutra, which is a very ancient work, attributed to Badarayana, a sage who lived in the first century BCE, but which may be even earlier. It summarises the teaching of the Upanishads about the Ultimate Reality, Brahman.

The last years of Sankara's short life were spent wandering throughout India, teaching Advaita philosophy and challenging rival teachers. He had a particularly heated debate with Mandana Misra, whose wife acted as umpire. Mandana Misra taught that final release or *moksa* could only be obtained by practising the rituals prescribed in the early parts of the Vedic scriptures. Sankara, on the other hand, insisted that personal knowledge of Brahman was essential. In a succinct summary of his teaching, which we shall discuss more fully below, Sankara announced his position: 'Brahman, pure Existence-Consciousness-Bliss is the one ultimate Truth. It is he who appears as the entire world of multiplicity owing to the thick cover of ignorance, just as a shell appears as a piece of silver. Through the knowledge of Brahman the whole world is dissolved into its substratum, which is the same as one's own *Atman* or soul. This is the supreme liberation and is the cessation of future births. The crown of the Vedas, the Upanishads, is the authority in support of this proposition.'[5] The claim of Sankara's biographers, of course, is that he won the argument. We are not told what Mandana Misri had to say to his wife after the contest!

Sankara concentrated on explaining his philosophy to other holy men and intellectuals, realising it was too complicated for the ordinary devotee, although he wrote hymns for them. He avoided the cities, which were the stronghold of Buddhism. To ensure the continuing influence of his teaching, he established monasteries at the four corners of India: Sringeri in the South, Puri in the East, Dwaraka in the West, and near Badarinatha in the North. The abbots, who have the title 'Sankaracarya', still have great authority and are venerated by traditionally observant Hindus. I once had the privilege of an audience with one the Sankaracaryas, who lives in great simplicity. Although he is well versed in Western philosophy and presumably speaks good English, the conversation – through interpreters – was conducted in Sanskrit.

Towards the end of his life Sankara visited Kashmir. Tradition says that at the age of 32, he left Kedaranath in the Himalayas, where the shrine is said to date back to the eighth century, heading north towards Mount Kalisa, the abode of the god Siva. He was seen no more.

Sankara's literary output was enormous. Nearly four hundred works have been ascribed to him. Sankara starts with Brahman or the Real. Brahman is outside time, space and causality. Besides Brahman there is nothing. Any idea that there are other beings is a misapprehension. The self is not other than Brahman. His teacher Gaudapada said that to think there are separate souls is like considering the space inside a jar is other than Space itself. To realize this truth of identity is to gain spiritual release (*moksa*).

From that standpoint of realization, the world is seen to be unreal. The difficulty of disagreeing with this is that most of us have not gained realization. To us the world seems real enough, but so also when we are in a cinema or watching television, the characters on the screen seem real enough. Equally while we are asleep, dreams seem real. Sankara's own famous comparison is of a rope, which is mistaken for a snake. There is only a rope and no snake, but as long as the rope is thought to be a snake it is in effect a snake. In the same way the world is *maya*. In thinking the world is real we mistake the omnipresent reality of Brahman.

Sankara claimed support for his views from scriptural texts, such as 'thou art that' (*tat-tvam-asi*) in the Chandogya Upanishad or 'Atman is Brahman.' Yet, it is not so much scripture, as the mystical sense of oneness, to which meditation is claimed to lead, that is convincing for the Advaitin. Truth is self-authenticating. It is known in experience and does not need supporting arguments. The twentieth century saint Ramana Maharshi (1879-1950) has been spoken of as a living example of Advaita. An experience in which he sensed that he had died made him recognise that at death the body dies, but that the self is unaffected. His realisation that Atman is Brahman remained with him as a constant condition.

In one way, Sankara's teaching is simple, but it calls in question all our conventional ways of thinking about the world. It points to the experience of 'oneness with all that is' of which some other mystics speak. Yet, Ramanuja, to whom we turn next and other mystics affirm that the ultimate experience is of mystical communion with the Divine, not absorption into the Absolute.

Sankara himself wrote many hymns of great devotion to God. He recognised that many people had not advanced beyond the need for a Personal God. He recognised also the value of ritual. His life, wrote Swami Atmananda, was in fact, a complete synthesis of the various paths to God. 'He came down to the common man to raise him up.'[6]

Determined as he was to affirm his Advaita philosophical teaching, Sankara, accepted diversity of ways of worship and the multiplication of gods, images and temples consistently with the doctrine of one Brahman and many names and forms. He encouraged sectarian tolerance and liberal reform.[7]

Jawaharlal Nehru, the first Indian Prime-minister wrote in his *Discovery of India*, that 'Sankara synthesised diverse currents troubling the mind of India and built a unity of outlook. In his life of only 32 years he did the work of many long lives and left such an impress of his powerful mind and rich personality on India that it very evident right up to this day. He was a curious mixture of philosopher and scholar, agnostic and mystic, poet and saint, practical reformer and able organiser. On the popular plane he destroyed many a dogma and opened the door of his philosophical sanctuary to everyone who was capable of entering it irrespective of caste or creed.'[8]

CHAPTER NOTES

1. S. Radhakrishnan in his *History of Indian Philosophy*, Vol II, quoted by T.S. Rukmani, *Sankara: The Man and His Philosophy*, Shimla. Indian Institue of Advanced Study and Delhi, Manohar Publications, 1991, p. 1.
2. See below, chapter 4 about Vyasa.
3. G.C.Pande, *Life and Thought of Sankaracarya*, Delhi, Motilal Banarsidass, 1994, p. 43.
4. Quoted by Pande, p. 86.
5. Quoted by Pande, p. 279.
6. Swami Atmananda, *Sankara's Teachings in His Own Words*, Bombay, Bharatiya Vidya Bhavan 1960. p. 49.
7. p. 357.
8. Rukmani, p. 2.

35

Rabia

Rabia transformed the early asceticism of Islam into a mysticism of love. One of her biographers, Farid al-Din 'Attar (died 1230) said of her 'Rabia was unique, because in her relations with God and her knowledge of Divine matters she had no equal. She was highly respected by all the great mystics of her time', as she has been by subsequent mystics and scholars.

Islamic mysticism is called *Tasawwuf*, but is usually known as Sufism, which now has an influence well beyond the Muslim world.[1] The word Sufism, probably derives from a word for 'wool' - indicating the woollen garment worn by early Muslim ascetics. The English words 'fakir' and 'dervish' derive from the Arabic and Persian words for 'the poor' - another term used for these holy people. The mystics' desire was for direct personal experience of God's love and full union with the Divine.

Although the Prophet Muhammad was not an ascetic and disapproved of celibacy, subsequently, a number of pious people, afraid of the Judgement to come, chose a life of celibacy, poverty and asceticism as a reaction to the worldliness of the early Umayyad period (661-749 CE). They withdrew from the world, which they deemed 'a hut of sorrows.' Known as 'those who always weep,' they bewailed their sins. This ascetic movement was changed into mysticism by Rabia, who stressed the importance of love. Sufism, at first, was transmitted by small circles of followers led by a Shaykh. Later, as we shall see in chapter 53, mystical orders developed around the teaching of a founder-leader. The Mawlawiya order, for example, were followers of Jalal-ad-Din ar-Rumi (b. 1207)

Rabia al-Adawiyah was born in about 713. She was the fourth child - Rabia means 'fourth' - of poor parents, both of whom died young. When later there was a famine, the sisters became separated and one day Rabia was abducted and sold into slavery. Trying to escape, she slipped and dislocated her wrist. Even so, she said in a prayer 'I am not grieved by this, I only desire to please you.' A voice replied, 'Be not sorrowful, for on the day of Resurrection your rank shall be such that those who are nearest to God in heaven shall envy you.' She went back to her master and did the work she was told, even though she fasted in daytime and prayed for much of the night. Her master, getting up in the middle of a night, watched her praying. The lamp above her head seemed to be a halo. Next day, the master spoke kindly to her and set her free. Although clearly some of the stories about her early life are legendary, it is probable that Rabia had indeed been a slave. She is known by the tribal name al-Adawiyha not by the name of her father.

Now free, she went into the desert for a time and then came back and, living in a small cell, devoted herself to worship. She began to attract followers. She had many offers of marriage but refused them all.

My peace, O my brothers, is in solitude,
And my Beloved is with me always,
For his love I can find no substitute...
O my Joy and my Life abidingly...
I have separated myself from all created beings,
My hope is for union with Thee, for that is the goal of my desire.[2]

She lived in poverty and was reluctant to ask for anything. 'I should be ashamed to ask for worldly things from Him to whom the world belongs and how should I ask them from those to whom it does not belong?'[3] Accommodating herself to God's will, she accepted suffering and pain without complaint. Indeed she regarded illness as a reproach from her Friend. In a poem called 'Sayings of Rabia,' written in the nineteenth century by Richard Monkton Milnes, Lord Houghton, Rabia says,

'I know not, when absorbed in prayer,
Pleasure or pain, or good or ill.
They who God's face can understand
Feel not the motion of his hand.[4]

She was often seen weeping and had a fear of hell and rejection. But she insisted that neither fear nor hope should be the reason for her devotion, praying:

O my Lord, if I worship Thee from fear of Hell, burn me in Hell,
and if I worship Thee from hope of Paradise, exclude me thence;
But if I worship Thee for Thine own sake
Then withhold not from me Thine Eternal Beauty.[5]

On another occasion she prayed,

O my Lord, whatever share of this world Thou dost bestow on me,
bestow it on Thine enemies
and whatever share of the next world Thou dost give me,
give it to Thy friends.
Thou art enough for me.'[6]

There is a famous story of Rabia that one day she was seen by a number of holy people with fire in one hand and water in the other. 'What are you doing?' she was asked. 'I am going to light a fire in Paradise and to pour water on Hell so that both veils (i.e. hindrances to the true vision of God) may completely disappear from the pilgrims and their purpose may be sure and the servants of God may see Him, without any object of hope or motive of fear.'[7]

Interestingly an engraving of this scene has been found in a work, published in 1644, called *Caritée* by the French Quietist Camus. Rabia is not named in the book, but stories of her had been brought to France by Joinville, who was chancellor to King Louis IX of France.[8]

A number of miracles are attributed to Rabia, as to other saints, although she was anxious to avoid a reputation for wonder-working. When she was asked why she discouraged visitors, she replied, 'I fear lest when I am dead, people will relate of me what I did not say or do.'[9]

Rabia lived to be nearly ninety. As she felt death was near, she asked to be alone 'to leave the way free for the messengers of God Most High.' From outside, her friends heard a voice saying, 'O soul at rest, return to thy Lord, satisfied with Him, giving satisfaction to Him. So enter among my servants and enter into my Paradise.'[10]

Rabia had a decisive influence on the development of Sufism and was quoted by almost all the great Sufi teachers. The Sufi aim is by overcoming the self, or ego, to attain union with God. Although that union in all its fullness is only possible after death, it can in part be experienced in anticipation in this life. By following the Sufi mystic path, the seeker for God grows in penitence, patience, gratitude, hope, holy fear, voluntary poverty, asceticism, complete dependence upon God and finally love.

Let us see how Rabia embodied these virtues and what she said about them. Rabia had a deep sense of penitence. When she was asked 'Why are you always weeping?' she replied, 'I fear that at the hour of death a voice may say I am not worthy.'[11] Interestingly, she speaks of repentance as a gift of God not as a human initiative. Indeed, in one sense, repentance flows from the experience of God's forgiveness. She was a model of patience, as when she was a slave and when she suffered pain. All that happens, good and bad, she taught, was to be accepted from God with gratitude. When she met someone with a bandaged head who was complaining of his pain, Rabia asked him how old he was. The answer was 'thirty years old.' She then asked how long his head had been bandaged. 'Last night', was the reply. Well, said Rabia, 'for thirty years God has kept your body fit and you have never bound upon it the bandage of gratitude, but for one night of pain you bind it with the bandage of complaint.'[12]

Hope and holy fear go together. Some people seek God because they are afraid of punishment, others because they look forward to heaven. Rabia, as we have seen, felt both motives were unworthy and sought God for God's sake alone. She regarded the Qur'anic description of the pleasures of heaven as allegorical and when asked about Paradise, replied, 'First the neighbour, then the house.'[13] Al-Ghazali commenting on this said that Rabia meant that in her heart was no leaning towards Paradise, but only to the Lord of Paradise. God is important, not heaven.

Rabia's poverty was extreme, but it is not just giving up possessions that is implied, but complete self-loss or what Jesus meant when he said, 'Blessed are the poor in spirit.'[14] One of her acquaintances, Muhammad b 'Ami said of her in her old age, 'I went in to Rabia and she was a very old woman of eighty years, as if she were a worn-out skin almost falling down, and I saw in her house a reed-mat and a clothes stand of Persian reed, the height of two cubits from the ground and upon it were her shrouds and the curtain of the house was made of palm leaves, and perhaps there was a mat and an earthen jug and a bed of felt, which was also her prayer-carpet.'[15] Renunciation is the personal application of the conviction that God is One - the central affirmation of the Qur'an. It is the giving up of the self. Rabia could truly say, 'I have fled from the world and all that is within it. My hope is for union with Thyself: for that is the goal of my desire.'[16]

The final stage to be attained is love, which includes passionate longing for God, intimacy with God and the satisfaction of glorifying God and enjoying God for ever.[17] Her biographer, Attar, said she was 'a woman on fire with love and ardent desire ... consumed with her passion for God.'[18] Love at its height is a sense of being completely at one with God and for some of being absorbed into God. Its culmination is the vision of God's glory. Rabia wrote in one of her poems,

My hope is for union with You, for that is the goal of my desire.[19]

It is said that her last words were, 'I have attained to that which I beheld.' Her life of total devotion had reached its consummation.[20]

Rabia was by no means the only Muslim woman saint. To many people, as Annemarie Schimmel, a distinguished scholar of Islam, has said, the idea of a woman saint in Islam is a contradiction in itself. In fact there were quite a number of Muslim women saints. There is, as she points out, no Qur'anic basis for the claim sometimes made that in Islam women have no soul – whatever a few fanatics may have said. Moreover Islam has no concept of original sin. As a result no blame is attached to Eve of whom the Prophet said, 'God has made dear to me women and perfume, and my heart's delight is in prayer.' Sufism emphasises the importance of mothers and the Prophet said, 'Paradise lies at the feet of mothers.' Women's testimony was accepted in judging the authenticity of sayings of Muhammad. Well to do women sponsored some Sufis. The great mystical poet Ibn Arabi (d. 1240) was even educated by a woman saint called Fatima, of whom it was said that in her old age she still looked like a young girl transformed by Divine love.

The influence of some women on the development of Islam and especially the Sufis and also the Sufi emphasis on love needs to be better known. It would help to correct the often one-sided view of Islam prevalent in the Western world. As Rabia said, love for God leaves no place for any enemies.

CHAPTER NOTES

1. The Sufi Order in the West was founded in London in 1910 by Hazrat Inyat Khan (1882- 1927), who was succeeded by Pir Vilayat Inayat Khan. The Order holds services of universal worship and draws on the traditions of several religions. The majority of Sufis, however, are Muslim mystics.

2. Quotations in this chapter are from Margaret Smith, *Rabi'a the Mystic and Her Fellow Saints in Islam,* Cambridge, University Press, 1928, p. 12. A new edition was published by Oneworld Publications (Oxford), 2001.

3. Quoted by Smith, p. 21.

4. Quoted by Annemarie Schimmel in her Introduction to the 1984 edition of Margaret Smith's *Rabi'a.*

5. Quoted by Smith, p. 30.

6. Quoted by Smith, p. 30.

7. Quoted by Smith, p. 99.

8. Mentioned by Schimmel in her Introduction, p. xxvii.

9. Quoted by Smith, p 37.

10. A quotation from the Qur'an 89, 27-30.

11. Quoted by Smith, p. 11.

12. Quoted by Smith, p. 61.

13. Quoted by Smith, p. 71.

14. Matthew, 5, 3.

15. Quoted by Smith, p. 25.

16. Quoted by Smith, p. 87.

17. Different Sufi teachers vary the order or add additional stages.

18. Quoted by Smith, p. 97.

19. Quoted by Smith, p. 110.

20. Quoted by Smith, p. 110.

36

Manikkavacakar

The hymns of the Tamil saints of South India, which are too little known, are among the most intense and evocative devotional hymns to be found in any language. Tamil, one of the oldest languages in the world, which is spoken in South East India, is a musical language to listen to, but, with over two hundred characters, it is difficult to learn. Several of the saints have a good claim to be included in our 'one hundred.' I have chosen Manikkavacakar, perhaps because it was chancing upon a volume of his poetry in the library of Madras Christian College, forty years ago, that first introduced me to the spiritual richness of Saiva-Siddhanta, which emphasises devotion and surrender to the Lord Siva, the third God of the Hindu Trinity of Brahma, Vishnu and Siva. As a personal God, Siva is worshipped in many forms.

The philosophical writings of Saiva-Siddhanta are mostly in Sanskrit. There is also a wealth of Tamil poetry dating, from the 1st to the 10th century CE. Much of it is religious in character, consisting of devotional (*bhakti*) hymns addressed to Siva and Vishnu. The Siva Devotees are called the Nayanars, whose first representative was the poetess Karaikkal Ammaaiyar, who sang of the dancing Siva, known as Nataraja or Lord of the Dance. Manikkavacakar (9th century) spoke of Siva as lover, lord, master and guru and intimately described the sensory joys of merging with God.

Those who wrote in praise of Vishnu are called the Alvars, to whom God is the light of lights, lit in the heart. They had no sense of caste and wrote for ordinary people. Their religion was not one of renouncing the world and of asceticism, but full of joy and beauty. Antal, an 8th century poetess, was literally love-sick for Krishna, who was an avatar of Vishnu.

There are not many Prime Ministers who have become saints. Manikkavacakar was born near Madurai, in South India – a city dominated by its magnificent temple. Although there are various legends about him, our main source of knowledge is his poetry. His parents called him after the place of his birth, Tiru-Vathavur. He is usually known as Manikkavacakar, which means 'the ruby-worded saint' and sometimes he is referred to by the name of his finest poems, *Tiruvacagam*, which means divine utterance. His father was a Brahmin, a member of the learned priestly class.

Manikkavacakar was quickly recognised as having a prodigious intellect. The king, hearing of this, sent for him and developed a great affection for him. Quite soon, the King appointed him to be Prime Minister. The poet, however, whose real interest was the sacred writings, was uneasy with the irreligion and luxury of court life. The tension had to be resolved.

A messenger arrived at court to say that ships with many priceless horses from Arabia had arrived in a neighbouring kingdom. The king instructed his prime minister to go, with an enormous treasure, to buy some of these horses. Manikkavacakar set out in royal pomp, escorted by mercenary troops from neighbouring kingdoms, on a long and arduous journey. As, at last, Manikkavacakar drew near to the city, he heard from the woods the sound of solemn music. He stopped the cavalcade and sent a messenger to find out about the music. The answer was that a saint, with the appearance of the god Siva, was sitting nearby under a tree. Manikkavacakar dismounted, drew near to the saint and was transported with rapture. Bowing before the guru, Manikkavacakar exclaimed: 'Henceforth I renounce all desires of worldly wealth and splendour. To me, thy servant, viler than a dog, who worships at thy feet, grant emancipation from worldly bonds. Take me, as your slave, O King of my soul.'[1] In response, the guru initiated him and Manikkavacakar became one with the Divine. He took off his courtly garments and, now as an ascetic, smeared himself with white ash. The great sum of money entrusted to him by the king, he handed over to the guru to be given to the poor.

The nobles who had accompanied him were, not surprisingly, astonished and also shocked at the misuse of the royal treasure. They protested, but Manikkavacakar took no notice. 'Why would you bring me back to earth's false employments?' Eventually the nobles gave up and went back to tell the king that his favourite minister had renounced the world and become a *sannyasi* or wandering ascetic and holy man. The king, angrily, sent an order for his minister's return, but the new sannyasi replied, 'I know no king but Siva and were the messengers of Yaman, the god of death, to come to bear me away, my guru has overcome death.' Manikkavacakar then asked God for guidance and was told to go back and assure the king that the horses would soon arrive. The king, however, was impatient and had Manikkavacakar thrown into prison, where he wrote some moving laments. Thanks to Siva's intervention, the horses did arrive, although they turned out to be jackals in disguise, but eventually all was well. Manikkavacakar was restored to the favour of the king, who at last reluctantly agreed to his minister's request to abandon palace life and set out as a wandering holy man.

It is not necessary perhaps to continue the, at times, fanciful story of Manikkavacakar, who was eventually recognised as a saint. What is important, however, is that he led a revival of Saivism – the worship of Siva - which had been overshadowed by the spread of Buddhism and Jainism.

Fascinating as is the story of Manikkavacakar's life, his primary importance lies in his writing and teaching - but first a word about the Revd G.U. Pope, who translated his great poem, the *Tiruvacagam*.

In the preface, written on his eightieth birthday, Pope recalled that his first Tamil lesson had been in 1837. Years later he told the then Master of Balliol College, Benjamin Jowett, about the wealth of Tamil literature. The Master replied, 'Print it.' Pope objected that it would take too long and he had no patent of immortality. Jowett replied, 'To have a great work in progress is the way to live long. You will live till you finish it.'[2] Pope also tries to answer the question he had been repeatedly asked about why anyone should be interested in the ancient literature of another people. His answer – still relevant – is that people of different cultures will not understand each other without some appreciation of the religions that shaped those cultures. Moreover, the existence of this literature with its emphasis on God's free grace questions the claim often made by Christians that theirs is the only religion of grace. Indeed the Tamil devotees debated whether God's grace was like a cat, who carries her kittens or like a monkey to whom the kittens have to cling. Is any human effort needed to be saved or is it all the work of God's mercy?

Manikkavacakar repeatedly tells of his utter unworthiness and need of God's grace.

Thou ent'ring stood'st by me fast bound in sin;
As one who says, 'I'm sins's destroyer, come!'[3]

He accepted God's will, even when it involved suffering. He wrote,

When I gave all I have to you my God and King,
I gave you leave to treat me in any way you will.
If you should show your love for me
Or should you seem to sting;
Should I complain? O no, Lord;
I'll love and praise you still.
If God is my owner,
He can do anything he likes with me.
How dare I question him?[4]

He bewails those times when God is absent, but eventually knows the assurance of God's embrace. Glorious, exalted over all, the Infinite–

To me mere slave, lowest of all, Thou hast assigned
A place in bliss supreme, that none beside have gained or known!
Great Lord what can I do for Thee?[5]

Manikkavacakar's poem the *Tiruvacagam* is sung daily at the Saivite temples of South India and known by heart by many worshippers. There is a local saying that 'anyone whose heart is not melted by the *Tiruvacagam* must have a stone for a heart.'

CHAPTER NOTES

1. Quoted by R H Lesser, *Saints and Sages of India*, p. 37.
2. *The Tiruvacagam – The Sacred Utterances of the Tamil Poet, Saint and Sage, Manikka-Vacagar*, by G U Pope, Oxford, Clarendon Press, 1900.
3. *Tiruvacagam* The Sacred Cento, Hymn V, XXII (p. 52).
4. Quoted by Lesser, p. 39.
5. *Tiruvacagam* , The Sacred March, Hymn XLVI, VIII (p. 336).

37

Saicho and Kukai

Saicho and Kukai, both monks, established in the eighth century two of the most influential schools of Japanese Buddhism: Tendai and Shingon. Many subsequent schools derive from one or other of these traditions. A third monk Eisai was to introduce Zen Buddhism to Japan in the twelfth century.

Buddhism was first brought to Japan in 522 CE by some monks from Korea. Soon afterwards, Mahayana Buddhism was adopted as the official religion by the imperial court. Prince Shotoku, who was regent from 592-622, promoted Buddhism in support of his policy of centralizing power. In 607 he sent the first of a number of delegations to learn more about Chinese religion and culture. It was not, however, until the ninth century, largely thanks to Saicho and Kukai that Buddhism began to gain a popular following as well as imperial backing.

Saicho (also known, after his death as Dengyo Daishi) was born in 767 and became a monk at the age of fourteen. Once he had completed his studies he withdrew to Mt Hiei, which is near Kyoto. As he ascended the peak, he sang repeatedly,

> O Buddhas,
> Of unexcelled complete enlightenment,
> Bestow your invisible aid
> Upon this hut I open
> On the mountain top.

There he learned about the teaching of the Chinese master Che-yi (538-597), who believed that the *Lotus Sutra* was the most precious of the Buddha's teachings. The Lotus Sutra says that the Buddha nature exists in everyone and all that is necessary to win freedom from the world is the recognition of this truth. Che-yi also insisted that that knowledge of this truth only came after a long process of purification.

In 804, Saicho went to China to learn more about this teaching and he also gained some knowledge of the Ch'an teaching that was to become known in Japan as Zen. On his return, he established a small temple on Mount Hiei.

His teaching, which is known as Tendai Buddhism, is a synthesis of many Indian and Chinese Buddhist traditions which give pre-eminence to the Lotus Sutra. Dating to somewhere between the 1st century BCE and 2nd century CE, the Lotus Sutra is perhaps the most important Mahayana Buddhist text. In it, the Buddha is no longer just a human being but has supernatural powers and preaches in a mythological paradise, surrounded by thousands of followers. Like a father, he watches over human beings:

> *'I tell you, Shariputra,*
> *I, too, am like this,*
> *Being the Most Venerable among many saints,*
> *The Father of the World ...*
> *I tell you, Shariputra,*
> *You men*
> *Are all my children,*
> *And I am your Father.*
> *For age upon age, you*
> *Have been scorched by multitudinous woes*
> *And I have saved you all'.*[1]

Moreover, out of compassion for human beings, the Buddha, who has been enlightened from the beginning, manifested himself in human form as the Buddha Sakyamuni to show people the way to liberation. The great compassion of the Buddha is repeatedly emphasised, especially in the various stories and parables. The Buddha, for example, is compared to a father rescuing his children from a burning house. There is also a parable that resembles the story that Jesus told of the prodigal son, who was welcomed home by his father. In the Lotus Sutra, just as the father is dying, his son, who 'over fifty years since, from a certain city left me and ran away to endure loneliness and misery, whom I sought sorrowfully in the city' returns. 'Now' said the father, 'all the wealth which I possess belongs entirely to my son.' 'When the poor son heard these words, great was his joy at such unexpected news and he thought, "Without any mind for, or effort on my part, these treasures now come of themselves to me."' The father in the story is, of course, the Buddha and we are all his sons.[2]

It is also said that a child who presents an offering of flowers crushed in his or her tiny hand is closer to realization than a proud monk.

The Lotus Sutra, unlike the emphasis on personal salvation in the Theravada tradition, presents the ideal of the bodhisattva, who dedicates himself to the salvation of others.

Tendai accepted that all sutras and forms of Buddhism were paths to truth, but that deepest truth was in the Tendai teaching. This was based on three principles. The first is that all things are empty (*sunyata*). The second is that nonetheless all things have a 'real' if temporary existence. The third truth is that all things are simultaneously absolutely empty and also appearing as temporarily real. Finally, the transitory phenomenal world of appearances is reality as it really is, to be seen as the Buddha-nature and showered with the Buddha's grace.

Monks who came to Saicho at Mt Hiei were expected to undergo a strict twelve-year novitiate. In time Mt Hiei became an enormous monastery with hundreds of temples. It was razed to the ground in 1571 by the warlord Oda Nobunaga, who massacred many of the monks. The monastery was restored and is still an awesome and beautiful place, but it lacks its former glory. It was there that most of the religious leaders in subsequent centuries studied and the monastery, deservedly, has been called 'the cradle of Japanese Buddhism.'

After his death in 822, Saicho was given the title of Denghyo Daishi or 'Great Master of the Transmission of the Doctrine.' The founder of Tendai is still revered today. The founders of Jodo and Jodo-shin schools of the Nichiren tradition and of Zen all studied at Mt Hiei.

Some of those who studied at Mt Hiei also became followers of Shingon, which is an esoteric or secret form of Buddhism intended for the initiated, which was founded by Kukai. Kukai was born in 774 and by the age of fifteen he was studying Confucianism and Taoism. He was, however, disappointed by 'their down-to-earth character and their triviality.' He therefore turned to Buddhism and wrote *Sango Shiiki*, The Truth of the Three Teachings. He argued that Buddhism was more profound than Confucianism or Taoism, but that it contained many of the teachings of both of those religions.

In 804, hoping to strengthen his faith, Kukai travelled to China with

Saicho. There Kukai met Huei-kuo the seventh patriarch of the Chen-yen school. He recognised Kukai as his spiritual son and transmitted his secret teaching to him. On his return, Kukai became abbot of the important monastery at Nara, but in 816, he left to found a new monastery on Mount Koya. There he began to expound Chen-yen teachings, which are known as Shingon in Japanese. His teaching became very popular and he is said to have attracted 90,000 monks to Koya. Kukai died in 835, but he is believed still to be present in deep meditation in the sanctuary at Koya.

Kukai held that the Truth, in so far as it can be expressed, is best done through art, especially in a mandala, which is a symbolic representation of the universe. 'The esoteric teachings,' he said, 'are too profound to be expressed in writing, but with painting the obscurities may be understood. The attitudes and *mudras* (signs made with the hand) of the revered images arise from the Buddha's love, and one may attain the buddha-nature simply by looking at them... art is what reveals to us the state of perfection.'[3] Music and literature were, he said, also valuable, but the Vajra (Diamond) and the Garbha (Womb) mandalas were of central importance. This emphasis on art also did much to popularise the religion.

Drawing on the belief that the Buddha nature is present in each person, Kukai taught that only our passions stop us realising this. What is required, therefore, is to 'purify the heart and to become conscious.' 'It is within one's own heart that one must seek Enlightenment and Omniscience. Why is this? Because the heart is naturally perfectly pure.'

CHAPTER NOTES

1. *Lotus Sutra* 3 in *World Scripture*, p. 93.
2. *Lotus Sutra* 4 in *World Scripture*, p.365.
3. Quoted in the *Oxford Dictionary of Religions*, p. 891. No reference is given.

38

Ramanuja

Ramanuja was one of the most influential religious thinkers of Hinduism. He integrated popular Hindu devotion to a personal God with the philosophical speculation of Vedanta philosophy. Unlike Sankara, he upheld the relative reality of the world and soul, although they depend on God, in a system known as Vishistadvaita or 'Qualified non-duality.'

Ramanuja was born in about 1017 CE in Sriperumbudur, a village in Tamil Nadu, South India, near Kanchipuram – often just called Kanchi – which is a holy city with numerous beautiful temples. Ramanuja's grandfather on his mother's side was known for his holiness. Through his mother and her brother Mahāpura, Ramanuja was introduced to the teachings of Yamuna (918-1038 CE), the Vaishnava teacher who would most influence his thinking. Yamuna himself was the grandson of Nathamuni who in the middle of the tenth century compiled the best known collection of the devotional hymns of the Tamil Alvars.[1]

Ramanuja was himself deeply influenced from an early age by the devotion to the god Vishnu, which pervaded the home in which he grew up. These ecstatic hymns focused on the experience of deep devotion to God, with many descriptions of the beauty and greatness of the Lord. Here are two examples:

All places, shinning like great lotus pools on a blue mountain broad,
to me are but the beauties of his eye – the Lord of earth
Girt by the roaring sea, heaven's Lord,
the Lord of all good souls.
Day and night she knows not sleep

And

In floods of tears her eyes do swim
Lotus-like eyes! She weeps and reels,
Ah! How without thee can I bear;
She pants and feels all earth for Him.[2]

Under his father's guidance, at a young age, Ramanuja mastered the scriptures. His intellectual ability was quickly recognised and he was sent to Kanchi for schooling under a follower of the Advaita or Non-Dual philosophy of Sankara. This teaching jarred with Ramanuja's deep devotion to a personal God. Moreover, Ramanuja could not restrain himself from pointing out his teacher's mistakes. His teacher was so infuriated, that he set out with his students to the Holy Ganges, planning to drown Ramanuja in the great river. On the way, Ramanuja escaped into a thick forest, where he happened to meet a tribal couple, who were hunters. They showed him the way back to Kanchi. His teacher, on his return, feigned pleasure at finding Ramanuja safely back in the city. But when the king of Kanchi called upon the teacher to cure his daughter, who had an evil spirit, he was unable to do so. Ramanuja, however, was successful. At this point, Ramanuja was excluded by his teacher.[3]

Ramanuja returned home and looked for another guru. He approached Kanchipurna, who was known for his piety. But Kanchipurna belonged to the lowest caste and said it was not fitting for a Brahmin like Ramanuja to become his disciple. Ramanuja, in defiance of custom, did invite Kanchipurna to his house for a meal and was annoyed when his wife afterwards washed the house and all its possessions to cleanse it from defilement.

At Kanchipurna's direction, Ramanuja went to seek initiation from Mahapurna, a leading devotee of the god Vishnu. He left Kanchi for Srirangam, which is now in Tamil Nadu but met Mahapurna on the way at a place called Maduranthakam. Mahapurna now came to live with Ramanuja at Kanchi. After a while the women of the two families had a fierce argument.

Mahapurna, therefore, quietly made his way back to Srirangam. This upset Ramanuja. He sent his wife back to her mother's home, abandoned the world and committed himself to the austere life of a sannyasin. He became a priest at the famous and massive Varadarajaperumal Temple in Kanchipuram, which has a hall with one thousand pillars.

At this point, Ramanuja had a vision of the God Vishnu and his consort Lakshmi. He started to offer daily worship to them at the place where he had received the vision. He also started teaching and giving addresses in which he spoke of God's universal love for every person.

Ramanuja held that devotion to Vishnu was the way to release and was also the teaching of the Upanishads. Up until that time worshippers of Vishnu were not regarded as orthodox by leading Brahmin scholars.

When Yamuna, who was the head of the Vaishnavite monastery at Srirangam, was looking for a successor, he sent one of his disciples to bring Ramanuja to him at Srirangam. By the time Ramanuja got there the guru had died and his body was about to be cremated. Ramanuja, while paying respects to the dead body, noticed that three fingers of the guru's right hand were firmly closed. On enquiry, Ramanuja was told that the guru had had three unaccomplished tasks: to write a commentary on two ancient texts and to propagate the worship of Vishnu. Ramanuja vowed that, with God's grace, he would fulfil these tasks. He was now recognised as a leader of the Vaishnavite school of Hinduism and became head priest at the Ranganatha temple at Srirangam.

Like many Hindu holy men, Ramanuja circum-ambulated India from Ramesvaram, a pilgrimage centre close to Sri Lanka in the South, where there is a beautiful temple, along the West coast to the source of the holy river Ganges, near Badrinatha, returning along the East coast.

After a time, however, Ramanuja fell foul of the Chola king, who was an ardent worshipper of Siva. He ordered Ramanuja to come to him and affirm his faith in Saivism. His followers refused to let him go. Two of them went in his place. They refused the king's injunction and were blinded as a punishment. Meanwhile Ramanuja escaped, disguised in a white robe. He withdrew to Mysore, where he gained many converts to Vaishnavism.

Eventually after twenty years, he was able to return to Srirangam, where he organised the temple worship and founded over seventy centres to spread his teaching. According to tradition he died at the age of one hundred and twenty in 1137. Even today, there are figures of Ramanuja in Vaishnavite temples. The concluding prayer of Vaishnavites often includes the words, 'Let Ramanuja's commands prevail and continue.'

Ramanuja's main works are commentaries on the Vedanta sutras and the Gita[4] and one book in which he explained his own views.[5] When Ramanuja remembered his vow to write the commentaries he realised that he needed an ancient text, but had been unable to find a copy in his part of the country. He said to his followers, 'I am told one is preserved in Kashmir. I shall start for there today.'[6] When he got there, however, the advocates of Advaita, who opposed his views, were reluctant to give him access to the work. It is not quite clear whether his disciple Kuresa did gain access to it there or whether the book was smuggled out of the library for a while, but, in any case, Kuresa managed to memorise the text – to Ramanuja's great joy and gratitude.

Ramanuja's contribution to philosophy was his view that discursive thought is a necessary part of the search for truth and that the phenomenal world is real and provides real knowledge. In all this, he was sharply critical of Sankara and disputed his interpretation of the scriptures.

Ramanuja compares the relationship of matter and the soul to God to that of the body to the soul. The body modifies the soul, but both have a separate existence. Matter and the soul, likewise, constitute God's body, modifying it yet having a distinct existence. The goal of the human soul is to serve God, just as the body serves the soul. Ramanuja, therefore, accepted the reality of matter, the soul and God, although both matter and the soul are ultimately dependent on God – hence his view is called 'modified nonduality.' or *Vishistadvaita*.

Another philosopher, Madhva, in the thirteenth century, went further in emphasising the distinctions between matter, the soul and God – all of which, he held, are eternal. The final relationship with God, he said, is neither absorption, nor a relationship in which the soul, although still identifiable, becomes one with God. Madhva taught that just as the lover and beloved remain separate beings so the devotee and God remain distinct. Madhva established his main temple at Udipi, in Karnataka, where his philosophical tradition is still taught.

Ramanuja's philosophical views affirmed the appropriateness of theistic worship. Ramanuja, therefore, gave an intellectual basis to the devotional religion of the people (*bhakti*). He also transformed religion from ritual practice into divine worship and a way of pondering the unfailing love of God. Such devotion not only wins release from the cycle of rebirth, but brings the believer into the presence of God, a Paradise called Vaikuntha, where God is pictured as enthroned in heaven with his consorts and attendants.

Ramanuja's followers, the Srivaisnavas, eventually became divided between those who thought salvation depended only on God's grace and those who believed that human effort in response to that grace was also necessary – a dispute that has occurred in other religious traditions.

Ramanuja's influence, however, extends far beyond those who see themselves as his followers and has provided an intellectual grounding for India's rich variety of theistic devotion. The question of the relationship of the world, the soul and of God to each other is debated in many religious traditions. At issue is how we picture our ultimate destiny as human beings. Is death the end, or does the spirit merge with the Spirit of Life or is our destiny to be forever in the presence of God and in loving communion with the Divine?

It has been said that although Ramanuja himself became an ascetic 'his theology was an effort to combine social duties, religious worship, devotion and the practice of meditation and contemplation into one harmonious whole.'[7]

CHAPTER NOTES

1. See below in chapter 37.
2. Quoted by Surendranath Dasgupta, *A History of Indian Philosophy*, Vol 3, p. 131. The 'she', of course, is the soul longing for God.
3. Much of this information is based on K.A. Manavalan, *Lives of Alwars and Ramanuja*, Madras, Sri Ramanuja Sidhantha Centre, n.d. c. 1993. am.
4. *Sribhasya, Vedantadipa, Vedantasarah,* and the *Bhagavadgita-bhasya.*
5. The *Verdartha-samgrahah.*
6. Swami Ramakrishnananda, *Life of Sri Ramanuja*, Madras, Sri Ramakrishna Math, 1993, p. 189. The text was the *Bodhayana-vritti.*
7, Surendranath Dasgupta, *A History of Indian Philosophy*, Vol 3, p. 131.

39

Al-Ghazali

Al-Ghazali, 'the Proof of Islam', 'the Ornament of Religion', 'the Guide to True Faith,' as he has been called, is considered the greatest Muslim religious authority after the Prophet Muhammad. He has deeply influenced Islamic jurisprudence, theology, philosophy and mysticism. Perhaps his greatest achievement was to integrate the Sufi mystical tradition into mainstream theological thought, although some Orthodox theologians were very critical of his writings.

Abu Hamid Muhammad, better known as al-Ghazali (his name is sometimes spelt al-Ghazzali) was born in 1058 CE, in the North East of the Old Persian Empire at Tus (near Mashad in present day Iran). Tus was at that time a centre of scholarship and it was also the birthplace of the Persian poet Omar Khayyam(1048-1125), who was an older contemporary of al-Ghazali. Al-Ghazali's uncle had been a well-known scholar. His father, who was a spinner and seller of wool – a poor man but devout – died when his sons were young. He had committed them to the care of a Sufi friend and left money for their education. Afterwards they were moved to a *madrassa* or college, where their food was provided, as well as their education. Clearly al-Ghazali was a very bright student and maybe over-eager and ambitious. Later in life he wrote that a student should not pester a teacher when he is tired, nor, after the class, follow him, asking questions. He also said that a boy's bed should be hard and that he should take plenty of exercise and after school he should have time to enjoy himself. All work and no play, he wrote, 'will deaden a boy's heart and spoil his intelligence and make life grievous unto him.'[1]

He started the study of law while still a boy at Tus and then went on to Nishapur and Baghdad for further study. He was soon himself lecturing to students and starting to write. His reputation was such that at the early age of thirty-four, the Vizier appointed him to the chair of theology at the Nizamiyya College in Baghdad.

His soul, however, was not satisfied. His study of Sufism made him aware that no amount of knowledge is a substitute for experience. 'It became clear to me that what is most distinctive of mysticism is something which cannot be apprehended by study, but only by immediate experience (*dhawq* – literally 'tasting'), by ecstasy and by a moral change. What a difference there is between *knowing* the definition of health and satiety... and *being* healthy and satisfied.'[2] 'I apprehended', he continued, 'clearly that the mystics were men who had real experiences, not men of words and that I had already progressed as far as was possible by way of intellectual apprehension.'[3]

Examining himself, he recognised that the motive of his work 'was not a pure desire for the things of God, but that the impulse moving me was the desire for an influential position and public recognition. I saw for certain that I was on the brink of a crumbling bank of sand and in imminent danger of hell-fire unless I set about to mend my ways.'[4] But he was torn between desire to follow the Sufi way and a reluctance to abandon his position and his family. 'For nearly six months I was continuously tossed about between the attractions of worldly desires and the impulses towards eternal life.'[5] But then one day he found himself unable to lecture – 'my tongue would not utter a single word.'[6] God had intervened and he now sought refuge with God. He made provision for his wife and family and left Baghdad – ostensibly to journey to Mecca – but in fact to seek seclusion in Damascus, where he stayed for two years. Subsequently he journeyed to Jerusalem, and spent long hours at the Dome of the Rock and then he did travel to Mecca.

Eventually, as he said, 'the entreaties of my children drew me back to my home country' to Nishapur, where he had been a student. He spent ten years trying to live quietly, but 'the events of the interval, the anxieties about my family, and the necessities of my livelihood altered the aspect of my purpose and impaired the quality of my solitude, for I experienced pure ecstasy only occasionally, although I did not cease to hope for that; obstacles would hold me back, yet I always returned to it.'[7] During this time, he wrote his major work, *Ihya 'ulum al-din* ('The Revival of Religious Sciences') and other important books. Eventually in 1106, he returned as a lecturer to the Nizamiyya College at Baghdad, but only in obedience to God, not from personal ambition. He ignored those who opposed and slandered him, but in due course retired once more to Tus, where he established a college for students of theology. It was there that he died at the age of fifty-three, but as he had said, 'the mystic is always mindful of death, because he has been promised union with his Beloved and the lover never forgets such a promise.'

His brother Ahmad related that on the day of his death, after his ablutions, al-Ghazali asked for his shroud. He then took it, kissed it and laid it over his eyes, saying, 'Most gladly do I enter into the Presence of the King.' One story says that when he knew death was approaching, he asked to be left alone. Next morning when his friends entered they found a beautiful poem beside his still body:

> *Say to my friends, when they look upon me, dead,*
> *Weeping for me and mourning me in sorrow*
> *Do not believe that this corpse you see is myself.*
> *In the name of God, I tell you, it is not I...*
> *I am a pearl, which has left its shell deserted,*
> *It was my prison, where I spent my time in grief.*
> *I am a bird, and this body was my cage*
> *Whence I have now flown forth and it is left as a token,*
> *Praise be to God, Who hath now set me free...*
> *Think not that death is death, nay, it is life,*
> *A life that surpasses all we could dream of here,*
> *While in this world...*
> *Think of the mercy and love of your Lord,*
> *Give thanks for His grace and come without fear...*
> *I give you now a message of good cheer*
> *May God's peace and joy for evermore be yours.'*[8]

Although a brilliant scholar, al-Ghazali recognised the inadequacy of reason outside its appropriate spheres, which may have been one factor in the eventual decline of the pre-eminence in his day of Muslim philosophers and scientists. On three vital matters faith not reason has to decide: whether the world is eternal; whether God has particular knowledge of the individual; and whether the body is resurrected after death. Mystical knowledge – the experience of God – cannot be achieved by study. The ordinary person's devotion is as important as the scholar's learning. 'Trust the religion of the old women', he said at the end of his life. Such experience, if genuine, results in a transformed life.

Al-Ghazali gave very clear guidance on the stages of the mystic path – including detailed instructions on one's ablutions and how to remember God at all times. For example, 'a prayer with clean teeth is better than seventy prayers without clean teeth.' The soul, he held, is in the image of or a mirror of the Divine, but it has become tarnished and needs to recover its true beauty. The purpose of the mystic, therefore, is to set the soul free from its fetter, to purify the heart, to polish the mirror. Besides a simple and moral life, repentance is the beginning of the Way which gradually leads to the joy of intimate communion with God which also transforms the character of the devotee, who grows in patience and gratitude.

The ultimate longing is to be in God's presence and to contemplate the face of God. This is granted to the one who has been transformed by love. Love is for al-Ghazali the final stage of the mystic Way, because love allows the soul to share the Divine Nature. He wrote,

'It is reasonable to give passionate love to the One from whom all good things are seen to come. In truth there is nothing good or beautiful or beloved in this world, but comes from God's loving kindness and is the gift of his grace.'[9]

The one who claims to love God must show the signs of love, one of which is to have no fear of death. To lay down life itself for the sake of the Lord is the mark of sincerity in the lover. Indeed the lover finds whatever he does for the Beloved is easy. Another sign of the true lover of God is that he is always mindful of God. The one who loves God wants to share the light he has received with others.

Al-Ghazali's interests were wide ranging. He was sociable, he had an interest in gardens and plants and he loved animals and birds. He told the traveller not to overload or beat his animal and to dismount for a time in the morning and evening to give the animal a rest and to get some exercise himself. He seems to have enjoyed a game of chess and he had a deep love of music.

Al-Ghazali studied extensively and travelled widely. He, therefore, drew on a great range of learning and experience. He was influenced by Plotinus (c.250-270 CE) and Neo-Platonism in his idea that the material world is an emanation from God and in thinking of God not only as

Light but also as Supreme Beauty. Al-Ghazali, of course, often referred to the Qur'an and the traditions about the Prophet and to Muslim scholars such as Avicenna (980-1087).[10]He was probably acquainted with the Old Testament and some Jewish writers as well as with the New Testament, which was available in Arabic. He quotes from St Mark's Gospel and from Jesus himself, for example in comparing religious teachers to a shepherd who protects his sheep from the wolf and in asking what use is salt if it has lost its savour. In speaking of Christ, he held Christians were wrong to think of him as one with God. It was like those who suppose that the reflection in a mirror is the object itself. Christians, Al-Ghazali wrote, beheld the radiance of God's light shining in Jesus, but were mistaken in thinking the Divine nature could be one with human nature. Nonetheless he acknowledged what was true in other people's beliefs, even if one should point out where they err from the teaching of the Qur'an.[11]

Just as Al-Ghazali was influenced by others, so he influenced not only later Sufi writers, but also Jewish scholars such as Maimonides and perhaps the Zohar, which is the central text of Kabbalah - the Jewish mystical tradition. The great Christian scholar St Thomas Aquinas (1225-1274) studied Arabic writers and acknowledged his indebtedness to them. The poet Dante (1265-1321), who wrote of the Beatific Vision, quoted Al-Ghazali as one of his sources and the French mystic Blaise Pascal (1623-1662) knew of his writings and like Al-Ghazali held that truth can only be reached by love.

Al-Ghazali thought of himself as the 'renewer' of religion for the sixth Islamic century. The renewal of religion in every age depends on the supremacy of Love, as Al-Ghazali emphasised.

CHAPTER NOTES

1. Quoted from Margaret Smith, *Al-Ghazali the Mystic*, London, Luzac and Co, 1944, p. 12. Much of the information here is based on Margaret Smith's book.
2. Al-Ghazali, *al-Munqidh min al-Dalal*, 'What delivers from Error', translated by W.Montgomery Watt, in *The Faith and Practice of Al-Ghazali*, London, George Allen and Unwin, 1953, p.55.
3. *al-Munqidh min al-Dalal*, p.55.
4. *al-Munqidh min al-Dalal*, p. 56.

5. *al-Munqidh min al-Dalal,* p. 57.
6. *al-Munqidh min al-Dalal,* p. 57.
7. *al-Munqidh min al-Dalal,* p. 60.
8. Quoted by Margaret Smith, pp. 36-7. These verses are attributed to his brother Ahmad al-Ghazali, although there is some doubt about this.
9. Quoted by Margaret Smith, p. 178.
10. Avicenna, although he died shortly before Al-Ghazali was born, is discussed below in chapter 42, which concentrates on Islamic philosophers.
11. See Margaret Smith, pp. 114-116.

40

Abelard

By the late tenth century there was a hint of new life and renewal in Christendom. Gradually the faith was to spread to most of north-western and central Europe and to Russia. The expansion of Islam was checked and in 1096 the First Crusade was launched with the aim of winning back the Holy Land for Christianity. There was a growth of commerce and economic life, a revival of monastic communities and a quickening of intellectual activity.

Perhaps the most outstanding thinker of the eleventh century was Peter Abelard - at least in his own opinion! Peter Abelard at one time considered himself the most brilliant philosopher of his day. In his autobiography, *A History of My Calamities*, he wrote of his time as a teacher in Paris, 'I thought myself then to be the only philosopher in the world.'[1] His lover Héloïse was even more enthusiastic. 'What king or philosopher could equal your fame? ... What queen, what powerful lady did not envy me my joys and my bed?' she asked in one of her letters. Some of his contemporaries spoke of Abelard as one of the greatest teachers and thinkers of all time. His understanding of the Atonement is still appreciated today by Liberal Christians, but his teaching on the Trinity was condemned as heretical. It would have pleased Abelard that he comes first in the *Oxford Companion to Christian Thought*, although that is because the book is arranged alphabetically!

Peter Abelard, a son of a knight, was born in 1079 in France at Le Pallet in Brittany. Instead of following a military career, like his father, Abelard went to Paris University to study philosophy and logic. He engaged in bitter quarrels with two of his teachers. One of them, Roscelin of Compiègne, a Nominalist, held that universals, such as 'truth' or 'goodness' had no independent reality but were only words, whereas William of Champeaux, a realist, held that universals actually exist. Abelard brilliantly elaborated an independent position. He argued that words could be used significantly, but language by itself was unable to show the truth of things in the realm of physics. Abelard, who was an admirer of Aristotelian logic, taught in Paris and at nearby centres. When Abelard turned his attention to Biblical studies, he was equally contemptuous of his teachers.

Besides his public teaching, Abelard also had a private pupil called Héloïse, who was a brilliant student. She was the niece of one of the cathedral clergy, Canon Fulbert, who was in effect her guardian. Abelard and Héloïse fell in love and had a son called Astralabe. Under pressure from Canon Fulbert, they married, but Abelard insisted that this was done secretly. Soon afterwards, Héloïse took refuge in a nearby convent. Fulbert, then arranged for Abelard to be attacked and castrated. To hide his shame, Abelard became a monk at the royal abbey of Saint-Denis near Paris and forced a reluctant Héloïse to become a nun. Abelard repeatedly told her to accept Christ's love instead of his. She spurned his advice and said she would readily have gone to hell with him. Although Héloïse, in due course, became an abbess, she did not renounce her passionate love for Abelard, which she expressed in moving letters, which have survived. Brutally, he wrote to her, 'I gratified in you my wretched desires and this was all that I loved.'[2] She may have lived as a dutiful nun, but her heart was never in her calling. Her heart had been fatally wounded by Peter Abelard.

At the Abbey of Saint-Denis, where Abelard endlessly criticised the way of life of his fellow monks, he tried to restore his reputation for austerity. Aware that the Old Testament spoke of eunuchs as an abomination, he quoted a verse from the New Testament where Jesus commended those who had made themselves eunuchs for the sake of the kingdom of heaven.[3] Whereas up to this point, Abelard's primary interest had been in questions of logic and philosophy, he now concentrated on Biblical studies and ethically based theology. He made a collection of sayings from the Bible and the Church Fathers to show how they often contradicted each other. In the Preface to this book, which was called *Sic et Non* ('Yes and No'), as a logician and student of language, he showed how students could reconcile the apparent inconsistencies. He also wrote the first version of his *Theologia*. His choice of the word 'Theology' for his writing was significant. The usual name for the intellectual study of God was 'divinity', but for Abelard that meant 'reading of the divine books.' His purpose was to help his students understand Christian belief, 'for nothing can be believed unless it is first understood.' This was a deliberate reversal of the famous statement made by Anslem (1033-1109), a distinguished scholastic philosopher and Archbishop of Canterbury, that 'Unless you believe, you shall not understand.'[4]

The subject of Abelard's *Theologia* was the doctrine of the Trinity. This was asking for trouble. In the 1090s, Abelard's master Roscelin had been accused of heresy on this subject. Moreover Anselm had dedicated his refutation of Roscelin to Pope Urban II in 1098. Abelard's view of the Trinity, which is discussed below, was subsequently condemned as heretical and the book was burned at a council held at Soissons in 1121.

On his return to Saint-Denis, after the trial at Soissons, Abelard wrote a controversial book about the patron saint of the Abbey. He argued that St Denis of Paris was not to be identified with Denis of Athens. The latter, better known as Dionysius the Areopagite, had been converted by St Paul.[5] Certain writings, including *The Mystical Theology*, were at the time – wrongly - attributed to Dionysius the Areopagite. Demoting their saint, did not go down well with the community. To avoid being brought to trial before the king, Abelard left in the hope of pursuing a hermit's life. He was, however, pursued by his students and resumed teaching philosophy. His combination of teaching 'secular arts' with his profession as a monk was much criticised.

In 1125, Abelard accepted election as abbot of a remote monastery of Saint-Gildas-de-Rhuys back in his native Brittany – not that he wished to return there to live beside 'the waves of the horrifying Ocean where the last point of land afforded me no further flight.'[6] Meanwhile Héloïse had become head of a new foundation of nuns called the Paraclete. Abelard provided the community with a rule and a justification of the nun's way of life. He also sent them some hymns that he had composed. In the early 1130s, he and Héloïse edited a collection of their love letters and religious correspondence.

In 1135 Abelard went back to Paris, once again to teach there and to produce a new version of his *Theologia*. He also wrote a book on Ethics, a *Dialogue between a Jew, a Philosopher and a Christian*, and a *Commentary on St Paul's Letter to the Romans*. He was soon in trouble again and once more accused of heresy. His opponents recruited the very influential Bernard of Clairvaux (1090-1153), a monastic reformer and mystical writer, to lead the attack. The condemnation of his views, made at a council at Sens in 1140, was quickly confirmed by Pope Innocent III.

Abelard was granted refuge at the great monastery of Cluny in Burgundy, where thanks to the intervention of the Abbot, Peter the Venerable, he made peace with Bernard of Clairvaux. He gave up teaching and lived the last few years of his life as a Cluniac monk. In one of his hymns he imagines the bliss of those who have reached the heavenly Jerusalem.

O what their joy and their glory must be,
Those endless Sabbaths the blessed ones see!
Crown for the valiant; to weary ones rest;
God shall be all, and in all ever blest...

Now in the meanwhile, with hearts raised on high,
We for that country must yearn and must sigh,
Seeking Jerusalem, dear native land,
Through our long exile on Babylon's strand. [7]

After his death, probably in 1144, Abelard's body was first sent to the Community of the Paraclete. Peter the Venerable in a very sensitive letter told Héloïse that God was now cherishing Abelard 'in His bosom in your place as another you.' Lest Héloïse should think that this meant God had taken him away from her, Peter went on, that at the Last Trumpet and bodily Resurrection, 'he will be restored to you by His grace.'[8] When Héloïse died, their bodies at last lay together. Eventually their remains were moved to the cemetery of Père-Lachaise in Paris, where tourists sometimes stop to remember this passionate and tragic romance.

It was Abelard's teaching on the Trinity, as well as his arrogance, that got him into trouble. He held that when Christians speak of God's power and wisdom and love, they are talking of the Father and the Son and the Holy Spirit respectively, whereas traditionally all the attributes of God apply equally to all three persons. His teaching lay itself open to the charge of tritheism (belief in three gods). Certainly he insisted that the threefold nature of God (tri-unity) is of the very reality of God and not just how humans conceive God. Some modern theologians likewise insist that the doctrine recognises the necessity for interrelationship as an inseparable feature of Being.

Abelard's teaching on the Atonement – the doctrine of how the death of Christ takes away the sin of humankind - was also original. In the Middle Ages, following some of the early Fathers, it was usual to think of the Atonement in terms of a ransom paid to the devil to secure human freedom from sin and death. People were familiar with the need to pay a ransom to free a slave or to release a peasant from serfdom. But why did God need to pay a ransom to the devil and why his Son? These were the questions theologians tried to answer.

Late in the eleventh century, Anselm in his *Cur Deus Homo* ('Why did God become Man?') had offered a new theory of the Atonement. (Anselm, mentioned above, would have expected and perhaps deserved a chapter to himself and would certainly have resented being an addendum to Abelard). Anselm, who was born in Italy, came to Normandy to become a monk at Bec, one of the great centres of learning. In 1078 he was elected abbot of Bec. Subsequently, in 1093, he became Archbishop of Canterbury. His attempt to prove, rationally, the existence of God by the so-called 'ontological argument' is still discussed. Anselm said that because anyone can think 'of a being than which no greater can be conceived,' then such a being must in fact exist, as people could not think of that which does not exist. Our interest here, however, is in his attempt, in his book *Cur Deus Homo* (1097-8), to give a rational explanation of the death of God-made-man. Anselm argued that human sin is an offence to God, so sinners owe God a debt of honour. Yet because humans in any case are required to offer God perfect obedience, they have nothing with which to pay the debt. God could pay the debt, but does not owe it. Only a god-man or sinless man can pay it. Adopting a concept from Roman law, Anselm speaks of Christ by his death making satisfaction for the human sin. Later some theologians spoke of the debt as a punishment rather than a debt of honour. In either case, it is hard to see why God cannot just forgive human sin as a parent might forgive his or her child.

Anslem's and similar explanations of the Atonement are often labelled 'objective,' because they imply that the death of Christ changed God's attitude to sinful humanity. So-called 'subjective' theories speak of Christ's life and death as an example, which changes the attitude of humans towards God. Their fears are taken away by Christ's great love, which inspires them to love and obey him. This was the approach preferred by Abelard, although some modern scholars argue that Abelard was 'not a proponent of pure exemplarism.' Sometimes he does indeed speak of Christ's death as a ransom or as blood money. But, Abelard was also sharply critical both of the older ransom theory and of the new idea of 'satisfaction'. If Adam's sin required such a price, what was the price needed for the greater sin of killing God's son? He asked, 'How could man's tasting of a single apple be a greater sin than crucifying the Son of God?'[9]

Abelard, especially in his later writings, emphasized that Jesus Christ is the great teacher and example. He came to show us how to love. Awareness of the intense pain and suffering that Jesus endured out of his love for human beings should call forth from humans an answering love and devotion. 'Why were you made to suffer tortures for our crimes? Now make our hearts suffer for all of those things, so that our compassion may be worthy of your Forgiveness.'[10] This mutual love is the basis on which forgiveness and reconciliation takes place. Abelard often quoted the saying of Jesus, 'Much is forgiven to them that love much.'[11] He wrote to Héloïse, 'Are you not moved to tears and remorse by the only begotten Son of God in His innocence being scourged, blindfolded, mocked, buffeted, spat upon, crowned with thorns, and finally hanged between thieves on that shameful cross?' (She replied that her feelings were not within her control. The only sufferings that moved her were those of her beloved Abelard). In his *Commentary on the Romans*, Abelard's mature conclusion is that 'Our Redemption through Christ's suffering is that supreme love in us, which as well as liberating us from the servitude of sin, confers on us true freedom as children of God, so that we do everything out of his love rather than from fear. For he has shown us such grace that no greater can be found.'[12]

The great value of Abelard's approach is that it seeks to explain the Atonement in terms of personal relationships rather than legal transactions. The distinguished Mediaeval scholar, Sir Richard Southern, wrote that Abelard's reinterpretation of the Redemption 'contains one of the great new ideas of the twelfth century: it asserted that the Incarnation was efficacious, not in satisfying the just claims of God or the devil, but in teaching by example the law of love. It left out the whole idea of compensation to God for human sin, and threw the whole emphasis of the Incarnation on its capacity to revive man's love for God.' [13]

Abelard showed an interest in and sympathy for the Jews, which was unusual at the time. He may have asked advice from Jewish scholars in Paris about the interpretation of some passages of the Bible. In his *Dialogue between a Christian, a Philosopher and a Jew*, the Jew speaks movingly of his people's sufferings, although the Philosopher argues that the Torah (Law) adds nothing to the natural or moral law that anyone can recognise by the use of reason.

Abelard's surviving writings add up to more than a million words. It is not surprising that people have judged him in different ways. Peter the Venerable said of Abelard that he was 'without equal, without superior.' He was a person who in his day aroused strong feelings of admiration and hostility. In the nineteenth century he was often spoken of as a rationalist and an iconoclastic thinker. More recently, attention has been paid to his theological writings, to his desire to avoid heresy and his deep study of the Bible and the Church Fathers. The question is whether he used reason to explain Christian doctrine, as he would have claimed, or whether in fact he adapted Christian teaching to his philosophical views? Was his confidence in his own power of reason greater than his faith in the word of scripture? Abelard's close pupils called him 'the Philosopher' and a recent scholar, John Marenbon, agrees, saying that we should see Abelard as 'a constructive philosopher, both in ontology and epistemology, and more boldly and successfully in ethics.' [14]

His philosophical writings certainly continued to influence Christian thinkers for several centuries and his theological writings are still important. His tragic romance also highlights the tension that so many people still suffer in trying to harmonise their sexuality and their spirituality.

CHAPTER NOTES

1. Peter Abelard, *Historia Calamitatum*, lines 254-5, quoted by M T Clanchy, *Abelard: a medieval life*, Oxford, Blackwell, 1997, p. 3.
2. Quoted by Clanchy, p. 151.
3. Matthew, 19, 12.
4. See Clanchy, pp. 264 ff. See below more about Anselm.

5. Acts 17,34.

6. *Historia Calamitatum*, lines 249-58.

7. *English Hymna* 465, translation by J M Neale.

8. Quoted by Clanchy, p. 158.

9. See Clanchy, p. 285.

10. Quoted by Clanchy, p.9 from Abelard's Hymns No 44.

11. Luke 7,47.

12. Abelard, *Commentary on Romans*, lines 256-61.

13. R. W Southern, *St Anselm*, 1990, pp. 206-7.

14. John Marenbon, *The Philosophy of Peter Abelard*, Cambridge, University Press, 1997, p. 339.

41

Maimonides

Maimonides was the most important Mediaeval Jewish intellectual, but his influence was not confined to Judaism. His works of philosophy, translated into Latin, were studied by some of the great Mediaeval Christian theologians, including St Thomas Aquinas (c.1225-74) and Meister Eckhart (c.1260-1327). Even later, philosophers such as Spinoza (1632-77) and Leibniz (1646-1716) took notice of his writings. He earned his living, however, from the practice of medicine. There is still scholarly dispute about the details of his life and how to interpret his thought.

After the destruction of Jerusalem in 70CE, Jews, without a homeland, were widely scattered. A considerable number lived in Babylonia, which was an important centre of Jewish learning. When Benjamin of Tuleda visited Baghdad in 1170, he found 40,000 Jews living there, with numerous synagogues and places of study. Many others lived in areas ruled by Muslims and others dwelt in Christendom. By the twelfth century, Spain had a particularly vibrant Jewish community and it was there that Maimonides lived for the first part of his life.

Moses Maimonides, which is his Greek name, was also known as Rambam, a word made up of the first letters of the Hebrew for 'Rabbi Moshe Ben Maimon' or 'Rabbi Moses, the son of Maimon.' He was born in Cordova in 1135, seven years after the birth there of the great Muslim philosopher Averroes. As a boy he studied with his father, who was a learned scholar. There was no *madrasa* or so-called university in Spain until the late fourteenth century, when one was built in Granada. Students, therefore, studied privately under 'masters', who had a written license to teach what they had learned. Quite early Maimonides astonished his teachers by his intelligence and wide interests.

In Maimonides' early years, Jews in Muslim Cordova were given full religious freedom. This changed dramatically when the city was captured by the Almohads in 1148. Although they have been unfairly labelled 'barbarians', the Almohads could certainly be fiercely intolerant of views with which they disagreed. For example, the second

Almohad ruler, Ali ben Yusuf, ordered works of the Muslim philosopher al-Ghazali (d.1111) to be burned.

Jews now had the choice of converting to Islam or leaving the city. The Maimon family continued to observe their Judaism secretly at home, but in public they tried to behave like Muslims. It was indeed a troubling question for Jews how they should behave under an intolerant Muslim regime. A rabbi living in a non-Muslim land – perhaps Christian Spain –said that even the appearance of conversion to Islam was a complete denial of God. Maimonides strongly disagreed. He pointed out that this would mean there was no difference between a forced conversion and a willing one. He rejected the view that Islam was idolatrous. A Jew, he said, should recite the necessary formula of belief rather than choose death. He added that Muslims 'well know that we do not believe in this speech [the confession] and that the only intent is to save oneself from the king, to appease him with simple words.' When possible Jews should move to a place where they were free to practise their religion, but 'should dwell in their houses until they go out.'[1]

The family, it seems, stayed for another eleven or more years in Cordova, or perhaps at times in the nearby countryside. Maimonides continued his study of Judaism and of the sciences and started writing. His *Treatise on Logic* was written while still in Spain and he began work on his great *Mishnah Torah*. The necessary disguise and compromises eventually became too troublesome and the family did 'go out' to Fez in Morocco. Fez was also under the control of the Almohads, but as newcomers the family hoped to avoid attracting attention. When one of Maimonides' teachers, however, was arrested and executed for being a Jew, it was time for the family to move again. This time they went to Palestine, but the country was so poor that no suitable work was available. So the family now went to Egypt and settled near Cairo. Jews there were free to practise their religion, provided they were not Jews who had submitted to Islam and had reverted to Judaism. Maimonides was in fact accused of so doing, but was able to show that he had never really adopted Islam.

In the mid twelfth century, Egypt was the most flourishing and peaceful country in the Islamic world. The Fatimids, a Shi'ite dynasty, had conquered the country in the mid tenth century. They were very tolerant of both Jews and Christians. Maimonides arrived in Egypt as Fatimid rule was crumbling. In 1171 the famous Saladin (1138-1193) overthrew the dynasty in a bloodless coup and restored Egypt to Sunnite orthodoxy. For a time, Saladin's campaign to purge the country of Shi'ite practices caused some difficulties for non-Muslims, but these repressive measures were soon relaxed.

We know quite a lot about the Egypt in which Maimonides now lived thanks to the discovery in the nineteenth century of the Cairo Geniza, which was a great storehouse for discarded scrolls and other writings which were too worn to be used. Thanks to the Geniza, we can identify some ninety Jewish settlements at the time of Maimonides. Most of the Jews had come at various times from elsewhere – Palestine, Babylon, North Africa, Spain and from Byzantium. Jews shared in the general prosperity and often formed trading partnerships with Muslims. The Jewish community was self-governing, led by an official called 'Head of the Jews' – an office, which Maimonides held at two periods of his life. Yet despite his long residence in Egypt, Maimonides continued to sign himself 'Moses the Spaniard' and remained proud of the land of his birth. The Jewish population was at its peak. Estimates vary between 33,000 to 12,000 Jews plus some Karaites, who were members of a Jewish sect that relied only on scripture and rejected subsequent interpretation. Two years before Maimonides died in 1204 there was a devastating famine, followed by a plague.

In Egypt, Maimonides felt safe from persecution, but family problems soon assailed him. Shortly after he got there, his father died. Then his brother David, who was a jewellery merchant, died in a shipwreck – taking the family fortune with him. Maimonides had been dependent on his brother's wealth, but now had to find work. Maimonides, who insisted that a rabbi should earn his own living, turned to medicine and was soon so successful that he became court physician to the sultan Saladin. There was an Arabic saying at the time that 'Galen's medicine is only for the body, but that of [Maimonides] is for both body and soul.' He also had a private practice, lectured to other doctors and, as already mentioned, he played a leading part in Jewish communal life. It is no wonder that Maimonides complained that the pressures of his many duties deprived him of peace of mind and undermined his health.

Maimonides married late in life. His son Abraham also proved to be a good scholar. Maimonides died in 1204 and was buried in the Holy Land at Tiberias, where pilgrims continue to visit his grave.

Maimonides' writings were of two kinds: a systematic summary of Jewish law and works of philosophical speculation.

To recognise the importance of his *Mishnah Torah*, a brief explanation is necessary. Orthodox Judaism treats the written Torah ('Teaching' or 'Law') and its interpretation by the rabbis, known as the oral Torah, as of equal authority. Much of the early rabbinic discussion of legal issues had been collected by early in the third century in the *Mishnah*. Further discussions had been gathered together by the fifth century in the *Talmud*. Rabbis continued to discus the various opinions reflected in these collections. The fascinating debates, however, made it difficult for those Jews who were not scholars to know what God's law required of them. In his Introduction to the *Mishnah Torah*, Maimonides recognised the difficulties. 'In our days, severe vicissitudes prevail, and all feel the pressure of hard times. The wisdom of our wise men has disappeared; the understanding of our prudent men is hidden.' His aim, therefore, was to ensure that 'the entire Oral Law might become systematically known to all without citing difficulties and solutions of differences of view...but consisting of statements clear and convincing, that have appeared from the time of Moses to the present, so that all rules shall be accessible to young and old.'

Maimonides' codification has been described as applying the approach of Muslim schools of law to Jewish Oral tradition. The *Mishnah Torah* like Maimonides' other Jewish works brought order and brevity to the vast amount of detailed argument and opinions, which confronted any member of the Jewish community who wanted guidance on a practical or theoretical query. His students were expected to learn his *Mishnah Torah* and not bother with the *Talmud*. This, not surprisingly, infuriated traditional scholars - including the head or *gaon* of the Babylonian Jewish community in Baghdad.

Maimonides' opponents, however, rather than attacking his codification itself, focussed on his philosophical writings and Maimonides' supposed denial of the possibility of resurrection and immortality, which he rebutted in his *Treatise on Resurrection*.

But how far did Maimonides feel it necessary, because of this criticism, to disguise what he really thought? Many scholars hold that his outstanding philosophical work, the *Guide of the Perplexed* was carefully constructed to ward off naïve believers and potential enemies by concealing his actual opinions beneath a disguise of orthodoxy. Others hold that the *Guide* was not a book 'written by a Jew for Jews' but a work of philosophy, which engaged with the issues then being debated by contemporary philosophers, be they Jewish, Muslim or Christian. 'The fact that the author is Jewish ... is irrelevant,' writes Oliver Leaman.[2] Other writers think his intention was to make the wisdom of Judaism known more widely.

Maimonides had a detailed grasp of the works of his philosophical and theological predecessors, but as he wrote to Samuel ibn Tibbon who translated his works into Hebrew – Maimonides wrote in Arabic with Hebrew characters – 'The works of Aristotle are the roots and foundations of all works on the sciences.' He contrasted Aristotle with Plato, saying that the latter wrote in parables and did not really contribute anything that cannot be found in Aristotle. He referred to many other writers. Indeed he is more often critical of Jewish thinkers, having a higher opinion of Greek and Muslim authorities.

Maimonides himself said to the student to whom he dedicated the *Guide* 'you asked me to make clear to you certain things pertaining to divine matters... My purpose in this was that the truth should be established according to proper methods.' Maimonides' purpose was to explain in a logical and ordered way all that can be known about metaphysical problems. He was critical of the lack of logical rigour in the arguments of many theologians, who in turn were suspicious of philosophers. Maimonides' strategy was in keeping with the style of Muslim philosophers. Averroes in his *Incoherence of the Incoherence* adopted a similar approach.[3] It seems right then to judge his *Guide* as work of philosophy in its own right, not one in which his true views are concealed, although Maimonides saw no reason for the ordinary believer to struggle with issues which were beyond his grasp.

What place does reason play in the spiritual life? This is a perennial question. Maimonides was convinced that belief and reason went together. 'The foundation and support of all wisdom is the recognition that there is one original Being, and that all else exists only through the reality of his Being.' Another perennial question is whether we can speak of God directly. Can we describe God? Maimonides said we can speak of God's character as seen in God's relationship to the world and to human beings, but we cannot describe God as God is. Following what is known as the *'via negativa'* or 'negative way', Maimonides recognised that God is not another object that can be described. The mystery of Being transcends our human knowledge and so we speak of the Holy in negative terms, as in the hymn 'Immortal, Invisible.' Indeed Jews avoid using the name of God. Maimonides, therefore, said that the language we use of the Divine is 'analogical.' If, therefore, we speak of God as a 'Loving Father', for example, we borrow from our human experience, but know that the comparison is not exact.

In his treatment of religion, Maimonides criticised anything that could not stand up to reason. He said a miracle 'cannot prove what is impossible; it is useful only to confirm what is possible.' He believed in the common Jewish view that a human being has both a good and an evil inclination and can become 'righteous like Moses or evil like Jeroboam' (the first king of the northern state of Israel who is condemned in the Bible for setting up golden calves to be worshipped instead of the Lord).

Many commentaries have been written on Maimonides' *Guide of the Perplexed* and his work not only influenced subsequent Jewish thinkers, but also, as we shall see, the great Christian theologian St Thomas Aquinas (1225-74) and the mystic Eckhart (1260-1327).

Maimonides, however, is perhaps best known for his 'Thirteen Principles of Faith', which are often taken as a summary of what Jews believe. In the Orthodox Prayer Book they are printed after the Ten Commandments and spoken of as the 'Jewish Creed.'[4]

1. I believe with perfect faith that the Creator, blessed be his name, is the Author and Guide of everything that has been created and that he alone has made, does make and will make all things.

2. I believe with perfect faith that the Creator, blessed be his name, is a Unity, and that there is no unity in any manner like unto his, and that he alone is our God, who was, is, and will be.

3. I believe with perfect faith that the Creator, blessed be his name, is not

a body, and that he is free from all the accidents of matter, and that he has not any form whatsoever.

4. I believe with perfect faith that the Creator, blessed be his name, is the first and the last.

5. I believe with perfect faith that the Creator, blessed be his name, and to him alone, it is right to pray, and that it is not right to pray to any being besides him.

6. I believe with perfect faith that all the words of the prophets are true.

7. I believe with perfect faith that the prophecy of Moses our teacher, peace be upon him, was true and that he was the chief of the prophets, both of those that preceded him and of those that followed him.

8. I believe with perfect faith that the whole Law, now in our possession, is the same that was given to Moses our teacher, peace be upon him.

9. I believe with perfect faith that this Law will not be changed, and that there will never be any other law from the Creator, blessed be his name.

10. I believe with perfect faith that the Creator, blessed be his name, knows every deed of the children of men, and all their thoughts, as it is said, It is he that fashioneth the hearts of them all, that giveth heed to all their deeds.

11. I believe with perfect faith that the Creator, blessed be his name, rewards those that keep his commandments and punishes those that transgress them.

12. I believe with perfect faith in the coming of the Messiah, and, though he tarry, I will wait daily for his coming.

13. I believe with perfect faith that there will be a resurrection of the dead at the time that it shall please the Creator, blessed be his name,

and exalted be the remembrance of him for ever and ever.

Maimonides devoted his life wholeheartedly to the service of the Jewish community and to the wider society in Cairo. Moreover, he believed that by developing their intellectual powers to the full people could help turn a savage and irrational world into a reasonable one, conforming to the Perfect Mind of the Divine. This particularly was the Jewish vocation. Jews did not have state power, military force or even a land. They had brains. They were called to leaven the dough of humanity and to enlighten the gentiles.[5]

Maimonides' writings achieved this aim. Maimonides believed, with justice, that his work helped to make available all that Judaism, as a religion and a philosophy, has to offer to enable people to make a living conversion in the direction of God.

CHAPTER NOTES

1. Norman Roth in *Moses Maimonides and His Time*, Ed Eric L Ormsby, Washington, Catholic University of America Press, 1989, pp. 17-18, quoting from a letter by Maimonides.
2. Oliver Leaman, *Moses Maimonides*, London, Routledge, 1990. pp. 6-7 and passim. She refers critically to the views of Leo Strauss.
3. Leaman, pp. 9-10.
4. *The Authorised Daily Prayer Book of the Hebrew Congregations of the British Commonwealth of Nations*, (English translation by S. Singer), London, Eyre and Spottiswoode, 1962, pp. 93-95.
5. This paragraph is based on a passage in Paul Johnson's *A History of the Jews*, p. 187.

42

Avicenna and Averroes

The lasting contribution to human knowledge of Islamic philosophers, of whom Avicenna and Averroes were the most important, is often forgotten today. They also played a vital part in transmitting the works of the Greek philosophers Plato and Aristotle to the Christian West.

Avicenna, as Ibn Sina is known in the West, was born near Bukhara, which is now in Uzbekistan. Arab Muslim armies had come to the area in the late seventh and early eighth centuries. At that time the population was a mixture of Zoroastrians, Buddhists and some Christians and Jews. A mosque had been built in Avicenna's home town of Afsahana in 709. Four years later a mosque had been constructed on the citadel of Bukhara, where previously there had been a Zoroastrian fire temple. This mosque has recently been restored as part of the revival of religion since Uzbekistan's independence from Soviet rule.

Bukhara, which is strategically located on a large oasis on the banks of the Zarafshan River, grew from a cluster of villages which were united by its market and mosque. At the time Avicenna was born in 980 CE, Bukhara was ruled by the Samanids - the first great native dynasty that arose in Persia after the Arab conquest. The population was still religiously mixed when Avicenna was born, although Muslims by then were dominant.

Avicenna's father, who was in government service, was an Isma 'ili – a mystical grouping related to Shi'a Islam. Avicenna says he was never attracted to this movement. Even so, many thinkers congregated at his father's home and no doubt as a boy he listened to their conversations. He was a precocious child with an amazing memory. By the age of ten, he knew the Qur'an and many poems by heart.

Avicenna was sent to a local greengrocer to learn the new 'Arabic' arithmetic, with its distinctive use of the zero, which was replacing the Persian system of finger calculation. He was taught Islamic law, according to the liberal Hanafi tradition, by a noted jurist in the town. A resident tutor was employed to teach him philosophy, which included the study of Aristotle and Euclid. Avicenna then turned to medicine and the study of Galen, the second-century Greek physician.

Soon, by the age of sixteen, Avicenna was practising medicine and discovering new cures. His reputation was made when he successfully cured a Samanid prince. As a reward, Avicenna was given access to the royal library. In an age of manuscript literature, when books were rare and prized possessions, one can imagine his delight. 'I saw', he later wrote, 'books whose very titles are unknown to many, and which I never saw before or since.' When he came upon a new book, Avicenna went at once to the hardest passages to judge the author's scholarship rather than wasting time on the repetition of material with which he was already familiar.

Staying up much of the night, Avicenna devoted himself to philosophy, recording his arguments on papyrus cards. When defeated by some question, he relied on prayer, wine and his dreams, in which an answer sometimes came to him. He still, however, could not grasp the point of Aristotle's *Metaphysics*, even though he had read it forty times. He decided that metaphysics was unintelligible. He was, however, persuaded by a merchant to buy a little work *On the Objects of Metaphysic* by Al-Farabi (c.870-950), who was a logician and also a politician, at a knockdown price. Al-Farabi was one of many scholars by whom Avicenna was influenced. This suggested that there are ultimately three sciences: physics, which deals with bodies, mathematics, which relates to the abstract characteristics of bodies and metaphysics, which treates of being as such. So now at the age of eighteen, Avicenna had discovered the point of metaphysics. He was also actively engaged in legal debates.

By his late teens, Avicenna's central beliefs were clear. His knowledge, he said, was to mature, but his memory grew less elastic. His first work was written when he was seventeen and it laid the basis for his key arguments that the rational soul is real and immortal, although it has no physical existence. His first proper book was written when he was twenty-one.

For a time, after his father's death, Avicenna was employed by the government, but then he says, 'necessity compelled me to leave Bukhara and move to Gurganj'- 'necessity' was the impending collapse of Samanid rule. Mahmud of Ghazna, a Turkish leader who was strictly orthodox and suspicious of philosophers, took control of the area. Avicenna had to move from the city. Even so, he persisted with his writing. He was often in danger and when he was imprisoned in the castle of Fardajan, he wrote,

That I go in you see, so that's without doubt
What's uncertain is whether I ever come out.'

He was, in fact, there for four months. Soon after he was set free, in 1022, with his brother, his disciple and two slaves – all disguised as Sufis – he escaped to Isfahan. As he approached the city, he was met with fresh clothing, fine mounts and given furnished rooms and warmly welcomed by the ruler, Ala' ad-Dawlah. Here at last he had some peace and could concentrate on his writings, especially the completion of the *Kitab al-Shifa*, 'The Book of Healing for the Soul' and the *Qanun fi at-tibb*, 'Canon of Medicine.' This book, which became with Hippocrates and Galen, a standard European medical text, includes his own discoveries. For example, he found that ice-compresses cured his headaches. His literary output was prolific – much of it in Arabic and some in Persian. He composed the first work in Persian on the philosophy of Aristotle, he summarised his *Kitab al-Shifa*, in the *Kitab an-naja*, 'The Book of Salvation,' and produced nearly 200 treatises. A criticism that his learning did not include the niceties of the Arabic language led him to study it intensively for three years. He then wrote poems in various styles, had them bound, and presented them – to the amusement of other scholars - to his critic as some rare work that had just been found. Amongst all this activity, he regularly took part in the court scholarly assemblies on a Friday night.

The settled life in Isfahan was not to last. In January 1030, his baggage was plundered and the manuscript of *Kitab-al-Insaf* was lost. It was not destroyed, but only fragments now survive. He devoted the 1030s to his 'Books of Hints and Pointers.' When his patron Ala' ad-Dawlah came under attack, he accompanied him on his campaigns. In 1034 he fell ill of colic, but trying to keep up with Ala al-Dawla, he treated it too strenuously with eight enemas in a single day. This resulted in an ulcer and suppuration. His health deteriorated and he died at the age of 58 in 1037 in Hamadan.

We know many of these details because Avicenna dictated a short autobiography to his disciple Al-Juzjani, who continued the account down to his master's death. As far as we know he did not marry or have children, but, his disciple said the master was 'vigorous in all his powers, the sexual being the most powerful and predominant of his concupiscent faculties and he indulged it often' – even to the detriment of his health. He also enjoyed wine. He never claimed to be a paragon of Islamic piety.

In contrast to al-Ghazali, Avicenna believed it was possible to provide a philosophical basis for faith. He was influenced by the writings of the mystic Plotinus (c.205-70), who was the founder of Neo-Platonism. God is the necessary existent. As first cause and prime mover, God produces a single intelligence, which gives rise to other intelligences. The tenth pure intelligence governs the terrestrial world. He followed the Greek theory of four elements, earth, air, fire and water. The balance of elements is constantly being disturbed, but each seeks to return to its original position. Avicenna linked this with the soul's search for the divine.

Avicenna's works were translated into Latin and had considerable influence on Mediaeval Christian theologians, such as St Thomas Aquinas. 'The great insight of Avicenna as a philosopher was the recognition of the compatibility of contingency, by which Islamic thinkers tried to canonise the scriptural idea of creation, and the metaphysics of necessity, in which the followers of Aristotle had enshrined the idea that the goal of science is understanding why and how things must be as they are.'[1]

Study of Avicenna's philosophy, however, was banned for a time in the thirteenth century, but again permitted by Pope Gregory IX in 1231. Although he was given the honorific title of *ash-Shaykh ar-Ra'is* or 'The Leading Wise Man', his philosophical writings have been criticised by a number of orthodox Muslim theologians in the past.

The same was true of the last of the great Islamic philosophers Averroes, who was born in Spain nearly a century after Avicenna's death, at a time of political struggle between Almoravids and the Almohads and also of theological tension between the more open approach popular at Seville and the strict orthodoxy at Cordova (Cordoba).

Averroes or Ibn Rushd was born in Cordova into a family of distinguished lawyers and public servants. His grandfather was a noted legal thinker, some of whose writings still survive. He died in 1126, the year in which his even more famous grandson was born. Averroes' education gave him a good grounding in Arabic letters, jurisprudence, medicine and philosophy. His legal training was in the Malakite school of law, named after Malik b Anas (d.795), who gave considerable weight to a scholar's independent judgement, *ijtihad*. His theological training was according to the Ash'arite tradition, which so emphasised the power and influence of God over all things that it abandoned the objectivity of causality, ethics and the world as an eternal entity – views that Averroes was later to oppose.

His scholarship came to the attention of Ibn Tufayl (d. 1185), the leading philosopher of the period and court physician to the Caliph. In 1169 Averroes was introduced to the Caliph Abu Ya 'qub Yusuf by Ibn Tufayl. According to Averroes' own account of the meeting, 'the Prince asked me, "What is their (the philosophers') opinion about the heavens – Are they eternal or created?" Confusion and fear took hold of me, and I began to make excuses and deny that I had ever concerned myself with philosophical learning... The Prince of Believers (i.e. The Caliph) understood my fear and confusion ... and set me at ease until I spoke. He then learned what was my competence in that subject. When I withdrew he ordered for me a gift of money, a magnificent robe of honour and a steed.'

Later Ibn Tufayl, who was close to the Caliph, told Averroes, 'Today I heard the Prince of Believers complain of the difficulty of expression of Aristotle and his translators and mention the obscurity of his aims, saying, "If someone would tackle these books and summarise them and expound them, after understanding them thoroughly, it would be easier for people to grasp them."' Ibn Tufayl then said to Averroes, 'So if you have in you abundant strength for the task, perform it.' This, Averroes said, 'was what led me to summarise the books of the philosopher Aristotle.'

Between 1169 and 1195, he wrote commentaries on and summaries of most of Aristotle's works. All of the commentaries are included in the Latin version of Aristotle's complete works. These clearly presented commentaries exerted considerable influence on subsequent Christian and Jewish thinkers. Indeed Averroes became known in the Christian world as 'The Commentator.'

Soon after the decisive meeting with the Caliph, Averroes was appointed the religious judge of Seville and soon afterwards chief judge of Cordova. Then in 1182 he became physician royal at the court of the Almohad dynasty, at Marrakesh in Morocco. When the Caliph was succeeded by his son, who was nicknamed al-Mansurr, Averroes continued in favour. But in 1195, the new Caliph, yielding to public pressure, ordered Averroes' books to be burned, accusing him of heresy and irreligion. The teaching of philosophy and science was banned – except for astronomy, medicine and administration. On one occasion Averroes was driven from the mosque in Cordova by an angry crowd of worshippers. Averroes was hurt by this and by the reputation that he had acquired of being a bad Muslim. Averroes himself was exiled to Lucena, which is South East of Cordova. Averroes was quite soon restored to favour, but he died soon after these traumatic events in 1198, in Cordova, at the age of seventy- two.

Besides his Commentary on Aristotle, Averroes wrote a book on General Medicine. He also made a significant contribution to theological thinking. He wrote three treatises: *Fasl al-Maqal,* 'The Decisive Treatise,' in 1179, *Al-Kashf an Manahij Al-Adilla,* 'The Exposition of the Methods of Proof,' also in 1179 and a short tract dealing with God's eternal and unchanging knowledge of contingent entities. He also wrote in 1195 a systematic rebuttal of Al-Ghazali's 'Incoherence of the Philosophers' called 'The Incoherence of Incoherence,' *Tahafut al-tahafut.* Averroes held that the world is eternal, caused, but not created by God, who is eternal and uncaused.

At first, when his writings became known in Northern Europe in about 1230, a party of 'Averroists' emerged at the University of Paris. In 1270, however, St Thomas Aquinas directed a treatise against these views, saying that they implied that 'things are true according to philosophy but not according to the Catholic faith, as though there were two contradictory truths.' Averroes himself, if not those who used his name, had aimed to reconcile the two truths, saying that there was a single truth which may be presented in two ways. Certainly Mediaeval Scholasticism, which was the attempt of Christian thinkers to bring together, by the use of reason, the articles of faiths into a single system, was deeply influenced by the writings of Averroes, whether scholars agreed or disagreed with his views.

Still today in Islam and indeed other religions creative thinkers are viewed with suspicion. In the words of one modern scholar, 'Averroes' reputation within the Islamic community did not remain high after his death and there is little evidence that he influenced the development of thought within Islam until quite recently. He had a far more successful afterlife among the Jewish communities in the medieval world and a widespread effect upon the Christian world.'[2] A renewed interest in Avicenna and Averroes among Muslim scholars might help Islam as it seeks to relate constructively to the modern world.

CHAPTER NOTES
1. L E Goodman, *Avicenna*, London, Routledge, 1992, p. ix.
2. Oliver Leaman, *Averroes and his Philosophy*, Oxford, Clarendon Press 1988, p.5.

43

Hildegard of Bingen

Hildegard was a mediaeval mystic and talented musician, who has been described as one of the most significant women in Christian history. She was a polymath or scholar in many subjects. She was, in Fiona Maddocks' words says, 'a visionary, a theologian, a preacher; an early scientist and physician; a prodigious letter writer who numbered kings, emperors and popes among her correspondents.'[1] Hildegard, besides being a composer, was interested in painting and architecture and even invented her own coded language. She was courageous, perhaps overbearing, but sometimes overcome by her spectacular visions.

We know quite a lot about Hildegard, although some of the relevant material, such as her nearly four hundred letters, is still being edited. A biography, *The Life of St Hildegard*, was begun while she was still alive and completed within eleven years. It includes some autobiographical material, which Hildegard dictated in the 1170s when she thought she might be dying. There is also a letter about her by Guibert of Gembloux to his fellow monk Bovo and relevant material in the *Life of Mistress Jutta*, who was her teacher and abbess.[2]

Hildegard grew up at the beginning of the twelfth century, which was to be a time of new growth in both the economic and social life of Europe and in the intellectual and organizational life of the Church. She was born in 1098, not far from Mainz in Germany. Her parents were of noble descent and she was their tenth child. She was sickly from birth and even as a child she had visions. Just before her eighth birthday, she was placed in the care of Jutta, a holy woman who, although she lived a solitary life, had attracted so many followers that a small nunnery had sprung up nearby. Later, Hildegard was to criticise the twelfth century practice of dedicating young children to the monastic life against their will. Even so, Hildegard obviously had a good education as well as a pious one. She became familiar with the scholarly diet of the time, which included works by Aristotle and Augustine.

Hildegard took her nun's vows when she was about fifteen. When Jutta died in 1136, Hildegard was unanimously elected as head of the nunnery. In 1150, however, she decided to found her own monastery on the banks of the Rhine, near Bingen. Although often spoken of as an abbess, she never officially had this title, as her communities remained nominally under the jurisdiction of the Benedictine monastery at Disibodenberg.

Hildegard was clearly a very capable head of her communities. It was, however, her mystical visions which made her famous. In 1141, she said that she was commanded by God 'to write down what you see and hear.' Because of self-doubt, she was reluctant to do so. Soon after receiving this message, she was taken ill. 'Through this illness', she said, 'God taught me to listen better.' Encouraged by two trusted friends, she started to write and after ten years completed her first theological book, *Scivias* or 'Know Your Ways.' She insisted, 'these visions were not fabricated by my own imagination, nor are they anyone else's, I saw these when I was in the heavenly places. They are God's mysteries. These are God's secrets. I wrote them down because a heavenly voice kept saying to me, "See and speak! Hear and write."'[3] Another time, she wrote, 'Nor do I put down words other than those I hear in the vision, and I present them in Latin, unpolished, just as I hear them in the vision. For, I am not taught in this vision to write as philosophers write.'[4]

In 1146 – her first dateable writing – she sent a letter to St Bernard of Clairvaux (1090-1153), a monastic reformer and mystical writer who had great influence in Church affairs, asking for reassurance about her unpublished work. Soon afterwards, describing herself as 'a small insignificant figure,' she wrote to Pope Eugenius III, saying that 'The living Light has taught me.' She added that 'the same Light has not left me but burns in my soul as I have had it since childhood.' Pope Eugene III gave her his backing at the Synod of Trier in 1147-8. Soon she became known as 'the Sybil of the Rhine' and attracted followers from across France and Germany. She also undertook four preaching tours. This was– highly unusual as Benedictines were not permitted to leave their cloisters without special permission and only priests were allowed to preach.

Besides her *Scivias*, Hildegard recorded further visions in her *Liber Divinorum Operum*, or 'Book of Divine Works.' She also added her own interpretation of these mystical experiences and the manuscripts include some illustrations of them. Her other theological works were commentaries on the Bible and a book about human vices and virtues.

Rooting her ideas in what she called her 'vision', a religious experience of the 'living light', she set herself to write an encyclopaedic survey of theological knowledge. As a religious thinker, Hildegard is increasingly gaining in prestige. She was Orthodox in her beliefs, but her theology has a freshness that many today find attractive. In part this lies in the distinctively feminine aspect of her spirituality. She sees men and women as mutually interdependent, both equally reflecting the image of God. Her ideas too are linked to an ecology in which the human being is a part of nature, a microcosm of the wider workings of the universe.[5] She wrote, 'I am the fiery life of divine substance, I blaze above the beauty of the fields, I shine in the waters, I burn in sun, moon and stars.' She insisted that Love is the Power that informs and holds together the whole universe.

This approach is also reflected in her poetry. For example, she wrote:

Love abounds in all things,
Excels from the depths to beyond the stars,
Is lovingly disposed to all things.[6]

Another beautiful poem speaks of the Virgin Mary:

Because a woman brought forth death,
A bright Maiden overcame it,
And so the highest blessing
In all of creation lies
In the form of a woman
Since God has become man
In a sweet and blessed Virgin. [7]

If in her own day, Hildegard was famous as a visionary and a prophet, today she is probably better known for her music. This interest, however, is quite recent. It was only in the 1990 revised edition of the *New Oxford History of Music* (1952) that she first gets a mention. Hildegard's music captured public attention in 1981, when a long-playing record of her music was made. Called 'A Feather on the Breath of God', this collection of hymns, edited and directed by Christopher

Page and sung by members of Gothic Voices, won a coveted *Gramaphone* award. Several other recordings have since been made. Some scholars question whether she was actually the author or whether the work of other people was attributed to her, but she seems to have been known for her music during her lifetime.

In the Middle Ages music was believed to be a mirror of the divine order. Hildegard, in keeping with others before and after, saw the world as a hymn of praise to God. Even in the seventeenth century, the poet Addison (1672-1719) echoed this idea in his hymn '*The spacious firmament on high*', which concludes:

What though in solemn silence all
Move round the dark terrestrial ball;
What though nor real voice nor sound
Amid their radiant orbs be found;
In reason's ear they all rejoice,
And utter forth a glorious voice;
For ever singing as they shine,
"The hand that made us is Divine."[8]

The invisible and unheard music of the heavens, which the late Roman scholar Boethius (c.480-c.524) called *musica mundane*, or the 'Music of the Spheres', was thought to parallel the physical and emotional make-up of human beings, who in turn made their own music. Hildegard herself spoke of music as an allegory of the body and the soul.

Hildegard's *Symphony of the Harmony of Heavenly Revelations* includes 77 songs, of which 43 are antiphons, psalms or hymns of which the verses are recited alternately by two groups, and 18 responsories, anthems sung by a soloist or choir after a scripture reading. She also wrote a morality play, *Play of the Virtues*. This is a very early and rare example of an oratorio for women's voices. The only male part is that of the Devil, but because of his corrupted nature, he cannot sing. It has been suggested that this work may have influenced the Northern Italian founders of opera, but this is unlikely.

Hildegard was an authority on a wide range of other subjects. She is regarded as Germany's first woman doctor and scientist, thanks to her *Book of Simple Medicine* and her *Book of Compound Medicine*. The second book is particularly noted for its frank discussion of gynae-cology and sexuality, including a scientific description of the female orgasm. She was sharply critical of adultery, lesbianism and mastur-bation, but showed greater compassion than other religious leaders, nearly all of whom were male. In present-day Germany, she has become an inspirational figurehead for proponents of herbal medicine and alternative therapies

The high regard in which Hildegard was held provoked some jealousy. Sadly, her last years were soured by controversy. Hildegard allowed the burial at her convent at Rupertsberg of a noble man, who had been excommunicated. She understood that he had confessed his sins and been absolved and reconciled to the church before his death. The clergy at Mainz insisted that this was not the case and that the man's body must be exhumed from consecrated ground. Hildegard refused and the convent was placed under an interdict, which banned the sisters from singing the office and from receiving Mass. One of Hildegard's letters shows how painful it was for her to be deprived of music. 'Anyone who without just cause imposes silence on a church and prohibits the signing of God's praises will,' she wrote, 'lose their place among the chorus of angels unless they have amended their lives through penitence and humble restitution.'[9] The warning seems to have been enough to persuade the bishop to relent. The edict was lifted six months before Hildegard died at the age of eighty-one in 1179.

It is said that God confirmed her good standing before Him by a manifest miracle just before her death. Two arcs of brilliant and varied colour appeared over the room where she was lying. A full moon shone, illuminating the apex where the two arcs crossed. Circles and crosses seemed to bend toward the earth over the place where she had passed away. There was also a brilliant light upon the whole mountain. Although beatified, the process of canonization as a saint was never completed. Today, however, there is growing appreciation of Hildegard, not only for her many talents, but even more for the life story, of a woman who in an apparently misogynist period was able to assert herself as an influential and popular spiritual guide, from whom we can still learn today.

CHAPTER NOTES

1. Fiona Maddocks, *Hildegard of Bingen*, London, Hodder Headline, 2001, Review paperback edition p. ix.
2. See further, *Hildegard of Bingen; Selected Writings*, London, Penguin, 2001.
3. Quoted from Carmen Acevedo Butcher's *Hildegard of Bingen: A Spiritual Reader*, Paraclete Press, 2007, p. 63.
4. *Selected Writings* p. xx.
5. *Selected Writings* pp. xli-xlii.
6. *Hildegard of Bingen, Symphonia: A Critical Edition*, Ed and trans Barbara Newman, Ithaca, Cornell University Press, 1998 , p.120.
7. *Symphonia*, p.118.
8. *English Hymnal*, 297.
9. *Hildegard of Bingen*, p. 246.

44

Honen, Shinran and Nichiren

Honan, Shinran and Nichiren were all at some time students at Mt Hiei of Tendai Buddhism and each originated important schools of Japanese Buddhism. Honen and Shinran were founders of two 'Pure Land' schools, which teach faith in the mercy of Amida Buddha. They continue to claim many thousands of followers today in Japan and increasingly in America and other parts of the world. Nichiren was the founder of Nichiren Su, which also has many followers.

Honen has been called 'The Great Illuminator', 'The Perfect Light', or 'Highest Wisdom', by different Japanese Emperors and more prosaically by the *Encyclopaedia Britannica* as 'one of the outstanding figures in the history of Japanese religion.'[1] Honen himself, however, rejected government employment and official titles. When he went out, instead of taking a carriage, he always went on foot, wearing straw sandals. Yet it was under his leadership that Pure Land Buddhism emerged as an independent school of devotional Buddhism. Indeed the movement spread so rapidly that within a century of his death, the retired emperor Go-Fushimi (1288-1336) ordered a priest (later an abbot) called Shunjo to write an account of Honen's life. Shunjo said, 'I made careful enquiries about what I had heard about Honen and also critically examined all the old records and selected what I believed to be true.'[2] Although some material is legendary we have a more authoritative biography of Honen than of many of the people whom we have already met. Several subsequent biographies of Honen have been written.

Honen, whose childhood name was Seishi-Maru, was born in 1133 at Inaoka in Western Honshu in the South West of Japan. He was the son of a regional military chief. When he was only nine, his father, as he lay dying from an attack by a village headman, told his son not to waste his life trying to avenge him, but to enter the priesthood. My murder, the father said, was the result of some sin in a previous life. 'If you harbour ill-will towards your enemy, you will never be free from enemies.'[3]

When he was 15 – or some say 13 – he was sent to the capital Kyoto and then to Mt Hiei to the monastic centre of Tendai Buddhism, which as we have seen in chapter 37, was established by Saicho (767-822) and which gives pre-eminence to the Lotus Sutra.

Honen, later in life, was to be scathing about the Tendai tradition and its teachers. He said that almost everything he learned was the result of his own study of the scriptures and the commentaries. Increasingly Honen came under the influence of Pure Land Buddhism, which originating in China in the fourth century CE, taught that salvation was by the mercy of Amida Buddha (or Amitabha), who was a king, who, in the long distant past, heard the teaching of the Buddha of his age. He devoted himself to the welfare of others for many millennia and eventually he became a Buddha, known as Amida. He now sits on a lotus, emitting rays of golden light and resides in a transcendent realm, known as the Pure Land.

It was Amida Buddha who delivered Honen from evil passions and set him free from the bondage of birth and death. Honen said, 'I came upon this passage in the *Commentary on the Meditation Sutra* by Zendo[5] (613-81) "whether walking or standing, sitting or lying, only repeat the name of Amida with all your heart. Never cease the practice of it even for a moment. This is the very work which unfailingly issues in salvation, for it is in accordance with the original vow of the Buddha."' Honen also discovered that the Tendai monk Genshin Sozu (942-1017) had said, 'The thing essential to birth in the Land of Bliss is the practice of the *Nembutsu* ('Mindfulness of the Buddha').'[6] Originally in Pure Land Buddhism, the *Nembutsu*, was a form of meditation in which the Buddha Amida and his transcendent Pure Land were visualized, but by the time of Honen it had become an invocation, 'I take refuge in the Buddha Amida', which in Japanese is *Namu Amida Butsu* or in Chinese *Na-mo O-mi-to fo*.

This now became the message of Honen – that all that was required for rebirth in the Pure Land was to recite, with faith, *Namu Amida Batsu*. Even the wicked person, by reciting these words, may be reborn into the Pure Land. 'Ten repetitions, even one, will not be in vain.'[7]

Honen claimed that the Buddha had taught two ways to salvation. The Sacred Way (*Shodo*) required the practice of meditation, but this was too hard for most people. For them the only way was *Jodo* or total trust in Amida Buddha's assurance of salvation to all who call upon his holy name.

It was in 1198 that Honen, now 43, publicly proclaimed this message and set up his headquarters in Kyoto, the secular capital, and away from the religious authorities. They, however, soon resented the popularity of the new movement. Two of his closest followers were killed and some of his followers urged him to give up, but he replied, 'I could not live and not teach what I have been teaching, even if it meant my death.'[8] He was sent into exile to Shikoku Island, but after a year he was permitted to return to the mainland, but only allowed back to Kyoto in 1211, where the people gave him a warm welcome. He died early in the following year (1212). His dying words were, 'The light of Amida illumines all sentient beings throughout the ten quarters who call upon the sacred name, protects them, and never forsakes them.'[9] Earlier, he had written this beautiful evening prayer:

> *Ten times Amida's name shall pass my lips*
> *Ere I repose.*
> *My last long slumber shall begin some time,*
> *And when – who knows*[10]

Honen insisted that salvation was available to anyone, even the worst sinner. His enemies argued that such emphasis on the unconditional mercy of the Divine can be perverted into an excuse for lawless behaviour, often called antinomianism. Honen clearly rejected this. Although any sentient being, even one who has committed five deadly sins, may be granted salvation by calling upon Amida Buddha, he should not continue in his evil actions. 'The profound desire in the Buddha's heart is that you keep the ten cardinal precepts while you are calling on the sacred name ten times.'[11] Honen urged his followers to avoid criticism of the scriptures or of other Buddhist teachers Women also could receive salvation, which was contrary to the general opinion at the time. Once a harlot, who bewailed what she must have done in a previous life to be so degraded, asked Honen whether she could be saved. He replied,

'If you can find another means of livelihood, give this one up at once, but if you cannot … begin just as you are and call on the sacred name; for it is for just such sinners as you that Amida made that wonderfully comprehensive vow. So put your sole trust in it, without the least misgiving.'[12]

He urged people so to trust in Amida that they lived without anxiety.

'Whatever befalls, I have made up my mind not to be anxious about myself, and so, come life, come death, nothing troubles me.'[13]
Honen called for complete dedication.

'When a deer is being pursued by the hunters, it does not stop even to look around for its fellows or look back at its pursuers, but with all eagerness, hastens straight forward ... and escapes in safety. It is with the same determination that a man fully entrusts himself to the Buddha's power, and without any regard to anything else, steadfastly sets his mind upon being born into the Pure Land.'[14]

Honen's main work, *Senchaku hongan Nembutus-shu*, 'Book on the choice of *Nembutsu'*, was written in 1198. His community became known as the still influential Jodo School. His disciples carried the message to all levels of Japanese society.

One disciple, whose school was to become even larger than Honen's, was called Shonin Shinran (1173-1262). He was born near Kyoto. His family were of noble descent and his father Arinori Hino was a high court officer in the service of the Empress Dowager. The Fujiwara clan, to which he belonged, however, had seen their prestige decline as the military class gained political ascendancy over the older aristocracy. Shinran was orphaned at an early age. At the age of nine Shinran, who had early on wanted to devote himself to Buddhism, became a Tendai monk. For twenty years he studied on Mt Hiei, but despite rigorous asceticism, he failed to find the assurance of salvation. Illness prompted him to come down from Mt Hiei and to meditate for one hundred days in Kyoto. There he met Honen and became one of his pupils. Shonin quickly experienced salvation through Amida's all-embracing love for all creatures. So at the age of 29, as he later wrote, 'I Shinran, the simple-hearted man with shaven head, abandoned the practise of unessential work and found a home in the Orginal Vows of Amida Buddha.'

Four years later he was allowed to copy Honen's main work *Senchaku-shu* and to draw a portrait of Honen. When Honen was exiled in 1207 to Tosa Province, Shinran was also banished, but to Echigo. There in violation of the celibacy expected of a Buddhist monk, Shinran married Eshinni and had a child. He rejected the need for monastic rules and residence. He then established his own, now more numerous school, which became known as Jodo Shinshu. He rejected all ways of effort (*jiriki*), even repeated calling upon Amida. He stressed reliance upon the power of the other (*tariki*). One prayer, sincerely meant, was enough. 'If there is aroused even once in us one thought of joy and love through Amida's vow, we turn just as we are, with our sins and lusts upon us, toward nirvana.' Having attained rebirth in the Pure Land, a person should return to help others.

From 1212 to 1235, Shinran lived in Kanto in Eastern Japan, where he concentrated on spreading his beliefs and also compiled a six volume anthology called *Kyogyo-shinsho* or 'True Teaching, Practice and Realization of the Way.' In 1235 or 1236, he returned to Kyoto, where his followers were suffering constant oppression. To make matters worse, his oldest son Zenran tried, with his heretical teaching, to control the community. Shinran, in the most tragic event of his long life, had to disown Zenran. Even in his troubles, Shinran made no attempt to justify himself, relying solely on Amida. Shinran died quietly on November 28th, 1262 in Kyoto, where he had been born ninety years earlier. His followers commemorate his death for seven days each year, meditating on subjects mostly taken from 'The Life', which was written by Kakunyo Shonin (1270-1351), who talked to many of Shinran's disciples and travelled to the places where Shinran had lived or visited.

Another school Jishu or 'one universality' was founded by Ippen (1239-89), also known as Yugyo Shonin or 'wandering holy man.' He held that repetition of *Nembutsu*, even without faith, was enough. His school is known as Ji, which means 'Time', because followers would invoke *nembutsu* for six-hours a day.

Nichiren, the founder of Nichiren Su, also studied for a time at Mt Hiei, but subsequently he sought to restore what he considered to be the orthodox teachings of the historical Buddha.

Nichiro, who was born in 1222, was a son of a fisherman. When he was twelve, his family placed him in the care of a local Tendai monastery, where at the age of sixteen he was given the 'precepts name' of Zenshobo. He then spent ten years travelling to various centres trying to discover 'true Buddhism.' After that he settled for a time at Mt Hiei and began an intensive study of Tendai teaching. Because of his radical ideas, however, he was driven out of Mt Hiei and moved to Mt Koya to learn the secret teachings and practices of the Shigon School, which, as we have seen, was founded by Kukai (774-835). Eventually, Nichiren decided that true Buddhism had been taught by Saicho, the founder of the Tendai School, who had asserted the superiority of the Lotus Sutra over all other sutras.

Nichiren now returned to his home village and urged people to put their trust in the truth expressed in the Lotus Sutra, saying

'When you fall in an abyss, and someone lowers a rope to pull you out, will you hesitate to grab the rope because you doubt the competence of the helper? Has not the Buddha declared, "I alone am protector and saviour?" Here is the power! Here is the rope!... Our hearts ache, our sleeves are soaked with tears until we see face to face the gentle figure of the one who says to us, "I am your father."'[15]

The invocation or *mantra*, which he taught – called *daimoku* or 'sacred title' – was, 'I take refuge in the Lotus of the Wonderful Law Sutra.' This, as a calligraphic inscription on wood, became a focus of worship.

In 1260, Nichiren wrote a well-known work called 'Treatise on the Establishment of Righteousness to Secure the Peace of the State' (*Rissho ankoku-ron*). In this he denounced the government and condemned other schools of Buddhism as false and demonic. He warned that unless people converted to (his) true Buddhism, Japan would continue to suffer a series of natural disasters, such as the storms, earthquakes, famines and epidemics, which had hit the country at that time. Nichiren also predicted that Japan would suffer invasion by a foreign army, which did indeed happen in 1268, when a Mongol military force invaded Kyushu.

Not surprisingly his outspoken remarks annoyed the government and other Buddhist schools. Nichiren was exiled in 1261 to the Izu Peninsula, but was pardoned in 1264. Nichiren persisted in his views and was again arrested and sentenced to death. Tradition says that as the executioner raised his sword, it was struck by lightning. Nichiren's life was saved, but he was again exiled – this time to the isolated island of Sado. There he wrote his 'Treatise on Opening the Eyes' (*Kaimokusho*) and 'Treatise on Contemplating the True Object of Worship' (*Kanjin Honzonsho*).

Nichiren said of his time in exile,

'The spot among the mountains is cut off from the life of the world. There is no human habitation anywhere around... I am living in the loneliest isolation. Yet in my heart, in Nichiren's body of flesh, is hidden the great mystery which the Lord Sakyamuni (the Buddha) revealed on Vulture Peak and entrusted to me. My heart is a place where all Buddhas are immersed in contemplation, turning the wheel of truth on my tongue, being born from my throat, attaining Enlightenment in my mouth.'[16]

Nichiren was pardoned in 1274, but on his return, he retired from public life. He believed that the Vulture Peak - the mythical mountain on which the Buddha is said to have revealed the teachings found in the Lotus Sutra – was Mount Fuji or Fujisan. During his last years he established a monastery nearby on Mount Minobo, where his remains are now enshrined.

Nichiren died in 1282. His followers agreed that guardianship of his tomb should circulate among his six senior disciples, but when it was his turn Niko (1253-1314) declared that he and his successors would retain this task. Nichiko (1246-1332), however, objected and founded his own Daisekiji temple at the foot of Mount Fuji.

The Nichiren tradition, in which Nichiren is considered to be a bodhisattva or a Buddha, has both continued to grow and to subdivide. It is, as already mentioned, second to the Pure Land schools in the number of its adherents. There are today some twenty Nichiren Buddhist movements and about twenty 'new religions', including Rissho Kose Kai and Soka Gakkai, which spring from this tradition. As with other forms of Japanese Buddhism, there are now Nichiren centres and temples in different parts of the world.

CHAPTER NOTES

1. *Encyclopaedia Britannica*, 8, 1060.
2. *Honen the Buddhist Saint: His Life and Teaching* Rev Harper Havelock Coates and Rev Ryugaku Ishizuka, Kyoto, Chionin, 1925, pp. 87-8.

3. *Honen: His Life and Teaching,* p. 104.
4. See chapter 37
5. In Chinese Shan-tao.
6. *Honen: His Life and Teaching,* pp. 186-187.
7. *Honen: His Life and Teaching,* p. 395.
8. *Honen: His Life and Teaching,* p. 602.
9. *Honen: His Life and Teaching,* p. 638.
10. *Honen: His Life and Teaching,* p. 544.
11. *Honen: His Life and Teaching,* p. 78.
12. *Honen: His Life and Teaching,* p. 612.
13. *Honen: His Life and Teaching,* p. 400.
14. *Honen: His Life and Teaching,* p. 399.
15. Quoted in the *Oxford Dictionary of Religion,* p. 696.
16. Quoted in the *Oxford Dictionary of Religion,* p. 697.

45

Eisai and Dogen

Dogen and to a lesser extent Eisai established the two most important schools of Zen Buddhism: Sōtō Zen and Rinzai Zen. Although Zen Buddhism has flourished in Japan and spread from there to the West, it began in China.

Ch'an – the Chinese name for Zen – dates back to Bodhidharma, who probably lived in the fifth century CE. Bodhidharma was the twenty-eighth successor in the line from Sakyamuni Buddha himself. He came from India to southern China, but his missionary efforts there met with little success. He, therefore, wandered to the north and is said to have crossed the Yang-tse River on a reed. He settled at Shao-lin monastery, which had been built by the emperor in 477CE. There he sat motionless, facing a wall, for nine years. Verses attributed to him, although they are probably later, give a good summary of Zen

A special transmission outside the scriptures;
Not established on words and letters;
By pointing directly into the mind;
It allows one to penetrate the nature of things to attain Buddha-nature.[1]

On one occasion Bodhidharma was summoned to a private audience by the Emperor Wu – according to a story that has become part of Zen tradition. Emperor Wu had converted from Confucianism to Buddhism, which had first come to China in 61 CE. As emperor, Wu forbade cruelty to animals and tried to abolish capital punishment. He also arranged for the translation of Sanskrit texts. When he met Bodhidharma, the Emperor told him what he had done and the number of temples he had built in honour of the Buddha. He then enquired what 'merit' he would have gained by all that he had done. 'None at all,' Bodhidharma replied. The Emperor then enquired what was the first principle of Buddhism. 'Vast emptiness and nothing holy,' was the answer. Irritated, the Emperor then asked, 'Who are you who thus replies to me?' 'I do not know,' said Bodhidharma. The apparent rudeness was to make the point that Zen saw no value in speculative discussion and rejected the idea of earning merit.

Subsequently, because Ch'an divided into 'five houses and seven schools,' its importance in China declined. It was in Japan that Zen was to gain new vitality and to become a spiritual movement, which is still growing. But that was not to be until five hundred years later when Eisai went to China in 1168.

Eisai has come to be regarded as the founding figure of Zen in Japan and after his death he was given the title of Senko Kokushi. Eisai (1141-1215), sometimes also known as Yōsai, began his career by studying Tendai Buddhism at Mt Hiei. When Eisai went to China in 1168, he studied Ch'an and brought back the Lotus Sutra, which is one of the most important Mahayana texts. In 1187 Eisai made a second trip to China. He had hoped to go to India, but this proved impossible. He, therefore, stayed in China studying Ch'an and he received a seal of recognition. On his return to Japan in 1191, he built what was to become the first Rinzai Zen temple. Despite opposition, he also founded the Kenninji monastery in Kyoto. His book 'The Dissemination of Zen for the defence of the Nation' (*kozen gokoku ron*) called for an independent school of Zen Buddhism. Although he did not himself establish such a school, Rinzai-shu, which we will describe below, was based on his teachings, although it only developed as a school some fifty years after his death. Eisai was also the teacher of his more famous pupil Dogen and for that reason, although his own lineage died out, he is often regarded as the founding figure of Zen Buddhism. Eisai also introduced the cultivation of tea to Japan and wrote the first book on the merits of tea drinking. It may be that tea was helpful as a stimulant to keep meditators awake. There is a legend that tea derived from the eyelids of Bodhidharma. It is said that Bodhidharma tore his eyelids off so as to keep himself awake during his nine year-long meditation. He threw them to the ground, where they began to grow as tea.

Dogen Kigen (1200-53) was born into an aristocratic family, which was declining in status because of the changing political situation. He entered the Tendai Shu monastery at Mt Hiei at the age of thirteen. There he was assailed by the 'Great Doubt.'

The sacred texts affirmed that all beings are endowed with Buddha-nature. If so, why, Dogen asked, was such strenuous training and effort necessary to attain enlightenment? He, therefore, left Mt Hiei monastery and went to study under Eisai. He then went to China for further study and became a disciple of Jü-ching (Rujing) (1163-1268). There he attained enlightenment by realising the truth of 'Mind and body dropped off; dropped off mind and body.'

In 1227 Dogen returned to Japan. His efforts to spread the teaching of Zen were thwarted by opposition, so he retreated to what is now the Fukui Prefecture, where in 1243, he founded Eihei-ji, 'the monastery of Eternal Peace' – although its relations with Soji-ji, the other leading Soto monastery, have been far from peaceful. It was at Eihei-ji that Dogen wrote his major work 'The Treasury of the Eye of True Dharma' or *Shobogenzo*. It consists of ninety-five chapters of which *Genjo-Koan* is specially revered. His sayings were also collected. In the nineteenth century he was given the titles Bussho-dento Kokushi and Joyo Daishi. Before his death, he wrote

> *Fifty-four years lighting up the sky.*
> *A quivering leap smashes a billion worlds.*
> *Hah!*
> *Entire body looks for nothing.*
> *Living, I plunge into Yellow Springs.*

Dogen's teaching centred on the practice of *zazen*, or sitting. *Zazen* requires the practitioner to stop thinking. 'If you think you will get something from practising *zazen*,' the Suzuki Roshi of the San Francisco Zen Centre has said, 'already you are involved in impure practice ... If enlightenment comes, it just comes. We should not attach to attainment.'[2] Dogen himself quoted a Chinese master, who was asked by a monk, 'What does one think about while sitting?' The master replied, 'One thinks about not-thinking.' How does one think about not-thinking?' the monk persisted. 'Without thinking was the answer.'

Little can be added in explanation of *zazen* to Dogen's own teaching:

'If you wish to attain enlightenment, begin at once to practise *zazen*. For this meditation you need a quiet room; food and drink should be taken in moderation. Free yourself from all attachment and bring to rest the ten thousand things. Think not of good or evil; judge not on right or wrong; maintain the flow of mind, will and consciousness; bring to an end all desire, all concepts and judgements!

To sit properly, first lay down a thick pillow and on top of this a second round one. One may sit either in the full or half cross-legged position. In the full position one places the right foot on the left thigh and the left foot on the right thigh. In the half position, only the left foot is placed on the right thigh. Robe and belt should be worn loosely, but in order. The right hand rests on the left foot, while the back of the left hand rests on the palm of the right. The two thumbs are placed in juxta-position. Let the body be kept upright, neither forward nor backward. Ears and shoulders, nose and navel, must be aligned to one another. The tongue is to be kept against the palate, lips and teeth firmly closed, while the eyes should always be left open.

Now that the bodily position is in order, regulate your breathing. If a wish arises take note of it and then dismiss it! If you practice in this way for a long time, you will forget all attachments and concentration will come naturally. That is the art of *zazen*. *Zazen* is the Dharma gate of great rest and joy'.[3]

Dogen believed that in this way, a person recovered the natural condition of humanity, which is 'great rest and joy.'

Dogen did not reject religious rituals or devotion to the Buddha. A proper sense of reverence and gratitude was, he said, necessary to develop the Buddha-mind. He also made clear that *zazen* is not an escape from the world, but leads to the recovery of an all-embracing compassion. He said:

'There is an easy way to become a Buddha: abstain from all evils, do not cling to birth and death, work in unwearying compassion for all sentient beings, respect those over you, neither detest nor desire, neither worry nor weep, that is what is called "Buddha". Do not search beyond it.'

The important new emphasis in Dogen's teaching is that whereas it had been said that all things *have* the Buddha nature, Dogen said that all things *are* the Buddha nature. Enlightenment is, therefore, a matter of realization rather than attainment.

The Zen training in the Rinzai School is more daring. This tradition was founded by the Chinese master Lin-chi I-hsüan (d.867) and introduced into Japan, as we have seen by Eisai, although it only developed into a school after his death. Lin-chi was known for his use of ear-splitting shouting (*ho* or in Japanese, *katsu*) and striking with a 'wake-up stick' (*kyosaku*), as a way of startling a disciple into sudden enlightenment. As Lin-chi said, 'The important thing in the study of Buddhism is to achieve a true understanding.' Personal experience is more important than imitating the Buddha or speculating about belief. It was Lin-chi who originated the oft-quoted saying, 'If you meet the Buddha, kill the Buddha; if you meet the patriarch, kill the patriarch.'

Zen Buddhist masters continued the practise of shouting and striking and also made use of the *koan* or puzzle, which Nan-yüan (d. 930) is said to have been the first to use, although their use is probably earlier. The *koan* is a saying that cannot be understood by conventional ways of thinking and is intended 'to break asunder the mind of ignorance and open the eye of truth.' It requires the disciple to search 'like a thirsty rat seeking for water, like a child thinking of its mother.' The most famous *koan*, perhaps, is 'What is the sound of one hand clapping?' The answer is to thrust one hand forward without a word. Other well-known *koans* are, 'What was your original face before your parents were born?' or 'Has a dog Buddha nature?' The answer to the latter question is *Mu*, a Japanese word which means 'emptiness' and is closely related to the concept of *sunyata*, which we have come across in the thinking of the important Buddhist philosopher Nagarjuna (c. 150-250 CE).[4]

The intention of these Zen practices is 'that the conceptual reasoning mind reaches its absolute dead-end and the "bottom" of the mind is broken through, so that the flow of thoughts suddenly stops, in a state of no-thought, and realization erupts from the depths. There is no longer anyone to ask or answer the question, but only a blissful, radiant emptiness beyond self and other words or concepts (*dhyana*).[5]

Zen practice in its various forms encourages mindfulness, which 'greatly deepens the power of concentration and the ability to stay with one's life situation.'[6] This concentration is an important feature in physical performances such as judo (*jujitsu*), archery and ceremonial swordsmanship (*kendo*). It also evident in the use of the brush in calligraphy and painting, by which the Japanese artist conveys a mysterious sense of stillness in Nature. It is to be found too in the spacing of movements in the tea ceremony and the ancient No drama, when 'it is not the action on the stage which conveys the deepest meaning, but rather the pauses and silences.'[7] The *haiku*, a highly concentrated verse of seventeen syllables based on simple everyday observation, suggests in a similar way that the truth of experience cannot be adequately expressed in words. A famous example is this *haiku* by the seventeenth century Zen poet, Basho, written about a humble weed:

> *When I look carefully*
> *I see the* nazuna *blooming*
> *Under the hedge.*[8]

Zen has permeated many aspects of Japanese culture and its influence has spread more widely in the West during the last one hundred years. It has been applied to subjects that would have puzzled both Eisai and Dogen, such as *Zen and the Art of Motorcycle Maintenance* and *Zen and Creative Management*. But the person who claims to have understood Zen has probably misunderstood it. For, as Bodhidarma said, the starting point for Zen training is 'to cease cherishing opinions.'

CHAPTER NOTES

1. An alternative translation of the fourth line is: 'It allows one to see into [the nature of one's own nature] and thus attain buddhahood. 'Not established on words or letters' I find rather pointed as the file in which I first typed this chapter was when I opened it empty!
2. Quoted by Nancy Wilson Ross, *Buddhism, A Way of Life and Thought*, London, Collins, 1981, p. 155.
3. From Dogen's *Fukanzazengi*. The quotations are from the excellent articles in the *Oxford Dictionary of World Religions*.
4. See chapter 31.
5. Peter Harvey, *An Introduction to Buddhism*, Cambridge, Cambridge University Press, 1990, p. 275.
6. Richard Bakes, Abbot of the Zen Centre in San Francisco, quoted by Nancy Wilson Ross, p. 159.
7. Nancy Wilson Ross, p. 163.
8. Nancy Wilson Ross, p. 146.

46

Ibn 'Arabi

Ibn 'Arabi, who came to be known as The 'Revivifier of Religion' (Muhyi-ad-Din), gave to Sufism a philosophical basis. Earlier Sufi writings were mostly practical guides for followers of the Path or attempted descriptions of the mystical states, which the author had experienced. Ibn 'Arabi formulated the doctrines of Islamic mysticism and made them explicit. Al-Ghazali, as we have seen,[1] held that the unmediated experience of the Divine, which God bestows on special friends, should not be described in writings, but Ibn 'Arabi swept such restrictions aside and set down his 'unveilings, witnessings, and tastings' for all to read.

Ibn 'Arabi[2] (or Ibn al'Arabi, as his name is sometimes spelt) was born in Murcia, which is in Andalusia in Southern Spain, in 1165. His father was employed by the ruler of the city. When Murcia was captured by the Almohad dynasty in 1172, he took his family to Seville, where again he was taken into government service. Ibn 'Arabi's father was, therefore, able to provide for his son a good education and initiation into courtly manners, which stood him in good stead when later in life he had dealings with the Sultan and with the ruler of Aleppo in Syria. Ibn 'Arabi said that he had no special religious education and spent much of his early years in childhood pastimes with his friends. He was employed for a time as a secretary by the governor of Seville. He married a woman named Maryam, who was from an influential family.

In his early teens, he was overcome by a spiritual call that quickly led to a vision of God. He said that everything that he subsequently said and wrote was 'the differentiation of the universal reality comprised by that look.'[3] During that early period, he had a number of visions of Jesus, whom he called his first guide on the path to God.

When Ibn 'Arabi's father told his friend Averroes,[4] one of the most famous Muslim philosophers, about the change in his son, Averroes asked to meet him. This was before 'his beard had sprouted.' Ibn 'Arabi's account of the meeting highlights the gulf that he perceived between the formal knowledge of a rational thinker and the divine 'unveiling' to the mystic or, in Ibn 'Arabi's own words, the 'gnostic.'

Averroes, Ibn 'Arabi said, 'asked me "What kind of solution have you found through illumination and Divine inspiration?" I answered him, "Yes and no. Between the 'yes' and the 'no' souls take their flight from their matter and their necks become detached from their bodies." Averroes became pale. I saw him trembling.' Later in a vision, Ibn 'Arabi saw Averroes deep in study, 'I said to myself, "His deliberation does not lead him where I am myself."'[5]

Following his life-changing vision, Ibn 'Arabi dedicated his life to the spiritual path, although it seems he did not enter formal Sufi training until he was nineteen.

It was not till he was thirty that he left Spain for the first time, travelling to Tunis. In 1200, he had a vision, which instructed him to travel to the East and in 1202 he performed the hajj at Mecca. Thereafter, he continued to travel extensively in Turkey, Syria and Egypt. In 1223, he settled in Damascus, where he taught, wrote and gathered a circle of disciples. It was there that he died in 1240.

Ibn 'Arabi was an amazingly prolific author. Some 850 works have been attributed to him, although not all are authentic and some are short treatises. Even so he wrote so much that scholars who specialize in studying his works are unlikely to have read them all.

There are three works that are especially well known. The most influential book, perhaps, was 'The Ringstones of the Wisdoms', *Fusus al-hikam*, on which over the years, his students have written more that one hundred commentaries. Based on verses of the Qur'an and traditions about the Prophet Muhammad, Ibn 'Arabi shows that each of the twenty-seven prophets from Adam to Muhammad disclosed in his own person and prophetic career the wisdom implied by one of the divine attributes. The 'Meccan Openings', *al-Futuhat al-makkiyya*, which he was 'commanded' to write when he first visited Mecca, covers an incredible range of subjects, including theology, cosmology, spiritual anthropology, law, as well as an explanation of the inner meaning of Islamic rituals and the letters of the Arabic alphabet. The work has over 560 chapters. His 'The Interpreter of Yearnings', *tarjuman al-ashwaq* is a short collection of love poetry and was the first of his works to be translated into English. The poems were inspired by Ibn 'Arabi's meeting in Mecca with a beautiful and devout daughter of a famous scholar. This girl was for Ibn 'Arabi the embodiment of Wisdom, just as Beatrice, who guided the poet through Paradise, was to be for Dante (1265-1321).

The basic Sufi teaching, according to Ibn 'Arabi, is that of the transcendent unity of Being. This means that although God is absolutely transcendent, the Universe is not entirely separated from God. The 'Universe is mysteriously plunged in God.' To treat anything in the world as independent of God is to be guilty of idolatry. The Sufi aim is union with the Divine, which comes as a result of the love created in human beings for Divine Beauty. Such union is gradually attained by a disciplined moral life and the purification of the heart. For Ibn 'Arabi this union, which can never be adequately described, is not, as some Sufis imply, a ceasing to be, but the realization that our existence from the beginning belonged to God. We are each a ray of the Divine. He wrote:

'It is like light that is projected through shadow, a shadow which is nothing but the screen (for light) and which is itself luminous by its transparency. Such also is the man who has realised the Truth; in him the form of the Truth is more directly manifested than in the case of others.'[6]

Ibn 'Arabi speaks of a Universal Man, the logos, who is a revelation of the Divine Names. For him, every prophet is an aspect of the Supreme Logos and is himself a 'word of God.' Ibn 'Arabi taught the unity of the inner contents of all religions. This was accepted by most Sufis, but it is expressed more clearly and fully by Ibn 'Arabi. His approach did not mean one can by-pass the practices and beliefs of particular religious traditions, but that by penetrating to the heart of the outward rites and practices one discovers a spiritual unity that transcends them. As Seyyed Hossein Nasr (b.1933) has said, 'Essentially the "burning of images" or the rejection of the external and formal aspects of religion, means that one must first possess these images and formal aspects. One cannot reject what one does not possess.'[5] Ibn 'Arabi spent much of his life praying the traditional prayers of a Muslim, repenting of his sins before God and invoking the Divine Name. He came to see that to have lived one religion fully is to have lived them all. It was at the heart of the revealed forms of religion that he found the formless and the Universal, as he wrote in these beautiful words:

My heart has become capable of every form: it is a pasture for gazelles and a convent for Christian monks,

And a temple for idols and the pilgrims' Ka'ba and the tables of the Torah, and the book of the Qur'an.

I follow the religion of Love: whatever way Love's camels take, that is my religion and my faith.[6]

These words are often quoted by those who sense the transcendent unity of religions and seek a fellowship of faiths. Ibn 'Arabi speaks today to those, of all religions, who follow the mystics' path. It would be a mistake, however, to limit Ibn 'Arabi's influence to his mystical writings. Probably many Sufis, who admired him but who were not scholars, read little of these works, although his influence can be seen in popular Persian, Turkish and Urdu poetry. Moreover, the great majority of his writings are full of rational and convincing arguments and reflect his deep learning. This is why Muslim scholars, even if they did not agree with him, could not ignore him. Modernizers in the late nineteenth and early twentieth centuries were critical of him - as they were of Sufism – but many Muslims who reject 'fundamentalism' are now looking with renewed interest to the teachings of the 'Most Grand Sheikh.'

CHAPTER NOTES

1. See chapter 39
2. Much of the information is based upon William C Chittick, *Ibn 'Arabi, Heir to the Prophet,* Oxford, Oneworld, 2005.
2. Ibn 'Arabi, *al-Futuhat al-makkiyya,* 4 volumes, Cairo, 1911, II, 548, 14.
3. *al-Futuhat al-makkiyya* , I, pp 153-4.
4. See chapter 42
5. Quoted by Seyyed Hossein Nasr in *Three Muslim Sages,* Cambridge, Mass, Harvard University Press 1964, p.115. Seyyed Hossein Nasr is the subject of chapter 99.
6. Seyyed Hossein Nasr, p. 117.
7. *Tarjuman al-ashwaq,* translated by R A Nicholson. 1911, London; Wheaton, Ill: Theosophical Publishing House, 1978.

47

Francis of Assisi and Clare

St Francis of Assisi is probably the best loved Christian saint. More than anyone, he tried to imitate the life of Jesus and carry out the work of Jesus in the spirit of his Master. He witnessed that there is nothing in the world which should distract a person from that Love which is God. He is known for the saying *'ubi caritas, ibi Deus est'* – 'where love is, there is God.' Although his name is often linked with St Clare, who founded the Poor Clares, he is joined with St Catherine of Siena as the principal patron saint of Italy. He founded the Franciscan Order of Friars, which is still active in many parts of the world.

There are innumerable lives of St Francis. Indeed there are so many that Friars of the French Canadian Province are required to read a new one every year.[1] It is difficult to be sure from the various accounts of his life what is fact and what is pious legend.[2] The various stories, however, paint a picture of a man of great simplicity, holiness and compassion. His own a writings are few: two versions of the Rule, his Testament, dictated during his last illness, some letters and some songs of praise. Some other writings have been lost.[3]

Francis was born in 1181/2 at Assisi, a hill town in Umbria, which has retained its mediaeval character. His father, who was a cloth merchant, was away at the time. His mother had him baptized Giovanni, but his father, on his return, changed his name to Francesco. Francis went to a local school, where he learned to read and write in Latin. He also picked up some French. He seems to have been a lively youth and a leader of the young men of the town.

In 1202 Francis was taken prisoner in a war between Assisi and Perugia and held captive for almost a year. On his return he fell seriously ill. When he recovered, he tried to join the papal forces, but in a dream he was told to return to Assisi and await the call to a new kind of knighthood. He now started to spend a lot of time alone in prayer. Several special experiences then helped to shape the pattern of his future life. He had a vision of Christ in a grotto near Assisi. In Rome, he joined the beggars outside St Peter's basilica. On another occasion he gave money to a man with leprosy – an illness for which he had a great repugnance - and even kissed the man.

Then, when he was praying in the then ruined chapel of St Damiano, a little way down the hill on which Assisi is built, he heard the command, 'Go, Francis, and repair my house, which, as you see, is almost in ruins.' With the literalism which was characteristic of him, Francis hurried home, collected much of the cloth from his father's shop, and rode to the nearby town of Foligno, where he sold the cloth and his horse. His father summoned him before the civil authorities and then brought accusations against his son before the bishop. Before proceedings started, Francis 'without a word, stripped off his clothes even down to his breeches' and gave them back to his father, saying, 'Until now, I have called you my father on earth. But henceforth I can truly say: Our Father who art in heaven.' Francis was left standing just in his hair-shirt, until the bewildered bishop gave him a cloak. Francis went off to the woods above Assisi and then attended to the repair of the church of St Damiano.

Francis then repaired the chapel of St Mary of the Angels, Porziuncula, on the plain below Assisi. It was there in 1986 that the Day of Prayer for World Peace, which was convened by Pope John Paul II and in which leaders of all world religions took part, began.

On February 24th, 1208, the feast of St Mathias, Francis heard and took literally these words from the Gospel: 'Take no gold, nor silver, nor money in your belts, no bag for your journey, nor two tunics. Nor sandals, nor a staff; for the labourer deserves his food.'4 Francis, a layman, now set out as a wandering preacher and was soon joined by some followers. He wrote a simple rule for them, which had as its aim, 'to follow the teachings of Our Lord Jesus Christ and to walk in his footsteps.' They then went to Rome to ask the approval of Pope Innocent III, which after some hesitation, was given. This was on April 16th, 1209, which is recognised as the date of the official founding of the Franciscan Order. These wandering and begging preachers were soon known as 'friars' – a word related to the old French *frère* or brother. The Order expanded quickly and within ten years it attracted some 5,000 members. In about 1221, Francis also started a Third Order for lay people who could not leave their families.

Francis had a strong desire to visit the Holy Land, but his first attempt to do so was frustrated by being shipwrecked. In 1219, however, he did reach Egypt, where the Crusaders were besieging Damietta. Francis, who was appalled by the bloodshed, went on foot to the Saracen camp where he was received by the Sultan. But neither the Christians nor the Muslims listened to his plea for peace.

Francis had to hurry back because of disturbances in the fast growing Order. He now appointed a vicar to be in charge of the Order and, after considerable discussion a new and longer rule was drawn up and approved by Pope Honorius III in 1223.

In the summer of 1224, Francis withdrew to the mountain retreat of Alvernia, which is close to Assisi, to pray. There on September 14th, the feast of the Exaltation of the Cross, he received the stigmata – the same marks as those inflicted on Jesus when he was nailed to the cross. During his lifetime, Francis was careful to hide the stigmata, which became known after he died. His death occurred two years later, when, after a time of constant pain and growing blindness, he welcomed 'Sister Death.' As Brother Angelo and Brother Leo intoned the canticle of Brother Sun, Francis stopped them and added this verse,

Be praised, my Lord, for our Sister Bodily Death,
From whom no living man can escape.
Woe to those who die in mortal sin.
Blessed are they, whom she shall find in your most holy will,
For the second death shall not harm them.

As he was dying, he said, 'Let us begin, brothers, to serve the Lord for up to now we have made little or no progress.' On his last day, the Passion of St John was read to him. He died reciting Psalm 141, which includes the verse, 'Thou art my hope, my portion in the land of the living.' He was, at first, buried at the Church of San Giorgio, but four years later his body was moved to the crypt of the great Basilica di San Francesco, famous for its paintings by Giotto, which was severely damaged by an earthquake in 1997, but which has now been restored.

A few years before his death, Francis had founded a second order for women led by a local lady, known as St Clare (c.1194-1253). She and her companions, who became known as Poor Clares, were housed at the church of St Damiano. There, in the peaceful garden, Francis wrote his

'Canticle of Brother Sun' or 'Canticle of the Creatures.' Life there was very austere. The Poor Clares slept on humble straw mats. Clare was devoted to her nuns. She never left the convent at Assisi. Celano in his *Life of Clare,* wrote, 'In this little place, for the love of Christ, the Virgin Clare spent her life… In this hermitage for forty two years she broke the alabaster of her body with discipline, so that the Church could be filled with the fragrance of her scent.'[5] For some twenty-seven years she suffered from various illnesses and was often bed-ridden. It was a moving experience to visit the room in which she was so often confined. Yet despite her illnesses, Clare defended Assisi from attackers. In September 1240, she confronted the troops of Frederick II of Germany 'who came here and entered the cloister of the virgins… With a fearless heart she ordered to be brought, infirm as she was, to the door facing the enemies, preceded by the small silver box in which the body of the Holy of Holies was devotionally reserved. The troops, struck by the force of her prayer, very quickly left the place of San Damiano.'[6] Two years later the scene was repeated when imperial soldiers threatened the monastery and the city. This liberating event is still celebrated every year in Assisi on June 22nd.

At Christmas 1252, Clare, although in pain, remained on her mat sharing in ecstasy in the liturgy at the Basilica of St Francis. During the following year, she was visited by Pope Innocent IV. He gave her a document confirming the community's rule. Two days later on August 11th, 1253, after twenty eight years of illness, she died while singing, 'Go safely in peace my blessed soul… and you Lord be blessed for you created me.'[7]

St Francis is revered, primarily, because he embodied the simplicity and love of Jesus Christ. He dedicated his life of poverty to prayer, preaching the Gospel, caring for the poor and sick and working for peace. This is best expressed in the well-known prayer, somewhat doubtfully attributed to him:

Lord make me an instrument of your peace;
Where there is hatred, let me sow love,
Where there is injury, pardon;
Where there is doubt, faith;
Where there is despair, hope;

Where there is darkness, light;
Where there is sadness, joy.
O divine Master, grant that I may not so much seek
To be consoled, as to console,
To be loved, as to love;
For it is in giving that we receive;
It is in pardoning that we are pardoned;
It is in dying that we are born to eternal life..

Francis' love of nature and of birds and animals is famous. There are stories of him preaching to the birds and taming a wolf, who was threatening the inhabitants of Gubbio. He spoke of all creatures as his brothers and sisters, as, for example, in his beautiful 'Canticle of the Creatures,' which begins:

Praise be to my Lord God for all his creatures,
especially for our brother the sun,
who brings us day and brings us the light;
fair is he and shines with a very great splendour;
O Lord, he signifies you to us.

The twentieth century saw a great revival of interest in St Francis. This, however, it has been said, resulted in caricatures of a sentimental nature-lover or a hippy "drop-out" from society. They disguise his strength of character and determination. They also neglect his all-pervasive love of God and his identification with Christ's sufferings, which were central to everything that he did.

CHAPTER NOTES
1. Omer Englebert, *Saint Francis of Assisi,* Chicago, Franciscan Herald Press, 1965, p.vii.
2. For a summary discussion of the sources, see the entry on 'Francis of Assisi' by Regis J Armstrong in *The Oxford Companion to Christian Thought,* pp. 249-50.
3. Most of the material is collected in *St Francis of Assisi: Writings and Early Biographies,* Ed Marion A Habig, London, SPCK, 1972.
4. Matthew 10,9-10.

5. Celano, *Life of St Clare*, 10. The quotations are from the Guide for Visitors.
6. Celano, *Life of St Clare*, 21.
7. Sister Filippa, *Canonization Process of St Clair*, 8.

48

Aquinas

St Thomas Aquinas, known as the 'angelic doctor' was the greatest Christian philosopher of the Middle Ages and one of the greatest of all Catholic teachers. His writings shaped the doctrines of the Catholic Church and are still highly influential. Yet although he is spoken of as a philosopher, he would probably have thought of himself as a monk. Recently more attention has been paid to him as a spiritual master, who was a theologian and a contemplative as well as a philosopher.[1]

Thomas was born in 1224 or early in 1225 at the family castle at Roccasecca in southern Italy, not far from the great monastery of Monte Cassino, which is on the road between Rome and Naples. His father was Count of Aquino (hence Thomas' name Aquinas). When he was about six years old, Thomas, accompanied by a nurse, was sent to be educated at the monastery of Monte Cassino, where his uncle was abbot. His parents may have hoped that Thomas, their youngest son, would himself one day be abbot. In 1239 life suddenly changed for Thomas. Because the political situation was unsettled, Thomas returned to his family. He was then sent to the University of Naples, which had recently been founded by the Emperor. Great interest was being taken there in the Greek and Arabic scientific and philosophical works, which were just being translated by Michael Scot (d.1235). Cultural life in Sicily and Southern Italy at the time was vibrant and Aristotelian science, Arabic astronomy, and Greek medicine were all flourishing in Palermo, Salerno and Naples. In Paris, by contrast, the study of Aristotle's writings was officially still forbidden, but the repetition of the interdictions suggests that there was already considerable interest in them there as well in the writings of Averroes.

At Naples, Thomas got to know the Dominicans - as members of the 'Order of Friars Preachers' were already known – and decided to join them. The Dominican Order had been founded by St Dominic (1170-1221) in 1215. Like the Franciscans, the Dominicans lived a simple life, wandering and begging for alms, but their particular emphasis was on study and preaching, which may have attracted Thomas. By his decision, Thomas was breaking away both from the feudal world into which he was born and the settled monastic life of prayer, study and manual work, in which he had been schooled. Like St Francis himself, Thomas also wished to follow a life of poverty and simplicity. His family were horrified. As he set out to study at the famous University of Paris, he was 'kidnapped' by his parents and confined at home. They even, it seems, hoped a prostitute could tempt him to stray from the vow of celibacy. Thomas refused to give in to his family's demands and, after a year, they set him free to go to Paris, where he studied under Albertus Magnus (c.1206 – 1280), an outstanding scholar and theologian who came from Germany. It is noteworthy how international the intellectual world of Europe was at that time. Scholars, of course, were all fluent in Latin.

It was an exciting time to be in Paris, but a challenging one for a committed member of a religious order. Under the influence of the writings of Aristotle and the Muslim scholar Averroes, some people were emphasising the power of reason at the expense of faith. The reaction of the Church, as already mentioned, was, unsuccessfully, to try to ban this new learning. The great achievement of Thomas Aquinas, like his teacher Albertus Magnus, who was not afraid of the new learning, was to show that faith was not irreconcilable with reason. Faith was for Thomas the starting point for theology and indeed the very reason for theology or 'sacred doctrine.' Thomas would have seen his preaching and his many answers to the questions of those who consulted him as just as much theological work as the exposition of doctrines.

Not only was the Church being confronted by this rationalist criticism, the social framework was also changing. The unchanging agrarian society with its feudal structures, now had to compete with a growing urban society, where production was organised in trade guilds, whose members had a great sense of community. A market economy was developing and with it people became more interested in this world than the next.

After some three years in Paris, Thomas went to Cologne with his teacher Albertus, who was taking charge of a new faculty established by the Dominicans at the convent in Cologne. In 1252 Thomas returned to Paris and after gaining his masters degree started teaching in the Dominican schools, which were incorporated into the university. When

Thomas was first in Paris he had been known as 'the dumb ox.' This partly referred to his large size but also to the fact that he said very little. But now his intellectual powers were recognised. In 1259, he was appointed theological adviser and lecturer to the Papal Curia in Rome. After a time in Italy and elsewhere, he was sent back to Paris in 1268.

There, a sharp debate had been stirred up by scholars, such as Siger of Brabant (c.1235-84), who, influenced by the writings of Averroes, argued that faith and reason were contradictory. Thomas said that such a view not only compromised orthodoxy but also undermined a Christian interpretation of Aristotle. In 1270 the radical views of the followers of Averroes were condemned by Church authorities - although his followers may have misinterpreted him. Even the attempt by Thomas - which we shall consider more carefully later - to establish the autonomy of reason under faith, was discredited.

In 1272, Thomas returned to Italy to establish a Dominican house at the University of Naples. There was, however, no escape from theological controversy. A Franciscan friar Bonaventure, who had been a friend of Thomas in Paris, criticised those, including Thomas, who separated theology from philosophy. Thomas was known, however, for his courtesy and humility even during heated debates.

Late in 1273, Thomas underwent an astonishing transformation, after which he wrote nothing more. 'I cannot do any more,' he said to his companion, 'Everything I have written seems to me as straw in comparison with what I have seen.'[2] He was profoundly changed and lacked the robust energy, which was characteristic of him. Previously, he had always got up to pray long before anyone else was awake. Various explanations of what happened to Thomas have been advanced. It has been suggested that he suffered a serious cerebral stroke or that he was exhausted by over-work. An alternative view is that a mystical experience of God, who transcends all human language, made him aware of the inadequacy of his monumental theological work. Maybe Thomas intended to show that theology is never a closed system but points beyond itself to a Mystery that defies description – the grain of treasured experience to which the chaff of words can only point.

In 1274, Thomas was personally summoned by Pope Gregory X to the second Council of Lyons, which was an attempt to heal the split between the Latin churches in the West and the Greek Byzantine churches in the East. On the way, he was taken ill and stopped at the Cistercian Abbey of Fossanova, where he died on March 7th, 1274. Ironically, Thomas had said that no one could be an accomplished metaphysician before the age 50, but he himself died at the age of 49.

Three years later, in 1277, the masters of Paris, the highest theological authority in the Church, included twelve of Thomas' propositions in the 229 propositions that they condemned. Nonetheless, Thomas, who had lived a simple and austere life, was canonized a saint in 1323 and named a doctor of the Church in 1567. During the modernist controversies at the end of the nineteenth century, he was proclaimed the protagonist of orthodoxy.

Thomas' major writings included commentaries on Aristotle and the Bible, discussions on particular topics such as Truth or Evil and general treatises on doctrine. The latter, such as the *Summa Contra Gentiles* (Against the Gentiles) and the *Summa Theologiae* were in the form of questions and then arguments for and against.

The *Summa Theologiae* was intended as a moral theology, concerned with the living out of the Christian life understood as the human pilgrimage of return to God and eternal bliss. The Summa contains three parts and a supplement. The First part deals with the doctrine of God, the Trinity, the Angels and Man. In part two, which itself has two parts, he first talks of Man's Last End and of human passions and sin and then discusses human virtues. In the third part, Thomas writes about the Incarnation, the life of Christ and Baptism and Communion. Thomas describes Jesus as a wandering teacher, whose mission was to serve truth in a life of poverty, prayer and preaching. The Supplement deals with further sacraments and with the Resurrection.

Thomas also wrote a number of beautiful hymns, especially about the Mass, some of which are still sung today, as for example:

Thee we adore, O hidden Saviour, thee
Who in thy Sacrament art pleased to be;
Both flesh and spirit in they presence fail,
Yet here they Presence we devoutly hail.

O blest Memorial of our dying Lord,

Who living Bread to men doth here afford!
O may our souls for ever feed on thee,
And thou, O Christ, for ever precious be.[3]

Or

Of the glorious Body telling,
O my tongue, its mysteries sing,
And the Blood, all price excelling
Which the world's eternal King,
In a noble womb once dwelling,
Shed for this world's ransoming.

Thomas' essential contribution was to show that faith and reason were not contradictory. For Aquinas, the mystery of God is expressed and incarnate in human language; it (faith) is thus able to become the object of an active, conscious and organized elaboration in which the rules and structures of rational activity are integrated in the light of faith. Theology is knowledge that is rationally derived from propositions that are accepted as certain because they are revealed by God. In this Aristotelian sense it is a 'science.' The theologian accepts authority and faith as his starting point and then proceeds to conclusions using reason. The philosopher relies solely on the natural light of reason. Thomas' position required him to accept the fundamental consistency of the laws that govern the natural world. He, therefore, rejects a view of the natural world as an arena of God's direct action. For example, Aquinas does not agree with the view that God directly sends a flood or a plague. The natural world has a certain autonomy. This recognition was a necessary first step to the scientific study of the natural world, which has come to dominate Western society.

In the same way, political life also was seen to have its own autonomy. This meant that independent study of how society works and the art of statesmanship was now allowed, whereas in the past it had been enough only to quote maxims from the Bible about what was required of a just king. Thus Thomas was laying the foundations for modern Western society, which recognises a distinction between the sacred and the secular. Instead of consulting the Bible for information about the natural world or the organization of society, people should use their own power of reasoning. Thomas, in his own day, had his critics. Subsequently, some of the Reformation thinkers were more suspicious than he was of the power of reason. Still today his approach would be rejected by some so-called fundamentalists and rationalists, of course, would not accept his reference to faith.

Aquinas held that the existence of God could be demonstrated on the basis of the knowledge which we obtain through our senses and our reason, although he rejected Anselm's ontological argument that the existence of God is self-evident.[4] He also held that reason could show that God is one, good and infinite and that everything that exists has been created by God and is sustained by God. Human beings by the innate light of conscience, despite their sinfulness, could cultivate the four natural virtues of prudence, justice, courage and self-control. Only through God's grace, however, can a person receive the Christian virtues of faith, hope and love.

Believing that Jesus Christ was born of the Virgin Mary, Aquinas did not, however, accept the view, then being taught by the Franciscans, that Mary herself was conceived without the taint of original sin – a doctrine officially endorsed by the Roman Catholic Church in the nineteenth century. On the Atonement he held together the views of Anselm and Abelard, holding that Christ both made satisfaction for human sin and by his sacrificial love moved people to love him in return.[5] God's grace, Aquinas taught came to men and women through the sacraments and, as we have seen from his hymns, he had a deep devotion to Christ's presence in the Mass or communion service.

Aquinas rejected a sharp dualism of mind and body. He held that the criteria of human goodness are discovered by the study of human nature, which is essentially bodily and social. Indeed, despite his years of study and writing, he never forgot that a good life is more important that great knowledge. 'Clearly', he wrote, 'all cannot pass their time in laborious studies. So Christ gave us a law that in its brevity is accessible to all, and that no one thus has the right to ignore: such is the law of divine love, that "brief word" that the Lord declares to the universe.' Charity, which reflects the presence of the Holy Spirit, Thomas said, 'puts perfect joy within us... It also gives perfect peace.'[6]

The first biographer of Thomas, William of Tocco, who had known

Thomas well, said of him:

> 'Brother Thomas raised new problems in his teaching, invented a new method, used new systems of proof. To hear him teach a new doctrine, with new arguments, one could not doubt that God, by irradiation of this new light and by the novelty of this inspiration, gave him the power to teach, by the spoken and written word, new opinions and new knowledge.'[7]

Thomas made a profound contribution to the development of Christian thought and indeed to the development of the intellectual life of Europe. He was above all a man of prayer. 'Every time that he wished to study, to undertake a dispute, to teach, to write or dictate, he first withdrew into secret prayer and prayed pouring out tears, in order to obtain an understanding of the divine mysteries.'[8]

CHAPTER NOTES

1. Jean-Pierre Torrell gives the subtitle 'Spiritual Master' to the second volume of his study, *St Thomas Aquinas*, translated by Robert Royal, Washington DC, The Catholic University of America Press, 2003.
2. Quoted by Jean-Pierre Torrell in *St Thomas Aquinas*, p. 289.
3. *English Hymnal*, 331 Translated by Bishop J R Woodford.
4. See above chapter 40
5. See above chapter 40.
6. From the Hymn to Charity, quoted by Jean-Pierre Torrell, Vol 2, pp. 363-4. The 'brief word,' refers to Romans 9,28, according to the Vulgate.
7. Quoted from the *Encyclopaedia Britannica*, vol 18, p. 348.
8. Quoted by Jean-Pierre Torell, vol 1, p. 284.

49

Mother Julian of Norwich

Mother Julian of Norwich is often called the greatest of the holy people who are known as the 'Middle English mystics.' She emphasised the Love of God and had an optimistic view of humanity's ultimate destiny. There are still today Julian groups, who follow her pattern of contemplation, and she is highly regarded by Christian feminists.

Mediaeval spirituality in England focussed on the humanity of Jesus and the sufferings, which he endured during his passion and on the cross. It emphasised the wickedness of human sin and the terrors of punishment that would ensue. The importance of both penance and pilgrimage, which was vividly described in Geoffrey Chaucer's (c.1343-1400) *Canterbury Tales*, was stressed.

To set Mother Julian in context, it is helpful to know a little about the other four well-known Middle English mystics. There were, of course, also at the time several important mystics in Europe, such as the anonymous author of the *Theologia Germanica* and Thomas à Kempis (c.1380-1471), to whom the *Imitation of Christ* is attributed. The earliest of the English mystics was Richard Rolle (c.1300-49), known for his *The Fire of Love* and *The Mending of Life*. After a period of purgation, he said a person experiences 'the opening of the heavenly door'[1] which creates a deep longing for God. Eventually this leads on to mystical union with God. Of the author of *The Cloud of Unknowing*, which dates from about 1380, nothing is known. It is suggested that he may have been a member of the austere Carthusian order, where the rule of silence is observed and whose members spend most of their time alone. *The Cloud of Unknowing* emphasizes contemplation of God alone – beyond all images and sensual feeling.

Not much more is known about Walter Hilton, other than that he died in March 1395/6 as an Augustinian canon at the priory of Thurgarton – the Augustinian order also emphasized contemplation. The other woman among the Middle English mystics was Margery Kempe (c.1373-c.1440), who lived in the world. We know quite a lot about her because her autobiography, called the *Book*, was discovered in 1934. Margery was the daughter of a prominent citizen in King's

Lynn in Norfolk. She married and bore fourteen children, but eventually persuaded her husband to agree to her adopting a celibate way of life. This gave her more freedom, which she used to go on pilgrimage to the Holy Land, where she found herself crying uncontrollably at any mention of the passion of Jesus. Her unusual behaviour led on occasion to her arrest for heresy, but she was never convicted of this. Sometimes she has been compared unfavourably with Mother Julian, because of her hysteria and supposed hypocrisy, but today there is greater appreciation of her special calling. Margery Kempe mentioned that she went to Norwich to speak with 'Dame Jelyan,' writing, 'Much was the holy dalliance that the anchoress and this creature had by communing in the love of our Lord Jesus Christ on the many days they were together.'[2]

Of Julian of Norwich, who was probably born in November 1342, very little is known other than from her writings. The only certain date is that of her 'shewings' on May 8th, 1373. Even her name is uncertain, the name 'Julian' coming from the Church of St Julian in Norwich, which at the time was one of England's most prosperous towns. Two fragments of stone from where her cell stood are still to be seen in the church. Julian is mentioned in several wills - one bequest in 1416 was to Julian 'recluz' at Norwich. She probably was eighty or more when she died.

Julian differed from the other Middle English mystics in that she was an anchoress and a visionary. An anchoress is a hermit who lives in a walled up cell. Hers was attached to the Church dedicated to St Julian the Hospitaler, who was the hero of a romance, in which he accidentally killed his own parents when out hunting.[3] He and his wife then did penance by going to live by a ford and helping travellers across the river. One day they gave succour to a man almost dead from cold, who before he departed in glory told them that Jesus Christ had accepted their penance.

Julian's cell would have had a window opening on the church and another on the street, from which she gave counsel to the many people who came to her for spiritual guidance. We know the names of five anchoresses who subsequently occupied the cell, which was in use up to the Reformation in the sixteenth century.

Julian was also a visionary, who is a person who describes their spiritual experience as perceived directly by sight, sound and even touch and smell. They speak of actually seeing the person of their vision. The experience, which has more often been given to women mystics, is accompanied by a deep-felt conviction of its truthfulness for them and for others. The flowering of visionary literature took place between the twelfth to the fourteenth century in England and on the Continent. The visions may be of God or of Jesus on the Cross or of heaven or hell. There are three main types of vision. Some, where love is aroused and deepened, inspire new devotion; others provide teaching about a doctrine and thirdly some are visions of prophecy revealing God's love or hope for the world.

How is it to be known whether a vision is authentic? One test is whether the person who receives it is known to be living a devout and holy life. Sometimes the visions are accompanied by healing. Thirdly, their message should not contradict scripture or the teaching of scripture. The message they receive, may of course, be critical of Church teaching and practice. For example, Catherine of Siena (1347-80), as a result of her vision, was critical of abuses in the church and told Pope Gregory XI that he should return to live in Rome.[4]

Julian experienced her visions when she was thirty. She was suffering from a severe illness and believed that she was on her deathbed. A priest came and held a crucifix before her eyes. To her distress, her mother, who thought that she had died, closed her eyes 'and this greatly increased my sorrow, for despite all my pains, I did not want to be hindered from seeing (Christ) because of my love for him.'[5] Lying there, Julian had a series of intense visions of events in the Passion of Christ and on the next day a final vision. The visions ended by the time she overcame her illness on May 13, 1373. She recorded these visions soon after having them in her *Shewings* or *Revelations of the Divine Love*. Later, after a further revelation and twenty years reflection, she wrote a longer version in which her original experience of God was set in a Trinitarian theological context. Her *Shewings* is believed to be the first book written by a woman in the English language. In time, Julian became well known throughout England as a spiritual authority.

At the heart of the revelation which she received was an overwhelming sense of the love of God. She wrote,

'And from the time that [the vision] was shown, I desired often to know what our Lord's meaning was. And fifteen years and more afterward I was answered in my spiritual understanding, thus: "Would you know your Lord's meaning in this thing? Know it well, love was his meaning. Who showed it to you? Love. What did he show you? Love. Why did he show it? For love. Keep yourself therein and you shall know and understand more in the same. But you shall never know nor understand any other thing, forever."

Thus I was taught that love was our Lord's meaning. And I saw quite clearly in this and in all, that before God made us, he loved us, which love was never slaked nor ever shall be. And in this love he has done all his work, and in this love he has made all things profitable to us. And in this love our life is everlasting. In our creation we had a beginning. But the love wherein he made us was in him with no beginning. And all this shall be seen in God without end.[6]

'Love was his meaning,' she wrote. God's love reaches to our deepest need. This may not seem so startling to Christians today, when God's generous love is emphasised, but at the time – to judge by the medieval windows and paintings – the Last Judgement, with Christ as Judge, was a more prominent theme. Sermons were more often about the wrath of God rather than Divine mercy.

Julian, however, stressed the welcome God offered to the penitent. She wrote,

'Our courteous Lord shows himself to the soul, welcoming it as a friend as if it had been in pain and in prison, saying, "My dear darling, I am glad you have come to me in all your woe. I have always been with you and now you see me loving and we are one in bliss."'[7]

She also recognised that although 'peace and love are always alive in us, we are not always alive to peace and love.'[8] 'If God forgives us', she asked, 'who are we to withold forgiveness from ourselves?'[9] Her vision had shown her that 'God attached no more blame to us than if we were as pure as angels in heaven', but this seemed in conflict with the

Church's emphasis on sin.[10] She saw suffering as a means by which God could draw a person closer to Himself.

Julian was concerned that sometimes when we are faced with a difficult moral decision; it seems that no matter which way we decide, we will have acted from motives that are less than completely pure, so that neither decision is defensible. She finally wrote: 'It is enough to be sure of the deed. Our courteous Lord will deign to redeem the motive.'

Julian's deep conviction of God's love also gave her hope for the future of both society and the individual. Although she lived in a troubled time, which was marked by the terrible plague known as the Black Death and the turmoil of the Peasants' Revolt (1381), Julian's theology was optimistic. Whereas many preachers saw the Black Death and the Peasants' Revolt as a sign that God was punishing the wicked, Julian spoke of God's love in terms of joy and compassion as opposed to law and duty. She believed that God loved and would save everyone. Her words 'All shall be well, and all shall be well, and all manner of things shall be well' are famous. T. S. Eliot quoted them in *Little Gidding*, the fourth of his *Four Quartets*, and they also served as the title of the first novel by American writer Tod Wodicka. Its protagonist Burt Hecker may not be an anchorite, but he practises his own retreat as a medieval re-enactor, donning a tunic, humming plain-chant and even brewing his own potent mead. The song 'Julian of Norwich' by Sydney Carter (1915-2004) which begins 'Loud are the bells of Norwich' has the refrain.

All shall be well, I'm telling you
Let winter come and go
All shall be well again, I know.[11]

Her confidence in God's love was such that she seems to have believed that in the end God would reconcile all souls to himself - a doctrine known as 'universalism.' Speaking of her visions of heaven and hell, she said, 'To me was shown no harder hell than sin.'

The early Church Father Origen (c.185-c.254) was also a universalist, but after his death such teaching was condemned as heretical. Even though Julian's views were not typical, local authorities did not challenge either her theology or her authority to make such religious claims because of her status as an anchoress.

As part of her emphasis on God as compassionate and loving, she wrote of the Trinity in domestic terms. She compared Jesus to a mother who is wise, loving, and merciful. She said God is 'really our Mother as he is Father.' She saw God's motherhood in 'the foundation of our nature's creation.' Moreover Jesus' incarnation began in 'the taking of our nature, where the motherhood of grace begins.' She spoke metaphorically of Jesus in connection with conception, nursing, labour, and upbringing. She has, therefore, been heralded as a pioneer of Christian feminism, although Anselm (1033-1109) also had spoken of God as a mother.

Appreciation of Mother Julian of Norwich is still growing. There is a modern statue of her on the facade of the Anglican Cathedral at Norwich. Many visitors make their way to her shrine in Norwich.

In one of her visions Julian describes seeing God holding a tiny thing in his hand, like a small brown nut, which seemed so fragile and insignificant that she wondered why it did not crumble before her eyes. She understood that the thing was the entire created universe, which is as nothing compared to its Creator, and she was told, 'God made it, God loves it, God keeps it.' Astronauts from space have also said that Planet Earth is fragile and precious.

CHAPTER NOTES

1. Revelation 4,1.
2. *The Book of Margery Kempe,* ed Meech and Lane, Oxford, Oxford University Press, vol I, p. 42.
3. In one version, he did not kill them but was warned by a hart that he would kill them if he went on hunting.
4. Much of the material about visionaries is based on the article by David Perrin in *The New SCM Dictionary of Christian Spirituality,* p. 637-8.
5. Quoted in Robert Llewelyn, *With Pity Not With Blame,* London, Darton, Longman and Todd, 1982, p. 5. There are several editions of her *Shewings* for example by Edmund Colledge, OSA and James Walsh, London, SPCK, 1979.
6. Translated by Liz Broadwell, www.missionstclare.com
7. *Revelations of Divine Love,* chapter 40, quoted by Robert Llewelyn,

Love Bade me Welcome, London, Darton Longmann and Todd, p. 14.

8. Llewelyn, p. 20.
9. Llewelyn, p. 25
10. Llewelyn, p. 22.
11. Published by Stainer and Bell, London.

50

Tsong Khapa Losang Drakpa

The forced exile of the Dalai Lama and of many Tibetan monks has made Tibetan Buddhism better known than ever before. It has also given added importance to Tsong Khapa Losang Drakpa (1357 – 1419), who founded the dominant *Gelukpa* school of Tibetan Buddhism.

Tibetan Buddhism or *Vajrayana* is a distinct form of Buddhism, although closely related to Mahayana (Great Vehicle) Buddhism, which is the form of Buddhism prominent in China, Japan, Korea and Vietnam. *Vajrayana* Buddhism agrees doctrinally with most Mahayana teachings. It emphasises the gradual path to Buddhahood or emptiness and the ideal of the bodhisattva, who sacrifices himself in the service of others. There is also a use of rich psychological symbolism and of visualization in meditation.

To understand the significance of Tsong Khapa, it is necessary first to know something about the history of Tibetan Buddhism. The Bön Religion, a diversified shamanist tradition, is indigenous to Tibet. Buddhism seems to have first come to Tibet during the reign of King Songsten Gampo (c.609–50), who founded the Jokhang temple. In the following century, King Thi-Song Detsan (740-786) invited the highly educated monk Santirakshita (c.705-88) to begin the construction of the first Buddhist monastery in the country. Santirakshita, however, was unable to complete the task because of the interference of 'demons' – perhaps priests from the indigenous religions. Santirakshita, who was a philosopher, suggested to the king that he should ask for help from Padmasambhava (eighth century), who was an accredited Tantric[1] master at the Nalanda University in North-West India. Padmasambhava, the King was told, would be able to exorcise the demons. This Padmasambhava did as he made his way across Tibet. One by one the demons were turned into loyal protectors of Buddhist teaching. The Samye monastery was opened in 779 and for centuries it belonged to the Nyingma-pa Tibetan monastic order, to which Padmasambhava was closely linked.[2] At the same time, Buddhism was declared to be the state religion and the first seven Buddhist monks were ordained.

In the ninth century, Buddhism suffered a reversal. With the collapse of the monarchy in 842, traditional religions reasserted themselves and Buddhism was persecuted. A few people, secretly, remained faithful to the teachings of the 'Great Guru', Padmasambhava, whose writings were not rediscovered for many years. Although the earliest manuscripts of the *Bardo Thodol* or Book of the Dead - which gives instructions to those who want to go beyond death by changing it into an act of liberation - only date back to the fourteenth century, its teaching may derive from Padmasambhava himself.

From the eleventh century Buddhism once again became increasingly influential in Tibet, largely thanks to the arrival of the Indian monk Atisa (c.982-1054). He found Tibetan Buddhism, after the period of persecution, to be in decline. The monks only had a superficial knowledge of the faith. Tantrism, which teaches a way to transformation and freedom through uniting the male and female energies, was widespread. Tantrism focuses on ritual, visualization and symbols, but it may be misunderstood to sanction immoral sexual practices. Atisa emphasized monastic discipline and insisted that Tantrism must be grounded in a sound knowledge of the Buddha's teachings. Devotion to one teacher was also vital. Atisa said – in words that have influenced Tibetan Buddhism ever since - that without a teacher, 'the doctrine and the man will go separate ways.'

Tsong Khapa was born in Eastern Tibet. According to traditional biographies, his birth was the culmination of a long spiritual development that began in a previous life at the time of Gotama Buddha. Before his birth his parents had auspicious dreams, in one of which he chose the woman who would be suitable to be his mother. He received the layman's (*upāsaka*) vows when he was only two and the vows of a novice monk, when he was seven. Already he was devoting himself to the study of the Buddhist scriptures and to meditation. Quite early, he started to travel throughout Tibet and was willing to learn from teachers of different Buddhist traditions. His greatest teacher was master Rendawa (1349-1412) of the Sakya school, who was deeply versed in the teachings of Nagarjuna.[3]

When he was thirty-two, Tsong Khapa started writing his most influential works, *The Golden Rosary of the Good Explanations* and *The*

Great Expositions of the Stages of the Path. One purpose of his writing was to purify and reform Tibetan Buddhism. By 1409, he had enough followers to found his own monastery of Riwo Ganden ('Joyous Mountain'), where traditional rules were strictly observed. Eventually, this became a huge complex with some 4,000 monks. Subsequently, he founded Drebung and Sera monasteries, which were also near Lhasa, all of which were ransacked by the Chinese army in 1959. When I visited Tibet in 1996, they were being restored, partly so as to attract tourists. Monks, however, are immediately under pressure from the Chinese authorities when there is unrest in the country. Tsong Khapa's Monastic order, which is still the most influential, soon became known as '*Geluk*' (Virtuous Way). To differentiate his monks from those of the other schools, who wore red hats, his monks wore yellow hats.[4]

Monastic training is long and for those who achieve the higher 'geshe' degree intellectually very demanding. The primary method of examination is oral debate, in which a monk must be able to defend a philosophical position against all challenges. The debates, as I saw at the Sera monastery, are very lively, with monks enthusiastically jumping, pivoting, shouting and sometimes even pushing their opponents. The aim is to train monks to think on their feet and critically to examine what they believe.

In 1408, Tsong Khapa established the Great Prayer, a New Year festival in the Jokhang, which is Tibet's holiest temple. The Jokhang temple, as already mentioned, is the centre of old Lhasa and was built by the thirty-third king of Tibet in the early seventh century. It houses the statue of a previous Buddha, Aksobhya, which was given to the king by his Nepalese wife. The statue was broken by the occupying Chinese army, but in 1989 the two halves were reunited and re-consecrated.

In his middle fifties, Tsong Khapa's health deteriorated and just before he died at the age of sixty-two, he gave his final instructions to his disciples. His death was marked by auspicious signs and his body took on the appearance of the youthful bodhisattva Manjusri - and multicoloured rays of light poured forth from it.

Tsong Khapa's book, the *Great Exposition,* is based on Atisa's *A Lamp for the Path to Enlightenment.* Like Atisa, Tsong Khapa wanted scholarship and tantric training to go together. He insisted that only those with a profound knowledge of the scriptures should practice Tantric rituals and ensured that these accorded with the vows of a monk.

Tibetan Buddhism, which emphasises the value of compassion, holds up as an ideal the bodhisattva, who sacrifices himself for the welfare of all living beings. The Bodhissatva's vow can be an inspiration for us all:

May I become at all times, both now and forever,
A protector for those without protection,
A guide for those who have lost their way,
A ship for those with oceans to cross,
A bridge for those with rivers to cross,
A sanctuary for those in danger,
A lamp for those in need of light,
A place of refuge for those in need of shelter,
And a servant to all those in need.

The Tibetan Buddhist practice of *tonglen* (Tibetan for 'giving and taking') is also a good way to develop sympathy for other people. First, you focus on a suffering individual or group. Breathe in deeply and feel yourself drawing in all their emotional pain, right into your heart, making their grief your own. Then, as you breathe out, send love, warmth, kindness and compassion to people who are suffering – in the hope that their fear and pain will be replaced by courage and some acceptance.

Tsong Khapa is believed by many Tibetan Buddhists to have been an emanation of the Bodhisatvas, Avalokitesvara and Manjusri. Certainly his teaching has continued to inspire the non-violence and compassion which is characteristic of Tibetan Buddhism and is evident today in the behaviour and teaching of Tenzin Gyatso, the present Dalai Lama.

CHAPTER NOTES
1. Tantrism is explained later in the chapter
2. The monastery eventually passed into the control of the Sakya order.
3. See chapter 31
4. The names of the other monastic schools are *Nyingma, Kagyu and Sakya.*

51

Kabir

Kabir was an Indian mystic and devotional poet who wrote for ordinary people. He transcended religious differences, saying of himself, that he was 'at once the child of Allah and of Ram.' It has been said of him that he 'was one of the few truly universal saints... who appeals to anyone interested in serious things, of any age, country or religious persuasion.'[1]

Kabir is usually said to have been the son of a Hindu Brahmin widow, who abandoned her child – one tradition suggests a divine virginal conception. He was found by a childless Muslim couple, called Niru and Nimma, floating on a lotus leaf on or more plausibly beside the Lahara Tara Lake, which is near to the holy city of Varanasi (Benares). The usual date given for his birth is 1440, although this is uncertain. Niru and Nimma, who were weavers, brought up Kabir as a Muslim - *Al-Kabir*, 'the Great' is one of Islam's ninety-nine names for God.

Growing up in Varanasi, with its many temples, Kabir was bound to have some awareness of Hindu ideas and practices. He was particularly attracted to Ramananda (c.1360- c.1470), who was a follower of the great twelfth century theistic philosopher Ramanuja.[2] Ramananda, teaching in Hindi, the language of the people, encouraged devotion to Rama and his consort Sita.[3] Ramananda's influence is still felt today and among his later disciples were Mirabi (15th/16th century), a Rajasthani princess and poet, and Tulsidas (1532-1623), who retold the Ramayana in Hindi. Ramananda preached against caste and mixed freely with people of every sort. As a result, some of the fellow-disciples of Ramanuja refused to eat with Ramananda.

Yet when Kabir at first approached Ramananda and asked to be initiated as a disciple, Ramananda sadly declined, saying, 'You know it is impossible, my son. Only Brahmins can be initiated.' Such initiation consists of the guru placing his hand on the disciple and pronouncing a sacred mantra over him. Kabir was much upset, but early in the morning before it was light, he went to the river and sat down on the steps, where Ramananda was accustomed to come for his morning bath.

As Ramananda climbed down into the river, his foot fell on something soft and, in horror at having hurt a living-being, he called out *'Hai Rām'* (Oh God). Kabir, delightedly, stood up and said, 'Now you have pronounced your mantra over me. I am your disciple.' The old man blessed him and accepted him as a follower. Kabir sang of him in these words,

> *By the grace of God I found my teacher*
> *I walk now by his side.*
> *How can I forget him –*
> *Friend, philosopher and guide.*[4]

Kabir accepted from Hinduism belief in reincarnation and the law of *karma*. Although he often mentioned Krishna, the Divine Flute Player, Kabir rejected idolatry, the caste system and the emphasis which *sannyasin* (or holy men) put on asceticism.

Kabir had no time for ritualism.

> *O Servant, where dost thou seek Me?*
> *Lo! I am beside thee.*
> *I am neither in temple nor mosque: I am neither in Ka'ba nor in Kailash,*
> *Neither am I in rites and ceremonies, nor in Yoga and renunciation.*
> *If thou art a true seeker, thou shalt at once see Me:*
> *thou shalt meet me in a moment of time.*
> *Kabir says, " O Sadhu! God is the breath of all breath."*[5]
> Again, Kabir sang:
> *The images are all lifeless, they cannot speak;*
> *I know, for I have cried aloud to them.*[6]

Kabir, who was a family man, with a wife and children, rejected the wandering life and the physical austerities of the Hindu holy men.

> *'We can reach the goal without crossing the road.'*[7]

He earned his living as a weaver, although perhaps in reply to his wife's complaints that he spent more time on his devotions instead of on his work, he wrote,

Give me enough to feed myself
And feed my family too;
Nor let the beggar go unfed
That's all I ask of you.[8]

Kabir rejected caste distinctions:

Don't ask my caste or creed
These only cause division.
I serve God, my father
I am God's own son.[9]

From Islam, Kabir accepted the emphasis on the Oneness of God and the equality before God of all people. He was particularly drawn to the mysticism of the Sufis, as by his time, the poetry and philosophy of Rumi and other inspiring Sufis was well known in India.

His songs convey his longing for intimate communion with God, whom he calls a divine Friend, a Lover and a Teacher. 'Dear Friend, I am eager to meet my Beloved. When I am parted from my Beloved', he wrote, 'my heart is full of misery: I have no comfort in the day, I have no sleep in the night.'[10]

Kabir, as Rabindranath Tagore and Evelyn Underhill say in their introduction to his poems, 'belongs to that small group of mystics who have achieved what might be called the synthetic vision of God.' Such mystics have risen above the philosophical debates about whether the Absolute is impersonal or personal, transcendent or immanent. Brahma, he says, 'may never be found in abstractions.' 'Some contemplate the formless, and others meditate on form: but the wise man knows that Brahma is beyond both.' [11] Kabir recognised God as omnipresent – within the heart and pervading the world. 'O woman, what does it avail thee to dispute whether He is beyond all or in all?'[12] Kabir achieved a synthesis between the personal and cosmic aspects of the Divine Nature. Kabir avoided the 'excessive emotionalism,...which results from an unrestricted cult of the Divine Personality.'[13] Kabir was also 'protected from the soul destroying conclusions of pure monism.'[14] He says that: 'The creature is in Brahma, and Brahma is in the creature: they are ever distinct, yet ever united.'[15] He also said that the spiritual and the material world are 'no more that God's footstool.'[16] Kabir also combined the sense of God's transcendence with a passionate love for the divine bridegroom and friend. He sings of the ecstatic joy of being one with God. 'Dive thou into that ocean of sweetness: thus let all errors of life and death flee away.' 'I have come to the Sorrowless Land... Wonderful is that land of rest, to which no merit can win.' 'What a frenzy of ecstasy there is in every hour! ...(The worshipper) lives in the life of Brahma.'[17]

Kabir's love for God was reflected in a deep compassion for other people.

You may be very learned
You may teach very well;
But without compassion
You'll surely go to hell. [18]

He taught that 'Sweet words, like monsoon showers spread sweetness as the rose.' [19] 'Only selfless service,' he insisted, 'does the world deserve.'[20]

He emphasised the importance of humility. Kabir addressed the people, rather than the religious leaders. His songs are in the vernacular, using an early form of Hindi, which was widely understood. He may have been illiterate and he gave little attention to grammar or elegance, but his poems are full of imagery drawn from everyday life. For example,

'As a swan can sip the milk
From a milk and water drink.
So a saint extracts the good
And lets the evil sink.'[21]

Kabir's criticisms made him unpopular with both the Hindu and Muslim religious leadership and he met with considerable opposition. It is said that a beautiful courtesan was sent by some priests to try to tempt him, but instead she was converted by his pure love. Once, after a miracle of healing, he was brought by some Hindu priests before the Emperor Sikandar Lodi (d.1517) on the charge of claiming divine powers. Sikandar, a cultured and tolerant ruler, decided that as technically Kabir was a Muslim he should be given the theological latitude usually accorded to Sufis. In order to keep the peace in Varanasi, however, the Sultan exiled him from the city. This happened in about 1495, so Kabir spent the last twenty years of his life wandering from city to city in Northern India continuing to sing of the love of God until his hands were too feeble any longer to make the music, which he loved. He died at Maghar near Gorakhpur in 1518

Kabir's Hindu and Muslim disciples, neglecting his teaching, disputed about his body, which the Muslims wished to bury and the Hindus to cremate. As they argued, Kabir appeared before them and told them to lift the shroud and look at what lay beneath it. Instead of a corpse, there was a heap of flowers.

Many of Kabir's poems were collected into a book called *Bijak*, which was completed by 1570. Some of his poems were included in the *Adi Granth*, the holy scripture of the Sikhs. His poems influenced other religious teachers and devotees in North India, who belonged to what is known as the *Sant* (or holy) tradition, which was particularly influential from the fifteenth to the seventeenth centuries, but is still quite popular even today. There has been a revival of interest in his writings in recent years and his poems became more widely known thanks to the beautiful translation of them into English by Rabindranath Tagore (1861-1914), probably the greatest modern Indian poet. There has also been some critical study of Kabir and his works to re-situate him in his own time and context and to identify which of the many poems attributed to Kabir are authentic.[22]

Yet, even now Kabir transcends any attempt to label him. Charlotte Vaudeville says, 'Sometimes he is a Bhakta speaking the language of Yoga, as if Yoga were an interiorised form of Bhatki (loving devotion to God); sometimes he is a Yogi speaking... as if within the mysterious *Sahaja* state he had met infinite Love.'[23] Sister Rosemary SLG is right when she says 'Kabir, like God, is one-without-a-second and not even his own immediate followers share precisely his vision. He insists on immediate and personal experience, which in the last resort is secret and beyond words. We cannot see what he saw, but we can share his way of looking.'[24] Like so many of the holy people included in this book, Kabir points to a Mystery that cannot be adequately described, but who is known only in the experience of loving communion.

CHAPTER NOTES

1. R H Lesser, *Saints and Sages of India*, New Delhi, Intercultural Publications, 1992, p. 2.
2. See chapter 38.
3. See chapter 7
4. R.H Lesser, p. 8.
5. The Ka'ba is the focus for Muslim worship at Mecca. Kailash is a Himalayan mountain, which is sacred to Hindus. A *sadhu* is a holy person. The poem is from *Poems of Kabir*, translated by Rabindranath Tagore, London, Macmillan, 1962, p.1.
6. Tagore, p. 49.
7. Tagore, p. 79.
8. Lesser, p. 5.
9. Lesser, p. 1.
10. Tagore, p. 56.
11. Tagore, pp. xxvii-xxxi.
12. Tagore, p. 55.
13 Tagore, p. xxvii
14. Tagore, p. xxviii
15 Tagore, p. 77.
16. Tagore, p. 6.
17. Tagore, p. 9.
18. Tagore, pp. 17-24.
19. Lesser, p. 9.
20. Lesser, p. 10.
21. Lesser, p. 11.
22. Lesser. p. 16
23. See, for example, Charlotte Vaudeville, *Kabir*, Oxford, Clarendon Press, Vol I, 1974.
24. Charlotte Vaudeville, p.144.
25. Sister Rosemary, SLG, *Kabir, The Way of Love and Paradox*, Oxford, SLG Press, Convent of the Incarnation, Fairacres, 1977, Second edition 2006, p. 4.

52

Eckhart

Meister Eckhart, who founded the school of 'Rhineland Mysticism,' is considered by some people to have been the greatest German specu- lative mystic and one of the key figures in the history of Western mysticism. Eckhart's influence has been felt by German Protestantism, the Romantic Movement and by Idealist and Existentialist philosophers. Recently Matthew Fox, an advocate of 'creation spirituality' and the Post-Modernist thinker Jacques Derrida have written about his work. Some Zen Buddhist and Hindu spiritual teachers have also studied his writings. Many of his writings were in German and were influential in the development of the language.

Eck(e)hart, best known as Meister Eckhart, was born in about 1260, probably in the village of Tambach in Thuringia in Germany. 'Von Hocheim' is now thought to be a- surname, referring to his family, who were landowners, rather than to his place of birth. Eckhart entered the Dominican Order at the age of 15 and studied at Cologne, where the influence of Thomas Aquinas, who had only just died, was still strong. In his mid-30s, he became the senior figure of the Dominicans in Thuringia and subsequently, in 1303, their provincial leader in Saxony and then, in 1306, Vicar of the Dominicans in Bohemia. There is some uncertainty about his subsequent appointments.

In 1302 he received his master's degree from the University of Paris and was subsequently known as Meister or Master Eckhart. He was a theologian, preacher and author. His writings derive from his own personal mystical experiences. They are, however, complex and have been interpreted in different ways. His main works in German were *The Book of Divine Consolation*, which was dedicated to the Queen of Hungary, *The Nobleman*, and *On Detachment*. He also wrote *Commentaries on the Bible* and *Sermons* in Latin.

Eckhart in one sermon gave a summary of his message.

'When I preach, I usually speak of detachment and say that a man should be empty of self and all things; and secondly, that he should be reconstructed in the simple good that God is; and thirdly that he should consider the great aristocracy which God has set up in the soul, such that by means of it man may wonderfully attain to God; and fourthly, of the purity of the divine nature.'

Eckhart describes four stages of the union between the soul and God: dissimilarity, similarity, identity and breakthrough. Self-understanding is essential. 'To get into the core of God at his greatest, one must first get into the core of himself at his least; for no one can know God who has not first known himself. 'At first a person becomes aware that only God is real and that 'all creatures are pure nothingness' and their being derives from God. The 'noble man', therefore, regards worldly objects with detachment. Becoming detached from the sense of self and the illusion that individual things exist, a person becomes aware that the soul is an image of God. 'You must be in Him and for Him, and not in yourself and for yourself.' Eckhart often speaks of identity, but it is not entirely clear what he means. At times, he seems to have adopted the monist position that the soul and God are identical, whereas Orthodox Christian teaching is that however close the soul is to God, both retain their own identity. At times Eckhart seems to imply a total union of will and the unity of love. 'Jesus enters the castle of the soul... the core of the soul and the core of God are one.'

There is, however, a further stage beyond that of identity, when even the mental concept of God has to be abandoned. A person enters into the Emptiness beyond God, which at times Eckhart calls 'the Godhead.' Parallels to the philosophical speculations of the Hindu Sankara or the Buddhist Nagarjuna are clear.

Eckhart belonged to the tradition of what is known as 'Apophatic' theology and spirituality. Eckhart was influenced by Dionysius (c.500), an obscure Syrian monk, who taught that God could not be known by the intellect but only by mystical experience. He was also influenced by the Irishman, Erigena or John Scotus (c.810-c.877), who translated Dionysius' writings from Greek to Latin and commented upon them. The premise is that no language can adequately describe God. The Divine Mystery is beyond all human thought. Eckhart, therefore, delighted in wordplay in which the meaning of words falls apart so that the mind 'breaks through' to a new reality. Gradually images and ideas, which get in the way, are stripped bare and through a path of training (*ascesis*), which requires poverty, simplicity and solitude, the soul develops an inner stillness and emptiness. Suffering, of which the passion of Jesus Christ is the example, as another great mystic John of the Cross (1542-91) taught, leads to the 'dark night' of the soul in which all former spiritual attitudes and ideas are removed.

Eckhart, particularly, emphasised the vital importance of quiet and inner silence and passivity if a person wanted to move from 'natural' to 'supernatural' prayer. In the latter, the field of consciousness is cleansed of all objects – even the symbols of God.

> 'If a man will work on inward work, he must pour all his powers into himself as into a corner of the soul, and must hide himself from all images and forms, and then he can work. Then he must come into a forgetting and not-knowing. He must be in a stillness and silence: then it is heard and understood in utter ignorance. When one knows nothing, it is opened and revealed. Then we shall become aware of the Divine Ignorance, and our ignorance will be ennobled and adorned with supernatural knowledge. And when we simply keep ourselves receptive, we are more perfect than when at work.'[1]

When he was about 60, Eckhart became a professor at Cologne University. The Archbishop, who was a Franciscan and hostile to the Dominicans, accused Eckhart, who was by now very popular, of heresy. Eckhart replied by publishing a *Defense* in Latin, which gives a reasoned explanation of the articles that were challenged and denies any heretical intent. He asked for the case to be referred to the papal court at Avignon. Before judges, who had had no mystical experiences, he affirmed, 'What I have taught is naked truth.' Twenty eight propositions were condemned by a papal bull in 1329, but by that time, Eckhart was dead. His teachings were passed on, especially by Johann Tauler (c.1300-61) and Henry Suso (c.1295-1366), both Dominicans, although they lacked his intense intellectual power.

Evelyn Underhill, famous for her studies of Mysticism, speaks of Eckhart with the poet Dante (1265-1321), famous for his *Divine Comedy*, as the mystical and intellectual giants, of the early thirteenth century. Both have continued to inspire and fascinate by their genius.[2]

Several scholars, including Rudolf Otto (1869-1937)[3] and the

Buddhist D T Suzuki (1870-1966) have pointed to parallels between Eckhart and Buddhist and Eastern philosophies. Interestingly, Maurice O'Connell Walshe, one of the pioneer translators of Eckhart into English was a Buddhist. It was he who first introduced me to Eckhart's writings.

These parallels had already been noticed by the German philosopher Arthur Schopenhauer (1788-1860). He rejected the theories of Hegel and held that the will to live is irrational and that efforts to understand the world are doomed to failure. Schopenhauer saw Eckhart's vision as equivalent to that of Eastern mystics. He wrote,

'If we turn from the forms produced by external circumstances, and go to the root of things, we shall find that Sakyamuni (the Buddha) and Meister Eckhart teach the same thing; only that the former dared to express his ideas plainly and positively, whereas Eckhart is obliged to clothe them in the garment of the Christian myth, and to adapt his expression thereto...I say therefore that the spirit of (original) Christian morality is identical with that of Brahmanism and Buddhism.'[4]

This view that the mystical experiences of the saints of all ages is essentially one and the same, and that the differences are due to historical and cultural circumstances, is sometimes known as the 'Philosophia Perennis' or 'Perennial Philosophy.' Aldous Huxley (1894-1963), in the mid twentieth century wrote,

'Philosophia Perennis – the metaphysic that recognises a divine reality substantial to the world in all things and lives and minds; the psychology that finds in the soul something similar to or even identical with divine reality; the ethic that place's man's final end in the knowledge of the immanent and transcendent Ground of all being – the thing is immemorial and universal.'[5]

It is a view that was shared by many of the late nineteenth and early twentieth century pioneers of what was then called 'Comparative Religion.' Today, however, it is an approach which is rejected by those influenced by Post-modernism's suspicion of all universals.

The nature of mystical experience has itself become a field of study. Eckart, however, would have emphasised the importance of the experience rather than theories about it. In his *Sermons*, the metaphors are chosen for their ability to collide with and contradict one another. The explosion of language is a way by which – as in Zen – a new understanding is born. The process is often repeated in a single sermon, with the intention of transforming the listener's understanding so that the 'divine ground' breaks through and comes to 'birth' in the soul.

CHAPTERS NOTES

1. Quoted by Evelyn Underhill, *Mysticism*, London, Methuen, 1911; 1960 University paperback edition, p. 319.
2. *Mysticism*, p. 463.
3. Otto is mentioned in chapter 1.
4. A Schopenhauer, *The World as Will and Representation*, Vol II, Chapter XLVIII.
5. Aldous Huxley, *The Perennial Philosophy*, 1946, p. 1. See also Chapter 99.

53

Jalal-ad-Din ar-Rumi

Type the name 'Rumi' into Google and you get over a quarter of a million items. This is one indication of the inspiring worldwide influence of this Sufi Muslim mystic, poet and leader.

Jalal-ad-Din ar-Rumi is also known as Mawlana or Mevlana, which means 'Our Master.' He was born in 1207, probably on 30th September, in Balkh, which is now in North Afghanistan. His father Baha'ad-Din Walad, possibly a descendant of Abu Bakr, the first Caliph, was a noted mystical theologian, author and teacher. In 1219, when Jalal-ad-Din was twelve, the family left Balkh because their home city was threatened by invading Mongols. After a pilgrimage to Mecca, they eventually ended up in Rum (Anatolia) – hence his surname Rumi, by which he is often called. The family settled at first at Larinda. His mother died there, but it was also in Larinda that Rumi married and had a son. Soon afterwards the family moved to Konya, which was then the capital of the Western Sejuk Empire. His father taught in numerous religious schools (*madrassas*) there. When he died in 1231, he was succeeded by his son.

Rumi's life and work really divide into three distinct stages. During the first, he was a student of theology and then a teacher. All this was changed by his meeting with a wandering dervish called Shams ad-Din in 1244. Now, Rumi discovered the ecstasy of mysticism and spent his time dancing and listening to music. After Shams' disappearance, when he was supported by his friendship with Salah ad-Din Zarkub, he wrote the *Divan–i-Shams* (*The Collected Poetry of Shams*). During, the third period, following Zarkub's death, he was inspired by another disciple Husam ad-Din Chelebi. His great work the *Mathnawi* is called 'the book of Husam.' Rumi died on 17th December 1273 on what is known as his 'wedding night', when he was finally united with God.

During the first period, Rumi was widely respected as a teacher and even members of the royal court came to consult him. He insisted, however, that his classes were open to anyone. Aware that learned theologians often obscured the truth he tried to explain the teaching of Islam in simple terms. Some people criticized him for associating with people who had a bad reputation. He replied, 'Were my disciples good men of eminence, I would have been their disciple. Since they are bad men, they accept my leadership so that I may change them.'

Rumi himself, however, was soon to be changed by his meeting in 1244 with Shams, a sixty-year old Sufi, described as 'a weird figure, wrapped in coarse black felt', said by some to have 'an exceedingly aggressive and domineering manner.' There are various accounts of the meeting. Shams, it is said, asked Rumi, 'What is the purpose of wisdom and knowledge?' 'To follow and reach the Prophet,' Rumi replied. 'That is common place' Shams responded. 'What then is the purpose of knowledge?' Rumi asked. 'Knowledge is that which takes you to its source,' was Shams' answer. The difference is between knowing *about* God – theology - and knowing God – mysticism. Rumi, subsequently in his verses, makes clear the limitation of intellectual activity.

If in the world you are the most learned scholar of the time,
Behold the passing away of this world and this time.[1]
'What is Love?' he asked and replied:
The Sea of Not-Being: there the foot of the intellect is shattered.[2]

Rumi himself tells the story of a scholar who, being rowed across some water, asked the boatman whether he had studied grammar. 'No', the boatman replied. 'Well,' said the scholar, 'you have wasted half your life.' After a time a threatening storm arose. The boatman asked the scholar, 'Do you know how to swim?' 'No', he answered. 'Now your whole life has been wasted', the boatman retorted.

Under Shams' guidance, Rumi experienced the ecstasy of union with God. Having previously disapproved of music, now, in the words of his son, 'day and night he danced in ecstasy, raving like a madman.' Rumi gave up his teacher's gown and dressed as a dervish. 'He had been a mufti: he became a poet. He had been an ascetic: he became intoxicated by Love.' His students were horrified and jealous of Shams, who monopolised Rumi and deprived them of their teacher. Shams fled to Damascus, but, a compromise was patched up, and Shams returned to Konya. Trouble soon broke out again. Suddenly, in 1247 or 1248, Shams disappeared. According to some accounts he was stabbed by one of his enemies.

Rumi was devastated and at first refused to accept that Shams had died. 'Who dare say that the Immortal one met his death?'. The friendship with the goldsmith Zarkub helped him to cope with his loss. Like Alfred Lord Tennyson (1809-92) in his *In Memoriam*, Rumi voiced his grief in poetry. The *Divan* is supposedly written by Shams, but is, in fact, by Rumi. Rumi would have said that as soulmates they had become one. To him, Shams was the personification of the perfect man. The *Divan* is a collection of about 25,000 rhyming couplets.

Rumi's most famous work, the *Mathnawi*, composed while he was performing whirling dances, was dictated over nearly twelve years to Husam, during the third period of his life. It consists of over 25,000 verses. The *Mathnawi*, begins with a metaphorical song in which the reed, parted from the reed-bed, complains of its separation.

'*Everyone who is left far from his source*
wishes back the time when he was united with it.'[3]

In the same way, the soul longs to be reunited with God.

'*It is the fire of Love that is in the reed,*
'*Tis the fervour of Love that is in the wine.*'[4]

Elsewhere he wrote, 'We are the flute, the music you.'

The emphasis is on inner experience. 'I gazed into my heart; there I saw Him; He was nowhere else.' But to achieve this realization, the ego has to disappear.

The overwhelming emphasis of Rumi's writing is on the wonder of divine and human love.

'*Love is not contained in speech and hearing:*
Love is an ocean whereof the depth is invisible.'[5]

The union of love is complete. Yet, he is aware that in the closest union there is a duality. The two remain distinct even as they become one.

Love can transform suffering, which is a spiritual discipline.

'*By love bitter things become sweet.* (II, 1529.)
Through love thorns become roses.'[6]

He also said that God could be seen in the ugly as well as in the beautiful.

Many times, Rumi makes clear that the Divine love transcends religious differences. A Persian, an Arab, a Turk and a Greek, he said, all wanted to buy grapes, but each of them used a different word for the grapes and began to fight about this. They were deceived by appearances. The seventy two creeds and sects in the world do not really exist.

> 'The religion of love is apart from all religions:
> For lovers (the only) religion and creed is God.'[7]

> 'Not Christian or Jew or Muslim
> Not Hindu, Buddhist, Sufi or Zen
> Not any religion or cultural system.
> I am not from the east or the west...
> I belong to the beloved
> And have seen the two worlds as one.'[8]

He has God say, 'I am not sanctified by their glorification of Me. It is they that become sanctified.' Rumi wrote this haunting verse, which is often used as an invitation to prayer at interfaith gatherings:

> 'Come, come, whoever you are,
> Wanderer, Worshipper, Seeker of meaning.
> Our fellowship is not one of despair,
> Even though you have broken your vows a hundred times,
> Come, come, whoever you are.'

Although Rumi spoke of heaven and hell, he believed that in the end all beings, including even Satan, would be saved. 'I will kindle such a fire of Grace,' God said, 'that the least spark thereof consumes all sin.'[9]

Rumi emphasised the need for a spiritual guide and a companion. 'If anybody goes on the way without a leader, every two days journey becomes one of a hundred years.'

He stressed the need to live in the present. 'The Sufi is the son of the (present) time... It is not the rule of the Way to say "tomorrow."'[10] Complete trust in God is required, but this is no excuse for quietism and inactivity. We should work for our living, not depend on others. His emphasis was on the transformation of human desires and passions. Lust should be transmuted into love.

Rumi was not just a poet and a mystic. The psychoanalyst Eric Fromm said that 'He discussed the nature of the instincts, the power of reason over the instincts, the nature of the self, of consciousness, the unconscious and cosmic consciousness; he discussed the problems of freedom, certainty and authority.'[11] Despite his disparaging comments on the intellect, Rumi was a creative if not a systematic thinker, but there is not space here to discuss the philosophical reflections of his prose work, *Fihi ma fihi* (*What is within is Within*)

Rumi, as we have seen, highly valued dance and music as a way to stimulate the experience of union with God. After Rumi's death, his son, Sultan Walad, who wrote a biography which is the basis for much of our knowledge of Rumi's life, organised his followers into a loose fraternity, known as Mawlawiyya or Mevlevi Order, a name derived from one of the titles given to Rumi. In the West, the Order is usually known as the Whirling Dervishes. The Order gained great importance during the Ottoman Empire, but Ataturk, the modernising ruler of Turkey, banned all dervish orders in 1925. Visitors to Konya, however, can now observe the dances at what are, supposedly, cultural programmes, but which we found were was an intensely moving spiritual occasion. The dancers are dressed in long white skirts that represent their shrouds. Over them, they wear voluminous black coats symbolising their worldly tombs. Their conical felt hats represent their tombstones. The ceremony begins with the intoning of a prayer for Mevlana (as Rumi is usually called in Konya) and a verse from the Qur'an. A kettledrum booms and this is followed by the plaintive song of a reed flute. Then the highly ritualistic dance begins. It is repeated four times and the ceremony ends with another verse that seals the experience of mystical union with God.

Konya, a holy city, is naturally a place of pilgrimage. The Mevlana Museum is the former lodge of the whirling dervishes. Mevlana's sarcophagus, flanked by those of his son, Sultan Veld and of his father, is covered in velvet shrouds with rich gold embroidery. There is a huge turban as a sign of his spiritual authority. It is indeed a sacred place.

Jami (14919-92), a Sufi known as 'the seal of the poets' said that the

Mathnawi was the essence of the Qur'an in Persian. Rumi himself said of it, 'It is the grandest of gifts and the most precious of prizes… It is a light to our friends and a treasure for our (spiritual) descendants.' The number of those descendants is still increasing.

CHAPTER NOTES
1.   *Divan* I, 2845-7.
2.   *Divan* III, 4723-25.
3.   *Mathnawi*, 1,4.
4.   *Mathnawi*, 1,10.
5.   *Mathnawi*, 5,2728-36.
6.   *Mathnawi*, 2,1529.
7.   *Mathnawi*, 2,1750-70.
8.   *1,000 World Prayers* - a free translation.
9.   *Mathnawi* 1, 1848.
10. *Mathnawi*, 1,133.
11. Preface to A Reza Avasteh, *Rumi the Persian*, Lahore, Sh.Muhammad Ashraf, 1965, p.ix.

54

Sergius of Radonezh

St Sergius was the greatest spiritual leader and monastic reformer of Mediaeval Russia. He is one of the most venerated Russian saints and is patron saint of all Russia. His monastery at Radonezh – modern Zagorsk - is known as a symbol of religious renewal and national identity.

Bartholomew or Batholomew, as he was named at his baptism, was born in the ancient Principality of Rostov. The date of his birth is uncertain. It was perhaps in 1314 or maybe a few years later. Our knowledge of his life is based on the Mediaeval *Vita of St Sergii of Radonezh*[1]. His father Kiril belonged to the old Russian aristocratic order known as Boyar, which was abolished by Peter I. Kiril was in the service of the Prince. During Batholomew's childhood his father was impoverished. This was due partly to the repeated raids by Mongols and Tatars – Turkic-speaking tribes from Central Asia. It was also due to the frequent diplomatic missions which Kiril was required to undertake and partly because sovereign power was transferred to Moscow. The new regent appointed by the Moscow prince adopted repressive measures against the local leaders – killing some and confiscating the property of others, who were forced to leave the area. Kiril was one of the latter. He and his family moved to the small town of Radonezh, about forty miles north of Moscow – it is now the village of Gorodok.

From early youth, Batholomew wanted to be a monk, but he waited until his parents, who both in old age entered a monastery, had died. He did not, however, want to enter an established monastery but wished instead to go to a hermitage. He invited his elder brother Stefan, who had become a widower, to join him. Batholomew gave his share of the family property to his younger brother Peter, who was married. Although the area where Batholomew and Stefan settled was later to become the site of the Great Monastery of the Trinity, at the time it was a complete wilderness. The brothers constructed a small church and a cell in which to live. Stefan could not endure the solitude for long and left for Moscow, where he joined the Monastery of the Theophany

327

and in due course became confessor to the Great Prince of Moscow. Batholomew remained alone, but soon met the monk-priest Mitrofan, who encouraged Batholomew to become a monk, at which point he took the name Sergius. There is some uncertainty whether his brother Peter supplied him with food or whether he grew his own. There were springs of water in the area. Certainly he lived a very austere and simple life. At different times, Sergius was a cook, baker, miller, tailor and carpenter. Despite his ancestry, he is remembered as a 'peasant saint', who, as one Russian writer put it, 'smells of fresh fir wood.'[2]

Gradually other hermits joined him. Each lived in his own cell, but they needed an abbot or hegumen (the title given to the leader of a religious community in the Orthodox Church). They asked Sergius to take on this responsibility, but he refused. Mitrofan, therefore, took the position, but after his early death, Stefan agreed to serve as abbot. His monastery quickly became famous and, because of its strict rule, attracted many monks and material donations.

A big change occurred when Sergius introduced a communal way of life at the monastery instead of the original pattern whereby each monk lived by himself as a hermit. He also prohibited begging, which meant that the monks had to work to provide for their physical needs. At this point, after the death of the Great Prince of Moscow, Stefan returned but soon became the leader of some disgruntled monks, who disliked the changes. Sergius, to avoid a quarrel, silently departed. He then founded a new monastery, but, because some monks came to join him, the dispute with his brother was re-ignited. Metropolitan Alexis had to interfere and reinstated Sergius. The Metropolitan hoped that Sergius would succeed him, but he refused. After Alexis's death, Sergius, unwillingly got drawn into a dispute about who should be his successor.

Sergius' disciples, meanwhile, started to spread his teaching and to found monasteries. Sergius' teaching and practice, like that of St Theodosius of the Caves (d. 1074), whose monastery at Kiev became an example for monasticism in Southern Russia, was based on that of St Theodore the Studite (759-826). St Theodore, who defended the use of icons and whose monastery became a model for Eastern monasticism, was himself influenced by earlier spiritual teachers such as St John Climacus, (b. 525) who wrote the *Ladder of Divine Ascent*.[3]

There is a remarkable continuity in the spiritual life of the Orthodox Churches. Father Lev Gillet[4] identified six main elements in Orthodox spirituality: deep and continuing study of the scripture, which also is central to the liturgy; knowledge of the writings of the Early Church Fathers; encouragement of intellectual endeavour; the monastic way of life; the importance of liturgy; and the teaching of practices which encourage contemplation. The emphasis is on spiritual transformation, which leads to union with God and deification. An ancient prayer says that Christ became human so that human beings might become divine or share in the divine nature. Spiritual transformation, however, is not a selfish pre-occupation. Fr Lev Gillet insisted that the Orthodox virtue of *apatheia* does not mean 'apathy' in the modern sense but is in reality the state of a soul in which love towards God and other people is so ruling and burning as to leave no room for human (self-centred) passions.[5] The fruit of the Spirit is love, as is seen in the stories of the life of Sergius and of many other saints of the Orthodox Churches.

Through the presence of the Holy Spirit the believer comes to reflect the divine light. It was said by contemporaries of St Sergius, as it was later said of St Seraphim, that at times his physical appearance was transfigured by light. This emphasis on light in the Orthodox tradition is also apparent in this ancient hymn, which dates from at least the third century, which is sung every evening:

O Gladsome light, O grace
Of God the Father's face,
The eternal splendour wearing;
Celestial, holy, blest.
Our Saviour Jesus Christ,
Joyful in thine appearing.

Now, ere day fadeth quite,
We see the evening light,
Our wonted hymn outpouring;
Father of might unknown,
Thee, his incarnate Son,
And Holy Spirit adoring.

To thee of right belongs,
All praise of holy songs,
O Son of God, Life-giver;
Thee, therefore, O Most High,
The world doth glorify,
And shall exalt for ever.[6]

Sergius himself is said to have received a vision of the Virgin Mary with the two apostles, Peter and John. Sergius fell prostrate and for a time was unable to speak. Other monks thought he was dead, although some modern writers suggest that he had an epileptic fit.

When Sergius felt his death was approaching, he appointed Nikon to succeed him as abbot. Sergius died on 25th September 1392 and was buried in the church at the monastery of the Holy Trinity, which soon became a place of pilgrimage. Although the church was closed for a time by the Communist government, it was reopened in 1945 and continues to attract pilgrims and visitors to the impressive monastery at Zagorsk, which is an important centre of learning. After his death, miracles of healing were said to have occurred at his grave. He was canonized in 1452 and the cult was approved by Rome. The first church in his honour was built at Novgorod in 1460.

Besides reviving monastic life in Russia, which prepared the way for Russian colonisation of the vast Northern areas, Sergius also had a strong sense of his social and national responsibilities. Although he did not take part in political life, he is said to have encouraged Dmitri Donskoi, the Prince of Moscow, when he consulted him, to continue his armed revolt against the Tartars and to have blessed the Russian ruler before he went to fight the critical battle against the Tartars at Kulikovo. It is suggested that he hoped Russian lands would be united under the leadership of Moscow. Sergius also showed great compassion towards those in need and taught the peasants better ways of cultivating the soil.

It is no surprise that Sergius, who is sometimes likened to St Francis of Assisi, is one of Russia's best-loved saints as well as the country's patron saint.

CHAPTER NOTES

1. *Vita of St Sergii of Radonezh,* translated with an introduction by Michael Klimenko, Houston, Nordland Publishing International, 1980.

2. Quoted by Donald Attwater, *A Dictionary of Saints,* London, Penguin, 1965, p. 306.

3. See chapter 28

4 *Orthodox Spirituality,* by a Monk of the Eastern Church, Fellowship of Saint Alban and Saint Sergius, London SPCK, 1945, 2nd edtn 1978, p.1.

5. *Orthodox Spirituality,* p.15.

6. *English Hymnal,* 269.

55

Guru Nanak

The message of Guru Nanak, who was the founder of Sikhism and its first Guru, that God transcends the religious divisions created by humankind, is as much needed today as it was in the sixteenth century. As he emerged from his first deep communion with the Divine, he said,

'There is no Hindu:
There is no Mussulman (Muslim).'[1]

When asked which path he would follow, he replied, 'I shall follow God's path. God is neither Hindu nor Muslim.'

Nanak was born in 1469, some fourteen years before Martin Luther. He grew up in the Punjab, which, ruled by a weak Afghan dynasty, was half Hindu and half Muslim. His father, who was a Hindu, worked as the village accountant for the local Rajput chief, who had converted to Islam. Nanak's birth was marked by prodigies and by prophecies that he would not only adore God but would also lead many others to do the same. He was a precocious child, already interested in spiritual things. Very soon he was writing verse on his slate tablet. He learned Sanskrit and also Arabic and Persian. But he was dreamy and careless about the practical tasks he was given. Once he let the cattle, which he was supposed to be watching, wander into a farmer's field and trample down the crop. The family wondered if he was emotionally or physically ill.

The family was also baffled by his questioning of traditional religious rituals and his asking what they meant. When at eleven it was time for him as a high caste Hindu to put on the sacred thread, he enquired of the Brahmin priest what difference a thread would make. Was it not righteous deeds, Nanak asked, that distinguished one person from another? As he did not get a satisfactory answer, Nanak refused to wear the thread. He then recited to the Pandit and his father's guests this verse that he had composed:

Out of the cotton of compassion

Spin the thread of contentment,
Tie the knot of continence,
And the twist of virtue;
Make such a sacred thread;
O Pundit, for your inner self.[2]

As a young man Nanak went to work in Sultanpur, which was a great centre of learning. His brother-in-law, who worked for the Nwab, introduced Nanak to the Nwab, who offered him a job as a store keeper. Although he worked hard, he was constantly aware of the Divine Presence. He wrote,

God has His seat everywhere,
His treasure houses are in all places.[3]

And again,

If I remember Him, I live,
If I forget Him, I die.[4]

Quite soon Nanak gathered a few friends for meditation and the worship of God's Name. His sister admired him, but thought religion was only one part of life. Indeed Nanak himself said that the secret of religion was to live in the world without being overcome by it. His sister, therefore found him a suitable wife, called Sulakni. Nanak was nineteen when he married her. They had two sons.

Nanak spent more than eight years at Sultanpur. The transforming event in his life took place when he was nearly thirty. He failed to appear for work after his morning ablution in the local river. He was missing for three days and there were fears that he had been drowned. In fact he was in deep contemplation of God. One account said that he had been taken into the presence of God, who gave him a bowl of milk, saying it was nectar (*amrit*), which would give him 'power of prayer, love of worship, truth and contentment.' He was told to call others to experience the bliss of God's love.

Guru Nanak spent the next twenty or more years travelling and teaching. He is said to have travelled not only in India but to Afghanistan, Sri Lanka and even to Mecca. He had no use for ritual. He mocked the Hindu custom of throwing sacred water in worship toward the rising sun. In Mecca, he lay down with his feet towards the holy Ka'aba. He was woken by a Muslim who angrily reproved him for this profanity. He said 'Turn my feet to any direction where God is not present.' He stressed inner holiness. To Muslims he said,

Make mercy your mosque and faith your prayer mat,
Righteousness your Qur'an;
Modesty your circumcising, goodness your fasting,
For thus the true Muslim expresses his faith.'[5]

Pollution, he insisted to the Hindus, was a question of behaviour not of what you touched.

Pollution of the mind is greed,
The pollution of the tongue lying,
The pollution of the eyes is to look with covetousness
 upon another's wealth, upon another's wife
and upon the beauty of another woman,
The pollution of the ears is to listen to slander.[6]

Positively, he urged people to trust God and dwell on *Nam*, which is usually translated 'Name', but has a far richer meaning. *Nam* signifies the Divine presence, Reality and Truth. By living in harmony with the Divine Name, a person is freed from the circle of death and rebirth. Devotion to the Name is the way to liberation. Guru Nanak urged people to sing the praise of God. 'Oh my mind', Nanak said, 'love God as a fish loves water.'

The emphasis on the praise of God did not mean for Nanak, unlike Hindu holy men, indifference to or withdrawal from the world. Quite the contrary. He advocated willing and joyous acceptance of life. 'The body is the palace, the temple, the house of God: into it He has put His eternal light.' Liberation was to be won in the world, 'amid its laughter and sport, fineries and food.' He saw a divine purpose in family life and emphasised its value. Living in 'in the midst of wife and children,' he said, 'one would gain liberation.' He stressed the importance of service of others. 'By a life of service in this world alone will one become entitled to a seat in the next world' 'There can be no love of God without service.' In the community that he established in Kartarpur, where he settled in about 1521, after his travels, and where he stayed for the rest of his life, everyone was expected to work as well as join in the morning and evening hymn singing. 'They alone who live by their own labour and share the fruit with the others have found the right path.'

Because the world was God's creation Nanak was deeply concerned about social and economic problems of the time. He attacked the rampant corruption and abuse of power. 'The times are like a drawn knife... And righteousness hath fled on wings.' He criticised the rulers. He complained that religion was mostly formal and often hypocritical. 'Those who wear the sacred thread use knives to cut men's throats.' Indeed, although Nanak repeatedly spoke of God's power and justice, he did once ask, 'When there was such suffering, did you not feel pity, O God? Creator, you are the same for all.'

Nanak was disgusted by the treatment of women as inferior.

> *Of woman we are born, of woman conceived,*
> *To woman engaged, to woman married*
> *... By woman is the civilization continued...*
> *Then why call her evil from whom are great men born?...*
> *And without woman none should exist.*[7]

He rejected the view, common at the time that menstruation and child-birth were defiling. Among Guru Nanak's followers, women were treated equally.

Guru Nanak was not a systematic thinker. His teaching is set forth in verse. Many of his hymns are included in the *Adi Granth*, the Sikh holy book. His hymns were composed in Punjabi, the language of the common people. In fact, they were the first significant literary work in Punjabi.

It is perhaps paradoxical that someone who objected to religious labels should form his own community. Indeed to ensure that his followers continued to witness to his teachings, he appointed a successor. He did not, however, choose one of his sons, as he wished to avoid creating a dynasty. Instead Nanak appointed his devoted disciple Angad Dev (1504-1552) to follow him and to become the Second Guru. There were to be eight further Gurus. The tenth Guru, Gobind Singh

(166-1708) transferred the Guru's authority to the Community and to the Scriptures, often called the *Guru Granth Sahib.*

Guru Nanak has obviously been a major influence in the continuing history of the Sikh religion and community - the term Sikh is derived from the Sanskrit word for *shishya,* which means 'devoted follower.' As Sikhism has become much more widely dispersed so his influence is increasing and many who are not Sikhs have become aware of his radical teaching which challenges religious exclusivism and intro-version. There is One God who has at heart the welfare of all people.

Sikhs in their morning prayers continue to use the *JapJi,* which was composed by Guru Nanak, and which begins with these words:

There is One God
His Name is Truth
He is the Creator
He is without fear
He is without hate,
Immortal is His form
He is not born to die or be born again
By the Guru's grace, He is obtained.

He was true before time began and He
Was the Truth when time began.
True He is even now and
True He shall be hereafter...

How then shall the truth be known and how the veil
of false illusion torn?
Only by obeying, O Nanak, the will of the Lord.[8]

CHAPTER NOTES

1. *Guru Granth Sahib,* Rag Bhairon, p. 1136, quoted by Patwant Singh, *The Sikhs,* London, John Murray, p.1136.
2. *Guru Granth Sahib,* Asa, p. 471, quoted in *The Sikhs,* p. 19.
3. *Guru Granth Sahib,* Japji p. 5, quoted in *The Sikhs,* p. 21.
4. *Guru Granth Sahib,* Rehras, p. 9, quoted in *The Sikhs,* p. 22.
5. *Guru Granth Sahib,* Var Maji, 7, 1, quoted by Mary Pat Fisher, *Living*

Religions, Prentice Hall, 1999, p.396

6. *Guru Granth Sahib*, Asa, p. 472, quoted in *The Sikhs*, p. 26.
7. *Guru Granth Sahib*, Asa, p. 473, quoted in *The Sikhs*, p. 27.
8. *Guru Granth Sahib*, Japji p. 1, quoted in *The Sikhs*, p. 23.

56

Martin Luther

Martin Luther, who has been described as 'one of the pivotal figures of Western civilization as well as of Christianity,' set in motion the Reformation which divided Western Christians into Catholics and Protestants. Rejecting the traditional teaching of the Church on many points, he offered creative new interpretations, which are still significant today. His translation of the Bible into German was of great importance not only for the religious life of the people but also for the development of the German language.

Martin Luther was born on November 10th, 1483 at Eisleben in Thuringian Saxony in Germany to Hans and Margarethe Luther. The family soon moved to Mansfeld, where his father did well working in the copper mines and where he became a local councillor. Luther's childhood memories were of sombre piety and strict discipline. He went to the well-known University of Erfurt, where he talked so much that he was nicknamed 'the Philosopher.' His father expected him, after his degree, to become a lawyer and was angry to discover that his son, without asking him, had become a monk and joined the strictly observant Augustinian Order in Erfurt. Luther said later that he did this because on his return from a visit to his parents, he was overtaken by a thunderstorm and cried out in terror, 'Help, St Anne, and I'll become a monk.' He was ordained a priest in 1507 and then selected for higher theological studies at Wittenburg University, where in due course he became professor of Biblical theology – a position he held almost to the end of his life. 'In between lectures, in a manner of speaking, he began the Protestant Reformation.'[1]

At first, he zealously and happily took part in the disciplined life of the monastery, but he was increasingly troubled by his failure to live up to the rule of the Order. 'I scrupulously carried out the penances which were allotted to me. And yet my conscience kept nagging. It kept telling me: "You fell short there", "You were not sorry enough," "You left that sin off your list."[2] His inner turmoil was reinforced by his struggle to understand St Paul and in particular the phrase, 'the righteousness of God', which Paul uses in his *Letter to the Romans*. Luther understood this to mean God's concern for justice shown in punishing the sinner. As he recalled toward the end of his life,

'However irreproachably I lived as a monk, I felt myself in the presence of God to be a sinner with a most unquiet conscience... I did not love, indeed I hated, this just God, if not with open blasphemy, at least with huge murmuring.

He suddenly realised that Paul was not thinking of the justice that God demanded but of God's gift, whereby he treated the sinner as if he were just.

'At last I began to understand the justice of God as that by which the just man lives by the gift of God, that is to say, by faith, and this sentence, "the justice of God is revealed in the Gospel" is to be understood passively, that by which the merciful God justifies by faith, as it is written, "The just man shall live by faith." At this I felt myself to have been born again, and to have entered through open gates into paradise itself.'[3]

The accuracy of Luther's memory has been questioned, as the record of his lectures at the time shows his growing understanding of Paul's message and of the teaching of St Augustine. Be that as it may, central to his teaching was the affirmation that salvation was God's gift to be claimed by faith, not something to be earned by good behaviour. 'Justification by faith alone' became the watchword of the Reformation.

This new understanding of God's mercy is the theological background to his protest against the sale of indulgences. 'God's forgiveness for Cash' sounds even worse than 'Cash for Honours,' but it was not as simple as that. In the sacrament of penance the priest who pronounced God's absolution required the penitent to do something to show he or she was genuinely sorry – such as saying more prayers or going on a pilgrimage. You could, however, give money to the Church and in return be let off the required act of penance. This was known as an indulgence. There were rules to regulate this, but they were not entirely clear. The Papacy with a great need for money authorised more and more indulgences, including ones that let a person off some of the time they would otherwise have spent in Purgatory. When a Jubilee indulgence was announced by the Pope, Prince Frederick of Saxony would not allow it in his territory - partly because it would reduce the number of pilgrims to Wittenberg. Luther, objecting to the practice, especially the crude salesmanship of a Dominican called Johann Tetzel, in 1517 nailed his 'Ninety-Five' theses on the door of the church at Wittenberg.

Not only the Papacy but also the Archbishop of Mainz would loose money if people followed Luther's teaching and boycotted the indulgence. So Luther was quickly in trouble with the Archbishop. There were, over the next eighteen months, various inconclusive hearings, which did nothing to resolve the issues. Meanwhile, Luther had been studying the history of the papacy and had started to question its authority. Indeed at the Leipzig Disputation in 1519, he publicly rejected papal infallibility. Henceforth his authority was the Bible. All this time, Luther besides serious theological work, was busy writing numerous pamphlets, arguing his case with vehemence. As he admitted, 'I am hot-blooded by temperament and my pen gets irritated easily.' In June 1520 Rome issued a papal bull which condemned forty-one of Luther's propositions as heretical. In December, Luther burnt the bull. In January 1521, the Pope retaliated by formally excommunicating Luther.

It was now up to the secular arm to get rid of this heretic – but because of the complex political situation in Germany and the support he received from his prince, Luther was first required to appear in 1521 at the Diet of Worms, convened by the Emperor Charles V. As he approached Worms, he wrote in 1522, God 'saw into my heart that although I had known there were as many devils ready to spring upon me as there were tiles on the house-roofs, I would joyfully have sprung into their midst.' This was the theme of one of his great hymns - which was well translated by Thomas Carlyle (1795-1881) - which Luther published with a chorale that he had written in 1529:

A safe stronghold our God is still,
A trusty shield and weapon;
He'll keep us clear from all the ill
That hath us now o'ertaken...

And were this world all devils o'er,
And watching to devour us,
We lay it not to heart so sore;

340

Not they can overpower us.[4]

At the hearing, Luther was required to recant, but he replied 'Unless I am proved wrong by Scriptures or evident reason, then I am a prisoner in conscience to the Word of God. I cannot retract and I will not retract. God help me. Amen.' Although this is now questioned, tradition has it that he ended his defence with the stirring words, 'Here I stand. I can do no other.'

Despite Luther's moral victory, he was declared to be an outlaw whose writings were proscribed. On his way home Luther, after an arranged kidnapping, was secretly confined in the castle of Wartburg, near Eisenach. He remained there until, disobeying his prince, he returned to Wittenberg in 1522. He stayed there for the rest of his life, although he actually died at Eisleben, where he had been born. He was buried in the Church of All Saints in Wittenberg in February 1546.

His return to Wittenberg was by no means the end of his involvement in controversy and his theological work during this period, which we shall consider first, was of great importance in laying the basis for Lutheranism, which now has millions of adherents across the world.

He was a prolific writer. Some seven hundred works in his name, in 4,000 editions, were circulating in Germany by the time of his death. Some were pamphlets but others were substantial theological works or commentaries on the Bible. Much of his theology, on, for example, the doctrines of the Trinity and the Atonement, was traditional. He made two distinctive contributions: *Sola scriptura* (scripture alone) and *Sola fide* (faith alone). First, he asserted the authority of scripture over against the authority of the papacy, insisting that both the doctrines and practices of the church must be shown to derive from the scriptures. Luther, therefore, condemned innovations, such as indulgences. Secondly, he insisted that for a person to be righteous in God's eyes depended only on faith in God's saving grace in Jesus Christ and was not to be gained by human efforts to obey God's laws. Good works were the loving response to God's mercy, not a way of earning it. The cross of Christ was central to his thinking.

Luther, who allowed clergy to marry, rejected the clericalism of the Church. Affirming the 'priesthood of all believers,' he emphasised the dignity of life in the world rather than in a monastery.

Luther not only provided the theological basis for Protestantism, he also translated the Bible into German and wrote a number of hymns, some of which are still sung today. Although he had help from Philip Melanchthon (1497-1560) and some others, the German Bible was mainly Luther's work. The translation of the New Testament from Greek was published in 1522 and the translation of the Old Testament from Hebrew appeared in 1534. Luther was also concerned that children should be provided with a good education, especially as reading the scriptures had now become so important.

In the opinion of the poet Samuel Taylor Coleridge, 'Luther did as much for the Reformation by his hymns as by his translation of the Bible.' Some monks said the same: 'Luther has done us more harm by his songs than by his sermons.' He printed the first German hymn book in 1524 with eight hymns. By the following year, there were forty hymns, which were enhanced by Luther's skill as a musician. One, written for children on Christmas Eve, has fifteen verses. The first seven were sung by a man, dressed as an angel, the remaining verses were sung by the children and included this touching request:

Ah, dearest Jesus, holy child,
Make Thee a bed, soft, undefiled,
Within my heart, that it may be
A quiet chamber kept for Thee.[5]

Luther said of music that 'it is one of the most beautiful and noble gifts of God. It is the best solace to a man in sorrow; it quietens, quickens and refreshes the heart.'[6]

Luther was caught up in a number of controversies besides his struggle with the papacy. Believing that the secular power was ordained by God, he stressed the Christian duty of civil obedience and the sinfulness of rebellion against the lawful authority. He, therefore, strongly opposed the Peasant's War, that broke out in 1524, writing with unnecessary brutality a broadsheet entitled' 'Against the Murdering and Thieving Hordes of Peasants.' Luther wrote equally vehemently against the Jews. In his lectures on the Psalms (1514-15), he affirmed God's wholesale rejection of the Jewish people. His booklet *That Jesus Christ*

Was Born a Jew (1523) appeared more sympathetic. He was very critical of the way the Church had treated the Jews and suggested a more friendly approach would lead to their conversion. When this did not happen, he urged Christian authorities to expel those Jews who did not convert and in his intemperate *On the Jews and Their Lies* (1543) he urged rulers to confiscate rabbinical texts, forbid the rabbis to teach and to burn down synagogues and the homes of Jewish people and if necessary to drive them out of the country 'for all time.' The Nazis not only republished this writing of Luther but in the Holocaust carried out his instructions. Meanwhile many in the churches, aware of his teaching against civil disobedience, did all too little to oppose Hitler.

Luther was also engaged in arguments with other reformers about the communion service and the meaning of Jesus' instruction to his disciples to eat bread and to drink wine in 'remembrance of me.' According to the traditional doctrine of 'transubstantiation' the bread did indeed become substantially flesh, even if it still looked like bread, and the wine became blood, even if it still appeared to be wine. Luther agreed that the words of Jesus must be taken literally. Ulrich Zwingli (1484-1531), a more radical Swiss Reformer, argued that the service was an act of remembrance. Others, who rejected transubstantiation, insisted that there was a real or spiritual presence of Christ at the Lord's Supper.

Luther, a learned Biblical scholar, was a passionate person whose moods could change from deep depression to anger, to tenderness and to devotion. The vehemence of some of his language is offensive in these more ecumenical days. He would not, however, be shaken from his basic convictions, which many Protestants have reaffirmed in their own spiritual experience and which he expressed in a hymn, based on Psalm 130, which was sung at his funeral:

'Tis through Thy love alone we gain
The pardon of our sin;
The strictest life is but in vain,
Our works can nothing win;
That none should boast himself of aught
But own in fear Thy grace hath wrought
What in him seemeth righteous

Wherefore my hope is in the Lord
My works I count but dust,
I build not there, but on His word,
And in his goodness trust.
Up to his care myself I yield,
He is my tower, my rock, my shield,
And for His help I tarry.[7]

CHAPTER NOTES

1. *Encyclopaedia Britannica*,11,189.
2. Quoted by Owen Chadwick, *The Reformation*, Penguin, 1964, 45.
3. From an autobiographical fragment written in 1545.
4. *The Methodist Hymn Book*, London, Methodist Conference Office, 1933. No, 494.
5. *The Methodist Hymn Book*, 126, The English translation, by Catherine Winkworth, omits the first six verses.
6. Quoted by John Telford in *The New Methodist Hymn Book Illustrated*, London, Epworth Press, 1934, 5th Edition, p. 91.
7. *The Methodist Hymn Book*, 359, translated by Catherine Winkworth.

57

Thomas Cranmer

Thomas Cranmer's *Book of Common Prayer* has shaped both the devotion and the language of many English-speaking people for over four hundred years. He helped Henry VIII obtain the annulment of his first marriage and was one of the architect's of the English Reformation. He died a martyr's death under Queen Mary.

Cranmer was born on July 2nd, 1489 at Aslacton in Nottinghamshire. His father belonged to the lowest rank of gentry. After enduring 'a marvellous severe and cruel schoolmaster,' Cranmer went to Cambridge University in 1503. In 1510 or 1511 he was elected to a fellowship at Jesus College, but soon had to give this up because he married a relative of the landlady of the Dolphin Inn. For a time, he earned his living teaching at what was then Buckingham College (now Magdalene College, where I was to study 450 years later). As Cranmer's wife died in childbirth, he was restored to his fellowship at Jesus College. Cranmer then was ordained and concentrated on his studies, becoming a very well read theologian. He immediately took a sympathetic interest in the theological ferment in Germany caused by the writings of Martin Luther and by 1525 was praying for the abolition of papal power in England.

His involvement in national life was almost accidental. Because a severe plague was raging in Cambridge in 1529, he went to stay at a house in Waltham in Essex. The King was visiting the area and two of his chief councillors happened to meet Thomas Cranmer. Inevitably conversation turned to the question of the royal divorce and Cranmer argued in the king's favour. He was summoned to meet the king and accepted a commission to write a propaganda treatise based on scripture, the Fathers, and the decrees of general councils. Whatever Henry's romantic desires and the political machinations of the king, the emperor and the pope, the point at issue in ecclesiastical law was whether the King's marriage to Catherine of Aragon was valid. She had previously been married to Henry's elder brother Arthur who died in 1502. Marriage to a brother's widow was not allowed in Canon Law, but Pope Julius II, under pressure from Catherine's parents, had granted a special dispensation on the grounds that the marriage was not consummated. But was this the case? And did the pope have the authority to set aside 'God's law?' The fact that Henry had no male heir was taken as a sign that the Pope did not have that power.

This was the case Cranmer was required to argue. In return, he was provided with hospitality by Anne Boleyn's father and appointed archdeacon of Taunton. His treatise, when complete, was presented for debate at Oxford and Cambridge Universities, where it won general approval. Cranmer, himself, was part of a delegation to Rome, where he had a courteous if fruitless audience with the Pope. In 1532 he went to Germany where he made contact with some of the Lutheran theologians and the princes who were sympathetic to them. At Nürenberg he developed a particularly close relationship with Andreas Osiander, a theologian with rather more conservative views than Luther and with Osiander's attractive niece, whom Cranmer secretly married in 1532 – clergy at that time were still required to be celibate.

In the same year 1532 the elderly Archbishop William Warham died. In 1533, with backing of Thomas Cromwell who was now one of the King's chief advisers, Cranmer was appointed Archbishop instead of Stephen Gardiner, who was the obvious candidate. Cranmer quickly convened his court at Dunstable, declared the King's marriage to Catherine of Aragon null and void and pronounced the second marriage to Anne Boleyn, who was already pregnant, to be valid. Subsequently, Cranmer was involved in Henry's further matrimonial proceedings.

His lasting work was the changes he encouraged to the Church in England, which was now under royal rather than papal control. With Thomas Cromwell (1485-1540), he encouraged the publication of the Bible in English. It is hard for us to realise what a revolutionary step this was. All services at the time were in Latin and if you could lay your hands on a Bible that also was in Latin. Although Wycliffe (c.1329-84) had translated the Bible into English in the fourteenth century, the first printed edition in English of the New Testament, translated from the original Greek by William Tyndale (1594-1536), was not made until 1525. Copies had to be smuggled into England as it was illegal to import them. Indeed Tyndale's New Testament was ceremoniously burned in London in 1526 and ten years later he himself was burnt at the stake, praying as he died, that God would 'open the King of England's eyes.' Already, an English Bible had been printed on the Continent. This, a translation from the Latin and German versions, was the work of Myles Coverdale (1488-1568) and was known as 'The Great Bible.' It was the version which all parishes were then required to obtain. The frontispiece looks at first sight like 'The Last Judgment,' with Christ in the Centre, but in fact it is King Henry who is at the centre, distributing copies of the scriptures to his grateful people. These early versions were later superseded by the Authorised or King James Bible, which, making much use of Tyndale's work, was a translation from the original Hebrew and Greek, published in 1611.

Together with the English Bible, of which long portions had to be read at every service, Cranmer's Book of Common Prayer has shaped the worship of the Church of England and subsequently of the worldwide Anglican Communion.[1] Both also profoundly influenced the English language and many in previous generations knew much of the Bible and many of the Prayer Book collects or prayers by heart.

Not until Henry was dead and his only son Edward VI was enthroned was Cranmer able to work on the Prayer Book. Although the *Book of Common Prayer* was used for centuries and is still used in a number of churches today, Cranmer in fact wrote two prayer books in 1549 and, a more Protestant one, in 1552, and recognised that liturgy had to change with changing times. He was also aware that the Latin services were too complicated and wrote in his Preface that 'to turn the book only was so hard and intricate a matter, that many times there was more business to find out what should be read than to read it when it was found out.' The Prayer Book contains daily services for Morning and Evening Prayer, an Order for Holy Communion with readings for each Sunday, and services for Baptism, Weddings and Funerals. The Psalter, which is included, is in large measure Coverdale's version. Much of the material was translated and often adapted by Cranmer from earlier liturgies, but some of it was his own composition, as, for example, the beautiful prayer to be said on the Sunday before Lent:

O Lord, who hast taught us that all our doings without charity (love) are nothing worth: send thy Holy Ghost, and pour into our hearts that most excellent gift of charity, the very bond of peace and of all virtues, without which whosoever liveth is counted dead before thee: grant this for thine only Son Jesus Christ's sake. Amen.

It was not only the complexity of the services, which were a cause for complaint but also the scarcity of preaching. Cranmer, therefore, published a *Book of Homilies* to remedy this – today the preacher who lacks inspiration can find a sermon on the internet! No doubt with all the theological debate at the time there were also complaints that people did not know what they should believe. Cranmer dealt with this as well, producing his 42 articles, defining the theological position of the Church of England. These were later modified and reduced to the *Thirty Nine Articles*, to which for many years clergy of the Church of England had to subscribe. I nearly forgot to mention that under Edward VI, clergy were allowed to marry, so at last Cranmer's wife could make herself known, although the scurrilous story circulated by his opponents that he had her carried around with him in a chest with air holes is almost certainly untrue.

Cranmer, like other leaders of the Reformation, was deeply concerned that everyone should understand the faith, read the Bible and be able to participate in worship. Theologically he was also committed to Protestant teaching, especially that salvation was God's gift that only required faith. As to the presence of Christ at the Communion, he believed that this was a real presence, but he rejected transubstantiation, which, as already mentioned, was the doctrine that the bread and wine was literally changed into the body and blood of Christ.

Cranmer was remarkably hard working and a good scholar who continued to learn and if necessary to change his mind. He pleaded unsuccessfully with Henry for Sir Thomas More (1478-1535), Anne Boleyn (c.1504 – 1536) and Thomas Cromwell when they fell out of favour, even though he held obedience to the king was a Christian duty. He did not bear malice toward his enemies and refused to punish them. When Thomas Cromwell, in exasperation, warned him that 'the popish knaves' would have his eyes and cut his throat before he did anything about it, he merely shrugged his shoulders.

The prophecy was all too true. When Edward died young in 1553, he was succeeded by Mary Tudor (1516-1558, Queen 1553-1558). Mary was the daughter of Catherine of Aragon – Henry VIII's first wife - and a devout Roman Catholic. England, by royal command, reverted to Catholicism and obedience to the Pope. An abortive attempt had been made to supplant Mary by proclaiming Lady Jane Grey (1537-1554) as Queen. Cranmer reluctantly had been involved in this. When Mary became Queen he was accused of treason. His opponents, however, were more concerned to destroy him for promoting Protestantism. Once the law which allowed the secular arm to burn heretics had been reintroduced, Cranmer was forced to watch Ridley and Latimer being killed. In a humiliating ceremony, Cranmer was stripped of his episcopal and priestly orders. Great pressure was brought upon him to recant and deny his previous teaching. This Cranmer did and before his execution he was required publicly to read it. To the horror of the Queen and her advisers, Cranmer disavowed his recantations and emphatically denied Papal authority and the doctrine of transubstanti-ation. Then, approaching the fire, he put his right hand, which 'had offended' by signing the recantations, into the flames, which then consumed the rest of his body.

In the Collect that he wrote for the feast day of St John the Baptist, who was beheaded by a King Herod, Cranmer asked that God would 'make us so to follow his doctrine and holy life, that we may truly repent according to his preaching, and after his example constantly speak the truth, boldly rebuke vice, and patiently suffer for the truth's sake.' Perhaps more than he had bargained for, his prayer was answered. As a result, he is remembered not only for his lasting contri-bution to the Church of England, but as one of the early Protestant martyrs.

CHAPTER NOTES
1. The Book of Common Prayer was revised in 1662, when Charles II was restored to the throne. This is the version traditionally used in the Church of England, although optional variations were agreed in 1928. In the last forty years there has been extensive re-writing of the liturgies used in the Anglican Communion.

58

Ignatius Loyola

No life better illustrates the Catholic Reformation of the sixteenth century than that of Saint Ignatius Loyola.[1] His two major contributions were, first *The Spiritual Exercises*, which over the centuries has helped many people to grow in the spiritual life. Secondly and even more important he founded the Jesuits, a very powerful and influential Catholic teaching Order, which is still influential today. Some scholars have argued that Ignatius Loyola was even more influential than the leaders of the Protestant reformation, Luther and Calvin, because when the Thirty Years Wars of Religion ended with the Treaty of Westphalia in 1648, there were twice as many Catholics as Protestants in Europe and today the gap has grown even larger.

We know a lot about the life of Ignatius. He kept a spiritual diary and dictated a short autobiography. The first biography written by his friend and disciple Pedro de Ribadeneira was published in 1572. Much information is also available from Loyola's voluminous correspondence.

Ignatius Loyola's name was originally Iñigo Lopez de Onaz y Loyola, but it was changed to Ignatius when he started at the University of Paris. Ignatius was born in the ancestral family castle in the Basque area of Spain in 1491. He was the youngest son of a wealthy and noble family and at the age of fifteen, he became a page in the service to the treasurer of the kingdom of Castille. He was five foot two and as a young man he had shoulder length reddish hair. On one occasion, he got into a serious brawl and spent a time in the bishop's prison. In 1517, he became a courtier in the service of the viceroy of Navarre, who employed him on military and diplomatic missions. He is often spoken of as a soldier saint, but he only twice took part in military action. On the second occasion, in the vain attempt to defend the city of Pamplona against the French, Ignatius was hit by a canon ball, which broke his right leg and damaged his left leg.

This event changed his life. Up until then, in his own words, he had been 'a man given to the vanities of the world, whose chief delight consisted in martial exercises, with a great and vain desire to win renown.'[2] The French gave him emergency treatment and arranged for him to be taken back to the castle at Loyola. He had to undergo painful surgery to reset his broken bone, which, of course, was done without anaesthetics. Ignatius, like a true knight, showed no signs of pain, other than clenching his fists. For a time his life was in danger. During his long convalescence, he read a life of Christ and the lives of some saints, which was all the reading matter that the castle had to offer. The monk, who had edited the stories of the saints, spoke of the service of God in terms of holy chivalry. As a result of his reading and reflection, Ignatius determined to copy the austerities of the saints as a way of doing penance for his sins.

He made his way to the great monastery of Montserrat, which, perched on a hillside, is still a great place of pilgrimage. There he spent three days confessing the sins of his whole life. He hung his sword and dagger by the famous statue of the Black Madonna. Then after a night of prayer, he journeyed to Manresa, which is about thirty miles from Barcelona. He lived as a beggar, scourging himself and taking no care of his appearance. He spent long hours in prayer in a cave which is still to be seen in the chapel of the monastery, where I had the privilege of staying for a few days. There were times of great distress, but towards the end of his eleven months at Manresa, there were also moments of joy and interior light. One day, sitting beside the Cordoner River, 'the eyes of his understanding began to open and, without seeing any vision, he understood and knew many things, as well spiritual things as things of faith.'[3] Another vision was of the Trinity, which he pictured as three musical keys, different but in harmony. It was at Manresa, he made the first draft of his *Spiritual Exercises*, which, in its final form, was approved by Pope Paul III in 1548.

From Manresa, he set out in March 1523 on pilgrimage to Jerusalem, travelling from Barcelona, via Rome (where he spent Holy Week), Venice and Cyprus. The journey took him six months. He would have liked to settle there, but the custodians of the shrines rejected the idea. After a month visiting the holy sites, he started his voyage back, reaching Barcelona almost exactly a year after he had left the city. Recognising that it had not been God's will for him to stay in Jerusalem, he 'finally decided to study for a time in order to be able to help souls.'[4] He began his studies at Barcelona, but ended up in Paris in 1528, where he stayed for seven years, dependent on alms. His austere and unorthodox appearance and way of life, to which a few companions were attracted, on occasion got him into trouble with the authorities. He eventually gained the degree of Master of Arts.

Ignatius then returned to Spain. Partly, it was hoped that his 'native air' might help him recover his health – it seems that gall-stones caused him severe stomach pains. He also needed to settle the affairs of his companions, who were soon to come with him to Jerusalem, and he also wanted people who knew him in his youth to see how God had changed the old Iñigo. Whilst he was in his home-town, he got the people to introduce a new way of caring for the poor, so that they did not have to become beggars. Then he made his way to Valencia and got a ship, which despite a violent storm, managed to get to Genoa. From there he made his way to Venice, where his companions from Paris joined him, as they hoped to make a pilgrimage with him to Jerusalem. War between Venice and the Turkish Empire made this impossible. The companions spent much of the next eighteen months in prayer. On a brief visit to Rome, they were granted an audience with the Pope. During this time, Ignatius had another decisive spiritual experience. He seemed to see Christ, with the cross on his shoulder and beside him the Eternal Father. The Father said, 'I wish you to take this man for your servant.' Jesus took him and said, 'My will is that you should serve us.' In 1538, Ignatius and his companions again gathered in Rome, where on Christmas Day 1538, Ignatius, now ordained a priest, said mass for the first time in the Church of St Mary Major in Rome.

In the third and final period of his life, spent mostly in or near Rome, Ignatius' energies were primarily devoted to founding the Jesuits, or the 'Society of Jesus', as the Order is properly known. Pope Paul III gave his approval to the plan for a new order in 1540. As Head of the Order, Loyola spent a lot of time cultivating benefactors. He also had an enormous correspondence, on a wide range of matters, with which to deal. His own quarters consisted of four rooms: a bedroom, which was plain and neat, a workroom, a chapel and a spare bedroom for his personal assistant.

The Order quickly attracted recruits. There were nearly 1,000 Jesuits, divided into twelve provinces by the time Ignatius died in 1556. One of his most famous followers was St Francis Xavier who travelled to India and Japan. Xavier's letters, describing his experiences, were widely circulated in Europe. Missionary efforts in Africa were less successful. Many of the Society's members worked in schools and colleges and a particular contribution of Jesuits over the centuries has been as educators. Francis Xavier took control of a school in Goa in 1542. The first Jesuit school in Europe was established in 1545 at the request of the duke of Gandia. The real breakthrough came when the Jesuits took charge of a school in Sicily at Messina, which at the time was one of the largest cities in Europe. When Loyola died in 1556 there were 34 Jesuit schools. By 1615, the number had risen to 372 and continued to grow until 1773, when the Jesuits, who had become too powerful, were suppressed by Pope Clement XIV. The Jesuits were restored in 1814 by Pope Pius VII and resumed their educational work. There are twenty-one Jesuit universities in the USA as well as a good number of schools and colleges. There is a well known Jesuit saying, 'Give me a child until he is seven and he will be mine for life.'

In the *Constitutions* of the Society, members were not allowed to inflict physical punishment on themselves nor to wear penitential clothes. They were also not required to chant the daily offices, which gave them greater mobility and adaptability so that they 'were ready to live in any part of the world where there was hope of God's greater glory and the good of souls.' The Order was more authoritative than traditional monastic orders. The special vow of obedience to the pope, which Loyola called 'the cause and principal foundation' of the society was of great importance. Indeed the Jesuits have been called the Papacy's 'shock troops' of the Catholic Reformation.

The term 'Counter-Reformation' is now often avoided, as the movement for renewal was far more than a response to Luther and Calvin and other Protestants. There was indeed a widespread recognition of the need to correct the abuses to which Luther had pointed. The Council of Trent (1545) clarified the Church's teaching, especially on the sacraments, renewed the liturgy, and made the Church's central government more efficient. All this gave Catholics new energy and self-confidence.

The founding of the Society of Jesus and other new orders as well as the renewal in older orders such as the Augustinians and Carmelites, however, owed nothing to Protestantism. There was a widespread desire in the Church for a deeper spiritual life. Ignatius's own contribution in his *The Spiritual Exercises* was itself very important. The book is a series of exercises designed to help those who use it to conquer their will. A retreatant had to spend long periods of silence, interrupted only by the liturgy and communication with his director, who needed to be a person of considerable spiritual wisdom. The Exercises were divided roughly into four weeks. To begin with, after recollecting that God had made human beings to praise and serve Him for ever, the disciple was made to recognise his sinfulness and imagine, very vividly, the pains of hell – to hear the weeping of the damned, to smell the fumes and stench and to feel the flames. Later the retreatant was required to concentrate on the events of Jesus' ministry, as described in the Gospels. Thereby, imagining the events of God's mercy shown at Bethlehem and Calvary, he was to recognise his total dependence on God's mercy. The final week was one of joy – developing a 'heartfelt appreciation of all the blessings God has given me so far, so that, fully grateful, I may become completely devoted to God in effective love.'[5] Ignatius was clear that love had to be expressed in action.

Many Christians, who have never read *The Spiritual Exercises*, have been helped by Ignatius' emphasis on the imagination and the encouragement to try to picture the scene described in the New Testament and even to imagine the sounds and smells. In recent years, Ignatius' own method of one-to-one conversation and the process of personal discernment have been recovered and with it renewed interest in Ignatian spirituality.

Ignatius was clear that the deep devotion to Jesus Christ, which was cultivated by regular meditative reading of scripture should issue in total surrender and self-offering to Jesus. This is well illustrated in two famous prayers written by Ignatius Loyola:

Teach us, good Lord,
To serve you as you deserve,
To give and not to count the cost,
To fight and not to heed the wounds,
To toil and not to seek for rest,
To labour and not to ask for any reward
Save that of knowing that we do your will.[6]

Fill us, we pray, with your light and love that we may show forth your wondrous glory. Grant that your love may so fill our lives that we may count nothing too small to do for you, nothing too much to give and nothing too hard to bear.[7]

Ignatius himself, although frequently ill in his last years, never sought for rest but continued to direct his order until the day of his death on July 31st, 1556. The day before, sensing that death was near, he had asked his secretary Juan Polanco to obtain a final blessing for him from the Pope. Polanco asked if he could postpone doing that until he had finished some letters, which he needed to send that day to Spain. Ignatius told him to use his own judgment. Ignatius died early the next day without having received the last rites, which are usually administered to Catholics. He was buried that evening in the small Jesuit Church of Sancta Maria della Strada, which was subsequently rebuilt. St Ignatius Loyola was beatified in 1609 and canonized in 1622.

Today there are more than 20,000 Jesuits at work in 106 countries. The Order that he founded and his devotional book *The Spiritual Exercises* still continue to have a profound and widespread influence.

CHAPTER NOTES

1. John Patrick Donnelly, *Ignatius Loyola: the Founder of the Jesuits*, New York, Pearson and Longman, 2004, p. viii. See also *St. Ignatius' Own Story*: as told to Luis González de Cámara: with a sampling of his letters, translated by William J. Young, Chicago : Loyola University Press, 1980. *The Autobiography of St. Ignatius of Loyola, with Related Documents* / edited with introduction and notes by John C. Olin; translated by Joseph F. O'Callaghan, New York: Fordham University Press, 1992.
2. *Autobiography*, References here are to the 1943 translation, p.1.
3. *Autobiography*, p. 30.
4. *Autobiography*, p. 50.
5. Quoted by Donelly, p. 83.
6. 'Prayer for Generosity,' 1548.
7. In the *Lion Prayer Collection* ed by Mary Batchelor, Oxford, Lion Publishing, 1992, p.61

59

Mirabai and Tulsidas

Mirabai and Tulsidas are two outstanding poets who popularised devotional or *bhaki* Hinduism in North India in the sixteenth century. Their writings continue to inspire and enthuse millions of worshippers of the gods Krishna and Rama, who are avatars of Lord Vishnu.

Mirabai (also known as Meera, Mira and Meera Bai) was a princess. She was born in about 1504 AD, in the small state of Merta in Rajasthan in North India. The rulers were great devotees of Vishnu. Her father was descended from the founder of Jodhpur. As was customary with royal families, her education included knowledge of the scriptures, music, archery, fencing, and how to ride horses and drive chariots – she was also trained to wield weapons in case of a war.

Mirabai also grew up amidst an atmosphere pervaded by the worship of Lord Krishna. When she was just four years of age, she manifested her own deep devotion to Krishna. Mirabai is said to have watched a marriage procession in front of her residence. Mirabai, the child, spotted the well-dressed bridegroom and asked her mother innocently, 'Dear mother, who will be my bridegroom?' Mirabai's mother smiled, and half in jest and half in earnest, pointed towards the image of Sri Krishna and said, 'My dear Mira, Lord Krishna - this beautiful fellow – is going to be your bridegroom'. Soon after, Mirabai's mother passed on. As Mirabai grew up, her desire to be with her Krishna grew intensely and she believed that Lord Krishna would come to marry her. In due course, she became firmly convinced that Krishna was to be her husband.

Mirabai was soft-spoken, mild-mannered, gifted, sweet, and sang with a melodious voice. She was reputed to be one of the most extraordinary beauties of her time with her fame spreading to several kingdoms and provinces. The King of Mewar tried to arrange for her to marry his son, Rana Kumbha. Mirabai, however, could not bear the thought of marrying a human being when her heart was filled with thoughts of her Krishna. But unable to go against her beloved grandfather's word, she finally consented to the marriage. Mirabai was wed to Rana Kumbha in 1513, before she turned 14.

Mirabai it seems tried to be a dutiful wife, but she could not abandon her devotion to Krishna. After her household duties were over, she would go to the temple of Lord Krishna and worship, sing and dance there. This meant she mixed with people of all castes, which was not appropriate to her royal position and which horrified her mother-in-law. They wanted her to worship the family deity, Durga, but Mirabai refused, 'I have already given up my life to my beloved Lord Krishna'.

Mirabai's sister-in-law was jealous and spread rumours about Mirabai's behaviour, falsely suggesting that she was secretly in love. Her enraged husband ran with a sword to find her, but she had gone to the temple. A relative persuaded Rana to calm down and make sure that the rumours were true. When he went to the temple, he found her alone in her ecstatic mood talking and singing to the idol. Meera told him that it was Krishna to whom she was married. She wrote to her husband, the prince or *Rana* in these words:

Oh Rana, I must praise my Lord,
Whatever the world may say.
I follow my Guru and worship my Guru
And praise him night and day.[1]

Kumbha Rana was heart-broken but remained a good husband until his early death. She further shocked her in-laws by refusing to commit suttee or self-immolation on her husband's funeral pyre.

The abuse and physical violence now got worse and attempts were made to poison her. Mirabai sent a letter to a holy teacher asking for his advice. She wrote,

'Simply because I am constantly tortured by my relatives, I cannot abandon my Krishna. I am unable to carry on with my devotional practices in the palace. I have made Giridhar Gopala[2] my friend from my very childhood. I feel a total bondage with him. I cannot break that bond'.

Tulsidasji sent a reply:

'Abandon those who cannot understand you and who do not worship Rama, even though they are your dearest relatives... The

Gopis, the women of Mathura, disowned their husbands to go to their Krishna. Their lives were all the happier for having done so. The relation with God and the love of God are the only elements that are true and eternal; all other relationships are unreal and temporary'.

Mirabai left Mewar and returned to her native Merta, but her unconventional behaviour was no more acceptable there. So she set out on a number of pilgrimages, which took her to Brindavan (Vrindavana), the birthplace of Lord Krishna, to Mathura, with its many associations with Krishna and finally to Dwarka, with its beautiful temple by the seashore on the extreme Western tip of India. It was at Dwarka, which is one of the four most holy Hindu pilgrimage sites, that Krishna set up his capital after fleeing from Mathura. We were privileged to be there for the *darshan* (viewing) of Lord Krishna when we went there. In Dwarka, Mirabai devoted herself to the worship of the Lord Krishna and is said eventually to have been absorbed into his image. Her voice and the flute accompaniment were the only sounds that could be heard. She passed away in about 1547 CE.

Mirabai's legacy was a wonderful collection of devotional songs in Hindi and Gujarati. The songs are still popular in many parts of India. Some of her songs have been translated into English by Robert Bly and set to music by John Harbison.[3] Mirabai's poetry expressed her love for Krishna who was closer to her heart than her friends and family. She perceived Krishna to be her husband, lover, lord and master. The unique characteristic of Mirabai's poetry is her complete loving surrender to Krishna. Her longing for union with Krishna is predominant in Mira's poetry who said she wanted to be coloured with the colour of dusk (dusk being the symbolic colour of Krishna). She believed that in her previous life she was one of the several Brindavan milkmaids or *gopis*, who were in love with Krishna.

A Mirabai poem is traditionally called a *pada*, a term used by the 14th century preachers for a small spiritual song. This is usually composed in simple rhythms and carries a refrain within itself. Mirabai used the love poetry of the time, as a way of expressing her deepest emotions felt for her Lord. Here are two examples of her poetry:

> *That dark dweller in Brajj*
> *Is my only refuge.*
> *O my companion,*
> *Worldly comfort is an illusion,*
> *As soon you get it, it goes.*
> *I have chosen the indestructible for my refuge,*
> *Him whom the snake of death*
> *Will not devour.*
> *My beloved dwells in my heart all day,*
> *I have actually seen that abode of joy.*
> *Mira's lord is Hari, the indestructible.*
> *My lord, I have taken refuge with Thee,*
> *Your dasi.*

Or again,

> *Deep is my agony in this night of separation*
> *When will the streaks of golden dawn appear?*
> *The moonlight is no comfort to me*
> *If I sleep, I wake as if startled by a dream*
> *O merciful One, deprived of You, I lie in anguish*
> *Bless me then with a vision of Your face.*

Mirabai encouraged people to come together to sing songs of devotion. On one occasion the Emperor Akbar and his court musician came in disguise to hear Meera's devotional and inspiring songs. Both entered the temple and listened to Meera's soul-stirring songs to their heart's content. Before he departed, Akbar touched the holy feet of Meera and placed a necklace of priceless gems in front of the idol as a present.

Tulsidas was born a few years after Mirabai in Uttar Pradesh in 1532. He was a Brahmin by birth. It is said that Tulsidas, who was known as Tulsiram or Ram Bola as a child, did not cry at the time of his birth and that he was born with all his thirty-two teeth intact. His mother died in childbirth and his foster mother was bitten by a snake and died. The boy was, therefore, thought to be cursed and had to run away. Even the village priest would not help, but that evening a holy man called Narharidas came to the temple. He had pity on the boy and took him back to his hermitage. Narharidas then looked after him, taught him to read and write and initiated him into the worship of

Rama. Later Narharidas introduced him to Acharya Shesh Sanatana, a teacher who trained Tulsidas thoroughly in Sanskrit and the Vedas. The Acharya then sent Tulsidas out into the world to proclaim the love of Rama. His final words to his pupil were, 'You must be a householder like Rama.' Soon afterwards a marriage was arranged, although the father-in-law at first objected to Tulsidas' poverty, but was told that the young man was rich in learning.

Tulsidas's wife's name was Ratnavali. Their son's name was Tarak. Tulsidas was passionately attached to his wife and could not bear even a day's separation from her. Indeed, her friends teased her, saying, 'You have weaned Tulsi from Rama. Now he is a greater devotee of Ratna than of Rama.' One day his wife went to her father's house without informing her husband. Tulsidas went to look for her at his father-in-law's house. Ashamed, Ratna said to Tulsidas, "My body is but a network of flesh and bones. If you would develop for Lord Rama even half the love that you have for my filthy body, you would certainly cross the ocean of Samsara and attain immortality and eternal bliss". These words pierced the heart of Tulsidas like an arrow. He at once abandoned his home and became an ascetic.

Tulsidas set out on pilgrimage, on his way teaching people about the Ramayana, the great Sanskrit epic about Rama and Sita. He taught in Hindi, the language of the people, although this annoyed the more orthodox Brahmins. Later, under the directions of the monkey god Hanuman, Tulsidas wrote his own version of the story in Hindi, known as the *Ramacaritamanasa*, 'the Lake of the Deeds of Rama'. In Tulsidas' version, Rama became more human and attractive and easier to imitate. Tulsidas wrote in a pure Hindi and there is music to his verse. The *Ramacaritamanasa* was an immediate success and quickly became well known across North India. The book is probably, after the Bhagavad Gita, the best loved Hindu writing and is sometimes called 'the Bible of North India.' It includes this beautiful summary of the moral lesson of the epic. 'Those who regard other men's wives as mothers, and the wealth of others as more lethal than poison, who rejoice when others flourish and are deeply pained when they are afflicted, those to whom, you, O Rama, are dearer than life, in them is you're abode full of blessing.'

Tulsidas wrote eleven other books of hymns and poems, of which the *Vinaya Patrika* is the best known. In one of his own songs Tulsidas wrote,

> O Lord, in love I come
> Unto your lotus feet;
> I care not where I live
> Or what I have to eat.
>
> I need but you, O Lord;
> You are my lover true.
> My mind and heart are restless
> Until they rest in you.
>
> Men may praise or blame me -
> I do not fear them Lord.
> I only want you in my heart -
> You are my sole reward.

Tulsidas lived in Ayodhya for some time. Then he moved to Varanasi. One day a murderer came and cried, "For the love of Rama give me alms. I am a murderer". Tulsi called him to his house, gave him sacred food which had been offered to the Lord and declared that the murderer was purified. The Brahmins of Varanasi reproached Tulsidas, saying 'How can the sin of a murderer be absolved? How could you eat with him? If the sacred bull of Siva—Nandi—would eat from the hands of the murderer, then only we would accept that he had been purified'. Then the murderer was taken to the temple and the bull ate from his hands. The Brahmins were put to shame.

It is also said that some thieves came to Tulsidas's Ashram to take away his goods. They saw a blue-complexioned guard, with bow and arrow in his hands, keeping watch at the gate. Wherever they moved, the guard followed them. They were frightened. In the morning they asked Tulsidas, "O venerable saint! We saw a young guard with bow and arrow in his hands at the gate of your residence. Who is this man?" Tulsidas remained silent and wept. He realised that Lord Rama Himself had been taking the trouble to protect his goods. He at once distributed all his wealth among the poor.

On another occasion Tulsidas' blessings brought the dead husband of a poor woman back to life. The Emperor in Delhi heard of the miracle and sent for Tulsidas. When came to court, the Emperor asked the saint to perform some miracle. Tulsidas replied, 'I have no superhuman power. I know only the name of Rama'. He was then put in prison and told, 'You will only be released if you show me a miracle". Tulsidas then prayed to Hanuman. Countless bands of powerful monkeys entered the royal court. The emperor got frightened and said, 'O saint, forgive me. I know your greatness now'. He at once released Tulsidas from prison.

Tulsidas died in Varanasi in 1623, at the age of ninety-one. He is regarded as a reincarnation of Valmiki, the legendary author of the Ramayana.

Tulsidas' teaching derives from that of the philosopher Ramanuja. He believed in a Supreme Personal God, who was all-gracious.

I serve my God, my strength, my hope –
I live in Him alone
He may be called by different names
For me He's only one

This Supreme God took on human form for the blessing of humankind.

As salty sea-water evaporates
And comes down clean, pure rain,
So a sinner, meeting the Lord
Is cleansed from every stain.

He makes the dumb man talk
The lame man climb the hill;
So despite my sinfulness
He will love me still.

Because God took on a human body, the body is to be respected and Tulsidas rejected extreme asceticism. The Lord should be approached, he said, by faith, disinterested devotion and self-surrender. The devotee was to show love to all people:

Treat all people well.
Perhaps to your surprise,
The one whom you are meeting
Is God in some disguise.
And again,
If I forgive with loving kindness
I find my God within.

CHAPTER NOTES

1. The translations of the verses by Mirabai and Tulsidas are from R H Lesser, *Saints and Sages*, chapters 3 and 10.

2. One of the titles for Krishna.

3. Robert Bly, *Mirabai Versions*, New York, Red Ozier Press, 1984. Another translation is by A J Alston, *The Devotional Poems of Mirabai*, 1980.

60

John Calvin

Calvin as a theologian and church leader had a formative influence on the Protestant Reformation. Many Christians today, influenced by his theological and Biblical writing describe themselves as Calvinists or Reformed. He established a new scheme of civic and ecclesiastical governance. He made Geneva a central hub from which Reformed teachings spread across Europe and in due course to the Americas. It has been said that American culture, at heart, is thoroughly Calvinist.

Although John Calvin's name is forever linked with the Swiss city of Geneva, he was born in 1509 in France with the name Jean Chauvin. Calvin is derived from his Latin name Calvinus. His birthplace was Noyon in Picardy. His father, a member of the emerging middle class, was secretary to the bishop and as procurator was also responsible for much of the administration of the cathedral chapter. Calvin was educated with the young nobility of a family related to the bishop, and after elementary education in Noyon, went with them to study liberal arts in Paris. For some of the time he was at the Collège de Montaigu, where the Dutch Humanist Erasmus and the French author Rabelais had studied and where Ignatius Loyola, the founder of the Jesuit religious order and a leading member of the Catholic Counter-Reformation, was later to study. After gaining his master's degree, his father sent him for advanced legal studies at the university of Orléans and for a time he also studied at Bourges. Following his father's death in 1531, he returned to Paris, and joined some of the leading Humanists, who were studying the recently recovered treasure house of Greek and Roman literature. Calvin's first book was a carefully edited text *De Clementia* ('Concerning Clemency') by Seneca the Younger (c.4BCE-65CE), a Roman Stoic philosopher.

Soon after the publication of this book, Calvin was suddenly converted to Protestantism, but he gives us no details of his experience. At the time, it was illegal and dangerous to be a Protestant in France. Calvin, therefore, left France and, under the pseudonym of Martianus Lucanius, settled for a time in Switzerland at Basel, which was a Protestant centre, where he devoted himself to a study of the Bible and the Early Church Fathers and also the writings of Luther and other Reformers. His knowledge of Catholic teaching was mainly derived from the *Sentences* on theology by the Mediaeval scholastic theologian, Peter Lombard (1100-1160) and the *Decretum* on canon law by Gratian (died c. 1159).

The fruit of all this study was Calvin's best known work, *Institutes of the Christian Religion*, which was first published in 1536, and subsequently extensively revised. The definitive edition in Latin appeared in 1559 and in French in 1560. The first edition was an extended catechism, or summary of Christian teaching in the form of questions and answers. It was organised in the traditional way but its Protestant teaching was certainly new. By the final edition, the *Institutes*, had become a comprehensive and very influential handbook on Protestant dogma.

Before the first edition of the *Institutes* was published, Calvin had left Basel for Italy. His travelling in due course brought him to Geneva, where the city-state had just become Protestant, defying the bishop and ousting the cathedral clergy. Calvin was persuaded by a fellow Frenchman, William Farel, (1489-1565) a leader of the Genevan Reformation, to stay and help to establish Protestantism in the city. Calvin was appointed public lecturer on the Bible, with the task of explaining the reasons for the far-reaching religious changes to the educated citizens – which he also did in his book, *Instruction in Faith* (1537). He was soon also asked to preach and to help Farel prepare regulations on liturgy and morality. The City Council, however, refused to accept Calvin and Farel's creed and would not grant them the power to excommunicate those they suspected of heresy. The pair, in response, refused to celebrate the Lord's Supper at Easter. The city council, therefore, forced Farel and Calvin to leave the city in 1538.

Calvin left for Strasbourg. Thinking he should set an example to show his support for the marriage of clergy, he asked his friends to find for him a woman who 'was modest, obliging, not haughty, not extravagant, patient and solicitous for my health.' The choice was Idelette de Bure, a widow, whose first husband, by whom she had two children, had been a member of the radical Anabaptists. Calvin grew very fond of her and said that she was a helper in ministry, who never stood in his way, never troubled him about her children, and had a greatness of spirit. Sadly, she died quite young, in 1549, and their only child died at birth in 1542.

Without Calvin and Farel, Geneva soon began to descend into chaos. The new Protestant leaders were ineffectual and there was pressure on the city from the neighbouring state of Savoy to return to Catholicism. In 1541, they were invited back and Calvin was given the house of a former cannon, who had left a good wine cellar. With him came his wife whom he had recently married.

Although Calvin did not have a political position, his opinions carried great weight, although the City Council, to whom he was answerable, often disagreed with him. In the government of the Church, based on the example of the Acts of the Apostles, four orders of ministry were established: teaching doctors to study and expound the message of the Bible; pastors to preach and administer the sacraments; elders to ensure the people's godly behaviour and correct belief and if necessary to administer discipline; deacons to administer peoples' charitable gifts of money and to look after orphans, widows and others in need of help.

As a doctor, Calvin himself gave detailed commentaries on the scriptures – some of which he published, although others have only survived in the notes taken by students. The lecture hall still survives. Calvin also involved himself in the work of the preachers and in the work of the elders. The latter held a weekly consistory court, to which those with erroneous beliefs or whose behaviour was inappropriate were summoned. If they repented, they would get a severe reprimand. At worst, they could be excommunicated. The civil power would carry out the required punishment of unrepentant heretics. Some people were imprisoned for dancing, others reprimanded for immodest clothing or playing cards. More serious offenders, for example those convicted of sorcery, were handed over to city council for execution. Although it is disputed, it seems that Calvin did not criticise the use of torture, which was common at the time. Calvin believed that obedience to God was required in every aspect of life and his intention was to create a holy community in the city. In 1550, the magistrates authorised the clergy to make an annual visit to the home of each parishioner to see if the rules of the Church were being observed. Then, as now, attempts to impose 'good' behaviour on a society were a threat to personal liberty and human rights. The cruel death of the brilliant Spanish free thinker

Michael Servetus[1] (1511-53), who rejected traditional teaching about the Trinity, shows Calvin's dangerous intolerance, which is characteristic of religious people who are sure they are right.

The old picture of Calvin as almost a dictator is, however, misleading. The city council often rejected his suggestions and complained about over long sermons. He had his loyal followers, but he was more feared than loved. Some citizens were scurrilous in their abuse and rude notes were left in the pulpit. Some tennis players chose the square outside the church where he was preaching, hoping their noise would distract his audience.

Calvin's contribution to Genevan society was far-reaching. He encouraged efforts to revitalize secondary education in the city. He also persuaded the Genevan government to set up a theological academy in 1559, which eventually became the University of Geneva. Its first rector was Theodore Beza (1519-1605) another French man and a brilliant humanist scholar. Calvin would attend to quite detailed matters such as urging legislation to require rails on balconies, so as to protect small children. He was concerned for the plight of many Protestant refugees, fleeing from Catholic persecution, who made their way to Geneva. Quite often, on their arrival, he would invite them to his own home. He helped establish a fund to provide for them and thanks to his efforts a silk-weaving industry was introduced to give work to these refugees, many of whom, when they were able to return to their own countries, were influential in spreading Calvinism.

Calvin, in his later years became unwell and at times he had to be carried from his bed to preach or lecture. For many years he only ate one meal a day. When towards the end of his life, his friends urged him to cut down on his work, he replied 'What! Would you have the Lord find me idle when he comes?' He died in 1564. He asked to be buried without witnesses or ceremony in an unknown place. His tombstone is marked simply with the letters 'J.C.'

Calvin seems to have been as severe on himself as he was on others and, maybe, with his own strong self discipline, he was unsympathetic to human weakness, although always conscious that all people were sinners in need of God's forgiveness. He was a rather private person and it is difficult now to sense his charismatic power to inspire many people to risk their lives for their new religious convictions. His letters, of which more than 4,000 survive, do, however, show him to be more emotional than his public persona would suggest. He said of his grief at the massacre of over three thousand Waldensians in 1545, 'I write, worn out with sadness, and not without tears, which so burst forth, that every now and then they interrupt my words.'

'Union with Christ' lies at the heart of his teaching. He gave the highest degree of importance to 'that joining together of Head and members, that indwelling of Christ in our hearts – in short that mystical union' by which 'we put on Christ and are engrafted into his body.'[2] This unmerited relationship is made possible by the Holy Spirit. In the humanity of Christ, crucified and risen, our humanity has been turned back to God. By being bound to Christ in faith we are enabled to be reconciled to God.

Although Calvinism is often associated with the teaching of Predestination, Calvin's own emphasis was on the undeserved nature of God's gift of salvation. But why was that salvation given to some people and not to others – especially if those who received it had done nothing to merit it? The answer was that this was an act of divine grace and of God's choice. God, therefore, chose to save some people and to condemn others. This developed into the doctrine of double predestination – some people from all eternity were destined for heaven and others to hell. This doctrine was later rejected by John Wesley[3], the founder of Methodism and has also been rejected by many other Christians.

Calvin was convinced that the teaching of the Bible could reform every aspect of Christian life. The Scriptures, he said, 'should be read with a view to finding Christ in them.' 'God is nigh to us, face to face' in the mystery of preaching.[4] Through the Holy Spirit Christ is present in the Word as well as in the Sacrament of bread and wine.

Calvin stressed the corporate nature of the Christian life. One cannot have God as Father without having the Church as Mother. The believer was part of a God-fearing community. Indeed, society itself should reflect the values of the Gospel. Laity and clergy alike were called to incorporate every sphere of their lives into the service of Christ. Engagement with the world was emphasised instead of traditional monastic withdrawal. Rejecting the authority of the Pope, he also did not agree with the Lutheran teaching of obedience to 'the powers that

be.' Rather, Christians through their participation in society were called
to bring all human experience (secular and sacred) under the lordship
of Christ. This emphasis on involvement in the world has had a lasting
influence on Christianity, especially in North America.

CHAPTER NOTES
1. See below chapter 62.
2. *Institutes of the Christian Religion*, 3.12.10.
3. See chapter 68.
4. *Commentary on Haggai*, 1.12.

61

Servetus

Michael Servetus was a man of prodigious intellect, a scientist and a free-thinking theologian. Servetus is credited with the discovery of pulmonary circulation in the human body. He has been hailed as the first Unitarian and labelled a 'total heretic' – burned in effigy by the Catholic Church, and physically burned on Calvin's orders in Geneva. Servetus anticipated many of the questions discussed by critical Christian scholars in the last one hundred and fifty years. He was also a prophet of interfaith dialogue, writing 'for an additional audience of Jews and Arabs, Marranos and Moriscos.'[1]

Michael Servetus (or Miguel Serveto) was probably born in Villanueva in Southern Spain in 1511 on September 29th, the feast of St Michael and All Angels – hence his Christian name. His surname derives from the hamlet of Serveto in the Pyrenees, where his paternal ancestors had lived. Michael was born less than twenty years after the old Moorish kingdom of Granada had been conquered by the ardent Christian rulers, King Ferdinand and Queen Isabella. They had entered the fallen city triumphantly on 2 January 1492. Three months later, after a period of intense persecution of the Jews, the Edict of Expulsion was signed in Granada. By the end of the year the 200,000 Jews had left Spain and the country was *Judenfrein*. Vibrant, learned and cultured Jewish and Muslim communities were destroyed. Those who converted, the *conversos* or Marranos - a word derived from the Spanish for swine - were always suspected of harbouring their original faith and often fell foul of the Inquisition. Servetus' mother's family may have been *conversos*. 1492, the Year of the Expulsion of the Jews, was also to be the year in which Columbus set out on the journey in which he 'discovered' America.

Servetus' father, who was a notary at a nearby royal monastery, ensured a good education for his son, who became proficient in Latin, Greek and Hebrew. At the age of fifteen, Servetus entered the service of a Franciscan friar, who had been influenced by Erasmus. The friar encouraged Servetus to read the whole Bible in Hebrew and Greek manuscripts – the authoritative version of the Bible in use at the time, the Vulgate, was in Latin. Servetus then studied law at the University of Toulouse, where he seems to have mixed with some Protestant students. In 1529-30, he travelled with his patron Quintana, who was confessor to the Emperor Charles V (1500-1558), through Germany and Italy. He was however shocked by the worldly pomp of the papacy. After leaving his patron, Servetus visited Lyons, Geneva and Basel, meeting with some leaders of the Reformation, including Johannes Oecolampadius (1482-1531) and Martin Bucer (1491-1551). In July 1531 he published his controversial *De Trintatis Erroribus* ('On the Errors of the Trinity') and in the following year his *De Justitia Regni Christi* ('On the Justice of Christ's Reign').

To avoid persecution because of his radical views, Servetus then adopted the name of Michel de Villeneuve or Villovanus and found work as an editor of scientific works and published an annotated translation of the *Geographia* by the second century geographer and astronomer Ptolemy. He then studied medicine at Paris and matriculated in 1538. In a later work, he was to be the first European to describe the circulation of the blood.

Following his studies at Paris, Servetus, as we will continue to call him, practiced medicine near Lyons in France for some fifteen years, becoming the personal physician to the Archbishop of Vienne. He continued to write books about medicine and theology, including *Biblia Sacra ex Santis Paginini translatione* (1542) and then in 1553 *Christianismi Restitutio*, which was the book that led to his condemnation as a heretic. Charges were brought against him and he was arrested and imprisoned by the Catholic authorities in Vienne. He escaped just before he was condemned, but his effigy and his books were burned in his absence.

Intending to find refuge in Italy, Servetus, inexplicably, stopped in Geneva, where Calvin (1509-64), a leader of the Protestant Reformation, with whom he had exchanged acrimonious letters, was dominant. On August 13th, Servetus, rashly, went to hear a sermon by Calvin. He was recognised and arrested as soon as the service finished. Servetus was put on trial with Calvin leading the attack. Servetus wrote to the Council urging them to 'shorten the deliberations.' 'It is clear', he wrote, 'that Calvin for his pleasure wishes to make me rot in this prison. The lice eat me alive. My clothes are torn and I have nothing for a change, no shirt, only a worn out vest.'[2] The trial resulted in Servetus' condemnation on the charges of denying the Trinity and rejecting infant baptism. As Servetus was not a citizen of Geneva, legally the harshest penalty should have been banishment, but the government of the city consulted with other Reformed Swiss cantons, which all favoured his execution. Calvin supported this, although he asked for Servetus to be executed rather burned as a heretic. The Council rejected Calvin's request and on October 27th, 1553, Servetus, with his book chained to his leg was burned at the stake. To prolong his agony, new wood was used that took longer to burn. A few voices, however, were raised against imposing the death penalty for heresy and Servetus' execution damaged Calvin's reputation at the time and subsequently. Servetus' last words were, 'Jesus, Son of the Eternal God, have mercy on me.'

After the Execution, Calvin instructed the printer Robert Estienne to hunt for and destroy any remaining copies. It was thought that all the copies of the offending book were destroyed, but in fact, in what is an amazing story in itself, three copies survived.[3] 1665 a Hungarian count was browsing at a bookseller's in London, which at the time was the centre of the world book trade, because many libraries had been shipped to London to preserve them from the ravages of the Continental Wars of Religion. The count chanced upon an octavo which was over one hundred years old, but which did not have the author's or the printer's name. He recognized at once that it was Servetus' forbidden work. Eventually, the count gave it to the Unitarian Church in Transylvania.

Towards the end of the seventeenth century a second copy of *Christianismi Restitutio* was found in the library of a German aristocrat in Hesse. Some pages were missing, but at the end were hand-written notes by the chief accuser of Servetus. Yet, a few years later when the aristocrat wanted to show the book to the duke of Savoy, it was missing. The book reappeared in the library of an English collector Richard Mead in the 1720s. It was to be another one hundred and fifty years before a third copy was discovered in the library of the University of Edinburgh.

Although Orthodox Christian teaching affirms that there is One God in Three Persons, popular Christian teaching at the time of Servetus easily gave an impression of tritheism or belief in three gods. Roland Bainton has written that 'that pictorial representations showed the

Trinity sometimes as three identical old men, sometimes distinguished in that the Father wore a tiara, the Son carried a cross, and the Spirit a dove. Or again, one body was shown with three heads or one head with three faces.'[4]

An influential theologian Peter Lombard (d. 1160) had claimed in his *The Sentences* that the doctrine of the Trinity could be found on every page of Holy Writ. Servetus was amazed. 'To me', he said, 'not only the syllables but all the letters and the mouths of babes and sucklings, even the very stones themselves, cry out that there is one God the Father and his Christ, the Lord Jesus.'[5] Many modern Christian scholars agree that 'in the New Testament, there is no explicit Trinitarian statement.'[6]

Servetus stressed the unity of God. This laid him open to accusations of adopting early heresies which emphasised the oneness of God. He saw Father, Son and Holy Spirit as modes of operation rather than distinct persons and said that the Son was subordinate to the Father. For Servetus, the eternal Word, which was conjoined with the human Jesus, was a phase of God's activity, not a separate person in the Godhead. Likewise, the Holy Spirit is not a distinct Being. It is God's spirit moving in our hearts.[7] Servetus' position receives some support in contemporary theological debate. The argument is between those who speak of an 'essential' or 'immanent' Trinity, meaning that God is triune in God's inner essence or being and others who speak of an 'economic' or 'social' Trinity, referring to how God is seen by humans to relate to the world as creator, saviour and inspirer.

If the Son is only a mode of God's activity, there is a danger that his real humanity is called in question. Servetus tried to meet this by clearly distinguishing the Word, which is eternal, from the Son, whom he equated with the human Jesus to whom the Word is conjoined. To understand Servetus' thinking, we need first to appreciate his view of the relationship of humanity to God. There is an ancient saying that Christ became man so that we might become divine.[8] Servetus said that those who make a sharp demarcation between humanity and divinity 'do not understand the nature of humanity which is of such a character that God can communicate divinity to it.'[9] This was in sharp contrast with the pessimistic view of humanity to be found especially in Calvin and other Reformation thinkers, who held that only Christ's atoning death can save the faithful from the damnation which they deserve. Again, there are echoes of Servetus' approach among Christian theologians who reject a penal theory of the Atonement and those Protestant theologians, like Paul Tillich (1886-1965), who distinguished the human 'Jesus of Nazareth' from 'Jesus as the Christ' – meaning by Christ the principle of New Being or Divine Logos or Word. Moreover, the New Testament scholar James Dunn argues that 'to call Jesus "Lord" was evidently *not* understood in earliest Christianity as identifying him with God.'[10]

Servetus also believed that when all people have realised their divine potential through the Son, then Christ will give his Kingdom to God.[11] At that point, Servetus held, the Trinity in dispensation will terminate.[12] This was a rejection of the Reformers belief that only a few believers were predestined for salvation. Servetus hoped that in the end all beings would be reconciled to God – a hope shared by Universalists.

Growing up in an area where Jewish and Muslim influences had been strong, Servetus, even as a youth, was puzzled that Jews and Muslims did not accept Christianity and his writings were as much addressed to them as to fellow Christians.

Occasionally it has been suggested that Servetus was a Marranos – a forcibly converted Jew – and he was accused of being a Judaiser. Servetus certainly had a good knowledge of Hebrew and of Jewish history and thought. In the Introduction to the *Santes Pagnini's Bible*, which he edited (1545), he wrote that to understand the Bible one has 'to get a knowledge of Hebrew in the first place, and after that dilligently to apply yourself to the study of Jewish history before you enter upon the reading of the prophets.' He pointed out in the *Errors* that 'you must bear in mind that all things written about Christ took place in Judea and in the Hebrew tongue.'[13] This may seem obvious, but it was largely forgotten by the Church until quite recently. Even in his Christmas message for 2003, the then Bishop of Oxford, Richard Harries, reminded the faithful to 'Celebrate the Jew in Jesus this Christmas.'[14]

Servetus also argued that the prophetic writings should be interpreted as applying to the times when they were written not as foretelling the future. Modern Old Testament scholars would agree with this and also with his view that The Psalms of David were autobiographical and not prophetic.[15]

Servetus believed in a progressive revelation of God and saw at least 'a shadow of faith' in Judaism. He tried to gain a genuine under-standing of both Judaism and Islam. He certainly read the Qur'an and referred to the first Latin translation, which was printed in 1543.[16] Earlier in his life, he may have used a manuscript Latin translation or probably knew enough Arabic to read the Qur'an for himself.

Servetus can be seen as a forerunner of the interfaith dialogue, which is becoming increasingly common and as anticipating many contemporary Christian theological debates. He also may have influ-enced the sixteenth century Christian rationalism known as Socinianism, which in turn influenced both the growth of Unitarianism and the thinking of Isaac Newton, John Locke and the Cambridge Platonists. Such a seminal thinker, however, defies labels and is best remembered as a martyr for freedom of thought and liberty of conscience. This certainly is how both Voltaire (1694-1778) and Thomas Jefferson saw him. Voltaire, a French philosopher and champion of the Enlightenement, roundly denounced Calvin's treatment of Servetus - whom he called 'a very learned doctor', although also 'mad' and a 'fool'- as 'an assassination committed in ceremony.' Voltaire described the burning of Servetus in grisly detail. He wrote in a letter from his estate in Ferney, in 1759, 'I see from my windows, the city where Jean Chauvin, the Picard called Calvin, reigned and the place where he had Serveteus burned for the good of his soul.'[17] Thomas Jefferson (1743-1826), the Third President of the United Sates of America, who drafted the Declaration of Independence and the Statute of Virginia for Religious Freedom, feared that Presbyterian clergy wanted 'to rekindle in this virgin hemisphere the flame in which their oracle, Calvin, consumed the poor Servetus because he could not subscribe to the proposition of Calvin that magistrates have a right to exterminate all heretics to the Calvinistic creed.'[18]

In 1903, the city council of Geneva erected a small stone monument to Servetus, with these words on the back:

'Duteous and grateful followers of Calvin our great Reformer, yet condemning an error which was that of his age, and strongly attached to liberty of conscience according to the true principles of his Reformation and the Gospel, we have erected this expiatory monument.'

Servetus' champions were outraged and erected a sculpture in his memory, four miles South-east of Geneva and just across the border in France. It spoke of his fate as an insult 'to the Right of Nations.'[19] The French Senator August Dide said at the dedication of the statue, 'Glorifying Servetus ... we honour what is the most precious and most noble in our human nature: a generosity of heart, independence of the spirit, heroism of convictions.'[20]

CHAPTER NOTES

1. Jerome Friedman, *Michael Servetus: A Case Study in Total Heresy,* Geneva, Libraire Droz, 1978, p. 17. Marranos were Spanish Jews who had converted to Christianity and Moriscoe were Spanish Moors.

2. Lawrence and Nancy Goldstone's *Out of the Flames: The Remarkable Story of a Fearless Scholar A Fatal Heresy and One of the Rarest Books in the World,* New York, Broadway Books, 2002, p.316.

3. *Out of the Flames* tells the story of the book's survival.

4. Roland H Bainton, *Hunted Heretic, The Life and Death of Michael Servetus, 1511-1553.* The Beacon Press, Boston , 1953, p. 14. He refers to Alfred Hackel, *Die Trinität in der Kunst,* 1931; A N Didron, *Iconographie Chrétienne,* 1843 and Karl von Spiess, *Trinitätsdarstellungen mit dem Dreigesichte,* 1914. There are illustrations in Bainton's book.

5. *Errors,* 27b.

6. *Lutterworth Dictionary of the Bible,* pp. 934-5.

7. *Errors,* 31b.

8. This is echoed in the Church of England's new Collect for the First Sunday after Christmas, which includes the words 'grant that, as he came to share in our humanity, so we may share the life of his divinity.' *Common Worship,* The Archbishop's Council 2000, p. 381.

9. *Errors,* 11b

10. James D G Dunn, *The Partings of the Ways,* SCM Press 1991, p. 191.

11. See I Corinthians 15, 22- 28.

12. *Errors,* 81b-82a.

13. *Errors*, 1f, 13b.
14. Richard Harries in *The Door*, published by the Diocese of Oxford, Dec 2003, p. 1. See also my *Time to Meet*, London, SCM Press, 1990, p. 44ff.
15. J Muilenburg, *New Peake's Commentary on the Bible*, p. 475.
16. This was the translation made by Robert of Retina and Hermann of Dalmatia in 1143. It was published by Bibliander at Basel.
17. *Out of the Flames*, p. 258.
18. *Out of the Flames*, p. 294.
19. *Out of the Flames*, pp. 314-6.
20. *Out of the Flames*, p. 316.

62

Teresa of Avila and John of the Cross

St Teresa of Avila and St John of the Cross are among the greatest mystics of the Catholic Church. Together they founded the 'Disclaced' Carmelites, in which the austerity and contemplative character of the original Carmelites were restored.

'Teresa of Avila,' in the words of the Archbishop of Canterbury Rowan Williams, 'is one of the most accessible and attractive of all the great writers in the Christian mystical tradition.' 'Her very human attractiveness and the fascination of her unusual experiences of vision and rapture,' he adds, 'tends to obscure two salient facts about her. First, she was a woman reacting to a particularly difficult epoch in the history of the Spanish state and church; and second, she was an independent theological thinker.'[1]

Teresa of Avila, also known as Teresa of Jesus, was born in March 1515 at Avila in Spain. Her family were members of the minor nobility, but her paternal grandfather had been a Jewish convert to Christianity – a *converso*. In 1485, to their embarrassment, he had been found guilty at the Inquisition of Toledo of continuing secretly to practise Jewish customs. Even Teresa, because she was a Christian of Jewish descent, was sometimes viewed with suspicion.

Teresa describes her family as a happy and united one. Her father was a man of high principles, who, unlike most members of his class, refused to own slaves. From an early age, she was fascinated by the stories of saints and martyrs. At the age of seven, she and her brother Rodrigo ran away to seek martyrdom at the hands of the Moors, although their uncle spotted them outside the city walls and sent them home.

Her mother died when Teresa was thirteen. It is said that her father sent her to an Augustinian convent because he was worried by her flirtation with a cousin. At that time, she had no desire to be a nun, but in about 1535, she entered the Carmelite Convent of Incarnation, where ladies of the upper classes had comfortable quarters and their own servants. Teresa made her formal profession at the age of twenty-one. Teresa quickly developed a great love for mental prayer, but soon after becoming a member of the convent, she had a long period of illness and fell into a coma. It was a time of exhaustion and depression and she gave up private prayer. She was also irritated by the laxity of life at the convent.

Gradually she started once more to pray and engage in spiritual reading. Then, in 1554 she experienced a profound spiritual awakening, which was accompanied by changes in her own way of life. She adopted ascetic practices, so as to simplify her life and to focus her attention on Jesus Christ. She began also to seek reform in the Carmelite order and greater social justice. She also started to have visions and other mystical experiences. One vision, which has been much commented upon, was that of an angel with a fiery dart. The angel stood by her with an arrow in his hand with which he pierced her inmost parts; with its withdrawal she felt an exquisite mixture of pain and joy and an intense desire for God. The erotic overtones have been much discussed and are evident in the sculpture by Bernini of St Teresa in Ecstasy. More often her spiritual experiences were 'imaginative' visions of Christ's presence. At times she fell into a trance and on occasion experienced levitation. Teresa, now more afraid of sin, began to inflict mortifications on herself. Gradually she was motivated less by fear of God's judgement and more by gratitude for God's mercy and love. At first she questioned whether her experiences were inventions of the devil – indeed some of her peers suggested this. Her confessor, the Jesuit Francis Borgia, reassured her that her experiences were indeed from God. On St Peter's day in 1559, she became convinced that Christ, although invisible, was present to her in bodily form.

In her desire to see Carmelite life return to its original simplicity, with the authorization of Pope Pius IV, she opened the first convent of the Carmelite Reform, despite local criticism. There was opposition from many clergy, and the Inquisition at the time was acting with severity toward those practising mental prayer. The town authorities, who had banned begging, also, did not want another un-endowed house, which meant that the sisters' request for alms would be a financial drain on the citizens. Teresa, however, gained the support of the Carmelite Prior General from Rome. He visited Avila in 1567, and told Teresa to found more similar monasteries. In 1567, she also met a young Carmelite priest, Juan, better known as John of the Cross. He too was dissatisfied with the laxity of the Order. Teresa, therefore, persuaded him to undertake a similar programme of reform of male monasteries. John opened the first monastery of the Primitive Rule in 1568.

Teresa, in the remaining years of her life, despite opposition and illness, founded another sixteen convents in different parts of Spain. This involved long journeys, which she described in her *Book of the Foundations*. Members of the Primitive Rule became known as 'Discalced,' because they only wore sandals, whereas those who continued to follow what was called the Mitigated Rule were known as 'Calced,' because they wore proper shoes. The Discalced monks were required to observe complete poverty and not to have any possessions of their own. Three weekly disciplines of ceremonial flagellation were also prescribed. There was strict discipline. Minor misdemeanours included being late for meals, walking too fast or too slowly, and giggling. Serious offences included revealing confidential matters or laying violent hands on the Prioress. Teresa expected complete obedience. There is an amusing story of how she tested a senior sister, called Ursula. 'How ill you look', Teresa said to her, 'Off to bed with you at once.' The nun immediately did what she was told. When other sisters enquired how she felt she said, 'Poorly, very poorly.' When they asked, 'What's the matter with you?' she replied, 'I can't tell. Our Mother says I am ill.'[2] Although Ursula felt quite well, she obeyed what Teresa told her rather than her own body.

In 1575, a dispute arose between the rival Carmelite Orders. Teresa was grossly maligned to the Carmelite General, who, ordered her to go to a convent in Castille and told her to stop founding monasteries. Juan, or John of the Cross (1542-91), also was imprisoned in Toledo in 1577 and suffered cruel treatment.

It was in prison that John of the Cross wrote some of his most inspiring poems – so it seems fitting at this point to describe his writings. It says much for Teresa's perceptiveness that she recognised the special spiritual qualities of John, who was physically very small and retiring by nature. Indeed, it was only because of his admiration for Teresa, that John undertook the arduous and often unpopular work of monastic reform. In his writings, he claimed only to be supplementing what Teresa was writing. In fact, he made a distinctive contribution to the understanding of the mystical path. His writings are in some measure a reflection of his own experience, which he described in poetry.

Often his poems are in the form of a conversation of the Bride or the soul with the Beloved, who is the Lord. They have an amazing spiritual intensity as, for example, in this 'Song of the soul in intimate communication and union with the love of God:'

> *Oh flame of love so living,*
> *How tenderly you force*
> *To my soul's inmost core your fiery probe!*
> *Since now you've no misgiving,*
> *End it, pursue your course,*
> *And for our sweet encounter tear the robe!*

> *O cautery most tender!*
> *O gash that is my guerdon!*
> *Oh gentle hand! Oh touch how softly thrilling!*
> *Eternal life you render,*
> *Raise of all debts the burden*
> *And change my death to life, even while killing!...*

> *What peace, with love enwreathing,*
> *You conjure to my breast*
> *Which only you your dwelling place may call:*
> *While with delicious breathing*

> *In glory, grace, and rest,*
> *So daintily in love you make me fall!*[3]

In his writings, St John of the Cross, carefully analysed the three ways of the Christian life, which are often referred to as the 'classical spiritual itinerary.' The Purgative Way begins with growing awareness of sin and the need to change one's life, by giving more time to prayer and abandoning bad habits. The Illuminative Way is characterised by a move away from discursive meditation to contemplation or the prayer of stillness and silence. A sure sign of progress is the desire to 'remain alone in loving awareness of God, without particular considerations, in interior peace and quiet and repose.'[4] At first, the Illuminative Way may be associated with trances and raptures, but John says these should be acknowledged, but are not signs of particular holiness. Indeed the growth of holiness is marked by an ever-greater awareness of sin. The pilgrim 'feels so unclean and wretched that it seems God is against him and he is against God.'[5] The pilgrim's journey culminates in the Unitive Way, when he experiences the 'immediacy' of God's presence or the sense of being 'one with God.' 'The soul becomes divine, God through participation, insofar as is possible in this life.'[6] Even at this stage 'love can become deeper in quality ... and become more ardent.'[7]

John of the Cross died in 1591 on December 14th. His last words were, 'Tonight I will sing Matins in heaven.' He was beatified in 1675, canonized in 1726 and declared a Doctor of the Church in 1926.

Both John of the Cross and Teresa of Avila, as already mentioned, suffered much in their pursuit of reform and their contemplative mysticism was viewed with suspicion by some other Catholics. Teresa, from the convent at Castille to which she had been banished, sent repeated pleading letters to King Philip II of Spain. Eventually she met with success. The process before the Inquisition was dropped and her Carmelites were given independent jurisdiction, which was confirmed by Pope Gregory XIII. Teresa, whose health was broken, was then told to resume her work of reform. She set out again on exhausting journeys and in the last three years of her life she founded three more monasteries. On a journey back from Burgos to Avila, her final illness overtook her and she died late on October 4th, 1582 or, possibly, early on October 15th - No, it is not a misprint for October 5th, because her death coincided with the date on which the Catholic nations switched from the Julian to the Gregorian calendar, which meant that October 5th to October 14th never existed.

There is a macabre story that, after her death, Teresa's left hand was removed to be used as relic. It passed into the possession of the Carmelites of Ronda, but was stolen at the start of Spanish Civil War. It was later recovered at Malaga, in its bejewelled reliquary, and presented to General Franco, who kept it by him for four decades, before it was returned to Ronda. [8]

Teresa of Avila was canonized by Pope Gregory XV in 1622. Then, in

1970 she was recognised by Pope Paul VI as a doctor of the Church. St Catherine of Siena (1347-80) and St Thérèse (Teresa) of Lisieux (1873-97) are, with Teresa of Avila, the only three women among the more than thirty people who are recognised as doctors of the Church.

Much of the information about Teresa is based on her autobiographical *Life of Mother Teresa of Jesus*, written before 1567 and her *Book of Foundations*, in which she describes the establishment of her convents. The most treasured of her writings are her four works on the progress of the soul to God, especially *The Way of Perfection* (1583) and *The Interior Castle* (1588). *Spiritual Relations, Exclamations of the Soul to God* (1588) and *Conceptions on the Love of God* are shorter works. Some of her poems and letters also survive.

In her *Life of Mother Teresa of Jesus*, Teresa speaks of four stages in the ascent of the soul to God. The starting point is to 'settle yourself in solitude and you will come upon God in yourself.' The first stage is the 'heart's devotion', which requires a withdrawal of the soul from outward concerns, concentration on the passion of Jesus, and penitence. Then comes the 'devotion of peace', in which the will is lost in God, but reason and imagination are still not free from worldly distractions. Thirdly, 'devotion of union' is a supernatural, but not ecstatic state, in which reason becomes absorbed in God. The fourth state is 'the devotion of ecstasy or rapture,' in which all sense activity ceases and the soul and body are at one with God.

The Way of Perfection is addressed primarily to her nuns, describing the importance of poverty, discipline and avoidance of honours. Teresa reflects upon her experience of vocal prayer, mental prayer and the 'prayer of quiet.' She encourages the use of repetitive vocal prayer, such as the 'Our Father' or the 'Hail, Mary.' She also greatly values imaginative meditation on Gospel stories of Jesus. 'If you are happy', she wrote, 'look upon your risen Lord, and the very thought of how he rose from the sepulchre will gladden you... If you are suffering trials, or are sad, look upon him on his way to the Garden.'[9]

The *Interior Castle* is based on the metaphor of the soul as if it were a castle made of a single diamond. In the castle there are many rooms arranged in concentric circles. The seventh room is God, sitting at the very centre of the soul. The way of prayer is to enter more deeply into oneself, integrating the different aspects of the self, so that we become aware that at the centre of our being we are one with God. Teresa also speaks of spiritual marriage. Her emphasis is not now, as in earlier works, on emotional ecstasy. By spiritual marriage she means a union of the will with the will of God so that the soul is united with God in a loving compassion that seeks divine justice in the world.

It is sometimes claimed that mystical experiences are self-authenticating. For Teresa, however, 'mystical states' were far from providing a sort of 'paradigm of certainty.' They only had 'an authority within a frame of reference [i.e. Christian doctrine], which is to be believed on quite other grounds. Spiritual experiences quite properly are to be tested according to their consistency' with the Church's teaching.[10] Teresa never questioned the authority of the Church, although she objected to abuses. She was horrified by what little she knew of the Reformation.

For Teresa, to be a contemplative was essentially a matter of living in the world with a sustained awareness of the life and death of Jesus Christ. Her focus was more on the incarnation and the human life and passion of Jesus rather than on the exalted Lord. Her understanding of the way of life Christ required, depended not so much on books, but more on the 'living book' of lives lived in obedience to Christian teaching. For her, obedience to the reformed religious rule was the primary means of imitating Jesus.

Teresa was not a feminist in the modern sense. She took for granted society's opinion of women and spoke of a mature female saint as 'an honorary man.'[11] She recognised that the patriarchy of her day did not square with the stories of how Jesus related to women. She commented on his accessibility and readiness to be helped by women. She also appealed to the voice of Jesus against St Paul's injunction against women preaching. She did not support the view that female spirituality is characteristically passive.

Teresa was not a social reformer, although she mocked the nobility's obsession with dignity and titles and was critical of aristocratic neglect of the poor.[12] She also did not see the contemplative as a person who lived alone and was detached from society. Her contemplative life was the spring-board for her missionary vocation. In a life of much activity and many responsibilities, Teresa managed to remain centred on God. As she wrote,

Let nothing disturb you
Nothing frighten you,
All things are passing;
Patient endurance
Attains all things.
One whom God possesses
Lacks nothing
For God alone suffices.[13]

She also surrendered herself fully to the will of God:

Give me death, give me life.
Give me sickness, give me health,
Give me honour, give me shame,
Give me weakness, give me strength,
I will have whatever you give.[14]

Perhaps most famous of all is her recognition that Christ's work can only be done in the world by those who have surrendered themselves wholly to Him.

Christ has no body now on earth but yours,
No hands but yours,
No feet but yours.
Yours are the eyes through which
Christ's compassion looks out to the world;
Yours are the feet with which he is to go about doing good;
Yours are the hands with which he is to bless people now.[15]

Today the writings of both Teresa of Avila and of St John of the Cross are treasured by people of all faiths who seek to follow the path of holiness.

CHAPTER NOTES

1. Rowan Williams, *Teresa of Avila*, London, Geoffrey Chapman, 1991, p. 1.
2. Stephen Clissold, *St Teresa of Avila*, London, Sheldon Press, SPCK,

1979 p.109.

3. John of the Cross, *Poems*, translated by Roy Campbell, London, Penguin, 1960, p. 45.

4. John of the Cross, *Dark Night of the Soul*, 1580 2,5, 5.

5. John of the Cross, *Ascent of Mount Carmel*, 1579 2, 13, 2-4.

6. John of the Cross, *The Spiritual Canticle*, 1578, 22.3.

7. John of the Cross, *The Living Flame of Love*, 1583, Prologue 3.

8. Stephen Clissold, p.261.

9. *The Way of Perfection*, ii, 107.

10. Rowan Williams, p. 149.

11. *The Way of Perfection*, 7.8.

12. *The Way of Perfection*, 33.1 and *Spiritual Testimonies*, 2,8.

13. *1,000 World Prayers*, p. 28.

14. *1,000 World Prayers*, p. 115.

15. *1,000 World Prayers*, p. 147.

63

Akbar

Akbar, who was born in 1543, was a man of great and diverse ability and was the greatest of the Mughal emperors of India. Like the ancient Pharaoh Akhenaton, Akbar created a new religion, which he hoped would unite Muslims and Hindus in worship of the one God.

Abu-ul-Fath Jalal-ud-Din Muhammad Akbar – to give him his full name – was born on October 15th, 1542. Among his ancestors were the Mongol Conquerors Genghis Khan (c.1162-1227) and Timur or Tamerlane (1336-1405). His father Humayan came to the throne in 1530. He was expelled from Delhi, his capital city, by the Afghan usurper Sher Shar Sur, but eventually regained power in 1555. He died the next year, leaving two sons, of whom the elder was Akbar, who was thirteen. It was not until 1562 that Akbar took control, although in the meantime his position had been strengthened by the defeat of rivals for the throne.

Akbar was of medium stature with great physical strength. His complexion was dark and his voice loud. He had impressive eyes, which a Jesuit priest, described as 'vibrant like the sea in sunshine.' His manners were charming and he was 'great with the great, and lowly with the lowly.' He tried genuinely to rule justly, although at times he had a violent temper. As a boy he resisted the efforts of all his tutors to teach him and was illiterate and never able to sign his own name. Yet he was highly intelligent. He had a brilliant memory and learned a great deal from the books that were read to him. He had great curiosity and wide interests. He liked doing mechanical work in wood or metal. He was an artist and an architect. He collected a wide range of books and works of art. He was a successful general extending the empire to include Gujarat, Bengal and Kashmir.[1]

Akbar took a great interest in religion. He was brought up as a Sunni Muslim. He admitted that in his early years he had gladly persecuted heretics. One of his tutors, however, introduced him to the poetry of some Sufi mystics and from quite an early age he enjoyed the company of Hindu holy men. He was also said to have had visions of God.

Until the late fifteen seventies, Akbar faithfully observed the times of prayer and often went to the tombs of saints to pray. He also built a number of mosques. He had, however, already got to know some European Christians, learning a little about the faith from Father Julian Pereira, the vicar-general in Bengal. In 1579, he sent to Goa to ask for two priests to be sent to him to instruct him about Christianity. The two chosen were Father Rodolfo Aquaviva and Father Antonio Monserrate, both members of the Society of Jesus, which was founded by Ignatius Loyola (b.1491).[2] They arrived at Akbar's new capital city of Fathpur-Sikri in 1580.

By this time Akbar was showing greater tolerance towards Hindus. At first, this was probably dictated by political expediency and a desire to unite the diverse peoples in his empire. He married some Hindu princesses, abolished pilgrim dues, and was willing to employ some Hindus at a high level in the army and the administration. He was critical of Hindu ritualism and some customary practices. He tried to discourage widows throwing themselves on their husband's pyre; he allowed widows to remarry; and he tried to stop child-marriage.

Akbar also encouraged religious debate, for which he built at Fathpur-Sikri a special hall, known as the 'House of Worship.' At first the discussions were limited to scholars from different schools of Muslim theology. From about 1579, representatives of other religions – Hindus, Jains, Parsis (Zoroastrians) and Christians - took part.[3]

In the previous year Akbar had surprised and offended orthodox Muslims by himself mounting the pulpit and reciting verses by Faizi, who later became Chief Poet and who collected a fine library. Shaik Mubarak, a learned if independent theologian had sometime before suggested that Akbar should become the spiritual as well as the temporal head of the empire. In 1579, Shaik Mubarak prepared what has become known as the 'Infallibility Decree', which authorised the Emperor to make the final decision about any disputed question, provided that his ruling was in accordance with a verse from the Qur'an. The decree was imposed upon the unwilling Ulama or Muslim doctors of divinity. There was considerable unrest and rebellion in some parts of the empire. The Qazi of Jaunpur even ruled that rebellion was lawful, as Akbar had become an apostate.

1581 was a critical year for Akbar. Not only did he face Muslim opposition, but also traitors were plotting against him and rebels wanted to put his half-brother Muhammad Hakim of Kabul on the throne. Akbar's victory in Kabul meant that he returned to Fathpur-Sikri with absolute power. Almost at once, he declared a new religion, a pure monotheism, called *Tauhid Ilah* (Divine Monotheism) or *Din Ilahi* (Divine Religion). The claims of Muhammad to be an inspired prophet were put to one side and the authority of the Emperor emphasised. Prostration, until then reserved for the worship of God, was now also required by the sovereign. Some of the rituals were borrowed from Zoroastrianism.

Shaikh Mubarak's younger son Abul Fazl became the high priest of the new faith and confidant of the Emperor. Restrictions were imposed on Muslims. They were not permitted to name any children 'Muhammad' and they were not allowed to build new mosques or to repair old ones. Studies of the Muslim religion and law were discouraged. Hindus were mollified by the prohibition of beef and garlic.

Was Akbar motivated by the political aim of using religion to unite an empire whose members belonged to several different religions – Islam, Hinduism, Jainism, Zoroastrianism and a few to Christianity or nascent Sikhism? Did he suffer from megalomania and delusions of grandeur more acutely than most emperors? Was he motivated by a genuine encounter with God? He was said, as already mentioned, to have had mystical experiences. Many mystics have suggested that God is so wonderful that the language of every religion falls short. Akbar certainly had considerable curiosity about religion. He said once, 'I try to take the good from all opinions with the sole object of ascertaining the truth.'

Akbar's forty-nine year's reign came to an end in 1605. His contemporary Queen Elizabeth I of England reigned from 1558 to 1603. In September 1605 Akbar became ill with dysentery and there is some suggestion that he was poisoned. He was buried at Sikandra near Agra in a mausoleum which he had begun, but which his successor Jehangir rebuilt to a different design. When the Jats rebelled against the Emperor Aurangzeb, they attacked the mausoleum and dragged away the bones of Akbar and threw them into a fire. It is sad that the grave of this advocate of tolerance was desecrated by fanatics.

Akbar had few genuine followers and his religion died with him. Yet the hope that people can transcend their religious differences and come together in service of the one True God has not died. It inspired some of the early advocates of interfaith fellowship, such as the Hindu philosopher Dr S Radhakrishnan (1888-1975), who was a President of India, and Sir Francis Younghusband[4] (1863-1942), who founded the World Congress of Faiths.

Akbar became known to the Western world particularly thanks to the inspiring poem, 'Akbar's Dream' by Alfred Lord Tennyson. The notes that Tennyson made at the time show that the poet had a good knowledge of what Akbar had hoped to achieve. It begins with an inscription written by Abul Fazl for a temple in Kashmir:

'O GOD in every temple I see people that see thee,
and in every language I hear spoken, people praise thee.
Polytheism and Islam feel after thee.
Each religion says, 'Thou art one, without equal.'
If it be a mosque people murmur the holy prayer, and if it be
a Christian Church, people ring the bell from love to Thee.
Sometimes I frequent the Christian cloister, and sometimes
the mosque. But it is thou whom I search from temple to temple.
Thy elect have no dealings with either heresy or orthodoxy;
for neither of them stands behind the screen of thy truth.[5]

Heresy to the heretic, and religion to the orthodox,
But the dust of the rose-petal belongs to the heart
of the perfume seller.

Akbar begins by explaining to Abul Fazl his dislike of fanaticism
I hate the rancour of their castes and creeds,
I let men worship as they will, I reap
No revenue from the field of unbelief.
I cull from every faith and race the best
And bravest soul for counsellor and friend.
I loathe the very name of infidel.
I stagger at the Koran and the sword.
I shudder at the Christian and the stake;

Yet "Allah," says their sacred book, "is Love."

Then in the most famous passage, he tells Abul Fazl of his dream:

That stone by stone I rear'd a sacred fane,

A temple, neither Pagod, Mosque, nor Church,

But loftier, simpler, always open-door'd

To every breath from heaven, and Truth and Peace

And Love and Justice came and dwelt therein.

But Akbar then saw into the future and

I watch'd my son,

And those that follow'd, loosen, stone from stone,

All my fair work.

So easily fanatics can destroy painstaking efforts to achieve understanding, reconciliation and unity.

CHAPTER NOTES

1. Much of this information is taken from Vincent A Smith, *The Oxford History of India*, pp. 337-362.
2. See chapter 59, 'Loyola.'
3. It is unlikely that any Buddhists took part.
4. See chapter 85, 'Younghusband.'
5. Lord Alfred Tennyson made use of *The Ain I Akbari*, translated by H Blochmann, Calcutta, 1873-94, p. xxxii.

64

Guru Arjan Dev and Guru Gobind Singh

Guru Arjan Dev and Guru Gobind Singh had a decisive influence on the shaping of Sikhism as a world religion. Guru Arjan Dev (1563-1606), the fifth Sikh Guru or teacher, gave to Sikhism its main place of worship, the Golden Temple, and its scripture which is known as the *Adi Granth* or *Guru Granth Sahib*. The Guru's life and his martyr's death exemplify the highest virtues of Sikhism. Guru Gobind Singh (1666-1708), the tenth and last Sikh Guru, created the *Khalsa* or fellowship of the pure, which gave Sikhs the cohesion and confidence to withstand the attacks of their enemies and which has to this day ensured the survival of Sikhism through many vicissitudes.

Arjan Dev, who was born near Amritsar, now in the Punjab, was the youngest son of the fourth Guru. From an early age he showed a deep devotion to God, and to the envy of his brothers, he became the favourite of his father, who appointed Arjan Dev to be his successor. Arjan Dev was invested as Guru by Bhai (Brother) Budha, who was a highly esteemed devotee, on 1 September 1581.

Arjan quickly completed the excavation of the sacred pool at Amritsar, which his father Guru Ram Das (1534-81) had begun, and extended the town. He then superintended the construction of the Golden Temple, or Harimandir, which is the Punjabi for 'temple of God. The Harimandir, set in the sacred pool, is surrounded by water and approached by a narrow causeway. The Temple's location in water was to symbolise the synthesis of the spiritual and temporal realms of human existence. The fact that the base of the Temple is lower than the surrounding land is to emphasise faith's inner strength and confidence, which does not depend on lofty and magnificent buildings. When the sky is clear blue and the sun is shining on the gold of the temple, it is indeed a glorious sight, but it is even so a modest structure. Unlike most Indian temples, which have one east-facing door, the Golden Temple has four doors – one facing in each direction. This indicated that the Harimandir was open to members of all four castes, which in the Guru's words were 'equal in divine instruction.'[1] (Entry to some Hindu temples used to be restricted to members of the higher castes). The four doors also symbolized the universality of the Guru's message, expressed in this verse

The world is on fire: O God, save it in your mercy
Through whatever door we come to you.'

The four doors may also have indicated that people of all four castes were welcome at the shrine. At the temple, there was a community kitchen or *langar* where food was served to anyone who came, regardless of their caste or creed. Guru Arjan invited a famous Muslim holy man, the Sufi Mian Mir (1550-1635) to lay the cornerstone of the building.

Under Guru Arjan's leadership, Amritsar became not only a place of pilgrimage, but a centre of learning and the focus for all Sikhs. This was strengthened by his decision to collect the hymns of the Gurus and to place the scriptures in the Golden Temple.

Because his jealous elder brother was composing his own hymns, Guru Arjan decided to make a collection of the authentic hymns of previous Gurus. He already had his father's hymns with him and he persuaded an uncle to lend him the collection of hymns by the first three Gurus. He also made a public search for other compositions of previous Gurus. As a result, he had the laborious task of sifting genuine works from what was counterfeit. The selected material was then assigned to one of the thirty approved ragas or musical patterns. The hymns also had to be edited and transcribed. To this considerable collection Guru Arjan added over two thousand of his own compositions. The best known of these is his *Sukhmani* (Hymn of Peace), which is read daily in morning worship and also to the dying to comfort them. It emphasises the spiritual peace that comes from constant recollection of God's name. The *Hymn of Peace* consists of twenty-four poems of eight stanzas, each introduced with this refrain:

The Name of God is sweet sustenance,
Source of Peace and Joy within;
The Name of God brings perfect peace
To those who are truly devout.

In addition to the hymns of the Gurus there are hymns by fifteen Muslim and Hindu saints – some of whom were of low caste. All the hymns proclaim the power of God's name (*Nam*) to save all, regardless of caste or creed, who trust in God. The hymns call for constant devotion to God.

The *Adi Granth*, known also as the *Sri Guru Granth Sahib* in recognition of the belief that the book is the embodiment of the Guru, contains over six thousand hymns. The English translation by Gurbachan Singh Talib, which I have, consists of four large volumes. The completed work was ceremoniously installed in the Golden Temple on 16 August 1604. Quite recently, the celebration to mark the four hundredth anniversary of this event attracted over a million people and was attended by both the President and Prime Minister of India as well as dignitaries of many religions.

It is an interesting coincidence that 1604 is also a significant date in the history of the Bible – at least for those who speak English. In that year, King James I ordered a new translation to be made of the Bible into English, which became known as the Authorised Version or King James Bible.

The *Adi Granth* is placed on a platform in the Golden Temple and verses are chanted throughout the day. At night the holy book is placed in the Akal Takht, a nearby building which is the primary seat of the Sikh religious authority. Very early in the morning there is a ceremony at which the book is installed in the Golden Temple. It is customary for devotees to prostrate themselves in front of the scripture and, as they listen to the chanting, they sit on the ground so as not to be higher than the holy book.

Guru Arjan spent much of his time preaching in the Punjab. He had a sacred pool constructed at Tarn Taran, to which may people with leprosy came to be cared for by the Guru. As he travelled, he encouraged villagers to sink wells and one of these can still be seen in the city of Lahore.

Soon after the completion of the *Adi Granth*, Guru Arjan was summoned to the presence of the Mughal Emperor, Akbar (1542-1605), to whom complaints had been made that the book was derogatory to Islam. The book was opened at random and a passage read from a spot pointed out by the Emperor. The hymn was in praise of God as were the subsequent passages. Akbar was delighted and gave the Guru generous gifts.

The enthronement of Akbar's son, Jahangir, took place one week after his father's death on November 3rd, 1605 (two days before the Gun Powder Plot to blow up the English Parliament and to kill King James I). Jahangir was by no means so broad-minded. He regarded the Guru as heretical and disloyal and had him brought to Lahore. There he was tortured by being made to sit on red-hot iron plates and by having burning sand poured over him. He was then taken to bathe in the river, but the shock of cold water on his blistered body, was too much for him. Even as he walked to his death, he recited the words, 'Your will is sweet, Oh God; I only seek the gift of Your Name.' A Jesuit priest in Lahore wrote at the time, 'their good Pope died, overwhelmed by the sufferings, torments and dishonours.' He was the first Sikh martyr. One of his Sikh contemporaries wrote:

As fishes are at one with the waves of the river,
So was the Guru, immersed in the River that is the Lord.

With the growth of Sikh communities in Europe and North America, as well as in East Africa, Sikhism is becoming better known as a world religion with a universal message and its influence is growing. The Guru Granth Sahib again and again focuses on the glory of the One Supreme Being and the holiness of the Lord. The ideal to strive for is *sanjog* or the union of the individual self with the universal or the Absolute. The joy and ecstasy of this experience comes from the ever present remembrance of God. But the Guru Granth Sahib also makes clear that this mystical experience does not isolate the believer from the world but inspires him or her to seek to reduce suffering and evil. Oneness with the Divine is expressed in a sense of the oneness of all people – vividly shown in the *langar*, where all are fed without distinction of caste or indeed creed. At the Parliament of World Religions in Barcelona in 2004, a great *Langar*, was set up on the sea shore by the Sikh community, to which people of every faith came for free meals. This was indeed in the spirit of Guru Arjan, who wrote,

Some remember God as Ram;
Some call him Khuda;
Some use the name Gosain,
Some worship him as Allah.
Gracious Lord Almighty,
You are the source and cause of everything,
O Lord, Compassionate One,
Shower your grace on all…
Whoever does the will of God,
To him all things are revealed.'[2]

The persecution of Sikhs did not end with death of Guru Arjan Dev. The ninth Guru Tegh Bahadur (1621–1675) also died as a martyr and this had a profound effect on his son Gobind Rai, who was to become the tenth and last Guru, best known as Guru Gobind Singh.

The Mughal Emperor Aurangzeb (1618-1707) pursued a policy of persecuting non-Muslims. The governor of Kashmir was especially ruthless in implementing this policy and was using force to convert Hindu teachers (*pandits*) to Islam. They appealed for help to Tegh Bahadur, who pondered the matter deeply. Indeed, Gobind Rai, who was only nine, asked his father why he was so preoccupied. He replied, 'Grave are the burdens the earth bears. She will be redeemed only if a truly worthy person comes forward to lay down his head. Distress will be expunged and happiness ushered in.' 'No one', replied Gobind Rai, 'could be worthier than yourself to make such a sacrifice.' Guru Tegh Bahadur declared that if the Emperor could convert him to Islam, the pandits too would accept conversion. An angry Aurangzeb ordered the Guru to be brought to Delhi. Despite repeated torture, he told Aurangzeb, 'The Prophet of Mecca who founded your religion could not impose one religion on the world, so how can you? It is not God's will.' On 11 November 1675, the Guru's three companions were horribly killed before his eyes. Even this did not weaken his resolve and the Guru was publicly beheaded – on the spot where subsequently, when they captured Delhi, the Sikhs built the Gurdwara Sis Ganj in Delhi's Chandni Chowk. Guru Tegh Bahadur had demonstrated the truth of his own verse:

The truly enlightened ones
Are those who neither incite fear in others
Nor fear for anyone themselves.

The Guru's head was bravely recovered and after a perilous journey brought to his young son at Anandpur. As he wrote later,

He gave his head for men of faith without flinching
And chose martyrdom in the cause of righteousness.

His father's death shaped his son's future outlook and actions. Gobind Rai became convinced that the tyrant's injustice and cruelty had to be resisted by courageous warriors.

When all other means have failed,
It is but lawful to take to the sword.[3]

Guru Nanak had said 'truth is pure steel.' Gobind Singh put his trust more literally in the steel of the sword, writing;

You are the subduer of kingdoms,
The destroyer of evil armies...
I seek your protection,...
I cherish you, the saviour of creation,
Hail to you, O Sword.[4]

Before Tegh Bahadur died, he had symbolically appointed as his successor Gobind Rai, who was formally installed on 29 March 1676. As an adolescent he enjoyed martial games and was trained in swordsmanship. He learned several languages and had a gift for writing and was in due course to write his autobiography. He used his poems to teach love, morality and equality. While he gave the Sikhs a distinct identity, he also recognised the unity of the human race, writing:

Recognise all mankind as one,
Whether Hindus or Muslims,

The same Lord is the creator
And nourisher of all:
The monastery and the mosque are the same,
So is Hindu worship and Muslim prayer.
Men are all one.[5]

Gobind Rai's teenage years were ones of preparation. Then, in 1685 he accepted an invitation from the friendly Raja of Sirmur State, where he stayed for three years. As a young man, he was described as 'sharp featured, tall and wiry,' superbly dressed, wearing a plume-topped turban and always armed.

The next twelve years were ones of conflict, during which he fortified his base at Anandpur. From 1697 to 1700 there was some respite from fighting, which gave the Guru the opportunity to take measures that would give the Sikhs greater strength and unity. He convened a great gathering of Sikhs at Anandpur. On 30 March 1699, the Guru appeared in front of a crowd of some 80,000 with a naked sword and asked, 'Is there present a true Sikh who would offer his head to the Guru as a sacrifice?' There was an awed silence. He repeated the question twice. On the third occasion, Daya Ram arose and walked behind the Guru to a tent near by. Soon the Guru reappeared with his sword dripping blood. He asked for another head. This was repeated until five men had offered their lives to the Guru. Soon afterwards they were led back from the tent dressed in saffron-coloured raiment with neatly tied turbans and with swords at their side. He then initiated the 'The Five Beloved Ones' (*Panj Pyare*) with sweetened baptismal water (*amrit*), the nectar of immortality. Guru Gobind himself received initiation and now became known as Guru Gobind Singh. All five were called Singh and were required to wear five symbols of the Khalsa, all of which began with the letter 'k': *kes*, long hair and a beard; *kangha*, a comb to keep it tidy; *kara*, a steel bracelet; *kachch*, short breeches and *kirpan*, a sword. Their appearance distinguished them from both Muslims and Hindus and gave the Sikhs a visible and separate identity. During the next few days, some 50,000 Sikhs are said to have been baptised.

The khalsa of Singhs ('lions') and Kaurs, (the name for women which probably means 'princess') was to be a castless and disciplined community, which could resist the attacks of its enemies, give support to those in need and fight the oppressor. All people were to be treated equally, irrespective of caste and creed. They were not to cut their hair, or smoke, or have sexual relations outside marriage.

The remaining years of the Guru's life were ones of fighting and many remarkable acts of courage are recorded. His opponent Aurangzeb died in 1707 and the Guru himself was assasinated by two Pathan's in October of the following year. Before his death, he told his followers to revere as their Guru the scriptures, the *Adi Granth*, which is often called the *Guru Granth Sahib*. He assured them that 'Wherever there are five Sikhs assembled who abide by the Guru's teaching, know that I am in the midst of them: henceforth, the guru is the *Khalsa* and the *Khalsa* is the Guru.'[6]

It is paradoxical that a movement, which began with Guru Nanak who said that religious differences had no meaning in God's eyes, should itself have become a distinct religious community. His actions also pose the unanswerable question whether Truth is best served by martyrdom or by the sword. Yet without Guru Gobind Singh's courage and leadership, the Sikh community and faith might have been destroyed, whereas it is becoming increasingly influential as Sikhism is now generally recognised as a world religion, with many adherents in all parts of the world. Dr S Radhakrishnan (1888-1975) a philosopher and a President of India, saw in the creation of the *Khalsa*, the seeds of India's independence. Writing in 1956 he said, 'India is at long last free... This freedom is the crown and climax and a logical corollary to the Sikh Guru's and Khalsa's terrific sacrifices and heroic exploits.'[7]

CHAPTER NOTES

1. Quoted by Patwant Singh in *The Sikhs*, London, John Murray, 1999, p. 34. The comments here are based on Patwant Singh's explanation of the significance of the Golden Temple.

2. Quoted in *1,000 World Prayers*, p. 289.

3. A couplet from Gobind Singh's *Zafarnamah*, which was written in Persian. Quoted in the *Encyclopaedia of Sikhism*, Vol 2, p. 89.

4. Gobind Singh's, *Bachittar Natak*, quoted by Patwant Singh, p. 50.

5. From Gobind Singh's *Akal Ustat*.

6. Quoted in *The Oxford Dictionary of World Religions*, p. 543. no

reference given.

7. Quoted by Mary Pat Fisher, *Living Religions*, Upper Saddle River, NJ, Prentice-Hall, 1991, p 401.

65

George Fox

George Fox was born at a time of religious ferment in Britain. The Church of England from its beginnings under Elizabeth I, had met with opposition from both papists – followers of the then outlawed Roman Catholic religion who owed allegiance to the Pope – and from Puritans, who felt the Reformation in England had not gone far enough. Under King Charles I, an autocratic ruler who reigned from 1625 – 1649, Puritans felt increasingly alienated from the church by the increasing use of ritual. The victory of the Parliamentarians or Roundheads in the Civil War led to the execution of King Charles I, and the abolition of the Church of England. Puritans, with their emphasis on the Bible, abolished the celebration of Christmas Day and the observance of Saints Days. George Fox's radical views on religion, however, went too far for most Puritans.

George Fox rejected the conventional religion of his time and came to rely on the guidance of the Inward Light. This led him to found the Society of Friends, whose members are often known as Quakers. They have had a remarkable record in working for religious tolerance, social justice, peace and relief of those in need.

George Fox was born at Drayton-in-the-Clay (now known as Fenny Drayton) in Leicestershire, England in July 1624. Charles I was then king, but Fox was to live through the Civil Wars, the Commonwealth, Oliver Cromwell's rule and the reigns of Charles II and James II.

We know much about Fox's life from a running summary of it which he started dictating in about 1675. This was edited after Fox's death by Thomas Ellwood, a friend of the poet John Milton (1608-74). The Introduction was written by William Penn (1644-1718) a Quaker and a champion of religious freedom, who founded the American state of Pennsylvania. There is also a wealth of letters, pamphlets and other writings, but there are inconsistencies in the material, which have kept scholars busy.

Fox's father was called Christopher, an honest man, who was a weaver. His mother Mary's maiden name was Lago and 'of the stock of martyrs.'[1] Fox says, 'I had a gravity and stayedness of mind and spirit, not usual in children.' By the age of eleven I knew 'pureness and right-eousness.' We are not told about his education, but clearly he learned to read, as from an early age he was fascinated by the Bible. His literary style was plain. Some of his relations thought he should become a priest, but in fact he was 'put to work with a man, a shoemaker by trade, who dealt in wool and was a grazier and sold cattle.' Later in life, Fox pointed out that Abel, Noah, Abraham, Jacob, Moses and David were all keepers of sheep or cattle.[2] Fox comments that while he had this job, 'I used in my dealings the word verily, and it was a common saying among the people who knew me "If George says verily, there is no altering him."'

At the age of eighteen he left home hoping to find religious counsel, but he found no help from the priests whom he approached and his comments on them are unflattering – to put it mildly. One, who was ignorant of Fox's condition, told him to take tobacco and to sing psalms, but Fox hated tobacco and could not sing. He did not fare much better when he approached Puritan ministers. This was a time of much loneliness and sometimes of despair for Fox, but he also received what he called 'openings' or direct inspirations from God. He said of them, 'These things, I did not see by the help of man, nor by the letter, though they be written in the letter, but I saw them in the light of the Lord Jesus Christ, and by his immediate Spirit and powers, as did the holy men of God, by whom the holy Scriptures were written.' For example, in 1646, as he was going to Coventry, a consideration arose in him how it was said that 'all Christians are believers, both Protestants and Papists.' He continued, 'The Lord opened to me that, if all were believers, then they were all born of God and passed from death to life.' On another occasion, 'the Lord opened to me that "being bred at Oxford or Cambridge was not enough to fit and qualify men to be ministers of Christ."' Anyone who was guided by the Spirit was qualified to minister, including women – which was unheard of at the time. Indeed, he says that some people denied that women had souls. Another time it was opened to him 'that God, who made the world, did not dwell in temples made with hands.' He refused to apply the word 'church' to a building, speaking instead of a 'steeple-house.'

He continued to travel, mostly on foot, but felt weighed down by sorrows and temptations, although he was helped by the fact that Jesus too had been tempted. One day, he says, 'I was taken up in the love of God so that I could not but admire the greatness of his love.' Such experiences gave him confidence and he began preaching to individuals and groups. Fox was to be most successful at first in gaining adherents in the Lake District and later in Yorkshire and in London.

After a time in the Midlands, Fox went to the north of England. There he received a welcome from groups of Seekers, who belonged to a small seventeenth century sect. Seekers believed that the Church had been taken over by Antichrist or the Enemy of Christ[3], but that God would send fresh prophets to found a new pure church. Local congregations were gathered both by Fox and other itinerant men and women preachers, who called themselves the Publishers of Truth. This was in 1649 – a year, as already mentioned, that had begun with the Execution of King Charles the First on January 30th. It was a time of religious ferment, speculation and confusion. The Established Church, which people had been required by law to attend, had been abolished. There were no bishops to exercise control over those who set themselves up as preachers. All the government could do was to say that everyone must attend some place of worship, adding in 1653 that 'such as profess faith in God by Jesus Christ though differing in judgment from the doctrine, worship or discipline publicly held forth, shall not be restrained from, but shall be protected in, the profession of faith and exercise of their religion.'[4]

Such toleration did not extend to papists nor, always, to Fox himself. Fox got a harsh reception from some of those who heard him. In 1650, Fox was imprisoned in Derby for blasphemy. A judge, mocking Fox's exhortation to 'tremble at the word of the Lord', called him and his followers 'Quakers' – a name that stuck. He was again imprisoned in 1653 at Carlisle. There was even talk of putting him to death, but Parliament requested his release rather than have 'a young man... die for religion.' In 1653 Fox was again arrested, because of unfounded suspicions that his followers were plotting to restore the monarchy. Fox was taken to London for a meeting with the Lord Protector, Oliver Cromwell. Fox reassured Cromwell that he had no intention of taking up arms and explained the differences between his beliefs and those of more traditional Christian denominations. Fox records that on his leaving, Cromwell said 'with tears in his eyes, "Come again to my house; for if thou and I were but an hour of a day together, we should be nearer to the other," adding that he wished Fox no more ill than he did to his own soul.' Fox was once more at liberty. Much later, this incident was used as an example of 'speaking truth to power.' Fox met with Cromwell again in 1656, petitioning him to alleviate the persecution of the Quakers. By 1657 about a thousand Friends were in prison – as much for their rejection of accepted social conventions, which we shall look at in a moment, as for their religious views.

With the restoration of the monarchy, Fox was again accused of conspiracy – this time against Charles II. He was, however, released when he made clear that he was opposed, on principle, to the use of arms. He also wrote to Charles II giving him advice and, successfully, asking for the release of those Friends who were in prison. In 1661, after further problems, Fox and eleven other Quakers issued what is now known as the 'Peace Testimony', in which they committed themselves to oppose all outward wars, as contrary to the will of God. Meanwhile in New England, some Quakers had been executed, but Charles condemned this and allowed those who had been banished to return.

In 1669, Fox went to Ireland where he particularly attacked what he regarded as the excessive ritual of the Roman Catholic Church. Later that year Fox married Margaret Fell of Swarthmore Hall, Ulverston, in Lancashire. Margaret, whose first husband had died in 1658, was a lady of high social standing. She had herself been imprisoned for her beliefs. Their romance is the subject of the novel, *The Peaceable Kingdom: an American Saga* by Jan de Hartog.[5]

From 1671 to 1673, Fox travelled to the British colonies in the Caribbean and North America to strengthen and organise the Quaker communities there, especially in Maryland and Rhode Island. Later he made two short journeys to the Netherlands.

Fox's health began to deteriorate in 1684. He lived, however, to see the passing of the Act of Toleration, which put an end to the laws under which Quakers had been imprisoned. Those in jail were released at that time. And to some that came in and inquired how he found himself, he answered, 'Never heed, the Lord's power is over all weakness and death, the Seed reigns, blessed be the Lord.'[6] George Fox died in 1691 and was buried in the Quaker Burying Ground at Bunhill Fields in London.

Fox alienated many people by his attacks on 'the establishment' and by defying accepted patterns of behaviour. The Lord, he said, 'showed me that the physicians and doctors of physic were out of the wisdom of God, by which the creatures were made; and so knew not their virtues... He showed me that the priests were out of the true faith, which Christ is the author of ...He showed me also that the lawyers were out of equity and the law of God.' Fox refused to take up arms. He also would not swear on oath, which added to the problems when he came to court. He would not recognise class distinctions – refusing to doff his hat to anyone and insisting on calling everybody 'thou.' This, as he said, set the professionals 'all into a rage.' The Lord also told him not to bid people 'good morrow' or 'good evening' nor to 'bow or scrape' his leg to anyone. Fox was scathing about the immorality of his time and strongly objected to the tithes people had to pay to the church. His interest in social justice is shown in his complaints to judges about decisions that he thought were wrong. For example, he said that it was wrong for a woman convicted of theft to be executed.

Fox was a prolific writer. He dictated over five thousand texts, which were taken down in shorthand or longhand and then transcribed. He wrote very little himself and his own handwriting was laboured and is usually only found in corrections or annotations. It is suggested that he may have had a form of dyslexia. Nonetheless, his pen-box with its inkwell and sand sifter for blotting still survive. Many of his texts were letters offering guidance and encouragement to individuals. He also wrote open letters that were sent to groups of his followers and pamphlets and broadsheets. He also wrote two books, with fellow authors. Quite early on, Margaret Fell collected the texts and a good number survive.

Fox's emphasis was on the Light of God or of Christ in each person, who should rely on illumination or the Voice. Quaker meetings, therefore, even today are primarily times of quiet or listening for the Voice, whose message may be shared with others - although practice varies from meeting to meeting. 'That is it which must guide everyone's mind up to God,' he wrote, 'to wait upon God to receive the spirit from God. So the Spirit leads to wait upon God in silence, to receive from God.'[7] The Bible, spoken of as the words of God, was of secondary importance compared to the word of God speaking in a believer's life.

The scripture was to be interpreted in the light of this inner guidance and with help from other members of the gathering. Quakers saw no need for the outward rituals of baptism and communion. Business was discussed at 'meetings for worship for church affairs,' which all members could attend. No vote was taken. It is the role of the clerk to discern the sense of the meeting and to record it in a minute agreed by the group while still in session.

Fox spoke of Jesus as Son of God, emphasising his role as a Teacher. Quakers today vary from those who speak of Jesus as Lord and Saviour to those who hesitate to refer to themselves as Christian.

Friends believe themselves empowered by the Spirit in their day-to-day lives. The Quaker way has been described as practical mysticism. A Friend's whole way of life should reflect his or her convictions. There is a strong emphasis on the high importance of peace and non-violence, and the equality of all people. Friends have made a contribution to social and racial justice and to the peace, interfaith and environmental movements out of all proportion to their numbers. The emphasis on truth was shown in the way Quakers did business. Their objection to haggling led to goods having a fixed price. Their trustworthiness led to the establishment of a number of banks, such as Lloyds and Barclays.

William Penn in his long Introduction to George Fox's journal highlights Fox's importance and lasting influence:

'In his ministry he laboured to open truth to the people's under-standings, and to bottom them upon the principle and principal, Christ Jesus, the light of the world, that by bringing them to something that was of God in themselves, they might the better know and judge of him and themselves.

He had an extraordinary gift in opening the Scriptures. He would go to the marrow of things, and shew the mind, harmony, and fulfilling of them with much plainness, and to great comfort and edification. But above all he excelled in prayer... He was of an innocent life... He was an incessant labourer.'

CHAPTER NOTES

1. Quotations, unless otherwise indicated, are from edited extracts from the *Journal* in *George Fox Speaks for Himself*, edited by Hugh McGregor Ross, York, William Sessions, 1991, p. 107ff.

2. Josiah Marsh, *A Popular Life of George Fox*, London, Charles Gilpin, 1847, p. 364.
3. See the First and Second Epistles of John.
4. Quoted from the 1653 *Instrument of Government* in J R H Moorman, *History of the Church of England* p. 244.
5. Published by Scribner, 1972.
6. From William Penn's Introduction to George Fox's *Journal*.
7. *George Fox Speaks for Himself*, p. 20.

66

Ba'al Shem Tov and Elijah ben Solomon

At a bleak period in the history of European Jewry, two people, of very different approaches, helped to reinvigorate the Jewish community. One was Rabbi Elijah ben Solomon (1720-97), known as Vilna Gaon - a man of prodigious learning – who led a revival of Talmudic study. The other was Rabbi Israel ben Eliezer (c.1700-60), who is better known as Ba'al Shem Tov, which is a title probably meaning 'Master of the Good Name.'

Ba'al Shem Tov was an eighteenth century Jewish healer and holy man who has come to be seen as a central figure in the growth of the Hasidic[1] movement, in which mysticism became part of daily life and joy became a part of religion. Hasidism's pietism captured the imagination and loyalty of large numbers of Eastern European Jews in the nineteenth and twentieth centuries. Many Hasidic communities were destroyed in the horrors of the Holocaust, but today Hasidic groups are growing fast in Israel, America and Europe. The philosopher Martin Buber (1878-1965) did much to interpret Hasidism to twentieth century spiritual seekers.

By the time that the Ba'al Shem Tov was born, Poland had become home to a considerable number of Jews and an important centre of rabbinic scholarship. In the later Middle Ages, Jews had been expelled from some countries in Western Europe, including England in 1290 and Spain in 1492. During the sixteenth century the Jewish population in Poland grew rapidly from about 10,000 at the beginning to more than 150,000 by 1648. In that year, however, Bogdan Chmielnicki led a nationalist revolt of Ukranian Cossacks. For two months the Cossacks, who were Greek Orthodox Christians, moved from town to town, slaughtering Jews. The attacks, during the period known as 'the Deluge,' lasted till 1667. As a result, many Jews fled to Germany, Holland or Austria. Those who stayed were scattered across the Polish countryside.

Our main source for the life of Ba'al Shem Tov is the *Shivhei HaBesht,* or 'The Praises of Ba'al Shem Tov,' which contains more than two hundred stories about Ba'al Shem Tov and the people who were associated with him. It is best described as 'sacred biography', which means 'that it was not written to record the biography of a great person in the past but to persuade people in the present to behave in a certain way or to accept a particular doctrine.'[2] Dov Baer, the compiler of the *Shivhei HaBesht*, said in his Preface, 'I wrote it down as a remembrance for my children and their children, so that it would be a reminder for them and for all who cling to God, blessed be He, and His Torah, to strengthen their faith in God and his Torah and in the *zaddikim*, [holy Hassidic leaders] and so they would see how His Torah purifies the souls of its students so that a person can reach higher levels.'[3] Accepting that it was complied for edification, it is the stories in the *Shivei HaBesht* that are known to and loved by Ba'al Shem Tov's followers.

Israel ben Eliezer was born in about 1700 in a small fortress town in the province of Podolia, then in Ukraine, but now in Poland. His father, Eliezer, was a poor pious Jew. He was taken prisoner by the Turks during the Turkish-Polish war of 1676-1698 and held captive for many years. He and his wife, therefore, were quite old when they had a son and they both died while he was a child. As a result, the community provided for Israel and arranged for his education. He was a bright child but from time to time he played truant so that he could wander in the woods. Throughout his life he had a great love of Nature. In his teens, Israel was made an usher at the school. One of his duties was to bring the children to school and he often led them through the woods, singing to them as they walked.

He then was put in charge of some students. He is said to have spent much of the day sleeping, although it is also said that he got up at night to pray and to read. It was at this time that he got to know about Kabbalah, or Jewish mystical teaching - of which more in a moment.

At the age of seventeen, when he was already spoken of as 'an old bachelor', a wife was found for him, although she died very young. He then moved to a small town near Brody, which was then in Poland. There he became a teacher and after some reluctance on the part of her father, married the daughter of a well known scholar. The couple moved to the Carpathia mountains where Ba'al Shem Tov became a lime digger. Twice a week his wife would come to him with a cart onto which they would load the lime and she would take it to sell in the villages. It was a hard life, but it allowed Israel time to meditate and to enjoy once again closeness to Nature.

After seven years of this lonely life, Israel and his wife moved back to more populous centres and he tried to make a living as a private teacher and as a *shohet* or licensed ritual slaughterer. Eventually he asked for help from his brother-in-law, who set him up as an inn-keeper, although his wife did most of the work, while he sat alone in a hut by the river.

At the age of thirty-six, Israel ben-Eliezer became a *baal-shem*. might. A ba'al shem was a sort of 'shaman', who was a healer and a charismatic spiritual leader. He would write out charms and amulets and do some healing work. Israel ben Eliezer to whom this title was given is also known by the acronym Besht. Israel ben-Eliezer settled in Tlust in Eastern Galicia and soon made a name for himself as a faith-healer and fortune teller. After a time, he and his wife settled at Medziboz, near Brody, where they saved enough to buy a house. They had a son and a daughter. Ba'al Shem Tov mixed freely with people and soon became popular.

His importance, however, rests not on his work as a *baal shem*, but on his original religious teaching, which was recorded by his favourite disciple, Yacob Yosef – although we do not know how accurately.

At the time, the emphasis in Judaism was on keeping all the precepts of the Torah ('Teaching' or 'Law') as the way to the next world. But Ba'al Shem Tov did not want to wait: he longed to be united to God in this world, which Jewish mystical teaching, known as Kabbalah, said was possible. Kabbalah has a long history. Its earliest form, known as *Merkaba*, dates back as early as the first century CE and perhaps to the Dead Sea Scrolls. For a time many of the practitioners of Kabbalah lived in Spain, where the famous *Zohar* or 'Book of Splendour'– the central literary work of Kabbalah – first appeared. After the expulsion of the Jews from Spain in 1492, Safed, a town in the hills above the Sea of Galilee, became the centre of the movement. The most famous Kabbalist was Isaac ben Solomon Luria (1534-72), who taught that the world came into being by God's act of contraction, *zimzum*. The world, however, seeks to overcome its separation from God. This can be achieved through the super-soul, *neshamah*, which is an emanation of the deity lodged in the human body. In so far as the soul unites itself with God by keeping the commandments, it helps to unite the world with God.

Kabbalah was well known in eighteenth century Poland. As a teenager, Ba'al Shem Tov became acquainted with Luria's teaching and was influenced by Kabbalah, but his main emphasis was on individual salvation through which the world would be redeemed and he did not share Luria's emphasis on asceticism. 'Before one prays for general redemption, one must pray for the personal salvation of one's own soul.' Taking literally the verse 'the whole earth is full of the Glory of God', he believed that God's presence could be found wherever one looks for it. The world, he said, is the 'garment of God.' Faith involved 'cleaving' to God 'in all daily affairs.' [4]

Ba'al Shem Tov insisted that mere obedience to the commandments was not enough. They had to be observed with total concentration or *kavvanah*. He encouraged the study of Torah, which should not only be understood 'for its own sake', but also by contemplating the significance of each individual letter – a Kabbalist practice - which 'will make a man wise and radiate much light and true eternal life.' Ba'al Shem Tov, however, was uneasy with the stern discipline often demanded by teachers. He did not worry too much about the minutiae of keeping the commandments. He spoke of God's love and emphasised the need to rejoice in God. Religion should be a cheerful not a mournful business, although he and his followers were criticised by some rabbis for 'dancing, drinking and making merry all their lives.'

Those individuals who have superior spiritual qualities should not only teach people to worship God, they should not hesitate to help the sinner to repent. 'If you want to help a friend out of the mud', he said, 'don't be afraid of getting a little dirty.' He also suggested that holy people could help restore the souls of sinners who had died.

To gain the necessary emotional enthusiasm to sense his oneness with God in prayer, Ba'al Shem Tov would work himself up emotionally by shaking himself, singing and shouting. He explained this in a story. 'A man in danger of drowning makes all kinds of motions to save himself, and no one laughs at him. So when a man is praying and making violent movements he should not be laughed at because he is trying to save himself from the rushing waters, namely the evil spirits which try to disturb his thoughts in his prayer.' Prayer was for Ba'al Shem Tov the most precious means of reaching God. 'Prayer, as it were, touches the Holy One, blessed be He.' Prayer was not a matter of asking God for something, but the means by which a person communes with God. The holy person is one whose sense of God's presence is uninterrupted.

Ba'al Shem Tov gathered disciples around him, who in turn spread his message. When Ba'al Shem Tov died in 1760, Dov Baer became their leader and transferred the movement's centre to Mezeritz in the Ukraine. Not surprisingly, Ba'al Shem Tov met with opposition from traditional teachers.

The most authoritative opponent was Elijah ben Solomon (1720-1797), who was *gaon* or leader of the Jewish community in Vilna, in Lithuania. Elijah ben Solomon lead a revival of Talmudic study. He was an infant prodigy, delivering a homily in the synagogue at Vilna in Lithuania, at the age of six. His secular as well as his religious knowledge was amazing. His marriage at the age of eighteen brought him independent means, so he purchased a small house and devoted himself entirely to study. His sons said that he never slept for more than two hours a day. To avoid distractions, he closed the shutters during daytime and studied by candlelight. To stop himself falling asleep, he put his feet in a bowl of cold water. As his influence grew in Vilna, so his devotion to study increased. He was not against the Kabbalah or mystical tradition, as such, but insisted that everything should be subordinate to Jewish law.

Elijah ben Solomon regarded the Hasidic claims to ecstasy and miracles as a sham and would not accept that prayer was a substitute for scholarship. When the *Hasidim* began using unorthodox knives for *shehita* or ritual slaughter, there was a perfect pretext to demand their excommunication. The *Hasidim* responded in kind.

The controversies of his last years should not, however, obscure Elijah ben Solomon's important and lasting contribution to Jewish scholarship. He wrote more than seventy commentaries on the scriptures and Talmud and other Jewish writings. He believed completely in the eternity of the Torah and declared, 'Everything that was, is and will be is included in the Torah. And not only principles, but even the details of each species, the minutest details of every human being, as well as every creature, plant and mineral – all are included in the Torah.'

Ba'al Shem Tov has had a wider influence, but it has been said that many of those who appeal to Ba'al Shem Tov create him in their own likeness, rather than the other way round. Yet, as Moshe Rosman writes, 'The fact that there have been so many attempts to appropriate the Ba'al Shem Tov in the service of ideology and politics is testimony to the power of his image in Jewish collective memory. Perception of Israel Ba'al Shem Tov resonates through the ages and across the Jewish spectrum.'[5]

CHAPTER NOTES

1. Sometimes spelt 'Chasidic.'
2. Moshe Rosman, *Founder of Hasidism: A Quest for the Historical Ba'al Shem Tov*, Berkeley, University of California Press, 1996, p.153.
3. Rosman, quoting from *Shivei Ha-Besht*, I.
4. Deuteronomy 10, 20 says 'Thou shalt cleave to Him.'
5. Rosman, p. 211.

67

Mendelssohn

Moses Mendelssohn, whose writings ranged from aesthetics to metaphysics and from politics to religion, has been described as the first modern Jew. He encouraged members of the Jewish community in Germany to relate positively to the Enlightenment.

Moses was born in Dessau in Germany in 1729. He was, therefore, a younger contemporary of Ba'al Shem Tov and Elijah ben Solomon, whose followers despite their own bitter disagreements were to unite in opposition to the Jewish enlightenment or *Haskalah,* to which Mendelssohn made a vital contribution.

Mendelssohn's father Mendel Dessau was an ill-paid scribe who made a living copying scrolls. Moses was known as Moses Dessau in the Jewish community, but he chose to write as Moses Mendelssohn or son of Mendel. This was a small sign of his wish for fellow Jews to adapt to German society. His education was at first provided by his father and then by the local rabbi David Fränkel, who besides teaching him Torah and the Talmud, also introduced him to the work of the great Jewish philosopher Maimonides (1135-1204). In 1743, Fränkel moved to new work in Berlin and after a few months Moses followed him there.

Moses, in his early years, had a constant struggle against poverty, but was determined to become a scholar. He learned mathematics from a Polish refugee and found a Jewish physician to teach him Latin. He bought a Latin copy of *An Essay Concerning Human Understanding* by the British philosopher John Locke (1632-1704), who held that the experience of the senses was the only source of knowledge. Moses managed to understand it with the help of a Latin dictionary. He also learned some French and English. In 1750 a wealthy silk-merchant called Isaac Bernhard employed Mendelssohn to teach his children. Subsequently Bernhard made Mendelssohn his accountant and then his partner.

Berlin, under Frederick the Great, was a lively place to be. In 1754 Mendelssohn was introduced to the dramatist Gotthold Ephraim Lessing (1729-81), They were almost the same age and became good friends. Mendelssohn and Lessing met over a chessboard, just as later

Nathan in Lessing's play *Nathan the Wise* was to meet Saladin. Five years before his meeting with Mendelssohn, the young Lessing had produced his play *Die Juden*, which was intended to show that a Jew could be of a person of good character and a rational human being - an idea that most people laughed at as obviously untrue.

Jews at the time in Europe were still required to live apart in ghettos, to which Jewish doctors or businessmen, who had to mix with Gentiles during the day, would return at night. 'To educated Christians – or even uneducated ones' Jews at that time were, in Paul Johnson's words, 'figures of contempt and derision, dressed in funny clothes, imprisoned in ancient and ludicrous superstitions, as remote and isolated from modern society as one of their lost tribes. The gentiles knew nothing, and cared less, about Jewish scholarship.'[1] Added to this Christians, wrongly, continued to blame the Jews for killing Jesus Christ.[2]

Lessing encouraged Mendelssohn to publish his philosophical writings, although his *Philosophical Conversations* (1755) appeared anonymously. An anonymous satire, *Pope a Metaphysician*, published in the same year, was a joint work by Lessing and Mendelssohn. Mendelssohn, who was much admired for his conversation, soon became a welcome guest in Berlin society. Frederick the Great, although annoyed that Mendelssohn had criticised his poems, gave him 'right of residence' in Berlin, so that he did not have to live in the ghetto and suffer other restrictions to which Jews were subject.

In 1762, Mendelssohn married Fromet Guggenheim, who was to outlive him by twenty-six years. In the following year, Mendelssohn was awarded the Berlin Academy prize for an essay on the application of mathematical proofs to metaphysics – one of the other competitors was the great philosopher Immanuel Kant (1724-1804). Up to that time Mendelssohn had immersed himself in the scholarly pursuits of the Enlightenment, which with its emphasis on rationalism dominated eighteenth century thought.

In 1763 a young Christian student of theology came from Zurich to visit Mendelssohn, who was now quite famous. He insisted that Mendelssohn should tell him what he thought about Jesus. Mendelssohn said that provided Jesus had kept to Orthodox Jewish belief and practice, he 'respected the morality of Jesus' character.' Six years later, Lavater sent Mendelssohn a copy of an essay on Christian Evidences by Charles Bonnet. With this was a public challenge to Mendelssohn to refute what Bonnet had written or to 'do what wisdom, what love of truth and honesty must bid him, what a Socrates would have done if he had read the book and found it unanswerable.' Mendelssohn answered in an open letter, 'Suppose there was living among my contemporaries a Confucius or a Solon, I could according to the principles of my faith, love and admire the great man without falling into the ridiculous idea that I must convert Solon or Confucius.' Lavater later wrote warmly of Mendelssohn's 'keen insight, exquisite taste and wide erudition' but wished that he would recognise the 'crucified glory of Christ.' Subsequently, Lavater, in response to a letter from Mendelssohn, intervened to stop the expulsion of some Jews from Zurich.

Nonetheless, the controversy had absorbed so much of Mendelssohn's time that he was unwell for a while. When he recovered, Mendelssohn then decided 'to dedicate what remains of my strength for the benefit of my children or a goodly portion of my nation.' He sought to bring the Jews closer to 'culture, from which my nation, alas! is kept in such a distance that one might well despair of ever overcoming it.' One way of doing so was to encourage Jews to speak German fluently. At the time German Jews mostly spoke Yiddish - a mixture of German, Hebrew and Slavonic languages, which was written in Hebrew characters. The more learned Jews were well versed in Hebrew. Mendelssohn arranged for the first five books of the Bible – the Pentateuch – to be translated into High German and transliterated into Hebrew letters. Accompanying this was a Hebrew commentary, which highlighted the literary and moral qualities of the Bible. Mendelssohn himself did some of the translation and wrote much of the commentary. Traditional rabbis, however, reacted angrily to news of this intended publication. They saw it as a threat to the primacy of Talmudic study and a way of seducing readers to become interested in secular learning. Mendelssohn's chief collaborator was intimidated and withdrew. When the *Biur*, or commentary, appeared in 1783, it was banned in several communities, although welcomed by many young Jews who were eager to learn about a wider culture. Mendelssohn also seems to have supported the first modern school for Jews in Germany, where both religious and secular subjects were taught.

Mendelssohn also tried to persuade the majority population to accept Jews and allow them greater rights. His *On the Civil Amelioration of the Condition of the Jews* was published in 1781 and helped to promote tolerance. He followed this up by his book *Jerusalem* (1783), which argued that the state had no right to interfere with the religion of its subjects. Mendelssohn also said that while all Jews should obey the Torah, the Jewish religious authorities should not punish people for deviating from the Jewish religious law. The philosopher Immanuel Kant said it was 'an irrefutable book', which although 'slow in manifestation and in progress will affect not only your people but others as well.'

The case for tolerance had already been well argued by his friend Lessing in the dramatic poem *Nathan the Wise*, which appeared in 1779. Lessing celebrated the ethical basis of all true religion - identified as love and devoted service of others - which is to be found equally in Judaism, Christianity and Islam. Of the three representatives of the religions – Saladin for Islam, a Knights Templar for Christianity, and Nathan for Judaism - only the Jew, who was modelled on Moses Mendelssohn lived up to the ideal of full humanity and had the courage to speak the truth even to the mighty. The play emphasised that a religion of practical humanity united people of different faiths in brotherly solidarity and mutual tolerance.

Lessing and Mendelssohn's emphasis on tolerance was in tune with the time. The small number of Jews who had settled in America in the eighteenth century enjoyed full freedom from the beginning. It was taken for granted that the American Declaration of Independence, which stated that 'We hold these truths to be self-evident that all men are created equal, that they are endowed by the creator with certain unalienable rights, that among these are life, truth and the pursuit of happiness,' applied to Jews. In France, however, it was not so obvious that the French Revolution's claim that 'all men are born, and remain, free and equal in rights' included Jews. It was a matter of heated debate, but the armies of the French Republic, as they spread across Europe, brought emancipation to Jewish communities. Napoleon, who would not refer to Jews but only to 'French citizens of the Mosaic faith' subjected Jews in France to some discrimination, but these restrictions were swept away when the monarchy was restored. In other European countries Jewish emancipation took longer. Even at the start of the twentieth century, most of the large Jewish population in Poland, who were restricted to the 'Pale of Settlement,' still lived the traditional life of the ghetto. Jews in Russia continued to suffer from prejudice, persecution and periodic pogroms, which, at the end of the nineteenth century, drove many Jews to seek a new life in Western Europe or America.

Mendelssohn, personally and in his writings, anticipated the emancipated Jew of the nineteenth century. Unlike Locke, he did not draw a sharp distinction between the secular nature of the state and the spiritual role of the church. 'Our welfare in this life,' he wrote, 'is one and the same as our eternal felicity in the future.'[3] He insisted, however, that neither the church nor the state could coerce a person's beliefs. 'The state has no other means of acting effectively than the church does. Both must teach, instruct, encourage, motivate.'[4] The state, he accepted, could, if necessary use the sanction of force, but religious bodies should not - this got him into trouble with some Jewish authorities who exercised the power of excommunication. 'The state has physical power and uses it when necessary; the power of religion is love and beneficence.'[5]

In keeping with much Enlightenment thought, Mendelssohn upheld the essential rationality of religion and belief in God. This view is associated in Christianity with Sir Isaac Newton (1642-1727), the English mathematician and physicist. He and other Deists spoke of 'natural religion,' which left little room for miracles or an interventionist God. As we shall see Ram Mohun Roy's version of Hinduism and Sir Sayyed Ikbal Khan's approach to Islam were similar. Mendelssohn, in *Jerusalem*, suggested that Judaism was essentially a natural religion, containing no revealed truths, which were not available to unaided reason. The distinctiveness of Judaism, together with the belief that the Jews are God's chosen people, lay in the way of life commanded at Sinai. 'Judaism boasts of no exclusive revelation of eternal truths that are indispensable to salvation, of no revealed religion in the sense in which that term is usually understood. Revealed religion is one thing, revealed legislation another.'[6] The distinction is still often made between Christianity with its emphasis on right beliefs (orthodoxy) and

Judaism, which stresses obedience to the Torah as a way of life (ortho-praxy). Mendelssohn insisted that the Jewish way of life was of benefit to all people. His *Jerusalem* ends aftera reference to the Messianic prophecy of Zechariah that in the last days, 'many peoples and powerful nations will come to Jerusalem to seek the Lord Almighty and to entreat him,'[7] with the words, 'Love truth, love peace.'

Mendelssohn's final years were overshadowed by a controversy about 'pantheism.' This is the doctrine that God is, or is in, everything. At the time this view was especially associated with the Jewish philosopher Baruch Spinoza (1632-77), who had been excommunicated from the Jewish community in 1656. To the Orthodox, pantheism, which abolished the gap between Creator and the world that God created, was tantamount to atheism.

Mendelssohn planned to write a tribute to his friend Lessing. Before he achieved this, however, Friedrich Heinrich Jacobi, who had known both Lessing and Mendelssohn and who had corresponded with Mendelssohn on the subject, claimed publicly that Lessing was a pantheist and linked him with Spinoza. Others joined in the attack. Mendelssohn hastily composed a defence of his friend, entitled *To the Friends of Lessing: an Appendix to Mr Jacobi's Correspondence on the Teaching of Spinoza*. It is said that Mendelssohn was in such a hurry that he forgot to put on his coat before setting out on foot on a bitterly cold New Year's Eve to deliver the manuscript to the publisher. He caught a cold from which he died four days later on January 4th, 1786.

Mendelssohn was to be a role model for many Jews, as at last emancipated from the discrimination from which they had suffered for centuries, they began to play a full part in European life. To do so, some Jews, who came to belong to Reform or Progressive Jewish movements, initiated reform in Jewish worship and ways of life and insisted that they could hold together fundamental Jewish belief with contemporary ways of thinking. The constant danger, however, was of assimilation. Of Mendelssohn's own children, only two out of six, retained their Jewish faith. His grandson the brilliant musician Felix Mendelssohn (1809-1847) converted to Christianity. By the end of the nineteenth century, however, it was becoming clear that full participation in the life of Europe was no protection against anti-Semitism, which, under the Nazis was to claim millions of innocent lives and to destroy much of the rich cultural heritage of European Jewry.

How to be Jewish in the modern world is still a vital question for members of that faith. Writing also of Mendelssohn's near contemporaries, Elijah ben Solomon Zalman (1720-97), the *gaon* of Vilna, a prodigious Torah scholar and Ba'al Shem Tov (c.1700-60), the Hasid charismatic, Paul Johnson says, 'The fiery Talmud scholar, the mystic-enthusiast; the urbane rationalist – the whole of modern Jewry was to be written round these three archetypes.'[8]

CHAPTER NOTES

1. Paul Johnson, *A History of the Jews*, p. 299.
2. This teaching is known as 'deicide' and since the Holocaust has been repudiated by almost all Churches.
3. Moses Mendelssohn, *Jerusalem*, Berlin 1783, translated by Allan Arkush, Hanover, New Hampshire, University Press of New England, 1983, p.39.
4. *Jerusalem*, p. 61.
5. *Jerusalem*, p.45.
6. *Jerusalem*, p.97.
7. Zechariah, 8, 22.
8. Paul Johnson, p. 300.

68

John and Charles Wesley

John and Charles Wesley, both clergymen of the Church of England, inspired the Methodist movement, which soon became a worldwide church, now numbering some sixty million members in one hundred countries. John Wesley was the driving force, but some of Charles Wesley's hymns - such as the Christmas favourite 'Hark the herald angels sing' - are now sung by Christians of all denominations.

John and Charles' father, Samuel was himself a clergyman and rector of Epworth in Lincolnshire, although at one stage he had been a Non-Conformist minister. He and their mother Susanna encouraged their children's love of learning and devotion. John, the second son, was born on June 17th, 1703 and Charles on December 18th, 1707. In 1709, the rectory at Epworth was burnt to the ground. John was only just rescued in time, which is why later he described himself as 'a brand plucked out of the burning.'

John was educated at Charterhouse in London and then at Christ Church at Oxford University. He was ordained a priest in 1728 and after assisting his father for a while, he returned to Oxford in 1729 to take up his fellowship at Lincoln College. Charles went to Westminster School and then also to Christ Church. During the winter of 1728-9, Charles underwent a spiritual awakening and with two other undergraduates formed the Holy Club. They studied the scriptures 'methodically', received communion frequently, which was unusual at the time, and fasted twice a week. John, when he returned to Oxford, joined the Club and soon took charge. Its members now started to visit people in prison, teaching them to read, paying their debts and helping them to find work. They also distributed food and clothing to the poor.

Soon after his father's death, John was persuaded by the governor of the colony of Georgia in North America to go there, in the name of the Society for the Propagation of the Gospel (now USPG) to serve the spiritual needs of the colonists and to tell the indigenous people about the Christian faith. Charles, now ordained, went with him. But the venture was not a success. The mission to the Indians proved abortive; the colonialists disliked John's stiff high-churchmanship and his romantic interest in Sophia Hopkey, niece of a chief magistrate, came to nothing when she married another man.

The only blessing that John derived from the whole experience seems to have been his meetings with some Moravians – members of an evangelistic body of Protestant Brethren, which was descended in part from John Huss (c.1369-1415). Huss, a religious reformer in Bohemia and a precursor of the Reformation, was burnt as a heretic. The Moravians were committed to non-violence. They also emphasised the importance of hymn singing in worship and had published the first Protestant hymn book as early as 1501. A Moravian Church in America had just been established in 1734 and some Moravian missionaries were travelling to America on the same ship as the Wesleys. John was impressed by their quiet fearlessness when the ship was caught up in a great storm. In America itself, the Moravian leader Spangenberg asked John, 'Do you know Jesus Christ?' John answered, 'I know he is the Saviour of the world.' Whereupon Spangenberg asked again, 'True, but do you know that he has saved *you*?' It was not until their return to England, when they met again with the Moravians, who emphasised the need for personal faith, that John and Charles would be able to answer 'yes' to that question.

Charles had been the first to return to England. As he recovered from his exhaustion, he began to meet influential people and appeared at court before George II on behalf of Oxford University. Soon after John returned, Charles, who was still not at ease with himself experienced his 'Day of Deliverance' and on Whitsunday 21st May 1738, he wrote his first hymn, 'Where Shall My Wandering Soul Begin.' A year later he wrote his more famous hymn, 'O for a thousand tongues to sing.'

Meanwhile, John was at the time studying St Paul's *Letter to the Galatians*, which emphasises justification by grace through faith alone. Then on May 24, 1738 – three days after his brother's conversion - John, recalled, 'I felt my heart strangely warmed. I felt I did trust in Christ alone, for salvation; and an assurance was given me, that Christ had taken away *my* sins, even *mine*, and saved *me* from the law of sin and death.' One of Charles' hymns vividly expressed what his brother John experienced:

My chains fell off, my heart was free,

422

I rose, went forth, and followed thee.
No condemnation now I dread;
Jesus, and all in him, is mine.'[1]

Quite soon, John was persuaded by to preach in the open air by George Whitfield (1714-70), who had been a member of the Holy Club at Oxford and who was to become a great revivalist preacher. This John did at Bristol on April 1st, 1739 to a 'congregation' of 3,000 people. John had found his life's work.

As an itinerant preacher, John Wesley travelled nearly a quarter of a million miles - an average of 5,000 miles a year - mostly on horseback, across the length and breadth of the country. He preached, in all perhaps as many 50,000 sermons. He met with opposition from many church people who disliked 'enthusiasm.' He was supposed to get permission from the local vicar or rector before preaching in his parish. Once, when this was refused, he declared in words which have become famous, 'the world is my parish.' John also sometimes met with physical violence from the crowds. But in time this short slight figure, with a clean-shaven ruddy face, with bright eyes and snowy white hair, was to become almost a figure of veneration.

John gathered those who accepted Christ as Saviour into societies, which by his death were said to have 71,688 members. In 1784, John Wesley, now in his eighties, established an annual conference of 100 ministers to hold property and to give direction to the movement. Area circuits were also delineated each with a superintendent, to ensure the care and supervision of the members. In the same year the Methodist Episcopal Church was set up in the newly independent United States of America. John also wanted to send some priests to America, but the Bishop of London refused to ordain any of Wesley's preachers. He therefore took it upon himself to ordain some of his preachers, although in the Church of England, as in the Roman Catholic Church, only a bishop, who was Wesley was not, is authorised to ordain clergy. Wesley held that in the New Testament there was no distinction between bishops and elders. This was the step, which largely led to the separation of the Methodists from the Church of England, although it was only on John Wesley's death in 1791 that the Methodist Church was formally constituted.

Even before his death, there were divisions in the movement. George Whitfield, supported by the Countess of Huntingdon, created a separate body. There were to be other divisions in the nineteenth century, but the twentieth century saw the coming together again of most Methodist churches. John also became estranged from his brother Charles, who was so strongly against John's intention to marry his housekeeper Grace Murray, that Charles persuaded her to marry another preacher instead. In an emotional reaction, John married Mary Vazeille, a widow with four children, but she was to resent John's intimate concern for many of the young women who attended the Methodist societies. This may be one reason why John spent so much time travelling. Charles, by contrast, whose marriage was happier, quite soon gave up itinerant preaching and lived in Bristol and then in London, where he quite often preached at the City Road Chapel.

Recent biographers suggest that Charles' influence on the growth of Methodism has been underestimated. They emphasise his gifts of friendship and pastoral care.[2] Charles was known for his deep compassion for everyone. Charles also had a deeper love for the Church of England than John and disapproved of his brother taking to himself the authority to ordain priests. Charles, despite John's disapproval was buried in the churchyard of Marylebone Parish Church, with eight Church of England clergymen as his pall bearers.

John was essentially a preacher, not a systematic theologian and it was Charles' hymns which popularised the theology of Methodism. John's teaching is to be found in his sermons - the first four volumes of which remain among the 'doctrinal standards' of Methodism. His *Explanatory Notes on the New Testament* is another 'standard.' Other sources of information are his letters, his lengthy *Journal* and the decisions of Conference, where he was the dominant figure.

John, who translated a number of hymns and wrote a few himself, compiled *A Collection of Hymns For the Use of the People Called Methodist.* In his Preface, in October 1779, he comments on the poetry of the hymns:

'1. In these hymns there is no doggerel; no botches; nothing put in to patch up the rhyme; no feeble expletives. 2. Here is nothing turgid or bombast, on the one hand, or low and creeping on the other. 3. Here are no *cant* expressions, no words without meaning... We talk common sense.' Poetry, John, claimed, was a 'handmaid of Piety' and a 'means of raising or quickening the spirit of devotion, of confirming faith.'[3]

John Wesley called himself 'a man of one book.'[4] His authority was the scriptures, which, in the words of the spiritual writer Thomas à Kempis (c. 1380 – 1471), had to be interpreted in each generation 'in the same Spirit whereby they were given.'[5] Guidance as to their interpretation was to be found in the writings of the early Church Fathers. Although Wesley was suspicious of the influence on the church of the Emperor Constantine, who converted to Christianity, he did not question the creeds or the dogmas of the early Church councils.

Wesley's emphasis, however, was on the personal assurance of sins forgiven - although this was not a guarantee of never lapsing. Salvation was wholly dependent on God's free grace. The experience of pardon was guaranteed by the divinity of Christ and his atoning death. The doctrine of the Trinity was also an expression and affirmation of God's mercy. 'God the Holy Ghost,' he said, 'witnesses that God the Father has accepted the believer through the merits of God the Son - and having this witness, he [the believer] honours the Son and the blessed Spirit "even as he honours the Father."'[6]

Yet, despite his stress on God's free grace, Wesley quoted St Augustine's words, 'He who made us without ourselves, will not save us without ourselves.'[7] The believer, Wesley said, had to respond. Wesley, therefore, rejected the Calvinist teaching on Predestination and followed the teaching of the Dutch theologian Jacobus Arminius (1560-1609), who said that God wanted all people to be saved. This was one of the reasons for the break with George Whitfield. The believer also had to show a holiness of heart and life. As a result Methodists became known for their active compassion for the sick, the poor and the marginalised.

John Wesley preached the good news of God's free grace, but it was Charles, who by his hymn-writing, helped thousands to take this message to heart. As he wrote in the ever popular hymn 'Jesus, lover of my soul:'[8]

Plenteous grace with thee is found,
Grace to cover all my sin;
Let the healing streams abound,

Make and keep me pure within.

Although the Wesleys are primarily associated with the birth and growth of Methodism, their emphasis on personal conversion was also to influence the evangelical wing of the Church of England, especially members of the Clapham Sect, many of whom, such as William Wilberfore (1759-1833) became known for their social concerns and their missionary work. This would have pleased John Wesley who, although he engaged in debates about doctrine, recognised that Christians of different opinions could co-operate on practical action. As he wrote to a Roman Catholic, 'If we cannot as yet think alike in all things, at least we may love alike. Herein we cannot possibly do amiss. For of one point none can doubt a moment: "God is love; and he that dwelleth in love, dwelleth in God and God in him."'[9]

CHAPTER NOTES
1. *Hymns and Psalms*, 216.
2. See Gareth Lloyd, *Charles Wesley and the Struggle for Methodist Identity*, Oxford, Oxford University Press, 2007 and Gary Best, *Charles Wesley: a Biography*, London, Epworth, 2007.
3. From John Wesley's Preface, 20.10.1779.
4. Preface to his *Sermons*.
5. Thomas à Kempis, *The Imitation of Christ*, 1,5.
6. Sermon, 55.
7. Sermon 63 and 85.
8. *Hymns and Psalms*, 528.
9. From his Letters. The quotation is from I John 4, 16.

69

Seraphim of Sarov

St Seraphim is one of the most revered monks and mystics or holy men (*staretz*) of the Orthodox Church of Russia. The Liturgical chant praises him as 'an earthly angel and a heavenly man.' His life radiated the presence of the Holy Spirit and he encouraged lay people as well as monks to practise self-denial and contemplation.

Prokhor Moshnin, which was Seraphim's name before he entered monastic life, was born at Kursk in Russia in 1759. Kursk was a fortified town, which over the centuries had been destroyed several times by the Tartars. It had a hermitage and some two hundred miles away there was a large monastery in the forest of Sarov, to which many young men went and where Prokhor was in due course to become a monk.

Prokhor's father Isidor was a stonemason and brick-maker. His mother was called Agathia. As a child Prokhor had a bad fall, but recovered after a vision of the Virgin Mary, the Mother of God. As a boy he studied hard and directed there by a *staretz* (or holy man) he became a novice at Sarov when he was nineteen.

The monastery at Sarov was an old derelict fort, which St Theodosius (c.1002 – 74) used as the basis for a monastery. Later under Abbot John the monastery became a centre for relief of the poor and a place of pilgrimage. The regime there was austere, with total abstinence from meat and only one meal a day - except on Wednesdays and Fridays when a complete fast was kept. The day was fully occupied by choral prayer, manual work and study.

In the eighteenth century, when Prokhor was born, monasticism was under attack. Peter the Great abolished the Patriarchate and set up the Synod in its place. He also closed a number of monasteries. This policy was taken further by Catherine II. On her accession, 954 monasteries were still in existence, but 754 were closed during her reign and new ones could only be opened with government permission.

Prokhor, when he entered the monastery, was a well-built young man, with blue eyes, which reflected his joyous spirit. He would cheer up his fellow monks with words of encouragement – even whispering to them in chapel. He used to read the Bible, which he called 'the provi-

427

sioning of the soul,' standing before the icons. In 1780, Proktor fell ill, because of exaggerated austerity - of which later he told the devout to beware – and was bedridden for three years. During this period, he was consoled by visions of the Blessed Virgin and of the Apostles. In 1786, he took his monastic vows and was given the name Seraphim, by which he is always known, and which in Hebrew means 'fiery' or 'flaming,' and suggests a shining light-filled being. Seraphim was ordained priest in 1793 and, unusually for the time, celebrated the Eucharist every day.

In the following year, saddened by the death of the abbot, Seraphim withdrew to the forest. He grew most of his own food and shared it with the wild animals, including a huge bear, which kept him company and took food from his hand. He lived a life of extreme austerity and poverty. He had no bed and used a sack of stones for a mattress. At first he returned each Sunday to the monastery for the Eucharist and to receive some rations for the week. Near his retreat he created his own 'Holy Land' with, for example, a cave, which he called Bethlehem and a hill for Mt Tabor, so that he could enter more deeply into the events of the life of Jesus. During his life as a hermit there were times of rapture, but also fierce struggles with demons. 'They are hideous,' he said. 'Just as sinners cannot bear the brightness of angels, even so are evil spirits terrible to see.'[1]

In 1804 Seraphim was attacked by brigands, who thought the sack of stones was full of money. They left him for dead, but Seraphim dragged himself back to the monastery. There, without saying what had happened to him, he asked to be taken to the infirmary.

After five months Seraphim returned to his hermitage. Although only in his forties, he seemed prematurely aged. With a perpetual stoop, he now needed a walking-stick. At this time he got to know another *staretz*, called Nazarus, who had been one of the editors of the *Philokalia*, a collection of spiritual writings largely derived from Mt Athos, where Paissy Velitchkovsky had just translated it into Slavonic.[2]

When in 1807 the Abbot died Seraphim was offered the post, but he refused. Instead he submitted himself to the 'trial of silence.' For three years he spoke to nobody. 'No spiritual exercise,' he said later, 'can be compared with silence.' He also stopped going to the monastery for the Eucharist or to get food. Instead he lived on ground elder, which he said, was very nourishing. A new Abbot, however, was concerned that

Seraphim no longer came to the monastery and that he did not receive communion. Seraphim was ordered either to come every Sunday or, if he could not walk that distance, to come back permanently to the monastery. Seraphim obeyed the order, thus ending 15 years of solitary life. His cell at the monastery, however, was without bed, heat or lighting.

Another vision of the Virgin now led him to give up the solitary life – although he kept his door shut on Wednesdays and Fridays. He started gladly to welcome visitors, whom he usually called 'My Joy.' He also joined in the singing of the monks. Even so, he would still on occasion retreat to the forest. After 37 years preparation, he was now himself a *staretz*. He also became the spiritual director to a community of nuns at Diveyevo. Healing miracles were attributed to his prayers and levitation was witnessed by a disciple. Seraphim had a gift of insight by which he knew what was in a person's heart. When a proud professor came to visit him, he said, 'Teaching others is like casting stones down from the belfry, whereas putting into practice what one teaches is like carrying those stones up to the top of the belfry.' Even Tsar Alexander came to see him. At a time of growing unrest in Russia, Seraphim would remind soldiers of their duty to the Church and the country.

Seraphim was found dead on 14th January 1833. As his health deteriorated, he said, 'My life is drawing to a close, but if my body seems already dead, my spirit makes me feel like a new-born child.'[3] His death was discovered when, on his way to prayer, a monk smelled smoke. When he knocked on Seraphim's door, there was no answer. He told some other monks. One of them burst the door open. The room was dark and full of smoke. When a candle was brought they found the saint in his white cassock kneeling before the icon of the Virgin of Tenderness.

So many people attended his funeral that the candles went out for lack of air. It is said that at the hour of his death an extraordinary light lit up the sky and a monk near Kursk commented, 'It is the soul of Father Seraphim flying to heaven.'[4] After his death he is said to have appeared to the sisters of Diveyevo.

Seraphim was recognised as a saint by the Council of the Russian Church in 1903. Pope John Paul II also referred to him as a saint in his book *Crossing the Threshold of Hope*.[5]

Pilgrims soon started to flock to the monastery of Sarov, but under Communism all monasteries were closed. Sarov was closed in 1927. For a time it was used as a holiday camp for disabled and delinquent children, then as a concentration camp for deported clergy, and subsequently as a camp for felling timber, to which political deportees were sent. It was returned to the Russian Orthodox Church in 1992 and monastic life was re-established in 2006 – three hundred years after Sarov was originally founded. In 2003 President Putin and Patriarch Alexiy II visited Sarov to take part in the celebration of the 100th anniversary of St Seraphim's canonisation. In 1927 Diveyevo was also liquidated and the sisters dispersed, although at his canonisation, the Mother Superior had predicted that 'the relics of the saint will remain hidden for some time, but I am convinced that one day our dear *staretz* will come back to us.'

Seraphim wrote little. Two monks took notes and these *Instructions* were published in 1839 and reprinted in 1841, but were altered by Metropolitan Philaret who wrote, 'I have taken the liberty of correcting certain passages which are expressed in an unusual way, in order to avoid misunderstanding.' What we know of his teaching all points to his continuous sense of being filled with the presence of the Spirit through prayer. He urged disciples to concentrate on the Name of Christ and they would then begin to sense the Divine Light shining within them. 'When the mind and heart are united in prayer and the soul is wholly concentrated in a single desire for God,' he said, 'then the heart grows warm and the light of Christ begins to shine and fills the inward man with peace and joy.'[6] He focussed attention on Mary who was the supreme example of someone who has become a living temple of the Spirit. Unlike the Son who has a bodily presence – the Spirit hides and is only discerned in the lives of those open to his energy.

Seraphim insisted that the way of contemplation could be followed by lay people as well as monks. He said to his disciple Motovilov, 'The fact that I am a monk and you a layman is something that we don't need to consider... The Lord hears the prayers of a simple layman just as he does a monk's, provided they are both living in true faith and loving God from the depths of their heart.'[7]

Perhaps his best-known saying is 'Learn to be peaceful and

thousands around you will find salvation.' Certainly, many thousands have learned from his example that the way to such peace is through inner silence.

CHAPTER NOTES

1. Valentine Zander, *St Seraphim of Sarov*, translated by Sister Gabiel Anne with an introduction by Boris Bobrinskoy, Crestwood, N.Y., St Vladimir's Seminary Press, 1975, p.10.
2. See above, chapter 28.
3. Zander, p. 107.
4. Zander, p. 114.
5. Pope John Paul II, *Crossing the Threshold of Hope*, New York, Alfred A Knopf, 1994.
6. Zander, p. 103.
7. Zander, pp. xi-xii.

70

William Wilberforce

The name of William Wilberforce is forever linked to the Abolition of the Slave Trade. He was given a public burial in Westminster Abbey, where there is also a memorial to him. He was not, however, the only abolitionist and this was not the only social reform that he supported.

William Wilberforce was born on the 24th August 1759 into a long-established Yorkshire family. Early in the eighteenth century, his grand-father – another William Wilberforce had come to Hull, where he made his fortune from the Baltic trade. William was educated at first at Hull Grammar School. The very able headmaster, Joseph Miller, was to become a lifelong friend. The death of William's father, at the early age of thirty-nine, followed by his mother's illness, caused a dramatic and disagreeable change in his life. He was put in the care of an uncle and aunt, in their home at Wimbledon. He was happy enough there, but disliked the 'most wretched' boarding school at Putney, to which he was sent.[1] The aunt and uncle had joined the new and quickly growing Methodist movement, but when William's mother heard that William was about to follow their example, she took a coach to London, removed her son from her husband's relations and brought him back to Hull. William was deeply upset to be snatched away from his aunt and uncle, for whom he had a great affection. He was not even allowed back to his old school in Hull, but, to isolate him from any Methodist influences, he was sent as a boarder to Pocklington School, where at least, thanks to the family wealth, he was given a room to himself and special tutoring by the headmaster. During his holidays in Hull, he was introduced, almost by force, to the social life to the city.

Even so, William was shocked by the heavy drinking and licentiousness of his fellow students, when he began life in Cambridge at St John's College. Discouraged by his tutors from working too hard, Wilberforce himself came to spend a lot of time socialising and playing cards. It was during this time, when the American War of Independence was raging, however, that his interest in politics began. He would often travel to London to listen to debates from the public gallery in the House of Commons. Also often in the gallery was William Pitt – better known as Pitt the Younger – son of the first earl of Chatham. Pitt and Wilberforce quickly became firm friends and soon they were themselves to enter Parliament.

In 1780, Wilberforce - only just twenty-one –came top of the poll for Hull by a big majority. He took his seat in the House of Commons on 31st October 1780. Subsequently, he was for many years M.P. for the county of Yorkshire. Throughout his career, he sat as an independent. From the first Wilberforce was assiduous in attending the Commons, but was also welcomed into London society.

In the autumn of 1785, Wilberforce's life changed dramatically with his evangelical conversion to Christianity. His writings show a constant struggle to find more time for prayer and to lead a disciplined life. Thanks partly to Pitt's persuasion Wilberforce decided to continue as a Member of Parliament. He was determined to apply Christian principles to political action. He took the lead in persuading King George III to issue a Proclamation in June 1787 expressing concern at increasing immorality and calling on magistrates to prosecute those guilty of 'excessive drinking, blasphemy … and other dissolute, immoral or disorderly practices.'[2] Soon afterwards Wilberforce was invited by Sir Charles Middleton, a leading evangelical Member of Parliament, to visit him at his home at Teston in Kent. There, Wilberforce also met James Ramsay, vicar of a local parish, who, like Middleton had previously served in the Navy and also detested the slave trade. Two years before Ramsay had written his seminal *Essay on the Treatment and Conversion of African Slaves in the British Sugar Colonies.* In inviting Wilberforce, Middleton hoped to persuade Wilberforce to lead the Parliamentary campaign to abolish the slave trade.

Slavery was widespread in the Ancient world as it is still today – it was reckoned that in 2004, about twenty-seven million people were in some sort of forced or bonded labour, not to mention the sex slaves. With the 'discovery' of the New World, the need for slaves rapidly increased: first to mine gold and then to grow sugarcane. In 1510, King Ferdinand II of Spain gave permission for four hundred slaves to be taken from Africa to the New World. In 1562, Queen Elizabeth I gave her permission to Captain John Hawkins to capture and sell slaves provided they were not taken against their will![3] The trade grew rapidly.[4] It is reckoned that, in all, British ships transported about

2,600,000 slaves in 12,000 ships. Spanish, Portuguese and American ships all took their share of the trade. Portugal transported about 4,650,000 slaves. British ships set out from Liverpool or Bristol for Africa loaded with textile exports, which were exchanged there for slaves who were transported across the Atlantic to the Caribbean islands and to America. From there the ships returned to Britain with a cargo of sugar. It is estimated that from the seventeenth to the nineteenth century eleven million people were seized and transported across the Atlantic.

For each individual and his or her family enslavement was a tragedy. Moreover, the conditions on board ship and on the sugar plantations were quite appalling. Chained together, with no sanitation, little fresh air and bad food, large numbers of people died on the journey. Conditions on the plantations were almost equally harsh.

Of course, Wilberforce was not the first to abhor this vile trade. Even in the Middle Ages a Bishop Wulstan had travelled to Bristol to denounce the trade. In Westminster Abbey, besides the memorial to Wilberforce, there are also memorials to Granville Sharp (1735-1813) who was often called by his contemporaries the 'Father of the Cause'; to Thomas Clarkson, an indefatigable campaigner whose research was of vital importance; and to Olaudah Equiano (about 1745 – 1797), who was enslaved as a child and brought by his master to England, where he became a defender of black interests. In his autobiography, published in 1789, Equiano told the story of enslavement from the point of view of the enslaved.

Moreover, as Wilberforce began his career, the climate of opinion was changing. The growing emphasis on human rights called in question the very existence of slavery. The French philosopher Jean-Jacques Rousseau (1712-78) argued in *Le Contract Social* (1762) that men were born to be free and equal and that 'the words *slave* and *right* contradict each other and are mutually exclusive.'[5] The economic arguments for slavery were undermined by Adam Smith, who wrote in *The Wealth of Nations*, that 'the experience of all ages and nations, I believe, demonstrates that the work done by slaves, though it appears to cost only their maintenance, is in the end the dearest of any.'[6] Some Christian voices, were being raised against the evil of slavery, for example, by George Fox as early as 1671 and by John Wesley a century later.

The campaign for the abolition of the slave trade began in earnest in May 1787, with formation of a Society with this as its objective. Almost immediately slavery became a subject of debate in the newspapers. Public meetings were organised across the country. The Parliamentary campaign began in the next year, although notice of the debate was given by Pitt, as Wilberforce, who suffered from much ill health, was out of action. The debates are recounted in vivid detail by William Hague, a leading contemporary British politician, in his recent biography of Wilberforce and the information need not be repeated here.

Although the abolitionists were not unaware of the opposition that they would have to overcome, they can hardly have expected to wait twenty years before Parliament agreed to end the slave trade in Britain and the British colonies. It was to be another sixteen years before slavery itself was abolished in the British Empire. Why did it take so long?

Ship-owners and traders in Liverpool and Bristol, manufacturers of goods exported to Africa from the growing industrial towns and all owners of plantations in the West Indies had a vested interest in the continuance of the slave trade. Supporters of anti-abolitionists in Liverpool used to sing:

'If our slave trade had gone, there's an end to our lives,
Beggars all we must be, our children and wives,
No ships from our ports their proud sails e'er would spread,
And our streets grown with grass, where the cows might be fed.'[7]

It was argued that abolition would encourage revolt in the West Indies and would destroy the sugar cane plantations. It was also argued that abolition would merely benefit other naval powers and not reduce the number of slaves. Others suggested that the slaves were happy with their way of life! The plantation-owner William Beckford argued, as William Cobbett was to do later, that compassion should begin at home. The cabinet was divided and a majority in the Lords was against reform. Moreover, the French Revolution was also to make many in Britain more conservative and reluctant to support such a radical change.

William Wilberforce, although he could not have foreseen the dramatic events that were later that summer to take place across the Channel, was well aware of the difficulties ahead when on the 12th of May 1789, he launched his campaign with a three and a half hour long speech. He said he wanted to appeal to members' cool and impartial reason rather than to passion, although he asked how anyone could bare to imagine 'six or seven hundred of these wretches chained two and two, surrounded with every object that is nauseous and disgusting, diseased, and struggling under every kind of wretchedness?'[8] Wilberforce ended by an appeal to a higher authority. 'There is a principle above every thing which is political; and when I reflect on the command which says, "Thou shalt do no murder" believing the authority to be divine, how can I dare to set up any reasonings of my own against it?'[9] It was in Burke's words 'most masterly, impressive and eloquent ... perhaps not excelled by anything to be met with in Demosthenes.'[10]

Despite the strong evidence against the trade, which had already been presented to the Privy Council, by the time the debate was continued the opposition, as a delaying tactic, argued that the trade needed to be examined by the House of Commons itself. The Committee set up to do this made little progress and when, in 1791, Wilberforce again moved the abolition of the slave trade, it was once again defeated by a considerable majority. He promised, however, that 'Never, never, will we desist till we have wiped away this scandal from the Christian name, released ourselves from the load of guilt ... and extinguished every trace of this bloody traffic.'[11]

It was to be another sixteen years before the trade was abolished, although by an indirect and ingenuous Parliamentary manoeuvre rather than 'on general Abolition principles or ... on justice and humanity.'[12] In 1805 James Stephen wrote *The War in Disguise*, which argued that although Britain was a great maritime power, the colonies of her enemies were prospering because they were free to use the ships of neutral countries. He urged that the Navy should be free to search and seize neutral shipping. There was only one passing reference to the slave trade in Stephen's book. Yet, preventing neutral ships going to colonies of the enemies would not only stop them being able to import slaves, but by halting all their exports and imports, it would ruin their economies, thereby ending their demand for slaves. To ensure that the policy was effective, British ships had also to be forbidden from selling slaves to enemy colonies.

The Abolitionists were now only a step away from abolishing the British slave trade. The measure passed both Houses of Parliament in February 1807 and received the Royal Assent on March 24th and became law the following day. Although Wilberforce said that he was 'only one among many fellow labourers,' he received the acclaim that he richly deserved. To be effective, the Abolitionists had to win the day in Parliament. Wilberforce was a great Parliamentarian, an eloquent speaker and an astute tactician.

The hope of the Abolitionists was, in Clarkson's words, that destroying the trade, would be 'laying the axe at the very root' of slavery.[13] In fact the now illegal trade could only be completely halted when slavery itself was abolished. This was finally achieved for the whole of the British Empire when the Bill passed both Houses of Parliament in August 1833, freeing, at least technically, some 800,000 slaves. Wilberforce died at the end of the previous month, but just days before he received news that the Bill was sure to pass. 'Thank God', he said, 'that I should have lived to witness a day in which England is willing to give twenty millions sterling [in compensation to slave owners] for the Abolition of Slavery.'[14]

This was the cause above all to which Wilberforce devoted his life. Yet at the same time he was an active member for the important constituency of Yorkshire. He was very regular in his attendance at the Commons and a frequent speaker on a great variety of subjects. He had endless friends and guests and always charmed them by his witty and interesting conversation. He was forever trying to catch up with his enormous correspondence. He gave help to many individuals in distress and supported a wide range of good causes, including a Society for the Reformation of Manners and the Society for the Prevention of Cruelty to Animals. In opposition to the policy of the East Indian Company, he campaigned for missionaries to be allowed to spread the message of Christianity in India. He attacked the Game Laws, which imposed severe penalties, including transportation, for minor acts of poaching. Under the influence of Elizabeth Fry, he supported prison reform and campaigned to restrict capital punishment to the most serious crimes. He supported legislation to improve the working conditions of chimney sweeps and tried to limit the working day of children in the textile industry. He strongly supported efforts to improve and expand education.

Fear of revolution, such as his generation had witnessed in France, made him conservative on some measures. Wilberforce, for example, opposed an enquiry into the Peterloo massacre, in which eleven campaigners for Parliamentary reform were killed when the cavalry were sent into a vast crowd to arrest the leaders. His fervent Evangelical Christian beliefs at first led him to oppose Catholic emancipation, although he later changed his mind on this.

Like any politician, he was not free from criticism. He was sometimes accused of hypocrisy, of being blind to social evils at home, and being too close to the leaders of society. At times he was mocked for his Christian faith. He stands out, however, as a person who both in his public and family life was guided by his deep Christian beliefs. In his diaries, he repeatedly regretted his failure to spend more time in prayer and reading and also his failures in self-discipline.

Wilberforce's ability to live by and act upon his deep religious convictions, as much as what he achieved towards the Abolition of Slavery, ensure the continuing relevance of his example at a time when politicians are so widely and cynically viewed as self-seeking and corrupt. He showed, in William Hague's words,

'how a political career could be conducted differently, pursuing long-term objectives deeply rooted in certain principles, strengthened by his indifference to holding power by his under-standing of its transitory nature. As a result, he defied the axiom that political careers necessarily end in failure, going to his grave fulfilled by the knowledge of what he had helped to do, while those politicians to whom power alone is important decline in their old age into bitterness and despair... He showed unyielding reverence for truth, loyalty, integrity and principle as he understood it, setting an example that has stirred the hearts and elevated the minds of generations who followed.'[15]

Wilberforce not only achieved a reform that could not be reversed, he also showed that lasting change for the better is possible.

CHAPTER NOTES
1. William Hague, *William Wilberforce*, Harper Press, 2007.
2. Quoted by Hague, p. 107.
3. Hague, p. 116.
4. For a thorough study see Hugh Thomas, *The Slave Trade*, 1440-1870, New York, Simon and Schuster, and London, Picador (Macmillan Publishers) 1997. The estimated figures are on p. 805.
5. Jean-Jacques Rousseau, *Le Contract Social*, (the Social Contract) 1762, Bk I, Ch IV, quoted by Hague, p. 129.
6. Adam Smith, *The Wealth of Nations*, 1776, Book III, Chapter II, pp. 488-9, quoted by Hague, p. 130.
7. Quoted by Hague, p. 174.
8. Quoted by Hague, p. 179.
9. Quoted by Hague, p. 183.
10. Quoted by Hague, p. 184.
11. Quoted by Hague, p. 198.
12. Quoted by Hague, p. 332.
13. Quoted by Hague, p. 509.
14. Quoted by Hague, p. 503.
15. William Hague, p. 515.

71

William Blake

William Blake, although poor and unappreciated in his lifetime, has in the last century been increasingly recognised as a poet, artist, and visionary. He has been described as a 'man without a mask' and his writings, difficult as they are, are still disturbing, because they strip away the masks that we, as individuals and members of society, hide behind.

William Blake was born in London on November 28th, 1757, two years before William Wilberforce. It is interesting to compare the responses of these two dedicated men, from very different social backgrounds, to the big changes that were taking place in British society and to the protracted wars against the Americans and then the French.

William was the second of five children. His father was a hosier - a dealer in socks and underwear - and the family lived above the shop near Piccadilly. Although William was baptised at St James's Church, Piccadilly, the family were so-called Dissenters or Non-Conformists and not members of the Church of England. William did not go to school but was taught by his mother. He read widely. Later he himself was to teach his wife to read.

London was much smaller in his day and it was easy for William to go off on solitary rambles into the countryside. On one such walk, before he was ten years old, William had a vision in which he saw a tree full of angels. When he told his parents, his mother was more understanding than his father. William Blake, throughout his life, was intensely visual. He was what is now called 'eidetic'. What he imagined appeared to him to be as real as external objects. To him, his visions seemed to fill his outer rather than his inner eye.

Blake was keen to become a painter and at the age of ten was sent to a drawing school. He was then apprenticed to an engraver called William Ryland, but Blake did not like the look of the man's face. He is supposed to have said, he 'looks as if he will live to be hanged', which is what in fact happened to Ryland, who was hanged twelve years later for forgery.

Blake was, therefore, at the age of fourteen, apprenticed instead for seven years to James Basire, whose style of work was rather old fashioned. Basire had been commissioned to record the monuments in Westminster Abbey, so Blake spent long hours with him in the Abbey. Having completed his apprenticeship, Blake in 1779 was enrolled as a student at the Royal Academy, but he strongly disliked the President Sir Joshua Reynolds, who in any case did not think engravers had any place at the Academy, which should only be for painters. In 1782, Blake married Catherine Boucher and they set up house near Leicester Square. They had no children. In 1784, after his father's death, Blake moved back to the house next door to where he had grown up and opened a print shop. 1787, however, saw the death of his brother Robert and the failure of his business. Even so, Blake seems to have got enough work to earn a living by making engravings for publishers and by painting watercolours.

Blake was also, at this time, becoming friendly with some radical intellectuals, who opposed the war against the American colonies. Through them he was introduced to the writings of two very different thinkers: Emanuel Swedenborg (1688-1772) and Joseph Priestley (1733-1804).

Swedenborg was a Swedish scientist, philosopher and theologian. Swedenborg, who devoted his later years to writing some thirty volumes on the Bible, relied on what he had heard and seen in the world of spirits and angels and this confirmed Blake's confidence in his visions. The being of the Lord, Swedenborg said, cannot be described, but the Lord's essence consists of two primary qualities, love and wisdom. Such an approach suggested a mystical truth beyond creedal formulae. This thought was later to inspire Charles Bonney, who was a Swedenborgian and whose idea it was to convene the World Parliament of Religions - held in Chicago in 1893. Bonney said at the opening of the Parliament that 'every nation has some religion' and that there are 'common essentials of all religions, by which everyone may be saved.'[1] These ideas are reflected in Blake's early work *All Religions Are One*, which he wrote in about 1788.

Joseph Priestley (1733-1804) was in his early life a Unitarian minister and a teacher. He had a great interest in science, especially in electricity and was one of the discoverers of the element oxygen. Priestley was an enthusiastic supporter of the French Revolution. As the revolution turned violent, he himself became the object of violent abuse and attack for his continuing sympathy for its ideals. He therefore left England for America, where he became a friend of Thomas Jefferson (1743-1826), who drafted the American declaration of Independence and was the third President of the USA (1801-09). Blake himself started a work on *The French Revolution*, but it was never printed, probably because of a real fear of prosecution. For the Government had already accused Thomas Paine (1737-1809) - who had earlier argued for American independence from Britain - of treason for his *The Rights of Man* (1791-92) and *Age of Reason* (1793-94). Indeed, the Government, over the next thirty years, prosecuted more than one hundred booksellers just for stocking the *Age of Reason*. It is no wonder that Blake hid his revolutionary sympathies by using symbols of energy, such as Los and Orc, instead of the names of actual people and places.

Encouraged by his friends, Blake published his *Songs of Innocence* in 1789 – the year of the French Revolution. Blake engraved the text himself on small copperplates, with his own decorations, and printed and coloured them by hand. Five years later, he published his *Songs of Experience*. They were, however, unread and unknown for nearly seventy years, although it has been said, 'they were as formative for the culture of the twentieth century in Europe and America as the Bible and *Pilgrim's Progress* had been for an earlier age.'[2] Four years later, the *Lyrical Ballads* by the Romantic poets William Wordsworth (1770-1850) and Samuel Coleridge (1772-1834) were to attract wide attention. The different reception was perhaps not because of differences in style but because 'Blake's insight into the dilemmas of civilized city life and into the hierarchies of power among warring states and industrial societies left his contemporaries cold and spoke directly to today.'[3]

As public sympathy for the French Revolution drained away and Britain took up arms against the French, Blake found himself increasingly isolated. He continued to sympathise with the Revolution and even in 1801 he still dreamed that 'France and England will henceforth be as One Country.' He took the Sermon on the Mount literally and was, therefore, opposed to war. He was appalled by the attacks on Thomas Paine. He recognised, long before his contemporaries, that the industrial revolution was turning workers into animals and depriving them of creativity. 'The living and the dead,' he wrote, 'shall be ground in our rumbling mills.'

In the 1790s his style of writing changed. He wrote *the Marriage of Heaven and Earth* - a deliberate criticism of Swedenborg – in prose. His poetry changed from the lyrics of the *Songs* to a narrative form of unrhymed lines, which echoed the rhythm of the King James Authorised Version of the Bible. The obscure mythology was necessary because, as already mentioned, direct political or religious criticism had become dangerous and prosecution for sedition was an ever-present threat to authors, printers and booksellers.

As the economic depression of the war years worsened, aggravated by a series of bad harvests, people had little money to spend on engravings, which had become a luxury. Blake only scraped by because a few friends bought his works. In 1800 he was 'adopted' by William Hayley, who found a home and work for him at Felpham on the Sussex coast. The situation was, however, not as idyllic as it might appear. His wife was lonely in the country and the damp cottage made her rheumatism worse. The work he was given by Hayley was 'mere drudgery.' By 1803, he had decided they should move back to London, but matters came to a head after a contretemps with a soldier, who had come into the cottage garden uninvited. The soldier complained that Blake had assaulted him and that Blake had also made seditious remarks about the King. Blake was eventually cleared of the charge – but the soldier reappeared as a devious figure of treachery in Blake's last book *Jerusalem.*

Back in London, Blake worked on his two longest works, *Milton,* which he finished in 1804 and *Jerusalem,* which he completed in 1820. His vision of the ideal human life is the same as in *The Songs of Innocence* and *The Songs of Experience.* People needed to free themselves from conventional authority, including the hidden conventions that rule family life, such as hierarchies of seniority, sex and status. The good society, which Blake called the 'New Jerusalem', required not only political and social reform, but respect of people for each other and a new sense of harmony with the natural world. In *Milton* and *Jerusalem,* Blake, who never went north of London, showed that he was increasingly aware of the human degradation resulting from the Industrial Revolution with its 'dark Satanic Mills.'

In 1809, Blake held an exhibition of some of his paintings and wrote a thoughtful *Descriptive Catalogue*. The critic and essayist Charles Lamb (1775-1834) was one of the few people who visited the exhibition. Blake found it increasingly difficult to get work, although John Linnell commissioned watercolour drawings for an edition of the *Divine Comedy* by the Italian poet Dante (1265-1321).

In his final years Blake suffered from gallstones and wrote no more although he went on colouring books in bed. He died on August 12th, 1827. A neighbour said, 'I have been at the death, not of a man, but of a blessed angel.' Blake was buried in the Dissenters' Burial Ground at Bunhill Fields in an unmarked grave – although there is now a memorial. A memorial was also erected in Westminster Abbey to him and his wife in 1957.

To understand Blake, we need to remember that he lived in one of the most violent periods of English history. Changes, which had begun before he was born, gathered pace during his lifetime. Manufacturing changed from craftsmen working at home in villages to 'hands' employed in soul-destroying factories. Larger farms and enclosures were transforming the countryside. The population, which was less than seven millions in 1757 when Blake was born, had nearly doubled by the time he died in 1827. 'The cost of living more than doubled; wages did not. And all through these years walked the ironmaster war. Blake was born in the Seven Years' War. He learned to think as a man during the American War. His years of promise were turned to defeat in the war against the French Revolution. Defeat deepened to bitterness in the war against Napoleon from 1803 to 1815... And this war did not end at Waterloo. The Sedition Acts, the Combination laws, the suspension of Habeas Corpus were still riding with the yeomanry against the Manchester suffrage meeting at St Peter's Field in 1819[4]... A year before Blake died, Lancashire had its worst slump, and starving mobs broke a thousand looms in three days.'[5]

Blake, with his visionary insight, saw what was happening and drew images from his knowledge of myth to express his horror.

I stood among my valleys of the south
And saw a flame of fire, even as a Wheel
Of fire surrounding all the heavens: it went
From west to east, against the current of

Creation, and devour'd all things in its loud
Fury and thundering course round heaven and earth.'

The demands of the machines were destructive of the human being who was reduced to 'sorrowful drudgery to obtain a scanty pittance of bread.'[6] It was not until the second half of the nineteenth century that other prophetic voices, like John Ruskin (1819-1900), a British art critic and moral philosopher, and William Morris (1834-1896), a leader of the Pre-Raphaelites, spoke out against these evils, which Blake had foreseen – evils still to be seen in the degrading poverty of millions in the world today. Blake spoke of his own dedication in the well known words of *Jerusalem*:

I will not cease from Mental Fight
Nor shall my Sword sleep in my hand
Till we have built Jerusalem
In England's green and pleasant Land.

Blake saw both the political and the religious establishment as enemies because they tried to deny experience and thwart human fulfilment. He said, 'Prisons are built with stones of law, brothels with bricks of religion.'

Blake emphasised the importance of experience. Knowledge is not bounded by the senses, but it must be made actual through the senses.

'Some say that Happiness is not Good for Mortals, and they ought to be answer'd that Sorrow is not fit for Immortals and is utterly useless to any one; a blight never does good to a tree, and if a blight kill not a tree, but it still bear fruit, let none say that the fruit was in consequence of the blight.'

Blake affirmed, like the English poet and novelist D H Lawrence (1885-1930), the goodness of the physical and of human sexuality.

In a wife I would desire
What in whores I always found –
The lineaments of Gratified desire.

Abstinence sows sand all over
The ruddy limbs and flaming hair,
But Desire Gratified
Plants fruits of life and beauty there.[7]

Because religious authorities tried to inhibit human sexuality, people had to find other expression as in brothels. Love cannot be put 'in a golden bowl.'

Blake's intense dislike of the religious leadership was underlined by the contrast that he drew between Christ and the God of the Old Testament, to whom, in his view, the religious leaders paid homage.

'Thinking as I do that the Creator of this World is a very Cruel Being and being a Worshipper of Christ, I cannot help saying: "the son, O how unlike the father!" First God Almighty comes with a Thump on the head. Then Jesus Christ comes with a balm to heal it.'[8]

At least some Christians today would agree, as I do, with Blake's comments that religion has so often been life denying rather than life-affirming. For them, a favourite text are the words of Jesus, 'I came that they might have life and life in all its fullness.'[9] That life includes the physical as well as the spiritual. It is Blake's vision of the divine potential of humanity, that was thwarted by church and state, which underlies his vehement protests. 'Blake looked for man's fulfilment in that which at last makes him man alone, and alone makes him man: the sum of his mind, his feelings, his dignity, his knowledge of truth and of love, his reason in its widest sense: his belief in his own imagination.'[10] For this fulfilment, Blake recognised that a person, must 'be born again,' as Jesus said. Such rebirth transforms a person's view of life and society and allows them to recognise the Divine Image:

Mercy has a human heart,
Pity a human face,
And Love, the human form divine,
And Peace, the human dress.

Then every man, of every clime,

That prays in his distress,
Prays to the human form divine,
Love, Mercy, Pity, Peace.

In his refusal to reject aspects of human behaviour which society then –and perhaps still does – seek to repress, Blake's unitive vision, like that of other mystics, saw that the polarities of experience should be held together. In the *Songs of Innocence*, the symbol of Christ is the Lamb. In *Songs of Experience*, Blake constantly returns to the theme of 'The Tyger.' Blake recognises that energy, enthusiasm, commitment, and a willingness to fight for a cause are all parts of the divine scheme and do not necessarily contradict the harmony of nature as it is expressed in other creatures. 'The "Proverbs of Hell" say "the wrath of the lion is the wisdom of God" and "tygers of wrath are wiser than horses of instruction." In such opinions Blake tried to heal and even turn upside down the division between the good or the angelic and the bad or the Satanic.'[11]

Although many of Blake's insights were welcomed in the 'permissive sixties' and similar ideas are part of current debate, it is easy to see why Blake's radical vision was ignored by his contemporaries and why his totally new way of seeing the world and the ordering of society are still so challenging today.

CHAPTER NOTES

1. Charles Bonney, 'The Genesis of the World's Religious Congresses of 1893,' *New Church Review*, 1.1.1894, pp. 73-8, *passim*, quoted in Marcus Braybrooke, *Pilgrimage of Hope*, London, SCM Press 1992, p. 13.
2. *Encyclopaedia Britannica*, 1977, 2, p.1101.
3. *Encyclopaedia Britannica*, 1977, 2, p.1101.
4. The reference is to the Peterloo Massacre in Manchester in 1819 when the cavalry violently dispersed a crowd of radicals, killing a considerable number of people.
5. J. Bronowski, *William Blake*, Harmondsworth, Penguin Books, 1944, Pelican edition 1954, p. 185.
6. Blake's words describing his own experience.
7. Quoted by Bronowski, p. 192.

8. Quoted by Bronowski, p. 188.
9. John 10,10.
10. Bronowski, p. 197. John.
11. *Encyclopaedia Britannica*, 1977, 2, p.1102.

72

Sri Ramakrishna and Vivekananda

Interfaith dialogue today is widely recognised to be urgent. But this is quite recent. The beginnings of the interfaith movement date back to the World Parliament of Religions – mentioned in the previous chapter – which was held in Chicago in 1893. When on the opening day a Hindu monk, wearing orange robes, began his address with the words 'sisters and brothers of America' he was greeted with a peal of applause that lasted several minutes. 'I am proud', Vivekananda continued, 'to belong to a religion which has taught the world both tolerance and universal acceptance... We accept all religions as true.'[1] He had answered the challenge of Christian missionaries by implying that they were intolerant and narrow-minded.

Even more important than Swami Vivekananda was his *guru* or teacher, Sri Ramakrishna (1836-86). Gadadhar, who became known as Ramakrishna, was born in a rural village in Bengal. He was the fourth child of pious Brahmin parents - worshippers of Rama – who had a smallholding. In 1855, his eldest brother Ramkumar – 31 years his senior – became the resident priest at a new temple at Dakshineswar, just north of Calcutta. He asked his brother to join him. Within a year of the Temple's dedication, Ramkumar had died. Ramakrishna was then asked to take on the more demanding duties at the Kali temple, although there were complaints about his frequent trances during worship and his irregular attendance.

Ramakrishna longed for a vision of the Mother, Kali. He was almost excessively devoted to his spiritual practices. When he was on the point of suicide, he suddenly had a wonderful vision of the Mother. In due course, he followed other spiritual paths and had other visions, including one of Rama and then of Jesus and Muhammad.

The meeting with Jesus has been described in this way:

'For three days Ramakrishna did not set foot in the Kali temple. On the fourth day, in the afternoon... he saw coming towards him a person with beautiful large eyes, serene countenance, and fair skin. As the two faced each other, a voice sang out in the depths of Sri

Ramakrishna's soul: "Behold the Christ, who shed his heart's blood for the redemption of the world, who suffered a sea of anguish for love of men...It is he, the Master Yogi, who is in eternal union with God. It is Jesus, Love Incarnate." The Son of Man embraced the Divine Mother and merged in him. Sri Ramakrishna realized his identity with Kali, Rama, Hanuman, Radha, Krishna, Buddha, and Muhammad.'[2]

On the basis of his experience, Sri Ramakrishna claimed that it was the One Divine Reality, in different forms that he had experienced. This became the basis of the neo-Hindu claim that all religious paths lead to the same experience of unity with the divine. The differences, it is said, are in our cultural conditioning and the various languages and images we use to express an experience that is inherently ineffable. The philosopher Sarvepalli Radhakrishnan (1888-1975) put it like this, 'The seers describe their experiences with an impressive unanimity. They are near to each other on mountains farthest apart.'[3] Sri Ramakrishna himself said,

'A lake has several ghats (or steps down to the water). At one the Hindus take water in pitchers and call it *jal;* at another the Musalmans take water in leather bags and call it *pani.* At a third, the Christians call it *water.* Can we imagine that it is not *jal* but only *pani* or *water.* How ridiculous? The substance is one under different names, and everyone is seeking the same substance; only climate, temperament and name create differences.'[4]

Of all his disciples, the most influential was Narendranath Dutt, as Swami Vivekananda was originally known, who was born on January 12th, 1863.[5] As a student at the Scottish Presbyterian College in Calcutta, he asked a number of religious teachers, 'Sir, have you see God?' He usually got an evasive answer – but the principal suggested he should seek out Sri Ramakrishna, who gave him a direct answer. 'Yes, my son, I have seen God, just as I see you before me, only much more intensely.'[6]

Naren eventually became a follower of Sri Ramakrishna, who had from the first recognized Naren as his successor. A few days before his death from throat cancer, Sri Ramakrishna bequeathed his spiritual powers to Naren.

Following Ramakrishna's death, after a period of consolidation, Vivekandna left on a journey of almost seven years that was to take him throughout India and then to North America and Europe. During his journeys across India, Vivekananda became increasingly aware of the sufferings and struggles of India's people and hoped that in America he might find the material resources to help his people. Before setting out for the New World, he reached the tip of the Indian peninsula at Kanyakumari or Cape Comorin. A short distance from the shore there was a rock – now known as Vivekananda's rock - to which he was determined to swim through shark infested waters. There looking northward to Mother India, Vivekananda dedicated himself to 'My God, the afflicted: My God, the poor of all races,' A key part of his mission was to be commitment to social service and reform. As he wrote in a letter from America, he said, 'At Cape Comorin, I hit upon a plan. We are so many sannyasins wandering about and teaching the people metaphysics – it is all madness. Did not our Gurudeva use to say, "An empty stomach is no use for religion?"… Suppose some disinterested sannyasins, bent on doing good to others, go from village to village disseminating education and seeking in various ways to better the condition of all down to the *chandala* (a man of lowest caste)…can't that bring forth good in time?'[7]

By the time he reached Chicago, Vivekananda had lost the address of the place where the Parliament of Religions was to meet – in any case he was three months too early! He arrived by train late at night – with no one to meet him. He slept in a large empty box in a corner of the railway station. The next morning he wandered from door to door asking for directions and for help. Exhausted he sat down on the pavement ready to wait for whatever happened. Quite soon, a woman, in North Dearborn, Mrs. G W Hale, looked out of a window across the street and saw this man in oriental monk's robes. She went down, asked him if he was a delegate to the Parliament of Religions, offered him refreshment and then took Vivekananda to introduce him to the President of the Parliament, who was a personal friend.

Vivekananda, as mentioned above, claimed that all paths lead to God, and quoted Lord Krishna's words in the Bhagavad Gita, 'Whosoever comes to me, through whatsoever form I reach him, they are all struggling through paths that in the end always lead to me.'[8]

Vivekananda seized the moral high ground for Hinduism, implying that the missionary zeal or fanaticism of many Christians was narrow and intolerant. Instead of the missionary's denunciations of idolatry, Vivekananda claimed that the Hindu, who believes in reincarnation and that this life is one of many, saw even the simplest form of devotion as a stepping stone to knowledge of God. 'All religions from the lowest fetishism to the highest absolutism are but so many attempts of the human soul to grasp the Infinite.'[9] Appealing to evolution, Vivekananda said, 'Every religion is only an evolving of God out of material man. The same God is the inspirer of all. ... The contradictions are only apparent, says the Hindu. The contradictions come from the same truth adapting itself to the different circumstances of different natures.'[10] Vivekananda thereby sought to affirm the validity of the various paths within Hinduism and to emphasize the harmony of Hinduism with other religions.

This emphasis on experience or realization carries with it the suggestion that doctrines and rituals have only a relative importance – they are like 'fingers pointing towards the moon.' This, of course, is much disputed, and Ramakrishna and Vivekananda, unknowingly, initiated a major debate about the nature of mystical experience. Some scholars insist that spiritual experience cannot be separated from words. Others argue that there are varieties of mystical experience.

Vivekananda was impatient, as we have seen, with the time fellow monks spent on religious ceremonies instead of serving the needs of the people. 'One must learn sooner or later,' he told his fellow monks, 'that one cannot get salvation if one does not try to seek the salvation of his brothers...You must be prepared to go into deep meditation now, and the next moment you must be ready to go and cultivate these fields... You must be prepared for all menial services.'[11]

It is particularly significant that Vivekananda and other leading figures of neo-Hinduism have come to recognize disinterested service of the poor – *karma-yoga* – as one of the paths to God-realization and of equal standing to the other yogas, such as *Bhakti-yoga* or the way of devotion and *Jnana-yoga* or the way of wisdom.

Sri Ramakrishna and Swami Vivekananda in their mystical experience and realization of the Divine, sensed a oneness not only with spiritual seekers on other paths but with all humanity, especially the poor and needy, whose service can bring us into the presence of God.

CHAPTER NOTES

1. *The World's Parliament of Religions*, ed John Henry Barrows, Chicago, The Parliament Publishing Co, 1893, p. 102.

2. *The Gospel of Ramakrishna*, New York, Ramakrishna Vedanta press, 1942, p. 34.

3. S. Radhakrishnan, 'Fragments of a Confession' in *The Philosophy of Sarvepalli Radhakrishnan* ed A, Schlipp, p.62.

4. *The Gospel of Sri Ramakrishna*, p. 35.

5. *They Lived with God* by Swami Chetanananda, London, Shepheard-Walwyn, 1989, tells the story of many of Sri Ramakrishna's other disciples.

6. Nirvedananda, Swami, "Sri Ramakrishna and Spiritual Renaissance," *Cultural Heritage of India*, Vol. 4, ed. By Bhattacharya, Haridas Calcutta: The Ramakrishna Mission, 1955, p. 40.

7. Quoted by D.S Sarma, *Hinduism Through the Ages*, Bombay, Bharatiya Vidya Bhavan, n.d.

8. *The World's Parliament of Religions*, p. 102. See *Bhagavad Gita*, 9,23; 7,21.

9. *The Complete Works of Swami Vivekananda*, 5th edtn, Almora, 1931, vol 4, p. 331.

10. *The World's Parliament of Religions*, p. 977.

11. *Selections from Swami Vivekananda*, Calcutta, Advaita Ashram, 3rd Edtn, 1957, p. 340.

73

Sayyid Ahmed Khan and Muhammed Iqbal

How should Islam relate to the modern world? Two influential Indian Muslims Sir Sayyid Ahmed Khan and Sir Muhammad Iqbal gave rather different answers. Sayyid Ahmad Khan's approach was essentially defensive. He lived at a time when power in India was passing from the crumbling Mughal Empire to British imperialists and was deeply concerned to help Muslims relate to Western civilization. Muhammad Iqbal (1873-1938), who has been called 'one of the greatest minds that Muslim India produced,' affirmed the all-embracing sufficiency of Islam.

Sayyid Ahmad Khan, who was born on October 17th 1817, belonged to a distinguished family that claimed descent from the Prophet himself, through his daughter Fatima and his son-in-law Ali. The family migrated to Iran, then to Afghanistan and finally to India with the Emperor Shah Jahan in the seventeenth century. His maternal grand-father was a prime minister under Emperor Akbar Shah and had a lasting influence on his grandson Sayyid. He was also deeply influenced by his mother, who was known for her generosity and piety. His father was highly intellectual and mystically inclined. Sayyid had the traditional education of a member of the Muslim nobility. He had a female tutor, which was unusual, who taught him to read and understand the Qur'an. He learned Persian, Arabic and Urdu. His formal education was, however, cut short by the death of his father, which left the family in financial difficulty. Sayyid now had to earn a living and started work as a clerk with the East India Company in 1838. He then obtained legal qualifications and worked in the courts at Agra and elsewhere keeping the records and managing court business. In 1840, he was promoted to the title of *munshi* or secretary.

In the eighteen-forties he started writing on religious subjects in Urdu, which is a language widely spoken by Muslims in the Indian subcontinent. He was later to write *A Series of Essays on the Life of Muhammad* (1870) in response to a life of Muhammad by William Muir, which he said, 'cut his heart to pieces with its bigotry and injustice.' He wrote commentaries on the Qur'an and even on the Bible, which was probably the first such commentary to be written by an Indian Muslim. Sayyid Ahmad Khan emphasised the fact that both Christianity and Islam looked back to Abraham as their forefather.

During the Indian Mutiny of 1857, Sayyid Ahmad Khan, who lost several relatives in the turmoil, remained loyal to the British. Indeed he helped to save some British lives. Afterwards, however, he wrote a pamphlet on *The Causes of the Indian Revolt*, in which he fearlessly highlighted the weaknesses and errors of the British administration, which had led to so much discontent.

After the Mutiny, the East India Company was abolished and the British government, through the India Office, became directly responsible for ruling India. The Mughal dynasty and other princes lost what power they still had possessed.

Sayyid Ahmad Khan was deeply concerned that Muslims should relate positively to the new situation. One of his main objectives was to reduce the bitter enmity between the Muslim community and the British. He advised the British to appoint Muslims to assist in the administration. He hoped his book, *Loyal Muhammadans of India*, would give the British a more appreciative view of the Muslim community.

He also urged the Muslim community to take a positive approach to Western civilization. His greatest concern was with education and the need for Muslims to benefit from Western style education. He established schools at Muradabad (1858) - where he had been appointed to a senior position at the court - and at Ghazipur (1863). In 1864 he convened the first meeting of the Scientific Society to translate European works into the languages of India. He resisted Hindu attempts to replace Urdu by Hindi and said that the paths of Hindus and Muslims must diverge.

In 1867, Sayyid Ahmad Khan moved to Aligarh, where he acquired some land from the government for experimental farming, which was designed to encourage Indian farmers 'to adopt modern methods and to use seeds from India and cotton seeds from America.'

In 1869 Sayyid Ahmad Khan, who had been elected an honorary fellow of the Royal Asiatic Society of London in 1864, set out to visit Britain with his two sons and a younger friend. To pay for this, he had to mortgage the ancestral home in Delhi and take out a big loan. He spent seventeen months in England – mostly in London – and his time was occupied with political, literary and social occasion. He was 'in the society of lords and dukes at dinners and evening parties' and saw 'artisans and the common working-man in great numbers.' He was awarded the title of Companion of the Star of India by Queen Victoria. He also dined with the Secretary of State for India. For these occasions, he hired a carriage and horses, thereby adding to his financial difficulties.

On his return to India Sayyid Ahmad Khan started a periodical to 'educate and civilize' Indian Muslims. In 1876 he took early retirement and settled at Aligarh. It was there that he established in 1877 what is his most important and lasting monument, the Muhammadan Anglo-Oriental College. In 1920, it became Aligarh Muslim University. The college was based on the pattern of Oxford and Cambridge Colleges – following the Mutiny, Universities had already been established by the government at Calcutta, Bombay and Madras. The principal and the majority of the staff at Aligarh were British. Many of the Muslims who have been influential as politicians and thinkers in India graduated at Aligarh, including Pakistan's first two Prime Ministers. Dr Zakir Hussain (1897-1969), a former President of India, and Yusuf Ali (1872-1953), whose translation of the Qur'an into English has been widely used, also studied there.

Sayyid Ahmad Khan also instituted the Muhammadan Educational Conference, which held annual meetings in different Indian cities. Sayyid Ahmad Khan devoted the last years of his life to these projects. He was knighted in 1888 and in 1889 he received an honorary degree from the University of Edinburgh. Sir Sayyid Ahmad Khan died in 1898, and was buried inside the campus of his college. His funeral was attended by many of his students as well as by Muslim leaders and British officials.

Sayyid Ahmad Khan was convinced that the Muslims of India could 'not improve their lot unless they attain the modern knowledge and technologies that are a matter of honour for other nations in the language of those who, through the will of Allah, rule over us.' He had therefore to show that Islam and Western scientific thinking were not irreconcilable. 'I pondered over the Qur'an itself to understand the foundational principles of its composition and as far as I could grasp, I found no contradiction between these principles and modern knowledge.' He underlined the influence of Greek philosophers on classical Muslim thinkers and drew attention to the links with Judaism, which Islam shared with Christianity.

Sayyid Ahmad Khan believed in the Prophet and the Qur'an, but he claimed that reason was also an attribute of God and that Nature was God's handiwork. The Word of God must be in harmony with the Work of God. He therefore set out to provide, as he said in a speech in Lahore in 1884, 'a modern interpretation by which we should either refute the doctrines of modern sciences or show that they are in conformity with the articles of Islamic faith.' In fact, he was not interested in refuting modern science. Just as Ram Mohan Roy (1772-1833), the founder of the Brahmo Samaj, dispensed with idolatry and the miracles in his attempt to bring Hinduism up to date, so Sayyid Ahmad Khan, in his writings on the Qur'an, rejected the possibility of miracles. 'God,' he wrote, 'does not do anything that is against the principles of Nature that He has himself established.'[1] Intercessory prayer in which a person asks God for some blessing, he regarded as psychological rather than actual. He distinguished two types of verses in the Qur'an. Some have a precise meaning, but others are metaphorical. Of the latter he said, 'As the knowledge and experience of man increases and he gets a clearer perception of the world of nature, deeper meanings of these verses will be revealed to him and he will give new interpretations.'[2]

Sayyid Ahmad Khan has sometimes been seen as one of the earliest advocates of the 'Two-Nation theory', which eventually led to the partition of the sub-continent into India and Pakistan. Certainly his was a leading voice against making Hindi the second official language – the first was English – and wanted Urdu to be the 'lingua franca' of all Muslims. He was also opposed to talk of democratic self-government that would allow the Hindu majority a dominant position. He wanted the Muslims to retain at least some of the power, which they had had in his youth. Although the sub-continent was partitioned, there is still a large Muslim population in India.

The question of how to relate to science and the modern world has preoccupied all religions for the last two hundred years and is still a pressing problem for Islam. The Muslim world has also had to reassert itself after two hundred years or more of Western imperialism and the continuing economic and political dominance of Western powers.

Sayyid Ahmad Khan lived at a time when Mughal power had been eclipsed by the British Raj, when the self-confidence of Christianity expressed itself in a worldwide missionary endeavour and the discoveries of science had allowed people in the West to believe that progress was as inevitable as evolution. Sayyid Ahmad Khan may have made his faith in Islam too subservient to the then dominant Western civilization, but the isolationism of traditional Muslim leaders was no answer.

Muhammad Iqbal (1873-1938) was much more robust in his affirmation of Islam. Sir Muhammad Iqbal was born on November 9th, 1877 in Sialkot in what is now Pakistan. His early education was given by tutors at home. He went on to study at the Scottish Mission College in Sialkot, where he already showed his ability as a writer and poet. He then studied at the Government College in Lahore, where Sir Thomas Arnold, who taught Islam and modern philosophy at the College, took a keen interest in him. Encouraged by Sir Thomas, Iqbal travelled to England, where he gained a degree at Trinity College, Cambridge and also studied law at Lincoln's Inn.

Besides his legal work, Iqbal became increasingly interested in spiritual and religious subjects. He was influenced by philosophers such as Friedrich Nietzsche, Henri Bergson and Goethe, but the greatest influence was the Sufi poet Rumi.

Most of Iqbal's writings were in Persian, although some were in Urdu and others in English. For him, Islam was not merely a valid religion to stand alongside other faiths, but it was the root and branch of all religious experience. He tried to show that Islam provided the best code of conduct for a nation's viability. Although recognising that other religions offered similar values, he became increasingly critical of the materialism of the West, writing:

'The glitter of modern civilization dazzles the sight,
But it is only a clever piecing together of false gems.'

And again,

The wisdom or science in which wise ones of the West took such pride:

Is but a warring sword in the bloody hands of greed and ambition.'[3]

Iqbal took a keen interest in politics and was active in the Muslim League and a supporter of Jinnah. There were important differences, however, between the two. Iqbal believed that Islam should be the source of government, whereas Jinnah envisaged Pakistan as a secular state.

In 1933 Iqbal's health deteriorated and he spent his final years establishing an institution, known, as Idara Dar-ul-Islam, where studies in classical Islam and contemporary social science would be pursued. He died in 1938. He is highly regarded in Pakistan, where he is thought of as the ideological founder of the state.

Iqbal belonged to a different generation than Sayyid Ahmad Khan. The situation in which Muslims find themselves today is again different and varies from country to country. Yet the question of how to relate to modern civilization and the role of Islam in society are still live issues. There are many other influential Muslim thinkers in the last two hundred years who could have been discussed, but Sayyid Ahmad Khan and Sir Muhammad Iqbal were outstanding in recognising the central questions for Islam today, even if their answers were different.

CHAPTER NOTES

1. His ninth principle of exegesis.
2. Quoted by Dr S Abid Husain in *Islam*, Patiala, Punjabi University, 1969, 85.
3. Quoted by Vincent A Smith in *The Oxford History of India*, Oxford, p. 805.

74

Nakayama Miki

New religions are to be found in many parts of the world. To do justice to them would require another book. Independent Churches are a significant feature of African religious life. Several new religions have originated in the Far East. One of these is The Unification Church, which was founded in Korea by Reverend Sun Myung Moon (b.1920). Others, which we shall discuss in a moment, orginated in Japan.

Although at times all these movements have faced controversy and often opposition, they have attracted numerous followers in the West as well as in Asia. They indicate that there is a spiritual hunger in the modern world, which traditional religions have been unable to satisfy. All have emphasised the need for people of different faiths to work together for peace and the relief of suffering. It is perhaps worth remembering that all the 'world religions' were once 'new religions.'

In Japan both Shintoism and Buddhism have given birth to new religious movements.

The main religious traditions in Japan are Shintoism, an indigenous religion and Buddhism, which reached Japan early in the first millennium CE. Innovation is an accepted feature of Japanese religious life and there are numerous 'new religions.'[1] Many movements which began with some fresh religious experience or message from a medium have long since been incorporated into existing religions, but in some more recent cases such initiatives have led to the growth of separate religious bodies.

Japanese Buddhism gives plenty of scope for innovation since the proliferation of sects and independent temple organizations is accepted as a normal feature of religious life. Several of the new religions, therefore have developed from Buddhism, usually based in some way or other on the *Lotus Sutra*. Together they claim about a fifth of the population of Japan as adherents. Of these, the Reiyukai began as a movement caring for untended tombs and stressing the virtues of gratitude and loyalty towards ancestors. Today it boasts a huge central hall in Tokyo.

Several groups split off from the Reiyukai, however, in a series of organizational and doctrinal disputes. Of these the largest is the Rissho Kosei Kai (RKK) ably led for many years by the remarkable founding president, Nikkyo Niwano (1906-1999). He emphasized the exposition of the *Lotus Sutra*, which is regularly recited and studied as the doctrinal basis of the movement. It is notable that this is a lay movement. Its central buildings in Tokyo, which I visited when RKK hosted an international interfaith conference, are very impressive. Members share in a form of group counselling in which the individual's problems are analysed in Buddhist terms.

Soka Gakkai, which is also based on the *Lotus Sutra*, but with different doctrinal tendencies, is another lay movement, although linked with a monastic sect named Nichiren Shoshu, which claims a direct tradition back to Nichiren himself. Under the leadership of the third President Ikeda Daisaku (b. 1928) Soka Gakkai has grown rapidly.

Both Rissho Kosei Kai and Soka Gakkai are now established in many parts of the world and have made a major contribution to the search for international peace and interfaith understanding. It was an unforgettable experience for me to be shown round the Peace Park at Hiroshima by a survivor of the first atomic bomb who, after that terrible experience, had found new meaning in life as a member of RKK.

Three of the new religions originating from Shintoism were founded by women. Tenrikyo, the first Japanese 'new religion' was founded by Nakayama Miki, who is the subject of this chapter.

Two other new religions, which derive from Shintoism, were also founded by women. The first is known as the Teaching of the Great Origin (*Oomotokyo*). It was founded by Deguchi Nao (1837-1918), who, at the age of 55, was possessed by a spirit. The spirit's messages, which at first she scratched with a nail on the ground, spoke of a coming saviour, whom she later identified as Onisaburo. He was twice imprisoned during the Second World War and Omoto's buildings were destroyed. The religion was re-established and re-organised after the war under the name Aizenen (community of love and peace). It is now known as Omoto Aizenen and is a major independent religious group, which has a Shinto background combined with belief in a new revelation of its own.

The second new religion to be founded by a woman is the popularly

named 'Dancing Religion' (*Odoru Shokyo*), which also has the longer
formal name of Tensho Kotai Jingu Kyo. The foundress, named Sayo
Kitamura (1900-67), believed that a *kami* or spirit was speaking through
her abdomen, and these revelations are the basis of the religion's
teaching. She also initiated a form of ecstatic dance, which encourages
believers to experience a state of non-self (*muga*). In 1945, Sayo
Kitamura proclaimed herself universal Saviour and a successor to
Buddha and Jesus.

Too few women have been founders or leaders of a religion, so this
is perhaps the place to mention the Brahma Kumaris Spiritual
University, which is a movement teaching meditation. Although
founded by a man, the movement has flourished under the remarkable
leadership of three women known as Dadis. It has a beautiful and
tranquil headquarters at Mt Abu in India, but has many houses in
different parts of the world. Brahma Kumaris have been active in work
for peace and interfaith co-operation.

It is time now, however, to tell the story of Nakayama Miki, who was
born in 1798.[2] Miki grew up in a village near Nara. Her father was of a
minor samurai rank, but, in the hard times towards the end of the
Tokugawa regime, the family had to share in the work in the paddy
fields, which was usually left to the peasants. Miki was very devout and
wished to become a Buddhist nun, but she was forced to marry
Nakayama Zembei, who was from a local landowning family. It was a
difficult marriage which she bore with what followers of Tenrikyo
regard as admirable patience and virtue.

In 1837, Miki's eldest son suffered a severe pain in his leg and was
unable to work. The family called upon a healer, whose female assistant
would fall into a trance and receive instructions from a *kami* or spirit
about how to heal the patient. One day, the asistant was unable to come
and Miki offered to take her place. It is said that the *kami* entered into
her and identified himself through her lips as 'the true and original
God' and that he would use Miki as his shrine. She said the spirit was
Tenri-O-no-Mikoto, 'Divine King of Heavenly Reason', but she also
referred to it as Tsuki-Hi (literally "Moon-Sun", suggesting cosmic
unity) and, as Tenrikyo members still do, "God the Parent" (Oya).

Miki, after long discussions with her family, felt bound to obey. She
gave away her possessions, leaving the family very poor. Some people

thought she had gone mad. But then her spiritual healing began to help women in childbirth and to cure people of smallpox. Miki also began to lead simple worship, mainly in the form of chants to the Tenri deity. The restoration of the Meiji dynasty in the late 1860s suggested to Miki that God was striving to transform the world and bring help to the poor.

After the death of her husband she was claimed to have miraculous healing and prophetic powers. She and her daughter (Kokan) chose a life of poverty, giving away what they could to the less fortunate and founding a new religion.

From 1866 to 1882 Nakayama Miki wrote what she deemed the revelations of 'God the Parent' – God had no gender - believing herself to be God's mouthpiece and shrine. In Tenrikyo there are three successive levels of understanding of the nature of God: the first is Kami which is God as understood in every day terms, the second is Tsukihi (lit. Moon-Sun), or God as the creator of nature and natural laws, and lastly Oya (Parent), or God as the parent of human beings. These terms refer to three successive levels of people's understanding of one single God as they grow in spiritual maturity.

Miki was inspired to build a sacred pillar or *kanrodai*, in her yard where she believed creation had begun. She encouraged a life of charity and designed various spiritual dances. She was repeatedly imprisoned on the initiative of the Buddhist sects, which she and her followers criticised as dispensing false teachings, and in later years Tenrikyo became more assimilated to State Shinto in its ceremonial and teaching, though some accounts say that Nakayama Miki herself opposed this assimilation. She died in 1887. Her followers believe that she still resides at her former home, where a temple has been built over the sacred pillar. Pilgrims come from around the world to Tenri City to visit the shrine.

In its gatherings, Tenrikyo utilizes traditional musical instruments to play music from the Mikagura-Uta, a body of music, dances and songs created by the foundress. Most of the world's foremost authorities on Gagaku music (the ancient classical Shinto music of the imperial court of Japan) are Tenrikyo followers, and Gagaku music is actively promoted by Tenrikyo, although strictly speaking the Mikagura-Uta and Gagaku are separate musical forms.

Some critics have questioned her divine inspiration, saying she took inspiration from an amalgam of Buddhism, Shintoism and Japanese shamanism to create a religion that could satisfy the emotional needs of a 40-year-old Japanese woman in a troubled marriage. Members of Tenrikyo, however, insist that her teachings were totally original and her thinking uniquely inspired. Tenrikyo's relationship to both Buddhism and Shintoism has been uneasy. Since the Second World War, the movement has made clear its separation from State Shintoism and is now recognised to be an independent religion.

Today, Tenrikyo is estimated to have about two million followers world-wide, with one and a half million of those in Japan. The focus of the religion is to attain *yoki yusan* or *yoki gurashi* (joyous life) on Earth through charity and abstention from greed, selfishness, hatred, anger and arrogance. Members are encouraged to do voluntary work as a sign of gratitude and to adopt a constructive attitude towards troubles, illness and difficulties without placing judgement on what has happened in the past. Many metaphors from building and carpentry are used in Tenrikyo teachings, which view the construction of a better world as a step-by-step process in which people can make small steps towards progress through working together collaboratively. There is a Tenrikyo saying, 'Just being alive makes me happy! What a waste it would be not to show some initiative.'

CHAPTER NOTES

1. This section is in part based on an article by Michael Pye in *Eerdmans' Handbook to the World's Religions*, 1982 First American Edition, Grand Rapids, William B. Eerdmans Publishing Company.
2. There is a useful section on Nakayama Miki (her names are sometimes reversed) in *Japanese Religions*, Ed, Robert S Ellwood and Richard Pilgrim, Enlewood Cliffs, N.J., Prentice-Hall, 1985. pp. 80-82.

75

Baha' Allah

Baha' Allah, the 'Glory of God', was the founder of the Baha'i religion, which declares God's message of the oneness of humankind and the fundamental oneness of religion. Although the number of Baha'is is still quite small, they are to be found in almost every country of the world

Baha' Allah was preceded by the Bab – 'the Gate,' as Sayyid 'Ali Muhammad of Shirazi (1819-50) came to be known. He founded the Babi faith in 1844, which in turn sprang from Shi'ah Islam. He proclaimed the coming of 'Him Whom God Shall Make Manifest' or the messianic Hidden Imam, with whom later he identified himself.

The Bab attracted a number of followers from all parts of Persia. The Bab attempted to promulgate a new system of holy law, thus by implication starting a new religion. This met with strong opposition from the orthodox religious leaders who, because Islam holds that Muhammad was the final Prophet, regarded talk of a new prophet as heresy. The government was also alarmed. The Bab was arrested, imprisoned and eventually in 1850 condemned to death. He was taken to a public square and suspended by ropes against a wall. A regiment of several hundred soldiers fired a volley, but when the smoke cleared, the large crowd saw that the ropes had been cut, but that the Bab's body was not there. He was found unhurt nearby, calmly talking to some of his disciples. The execution was repeated – this time with the intended result. In the ensuing persecution, some 20,000 of his followers were killed. Lord Curzon, a Viceroy of India, said later of Babism, 'it is a creed of charity and almost of common humanity.'[1] Although the Babi movement continued into the twentieth century, it was soon to be eclipsed by the Baha'i faith, founded by Baha' Allah.

Mirza Husayn 'ali Nuri, as Baha' Allah (sometimes Bahaullah) was originally known, was born at dawn on November 12th, 1817 in Tehran. 'At this very hour' as one religious devotee said at the time, 'the light of the Promised One has broken shedding illumination upon the world.'[2] From childhood, Baha' Allah was of a deeply religious nature and declined to follow the wish of his father - a rich and influential land

465

owner and a government official - that he too should enter government service. Baha' Allah determined to devote himself to a religious life, but he did not have formal religious teaching. Rather he spoke as an inspired genius.

In 1844, Baha' Allah became a Babi. Two years after the Bab's martyrdom, some of the Bab's followers tried unsuccessfully to assassinate the Shah of Persia. One of those arrested, although he was ignorant of the plot, was Baha' Allah. He was thrown into an underground cell at the Black Pit, which was a notorious jail in Tehran. It was there that he became aware of his mission as a messenger of God, suggesting in some of his odes that he was the Central Figure of the movement initiated by the Bab.

Baha' Allah was released from prison in January 1853 and exiled to Baghdad. There he started to revive the Babi community, but disagreeing with his half-brother's style of leadership, he withdrew to live a life of religious seclusion in the mountains of Kurdistan. When he returned to Baghdad in 1856, he soon became the leader of the Babi exiles there. This alarmed the Persian government, which asked the Ottoman rulers to remove him. Before they took him to Constantinople, Baha' Allah spent twelve days in the garden of Ridvan (Rezvan) near Baghdad. There, to a small number of followers of the Bab, Baha' Allah declared that he was the messenger of God, whose coming the Bab had predicted.

After a short time in Constantinople, Baha' Allah was moved to Adrianople (Edirne) in European Turkey. There, in 1866 - which marks the beginning of the Baha'i Faith as a separate religion - Baha' Allah made a public claim to be a Divine Manifestation as foretold by the Bab. Not only, he affirmed, was the Second Coming of Christ realized in his person, but indeed he was the Promised One of all religions. Most of the Bab's followers acknowledged Baha' Allah, although a few sided with his embittered half-brother, who persuaded the Turkish government to exile Baha' Allah to Akko (Acre). There in an army barracks which had been converted into a jail, he was imprisoned for a while, although after a time he was given more freedom and allowed to live in the nearby countryside, ending his days in the mansion of Bhaji. Today it is a holy place, with gardens of outstanding beauty, which I have had the privilege of visiting. He died there in 1892.

Baha' Allah was a prolific writer and his words are now regarded by the faithful as direct revelations from God. Some 15,000 'tablets' have been collected. He ranged over a wide variety of subjects, but a distinct progression in what concerned him can be recognised. His earliest writings (c. 1852-6) consist of a number of poems of praise and a Commentary, from a Babi perspective, on the Qur'an. In the later Baghdad period (1856-63) his message became distinctively his own. In *The Hidden Words* (*Kalimat-I Maknunih*, 1857-8) he emphasized the practical, moral and spiritual demands of man's relationship with God. In *The Book of Certitude* (*Kitah-i-Iqan*, 1862) he outlined the doctrine of prophetic succession, which I will elaborate in a moment, and described the basic requirements for those who wish to become 'true seekers' after God. During the time at Adrianople (1863-8) he concentrated on the pattern of life appropriate to his followers and prepared the first of his letters to the rulers of the world. He continued these themes during the Akka period (1868-92) and made clear the major precepts and principles of his teaching in a variety of writings, including *Splendours* (*Ishraqat*) and his *Tablet to the Christians* (*Lawh-i-Aqdas*).[3]

God, Baha' Allah said, is and always has been the Creator and there never was a time when the universe did not exist. The purpose of human life is to know and worship God and to carry forward an 'ever-advancing civilization, which had now reached the stage at which the unity of humankind was a necessity.' Baha' Allah taught that God is unknowable and beyond every human attribute, but has chosen to reveal himself through his messengers, among whom are Abraham, Moses, Zoroaster, Buddha, Jesus, Muhammad and the Bab. Adam is also included, not as the first man, but as the first Manifestation of God in human development. Many Baha'is add the figure of Krishna. They are all exponents of 'Him who is the central Orb of the Universe.' In addition there are other moral reformers and sages, such as Confucius and minor prophets who aid the spiritual renewal of humanity, but who do not bring a new and independent Divine revelation.

The essential message of the Manifestations of God is one, Baha' Allah said, but each Messenger has a distinct individuality and a definitely prescribed mission. The Bab is the manifestation for this age, although a thousand or more years hence other manifestations may appear. Revelation is, therefore, progressive and continuing. 'Religion' as his successor Abdu'l-Baha said, 'is the outer expression of the divine reality. Therefore it must be living, moving and progressive. If it be without motion and it is non-progressive; it is dead.'[4]

Baha' Allah addressed a variety of 'tablets' to the rulers of Persia, Turkey, Russia, Prussia, Austria and Britain and to Pope Pius IX. The Letter to Queen Victoria can serve as an example. He called on rulers to listen to and to obey God. He commended her for entrusting 'the reins of counsel into hands of the representatives of the people.' He urged such representatives to work together for the benefit of all people. He deplored the increasing expenditure on arms and pleaded for peace. 'O rulers of the earth! Be reconciled among yourselves, that ye may need no armaments save in a measure to safeguard your territories ... Should any one among you take up arms against another, rise ye all against him, for this is naught but manifest justice.'[5]

Baha' Allah appealed to the Pope to 'rend the veils asunder' and to recognise that 'He who is the Lord of Lords is come, overshadowed with clouds... The Word which the Son concealed is made manifest.'[6] In his *Tablet to the Christians* Baha' Allah warned Christians not to make the same mistake as the Pharisees in judging Christ. He had suffered for the sake of the world, like Christ. He had, he said, the same Spirit as Christ and that in him the promises in Scripture of Christ's return had been fulfilled. Baha' Allah's interpretation of scripture is symbolic rather than literal. He predicted the downfall of Christian leaders, but called on Christians to proclaim God's cause, praising those who had been faithful. 'O concourse of priests! Leave the bells, and come forth from your churches. It behoveth you, in this day, to proclaim aloud the Most Great Name among the nations. Prefer ye to be silent, whilst every stone and every tree shouteth aloud: "The Lord is come in His great glory!"'[7]

Baha' Allah told the individual believer, to quote a few sample admonitions,

Be generous in prosperity, and thankful in adversity,

Be worthy of the trust of thy neighbour, and look upon him with a bright and friendly face.

Be a treasure to the poor and admonisher to the rich, an answerer of the cry of the needy...[8]

By the time of Baha' Allah's death in 1892, the Baha'i religion had spread beyond Persia to other parts of the Ottoman Empire to India, Egypt and Sudan. In the following year, the new religion was referred to at the Chicago World Parliament of Religions by a Presbyterian minister who was working in Syria. He told how Professor Brown, who was an Arabic specialist at Cambridge, had visited Baha' Allah two years before his death. Professor Brown himself had said,

'The face of him on whom I gazed I can never forget, though I cannot describe it. Those piercing eyes seemed to read one's very soul... a mild dignified voice bade me be seated, "Praise be to God that thou hast attained... Thou hast come to see a prisoner and an exile... We desire but the good of the world ... That all nations should become one in faith and all men as brothers; that the bonds of affection and unity between the sons of men be strengthened; that diversity of religion should cease, and differences of race be annulled – what harm is there in this? ... Do not you in Europe need this also? Is not this that which Christ foretold?"'[9]

Before his death, Baha' Allah appointed his son, 'Abdu'l-Baha, 'Servant of the Glory' (1844-1921) to be his successor. 'Abdu'l-Baha did not claim to be a prophet of God, like his father, but believed that he was divinely guided in his leadership and was the authorised interpreter of his father's writings, which he collected. When he visited London in 1911, some liberal Christians greeted him with enthusiasm. The minister of the City Temple, where Abdu'l-Baha preached, declared, 'The Baha'i movement is almost identical with the spiritual purpose of Christianity.'[10] At St John's Church, Westminster, the Archdeacon knelt with his congregation to receive Abdu'l-Baha's blessing.[11] Pioneers of the interfaith movement have welcomed the Baha'i emphasis on the unity of religions, but other Christians, especially Evangelicals, have criticised Baha'is' for denying the uniqueness of Jesus and accused them of syncretism or mixing religions.

Abdu'l-Baha appointed his eldest grandson, Shoghi Effendi Rabbani (1896-1957) to be his successor. Soon after his death, the Universal House of Justice, based at Haifa in Israel, was chosen to be the supreme ruling body of the Baha'i Faith.

Central to the Baha'i religion is a vision of a new world order. In this there will be complete world unity and peace and society will be grounded on moral and religious principles. The resources of the world will be shared for the betterment of all. God has created all human beings 'as the leaves of one tree and the drops of one ocean.'

Baha' Allah deserves a high place among those who will influence the future story of the human spirit. In his teachings, he anticipated many of the creative developments of the twentieth century: the peace movement, the growth of interfaith fellowship, equal rights for women, and the establishment of the International Court of Justice and the United Nations. His 'tablets' could well be required reading for our present world rulers.

Baha' Allah assured Professor Brown, 'Yet so it shall be; these fruitless strifes, these ruinous wars shall pass away, and the "Most great peace" shall come... Let not a man glory in this that he loves his country; let him rather glory in this, that he loves his kind.'[12]

All people of faith would surely pray that Baha' Allah's prophecy of a

'Most Great Peace' will be fulfilled?

CHAPTER NOTES

1. Quoted by George Townshend in *The Promise of All Ages*, London, Lindsay Drummond, no date c. 1941, from Lord Curzon, *Persia and the Persian Question*, p. 501. Other material is based on Michael W Sours, *A Study of Bahaullah's Tablet to the Christian*, Oxford, One World, 1990; Gary L Matthews, *He Cometh With Clouds*, Oxford, George Ronald, 1996 (With good bibliography) and Francis J Beckwith, *Baha'is*, (Minneapolis, Bethany House Publishers, 1985.

2. Townshend, p. 159.

3. This is based on the outline by Peter Smith in *The Baha'i Religion*, George Ronald, Oxford, 1988, pp. 5-6.

4. From *The Promulgation of Universal Peace*, Smith, p. 80.

5. From *The Letter to Queen Victoria*, Smith pp. 65-7.

6. Quoted by Gary L Matthews in *The Challenge of Baha'u'llah*, Oxford, George Ronald, 1993, p. 61.

7.   Michael W Sours, *A Study of Bahaullah's Tablet to the Christian*, p. 21.

8.   *Gleanings from the Writings of Baha'u'llah*, 1935 Available from Baha'i Centres.

9.   Townshend, pp. 23-4, quoting from Professor Brown, *A Travellers's Narrative*, pp. xxxix-xl.

10. *Abdu'l-Baha in London*, London, 1912, republished by the Baha'i Publishing Trust in 1987, p. 17.

11. *Ibid*, p. 21.

12. Townshend, pp. 23-4, quoting from Professor Brown, *A Travellers's Narrative*, pp. xxxix-xl.

76

Te Whiti-O-Rongomai

Te Whiti-O-Rongomai, the Maori leader of the village of Parihaka in New Zealand, resisted the seizure of Maori land by non-violent means. He has been described as the forerunner of Mahatma Gandhi, who knew of his example, of Martin Luther King and of Nelson Mandela.[1] He also can stand for all the victims of European colonisation in so many parts of the world.

Some background history of New Zealand is necessary to understand the importance of Te Whiti-O-Rongomai. Polynesian people, known as Hunters of the now extinct Moa bird, reached New Zealand by 800 CE. A second wave of migration in the middle of the fourteenth century marked the beginning of the 'Classic' period of Maori culture. Agriculture was developed, including the cultivation of the sweet potato, yam, taro and gourd. Maori social organisation was based on descent from members of 'a great fleet,' said to have arrived in fourteenth century. The tribe, based on common ancestry, with local sub-tribes and families, were the main social units. The village square, with a carved public meeting house, was the social and ceremonial core of the village and was used for public meetings and some ceremonies. Religion and Magic pervaded all aspects of Polynesian life. Humans had to beware of attracting adverse *mana*, with which all things – animate and inanimate – were endowed and of offending the supernatural beings, many of whom were malevolent, who inhabited the universe. Not only the great gods, such as Tangaroa, Tu and Lono, but also many lesser gods had to be worshipped in the correct way, often by priests.

The first European to arrive in New Zealand was a Dutch sailor called Abel Janszoon Tasman in the middle of the seventeenth century. Just over a century later, between 1769-70, the British Naval officer James Cook circum-navigated the two major islands and charted them with remarkable accuracy. By the end of the eighteenth century, whalers and traders had reached New Zealand. In the early nineteenth century several Christian churches began missionary work and the majority of Maoris now are Christian, although two indigenous religious systems, the Ratana Church and the Ringatu Church continue to attract followers.

In 1841 New Zealand was annexed by William Hobson, the first governor – South Island by right of discovery and North Island by right of cessation from Maori chiefs. Under the Treaty of Waitangi in February 1840, the Maori chiefs ceded sovereignty in return for a guarantee by Her Majesty the Queen of England to respect their 'exclusive and undisturbed possession of their land and estates, forests, fisheries and other properties... so long as it is their wish and desire to retain the same in their possession.'[2] The chiefs agreed to sell land only to the Crown. The treaty, as one member of the New Zealand Parliament said later, was quickly 'relegated to the waste-paper basket.'[3] With a combination of propaganda, trickery and brutality, the Maoris, who were often demoralised by new illnesses and by alcohol, were progressively deprived of their land. Some Maoris offered violent resistance, which gave the settlers an excuse to attack the Maoris and seize more of their land.

In North Island several tribes of the Waikato area elected Te Wherowhero as their king. Not all Maoris accepted his authority or the use of violence, but almost all refused to sell land to the Crown. The so-called 'King movement' was decisively defeated in 1865 and its members took refuge in 'King country' in the west central part of North Island. Although a few settlers sought to defend the rights of the Maoris, the majority were more interested in seizing all their land. Some called for the complete destruction of the Maoris - anticipating the cruel genocides of the twentieth century, which were the fate of indigenous people in many parts of the world and was the intention of the Nazis in their massacre of the Jews during the Holocaust. An editorial in the *Wellington Independent*, said, 'we must smite and spare not... They are determined to fight and we, in self-protection, must treat them as a species of savage beasts, which must be exterminated to render colonisation of New Zealand possible.'[4]

It was in this context that Te Whiti-O-Rongomai became leader of Parihaka. Te Whiti's date of birth is uncertain. He was born at Ngamotu, in Taranaki. He said that his name was taken from the sacred hill of Puke Te Whiti.[5] He was descended from a long line of chiefs, priests and warriors. He was steeped in ancient Maori learning and also in the teachings of the Bible. Te Whiti was a pupil of the Lutheran missionary Johannes Riemenschneider and was baptised Erueti (Edward), although he did not use this name. After leaving school he set up a flour mill at Warea. In September 1862, with some other Maori leaders, he ensured the safety of the passengers from the wrecked ship the *Lord Worsley*. Even though imperial troops burned his village, it seems unlikely that Te Whiti joined in the fighting of the 'King' movement against the army - although he granted asylum to many of those who had fought in Maori wars. Te Whiti would not allow his people to take up arms. Instead he moved the settlement inland to Parihaka.

Te Whiti rejected both negotiation with the Crown and rebellion. Instead he adopted a policy of civil disobedience and passive obstruction. He refused to allow government officials to survey the Land. Instead, Maoris began to plough up the pastures, which the settlers had claimed for themselves. 'Go, put your hands to the plough,' Te White told his followers. 'Look not back. If any come with guns and swords, be not afraid. If they smite you, smite not in return... If any man molests me, I will talk with my weapon – the tongue.'[6] As soon as the Armed Constabulary started to arrest the ploughmen, more appeared. Some settlers called for the destruction of the Maoris, but the government backed down and set up a Royal Commission to investigate the grievances of the Taranaki Maoris. Governor Gordon admitted to the British Colonial Office that if the intention of the ploughmen was to attract attention, they had been 'completely successful.' The ploughmen were sentenced to two months imprisonment and then required to find surety of £200 – an impossibly large sum - as a guarantee of their subsequent good behaviour. Acts were then rushed through Parliament depriving other ploughmen, many of whom had been shipped to South Island, of their right to trial (all too like Guantanamo Bay). Meanwhile the Royal Commission made clear that it had no intention of discussing the legality of the confiscation of Maori Land.

Pending the Commissions' report, the *status quo* as far as the land was preserved. Permission, however, was given 'to repair' the roads – in fact to make new roads through the lands where the Maoris grew their food. To protect their land from the settlers and their crops from stray animals, the Maoris put up fences. These were repeatedly pulled down by the Constabulary and as often re-erected by the Maoris. The Government refused to authorise gates and warned that anyone who re-erected a fence would be arrested. Te Whiti's reply was that when a fence was destroyed, it would be put up again. The fencers, who offered no resistance, were in turn taken prisoner. Harsh new laws, threatening two years hard labour, were introduced by John Bryce, the Native Minister, outlawing any action that hindered the occupation of the land. One Opposition member of Parliament protested that the Bill 'amounted to a general warrant for the apprehension of all persons, of all ages and sexes, for offences which were not named at all – in fact they might be arrested for no offence.'[7]

The people of Parihaka, nonetheless, persisted. But when the women and young children courted arrest, the Government gave way and ordered that there should be no further arrests. Bryce, who had actively led the Constabulary, resigned. There were, however, already over four hundred people in jail – about half of them ploughmen and half of them fencers. The cost was worrying the Government. The West Coast Commission observed that the land being taken was valued at three-quarters of a million pounds and 'now certainly has cost the country a great deal more than that.'[8] In Britain, Charles Bradlaugh, a radical Member of Parliament asked why the Parihaka prisoners were being held without trial. When a trial was held, prisoners were sentenced to two years hard labour for non-violently resisting the seizure of their land. Even so, children continued to take down the fences until the Government ordered that, to keep animals from destroying the Maoris' crops, a slip-rail should be placed wherever the road went through a fence. The Royal Commission questioned the imprisonments and gradually the ploughmen and fencers were released. When the Commission finally issued its report Ti Whiti refused to read it, suspecting rightly that its recommendations would deprive the Maoris of much of their land.

In any case, Bryce was soon back in office as Native Minister and the Constabulary were again at work. On November 5th 1881, Bryce led 1,600 members of the Armed Constabulary and Militiamen to Parihaka. Two days before, Te Whiti insisted, 'I stand for peace. Though the lions rage, I am for peace... I will go into captivity... The future is mine.'[9]

When the troops arrived they were welcomed by the inhabitants of the village, all of whom were sitting packed together on the ground, with Te Whiti in the middle. Finally, a constable forced his way through the crowd. Te Whiti with his colleague Tohu came forward with great dignity and without resistance to be arrested. The remaining villagers were ejected and many of their homes destroyed. They were held without trial for a year, until the Governor Sir Arthur Gordon insisted on their release.

In 1883, Te Whiti and Tohu were welcomed back to Parihaka, where their influence was in no way diminished. Relations between the two leaders, however, were strained. Tohu had lost hope of a peaceful solution and took no further part in protests, whereas Te Whiti continued with passive resistance. The situation continued to be tense and troubled and during the following years there were further non-violent protests. Te Whiti, also, spent further periods in prison, during one of which his wife died. Te Whiti was not allowed to attend the funeral. Nonetheless, despite all he had suffered, Te Whiti did not abandon his commitment to non-violence and preserved his community until his death in November 1907.

It was another twenty years before the justice of his cause was recognised. In 1926, a Royal Commission acknowledged the wrong done to the people of Taranaki. The wars, it admitted, were 'unjust and unholy wars' for land to which the Crown had no right.[10] The compensation, which amounted to two and a half pence per acre, plus some money for those whose homes had been destroyed, was far from generous, but Te Whiti's moral victory was clear – even if the Commissioners never mentioned him by name.

Te Whiti's basic beliefs were simple. He held that the Maoris should be left to their own way of life and that no land should be sold to the Europeans. He argued that both rebellion and negotiation had failed and was committed to non-violent civil disobedience. Te Whiti also prophesied that a 'Day of Reckoning' would come when all Europeans would voluntarily leave the country. Even today people of Parihaka chant the words of the Biblical prophet Isaiah:

'And the days of thy mourning shall be ended.
Thy people also shall be all righteous:

they shall inherit the land for ever.'[11]

Nowhere, however, have indigenous or aboriginal peoples been fully compensated for what they lost during the colonial era. Even so, it can be argued that the non-violent civil disobedience of Te Whiti achieved more than violent rebellion. The marble column erected above his grave has the words

> He was a man who did
> Great deeds in suppressing
> Evil so that peace may
> Reign as a means of
> salvation to all people
> on earth.

CHAPTER NOTES

1. By the historian Te Miringa Hohaia. See www.pukeariki.com.
2. From Article 2 of the Treaty of Waitangi, 1840.
3. Colonel Robert Trimble in a speech defending the destruction of Parihaka, *Hansard*, June 2nd, 1882, quoted by Dick Scott, *The Parihaka Story*, Auckland, Southern Cross Books, 1954, p.10.
4. *The Parihaka Story*, p. 17.
5. In a speech made in 1900. see www.pukeariki.com.
6. *The Parihaka Story*, p. 46.
7. Sir George Grey, quoted in *The Parihaka Story*, pp. 63-4.
8. Quoted in *The Parihaka Story*, p. 6.
9. *The Parihaka Story*, p. 89.
10. *The Parihaka Story*, p. 149.
11. Isaiah 60, 20-21.

77

Rudolf Steiner

Rudolf Steiner founded Anthroposophy, Waldorf education and biodynamic agriculture. He was an amazingly creative man, who was a philosopher, literary scholar, educator, artist, playwright and social thinker. His ideas on many subjects have had a continuing influence, including alternative medicine and organic farming. The German edition of his collected works runs to over three hundred volumes.

Rudolf Steiner was born on 27th February 1861 in Murakiraly, which was then in Austria, but now is known as Kraljevec in Croatia. His father, Johann, had been a huntsman, but at the time of Rudolf's birth he was a telegraph operator on the Southern Austrian Railway. After a couple of moves, the family settled at Pottschach in the eastern Austrian Alps, where Johann was appointed stationmaster.

Rudolf's higher education was at the Technical University in Vienna, where he studied mathematics, physics and philosophy.

One of his teachers mentioned his name to the editor of a new edition of the works of Goethe (1749-1832), Germany's most famous writer, and Steiner was asked in 1882 to become the scientific editor. Subsequently, Steiner was asked to edit the Goethe archives in Weimar. He also wrote two books about Goethe and helped to edit works by the German philosopher Arthur Schopenhauer (1788-1860). Steiner was also asked to help with the archive of Nietzsche (1844-1900). He had a memorable meeting with the great man. Steiner wrote in his autobiography, 'Nietzsche's ideas of the "eternal repetition" and of "supermen" remained long in my mind. For in these was reflected that which a personality must feel concerning the evolution and essential being of humanity when this personality is kept back from grasping the spiritual world by the restricted thought in the philosophy of nature characterizing the end of the nineteenth century.' 'What attracted me particularly was that one could read Nietzsche without coming upon anything which strove to make the reader a "dependent" of Nietzsche's.'[1]

Earlier, in 1886, Steiner, who was to have a great interest in the education of the young had been employed by the Specht family to tutor their four boys, one of whom was autistic. With the help of

Steiner's exceptional tutoring this boy attended high school, college, medical school, and became a doctor.

In 1897, Steiner left Weimar and moved to Berlin to become, chief editor and active contributor to the literary journal *Magazin für Literatur*. Steiner's support for the French novelist Émile Zoa (1840-1902), who defended the army officer Alfred Dreyfus, who was Jewish, from anti-Semitic accusations of treason, as well as Steiner's friendship with an anarchist upset some readers. As a result the circulation declined and Steiner left the magazine, but not before an article of his on 'Goethe's Secret Revelation' caught the eye of a leading member of the Theosophical Society. Steiner was asked to lecture to the Society and became head of its newly formed German section in 1902.

The Theosophical Society was founded in New York in 1875 by Mrs H P Blavatsky (1831-1891) and Colonel H S Olcott (1832-1907). The Society's aim was to further the cause of world harmony, to study comparative religion and to investigate the spiritual element in human beings and the world. The Society helped to encourage in the West an appreciation of Hinduism and Buddhism and an interest in reincarnation. The emphasis on a secret or esoteric wisdom, which it is claimed is to be found in all religions, received a more mixed response. After the death of Mrs Blavatsky, Annie Besant (1847-1933) became the leader and the headquarters, with its extensive library, moved to a beautiful setting at Adyar, near Madras, where it is still active. Annie Besant appointed Steiner to head the Esoteric Society for Germany and Austria. Marie von Sievers was named secretary. She became Steiner's second wife in 1914; his first marriage to Anna Eunicke, a widow, had previously ended in a divorce. Under Steiner's leadership the Theosophical Society grew quite quickly. Instead of Mrs Blavatsky's emphasis on Eastern wisdom, Steiner gave more attention to Western esoteric and philosophical traditions. This and differences about Jiddu Krishnamurti (1895-1986), whom Annie Besant believed to be the long-awaited 'World Teacher' or Maitreya of Buddhism or Messiah, led Steiner to leave the Theosophical Society and found his own movement known as Anthroposophy.[2]

Anthroposophy, says Roy Wilkinson who has written extensively about Steiner, is difficult to define. 'It is not a system, nor a collection of theories, nor a cult, doctrine or dogma, code or sect. It is too universal.'[3] The term is derived from two Greek words: *anthropos*, which means man and *Sophia*, which means wisdom. Anthroposophy, therefore, 'is a body of knowledge concerning the spiritual in man and in the universe.'[4] It is a spiritual science not a faith. In the ancient world thoughts were considered to be realities which came to man from the spiritual world. Steiner, likewise, came to believe in spiritual perception, independent of the senses or what he called 'knowledge produced by the higher self in man.' Steiner applied his training in mathematics and science to produce rigorous, verifiable presentations of his spiritual experiences. He believed that through freely chosen ethical disciplines and meditative training, anyone could develop the ability to experience the spiritual world, including the higher nature of oneself and others. If we develop organs of perception sufficiently we will discover spiritual laws, just as much as by observation of the physical world we discover the laws of Nature. This spiritual science needs to be applied to how we live.

The Anthroposophical Society grew rapidly. Because of the need for a home for the annual conferences, it was decided to build a theatre and organizational centre at Dornach in Switzerland. The building, called the Goetheanum, was designed by Steiner himself. During the First World War, the sound of gunfire could be heard across the border, but even so, people from all over Europe came to work on the building's construction. In 1919, the Goetheanum staged the world premiere of a complete production of Goethe's *Faust*. On New Year's Eve of 1922/23, the wooden building was burned down by arson. Steiner, at once, set about rebuilding it – this time in concrete. This was completed in 1928, three years after Steiner's death.

In 1923, Steiner founded the School of Spiritual Science, intended as an open university for research and study. The University has grown steadily and is especially active in the fields of education, medicine, agriculture, art, literature, philosophy, sociology and economics – indeed the many fields in which Steiner himself was interested.

The first school that Steiner established was at Stuttgart in 1919 – a time of dramatic change in Germany. The Kaiser had abdicated and the ruling class had been swept from power, but the new democratic system had yet to be established. There was also a fear that the Bolshevik revolution in Russia could spread to Germany. Steiner felt called to start a movement to establish a system of government based on justice, compassion and fairness for all. He lectured widely about this new movement, which after some initial popularity soon met with serious opposition.

A group of industrialists in Stuttgart, however, who heard Steiner speak about new co-operative forms of business, decided to merge their factories into an economic enterprise based on his principles. He was also asked by the owner of the Waldorf Astoria cigarette factory to found a school for the children of the workers at the factory. This is why many Steiner schools are known as Waldorf schools.

Steiner believed that education should be designed to meet the changing needs of a child as they develop physically, mentally and emotionally. He held that education should help a child achieve his or her full potential rather that being pushed towards the goals set for them by adults or governments. Learning should be encouraged for its own sake not to pass examinations. Steiner argued that up to the age of seven, children should be encouraged to play, draw and appreciate nature. He did not think children should be taught to read until they were seven and that they should be taught to write first. They should have one teacher during their early years. Teaching should encourage children to find links between art and science.

There are now over eight hundred Rudolf Steiner or Waldorf schools in different parts of the world. They are still noticeably different from more traditional schools, although his ideas have had a wide influence, especially on the movement for home schooling.

Steiner's work on biodynamic agriculture helped to prepare for the growth of organic farming. In 1924, a group of farmers asked him for advice. He encouraged farmers to 'individualise' their farms and to bring in as few materials from outside as possible. A farm should produce what it needed in terms of manure and animal feed. Steiner disliked the use of artificial or chemical fertilisers. But above all he felt that farmers had lost a sense of their spiritual relationship to Nature.

Steiner was also interested in the arts. He designed seventeen buildings, including the two Goetheanums. He also developed the art of Eurythmy, sometimes referred to as 'visible speech and visible drama.' He believed there are archetypal movements or gestures that correspond to every aspect of speech. Steiner himself wrote profound

'Mystery Dramas.'

Steiner also worked with doctors to develop a new approach to medicine and helped to prepare for the development of alternative medicine, especially by his guidance to the Weleda pharmaceutical company, which now distributes natural medical products world-wide.

In 1899, Steiner had what he called a life-transforming inner encounter with the being of Christ. He held that Christ's being and mission had a central place in human evolution. He wrote,

'The being of Christ is central to *all* religions, though called by different names by each. Every valid religion is valid and true for the time and cultural context in which it was born. Historical forms of Christianity need to be transformed considerably in our times in order to meet the on-going evolution of humanity.'[5]

For Steiner, Christ's incarnation was a historical reality, but, like some modern theologians such as Paul Tillich (1886-1965), he distinguished 'Christ' as the mediating principle in every religion from the incarnation of the 'Christ' in Jesus. Unlike most Christians, Steiner believed in reincarnation and karma.

In the 1920s, Steiner was approached by a Lutheran pastor in Berlin, who wanted advice on how to develop a more modern from of Christianity. Some other Protestant and Catholic pastors were also interested and the 'Christian Community' was formed. The centre of the community's life is a morning Eucharist, or communion service of bread and wine known as The Act of Consecration of Man. Steiner made clear however that the Christian Community was independent of the Anthroposophical Society, which was based on spiritual science rather than faith.

Steiner from an early date opposed anti-Semitism and he came under increasing attack from the National Socialists and was singled out for abuse in an article by Hitler. Steiner himself warned of the dangers of the National Socialists coming to power.

Steiner travelled extensively, lecturing to a wide range of audiences. The loss of the first Goetheanum seriously affected his health and by 1924, he was too weak to continue lecturing. He died on March 30th, 1925.

The Anthroposophical Society and the Rudolf Steiner schools continue today, as do other movements he helped to develop. Many of his ideas have been taken up in so-called 'New Age' movement, which includes a diverse set of organizations and an amorphous collection of ideas. Organic farming, alternative medicine, teachings from Eastern religions and esoteric wisdom - all interests of Steiner – are combined to offer a contemporary spiritual alternative to the traditional religions. Steiner's influence, however, has been far wider. He was a seminal thinker and many of his ideas have influenced people who have never heard of his name.

CHAPTER NOTES

1. Rudolf Steiner, *The Story of My Life*, London, Rudolf Steiner Press, 1924-5, chapter 18.
2. In 1911 Krishnamurti was made head of 'the Order of the Star', but later repudiated any claim to divinity. Instead he taught that truth can only be obtained by self-knowledge and self-awareness which is to be learned through meditation. He urged people to reject barriers of nationality, race or religion.
3. Roy Wilkinson, *Rudolf Steiner, An Introduction to his Spiritual World-view, Anthroposophy*, Forest Row, Temple Lodge Publishing, 2001, p. 15.
4. Wilkinson, p. 15.
5. In Carlo Willmann, *Waldorf Padagogik: Theologische and religionspad-agogische*, Cologne.

78

Freud and Jung

Sigmund Freud and Carl Jung might seem unlikely candidates for inclusion in this book, but their influence on our understanding of our psychological structure and of the functioning of the mind has been enormous and has profoundly affected the way we see ourselves and think about religion. Both grew up in homes in which religion played a part.

Sigmund Freud was born in 1856 in Freiberg in what was then Moravia (now Pribor in the Czech Republic). His parents were Jewish. One memory that haunted him was of his father telling how his new fur hat had been knocked off by a Gentile who shouted at him, 'Jew - get off the pavement.' The twelve year-old Sigmund asked his father how he had reacted. He replied, 'I stepped into the gutter and picked up my hat.' This permanently damaged Sigmund's respect for his father.

Three other events in his childhood stood out in Freud's memory. One was his sense of jealousy when his brother Julius was born. He admitted having evil thoughts towards his sibling and felt guilty for years when the baby died at only eight months. Freud, later, was to write about sibling rivalry. Freud also later in life admitted that, as a child, he had been sexually aroused by seeing his mother naked. It was this that led him to speak of infantile sexuality. The fourth recollection, which often recurred in his dreams, was of deliberately urinating in his parents' bedroom when he was seven or eight years old.

Freud became a medical student at the University of Vienna in 1873. He specialised in neurology so that he could learn more about human nature. His studies were unexpectedly interrupted when he fell in love with Martha Benays. They were betrothed in 1882, but because of Freud's poverty, the marriage was delayed until 1886. During their engagement, he wrote over nine hundred loving letters to her.

Freud held various posts for a short time. His interest soon moved to psychopathology and in 1900 he published his seminal work *The Interpretation of Dreams* (*Die Traumdeutung*), in which he argued that dreams, like neuroses, such as depression, anxiety or phobias, are disguised manifestations of repressed sexual desires.

In 1902, Freud was appointed Extraordinary Professor of Neuropathology at the University of Vienna and soon wrote *The Psychopathology of Everyday Life* (1904) and *Three Essays on the Theory of Sexuality* (1905). These works met with fierce opposition.

Alfred Adler (1870-1937) and Carl Jung (1875-1961) worked with Freud for a time, but then broke away. Adler rejected Freud's emphasis on sexuality and suggested that much behaviour results from efforts to compensate for feelings of inferiority. Jung, as we shall see, also disagreed with Freud's insistence on the sexual basis of neurosis.

Freud nonetheless continued with his work. He elaborated his theories of the division of the unconscious mind into 'Id,' which is the reservoir of instinctive responses, 'Ego,' which is the portion influenced by the external world and 'Super-Ego, which is 'the inhibitions of instinct characteristic of man.' His controversial book on religion, *The Future of an Illusion*, was published in 1927. Freud escaped from Vienna, just before Austria was annexed by the Nazi regime, under which psychoanalysis was banned. He settled with his family in Hampstead in London, but died there of cancer after only a year.

Religion, for Freud, was a collective expression of neurosis. It was used, he said, by individuals to escape from the realities of a hostile and indifferent universe. Relying on an attitude of *als-ob*, 'as if', people create an illusory world of make-believe, in a heaven and in a God, which they project. In a long correspondence with Oskar Pfister, Freud constantly reviewed his estimate of religion, but continued to maintain its essentially neurotic character. His views have not gained wide acceptance but have increased awareness that some manifestations of religion are unhealthy.

In a much earlier work *Totem and Taboo* (1913), Freud had argued that religious solidarity and restraints begin in a primeval rebellion of the sons against the father. In his *Moses and Monotheism* (1939) he suggested that Moses wanted the Hebrews to accept the ethical monotheism of Pharaoh Akhenaten,[1] but that they preferred the magic they were used to and killed Moses. The Mosaic monotheism, however, Freud held did eventually reassert itself. Again, these views have found little scholarly support.

Freud believed that just as Copernicus (1473-1543), who showed that the Earth moved round the sun, had displaced humanity from the centre of the universe and Darwin (1809-1892), with his theory of evolution, had taken away the idea than humans were different to animals, so he had shown that the mind is not subject to human control, but is the product of unconscious forces. Freud also treated religion from the standpoint of human behaviour, so helped to prepare the way for sociological and phenomenological approaches to the study of religion, which focus on the role of religion in society and in the life of the believer, but make no assumptions about whether or not there is a Divine or metaphysical Reality.

Jung's approach to religion was rather similar. 'It is not for psychology, as a science, to demand a hypostatisation of the God-image. But the facts being what they are, it does have to reckon with the existence of a God-image.'[2]

Carl Jung was born in Switzerland. His was a lonely childhood, although it was enriched by his vivid imagination. Carl, as a boy, tried to communicate to his father, who was a Protestant minister, his own experience of God, but father and son never managed to understand each other. His father in fact seemed to be losing his faith as he grew older. It was assumed, nonetheless, that Carl would also become a clergyman. Instead he studied medicine and became a psychiatrist. He joined the staff of the Berghölzli Asylum in Zurich, where, under the direction of Eugen Bleuler, research into mental illness of lasting importance was being carried out.

Jung in his early *Studies in Word Association* (1904-9) coined the word 'complex.' His studies in Dementia led to his meeting Freud and working with him for a time, but Jung's *Psychology of the Unconscious* (1912) lead to a break. Jung then moved back to Zurich and developed his own school of Analytical Psychology.

His first achievement was to differentiate two types of people the extrovert, who was outward looking, and the introvert, who was inward looking. He also gave attention to the significance of dreams. As a boy Jung had had very vivid dreams. He later developed the theory that these experiences came from an area of the mind, which he called the collective unconscious, which, he said, was shared by everyone. From this collective experience of humankind, the individual inherited ideas or archetypes in his or her unconscious. The collective unconscious, he claimed, was the source of dreams, myths and religion.

He wrote:

'I am so profoundly convinced of this homogeneity of the human psyche that I have actually embraced it in the concept of the collective unconscious, as a universal and homogeneous substratum whose homogeneity extends even into a world-wide identity or similarity of myths and fairy-tales; so that a Negro of the Southern States of America dreams in the motifs of Greek mythology and a Swiss grocer's apprentice repeats in his psychosis the vision of an Egyptian Gnostic.'[3]

Jung devoted much time to reflecting on how psychology related to religion. He found that sometimes obscure or neglected texts shed light on his own or his patients' dreams. Jung saw Christianity as part of a historic process, which was necessary for the development of consciousness. But he also thought that movements such as Gnosticism and alchemy, which the Church regarded as heretical, were also manifestations of unconscious archetypal images, which were not fully expressed in traditional forms of Christianity.

With other scholars such as the French anthropologist Claude Levi-Strauss (b.1908) and Mircea Eliade (1907-86), a philosopher of comparative religion, Jung showed the deep significance of Myth – which is concealed by the popular tendency to assume a myth is untrue or just a made-up story.

Jung, although he was not much interested in organised religion, believed that people were naturally religious and that the religious instinct was as powerful as the instinct for sex or for aggression. He was not, however, as already mentioned, particularly interested in metaphysical speculation, but in the role of religious symbols in helping people live a healthy and balanced life. He ended his *Psychology and Religion* (1938) by saying:

'Nobody can know what the ultimate things are. We must, therefore, take them as we experience them. And if such experience helps to make your life healthier, more beautiful, more complete and more satisfactory to yourself and to those you love, you may safely say: "This was the grace of God."

Jung held professorial positions at Zurich and then at the University of Basle. His last years were spent in the beautiful home that he and his wife Emma had had built by the lakeside in Zurich, where he died on June 6th, 1961, at the age of eighty-five. In an interview given in the year before he died, Jung again said, 'If you should find in yourself... an ineradicable tendency to believe in God or immortality, do not allow yourself to be disturbed by the blather of so-called "free-thinkers."' Jung, thus, helped many religious believers to see that faith and psychiatry were not necessarily in opposition.

CHAPTER NOTES
1. See chapter 5.
2. *Collected Works*, viii, para 528.
3. *Collected Works.*

79

Tagore

Rabindranath Tagore was India's greatest modern poet, who wrote in Bengali and English. In 1913 he was awarded the Nobel Prize for Literature - the first Asian to win a Nobel Prize - for his *Gitanjali*. He promoted Indian cultural and spiritual values both in India and Europe as a counterbalance to the materialism, which was dominant in the West.

Rabindranath Tagore was the youngest of the thirteen surviving children of Debendranath Tagore and Sarad Devi. He was born into a princely, wealthy and land-owning family. His father, Debenranath (1817-1905) was a philosopher and active religious reformer, who was known as Maharishi or 'great sage'.

To understand the context in which Rabindranath Tagore grew up it is necessary to know something about what is sometimes called the Hindu Renaissance or Neo-Hinduism, which was initiated by Ram Mohan Roy (1772-1833) and in which Debendranath Tagore played a significant part.

Ram Mohan Roy belonged to a respected Brahmin family in Bengal. He was a fine linguist who besides Bengali and English also learned Sanskrit, Arabic and Persian. For a time he worked for the East India Company. He was impressed by Western achievements and recognised the need for reform. In his earliest work *Tuhfat-Ul-Muwahhidin*, he argued that reason showed the necessity for belief in One Supreme Being. Later, Ram Mohan Roy put more emphasis on the Hindu scriptures - especially the Upanishads - many of which he translated. He argued that Hindu belief and practice in his time had degenerated from the pure teaching of the scriptures and needed reform. He, therefore, founded in 1828, the Brahmo Sabha, later known as the Brahmo Samaj. This taught the worship of the one True Formless God. It was a pure monotheism and images were abandoned. Ram Mohan Roy's primary concern was for the reform of morals. He opposed caste, polygamy, suttee – the custom by which a widow would burn herself to death on her husband's pyre - and the prohibition of the remarriage of widows. He emphasised the importance of improved education. Ram Mohan

Roy had a high regard for the moral teaching of Jesus. In 1820, he published his *Precepts of Jesus: the Guide to Peace and Happiness.* The supernatural is excluded. There is no reference to the Virgin Birth, the miracles, the Crucifixion or the Resurrection. 'I feel persuaded,' Ram Mohan Roy wrote, 'that by separating from the other material contained in the New Testament, the moral principles found in that book, these will be more likely to produce the desirable effect of improving the hearts and minds of men of different persuasions and degrees of under-standing.'[1] His book was welcomed by Unitarians but criticised by Christian missionaries at Serampore. Their comments led to Ram Mohan Roy giving greater attention to the person of Jesus.

Besides working for the reform of Indian society, Ram Mohan Roy also campaigned against the injustices of British rule. In 1830, having been given the title *Raja* or prince by the titular Moghul emperor Akbar II, Raja Ram Mohan Roy travelled to Britain to inform the king and parliament of these grievances. It was a time when reform was in the air in Britain – the Reform Act was passed in 1832. Ram Mohan Roy died while in Britain and is buried at the Arnos Grove Cemetery in Bristol. The Indian High Commissioner still usually attends a memorial service on the Raja's birthday.

Debendranath Tagore, like Ram Mohan Roy, had a wide knowledge of India's classical literature was well as of Western philosophy. He spoke out strongly against suttee and other social evils. He encouraged efforts to ensure an education for all Indian children. He founded Santiniketan (The Abode of Peace), which his son was to develop into an important educational centre. He also strongly opposed idolatry, but had a firm belief in the One God. Indeed, when some students returned from the Hindu holy city of Benares (Varanasi) saying that the Upanishads taught the identity of the individual self and the Universal Self,[2] Debendranath was moved to reject the infallible authority of the scriptures. 'When in the Upanishads I came across, "I am He," and "Thou art That," then I became disappointed in the Upanishads also.'[3] It was eventually agreed that 'the Vedas, the Upanishads, and other ancient writings were not to be accepted as infallible guides, that reason and conscience were to be the supreme authority and the teachings of the Scriptures were to be accepted only insofar as they harmonised with the light within us.'[4] The inner light became the authority of the Samaj.

Debendranath said,

> 'I came to see that the Pure Heart filled with the light of intuitive knowledge – this was its basis. Brahma reigned in the pure heart alone. The pure unsophisticated heart was the seat of Brahmoism. The rishi of old records his experience, "the pure in spirit enlightened by wisdom sees the Holy God by means of worship and meditation." These words accorded with the experience of my own heart, hence I accepted them.'[5]

Rabindranath Tagore was later to echo his father's opinion when he wrote, 'To me the verses of the Upanishads and of the Buddha have ever been things of the Spirit... as being instinct with individual meaning for me, as for others, and awaiting for their confirmation my own special testimony.'[6]

Debendranath's view of the authority of scripture, which is a matter of debate in every religion, was not welcomed by all the members of Brahmo Samaj and lead to divisions in it.

Rabindranath Tagore, who was born in 1861, grew up in a highly intellectual and cultured home in the rambling Jorasanko house in Calcutta (Kolkata), where the spiritual values of Hinduism and other religions were esteemed, but orthodox traditions and practices were critically scrutinized. His mother died when he was in his early teens. He never paid much attention to his tutor. After the sacred thread or *upanayana* coming-of-age ceremony, he toured India with his father for several months, visiting Santiniketan and the Sikh holy city of Amritsar, before staying for a time at the Himalayan hill station of Dalhousie. There he read biographies, studied history, astronomy, modern science and Sanskrit. He also studied the work of Kalidasa, who lived somewhere between 350 and 460 CE, whose Sanskrit poetry has never been surpassed. Rabindranath himself started to write poetry. As a joke he pretended that one work, which he wrote at the age of sixteen, was written by a newly discovered seventeenth century poet. His story 'Bhikharini' or 'The Beggar Woman', also composed in 1877, was the first short story to be written in Bengali. He wrote several other poems at this time.

For a time Rabindranath hoped to become a barrister. He went to a public (fee-paying) school in Brighton in 1878 and then studied law at University College, London, but returned to India in 1880, without a degree. In 1883 he married Mrinalini Devi. Then when he was about thirty, he went to manage the family's vast estates is Shilaidaha, which is now in Bangladesh. Rabindranath lived in close contact with the villagers and sympathised with their poverty and backwardness. This was to be the theme of his *Galpa Guccha* (1912), which was a collection of stories 'on humble lives and their small miseries.' He also came to love the Bengali countryside and the river Ganges. It was a creative time and he published several collections of his writings.

In 1901, Rabindranath moved to Santiniketan in West Bengal to found an ashram and in due course a university. It was, however, at first a sad time for him. His wife died and also two of their five children. His father also died in 1905. He continued to write, mostly in Bengali, although he translated some of his works into English, especially his widely appreciated *Gitanjali: Song Offerings*, which helped him to win the Nobel Prize. In 1915 he received a knighthood, but he surrendered it as a protest after the Jallianwallah Bagh Massacre in Amristsar. In this tragic event nearly 400 people were killed and many more injured when troops under the command of General Dyer fired without warning on the protesting but unarmed crowd. The carnage was made worse by the fact that the crowd were unable to leave the confined space because the only exit was blocked by British troops. A memorial marks the site of the massacre, for which General Dyer was eventually censured.

Tagore developed Santiniketan, ('the Abode of Peace') on which he spent his Nobel Prize money, both as a centre for agricultural development, indigenous crafts and for the arts – music, dance and drama. He insisted that it was to be open to both men and women. There was at the time no temple because Tagore wanted to emphasize that religions were equal in the quest for peace. Prayer and meditation normally took place, as in Vedic times, in the open air. This is the morning prayer, which students were expected to recite:

Thou art our father. Do Thou help us to know Thee as Father. We bow down to Thee. Do Thou never afflict us, O Father, by causing a separation between Thee and us. O Thou Self-revealing One, O Thou Parent of the Universe, purge away the multitude of our sins, and send unto us whatever is good and noble. To Thee, from Whom spring joy and goodness, nay, Who art all goodness Thyself, to Thee we bow down now and for ever.'[7]

Santiniketan is now a university, financed by the Indian government, and has played a leading role in the revival of traditional Indian culture. Tagore was critical of teaching by rote, which was common at the time. He lampooned it in a short story, where a bird, which eventually dies, is put in a cage by tutors and force-fed pages torn from a book.[8]

Throughout the 1930s, Rabindranath Tagore continued to be an important public figure. He protested about India's 'abnormal caste consciousness' and supported efforts to admit Dalits – members of the lowest social group – to Hindu temples. He supported the movement for Indian independence, although at times he was critical of Gandhi. He continued to write poems and dance-dramas. His last four years were marked by chronic pain and two long periods of illness. His writings from this time are preoccupied with death. He died on the 7th of August 1941, in a room at the house where he had grown up.

Tagore travelled extensively, visiting more than thirty countries on five continents, and thereby familiarising non-Indian audiences with his writing and political ideas. The missionary Charles Frere Andrews, who was also influenced by Gandhi, was a close colleague. The Anglo-Irish poet William Yates and the American poet Ezra Pound were among those who were impressed by Tagore's work.

Tagore is best known for his poems, but he also wrote novels – some of which have been adapted as films by the director Satyajit Ray - essays, short stories, dramas and a large number of songs. Tagore was also a painter and a musician.

Tagore's reputation was eclipsed for a time after his death, but his very varied writings and wide influence is now much more appreciated. His faith was based primarily upon his personal experience of God, as is expressed in this poem:

Have you not heard his silent steps?
He comes, comes, ever comes.
Every morning and every age, every day

and every night he comes, comes, ever comes.
Many a song have I sung in many a mood of mine,
But all their notes have always proclaimed,
"He comes, comes, ever comes."
In the fragrant days of sunny April through the forest path
He comes, comes, ever comes.
In the rainy gloom of July nights on the thundering chariots of clouds
He comes, comes, ever comes.
In sorrow after sorrow it is his steps that press upon my heart
and it is the golden touch of his feet that makes my joy to shine.[9]

Tagore's was a very personal interpretation of Hinduism. It has been attractive to a number of Westerners, who are fascinated by the 'spirituality of India.' Moreover his emphasis on Divine love resonates with Christians. Tagore, however, believed that Indian spiritual values were higher that those of the materialistic Western society. He was critical of the nationalism that had been imported into India from the West. He described it as 'organised selfishness.'[10] 'The naked passion of the self-love of nations in its drunken delirium of greed, is dancing to the clash of steel and the howling verses of vengeance.'[11] He was a world citizen. This is reflected in his haunting words,

On the seashore of endless worlds,
Children meet with shouts and dances[12]

Tagore was not a systematic thinker. 'I am a singer myself and ever attracted by the strains that come for the House of Songs.[13] He was deeply influenced by Hindu scriptures, especially the devotional or *bhakti* traditions. He spoke of God as 'Lord of my life' and as 'Brother' and 'Friend.' Tagore was an original thinker, who rejected many Orthodox doctrines, including karma - or the moral law of cause and effect, which determines a person's future birth. He also rejected Maya, which is the belief that the world is ultimately unreal. Tagore, like other influential spiritual teachers in the twentieth century, insisted that it is in the world that God has chosen to reveal himself and it is there in the service of the poor that God is to be found.

Here is thy footstool and there rest thy feet
where live the poorest and lowliest and lost.[14]
Or again,
Leave this chanting and singing and telling of beads!
Whom doest thou worship in this lonely dark corner of a temple
with doors all shut?
Open thy eyes and see thy God is not before thee!
He is where the tiller is tilling the hard ground
and where the path maker is breaking stones
Put off they holy mantle and even like him
come down on the dusty soil!
Meet him and stand by him in toil and in sweat of thy brow.[15]

In the end, it not so much his achievements for which Tagore will be remembered, remarkable as they were – his literary output was amazing – but for his quiet confidence in the unfailing presence of the Lord:

'Through birth and death in this world or in others, wherever thou leadest me it is thou, the same, the one companion of my endless life who ever linkest my heart with bonds of joy to the unfamiliar.'[16]

CHAPTER NOTES

1. Ram Mohan Roy, *The Precepts of Jesus*, 1820, Introduction.
2. This was the Advaita or Non-Dualist position taught by Sankara.
3. Debendranath Tagore, *The Autobiography of Maharshi Debendranth Tagore*, Calcutta, pp. 160-1.
4. Introductory chapter by S N Tagore in *Autobiography*, p.5.
5. *Autobiography*, p. 161-2. The quotation is from the Mundaka Upanishad, III, 1-8.
6. Rabindranath Tagore, *Sadhana* (1920), Preface, p. viii.
7. Quoted in E.J Thompson, *Rabindranath Tagore: His Life and Work*, Calcutta, YMCA Publishing House, no date, c. 1923 revised edition, c.1961, p. 77.
8. Rabindranath Tagore, *The Parrot's Training*.
9. Rabindranth Tagore, *Gitanjali*, in *1,000 World Prayers*, Ed Marcus

Braybrooke, O Books, 2003 p. 23.

10. Rabindranath Tagore, *Nationalism*, 1918 Quoted by Eric Sharpe in *Hinduism*, Ed J R Hinnells and E J Sharpe, Newcastle-upon-Tyne, Oriel Press, 1972, p. 96.

11. Quoted by Sharpe, p. 96.

12. *1,000 World Prayers* p. 298.

13. Quoted by Sharpe, p. 96.

14. *1,000 World Prayers*, p. 230.

15. *1,000 World Prayers*, p. 311.

16. *1,000 World Prayers*, p. 261.

80

Black Elk

Black Elk was a famous Medicine Man or Holy Man of the Oglala Lakota Sioux Native Americans, who for a time in the sixties became a cult hero among young Americans. Black Elk in his long life saw his people, who roamed freely across the country when he was boy, defeated by the American settlers and confined to a Reservation. He experienced a number of visions and exercised a spiritual and healing ministry among his people. Later in life Black Elk became a Christian, but continued to practise some traditional ceremonies, which he believed had come from God. He also toured the USA and much of Europe as part of 'Buffalo Bill's Wild West Show.'

The importance of Native American Spirituality with its deep appreciation of human beings' inter-dependence with Nature is increasingly appreciated today. There are, however, few literary sources.[1] This is partly why Black Elk is so significant, because as an old man he shared much of the story of his life with John G Neihardt, who first met him in 1930. His chief purpose, he said, was to 'save his great Vision for men.'[2] He also described some of the Sioux rituals to Joseph Epes Brown.[3] At the time of the publication of his conversations with John G Neihardt in 1932, there was little interest. The book was quickly 'remaindered.' A copy, however, later reached Carl Jung who took an interest in it. It was reissued in 1961 and was then greeted enthusiastically, especially by the young. The book in the words of the *Christian Herald* became 'the current youth classic.'[4]

Black Elk was born in about 1863. His first vision came when he was only a five-year old child. He heard a kingbird which seemed to be saying, 'Listen! A voice is calling you!' Then, he said, 'I looked up at the clouds and saw two men who sang this sacred song,

'Behold, a sacred voice is calling you;
All over the sky a sacred voice is calling.'[5]

Later when he was nine he had what he called 'The Great Vision,' which is reminiscent of the Biblical prophet Ezekiel's vision of the Chariot of the Lord.[6] His body began to ache and he fell into what appeared to his family to be a coma. In his visions he saw a bay horse who said, 'Behold me! My life story you shall know.' Then the horse wheeled North to where the great white giant lives; then to the East where the sun shines continually, to the South and to the West. Then after the dance of the horses, he saw, through the clouds six old men sitting in a row. The oldest of the Grandfathers said, 'Come right in and do not fear. We have called you here to teach you.' He was then given spiritual power by the Grandfathers. After that a voice said, 'Black Elk behold they have given you the centre of the nation's hoop to make it live.' Then as I rode to the centre of the village the Voice said, 'Give them now the flowering stick that they may flourish, and the sacred pipe that they may know the power that is peace, and the wing of the white giant that they may have endurance and face all winds with courage.'[7] Then the voice said, 'Behold the circle of the nations hoop, for it is holy, being endless, and thus all powers shall be one in the peoples without end.'[8]

When the vision was over, his parents told him he had been sick for twelve days, lying all the time as if he were dead. Later, Whirlwind Chaser who helped to cure him said, 'your boy is sitting in a sacred manner. I do not know what it is, but there is something special for him to do, for just as I came in I could see a power like a light all through his body.'[9]

Black Elk as a youth took a full part in the life of the people and described vividly his excitement when, as a boy of thirteen, he killed his first bison. Later in life, he was disgusted at the way the Whites killed the bison just for sport. 'They just killed and killed because they liked to do that. When we hunted bison, we killed only what we needed.'

By the time he was 17, Black Elk was becoming so anxious about the voices he heard that he was afraid whenever he saw a cloud coming. His parents were worried that he was ill again – so they asked an old medicine man to see him. Black Elk described his vision to the medicine man, who told Black Elk to arrange for a horse dance and then the fear would leave him. His parents made the necessary arrangements. Black Elk himself was told not to eat anything before the ceremony and to purify himself in a sweat lodge and then to wipe himself dry with sage.

Sixteen horses took part in the dance. Four black horses to represent the West; four white horses for the North; four sorrels or light brown horses for the East and four buckskin or greyish yellow horses for the

South. There was a bay horse for Black Elk to ride.

After the horse dance was over, Black Elk said 'I felt very happy, for I could see that my people were happier. Many crowded round me and said that they or their relatives who had been feeling sick were well again and they gave me many gifts. Even the horses seemed to be healthier and happier after the dance.' After this, he recalled, the medicine men would talk to him and he started to get up very early to see the rising of the day-star.

Soon, however, tragedy was to befall the people. Many of them were forcibly moved to a reservation. When Black Elk went back to his own people, few of them knew about the horse dance or about his vision. Looking back, Black Elk voiced a sense of sadness about his vision. 'I wish and wish my vision could have been given to a man more worthy. I wonder why it came to me, a pitiful old man who can do nothing. Men and women and children I have cured of sickness with the power the vision gave me; but my nation I could not help.'[10] He always insisted that it was not his power, which healed people, but the power that came through him.[11] His first cure happened when he was only nineteen.

Life in the reservation was very different from what Black Elk had been used to. The people had to live in little square grey houses of logs, although Native Americans had always lived in circles, because the Power of the world always works in circles. 'In the old days when we were a strong and happy people,' Black Elk recalled, 'all our power came to us from the sacred hoop of the nation so long as the hoop was unbroken, the people flourished. The flowering tree was the living centre of the hoop, and the circle of the four quarters nourished it.'[12] Many of the people were hungry because little of the money sent by 'Great Father in Washington' reached them.

Black Elk was then recruited for 'Buffalo Bill's Wild West Show.' This involved travelling through much of America and then to Europe. Black Elk hoped to learn more about the world, but he saw that the White people, 'would take everything from each other if they could, so that there were some who had more of everything than they could use, while crowds of people had nothing at all and maybe were starving. They had forgotten that the earth was their mother.' When they visited a prison he was shocked to see that 'Men pointed guns at the prisoners and made them move around like animals in a cage.'[13] In England, they performed before Queen Victoria. After their dance she said, 'I am sixty-seven years old. All over the world I have seen all kinds of people; but today I have seen the best-looking people I know. If you belonged to me, I would not let them take you around in a show like this.'[14] In Manchester Black Elk and some friends got left behind, so they went back to London and joined 'Mexican Joe' in London and then in Paris.

Black Elk was glad eventually to get home and his family were delighted. He was, however, distressed to see how the living conditions and morale of his people was deteriorating. Many were dying of whooping cough. Black Elk's power had deserted him while he was abroad but he was relieved when it came back to him on his return home. He had another vision in 1890, when he saw another heavenly world. That evening he prayed, 'Father, Great Spirit, Behold me! The nation that I have is in despair. The new earth you promised you have shown me. Let my nation also behold it.'[15]

He had another vision of a man standing with arms held wide in front of him... He was not a Wasichu (white man) and he was not an Indian. His hair was long and hanging loose, and on the left side of his head he wore an eagle feather... He spoke like singing, "My life is such that all earthly Beings and growing things belong to me. Your Father, the Great Spirit, has said this. You too must say this.'[16]

1890 was a disastrous year for his people. They were attacked at what is remembered as the Massacre or Butchering at Wounded Knee. Black Elk tried to encourage his people, but in vain. The soldiers slaughtered men, women and children. 'When I look back now from this high hill of my old age,' he said to John G Neidhardt, 'I can still see the butchered women and children lying heaped and scattered all along the crooked gulch – an American term for a small ravine cut by a torrent - as plain as when I saw them with eyes still young. And I can see that something else died there in the bloody mud, and was buried in the blizzard. A people's dream died there. It was a beautiful dream.'[17] Black Elk hoped that 'some little root of the sacred tree still lives.' His words, which have been recorded, have ensured that the vision has not been forgotten.

Already before the Massacre of Wounded Knee, Jesuit missionaries – the 'Black Robes' - had come to the reserves, despite opposition from the government. Some of the Jesuits learned the Lakota language. Black Elk's first wife, whom he married in 1892, became a Catholic and all three of their children were baptized. Black Elk himself, soon after his wife's death, was also baptized. Black Elk taught himself to read and immersed himself in study of the Bible. He became a catechist, but continued many traditional practices, saying, 'God prepared us before the missionary came. Our ancestors used the pipe to know God. That's a foundation! But from the old country came Christ from heaven – a wonderful thing – the Son of God.'[18] He died on August 17th, 1950. That night, the sky was filled with a brilliant display of the northern lights.

Black Elk was a man of prayer. 'Never fail to pray everyday,' he said, 'God will take care of you and reward you for this.' In one of his prayers he reflected on the joys and sorrows of life:

'You have set the powers of the four quarters of the earth to cross each other. You have made me cross the good road and road of difficulties, and where they cross, the place is holy. Day in, day out, you are the life of things.'[19]

Perhaps best known is his prayer called 'Sunset,' with its universal vision:

'Then I was standing on the highest mountain of them all, and round about beneath me was the whole hoop of the world. And while I stood there I saw more than I can tell and I understood more than I saw; for I was seeing in a sacred manner the shapes of all things in the spirit, and the shape of all shapes as they must live together like one being.

And I saw the sacred hoop of my people was one of the many hoops that made one circle, wide as daylight and as star-light, and in the centre grew one mighty flowering tree to shelter all the children of one mother and one father. And I saw that it is holy.

But anywhere is the centre of the world.'[20]

Yet as Black Elk said, 'It is hard to follow one great vision in this world of darkness and of many changing shadows. Among the shadows men get lost.'[21]

CHAPTER NOTES

1. The authenticity of the speech attributed to Chief Seattle (also Chief Sealth) is too much in doubt to refer to it.
2. *Black Elk Speaks: being the life story of a Holy Man of the Oglala Sioux (as told to John.G.Neihardt)* (1932), London, Barrie and Jenkins, 1972, p. ix.
3. *The Sacred Pipe: Black Elk's Account of Seven Rites of the Oglala Sioux,* recorded and edited by Joseph Epes Brown, Oklahoma, University of Oklahoma Press, 1988.
4. *Black Elk Speaks,* p. 10.
5. *Black Elk Speaks,* p. 15.
6. Ezekiel,1, 4ff.
7. *Black Elk Speaks,* p. 34.
8. *Black Elk Speaks,* p. 35.
9. *Black Elk Speaks,* p. 49.
10. *Black Elk Speaks,* p. 184.
11. *Black Elk Speaks,* p. 208.
12. *Black Elk Speaks,* p. 198.
13. *Black Elk Speaks,* p. 221.
14. *Black Elk Speaks,* p. 225.
15. *Black Elk Speaks,* p. 248.
16. *Black Elk Speaks,* p. 249.
17. *Black Elk Speaks,* p. 276.
18. Quotation from *Nicholas Black Elk, Catechist* by Caroline and Rod Lorenz, www.peace.mb.ca.
19. From www.indians.org.
20. From www.indians.org.
21. *Black Elk Speaks,* p. 254.

81

Gandhi

Gandhi has become an icon for all those who hope that social and political change can be achieved by non-violent means. He was the pre-eminent leader of India's struggle for independence, who based his political campaigns on his deep moral and spiritual convictions. Gandhi wrote and said so much and so much has been written about him that his influence has been multi-faceted.

Mohandas Karamchand Gandhi – Mahatma is a title which means 'Great Soul' - was born in the extreme West of India at Porbandar, beside the Arabian Sea, in 1869 on October 2nd - a day which is now observed as 'The International Day of Non-Violence.' Visitors can still see the modest three storey house where he grew up. Porbandar was the capital of a small principality in Gujarat where the local prince was the nominal ruler, although under the watchful eye of the British. Gandhi's father was the chief minister or *dewan*. Gandhi's mother, a devotee of the god Vishnu, spent much time in the temple and cared tirelessly for anyone in the family who was ill. The Jain religion was – as it still is – influential in Gujarat and Gandhi would have been steeped in its teaching of non-injury to all living beings, which implied vegetarianism, and its emphasis on mutual respect between members of different religions.

Gandhi's early education was limited - and he lost a year when he was married at the age of 13 – he was later to be strongly critical of child marriage. There was a period of adolescent rebellion, when he smoked, dabbled with atheism and ate meat, but after each escapade he promised not to repeat the offence – a promise that he kept. In 1887, he just managed to matriculate at the University of Bombay and started studying at Samaldas College in Bhavnagar. Gandhi himself wanted to be a doctor, but his family decided that he should be a barrister. It was, therefore, arranged for him to study in England, although it was an effort to raise enough money and his mother's anxieties were only assuaged when Gandhi vowed, while in England, not to touch wine, women or meat. Defying caste rules, which forbade travel overseas, Gandhi sailed for England in 1888.

Gandhi joined the Inner Temple and took his studies seriously. Adapting to Western clothes and English etiquette was a trial and his vegetarianism created real difficulties for him. He was also short of money. On the boat, he recalled, 'I was innocent of the use of knives and forks and had not the boldness to inquire what dishes on the menu were free of meat. I therefore never took meals at table but always had them in my cabin.'[1] In time he discovered there were some English vegetarians and he joined the London Vegetarian Society. Some of its members introduced him to the Bible and to Sir Edwin Arnold's *The Song Celestial*, which was a translation of the *Bhagavadgita*, the best loved Hindu scripture, which Gandhi had not previously read.

On his return to India in 1891, he was very upset to discover that his mother had died. Because there were too many lawyers, it was hard for him to find work. He, therefore, accepted a year's contract from an Indian firm in South Africa. Almost immediately he encountered racial prejudice. In a Durban court, he was asked to remove his turban. He objected and left the courtroom. Soon afterwards, travelling to Pretoria, he refused to move from his first class carriage for which he had bought a ticket. He was, therefore, unceremoniously thrown out of the train and left shivering overnight at Pietermaritzburg Station. Later in the journey, he was beaten up by a white driver because he would not travel on the footboard to make room for a white passenger. He soon found he was also barred from hotels, which were 'for Europeans only.' These experiences stirred a new self-assertiveness in Gandhi, who refused to accept injustice. On the cold station he reflected about his duty. 'Should I fight for my rights or go back to India or should I go on to Pretoria without minding the insults... The hardship to which I was subjected was superficial – only a symptom of the deep disease of colour prejudice. I should try, if possible, to root out the disease and suffer hardships in the process.'[2]

Although Gandhi studied the condition of his fellow countrymen in South Africa, he himself intended to return to India. But, at a farewell party, he discovered that there was a move to deprive Indians of their right to vote. 'This is the first nail in our coffin' he told his hosts. He was persuaded to lead the protest campaign and in 1894 he founded the Natal Indian Congress. Except for a short visit to India to fetch his wife and children, Gandhi stayed in South Africa until 1914. General Smuts said of his departure, 'The saint has left our shores, I hope for ever.' It was in South Africa that Gandhi first developed the non-violent technique of *Satyagraha* or 'firmness in truth.' He established a community at the Phoenix Settlement and he began to give serious attention to religion.

It was not until the end of the First World War that Gandhi became involved in the struggle against British rule. But by 1920 he had become the dominant figure on the Indian political stage and remodelled the Indian Congress into an effective instrument for change. The next twenty years were occupied by protests, negotiations, fasts, and times in prison.

In 1918 Gandhi led the protests against an oppressive tax, which was levied at the height of a famine. He was imprisoned, but so many people protested that the authorities released him, but too late to stop his fame spreading throughout India. In 1921, under his leadership, non-violent protest against British rule was extended to include a boycott of British-made goods – and especially textiles. Instead, Indians were urged to wear homespun cloth or *khadi* and to spend time each day spinning it. Yet fearing that the campaign would turn violent, Gandhi abruptly halted it. He was, however, arrested and sentenced to six years imprisonment for sedition – although he only served two years of his sentence.

Gandhi returned to the fray in 1928, when the British government appointed a constitutional reform commission. Indian political parties, however, all boycotted it. Gandhi called on the British to grant India dominion status or face a new campaign of non-violence. The British made no response, so at the end of 1929, the flag of India was unfurled in Lahore. Gandhi launched a new *satyagraha* against the salt tax and led the famous Salt March from Ahmedabad to Dandi - 248 miles – where people could make salt for themselves. The British imprisoned over 60,000 marchers. The British government then decided to negotiate and Gandhi came to London for a round table conference, but this was a disappointment as it focused on the position of the Indian princes and Indian minorities rather than on the transference of power.

In 1934 Gandhi resigned from the Congress Party, as he felt its leading members had adopted non-violence as an expedient and not as the fundamental creed it was for him. Gandhi went to live at Sevagram, a village in central India. He now focussed on a 'constructive programme' of building the nation 'from the bottom up' – with an emphasis on education, weaving and other cottage industries and above all an end to untouchability. He returned to head Congress in 1936.

When War broke out in 1939, Gandhi at first offered the British 'non-violent moral support,' but in 1942, at the height of the Second World War, he launched the *Quit India* campaign, calling for an immediate British withdrawal from India. This was met by the imprisonment of all the Congress leadership. Gandhi was held for two years at the Aga Khan Palace in Pune (Poona). During this time, both his secretary Mahadev Desai and his wife died and he himself suffered a severe bout of malaria. Popular outrage expressed itself in some violent protests which were sternly suppressed. Relations between Congress and the British were at breaking point and made worse by the policy of 'divide and rule adopted' by the British in their support of the princes and in efforts to set Hindus and Muslims at loggerheads.

The end of the war and the election of a Labour Government in Britain created a new situation, which resulted in August 1947 in Independence – but of a sub-continent divided between Pakistan, where Muslims were the great majority, and India, a secular state, of which the great majority were Hindus. Gandhi deplored the division and did what he could to halt the bloody communal violence. In September 1947, his fasting stopped the rioting in Calcutta and in January 1948 he shamed the city of Delhi into a communal truce, but a few days later on his way to evening prayers he was shot dead by a young Hindu extremist. 'The light has gone out of our lives, and there is darkness everywhere... Our beloved leader, Bapu as we called him, the father of the nation, is no more', Prime Minister Jawaharlal Nehru told a shocked nation. Gandhi's last words are said to have been *He Ram* - 'My God' – and these words are on his memorial at Raj Ghat in New Delhi.

Gandhi's three major campaigns in 1920-22, 1930-34 and 1940-42 were well designed to create that process of self-doubt and questioning that was to undermine the moral defences of the British. At the time, most of the British saw him at best as a utopian visionary or at worst as a cunning hypocrite whose profession of friendship for the British hid his wish for the subversion of the Raj. A few Christian missionaries, such as C F

Andrews (1871-1940) and some Labour politicians such as Reg Sorensen (1891-1971), who was an MP for thirty years, had a high opinion of him. By the centenary of his birth, however, he had many more admirers and a statue was erected to his memory in London in 1969.

Gandhi was deeply committed to social change by non-violent means. 'An eye for an eye,' he said, 'makes the whole world blind.' His emphasis was on the positive power of sacrificial selfless love, rather than 'non-violence.' He combined the idea of *ahimsa*, which he learned from the Jains of his native Gujarat and the sense of duty for duty's sake,[3] which is taught in the *Bhagavad Gita*. Gandhi was equally inspired by Jesus' Sermon on the Mount. He was also influenced by three outstanding and original thinkers: the American essayist and Transcendentalist philosopher, Henry David Thoreau (1817-1862), who for a time lived a simple life in a shack in the woods; the British art critic John Ruskin (1819-1900); and the Russian novelist and advocate of reform, Leo Tolstoy (1828-1910).

Gandhi's chosen term was *Satyagraha* - the force of truth – because it had a positive meaning, whereas to him 'pacifism' was a negative term describing a negative response to oppression. Pacifism was also an English word![4] 'Truth (*satya*),' he said, 'implies love, and 'firmness' (*agraha*) engenders and therefore serves as a synonym for force. I thus began to call the Indian movement "Satyagraha", that is to say Force which is born of Truth and Love or non-violence, and gave up the use of the phrase "passive resistance."' *Satyagraha* involves the acceptance of suffering for oneself and the desire to do good to one's adversary. '*Satyagraha* postulates the conquest of the adversary by suffering in one's own person.'[5] Gandhi's aim was not to defeat the opponent but to appeal to his or her higher nature.

Are there limits to non-violence? Gandhi admitted, 'I have to concede that even in a non-violent state a police force may be necessary... (but) police ranks will be composed of believers in non-violence.'[6] In 1940, when it looked likely that Britain would be invaded by Nazi Germany, he suggested to the British people that they should lay down their arms and, if not allowed free passage from their homes, they should let themselves be slaughtered, but refuse to give allegiance to the Nazis.[7] He was aware, however, that such a level of non-violence required great faith and courage. Non-violence, he insisted, was not a cover for cowardice. Gandhi asked, 'What difference does it make to the dead, the orphans, and the homeless, whether the mad destruction is wrought under the name of totalitarianism or the holy name of liberty and democracy?'

Although during his life-time, he attracted attention as a politician, increasingly it is recognised that Gandhi's political campaigns were an expression of his deep religious commitment. Unlike many Hindu holy men, Gandhi did not withdraw to a cave in the Himalayas. He insisted that he could only meet God in the service of the poor and once said that he carried his cave with him. He also said that he thought hand-spinning was superior to the practice of denominational religion. Gandhi's *Talisman* emphasises the priority that should be given to care for the poor: 'Recall the face of the poorest and most helpless person whom you have seen,' he wrote, 'and ask yourself, if the step you contemplate is going to be of any use to *him*... Will it (help) the hungry and spiritually starved millions of our countrymen?'[8]

His was not a dogmatic faith and Gandhi spoke of his religion as the quest for Truth. At his ashrams, Gandhi encouraged readings from the scriptures of the world. He opposed conversions and wished instead that the Hindu would become a better Hindu, the Muslim a better Muslim and the Christian a better Christian. He had a deep reverence for Jesus, whom he called a supreme *satyagrahi*, but he did not regard Jesus as the only Son of God. 'He is as divine as Krishna or Rama or Muhammad or Zoroaster.'[9] He saw Jesus' death on the cross as a supreme example of self-giving. After his death, his favourite hymn 'When I survey the wondrous cross' was played on All India Radio.

Gandhi had views on almost all subjects, including diet, mudpacks and nature cures.[10] He tried to live as simply as possible and my lasting impression of his room, which has been preserved at the ashram in Ahmedabad, is of its extreme simplicity and his lack of material posses-sions. But he realised this was not easy. Gandhi asked himself, 'Was I to destroy all the cupboards of books I had?' Although Cottage industries continue in India, its economic growth has been based on industriali-sation of which he would not have approved. Indeed in India there is more criticism of some aspects of his teaching than elsewhere. His early marriage coloured his attitude to sex. His treatment of his wife Kasturbai often seems to have been unkind, although he said 'Woman is the incarnation of ahimsa or infinite love... It is given to mothers to teach the art of peace to the warring world thirsting for that nectar.'[11] Gandhi was aware that he had failed his eldest son - whose story is told in the film *My Father Gandhi* - who died as a destitute soon after his father's assassination.

The continuing influence of Gandhi is widespread and diverse. Perhaps most important of all is the hope that he inspires that moral values are the essential basis on which a healthy and non-violent society should be built. 'When I despair,' he said, 'I remember that all through history the way of truth and love has always won. There have been tyrants and murderers and for a time they seemed invincible, but in the end, they always fail – think of it – always.'[12] This hope never failed him and as he himself said, 'I can see that in the midst of death life persists, in the midst of untruth truth persists, in the midst of darkness light persists.'

CHAPTER NOTES

1. M.K. Gandhi, *An Autobiography or The Story of My Experiments with Truth*, Ahmedabad, Navajivan Publishing House, 1927 (Reprint 2000), p. 37.

2. *An Autobiography*, p. 94.

3. *Nishkarma karma.*

4. See Peter D Bishop, *A Technique for Loving*, SCM Press 1981, p. 51ff and p. 83.

5. *The Selected Writings of Mahatma Gandhi*, Vol. III, Ahmedabad, 1968, 157.

6. *Harijan*, 1.9.1940. See also M. K Gandhi, *For Pacifists*, Ed Bharatan Kumarappa, Ahmedabad, Navajivan Publishing House, 1949.

7. M K Gandhi, *Non-violence in Peace and War*, Garland Publishing, Ahmedabad, 1948-9.

8. M K Gandhi, *My Religion*, Navajivan Publishing House, Ahmedabad, 1955, p. 52.

9. M K Gandhi, *Christian Missions*, p. 112.

10. A good anthology of Gandhi's sayings and writings is *The Mind of Mahatma Gandhi*, Ed R K Prabhu and U R Rao, 1945.

11. *Harijan*, 24-2-40, p. 13.

12. *Autobiography* from Wikipedia.

82

Albert Schweitzer

Albert Schweitzer, who was an outstanding theologian and a brilliant organist, is best remembered for his work as a missionary doctor at Lambaréné in Equatorial Africa and for his commitment to 'Reverence for Life.' Although today Christian missionary work in Africa and Asia in the nineteenth and early twentieth century is subject to critical questioning, it was highly influential and Schweitzer may be taken as a representative of this movement.

Albert, who was born on January 14th, 1875, was the second child of the pastor of the small evangelical Christian congregation of Günsbach in a predominantly Catholic area of Upper Alsace. Although now in France, Alsace-Lorraine was incorporated into the German Empire after France's defeat in the Franco-German War of 1870-71 and was therefore under German control during Schweitzer's childhood and early adult life. Alsace-Lorraine was returned to France in 1919 after World War I.

Albert said that he had a happy childhood, clouded only by his father's frequent illnesses. His father began to give him music lessons when he was only five and by the age of eight Albert was playing the organ. Albert's grandfather had been greatly interested in organs and organ-building. Albert was only nine when he first played the organ for a service at Günsbach. He began his education at the Günsbach village school and later moved to the Gymnasium at Müllhausen in Alsace, during which time he lodged with his great uncle who was his godfather. His chief interests were history and natural science as well as organ music. Before going on to Strasbourg University in the autumn of 1893, Schweitzer spent time in Paris where he received tuition in organ playing from the famous French organist and composer Charles Marie Widor (1844-1937). At Strasbourg University, Schweitzer studied Theology and Philosophy. His own reading of the Gospels convinced him, against the accepted scholarly interpretation at that time, that 'Jesus had announced no kingdom that was to be founded and realised in the natural world by Himself and the believers, but one that was to be expected as coming with the almost immediate dawn of a super-natural age.'[1] This was later to become the thesis of his famous book *The*

Quest for the Historical Jesus. Schweitzer continued his musical studies and played the organ sometimes at St William's Church in Strasbourg, which was a centre for the growing interest in the music of Bach.

In 1898 he received his doctorate in philosophy and began to lecture on the subject. In the following year he also gained his doctorate in theology. At the same time, he was a preacher at St Nicholas Church.

Schweitzer made his name as a theologian with his masterly study *Von Reimarus zu Wrede* (1906), which was translated into English as *The Quest for the Historical Jesus* (1910). The book was a thorough summary of nearly two hundred years of critical study of the life of Jesus. John Samuel Reimarus (1694-1768), with whom he began, assumed that Jesus shared the expectations of his Jewish contemporaries that the Messiah's coming was imminent. William Wrede, however, with whom Schweitzer ended his study, denied that Jesus had any eschatological expectation about the end of the world and moreover denied that Jesus actually thought of himself as the Messiah – it was a title given to him by his disciples after his death. Schweitzer summarised many other studies, suggesting in a well know phrase, that scholars looked into the deep well of history and saw in Jesus a reflection of themselves.

Schweitzer, who held that the Gospels of Mark and Matthew are historically reliable, argued strongly that Jesus did share the 'eschatological Messianic thought-world of late Judaism.'[2] Jesus was, consequently, mistaken in his expectation that the world was about to come to an end. His message of love had therefore to be disentangled from the thought world of his day and re-clothed in the world-view of today.[3] Schweitzer dismissed speculation about who Jesus was as unhelpful. The only thing that Jesus required of his followers was that they should actively and passively prove themselves men who 'had been compelled by Him to rise from being as the world to being other than the world, and thereby partakers of his peace.'[4] Schweitzer ended his book with these well-known words:

'As one unknown and nameless He comes to us, just as on the shore of the lake he approached these men who knew not who he was. His words are the same, "Follow Thou Me!" and He puts us to tasks which He has to carry out in our age. He commands. And to those who obey, be they wise or simple, He will reveal Himself through all that they are privileged to experience in His fellowship of peace and activity, of struggle and suffering, till they come to know, as an inexpressible secret, Who He is ...'[5]

His book transformed critical New Testament studies by putting the question of eschatology (the end of the world) at the centre of debate. Schweitzer also suggested that a historical biography of Jesus was impossible. His views have been much argued about and are now rejected by a number of scholars, but he set the agenda for New Testament studies for much of the twentieth century. It is now widely recognised that the Messianic expectations of Jesus' contemporaries were far more varied than Schweitzer allowed. A later book on *The Mysticism of Paul the Apostle* (1931) again emphasises the eschatological context of Paul's thought.

In the same year that his major theological work was published, Schweitzer's important study of John Sebastian Bach also appeared. Later, he worked with Vidor, on editing the works of Bach.

Schweitzer maintained both his musical and theological interest throughout his life and in later years lectured and gave organ recitals to raise money for his missionary work. In the same year that his works on Jesus and Bach were published, he announced his intention to become a missionary doctor and devote his life to philanthropic work – indeed, to devote himself as had written, 'to the tasks which Jesus has to carry out in our age.'

Initially, Schweitzer thought of working with tramps and discharged prisoners – but then he came upon an article in a magazine of the Paris Missionary Society about the 'needs of the Congo Mission.' The writer, after saying that there were not enough people to carry on the work in Gabon, hoped that his appeal would bring some of those 'on whom the Master's eyes already rested,' to offer themselves for this urgent task. As Schweitzer said, 'My search was over.'[6] Instead of talking about the religion of love, Schweitzer now wanted to put it into practice.

Schweitzer devoted himself with characteristic energy for the next six years to the study of medicine. There were, however, some doubts among members of the Paris Missionary Society whether Schweitzer was sufficiently orthodox for them to sponsor him. On his promise not to say anything that would cause offence to missionaries or their converts – 'd'être muet comme une carpe'[7] - Schweitzer's offer to work at Lambaréné, at his own expense, was accepted. Once in Africa, he was soon invited to preach and share in the ministry of the Church there.

By 1913, Schweitzer and his wife Hélène Bresslau, an accomplished scholar, who had trained as a nurse, whom he had married in 1912, were ready to leave. They said goodbye to Günsbach on Good Friday 1913 and embarked at Bordeaux on March 26th - with their seventy packing cases and a piano, presented by the Paris Bach Society! They were given a hearty welcome when they reached Lambaréné, which was then in the Gabon province of French Equatorial Africa. On the forested banks of the Ogowe River, with the help of the locals, Schweitzer built a hospital. Keeping a close eye on every detail, his style was both patriarchal and business-like. He was quickly besieged by sick people – some travelling as much as two hundred miles to seek his help.

War, however, was soon to interrupt his work. As a German alien working in French territory he was interned and then brought back to France as a prisoner of war – during which time he set to work on his *Philosophy of Civilization* (1923), in which he describes his personal philosophy of 'Reverence for Life.'

It was not until 1924 that he returned to Africa, reaching Lambaréné on Easter Eve. For health reasons, his wife stayed in Europe. Most of the buildings had collapsed or been buried by grass and creepers. The hospital was rebuilt, with Schweitzer acting as a 'doctor in the mornings and as a master-builder in the afternoons.'[8] Later the hospital was rebuilt on a better site, but because of the possibility of floods, it had to be erected on piles. When the new enlarged hospital was finished, early in 1927, Schweitzer says that he was greeted at every turn with the words, 'It is a good hut, Doctor, a good hut.'[9] Then land was cleared on which fruit and vegetables were grown. At last Schweitzer had a chance to return to Europe.

Much of the following two years Schweitzer spent travelling, giving lectures and organ recitals. He also recruited doctors and nurses for the hospital. His spare time was spent finishing his book *The Mysticism of Paul the Apostle*. Schweitzer insisted that Paul's writings had to be understood in the context of Jewish Messianic speculation and more specifically Paul's belief that Jesus was the Messiah whose return was imminent. Schweitzer rejected the view common at that time that Paul's thought was Hellenistic. 'There is in St Paul, no Greek element at all. He does, however, give the Christian belief a form in which it can be assimilated by the Greek spirit.'[10] For Paul the mystical union with Christ was essentially an ethical one.

In 1929, Schweitzer returned again to Lambaréné. This time his wife accompanied him, although she had to return, the following year, because of her health.

In 1932, Schweitzer returned to Frankfurt to give the address at the city's celebration to mark the one hundredth anniversary of Goethe's death. He went back to Africa the following year. In the year 1934, six hundred and twenty two operations were performed at the hospital. Later that year, Schweitzer was again in Europe and delivered the Hibbert Lectures in Oxford on *Religion in Modern Civilization* and the Gifford Lectures in Edinburgh on *The Problem of Natural Philosophy and Natural Ethics*. In 1937 he went back to Africa for the sixth time. To his delight, he came upon 'a spring of water which never runs dry.'[11] Schweitzer returned to Europe in 1939, but with war imminent, he immediately went back to be with his people in Lambaréné. Many of the natives asked him, 'How can it be possible that whites, who brought us the Gospel of Love, are now murdering each other, and throwing to the winds the commands of the Lord Jesus?' A question, to which Schweitzer says he was helpless to provide an answer.[12] Somehow, amidst all the difficulties and deprivations of war, Schweitzer struggled on and kept the hospital going. It was ten years before he could come back to Günsbach for some respite from his unremitting toil.

In the following years he kept travelling back and forth from Lambaréné to Europe as long as he could. He paid one visit to the USA. Schweitzer died on September 4, 1965 at his beloved hospital in Lambaréné, Gabon. His grave, on the banks of the Ogooue River, is marked by a cross he made himself.

In 1952, Schweitzer was awarded the Nobel Peace Prize for his message of 'Reverence for Life.' His 'Problem of Peace' lecture is considered one of the best speeches ever given.

From 1952 until his death Schweitzer worked against nuclear tests and nuclear weapons with Albert Einstein and Bertrand Russell. In 1957 and 1958 he broadcast four speeches over Radio Oslo which were published in *Peace or Atomic War*. In 1957, Schweitzer was one of the founders of The Committee for a Sane Nuclear Policy. On April 23, 1957, Schweitzer made his "Declaration of Conscience" speech, which was broadcast to the world over Radio Oslo, pleading for the abolition of nuclear weapons. He ended his speech, saying

'The end of further experiments with atom bombs would be like the early sunrays of hope for which suffering humanity is longing.'

In describing his belief in 'Reverence for life', Schweitzer wrote that two perceptions cast their shadow over his life. One was the realization that the world is inexplicably mysterious and full of suffering. The second was the fact that he had been born into a period of spiritual decadence. He hoped by encouraging people to think to make them less shallow and more moral. The scepticism of the modern world, he insisted could not be met by authoritative truth, which merely covers up the problem. 'It is only by confidence in our ability to reach truth by our own individual thinking that we are capable of accepting truth from outside' and can counter the prevalent scepticism. The need was for elemental thinking, which starts from the fundamental questions about the meaning of life. The Mystical tradition was elemental but its ethical content was too slight. 'The truth of a world-view must be proved by the fact that the spiritual relation to life and the universe into which that world view brings us makes us into inward men with an active ethic.'

'The Idea of Reverence for Life', he held,

'offers itself as a realistic answer to the realistic question of how man and the world are related to each other. Of the world man knows only that everything that exists is, like himself, a manifestation of the Will-to-Live. With this world he stands in a relation of passivity and activity. On the one had he is subordinate to the course of events which is given in this totality of life; on the other hand he is capable of affecting the life which comes within his reach by hampering or promoting it, by destroying or maintaining it.'

Reverence for Life, Schweitzer wrote, contained Resignation, World and Life-Affirmation and the Ethical. 'It is the ethic of Love. It is the ethic of Jesus.' 'The stronger the reverence for natural life, the stronger grows also that for spiritual life.' 'To the person who is truly ethical all life is sacred.' This meant, as Schweitzer recognised, the inescapable choice of sacrificing one life in order to save others. 'Every time I have under the microscope the germs that cause the disease, I cannot but reflect that I have to sacrifice this life in order to save other life.' Schweitzer was much respected for putting his theory into practice in his own life. He was, for instance, a well-known cat lover, who, although left-handed would write with his right hand rather than disturb the cat who would sleep on his left arm.

Schweitzer claimed that his emphasis on Reverence for Life was in harmony with the essential message of Jesus. He considered his work as a medical missionary in Africa to be his response to Jesus' call to become 'fishers of men.' He also hoped it would be a small recompense for the historic guilt of European colonizers, which he strongly denounced, asking

'Who can describe the injustice and cruelties that in the course of centuries they [the coloured peoples] have suffered at the hands of Europeans? . . . If a record could be compiled of all that has happened between the white and the coloured races, it would make a book containing numbers of pages which the reader would have to turn over unread because their contents would be too horrible.[13]

Schweitzer was a towering personality – an immensley strong man, physically, mentally and in his convictions. He said he could not have survived without strong nerves. His capacity for long and sustained hard work was remarkable. He cared deeply for the people of Gabon where he worked, but like many missionaries, his attitude was paternalistic and the medical care might seem rather basic compared to that of a modern hospital. Yet it is a mistake to ignore the great service of many medical and educational missionaries, even if their assumptions of cultural and spiritual superiority are unacceptable today. Schweitzer also said that the hospital should relate to the culture of the people whom it served. Schweitzer's comments on other world religions show a lack of personal knowledge and sympathy.

Yet while criticisms can be made of both his writings and his work, they should not obscure the powerful contribution he made to music, theology, medical care for the people of Gabon and as an advocate of nuclear disamament and racial justic. His devotion to Jesus may have been unorthodox but his commitment of the ethic of love that Jesus proclaimed has few parallels

CHAPTER NOTES

1. Albert Schweitzer, *My Life and Thought*, London, Guild Books, 1955 (George Allen and Unwin, 1933), p.16. See also his, *On the Edge of the Primeval Forest* and *More from the Primeval Forest*, London, Collins, Fontana Books, 1956 and 1958.
2. *My Life and Thought*, p. 49.
3. *My Life and Thought*, p. 53.
4. *My Life and Thought*, p. 57.
5. *Von Reimarus zu Wrede*, 1906. *The Quest for the Historical Jesus*, Translated by W. Montgomery, First English Edition, London, A. & C. Black, 1910, p. 403.
6. *My Life and Thought*, p. 83.
7. 'To be as silent as a fish', *My Life and Thought*, p. 129.
8. *My Life and Thought*, p. 182.
9. *My Life and Thought*, p. 186.
10. *My Life and Thought*, p. 191.
11. *My Life and Thought*, p. 226.
12. *My Life and Thought*, p. 237.
13. Material in this and the preceding paragraph is taken from the Epilogue of *My Life and Thought*.

83

Aurobindo

Sri Aurobindo, a poet, philosopher and seer, was at first a champion of Indian nationalism. After a decisive spiritual experience, he abandoned politics. He then concentrated on developing a philosophy in which the concept of evolution, given a spiritual meaning, has a central role. Through the practice of Integral Yoga, humans can prepare for the full realization of the Supreme Being, which is the ultimate goal of the cosmic process. His approach has significant similarities to that of The French Catholic priest Fr Pierre Teilhard de Chardin.

Sri Aurobindo Akroyd Ghose (pronounced 'Ghosh') was born in Calcutta on August 15th, 1872. His father, Dr Ghose, had lived in Britain and had studied at Aberdeen University. He was determined that his children should have a British education. Sri Aurobindo was, therefore sent, first to Loreto Convent school in Darjeeling and then to England. There he lived at the home of a clergyman, who was also his tutor. He gained entry to St Paul's School in London, where he excelled at Greek and Latin and won a scholarship to King's College, Cambridge. There he studied classical philology and learned three modern European languages.

He returned to India in 1893 and had various administrative and teaching jobs. In the early years of the twentieth century the Viceroy Lord Curzon insisted on dividing the unwieldy Bengal Presidency, which by then had a population of 78 millions. There was widespread opposition, and relations between the educated Indians and the British were irreparably damaged, although the partition was, in fact, eventually revoked. Sri Aurobindo took an active role in opposing the Partition. He immersed himself in politics and became a leader of a group of Indian nationalists known as Extremists, who were willing to use violence to obtain complete independence. He helped to found the Jugantar party, became editor of a nationalist Bengali newspaper, and began a serious study of Indian history and culture. In 1908, he was imprisoned on suspicion of plotting armed revolt. In court, the English trial judge happened to have been a fellow student at Cambridge. His defence lawyer said that long after the trial, Sri Aurobindo would be remembered as 'a poet of patriotism' and that he was standing 'not only before the Bar of the court, but before the High Court of History.' Sri Aurobindo was acquitted. Soon afterwards, he settled in the French colony of Pondicherry.

During his time in prison, he had a decisive spiritual experience. While studying the Bhagavad Gita, the most famous Hindu devotional writing, he heard a Divine voice, saying,

> 'Something has been shown to you in this year of seclusion, something about which you had your doubts and it is the truth of the Hindu religion. It is this religion that I am raising up before the world. It is this that I have perfected... When you go forth, speak to your nation, that it is for the *Sanatana Dharma* ('Holy Teaching') that they arise... I am giving them freedom for the service of the world... It is for the *Dharma* that India exists.'[1]

Philosophy and Hindu teaching now absorbed his energies. After four years of concentrated study at Pondicherry, he started a monthly review, *Arya*, in which most of his writings first appeared in serialised form. These were eventually revised and published. His most important work is the lengthy *The Life Divine* (1940). His much shorter *The Mother* (1928) was a guide to the practice of Integral Yoga. His greatest literary achievement was the blank verse spiritual poem, *Savitiri* (1950), which has about 24,000 lines. Much of his correspondence with disciples was published in three volumes of *Letters on Yoga* and there were other works on aspects of Hinduism.

In Pondicherry, Sri Aurobindo established an ashram, which I visited many years ago. The running of this, especially after Sri Aurobindo retired into seclusion in 1926, was largely in the hands of 'the Mother' as Mirra Richard (b. Alfassa) came to be known. She was born in Paris in 1878 to Turkish and Egyptian parents. She first visited Pondicherry in 1914 and settled there in 1920. When families with children joined the ashram, she established the Sri Aurobindo International Centre of Education, which pioneered significant educational developments that have a similarity to those advanced by Rudolf Steiner. The mother herself lived at the ashram, where she died on November 17th, 1973. Her room and that of Sri Aurobindo are visited by devotees. Sri Aurobindo, who died in 1950, lived to see an independent India. The Mother did much to facilitate the merging of Pondicherry into the new India.

In the 1960s, she started an international township, known as Auroville, near Pondicherry. Auroville, which was sponsored by UNESCO, is intended to be a 'universal town where men and women of all countries are able to live in peace and progressive harmony above all creeds, all politics and all nationalities. The purpose of Auroville is to realise human unity.' The Charter says that

1. Auroville belongs to nobody in particular.
   Auroville belongs to humanity as a whole.
   But to live in Auroville, one must be the willing servitor
   of the Divine Consciousness.
2. Auroville will be a place of unending education, of constant progress, and a youth that never ages.
3 Auroville wants to be the bridge between the past and the future. Taking advantage of all discoveries from without and from within, Auroville will boldly spring towards future realisations.
4. Auroville will be a site of material and spiritual researches for a living embodiment of an actual Human Unity.[2]

Auroville now has about 1,700 members from 35 countries.

The concept of evolution is central to Sri Aurobindo's philosophy. 'The sum and substance of all he says', writes K N Gupta, 'is that man is growing and has to grow in consciousness till he reaches the complete and perfect consciousness, not only in his individual, but in his collective, that is to say, social life. In fact the growth of consciousness is the supreme secret of life, the master key to earthly evolution.'[3]

Sri Aurobindo held that at the heart of all things there is a Consciousness-Force that is evolving to ever higher forms of being. Just as there is evidence of a physical evolution, lower forms of life evolving into higher forms, so there is an inner evolution, the evolution of the Spirit, which is at work at the various stages of existence. No evolution was possible, however, unless that which evolves is already present in the process at every stage. The ascent, therefore, Sri Aurobindo said, presupposes a primordial descent of the Eternal Spirit in earthly forms.

There is therefore a double process. The Divine descends from pure existence through the play of Consciousness-Force and Bliss and the creative medium of Supermind into cosmic being: we ascend from matter through a developing life, soul, mind and the illuminating medium of Supermind towards the divine being. The knot of the two, the higher and lower hemispheres, is where mind and Supermind meet with a veil between them. As the veil rends, the mind recovers its divine light in the all-comprehending Supermind.

This development is the destiny of humanity as a whole, although it must be realised in the individual. Sri Aurobindo wrote,

> 'Not individuals only... in time the race also in a general rule of being and living, if not in all its members, can have hope, if it develops a sufficient will, to rise beyond the imperfections of our present very undivine nature and to ascend at least to a superior humanity, to rise nearer, even if it cannot absolutely reach a divine manhood or supermanhood.' [4]

Sri Aurobindo envisages the emergence of a new humanity beyond the present stage of evolution. At first a few will attain the gnosis in different parts of the world. Gradually the number will increase and small islets of Gnostic communities will be established. Although withdrawn from the mass of humanity, these communities will exercise a powerful influence on the rest of humanity, so that it too may enter into the destiny that awaits it from eternity.

There are interesting parallels between the thinking of Sri Aurobindo and Teilhard de Chardin, who is the subject of the next chapter. When Teilhard was told of Sri Aurobindo's work, he commented, 'this is comparable to my own work, but for the Indian tradition.'[5] Sri Aurobindo spoke of 'the hope of the kingdom of heaven within us and the city of God upon earth.'[6] Teilhard wrote of the need 'to promote in equal measure the mastery of the world and the kingdom of God.'[7] R C Zaehner (1913-74), a Spalding Professor of Eastern Religions at Oxford, wrote that

'In their separate traditions, they represent something totally new in mystical religion. Both not only accepted the theory of evolution but enthusiastically acclaimed it, indeed were almost obsessed by it... Both were deeply dissatisfied with organised religion and both were vitally concerned not only with individual salvation or "liberation" but also with the collective salvation of mankind.'[8]

Despite their differences, Zaehner highlights areas of agreement. First, spirit takes precedence over matter. Secondly, if this is so, it follows that spirit must always have been present in matter in a rudimentary form. Third evolution is a progressive unification, an ever-increasing spiritualization of matter. Fourth, the goal of evolution must be the integration of matter in a final harmony and its convergence on to a centre of attraction, which is supra-mental and divine. Fifthly, the only conceivable agent of such convergence is an as 'yet unfounded law of love.'[9]

The Integral Yoga that Sri Aurobindo taught, drawing eclectically on various traditions, was intended to enable the practitioner to attain conscious identity with the Divine, the True Self and to transform his body, mind and life so as to become a fit instrument for a divine life on earth. He recognised that the spiritual discipline was long and difficult. The guiding principle is complete surrender to the Divine, as only the Divine can transform and divinise human consciousness. Sri Aurobindo spoke of a 'triple labour of aspiration, rejection and surrender.'

Sri Aurobindo, with the importance he attached to art and culture, recognised that profound and beautiful poetry, sinking 'deep into the soul' could be a powerful aid to the change of consciousness.

Sri Aurobindo was deeply versed in the culture and scriptures of India. He emphasised the hidden spiritual meaning of the Vedas – the earliest Hindu scriptures. He wrote in *The Foundations of Indian Culture*:

'The fundamental idea of all Indian religion is one common to the highest thinking everywhere. The supreme truth of all is that there is a Being or an existence beyond the mental and physical appearances we contact here. Beyond mind, life and body there is a Spirit and Self containing all that is finite and infinite... a supreme Absolute, originating and supporting all that is transient...All life and thought are in the end a means of progress towards self-realisation and God-realisation.'[10]

It is important to remember that Sri Aurobindo was writing at a time when the theory of evolution was thought to have undermined religious belief and when scientific materialism left no room for the spiritual. In his thinking Sri Aurobindo integrated Eastern and Western religious traditions. His spiritual interpretation of evolution has offered an optimistic way of understanding the whole cosmic process as motivated by Divine Love. He has influenced creative thinkers in many parts of the world and in India many people view him as one of the great *rishis* or spiritual seers of modern times.

CHAPTER NOTES

1. Quoted by T M P Mahadevan, *Outlines of Hinduism*, p. 232.
2. From the Auroville website. www.auroville.org.
3. K N Gupta, *The Message of Sri Aurobindo and the Ashram*, Pondicherry, 1955, p. 2.
4. Aurobindo, *The Life Divine*, p. 854, quoted in Marcus Braybrooke, *Together to the Truth*, Madras Christian Literature Society, 1971, p. 138.
5. A comment to Jacque Masui, quoted in Ursula King, *Towards A New Mysticism*, London, Collins, 1980, p. 96.
6. Sri Aurobindo, *The Human Cycle*, Pondicherry 1962, p.165.
7. Teilhard de Chardin, *Writings in the Time of War*, London, Collins, 1968, p. 91.
8. R C Zaehner, *Evolution in Religion: A Study in Sri Aurobindo and Pierre Teilhard de Chardin*, Oxford, Clarendon Press, 1971, pp. 3-4.
9. *Evolution in Religion*, pp. 37-8.
10. Sri Aurobindo, *The Foundations of Indian Culture*, p. 125.

84

Teilhard de Chardin

Pierre Teilhard de Chardin, a distinguished palaeontologist and theologian, tried through his writings, mostly published after his death, to bring the two worlds of science and religion together.

Teilhard's unitive vision covered an amazingly wide canvas. Professor Ursula King has said of Teilhard that

'His work contains challenging reflections on God and the world, the figure of Christ, science and religion, on ecological responsibilities, interfaith encounter, the greater unification of humanity, the place of the feminine and of love in creating greater unity, and the central importance of spirituality and mysticism in religious life. His new mysticism of action is directed to both the creative transformation of the outer and the inner world and the deepest communion with the living God of love, intimately present throughout the creation. More than anything else it is his powerful affirmation of the Incarnation and his vision of the universal cosmic Christ within an evolutionary perspective that reaffirm the core of the Christian faith for our scientific age.'[1]

Pierre was born on May 1st 1881, in the volcanic Auvergne region in central France. His father, a gentleman farmer, was interested in geology and encouraged his children to collect fossils, stones and other specimens of nature. His mother was a devout and holy woman. So from an early age he found himself 'rooted in two domains of life usually considered antagonistic.' 'Through my education and intellectual formation,' he wrote, 'I belong to the "children of heaven", while by temperament and owing to my professional studies I am "a child of earth."' His life's work was to seek to reconcile these two worlds and he tried not to erect any walls between these two areas of his interior life. 'I have found that far from destroying each other, each has served to reinforce the other.'[2]

Teilhard received a good classical and scientific education at the Jesuit College of Mongré, where he boarded from the age of 10 to 18. For some of the time, because the Jesuits were exiled from France, he studied at Hastings, on the south coast of England. He entered the Jesuit novitiate at 18 and was ordained priest at the age of 21 in 1912. During World War I, however, he chose to be a stretcher bearer rather than a chaplain. He was awarded the Legion of Honour for his bravery. Before the War, he had taught for a time at the Jesuit College in Cairo. After the War, he obtained a doctorate for his scientific research and then taught geology at the Catholic Institute of Paris. In 1923 he was invited by a fellow Jesuit researcher to join a fossil expedition to the Ordos desert in China. It was a decisive experience and the visit also led him to write his 'Mass on the World.' Subsequently, he spent most of his scientific career in China, including the period of World War II. It was in China that he wrote *Le Milieu Divin* (1927) and *The Phenomenon of Man* (1938-40), both of which were published after his death.[3]

After the Second World War, Teilhard returned to Paris, but opposition in Church circles made life so difficult that he accepted a research position in the USA, spending his last years at the Wenner-Gren Foundation in New York City. He made two archaeological expeditions to South Africa. He died on Easter Sunday, April 10th, 1955. Only twelve people attended his funeral.

His scientific work was already recognised. He had been involved in the discovery of Peking Man's skull. In addition, he enlarged the field of knowledge on Asia's sedimentary deposits and stratigraphical correlations, and also on the dates of its fossils. Publication of his religious and philosophical writings was banned by Church authorities during his lifetime. After his death they quickly attracted wide attention, although this has faded in recent years.

Teilhard's writings are an attempt to heal his inner tension between what he called his 'cosmic sense' and his 'Christic sense.' At first, he could find no way in which to bring the two together. In time, he came to see that Christ had a cosmic function and that the evolution of the cosmos had to be seen as a movement orientated upon a cosmic central point. 'With the passing years I have been aware, with ever greater clarity and depth of feeling, of that confluence as the key to every advance – and, be it said, to every conflict too – in my inner life.'[4] He believed in science, he said, but science had only looked at the world from *without*. It was necessary also to look from *within*.

It was as a student that he read *L'Évolution Créatrice* (*Creative Evolution*) by Henri Bergson (1859-1941), which was published in 1907, and which interpreted evolution as the result of the continuous operation of an *élan vital*. This book helped Teilhard understand the meaning of evolution for the Christian faith. He held that the stuff of which the universe is formed increases in complexity as it evolves. It also increases in consciousness. Humanity is one peak in the process, which moves through ever more closely knit social relationships towards the Omega Point, which from a theological standpoint, he identified with Christ. Evolution, he argued, results from an inward tendency rather than adaptations to the environment induced by the external struggle for the survival of the fittest.

There have been, in Teilhard's view, several critical points in the curve of evolution, such as the primordial emergence of matter, followed by the emergence of amphibians, then reptiles and then mammals. Life moves constantly forward in a spiral from one zoological layer to another, with something always carried forward. At the heart of the process, carrying it forward is the rise of consciousness. Consciousness is to be found everywhere, but in man – a being who is the object of his own reflection - evolution takes a new step forward. Teilhard wrote,

> 'Can we ... hesitate to admit that man's possession of it [self-reflection] constitutes a radical advance on all forms of life that have gone before him? Admittedly the animal knows: *But it cannot know that it knows:* that is certain... We are separated by a chasm – or a threshold – which it [the animal] cannot cross. .. It is not merely a matter of change of degree, but of a change of nature.'[5]

Every aspect of life – sexual attraction, reproduction, and the struggle for survival is changed as the threshold of reflection is crossed.

The evolutionary process, however, does not stop with human beings. The growth of consciousness means ever greater interaction and unification. Teilhard refers to this as the 'noosphere.' The word, which Teilhard invented from the Greek word for mind, means literally 'the realm of the mind.' But for Teilhard it meant much more. The noosphere is 'a layer of thinking and interacting that connects people around the whole globe.' It 'marks a new stage in human evolution' and binds people together by love – a universal love for the whole. 'How is it', he wrote, 'that we are not more sensitive to the presence of something greater than ourselves moving forward within us and in our midst?'[6]

This new stage in evolution towards the ultimate goal or Omega point is not automatic and the outcome cannot be taken for granted. It requires human co-operation, responsibility and co-creativity. The model of the noosphere provides a particularly creative perspective on racial, cultural, and religious pluralism in the new context of global complexity.[7]

Teilhard unites his commitment to evolution and to Christianity by seeing Christ as the Omega point - when science and mysticism fuse together. Christ not only embodies universal love, but also is linked not just to the moral universe but organically to the cosmos. This gives meaning to the words at the beginning of St John's Gospel that all things were made through the Logos [Christ].[8] Emphasizing the Incarnation of Christ – and therefore God's presence in the physical – Teilhard says that it is through Christ that the world acquires ultimate unity and cohesion. Indeed, Christ is the very meaning of the whole evolutionary process and the source of power and energy, which draws all things to itself.[9] As a result, whereas Orthodox Christians speak of two natures in Christ: the human and the divine, Teilhard added a third, 'the cosmic.' Indeed, he once described himself as 'the apostle of the cosmic (or universal) Christ.'

To see Christ as the Omega point, meant that Christianity was of vital importance. The Catholic Church, in particular, was intended to be a channel of the essential unitive power of love. It was, Teilhard said, a 'phylum' – a scientific term used of the next class up in the animal kingdom. Teilhard, however, increasingly recognised the importance of other religions and of their coming together in what is now known as the interfaith movement. At the inaugural meeting of *L'Union des Croyants* - the French sister organization of the World Congress of Faiths, which was founded in 1936 by the explorer and mystic Sir Francis Younghusband, who is the subject of the next chapter - a paper written by Teilhard was read by René Grousset. (Teilhard was not allowed to speak publicly). He spoke of *L'Union des Croyants* as 'the summit movement of tomorrow.'[10] Despite their differences, he said that people of different faiths could come together to build a common future. *L'Union des Croyants* could draw together and rekindle the faith of those who in varying forms believed:

'That there is a future and a goal for the world, ahead of Man;

That this future and this goal depends on the union, at once organic and mental, which will establish itself some day on our planet between all individuals, all races and all nations on Earth;

And that this union itself, so conditioned as it is by the progress around us of technology and socialism, can only be achieved with the vision and under the influence of a supreme centre, which is at once attractive and personal.'[11]

Certainly in his early days, Teilhard was critical of Eastern religions, especially the Advaita or non-Dual teaching of Sankara. Later, however, although he spoke of a 'universal' Christ, he recognised that humanity's understanding of the Divine was incomplete and on-going. There is a note in one of his writings that 'Christ would not be complete if he did not integrate Shiva.'[12] In *The Future of Man,* he wrote, 'A tendency towards unification is everywhere manifest and especially in the different branches of religion. We are looking for something that will draw us together, below or above the level of that which divides... Not through external pressure but only from an inward impulse can the unity of Mankind endure and grow.'[13]

Although Teilhard's thinking may appear speculative and abstract, he made a close link between mysticism and action – partly because the evolving future was dependent upon human choices and actions. As Ursula King has written, 'For Teilhard all forms of mysticism found their highest expression in a mysticism of action, a dynamic and activating centre burning with the fire of love, a mysticism deeply grounded in Christian incarnational theology.'[14]

Teilhard's views were regarded with suspicion by Catholic authorities. It was felt that he did not take the reality of evil seriously enough and that in his emphasis on Christ's incarnation, he neglected Christ's atoning death. His views were never actually condemned by the Vatican but advice was given to read his books with caution. After his death, as his books became known, there was at first considerable excitement among some Christians. His ideas had some influence on Vatican II and helped to shape the important document *Gaudium et Spes*. Although less attention is paid to him today, much of his thinking was seminal and his ideas will continue to inspire Christian thinkers.

One of those who has been most influenced by Teilhard was the American Passionist priest Father Thomas Berry (b. 1914), a leading environmental theologian or 'Earth-scholar', as he prefers to call himself. Berry insists that religions have to recognise that that 'the universe is now experienced as an irreversible time-developmental process... Not so much a cosmos as a cosmogenesis.'[15] This implies that human beings are co-creators with God. For weal or woe, the future is in human hands. 'The first great contribution this new perspective makes to religious consciousness', writes Father Berry, 'is the sense of participating in the creation process itself. We bear within us the impress of every transformation through which the universe and the planet have passed.'[16] 'We are earthlings. The Earth is our origin, our nourishment, our support, our guide. Our spirituality itself is Earth-derived.'[17]

This new appreciation of our part as humans in the evolving cosmos means that human beings have to see themselves as part of the earth community and recognise that all life is bound together. Just as astronauts, such as David Brown and Kalpana Chawla, who both died in the Columbia spacecraft disaster, emphasised the magical beauty of planet Earth, seen as a whole from space, so mystics who have explored inner space proclaim the same message of unity. Teilhard de Chardin himself said, 'I live at the heart of a single, unique Element, the Centre of the Universe, and present in each part of it; personal Love and cosmic Power.'[18]

CHAPTER NOTES

1. 'Teilhard de Chardin' by Ursula King in *The Oxford Companion to Christian Thought*, p. 696.
2. These remarks are from an essay Teilhard de Chardin wrote in 1934, which is quoted by N M Wildiers in *An Introduction to Teilhard de Chardin*, London, Collins Fontana, 1968, p. 13.
3. The English translation of *The Phenomenon of Man* was published in 1959 and of *Le Milieu Divin* in 1960.

4. *The Heart of the matter (Le Coeur de la Matière,* 1950) translated by René Hague, , , London, Collins, 1978, p. 24.

5. Quoted by Maurice Keating and H R F Keating in *Understanding Pierre Teilhard de Chardin,* London, Lutterworth Press, 1969, p. 45.

6. *Understanding Pierre Teilhard de Chardin,* p. 47.

7. Ursula King, *Christ in All Things,* London, SCM Press, *passim.*

8. John 1, 3.

9. See further *An Introduction to Teilhard de Chardin,* p. 138.

10. Quoted by Ursula King in *Towards A New Mysticism,* London, Collins, 1980, p. 268.

11. From *Le Congrès Universal des Croyants* by Solange Lemaître in a cyclostyled paper, quoted by Marcus Braybrooke in *Faiths in Fellowship,* London, World Congress of Faiths, 1976, p. 28.

12. Ursula King, *Towards A New Mysticism,* London, Collins, 1980, p. 98.

13. Pierre Teilhard de Chardin, *The Future of Man,* London, Collins, 1965 p. 196-200.

14. Ursula King, *Christ in All Things,* p. 85.

15. Dr Thomas Berry, 'The Cosmology of Religions', in *A Source Book for Earth's Community of Religions,* CoNexus Press, 1995 edtn, p. 95.

16. 'The Cosmology of Religions', p. 96.

17. Thomas Berry quoted in 'The Cosmology of Religions', p. 98. See also, Thomas Berry, 'The Spirituality of the Earth' in *Celebrating Earth Holy Days,* Ed. Susan J Clark, Crossroad, 1992, pp. 69-82.

18. Teilhard de Chardin, quoted in 'The Cosmology of Religions', p. 97.

85

Francis Younghusband

Sir Francis Younghusband, a man of many interests, is best known as an explorer and mystic. He was the first European to cross the Gobi Desert. A pioneer of interfaith fellowship, which has transformed the relationship between religions from competition to co-operation, he founded the World Congress of Faiths in 1936.

Francis Younghusband, perhaps appropriately, was born in India, on 31 May 1863. His mother soon returned with her baby to Bath in England. When Francis was four and a half she left him in the care of two unmarried sisters who imposed a strict Christian discipline on him. In 1873 he travelled to India with his parents, but in 1876 came back to school at Clifton College in Bristol. In 1881 he entered Sandhurst to train as an officer in the British army and in the following year set sail for service in India. The highlights of his military career were his exploration of the Himalayan passes and journeys of exploration to Manchuria. Even at this period, he was already interested in religion and was reading widely.

Younghusband came to public notice when he led a military mission to Tibet in 1903. There is still controversy about the expedition, especially the slaughter of over six hundred scarcely armed Tibetan defenders. Yet, it was after he had reached Lhasa and signed a peace agreement that Younghusband had a decisive spiritual experience.

The day after signing a treaty with the Tibetans, he went off by himself to the mountains, feeling elated by the good will of his former foes. But then, he wrote later, 'elation grew to exultation, exultation to an exaltation which thrilled through me with overpowering intensity... I felt in touch with the flaming heart of the world... A mighty joy-giving Power was at work in the world... Never again could I think evil. Never again could I bear enmity.'[1]

In December 1909, Younghusband sailed back to Britain from India and was not to return there for nearly thirty years. He dabbled in politics and in journalism. He was a member of several London societies, including the Royal Geographical Society, as President of which he supported Mallory's attempt to climb Mt Everest.

Younghusband also continued his interest in religion. He played a big part at the Religions of Empire Conference – the first major inter-faith gathering to be held in Britain - which met in London in 1924. He was also a founding member of the Society for Promoting the Study of Religions, which resulted from that Conference.

It was, however, indirectly a link with the 1893 World's Parliament of Religions, held in Chicago that prompted Younghusband to found the World Congress of Faiths in 1936. There had been no follow up to the World's Parliament of Religions until, in 1933, another, now almost forgotten interfaith gathering, which Younghusband attended, was held in Chicago, in direct imitation of the 1893 event. It was arranged by The Fellowship of Faiths. The organizers, Das Gupta, who was a follower of Rabindranath Tagore, and Charles Weller, a social worker encouraged Younghusband to arrange a similar international congress in London. This he did in 1936, although Younghusband, who liked to be his own boss, soon made clear the independence of the World Congress of Faiths.

When the World Congress of Faiths was convened at University College, London, more than seventy years ago, it was a highly unusual and controversial event. Few religious leaders attended or even gave their support. Younghusband, however, did persuade world-famous scholars, such as Yusuf Ali, translator of the Qur'an, the philosopher C E M Joad, the Buddhist scholar Dr D T Suzuki and the Hindu philosopher Dr Radhakrishnan to participate.

A continuing body was set up, known as the World Congress of Faiths. Conferences were held in Oxford (1937), Cambridge (1938) and Paris (1939). Even during the Second World War, conferences were held and Younghusband started a Chairman's Circular letter, which developed into the journal *Forum* and then *World Faiths* – predecessors of the present journal *Interreligious Insight*. The war, inevitably, stunted the congress, although it backed Bishop Bell's suggestion that the proposed United Nations should have a religious advisory council, for which some people still today are campaigning. Younghusband also focussed on the moral values which are shared by all the great religions - anticipating later work on the Global Ethic. Talk of a new world order was a recurrent theme. Indeed the title of the 1941 conference in Oxford was 'World Religions and World Order.'

Younghusband was active until the end of his life. He was taken ill at the 1942 Birmingham Conference and died a couple of weeks later on 31 July 1942. Friends from different faiths spoke at his memorial service, held at St Martin-in-the-Fields. It was perhaps the first public inter-faith service. The Congress, still inspired by Younghusband's vision, continues its educational work and has encouraged co-operation among the growing number of international interfaith organisations.

Although it was his mystical awareness that inspired Younghusband's deep commitment to interfaith work, he did not dwell on this in the run-up to the 1936 Congress. Instead he talked about his travels in Asia, which had brought him into close contact with Hindus, Muslims, Buddhists and Confucians. 'I had deep converse with them on their religions' he said in a broadcast. 'It forced me to see a beauty in the depths of (their religions).'[2] He also spoke of the time when he had been run over in Belgium. 'No one enquired... whether my religion was Hindu, Muslim or Christian, and if Christian whether I was Orthodox, Catholic or Protestant... They sprang to my help because of their fellow feeling. I was a human like themselves. What hurt me hurt them.'[3]

Nonetheless, it was his mystical awareness that was Younghusband's deepest motivation. One of his books called *Modern Mystics*[4] began with a chapter on Keshub Chander Sen, Ramakrishna and Vivekananda. Younghusband also attended the observation in India of the centenary of Ramakrishna's birth – the conference badge is still in the WCF archives.

Younghusband was a prolific author, who wrote both about his travels and about religion. On his return to England in 1910, Younghusband took part in the two general elections of that year and also wrote two books – *Kashmir*[5] and *India and Tibet*[6]. He also started on a religious book. It was originally to be called *The Inherent Impulse*, but the accident in Belgium led Younghusband to question whether a loving God chose to send suffering. 'Can we', he asked, 'really believe suffering is deliberately caused by a just and merciful Providence for our welfare.' As a result, he revised the book, which was published in 1912, with the title *Within*.[7] Two years later, in his *Mutual Influence*,[8] his most 'humanist' book, he was very critical of Christianity and rejected the doctrine of original sin.

For Younghusband, Jesus Christ was the highest manifestation of God yet known to us in terms of human personality, but he did not accept the unique divinity of Christ. 'Christ', he says in *The Gleam* (1923)[9] 'was plainly a development along the line of the holy men of God.' In a drama called *The Reign of God* that he wrote in 1930, he emphasised Jesus' role as the Inaugurator of the kingdom of God and avoided speculation about the nature of Christ.[10] He saw him as the Leader of a new type of humanity. He went further and in his *Mother World* (1924), which had the subtitle, *in Travail for the Christ that is to be*. The world, he said, was 'groaning and travailing to bring forth a leader.'[11]

Mother World is also interesting because in it Younghusband spoke of the Earth as a self-regulating entity, which seeks an optimal environment for the maintenance of life. Here he anticipated James Lovelock's (b. 1919)'Gaia' theory, which emphasises ecological inter-dependence and sees the planet as a living organism, which defends its own physical integrity.[12] Younghusband thought the world should be seen as a benevolent deity. People are 'in God and God is in them just as the ovum is in the mother and the mother is in it.' His feminizing of the divine principle was, in the 1920s, very radical. The physicist J S Haldane thought the book broke new ground, because it saw the universe as spiritual rather than mechanical.[13]

In *The Living Universe* (1927)[14], Younghusband developed the idea that the Universe is alive. His theme was that the whole universe is spiritual both in its totality and in its parts. The substance of all that is called material is energy and where there is energy there is life and life is spirit. Humans are integral, inescapable units of the World-Soul 'We have the capacity of thrilling in living response to the movement of the Eternal Spirit, which pervades all things.'[15] It is worth noting Younghusband's very considerable knowledge of natural sciences. Younghusband also believed that life on other planets is highly likely.

Today, 'social cohesion' and 'interfaith dialogue' are the watchword. International and national interfaith conferences are common, but for many years, the World Congress of Faiths (WCF) was a solitary voice calling for a fellowship of faiths. Even now few people share the far-sighted vision, which Younghusband expressed in these words:

'When I speak of fellowship I have found subtler and deeper meanings emerge as I study the idea more closely. It is not exactly either friendship, or companionship, or neighbourliness, or co-operation, though these may develop from it. And the sentiment from which it springs is something more than compassion, for compassion concerns itself with unhappiness alone rather than with both happiness and unhappiness. Even sympathy is associated rather with suffering than with enjoyment. At its intensest and highest, fellowship seems to be a communion of spirit greater, deeper, higher, wider, more universal, more fundamental than any of these – than even love.'[16]

The Observer, a distinguished British Sunday newspaper, said in its obituary, 'Sir Francis was sure that a new Renaissance, more glorious than any that went before it, was upon us. This is the marriage of East and West.'[17] It was to be at least another fifty years, however, before others began to talk of such a marriage.

CHAPTER NOTES

1. Francis Younghusband, *Vital Religion*, John Murray, London, 1940, pp.3-5.
2. Quoted in Marcus Braybrooke, *A Wider Vision*, Oxford, Oneworld, 1996, p. 19
3. Quoted in *A Wider Vision* p. 20.
4. Francis Younghusband, *Modern Mystics*, London, John Murray, 1935.
5. Francis Younghusband, *Kashmir*, London, John Murray, 1909.
6. Francis Younghusband, *India and Tibet*, London, John Murray, 1910.
7. Francis Younghusband, *Within*, London, Williams and Norgate, 1912.
8. Francis Younghusband, *Mutual Influence*, London, John Murray, 1915.
9. Francis Younghusband, *The Gleam*, London, John Murray, 1923.
10. Francis Younghusband, *The Reign of God*, London, John Murray, 1930.
11. Francis Younghusband, *Mother World*, London, Williams and Norgate, 1924.

12. James Lovelock *Gaia*, Oxford, Oxford Paperbacks 1982 and other related books.
13. Patrick French, *Younghusband: the Last Great Imperial Adventurer*, HarperCollins, 1994, p. 318.
14. Francis Younghusband, *The Living Universe*, London, John Murray, 1933.
15. George Seaver, *Francis Younghusband*, London, John Murray, 1952, p.234.
16. Quited in *A Wider Vision*, p. 48.
17. Quoted by Seaver, p.331. Bede Griffiths' book called *Marriage of East and West* was published in 1982. See further chapter 87.

86

Pope John XXIII

Angelo Giuseppe Roncalli, who was to become Pope John XXIII, was born on 25th November, 1881, to a peasant family near Bergamo, in Northern Italy. He was the fourth in a family of fourteen children. The family, he said, was 'so poor the children had no wine.' 'There are three ways of ruining oneself,' Angelo recalled, 'women, gambling and farming. My father chose the most boring.'

Angelo was a bright boy and was sponsored for an education at the Bergamo seminary, which carried out a severe religious training. It was there that he began the practice, which he continued into old age, of making spiritual notes. These were later collected in the *Journal of a Soul*.[1] In 1896, he was admitted to membership of the Secular Franciscan Order. Quite soon afterwards he started his training to be a priest and was a student at the Pontifical Seminary in Rome from 1901 to 1905. He was ordained in 1904.[2]

In the following year he became secretary to the recently appointed Bishop of Bergamo and travelled with him in his pastoral visitations. It was a chance for Angelo to discover at first hand the workings of the Church, which at the time was fearful and inward looking. In 1871, the Vatican had lost its papal states to the recently formed nation state of Italy and had been restricted to its current borders. Pope Pius IX had proclaimed himself a 'prisoner of the Vatican' and had taken a defensive stance toward the modern world. In his decree *Non expedit* ('It is not expedient'), Pope Pius IX had forbidden Italy's Catholics from taking any part in national politics. Pope Pius X (1903-1914) strongly opposed so called 'Modernist' tendencies, especially critical study of the scriptures. The Bishop of Bergamo, however, was a reformer who sought to re-involve the Church in the world. The Bishop was staunchly pro-labour and founded organizations for working women (of which Fr Angelo was secretary) and sided with the union during a local iron workers' strike. The elegant aristocratic bishop and his rotund peasant secretary, who complained 'my miserable body is growing fat and heavy,' were inseparable for ten years. The Bishop died in 1915 and Pope Pius X, who was succeeded by Benedict XV, died soon afterwards. For a time Angelo continued to teach at the seminary in Bergamo.

By this time, however, Italy had entered World War I against Austria and Germany. Roncalli, as we should now call Angelo, was called up to serve in the medical corps, as a stretcher-bearer and chaplain. He put on army uniform and, in what he later described as 'a moment of weakness on my part', grew himself a fat bristly moustache.

When the war ended, Roncalli opened a student house and was appointed spiritual director of the seminary. He was called to Rome in 1921, but quite soon was out of favour. When he became pope, he looked up his file and found that he had been suspected of 'Modernist' tendencies. He was made a bishop but effectively banished to Bulgaria. He had the grand title of 'Apostolic Visitor', but it meant little. Bulgaria is mostly an Orthodox Christian country with a small minority of Catholics. The Vatican had not felt it necessary to send an emissary there in six hundred years! Roncalli's life there was difficult. 'My ministry,' he recorded, 'has brought me many trials. But, and this is strange, these are not caused by the Bulgarians for whom I work but by the central organs of ecclesiastical administration. This is a form of mortification and humiliation that I did not expect and which hurts me deeply.' He made dozens of recommendations that were never followed and spent months trying to found a seminary, which would never be built. The one recommendation that the Pope followed was to appoint a Bulgarian as exarch – equivalent to a bishop - for those Catholics who used an Orthodox liturgy. Roncalli, as a result, was left with no pastoral duties to perform.

After ten years of frustration in Bulgaria, Roncalli got a new assignment, as delegate to Turkey, another long-neglected outpost. Again, Catholics were in a minority, but Roncalli established good relations with members of the Orthodox church and with Muslims, who were under some pressure from the unsympathetic secular government of the young Turkish republic. Roncalli was in Turkey when World War II broke out, and he devoted himself to the care of refugees, especially Jews. He obtained transit visas to Palestine for some; to others he issued baptismal certificates that would enable them to pass as Christians, with the understanding that no baptisms need be performed. Chaim Barlas of the Jewish Agency's Rescue Committee wrote: 'to the few heroic deeds which were performed to rescue Jews belong the activities of the apostolic delegate, Monsignor Roncalli, who worked indefatigably on their behalf.' Rabbi Isaac Herzog of Jerusalem wrote: 'Through [Roncalli] thousands of Jews were rescued.'

The end of World War II saw a big change in Roncalli's career. De Gaulle insisted that the Papal Nuncio in France, who had collaborated with the Vichy government, must go. The Vatican had to find a suitable replacement, and fast, so that the new nuncio was there in time for the traditional New Year's greeting to the President. Suddenly Roncalli's very obscurity was an advantage; no one knew of anything to object to in his appointment. Robert Schuman, the French premier, said of him: 'He is the only man in Paris in whose company one feels the physical sensation of peace.'

In 1953 Roncalli was made a cardinal and appointed patriarch of Venice. His address to the diocesan synod in 1957 gives a glimpse of the future pope: 'Authoritarianism suffocates truth, reducing everything to a rigid and empty formalism that is dependent on outside discipline. It curbs wholesome initiative, mistakes hardness for firmness, inflexibility for revealed dignity. Paternalism is a caricature of true fatherliness. It is often accompanied by an unjustifiable proprietary attitude to one's victim, a habit of intruding, a lack of proper respect for the rights of subordinates.'

Pope Pius XII died on October 9, 1958, and the conclave to elect a new pope began two weeks later. Roncalli was elected on the twelfth ballot – he had arrived in the Vatican with a return ticket to Venice! Many people thought that he had been elected as a *papa di passagio*, a 'stop-gap pope' as he was seventy-seven years old when he was elected. They were soon to be proved wrong.

His choice of the name John was unexpected, as it had last been used during the thirteenth century schism by a would-be Pope John XXIII, who was eventually regarded as an Antipope. Pope John XXIII explained why he chose the name:

'A name sweet to us because it is the name of our father, dear to me because it is the name of the humble parish church where I was baptised, the solemn name of numberless cathedrals... Twenty-two Johns of indisputable legitimacy have [been pope] and almost all had a brief pontificate' – a reference to his own age.[3]

Pope John's first public address was to the leaders of nations:

> 'Look at the people entrusted to you and listen to their voices. What do they seek? What do they implore of you? Not these new monstrous instruments of war which our times have produced and which can annihilate us all - not these, but peace.'[4]

On Christmas day 1958, Pope John became the first Pope to leave Vatican territory since 1870 when he visited children who were suffering from polio and then went to visit patients in a hospital. On the following day he went to Rome's Regina Coeli prison, where he told the prisoners, 'You could not come to me, so I came to you.' He wrote in his diary 'great astonishment in the Roman, Italian and international press.'

Soon after coming to office Pope John made the momentous decision to call the Second Vatican Council, which we shall consider shortly. The importance of the Council, however, should not obscure the impact made by the radiant goodness and simplicity of Pope John.

In September 1962, he was diagnosed with stomach cancer. He kept this from the public for eight months, but in April 1963 he hinted at this when he said, 'That which happens to all men will happen soon to the pope who speaks to you today.' On May 11th, 1963, he was awarded the Balzan Prize by the President of Italy for his work for peace. He died on June 3rd 1963 at the age of 81. I can still remember how his final days dominated the headlines of the world's press. He is remembered, affectionately, in Italy as 'Il Papa Buono' – the 'good Pope' - and by many across the world as 'the most loved Pope in history.' He was buried on June 6th and beatified on September 3rd, 2000.

The Second Vatican Council, which he convened, although he did not live to see it complete its work, brought radical changes to the life of the Roman Catholic Church and transformed that Church's relationship with both Christians of other denominations and with members of other world religions.

In terms of the life of the Church, perhaps the most noticeable change was the increased use of the vernacular in worship and the greater participation of lay people in the liturgy. The collegial authority of the bishops with the Pope was affirmed. The central place of Scripture was underlined and a more open approach to Biblical criticism was allowed.

While affirming the Catholic Church's position as 'the pillar and mainstay of the truth,' it was also recognised that 'many elements of sanctification and truth are found outside its visible confines.' All human beings are called to belong to the Church, but 'the Church knows that she is joined in many ways to the baptized who are honoured by the name of Christ, but who do not profess the Catholic faith in its entirety or have not preserved unity or communion with the successor of Peter.'[5] The document then went on to extend this to 'those who have not yet received the Gospel.'

Perhaps the most historic document was *Nostra Aetate,* 'In our Age,' which deserves extensive quotation.[6] This not only began the amazing transformation of Catholic-Jewish relations, which has taken place in the last forty years. It opened the door to dialogue with members of other faiths.

After the horrors of the Holocaust and a growing recognition of Christians' share of responsibility for anti-Semitism, the document made clear that Jews as a people were not to be blamed for the death of Jesus Christ.

'True, the Jewish authorities and those who followed their lead pressed for the death of Christ; still, what happened in his passion cannot be charged against all Jews, without distinction then alive, nor against the Jews of today.'

It recognised that Jesus voluntarily accepted the way of the Cross. The Document also indicated that God's new covenant in Jesus did not imply the abolition of God's earlier covenant with the Jews. It said;

'Although the Church is the new people of God, the Jews should not be presented as rejected or accursed by God, as if this followed from the Holy Scriptures... Further in her rejection of every persecution against any man, the Church, mindful of the patrimony she shares with the Jews and moved not by political reasons but by the Gospel's spiritual love, decries hatred against Jews at any time and by anyone.'

The document also made special mention of Muslims:

'The Church regards with esteem also the Muslims. They adore the one God, living and subsisting in Himself; merciful and all-powerful, the Creator of heaven and earth, who has spoken to men; they take pains to submit wholeheartedly to even His inscrutable decrees, just as Abraham, with whom the faith of Islam takes pleasure in linking itself, submitted to God. Though they do not acknowledge Jesus as God, they revere Him as a prophet. They also honour Mary, His virgin Mother...'

The Document set these more detailed references to Judaism and Islam in the context of an appreciative reference to other world religions:

'From ancient times down to the present, there is found among various peoples a certain perception of that hidden power which hovers over the course of things and over the events of human history; at times some indeed have come to the recognition of a Supreme Being, or even of a Father. This perception and recognition penetrates their lives with a profound religious sense.

Religions, however, that are bound up with an advanced culture have struggled to answer the same questions by means of more refined concepts and a more developed language. Thus in Hinduism, men contemplate the divine mystery and express it through an inexhaustible abundance of myths and through searching philosophical inquiry. They seek freedom from the anguish of our human condition either through ascetical practices or profound meditation or a flight to God with love and trust. Again, Buddhism, in its various forms, realizes the radical insufficiency of this changeable world; it teaches a way by which men, in a devout and confident spirit, may be able either to acquire the state of perfect liberation, or attain, by their own efforts or through higher help, supreme illumination. Likewise, other religions found everywhere try to counter the restlessness of the human heart, each in its own manner, by proposing "ways," comprising teachings, rules of life, and sacred rites. The Catholic Church rejects nothing that is true and holy in these religions...'

Pope John XXIII did not live to see the formulation of *Nostra Aetate*, but it breathes his spirit of openness and embracing love and marked a highly significant step forward in the growing dialogue and co-operation of the world religions. This was taken even further by Pope John Paul XXIII who invited other religious leaders and interfaith activists to join him in the memorable Day of Prayer for Peace at Assisi in October 1986, which my wife Mary and I had the privilege of attending.

CHAPTER NOTES

1. Pope John XXIII, *Journal of a Soul*, translated by Dorothy White, London, Geoffrey Chapman, 1965.
2. Much of this information is based on a Homily by Pope John Paul II, in *L'Osservatore Romano Weekly Edition in English*, 6 September 2000, www.vatican.va/news_services/liturgy.
3. *L'Osservatore Romano Weekly Edition in English*, 6 September 2000
4. Quoted in Peter Hebblethwaite, *Pope John XXXIII: Shepherd of the Modern World*, London, Image Books, 1983, p. 303.
5. *Lumen Gentium*, 15 The documents of the second Vatican council are available at www.vatican.va/archive/hist_councils/ii_vatican_council.
6. *Nostra Aetate*.

87

Bede Griffiths

Fr Bede Griffiths was a Catholic monk whose deep immersion in Hindu spirituality led him to discover a new vision of reality, the heart of which would be an emerging cosmic religion. 'We are emerging now' he said, 'into this new consciousness where we realise the unity of creation, the unity of humanity.'[1]

Alan Richard Griffiths, the fourth child of middle-class, Church-going English parents, was born on December 17th, 1906. He chose the name Bede, by which he is better known, when he became a monk. He was educated at Christ's Hospital and then at Oxford, where C S Lewis (1898-1963), the Christian writer and scholar made famous by the film *Shadowlands*, was one of his tutors. Griffiths spent much of his time at University walking in the country and reading the Romantic poets. His religion at this time, he said, was a 'worship of nature,' resulting from a peak experience, of which he wrote:

'Suddenly we know that we belong to another world, that there is another dimension to existence. It is impossible to put what we have seen into words; it is something beyond all words which has been revealed.'[2]

After he left Oxford, Alan Griffiths lived with two others in a very simple community at Eastington, rejecting as far as possible the paraphernalia of modern civilization, with which he was always uneasy. After a time, however, in Griffiths' words, 'a division began to take place among us' and the three members of the community went their separate ways, although they kept in touch throughout their lives.

After Eastington, Griffiths was unsure of almost everything. He returned home and earned some money by private tutoring, but had plenty of time to read the Bible. When he enquired about ordination, he was told he needed wider experience of life and went to help at the Oxford Mission in Bethnal Green. He liked the work, but could not stand London. He lived very austerely and was weakened by fasting and long hours of prayer.

He was advised to go on a retreat, at which he experienced the love of God. 'Repentance...came over me like a flood.'[3]. 'Now I felt that love had taken possession of my soul.'[4] For a time, he worked on a farm. Soon, he felt impelled to join the Roman Catholic Church. Then, in December 1932, the priest took him to visit Prinknash Abbey, a Benedictine monastery in Gloucestershire. It was love at first sight. Alan, soon to become Bede, quickly decided he wanted to become a monk. He made his solemn profession in 1937 and was ordained in 1940.

During his years as a monk, he continued the study of Eastern religions, which he had begun at Oxford. In the early 1950s, he learned that Fr. Benedict Alapatt, an Indian Benedictine living in Europe, wanted to start a monastic community in India. At first, Bede's Abbot rejected his request to accompany Fr Benedict Alapatt, but eventually in 1955, Bede was allowed to go and they formed a small monastic community in a village called Kengeri, following the Benedictine pattern with which Bede was familiar at Prinknash.

Late in November 1956, Bede moved to Kerala to a new community, which used the Syrian rite. Bede was there from late 1956 to the summer of 1968 but his relationship with the prior, Fr Francis, was never easy. It became increasingly clear that the two monks needed to go their separate ways. The situation was resolved when Abhishiktananda (1910-1973), the French monk originally known as Fr. Henri le Saux, decided to retire to the Himalayas. Abhishiktananda asked Fr Francis to take over his ashram, but Fr Francis, persuaded Bede to go instead to Shantivanam, where he was to live for the rest of his life, although in later years he travelled widely.

Shantivanam is a village in South India, near Tirachirapalli – usually known as Tiruchi or Trichy. Shantivanam means 'forest of peace.' The village itself is on a busy main road, but once you go down the short lane to the ashram, with its mango trees and Palmyra palms and with the sacred river Cavery meandering along one boundary, there is a deep sense of peace. This is where two French priests Fr Jules Monchanin, who became Swami Paramarubyananda (The Bliss of the Supreme Spirit), and Fr Henri le Saux, or Swami Abhishikttananda[5] (The Bliss of Christ), settled in 1950. They called their ashram 'Saccidananda', which is a Hindu name for the Ultimate Reality, God.

Saccidananda unites three Sanskrit words: *sat,* which means 'being'; *cit,* which means 'consciousness' or 'awareness' and *ananda,* which means 'bliss'.

Already in the 1950s, the two Frenchmen had adopted a simple Indian style of life. They wore the *kavi* habit of a Hindu *sannyasi,* they slept on the ground and ate with their fingers. Bede immediately felt at home at Shantivanam. He made some improvements – installing electricity, running water and lavatories. He also had some of the land cleared and planted more fruit trees and vegetables. In the early years there were times of intense loneliness, but late in 1971 he was joined by two young monks, Amaldas and Christudas.

By the mid-seventies, especially after the publication in 1976 of *Return to the Centre,* Bede was becoming quite well known and attracting a growing number of visitors to the ashram. But Bede was also under attack from some conservative Catholics who thought he was undermining the Church and from some Hindus who objected to his 'deceitful' borrowings from Hinduism.

In 1990, Bede suffered from heart failure and a slight stroke. On January 25[th,] he felt a blow like a 'sledge hammer,' but it was accompanied by a deep spiritual experience 'in which the feminine came and hit me.'[6] Bede was now open to the feminine, all barriers were broken down. Two images summarised his experience: Christ Crucified and the Black Madonna, who also reflected the Hindu goddess Shakti and the Earth Mother. 'I feel it was this Power' he wrote, 'which struck me. She is cruel and destructive, but also deeply loving, nourishing and protecting.'[7]

Bede knew the experience had changed him and said he had grown more in two years after the stroke than in the previous 84 years. This is how, on reflection, he spoke of what happened:

'On the psychological level it was 'a death of the mind' – a breakdown of the left-brain rational mind and an awakening to the feminine intuitive mind. But on the spiritual level it certainly left an impression of *advaita* – a transcendence of all limitations and an awakening to the non-dual reality. This has left an indelible impression on me. I am seeing everything in a new light.'[8]

Initially after his recovery, Bede said he would not travel again but planned to retire to his hermitage. But soon 'I felt the call and the need.'[9] The next two years were taken up by a hectic round of travel. Then on Dec 20, 1992 at the midday office he was taken ill and after a period of considerable pain he died on 13th of May 1993. His last words were 'God the Father, God the Son, God the Holy Spirit, I surrender to you.' As he died, the disciples gathered round his bed and sang a Sanskrit chant that he loved '*Christa jaya jaya, Namo, Namo*, Praise be to you, Oh Christ, Hail, Hail, Praise be to you, Oh Christ.'[10]

In his teaching, Bede emphasised two sources of knowledge. Even before he set out for India, Bede recognized the importance of non-rational ways of knowing. At Shantivanam, he gave greater emphasis to contemplative or mystical knowledge or what he often calls 'intuition,' although he continued to uphold the value of reason and the experience of the senses. Bede also referred to intuition as the feminine power of the mind, but argued for an eventual transcendence of male and female.

The language of human love, he said, pointed to the experience of the mystic. In *The Marriage of East and West*, he spoke of a mystical experience beyond darkness and all differentiation where 'the soul becomes self-luminous or rather discovers that it is itself but the reflection of a light which shines forever beyond the darkness... It is the discovery of this infinite, eternal, unchanging being, beyond the flux of time and change, beyond birth and death, beyond thought and feeling, yet answering to the deepest need of every human being, which is the goal of all religion and of all humanity.'[11]

Bede's personal journey of faith meant that he inevitably had to reflect on the relationship of Christianity to other world religions – a subject that has been much debated in the Church during the twentieth century.[12] Traditionally the Church had claimed a monopoly of the Truth and that God was fully revealed only in Jesus Christ. Even in his early thinking about other religions, Bede, with the value he put on intuitive knowledge recognised that Truth is mediated spiritually not religiously. Indeed, his own awakening to God in Nature was quite apart from any religious commitment. He therefore had no problem in recognising that there may be a revelation of God in other religions. He regarded all who live by the 'Natural Law' of reason and conscience, which is to be found in the hearts of all people, as members of the church.[13] He sometimes spoke of other religions as finding their fulfilment in Christianity, which would not replace other religions, but potentially include them.

In the third period at Shantivanam, as he opened himself to the *Advaita* philosophy of Sankara, Bede moved from 'fulfilment', to 'complementarity.' 'The divine mystery,' he wrote, 'the eternal Truth, has been revealing itself to all men from the beginning of history. Every people has received some insight into this divine mystery... These insights, insofar as they reflect the one Reality, are in principle complementary. Each has its own defects both of faith and practice, and each has to learn from others, so that they may grow together to that unity in Truth which is the goal of human existence.'[14] 'At the deepest level I don't find anything incompatible. The deeper you go into Hinduism or Buddhism, the more you see how there's a fundamental unity with Christianity.'[15]

The aim of the ashram, therefore, was to encourage 'an organic growth in which each religion has to purify itself and discover its own inmost depth and significance and then relate itself to the inner depth of the other tradition.' This was reflected in the liturgy, in which features of Hindu temple devotion were incorporated into the Christian mass. Bede also encouraged Christians to use other scriptures besides the Bible for their meditation.[16]

Bede hoped that the meeting in depth of the great religions would lead 'towards ...that unity in truth, which is the ultimate goal of mankind.'[17]

In his introduction to *Universal Wisdom*, he wrote, 'This is the destiny of all humanity to realize its essential unity in the Godhead, by whatever name it is known, to be one with the absolute Reality, the absolute Truth, the infinite, the eternal Life and Light. But this unity cannot be known without the pain of self-sacrifice; it demands 'Nothing less than all.'[18]

Such a view inevitably meant that Bede had to rethink traditional Christian claims for the uniqueness of Jesus Christ. Bede is clear that the historical Jesus is a symbol of the Christ or Logos (Word of God) – but not exhaustively so. 'The Buddha, Krishna, Christ – each is a unique revelation of God, of the divine Mystery.'[19]

Bede's emphasis on an ultimate unity did not lead him to disguise the differences between religions and he put forward a Christian version of *advaita*. *Advaita* or non-duality is especially associated with the great Hindu philosopher Sankara, who said that in the light of ultimate experience, all differences disappear and the world is essentially *maya* or unreal. Bede stressed the importance of Christians relating to this teaching, based on mystical knowing, which is an experience of the soul in its inmost depths. Yet Bede found Sankara's teaching unsatisfactory. He was more sympathetic to the Hindu thinkers Ramanuja and Madhva, who rejected Sankara's strict non-dualism, and also to Sri Aurobindo's writings, but found their views also to be inadequate. Towards the end of his life in a letter to Russill and Asha, a young couple who came to live at the ashram with whom Bede formed a close attachment, he accepted that people may come to 'final reality through Hindu advaita or Buddhist sunyata' but added that 'for a Christian the way is through Christ and the Church. I should add that for me there is a Christian Advaita in which the mysteries of faith are not lost, but finally realized.'[20]

In Bede's Christian Advaita, which is based on the Christian doctrines of Creation, Incarnation and the Trinity, a difference remains between lover and loved, God and the soul, even in the highest realization. Communion is different to identity. Moreover, Bede affirmed the reality of the world and its differentiation from God.

Griffiths later explained his theory of *advaita* by reference to marriage which entails oneness and two-ness, unity and distinction. He spoke some sixty years later of his night of conversion as being overwhelmed by love 'total... like a marriage.[21]

Bede, like many other prophetic writers of the twentieth century, felt a new age was emerging. New psychological and scientific thinking were evidence of this, he said, and a materialistic and mechanistic model of the universe was being recognised as inadequate. He tried to outline some features of the new age.

1. It will be based on a new relationship to the world of nature in which humans see themselves as part of the physical organism of the universe.
2. This sense of communion with an encompassing reality will

replace the attempt to dominate the world and more eco-friendly forms of technology will be developed.

3. A new type of human community will emerge with decentralised societies moving away from big cities. There will be an integrated education of body, soul and spirit.

4. People will return to the perennial philosophy.

5. Christians will reunite, under a reformed papacy and a new theology will reflect the insights of the religions of the East.

For Bede, an emerging universal religion was at the very heart of this new world culture. In his ashram, in his writings and in his life he dedicated himself to nurturing the necessary new spirituality. Whether the future will see a convergence of religions or a clash of civilizations is perhaps the fundamental choice for humanity at the start of the Third Millennium.

CHAPTER NOTES

1. In a talk given at Melbourne on 17.5.1992, quoted by Shirley du Boulay, *Beyond the Darkness*, London, Rider, 1998.

2. Bede Griffiths, *The Golden String*, Fontana edtn 1964, p. 11.

3. *The Golden String*, p.106.

4. *The Golden String*, p.108.

5. See further Shirley Du Boulay, *The Cave of the Heart*, New York, Orbis, 2005.

6. Quoted by Judson B Trapnell, *Bede Griffiths: A Life in Dialogue*, State University of New York, Press, 2001, p. 2. .

7. In Judy Walter's journal. Quoted in *Beyond the Darkness*, p. 228

8. Letter to Sister Pascaline Coff OSB 15.4.90, quoted in *Beyond the Darkness*, p. 231.

9. Quoted in *Beyond the Darkness*, p. 239.

10. Quoted in *Beyond the Darkness*, p. 263.

11. *The Marriage of East and West*, London, Collins, 1982, p. 167.

12. See Paul Knitter, *Introducing Theologies of Religions*, New York, Orbis, 2004.

13. Quoted in *A Life in Dialogue*, p. 103.

14. *Vedanta and Christian Faith*, 1973 edition, author's Preface. Quoted in *A Life in Dialogue*, p.185.

15. Griffiths, 'On Poverty and Simplicity' –. quoted in *A Life in Dialogue*, p. 188.
16. See his *Universal Wisdom*, London, HarperCollins, 1994.
17. 'The One Mystery', *Tablet* 228/6975 9.3.74 223. see *Beyond the Darkness*, p.176.
18. *Universal Wisdom*,London, HarperCollins, 1994, p. 39 – 40.
19. *Return to the Centre*pp. 86-7 Quoted in *A Life in Dialogue*, p. 151.
20. Letter to Russilll and Asha 18.3.90, quoted in *Beyond the Darkness*, p. 235.
21. *Golden String* p. 108.

88

Kahlil Gibran

'Could we have a reading from Kahlil Gibran at our wedding?' a rather nervous couple asked me.' 'Oh yes, everyone has it,' I replied rather too quickly – not recognising that the couple thought they were being daring and original. *The Prophet* by Kahlil Gibran is highly popular and it is said that after Shakespeare and Lao-tzu, he is the best selling poet of all times. Yet people often know very little about the author.

In part, this was deliberate. Before the publication of *The Prophet*, Kahlil Gibran read some extracts in public, which attracted wide approbation. 'I am a false alarm', he said to his friend Mikhail Naimy – implying that he did not live up to what he had written.[1] Does a person's own behaviour affect the influence of what he or she writes? 'Practise what you preach' it is said, but in this book I have tried to assess a person's influence and not to usurp role of the Recording Angel. Robin Waterfield in his biography of Kahlil Gibran wrote, 'He hobnobbed with the rich and famous of Boston and New York – and claimed affinity with the poor of the world. He suffered devastating personal tragedies and yet is known for the peace and optimism of his most popular work.'[2] Gibran once said, 'The difference between a prophet and a poet is that the prophet lives what he teaches, and the poet does not. He may write wonderfully of love, and yet not be loving.'[3]

On other occasions, however, he expressed the desire to live what he said and to practice the ideals of *The Prophet*. Gibran's own epitaph was 'Even the most winged spirit cannot escape physical necessity.'[4]

Details of Kahlil Gibran's life are scarce. Partly this is because his recollections do not always seem to be accurate. Moreover now that the village where he was born has become famous stories of his early life have increased.

Kahlil Gibran was born in 1883 at Bisharri, a small isolated village, which overlooks the 'Sacred Valley' in the foothills of Mount Lebanon (*lubnan* is the Semitic word for white). Lebanon only became an independent country after the Second World War. At the time when Khalil grew up it was part of the Ottoman Empire. His family were

Maronites – members of a Syrian Christian body founded by a fourth century hermit called Maro. In the controversies about the nature of Jesus Christ as God and man, they held that Jesus had both a human and a divine nature, but only one will – a position eventually declared heretical. At the time of the Crusades, however, the Maronites united with Rome and are now one of the Eastern Catholic or Uniat Churches, which have limited autonomy. Others in the area were Muslim or Druze, a small independent religious group with Ismaili origins.

The family seem to have been quite poor, living in a crumbling stone house with a mud roof. When the roof collapsed, they moved into one floor of a communal building. Gibran's father was described as 'irascible' and 'imperious' - a heavy drinker and a gambler. He was arrested for financial irregularities. His mother was a devout Christian. In 1903 the family, but not the father, emigrated to America, but Gibran left part of his heart in Lebanon. 'Much of what he gave to the world,' Suheil Bushrui has said, 'he owed to his homeland.' Bushrui mentions Lebanon's 'geographical position and its admixture of ethnic groups... its sacred cedar grove...and the lofty snow-capped mountains soaring into heaven... Perhaps most of all he was indebted to Lebanon for his awareness of the inestimable benefits that flow from the harmonious coexistence of different peoples and faiths.'[5] A few months before his death, Gibran wrote to a friend, 'I wish to go back to Lebanon and remain there forever.'[6]

The family settled in Boston - by 1910, there were over 100,000 Syrians in the USA. Kahlil Gibran was twelve and did well at school. His ability, especially his drawings, attracted the attention of an artist who belonged to the so-called 'Decadent' school of painters and poets. Gibran sat as a model for Fred Holland Day, who was a member of the 'Decadent' school. Day and his friends introduced Gibran to Romantic and Pre-Raphaelite literature.

When he was fifteen, his family sent Kahlil Gibran back to Syria to complete his education in Beirut. There he immersed himself in Arabic literature and helped produce a student magazine. One of his Boston friends, Josephine Peabody, who admired his paintings, kept in touch with him.

In 1902, Kahlil Gibran's sister Sultana died. He hurried back to America to join the family. Sadly, the next year his brother Peter and then his mother died. When his father died in 1909, Gibran 'wept bitterly' even though their relationship had never been easy. Gibran noted that 'his friends wrote saying that he blessed me before the end came.'[7]

Kahlil Gibran, now settled in the USA, started writing, with help and encouragement from Mary Haskell, with whom for some years he had a close relationship. His first novel, *The Broken Wings*, set in Lebanon, was published in Arabic in 1912 and subsequently in English. Although mostly known for *The Prophet*, to which we shall return, which was published in 1922, Kahlil Gibran's other writings are extensive. The *Treasured Writings of Kahlil Gibran*, which I possess, although not his complete works, has over 900 pages. His works consist mainly of short poems, prose poems and short stories. Numerous letters have subsequently been published.

In his early writings Kahlil Gibran sees love as a means of self-realization and only later thinks of it as a catalyst for broader change. Human beings are bound in degrading ways to the world with its man-made laws, but can find freedom and discover their greater selves by allowing Love into the heart. 'Behind all this creation, there is Eternal Wisdom… Man in his Divinity I saw standing like a giant in the midst of wrath and destruction.'[8] Through love, a person can realize his or her potential, which is nothing less than divinity. It is a freedom that, recognising that life is one, withholds judgment on others.

Convinced that Christ had come to help the poor and oppressed, Gibran was critical of the wealth and power of the Church. In *Kahlil the Heretic*, the heretic says,

'"Vain are the beliefs and teachings that make man miserable… It is man's purpose to be happy on this earth and lead the way to felicity and preach its gospel wherever he goes… This is the truth, which I have learned from the teachings of the Nazarene… This is the deep secret, which the beautiful valleys and fields revealed to me. This is the religion as the convent should impart it; as God wished it; as Jesus taught it." Then the heretic recalled how he had addressed the monks, asking, "Why are you living in the shadow of parasitism, segregating yourselves from the people who are in need of knowledge? … Let us restore to the needy the vast land of the convent."'[9]

Although scornful of the hypocrisy and wealth of religious institutions, Gibran, in an Arabic work *Iram al 'Imad*, 'Iram, ('City of Lofty Pillars') dreamed of the unity of religions. He was so critical of the Church that he refused the last rites, but he was fascinated by the person of Jesus. Mary Haskell's journals refer to many discussions with him about Jesus. Gibran told her about his recurring dreams of Jesus Christ. In *Sand and Foam*, Gibran wrote, 'Once every hundred years, Jesus of Nazareth meets Jesus of the Christians in a garden among the hills of Lebanon, and they talk long. And each time Jesus of Nazareth goes away saying to Jesus the Christian, "My friend, I fear we shall never, never agree."'[10]

Towards the end of his life, Gibran wrote *Jesus Son of Man*, which was published in 1928. The author emphasizes the humanity of Jesus, whom he placed in everyday surroundings. He imagines what Jesus' contemporaries would have said about him and this gives freshness to his work. Nathaniel probably speaks for Gibran when he says:

'I am sickened and the bowels within me stir and rise when I hear the faint-hearted call Jesus humble and meek, that they may justify their own faint-heartedness; and when the downtrodden, for comfort and companionship, speak of Jesus as a worm shining by their side...It is the mighty hunter I would preach and the mountainous spirit unconquerable.'[11]

Barabbas makes the sad remark, 'His crucifixion endured but for an hour. But I shall be crucified unto the end of my years.'[12] John son of Zebedee speaks of Jesus as 'Christ the Gracious.'[13] Gibran relating Jesus to other 'avatars', says, 'Many times Christ has come to the world and he has walked many lands. And always He has been deemed a stranger and a madman.'[14]

Jesus the Son of Man was one of Gibran's last works. By the early nineteen thirties, Kahlil Gibran was terminally ill. Although in *The Prophet* Gibran, who had a firm belief in reincarnation said that there is no such thing as death, in *The Procession* he wrote:

And death on earth, to sons of earth
Is final, but to him who is
Ethereal, it is but the start
Of triumph certain to be his.[15]

Gibran died in April 1931. After his death, there were disputes by rival claimants to be his literary executor and over the royalties which he left to his native village of Bisharri. He died in New York, but his body was transported to Boston for burial there and later exhumed and taken to Lebanon to be buried in a ruined monastery – now a centre for pilgrims – near Bisharri.

When asked how he came to write *The Prophet*, Kahlil Gibran replied, 'Did I write it? It wrote me.'[16] It was the product of many years of reflection, starting in 1912. Gibran waited for moments of inspiration to come. His close friend Mary Haskell read every word of it and helped him with the 'spacing' of the sentences, taking the Book of Job as the model. Even as late as 1922, when it was published, he and Mary were worried that it was 'too preachy,' but as early as 1914 he had said of his style, 'I do not explain or discuss. It is just said – with authority. Analysis does not live and it is not delicious to us.'[17] The book is deliberately short. The 'reallest' books, he said, are short.

The language, which echoes that of the Gospels, especially in the cadences of the King James Authorised version, is clear and the words simple. The vagueness is intentional and allows the reader, as Gibran said, space 'to have his or her say as well.' The book deals with the deepest concerns of the human heart. Its message is love. His friend Mary said, 'it is the most loving book ever written.' She also said that 'generation after generation will find in the book what they would fain be.'[18]

Yet, if the words recall those of Jesus, Almustafa is more reminiscent of the Prophet Muhammad. The form is influenced by Nietzsche's *Thus Spake Zarathustra*, although by the time he wrote it Kahlil Gibran's message that 'You are far greater than you know, and all is well', was very different to Nietzsche's, although he had been influenced by him as a young man. William Blake also had a strong influence on Gibran.

Initial reviews of *The Prophet* were lukewarm, except for the *Chicago Evening Post*, which praised it as a 'little Bible.' Literary critics and intellectual have also been disparaging, dismissing it as platitudinous, over-sentimental and trite, but, says Robin Waterfield, 'these are arrogant criticisms of hard-hearted individuals.'[19]

Almustafa's words about marriage are so well known that it may be more interesting to quote another passage that he wrote:

> Here love begins to render the prose of Life into hymns and canticles of praise, with music that is set by night, to be sung in the day. Here Love's longing draws back the veil, and illumines the recesses of the heart, creating a happiness that no other happiness can surpass but that of the Soul when she embraces God. Marriage is the union of two divinities that a third might be born on earth. ...
> It is that higher unity which fuses the separate within the two spirits. It is the golden ring in a chain whose beginning is a glance, and whose ending is eternity.'[20]

Love, human and divine, was for Gibran the deepest meaning of life. He wrote,

> *We shall pass into the twilight,*
> *Perchance to wake to the dawn of another world.*
> *But love shall stay,*
> *And his finger-marks shall not be erased...*[21]

CHAPTER NOTES

1. Robin Waterfield in *Prophet: the Life and Times of Kahlil Gibran*, London, Allen Lane, 1998 quotes this passage on p. 3.
2. Waterfield, p. xi.
3. Kahlil Gibran, *Sand and Foam*, New York, Alfred Knopf, 1928, p. 64 Also *Beloved Prophet: the Love Letters of Kahlil Gibran and Mary Haskell and her Private Journal*, ed Vikrginia Hilu, London, Quartet, 1973, p. 392.
4. *Sand and Foam*, London, Heinemann, 1954, p. 64.
5. Suheil Bushrui, *Kahlil Gibran of Lebanon*, Gerards Cross, Colin Smthye 1987. I quote from a copy of the book signed by the author. His comments on 'harmonious co-existence', sadly, no longer apply.

6. Kahlil Gibran, *A Self Portrait,* translated and edited by S S Bushrui and S H al-Kuzbari, Burnt Mill, Longman, 1983, p. 93.

7. Bushrui, p. 31.

8. *The Treasured Writings of Kahlil Gibran,* translated by Anthony Rizcallah Ferris and edited Martin Wolf, New York, Castle (Books sales Inc) 1985 edtn pp. 478-9

9. *The Treasured Writings of Kahlil Gibran,* pp. 298-9.

10. *Sand and Foam,* p. 77.

11. *Jesus the Son of Man: His Words and His deed as told and recorded by Those who Knew Him,* New York, Alfred Knopf, 1928, (London, William Heinemann, 1954), p .63.

12. *Jesus the Son of Man,* p. 192.

13. *Jesus the Son of Man,* p. 46.

14. *Jesus the Son of Man,* p. 43.

15. *The Procession,* New York, Arab-American Press, 1947, p. 42.

16. Quoted in M S Dasudi, *The Meaning of Kahlil Gibran,* Secaucus, Citadel Press, 1975, 49.

17. Entries in Mary Haskell's diaries for 4.10.1914 and 7.10.1920, quoted by Waterfield, p. 258.

18. Mary Haskell's diaries, 20 August 1920.

19. Waterfield, p. 258.

20. From *The Words of the Master,* in *The Treasured Writings,* pp. 475-6.

21. Kahlil Gibran, *The Earth Gods,* London, Heinemann, 1969, p. 44.

89

Martin Buber

Martin Buber has been described as 'one of the most influential figures in twentieth century spiritual and intellectual life' and as 'one of the last great figures of German Jewry.'[1] His writings have had a lasting impact on Christian as well as Jewish thought.

Martin Buber, whose Hebrew name was Mordechai, was born on February 8th, 1878 in Vienna, Austria. Both his parents were assimilated Jews. His father Carl was a scientist specialising in soil and plant management. When Martin was only three, his mother left Carl. As a result, Martin was brought up by grandparents, who lived in Lemberg, - now Lvov in the Ukraine. His grandfather Solomon Buber (1827-1906) was a wealthy philanthropist and scholar. His grandmother, Adele, whose family wealth gave Martin financial security until the German occupation of Poland in 1939, was more in tune with the Enlightenment movement, which wanted to relate Jewish life more closely to contemporary European culture. Although Buber learned Hebrew from his grandfather, he was more attracted by his grandmother's interests and was particularly drawn to the Romantic poetry of Freidrich Schiller (1759-1805). Martin went to a grammar school, which encouraged his wider interests and gave him a good grounding in the classics. He spoke the local languages – Hebrew, Yiddish, Polish and German – and learned Greek, Latin, French, Italian and English.

In 1892, Martin returned to his father's house. He gave up observing Jewish festivals and religious practices. Instead he started reading philosophical works by Immanuel Kant (1724-1804), Søren Kierkegaard (1813-55) and Friedrich Nietzsche (1844-1900). He was particularly influenced as a young man by Nietzsche's devastating criticism of modern culture. In 1896 he went to study at Vienna, which was a lively centre of intellectual activity and artistic achievement. Sigmund Freud (1856-1939) had only published his theories on psychoanalysis a few years earlier. The philosopher Ludwig Wittgenstein (1889-1951) was only seven years old. Martin also spent time at the universities of Berlin, Leipzig and Zurich. It was in Zurich that Buber met and, in 1901, married Paula Winckler, who was a convert to Judaism and a keen supporter of Zionism. Buber's doctoral thesis was on the two great Christian mystics Nicholas of Cusa (c.1400-64) and Jakob Boehme (1575-1624).

Theodor Herzl (1860-1904), the founding advocate of Zionism - the movement for a Jewish national home - was also based in Vienna at this time, working as a journalist. In 1902 Buber who was already himself interested in Zionism, was invited by Theodor Herzl to edit the Zionist weekly paper, 'Die Welt.' Differences soon emerged and Buber resigned. Buber's emphasis was on spiritual renewal and he wanted immediate agricultural settlements in Palestine, whereas Herzl was more concerned to gain a recognised Jewish homeland by diplomatic means.

Buber himself now took up the study of Hasidism, a charismatic Jewish movement initiated by Ba'al Shem Tov in the eighteenth century. Buber's books, especially his *Tales of Rabbi Nachman* and *Tales of the Hasidim* and *The Legend of Baal Shem*[2] helped to make this movement more widely known, which now has its strongest support in New York and Israel.

In 1910 to 1914, Buber studied and wrote about myths. Partly based in Berlin, Buber also had a house in Heppenheim, near Frankfurt, which is now the headquarters of the International Council of Christians and Jews. In 1916 Buber started editing – until 1924 - a monthly magazine called 'Der Jude' ('The Jew'), and renewed his interest in Zionism.

In 1930, Buber became an honorary professor at Frankfurt University, but resigned in protest immediately Hitler came to power in 1933. In 1935 he founded the Central Office for Jewish education, which became increasingly important, as Jews were banished form public schools and colleges. In 1937, he left Germany to settle in Jerusalem, where he lived, teaching and writing until his death on June 13th, 1965. By that time he had become an international figure, giving lecture tours in Europe and North America and being honoured by various awards, including the Israel Prize in 1958.

Buber's most influential book was *Ich und Du* (*I and Thou*).[3] In this work, Buber moved away from some of his earlier language about the mystical union of God and human beings, to emphasise relationships. He distinguished two patterns of relationship: 'I-Thou' and 'I-It.' The 'I-Thou' relationship between human beings, in which both parties enter into the fullness of their being, is rare, but may occur in great love or an ideal friendship. Much of the time, as humans, we only share part of our self with others. In our relationship with the material world we adopt an objective or an 'I-It' relationship, which Buber acknowledged was necessary for scholarly work and scientific research.

It is in our meeting with God, Buber maintained, that a true 'I-Thou' relationship is possible. Indeed it is God, 'the Great Thou' who makes personal relationships possible. Often, however, we treat God as an object, either by concentrating on dogmas or teaching about God, or by making God a lawgiver or by focussing on religious organizations.

Later in life, Buber somewhat modified his views. His friend and fellow Jewish philosopher Franz Rosenzweig (1886-1929), especially famous for his book, *The Star of Redemption*, commented that 'Buber gives more recognition to the "Thou" than anybody before him, but he wrongs the "It."' Buber replied, that had he lived in a time when the 'I' was flourishing he would have given more attention to the 'It.' Whereas Rosenzweig, who came near at one point to converting to Christianity, became an ever more practicing Jew, Buber felt free to find his own expression of his faith. Buber has also been criticised for the preponderance of abstract nouns in his writing and certain vagueness in his thought. It has also been observed that the proponent of 'I-Thou' allowed very few people to address him by his first name.

Buber's emphasis on the 'Thou', however, remains highly important at a time when so many relationships are impersonal and officialdom and electronic communication are dominant. In the sixties, when Buber was becoming known in America, his ideas were seized upon by the student movement with its emphasis on spontaneity, authenticity and anti-establishment sentiment. It was at this time also that his works on Hasidic Judaism were translated into English.

Buber's book reflects the age-old mystical emphasis on direct experience of the Divine, which can be obscured by doctrines and ritual. It had an important impact on religious thinking – both Jewish and Christian. John Robinson, Bishop of Woolwich, quoted him in his popular book *Honest to God* (1963), which started a stormy debate about how Christianity should be understood in the modern secular society of the sixties. It has been said that Buber 'inaugurated a Copernican revolution in theology... against the scientific-realistic attitude.'[4]

Buber's lesser known *Good and Evil* (1952) which is based on five of the Psalms, is a significant discussion of the subject. It may be surprising today that Buber said comparatively little about the Holocaust, but the enormous growth of Holocaust literature did not start until the late sixties. Buber said that just as Job received no intellectual answer to his remonstrating with God, so contemporary Judaism would receive no answer to its questions about the Holocaust. God, however, appeared to Job and the only reassurance today was to see God. For this to happen, people needed to call for God's help just as Job had done. Buber wrote, 'Though His coming appearance resembles no earlier one, we shall recognize again our cruel and merciful Lord.'

Buber applied his distinctive approach to the Bible, which he translated into German and on which he wrote a number of commentaries. He saw the Bible as originating in the ever-renewed encounter between God and his people. This meeting, he said, could give rise to a tradition, which authentically reflected this experience and another that distorted the encounter to serve later ideological aims. He dismissed most of the legal prescriptions of the Talmud - the collection of ancient Rabbinical legal discussions – as 'spurious' and obscuring a living relationship with God. Orthodox Jews, not surprisingly, viewed his teaching with suspicion.

Buber, whose doctoral thesis, as we have seen, was on two Christian mystics, was an early proponent of Jewish-Christian dialogue. He referred to Jesus as 'my brother.' In his book *Two Types of Faith* (*Zwei Glaubensweisen*) (1950) Buber highlights the distinctive nature of both Judaism and of orthodox Christianity. In Judaism there is a persevering trust in God, thought of as both utterly transcending creation and yet immediately present to his covenanted and faithful people. In Christianity there is belief in a gospel, a message in whose development Paul played a major role, that God's redemptive love has been displayed above all in the person who became known and preached as Jesus Christ, the crucified and risen Son of God.

Buber said he did not believe in Jesus but he shared Jesus's faith. Buber did not believe in Jesus as a Messianic figure, but he did believe in Jesus' Judaic faith in God. He thought that the Jewish community, in the course of its renaissance, would recognize Jesus, not merely as a great figure in its religious history, but also in the organic context of a

Messianic development extending over millennia, whose final goal is the Redemption of Israel and of the world. 'But I believe equally firmly that we will never recognize Jesus as the Messiah Come, for this would contradict the deepest meaning of our Messianic passion. In our view redemption occurs forever, and none has yet occurred. Standing, bound and shackled, in the pillory of mankind, we demonstrate with the bloody body of our people the unredeemedness of the world. For us there is no cause of Jesus; only the cause of God exists for us.' Buber's radical beliefs about the Messiah and Christianity were different to those of traditional Judaism. Yet for him, Jesus was a man, a Jew, and a social activistfrom whose life Jews could learn. [5]

Buber, as have seen was an early supporter of Zionism, but already in the nineteen-twenties, he advocated a bi-national Jewish-Arab state. The Jewish people, he said, should make clear their 'desire to live in peace and brotherhood with the Arab people and to develop the common homeland into a republic in which both peoples will have the possibility of free development.'[6] Buber, going beyond nationalist sentiment, looked for the creation of an exemplary society in which Jews and Arabs could live together. In 1925, he shared in the Creation of 'Brit Shalom' (Covenant of Peace), which advocated a bi-national state and maintained this hope until the end of his life. At the time of violent riots in 1928 and 1929, he opposed the arming of Jewish settlers and opted for the minority pacifist position. In debates about immigration quotas, Buber argued for parity rather than the attempt to achieve a Jewish majority.

Buber took a particular interest in the *kibbutz* movement and wrote about it in his *Paths in Utopia*. Living through the early and dangerous years of the newly born state of Israel, Buber was conscious that his continuing hope for a bi-national state was a minority view, but he held to his views, believing that a person should be true to his or her beliefs, whether or not they were popular. It was fitting that, at his state funeral in Jerusalem in 1965, a delegation of the Arab Students' Organization placed a wreath on the grave of one who had striven for peace between Israelis and Palestinians.

Buber was a prophetic and often isolated thinker, who rose above the controversies of his time. He has been described as one of the founder figures of the epoch, which began with the First World War. He strove for a position beyond individualism and collectivism. He also, more than perhaps any other modern thinker, acknowledged both the terrible misuse but also the indispensability of the word God. 'Yes, it is the most heavy-laden of all human words. None has become so soiled, so mutilated...But we may not give it up.' He recognized that spiritual renewal was essential to ensure that religion is a blessing and not a curse for humanity.

CHAPTER NOTES

1. *Encyclopaedia Britannica*, 1977, 3, p. 358.
2. Although written in the first decade of the twentieth century, these books were not translated into English until after the Second World War. For more information on Ba'al Shem Tov see chapter 77.
3. *Ich und Du* was published in 1923. The first English translation was published in 1937. Walter Kaufman, a critic of Buber, who produced a second translation of the work, preferred 'You' – arguing that 'Thou' was archaic and impersonal.
4. Johannan Bloch in *Martin Buber. Bilanz Seines Denken*, Ed Hayyim Gordon, Freiburg, 1983, p. 42.
5. Martin Buber, *Two Types of Faith*, London, Routledge and Kegan Paul, 1951, *passim*. See also Maurice Friedman, *Encouner on a Narrow Ridge: A Life of Martin Buber*, New York, Paragon House, 1991,p. 293
6. Martin Buber, *Between Man and Man*, Routledge, 1947, 2002, pp. 250-51.

90

Mother Teresa

Mother Teresa, who devoted most of her life to the poorest of the poor, founded the Missionaries of Charity. Even in her lifetime she became an icon of sacrificial service and soon after her death, the Holy See began the process of beatification.

Agnes Gonxha Bojaxhiu was born on 26th August 1910, although she regarded the following day when she was baptised as her 'true birthday.' She was born in Skopje, which was then under Turkish rule. Her parents were Albanian and I was present at the unveiling of a statue of her in Tirana, which is the capital of Albania. Skopje is, however, now the capital of the Republic of Macedonia.

Agnes' father, who was involved in politics, died when she was only eight. After his death, her mother brought her up as a Roman Catholic. She was fascinated by stories about missionaries and by the age of twelve wanted to commit herself to a religious life. At the age of eighteen, she left home and went to Ireland, where she learned English at the abbey of the Sisters of Loreto, who ran schools in India. In 1929 she went to India and began her novitiate at Darjeeling. She took her first vows in 1931, when she chose the name Teresa, after Teresa (or Thérèse) of Lisieux (1873-1897), who had been declared patroness of Missions in 1927.

In the nineteen thirties Teresa moved to Calcutta (Kolkata) to teach at the Loreto convent school, which was in the east of the city. She took her solemn vows in 1937.

Teresa was happy teaching, but was increasingly troubled by the near-by poverty, which was made worse by the famine of 1943 and the violent clashes between Muslims and Hindus prior to Independence.

On September 10th, 1946 Teresa experienced what she later described as 'the call within a call' as she was travelling to Darjeeling for her annual retreat. 'I was to leave the convent and help the poor while living among them. It was an order. To fail would have been to break the faith.'[1] She did some training in nursing and moved into the slums. Instead of her nun's habit, she wore a simple white cotton cloth with a blue border and she also became an Indian citizen. In 1948 She

565

started a school, but soon concentrated on caring for the needs of the destitute and starving, especially those close to death. It was a difficult transition, as she noted in her diary. 'The poverty of the poor must be so hard for them. While looking for a home I walked and walked till my arms and legs ached. I thought how much they must ache in body and soul, looking for a home, for food, for health. Then the comfort of Loreto came to tempt me. "You have only to say the word and all that will be yours again," the Tempter kept on saying... Of free choice, my God, and out of love for you, I desire to remain and do whatever be your Holy will in my regard. I did not let a single tear come.'[2]

In 1950, Teresa received permission from the Vatican to start a diocesan congregation that would become the Missionaries of Charity. Its mission was to care for 'the hungry, the naked, the homeless, the crippled, the blind, those with leprosy, all those people who felt unwanted, unloved, uncared for throughout society, people that have become a burden to the society and are shunned by everyone.'[3]

The first Home for the Dying was opened in 1952 in a place made available by the city authorities. The aim was to provide a 'beautiful death for people who lived like animals to die like angels – loved and wanted.'[4] Later, Mother Teresa opened a home for children. Soon homes were being opened across India and the first home overseas was opened in Venezuela in 1965. In 1982, at the height of the siege of Beirut, Mother Teresa managed to achieve a temporary cease-fire so that she could rescue thirty-seven children who were trapped in a hospital close to the front line. Later, with the collapse of Communism, her work expanded in Eastern Europe and she went back for the first time to Albania, the land of her birth, to open a home in Tirana. The Order has grown enormously with, by the time of Mother Teresa's death in 1997, over five hundred missions in more than one hundred countries.

In 1963 an Order of Brothers was founded and a contemplative branch of Sisters in 1976. There are various groups of Co-Workers, including one for those who are sick and suffering, who are linked to an active brother or sister. They are encouraged to offer their suffering as a sacrifice and as a way of sharing in the passion of Christ. 'Suffering in itself is nothing, but suffering accepted together and borne together is joy.' Many of the Sick and Suffering Co-workers were helped to find meaning in their pain. One Brother wrote, 'We cannot escape it (suffering) and we must do all we can to help one another find a purpose in it. If we can find a purpose for accepting his cross as Jesus Christ accepted his own then one will never feel alone.'[5] This emphasis on the redemptive power of suffering is one strand in Christian devotion.

Her work gained increasing recognition both in India, where in 1980 she received India's highest civilian award, the Bharat Ratna. Her work also became more widely known elsewhere, helped in part by a film made by the well known British broadcaster Malcolm Muggeride called *Something Beautiful for God*. A book of the same title was published in 1971. In the same year she received the first Pope John XXIII Peace prize and in 1979 she was awarded the Nobel Peace prize.

Mother Teresa suffered heart attacks in 1983 and 1989, but her offer to resign as head of the Missionaries of Charity was turned down by its members. Her health continued to decline and she died on September 5th, 1997 – just after her eighty-seventh birthday. In the West, her death was overshadowed by news of the sudden death of Princess Diana, but she was given a state funeral by the Indian government in gratitude for her services to the poor of all religions in India.

Like so many of the great spiritual figures of the twentieth century, Mother Teresa expressed her deep devotion to God, not by retreating to a hermitage but by her service of those most in need. Her care for others was an expression of her love for Jesus, as in this prayer, which begins:

> *Lord, open our eyes,*
> *That we may see you in our brothers and sisters.*[6]

The daily prayer of her Co-Workers is,

> *Make us worthy, Lord, to serve our fellow human beings throughout the world who live and die in poverty and hunger.*
> *Through our hands, grant them this day their daily bread; and by our understanding love, give them peace and joy.*[7]

Mother Teresa insisted upon the vital importance of prayer. 'Everything starts from prayer', she said. 'Without asking God for love, we cannot possess love and still less are we able to give it to others.'[8] 'We do nothing', she said, 'he does everything. God has not called me to be successful. He called me to be faithful.'[9]

Criticisms have been made of her work. Many people who are not Roman Catholics disagreed with her determined opposition to divorce and abortion, but in this she was faithful to the teaching of her Church. Her own response to criticism was, 'No matter who says what, you should accept it with a smile and do your own work.'[10]

Others have said she did nothing to tackle the causes of poverty or 'to alleviate the conditions of the poor. She just took care of the sick and dying and needed them to further a sentimentally-moral cause.'[11] She certainly, however, highlighted their plight and drew international attention to the need for radical change.

At a time when some Hindu groups were very suspicious of efforts to convert the poor to Christianity, Mother Teresa was accused of this. She herself, however, insisted that 'I've always said we should help a Hindu become a better Hindu, a Muslim become a better Muslim, a Catholic become a better Catholic.'[12] On one occasion, she was overheard to say to someone who was terminally ill, 'You say a prayer in your religion, and I will say a prayer as I know it.'[13] One of her prayers begins,

Some call Him Ishwar, some call Him Allah, some simply God, but we all have to acknowledge that it is He who made us for greater things: to love and be loved. What matters is that we love. We cannot love without prayer, and so whatever religion we are we must pray together.'[14]

On the other hand, Mother Teresa is reported to have said on another occasion, 'I'm not a social worker. I don't do it for this reason. I do it for Christ. I do it for the church.'[15]

Mother Teresa, who wrote numerous letters of spiritual counsel, asked that they should be destroyed when she died. Many of them, however, were published in 2007 in *Come Be My Light*. In one of them to Michael van der Peet, she wrote, 'Jesus has a very special love for you. As for me, the silence and the emptiness is so great, that I look and do not see – listen and do not hear – the tongue moves (in prayer) but does not speak... I want you to pray for me - that I let Him have a free hand.'[16] The Editor compared her experience to the 'dark night of the soul,' which St John of the Cross and other saints have mentioned. Some of the media spoke of her 'crisis of faith.'[17]

If there were times of darkness, they do nothing to lessen Mother Teresa's example and achievements. She could be tough in her advice to others and certainly was hard on herself. Yet, in the words of Nawaz Sharif, a Prime Minister of Pakistan, she was 'a rare individual who lived long for higher purposes. Her life-long devotion to the care of the poor, the sick, and the disadvantaged was one of the highest examples of service to our humanity.' An American public opinion poll ranked her as 'the most admired person of the twentieth century' and Javier Pérez de Cuéllar, a Secretary-General of the United Nations, said of her, 'She is the United Nations. She is peace in the world.'[18]

CHAPTER NOTES

1. Quoted by Joan Graff Clucas, *Mother Teresa*, New York, Chelsea House Publications, p. 39.
2. Quoted by Kathryn Spink, *Mother Teresa: A Complete Authorised Biography*, HarperCollins, p. 284.
3. Spink, p. 284.
4. Spink, p. 55.
5. Kathryn Spink, *A Chain of Love: Mother Teresa and her Suffering Disciples*, London, SPCK, 1984, p. 14.
6. *1,000 World Prayers*, Marcus Braybrooke (ed.), p. 315.
7. *1,000 World Prayers*, p. 311.
8. Mother Teresa, *Everything Starts from Prayer*, Ed. Anthony Stern, Ashland, Origon, White Cloud Press, 1998, p. 1.
9. *Everything Starts from Prayer*, p. 129.
10. Quoted on the Wikipedia entry.
11. Victor Bamerjee,'A Canopy Most Fatal' in the *Indian Telegraph*, 8.9.2002.
12. *Everything Starts from Prayer*, p. xv.
13. *Everything Starts from Prayer*, p. xvi
14. *Everything Starts from Prayer*, p. 11.
15. CBS News, 9.10. 2003.
16. Brian Kolodiejchuk, *Mother Teresa: Come Be My Light*, New York, Doubleday, 2007.

17. For example, *Time* and *The Daily Telegraph*.
18. *ChristianMemorials.com*.

91

Yukitaka Yamamoto

Yukitaka Yamamoto, the ninety-sixth Shinto Priest of the Tsubaki Grand Shrine in Japan, was a dedicated worker for world peace and for interfaith co-operation. He was President of the International Association for Religious Freedom from 1996-1999 and helped Westerners to understand Shrine Shintoism.

The indigenous religion of Japan has no founder. The name Shintoism is a combination of *Shin*, which is the Chinese character for god and *Tao*, which is the ordinary word for 'road', but also has the sense of way of life or way of God. Shintoism is also referred to as *Kami no Michi* – the way of the kami, or spirits, which are present in Nature. The indigenous religion only acquired the name Shintoism when the arrival in Japan of Buddhism - which was called Butsudo - made it necessary to distinguish it from the new religion.

Shintoism also has no formal scripture, although a text known as the *Kojiki*, complied between 682 and 712 CE, records the early myths and traditions of the people. It is said that the original deity who emerged from the waters that covered the earth gave birth to many *kami*, of whom two – *the Amatsu Kami* – were told to organise the material world. They created the Goddess of the Sun – the *Kami Amaterasu* – to rule the earth and they also gave birth to the ancestors of the people of Japan.

Shintoism, with its deep sense of natural beauty, reflects the spiritual awareness of a people who lived close to Nature. They organised their lives around the changing seasons, honouring the sun and moon and lightning. Mount Fuji or *Fuji-san*, the highest of the volcanic peaks, is regarded as a sacred embodiment of the divine creativity that in past ages formed the islands of Japan. This affinity to Nature, despite the modern industrialization of Japan, is still preserved in Japan's rock gardens, tea ceremonies, poetry and art.

Shintoism encourages people to live 'according to the kami' and in harmony with Nature. This, to which the name *Kannagara* may be given, is not an exclusively Japanese or Shinto idea, but, according to Yukitaka Yamamoto,

'A concept with universal significance and applicability. *Kannagara* has to do with spirit, and with bringing the spirit of man and his activities into line with the spirit of Great Nature. The Spirit of Great Nature may be a flower, may be the beauty of the mountains, the pure snow, the soft rains or the gentle breeze. *Kannagara* means being in communion with these forms of beauty and so with the highest level of experiences of life.'[1]

The *kami* are most powerfully present in places of great beauty such as mountains or waterfalls. It is therefore at such places that, to honour the *kami*, the Japanese have built shrines, which may include the grave of a *kami*. This is the case at the Tsubaki Grand Shrine. The shrine, which is at the foot of Mount Takayama and Mount Hikiyamai, is very ancient. It was in this area that Sarutahiko Okami, the head of the earthly *kami*, who was the pioneer of the way of rightness and justice, lived and died. The *Kojiki* indicates that, after his death, a shrine was established around 300 CE, on the order of Princess Yamatohime-no-Mikoto - a descendant of the *kami* of the Sun, Amaterasu - to enshrine the soul of Sarutahiko Okami. The shrine had to be restored in the sixteenth century, because it had been razed to the ground by Oda Nobinaga (1534-1582), who persecuted many religious groups. By the time Yukitaka Yamamoto became a priest at the shrine, more work was urgently needed, as the roof was beginning to collapse and there was rot under the main worship sanctuary. One of Yukitaka Yamamoto's great achievements was the restoration of the shrine.

Because of the significance of Sarutahiko Okami and because of its antiquity, the Tsubaki Grand Shrine is one of the most important Shinto shrines in Japan, although it has never been associated with State Shintoism, which was a militaristic perversion. Indeed, Yukitaka Yamamoto says that because of the importance of Sarutahiko Okami in Japanese mythology, 'Tsubaki Grand Shrine has shown its ability to think and behave independently of the government at more than one crucial time in Japanese history.'[2]

But it is time now to say more about Yukitaka Yamamoto, who never expected to be a priest. Yukitaka Yamamoto was born at the Tsubaki Shrine in 1923. His father Yukitero Yamamoto was the 95th High Priest, having married Hisao, who was the daughter of the 94th priest.

Yukitaka was a twin. He also had an elder brother and a younger brother as well as his twin brother and one sister. Although, Yukitaka recollected, 'I did not know we were poor,' the family, in fact, was very poor. Only three times, as a child, did Yukitaka receive new clothes. The family only ate white rice at festivals. His father, however, defied custom by sometimes getting red meat, because he wanted his children to have strong bodies. The children had to collect wood from the forests and water from the stream. There was no electricity or running water.

Yukitero Yamamoto decided that Yukitaka's elder brother and his twin brother should become priests. This meant that Yukitaka and his younger brother would have to find other work. At the age of six, Yukitaka started at the local elementary school and then went on to a middle school, which involved cycling more than twelve miles in each direction. At the school Yukitaka became captain of the Kendo team – Kendo is a traditional Japanese martial art in which two contestants, wearing protective armour, fight with bamboo swords. He also set a record for the 10,000 metres race.

On leaving school, Yukitaka, who wanted to travel, won a scholarship to a specialist college called Takuna Juku, where people were trained, supposedly, to go to countries like Indonesia to assist in developing the region. The discipline was that of a military college. Yukitaka Yamamoto was only just eighteen, when the Japanese attacked Pearl Harbour. The war started around the time he left Middle School. As a result on graduating from Takuna Juku in August 1942, Yukitaka Yamamoto joined the navy and became a political officer. He was posted to New Britain Island, just east of Papua New Guinea, to serve at the Naval base of Rabaul, where he landed on December 25th, 1942.

The tide was already turning against the Japanese. By September 1943, the Japanese had lost Eastern New Guinea, the Northern Solomon Islands and the Marshall Islands, which are in the Pacific. The USA was operating a two prong attack, with General Douglas MacArthur advancing in the south and Admiral Chester William Nimitz advancing in the north. Yukitaka Yamamoto had very quickly become convinced of the pointlessness of war. In March 1944, Rasbaul was heavily bombarded and Yukitaka Yamamoto like many others was moved to Northeast New Guinea, but in April, American and Australian forces landed. About fifteen thousand Japanese fled from Hollandia into the jungle. Most of them died there of hunger or disease – some were eaten by crocodiles. Yukitaka Yamamoto comments that for nearly two years he did not have a single grain of rice. He ate nuts, berries and buds of trees and grass. Some of the fleeing Japanese gave up and a few made it back to Hollandia. About three hundred pushed on and Yukitaka Yamamoto was one of only three to survive. Yukitaka Yamamoto said,

'I remembered how I had been trained not to be a soldier but to be a worker in the development of Greater East Asia… and that we would free the nations of Pacific from colonial overlords. Instead we were locked in deadly combat with the United States… We had been completely deceived. Here I was in the midst of a gruesome conflict creating meaningless death and destruction…Coming face to face with the sufferings and privations of war is the best source of motivation to seek peace.'[3]

Yukitaka Yamamoto tells of his terrible memories, including seeing human beings eat the flesh of other human beings. 'I can never forget the bitterness, sadness and horror of those days,' he wrote later. 'They forced me to think profoundly about what mankind must do to prevent such a diabolical cataclysm from ever taking place again.'[4]

The war officially ended on August 15th, 1945, but Yukitaka Yamamoto knew nothing of this. In the forest, he and his companions found themselves under attack by poisonous darts from natives. At the end of August they found pieces of paper that said the war was over - but they did not believe the news. Three months later, Yukitaka Yamamoto and a few other Japanese fugitives decided to come down from the mountains. They surrendered to some American soldiers who shook hands with them and arranged for medical checks. But Yukitaka Yamamoto was to remain a prisoner of war until June 1946, when he at last returned to Japan, although he was not discharged from the navy until September, having spent the time trying to help settle some of the returning soldiers – a task that underlined for him the terrible cost of war in human terms.

Yukitaka Yamamoto, already knew from vivid dreams, that his elder brother and his twin brother had been killed in the war. It fell to him, therefore, to train to be a priest and he entered Kogakuin University near Ise, where there is a famous shrine. In his early years as a priest, working alongside his father, there was little to do. Although his father had refused to co-operate with State Shinto, many people had misgivings about anything associated with Shinto. There were, therefore, few visitors to the shrine, so Yukitaka Yamamoto, for a time, helped develop a local agricultural co-operative. In 1955, Yukitaka Yamamoto decided to devote the rest of his life to the search for inner truth and understanding and to concentrate on his work as a priest at Tsubaki Grand Shrine.

Yukitaka Yamamoto especially valued the discipline of *misogi harai*, or water purification. He revived the full ritual in 1959 and practised it on a regular basis. For the *misogi*, a person puts on a loin cloth and a headband. After exercises to shake up the soul and other rituals of purification, one enters the waterfall to commune with the *kami*. One then takes the weight of the water on the back of the neck, allowing it to cover the body and wash away impurities. At the same time the bather shouts out 'Purify my soul – wash my soul – purify the six elements of existence.' When my wife and I visited Tsubaki Grand Shrine, we were privileged to be invited to take part in the *misogi* purification. My wife particularly remembers the sense of oneness with Nature that she experienced. Yukitaka Yamamoto continued with this discipline for several years.

Even before the war, some Americans had made contact with shrine. By 1968, Yukitaka Yamamoto was thinking about visiting the USA and was greatly helped in his preparations by Dr Shininchiro Imaoka, who was a Japanese Unitarian minister and founder and first President of the Japanese Free Religious Association. Dr Imaoka, who died at the age of 106 in 1988 was known for his generosity. His son said, 'My father was a very bad father. He gave away everything. During the war, my mother had to hide food so we would not starve.' It was he who was to introduce the Tsubaki Grand Shrine as well as the new Buddhist movement Rissho Kosei Kai - founded by Dr Nikkyo Niwano – to the International Association for Religious Freedom (IARF). IARF is one of the oldest interfaith organisations, dating from early in the twentieth century. Originally IARF mainly concentrated on issues of religious freedom as they affected Liberal or Free Christians and Unitarians in Europe and America, but by the late sixties IARF was reaching out to liberal members of other religions. For example, Dr Dana Greeley, an outstanding Unitarian leader, was also working at this time with Japanese religious leaders in setting up the World Conference on Religions and Peace (WCRP) to mobilise people of faith in opposition to nuclear weapons. The first WCRP Assembly was held at Kyoto, Japan, in 1970.

In America, Yukitaka Yamamoto attended a meeting of the Universalist Unitarian Association, where, for the first time, he spoke about Shintoism to a non-Japanese audience. Subsequently he has helped to make Shintoism better known in the West and there is now an American Tsubaki Shrine at Stockton in California.

'More than once,' Yukitaka Yamamoto recalled in his biography 'I had difficulty explaining that State Shinto and the local, traditional and authentically spiritual Shrine Shinto were two totally different things.'[5] After Japan's military successes against China and Russia early in the twentieth century, the government used Shinto, which had earlier been formally separated from Buddhism, as a unifying ideology to strengthen its hold on society. The union of religion and state, as taught by State Shinto, Yukitaka Yamamoto has said, was a 'perversion of the true thought of Shinto, which is about *kannagara*, or the way of the divine as perceived by the Japanese spirit.'[6] The aim of Shinto rituals is to bring the divine into direct relation with humans. For instance, in some ceremonies branches of evergreen trees, on which the spirits have alighted, are used to transfer blessings to the worshipper. Shinto temples are simple, usually of unadorned wood. Shinto beliefs too are simple, compared to the complex doctrines of some other religions. Shintoism is sometimes described as polytheistic, but Yukitaka Yamamoto has written that this is misleading. 'There is ultimately only one *kami* and all *kami* share the same quality but the one *kami* can divide into several parts and these can function in different places at the one time.'[7]

Reverence for one *kami* should imply reverence for all *kamis*. Followers of Shintoism should, therefore, relate happily to members of other faiths. Yukitaka Yamamoto insisted that 'a Shinto believer who denounces other religions is not a real Shinto believer.'[8] With such beliefs, it was natural that Yukitaka Yamamoto should feel at home with members of the International Association for Religious Freedom. In

1969 Yukitaka Yamamoto attended the IARF Congress at Boston, where he became a member of IARF, of which in 1996 he became President. He voiced the universalism inherent in the movement when he said, 'We are children of the sun dependent equally upon the sun's light and heat for our survival... and brothers and sisters in our common humanity.'[9]

Yukitaka Yamamoto's sense of human unity and commitment to peace has been characteristic of other influential Japanese religious leaders of the second half of the twentieth century, such as Dr Daisaku Ikeda and Rev Nikkyo Niwano, who have already been mentioned.[10]. All of them have been shaped by the horrific experience of war and of the devastation caused by the dropping of atomic bombs on Hiroshima and Nagasaki.

Daisaku Ikeda, the President of Soka Gakkai International, was inspired by the Bodhisattva's example of total dedication to the relief of suffering, but he also recalled how deeply he was affected by his mother's example. Soon after she had been told that her eldest son had been killed in action in Burma, an American pilot parachuted to earth near their house. Japanese soldiers seized him and began to beat him and kick him. Daisaku's mother protested, saying, 'Think how worried the American's mother must be about her son.'

Revd Nikkyo Niwano, the founder of Rissho Kosei kai, was inspired by the Lotus Sutra, which presents the concept of peace. Nikkyo Niwano spoke for Yukitaka Yamamoto and other Japanese religious leaders, when he wrote 'a world of great harmony will appear when all nations, all races, and all classes come to live in accordance with one truth, so that discrimination among them vanishes, discord and fighting do not occur, and all people work joyfully, enjoy their lives, and promote culture.[11]

CHAPTER NOTES

1. Yukitaka Yamamoto, *Kami No Michi: The Way of Life*, Stockton, CA, Tsubaki America Publications, 1987, p. 74.
2. Yukitaka Yamamoto, p. 54.
3. Yukitaka Yamamoto, p. 25.
4. Yukitaka Yamamoto, p. 26.
5. Yukitaka Yamamoto, p. 63.
6. Yukitaka Yamamoto, p. 66.

7. Yukitaka Yamamoto, p. 82.
8. Yukitaka Yamamoto, p. 83.
9. Yukitaka Yamamoto, p. 67.
10. See chapter 74.
11. Nikkyo Niwano, *A Buddhist Approach to Peace*, Tokyo, Kosei Publishing, 1977, p. 65.

92

Elie Wiesel

Elie Wiesel, who survived the concentration camps as a teenager, has been a witness to the world about the unbelievable horrors of the Holocaust or Shoah. He has insisted that 'victims need above all to know that they are not alone.'[1] He is a novelist and political activist

Elie Wiesel was born in 1928 in Transylvania in Sighet, now known as Sighetu Marmatiei, which was then in the Kingdom of Romania, but is now part of Hungary. His father Shlomo, who was an Orthodox Jew of Hungarian descent, ran his own grocery store. Shlomo was an active and trusted member of the local community. Elie's mother Sarah was the daughter of a nearby farmer, who was a Hasid or member of a charismatic Jewish religious movement of which Ba'al Shem Tov (1700-60) - whom we have met in chapter 66 - was one of the first leaders. His mother encouraged Elie to study the Torah (Jewish teaching) and Kabbalah (Jewish mysticism). His father, who was more of a humanist, 'a cultured man and rather unsentimental'[2] encouraged him to learn Modern Hebrew and to read widely. Elie had two older sisters and one younger one. As an adolescent, Elie was a deeply observant Jew. 'By day I studied Talmud,' he wrote, 'and by night I would run to the synagogue to weep over the destruction of the Temple.'[3]

The town of Sighet was again annexed by Hungary in 1940. In 1944 Elie and his family were placed in the larger of the two ghettos in Sighet. Then German soldiers arrived. At first life seemed fairly normal, then late one night his father came home and said one word, 'Transports.' Next day, the Hungarian police began clearing the ghetto. Elie watched the first people to be deported. No one knew where the people were going. 'The secret was well kept.' All too soon, Elie and his family were being crowded into the cattle cars - eighty to each one. After a hellish journey they arrived. 'Someone near a window read to us "Auschwitz". Nobody had ever heard that name. The train did not move again.'[4]

By giving his age as eighteen, Wiesel escaped being taken straight to the gas chambers. On the first night, the group he was marching with came closer and closer to the pit from which an infernal heat was rising.

He wrote,

> Never shall I forget that first night, the first night in camp, which has turned my life into one long night, seven times cursed and seven times sealed.
> Never shall I forget that smoke.
> Never shall I forget the little faces of children, whose bodies I saw transformed into smoke under a silent sky.
> Never shall I forget those flames that consumed my faith forever.
> Never shall I forget that nocturnal silence which deprived me for all eternity of the desire to live.
> Never shall I forget those moments that murdered my God and my soul and turned my dreams to ashes.
> Never shall I forget these things, even if I am to live as long as God himself.
> Never.[5]

Later in the book, Wiesel describes, in a famous passage, the time when two adults and a young boy were hanged by the SS:

> '"Where is merciful God? Where is He?" Someone behind me was asking ... Then came the march past the victim. [The adults were dead], but the child, too light, was still breathing and [for half an hour he remained] writhing before our eyes. Behind me, I heard the same man asking, "For God's sake, where is God?" And from within me I heard a voice answer: "Where is He? This is where – hanging from this gallows." That night the soup tasted of corpses."'[6]

Christians, with their belief that Jesus, the Son of God, died on the cross, sometimes take Wiesel to mean that God was to be found in the suffering, but the context suggests that it was Wiesel's faith in God that died at that time. For Wiesel then goes on to describe his feelings of rebellion as some ten thousand men came to participate in the solemn service on the eve of *Rosh Hashanah* (the Jewish New Year). 'Why would I bless God's name? 'I was the accuser, God the accused. My eyes had opened and I was alone, terribly alone in a world without God, without man.' On *Yom Kippur*, (the Day of Atonement), Wiesel did not fast. As I swallowed my ration of soup, I turned that act into a symbol of rebellion, of protest against Him'[7]

It was not until some years after his time at Aushwitz that Wiesel wrote of his experiences in the concentration camps. At Auschwitz the number A-7713 was tattooed into his left arm. He was separated from his mother and sister Tzipora, who are presumed to have been murdered. Wiesel managed to stay with his father for a year, but his father died after they had been marched to Buchenwald only months before the camps were liberated.

There is a certain ambiguity and development in Wiesel's writings. In his early novels *Night, Dawn* and the *Accident,* he expresses his despair and the emptiness of a world without God. Later, in *Town Beyond the Wall,* he wrestles with the question of how man is to live in a post-Holocaust world. Later, in *The Gates of the Forest,* he considers the role of tradition. In *The Oath,* he transcends despair and investigates the consequences of his vision of a world in which the loving God of Israel is absent. In the cantata *Ani Maamim,* he wrestles with problem of theodicy – of why a good God allows suffering. In a later work, *The Trial of God,* Berish begins the prosecution by accusing God of cruelty and indifference. Towards the end Berish declares,

'I lived as a Jew, and it as a Jew that I shall die – and it is as a Jew that, with my last breath, I shall shout my protest to God! And because the end is near, I shall shout the louder! Because the end is near, I'll tell Him that He's more guilty than ever.'[8]

It has been said that 'Wiesel seems to adopt contradictory positions. On the one hand, he argues that God is indifferent to suffering...On the other hand he adopts a Job-like stance.'[9] Perhaps the same consistency is not to be expected of a novelist as of a theologian or a philosopher. At times in his writings, Wiesel held that God needlessly permitted the Holocaust. It was an event, which no possible good-to-come could justify. His experiences led to loss and despair and his own faith was challenged. He spoke of the death of the self who believed in God. Yet he also suggests that God was on trial as well. In true Jewish manner he asserted that one must "never give up, never yield to despair." He adopts the stance of the wrestler with God. Wiesel believed that wrestling with God, protesting against Him, was the only legitimate response, not giving up on God completely.

After the war Wiesel was placed in a French orphanage and was reunited with his older sisters Hilda and Bea. He learned French and studied at the Sorbonne. For a time he taught Hebrew and then worked as a choirmaster before he became a professional journalist. He refused, however, to write anything about the Holocaust – there were no words to describe it. Then in 1952 he met François Mauriac, who was Nobel Laureate in Literature. Mauriac persuaded Wiesel to write about what he had seen and endured. Wiesel wrote some nine hundred pages in Yiddish and wrote a much shorter version in French. But, despite Mauriac's best efforts, both the French and the English versions were rejected by major French and American publishers. Eventually a French version – with even more cuts – was published by Éditions de Minuit in 1958. *Night* has, of course, become a best seller.

By the time the book was published, Wiesel had moved to New York. He became an American citizen. His writings soon gained him recognition and he has won many literary prizes. He has taught at Universites and is a well-known public speaker, especially on many aspects of the Holocaust.

The driving force for Wiesel, the compulsion that made him put pen to paper, was the need to record the story of the Holocaust for posterity. As a survivor, he felt he had to tell the story. He had no choice. The story had to be remembered for three reasons. Firstly, the dead are owed a debt by the living and deserve to be remembered. Those whose names are not known must also be remembered. Secondly, by never forgetting we will never allow it to happen again. Thirdly, in remembering the past, it is re-created. Then it is possible to mourn the dead properly.

Wiesel recognised and stressed the importance of being a messenger. He explained that he went through a five-step process to recognise this role.

1. The event took place. One must speak.
2. The event defies description. One cannot speak.
3. The event suggests an alternative. One could *choose* silence.
4. The event precludes silence. One *must* become a messenger.
5. The event suggests a certain kind of message. One can be a

'teller of tales'.

The Holocaust was a defining event in twentieth century history. It gave an impetus to the Zionist struggle for a land where Jews could determine their own future. Israelis, however, soon discovered that such freedom depended upon their own strength. The Arab world has been reluctant to make space for a Jewish state and in turn many Palestinians have been forced from their homes. The problems of the Middle East continue to dominate world politics.

Christians have become aware that false teaching about Jews, who were traditionally blamed for the death of Jesus – sometimes referred to as 'deicide' – contributed greatly to the suffering of Jews through the centuries and prepared the seed ground on which the evil weed of Nazism could grow. Anti-Semitism itself was a pseudo-scientific and baseless claim that some races – primarily Arians – are superior to other races.

The Holocaust has raised numerous questions about both human nature and its potential for evil and the character of God. If God is all-loving and all-powerful, how could God let such evil happen and allow his 'chosen people' to suffer such an atrocity? Both Jewish and Christian theologians have wrestled with these questions and attempted a variety of answers. Indeed, it has been said that all religious thought today has to start with the Holocaust.

Wiesel, as has been said, was a novelist not a theologian. He said, 'I have learned that there are no sufficient literary, psychological or historical answers to human tragedy, only moral ones.' He has ensured that the horror of the Holocaust will not be forgotten and has raised issues that others continue to struggle with.

Wiesel insists that the Holocaust was a unique event. He recognizes that others besides Jews were murdered by the Nazis, but adds, 'Not all victims were Jews, but all Jews were victims.' He is well aware that many other innocent victims have suffered in subsequent acts of genocide. Yet he believes that the Holocaust conveys a universal message, valid wherever injustice, oppression and hatred are to be found. Consequently, Wiesel is listened to by Jews and non-Jews alike. Wiesel urges men and women to speak out against injustice wherever it is found and not just to speak out against it but to act against it too.

'Take sides. Neutrality helps the oppressor, never the victim. Silence encourages the tormentor, never the tormented.'

Wiesel was awarded the Nobel Peace Prize in 1986. The citation deservedly said of him that he is: 'One of the most important spiritual leaders and guides in an age when violence, repression and racism continue to characterise the world, Wiesel is a messenger to mankind: his message is one of peace, atonement and human dignity.'

CHAPTER NOTES

1. Elie Wiesel, *Night*, which was first published as *La Nuit*, in 1958. References are to the translation by Marion Wiesel, London, Penguin, 2006, p. 120. From his Nobel Peace Prize Acceptance Speech.
2. *Night*, p. 4.
3. *Night*, p. 3.
4. *Night*, p. 27.
5. *Night*, p. 34.
6. *Night*, pp. 64-5.
7. *Night*, p. 66-9.
8. Quoted in Dan Cohn-Sherbok, *Holocaust Theology*, Lamp Press 1989, p. 101. In his chapter on Wiesel, Dan Cohn-Sherbok gives a good summary of Wiesel's novels.
9. Dan Cohn-Sherbok, p. 102.

93

Martin Luther King

Martin Luther King, the youngest person to be awarded the Nobel Peace Prize, helped to end racial discrimination and segregation in the USA by a campaign of non-violent civil disobedience which he led. A Baptist minister, he has been compared as an orator to Abraham Linclon. His example continues to inspire those committed to social change by non-violent means.

Martin Luther King was born on January 15th, 1929, in Atlanta, Georgia. By a mistake, his name was recorded as 'Michael King' on his baptismal certificate, but this was not discovered until 1934, when his father was applying for a passport. Martin Luther was the son of the Reverend Martin Luther King, Senior and Alberta Williams King. He had an elder sister. His father, like Martin's grandfather, was pastor of Ebenezer Baptist Church in Atlanta and had been involved in a struggle for voting rights in 1935. 'Of course', Martin said, 'I was religious. I grew up in the church. My father is a preacher, my grandfather was a preacher, my great-grandfather was a preacher, my daddy's brother is a preacher. So I didn't have much choice.'[1] Growing up, he was very conscious of the discrimination from which black people suffered. 'For a long time I could not go swimming, until there was a Negro YMCA. A Negro child could not go to any public park. I could not go to the so-called white-school. In many stores I couldn't go to a lunch counter to buy a hamburger or a cup of coffee. I could not attend any of the theatres.'

Martin was educated at Morehouse College, where he said, 'the shackles of fundamentalism were removed from my body.'[2] He then went to Crozer Theological Seminary, where he studied Gandhi's life and teaching seriously, but was also challenged by the critique of pacifism by the American theologian Reinhold Niebuhr (1892-1971). King thought Niebuhr mistook pacifism for non-resistance instead of non-violence. 'True pacifism,' King said, 'is not unrealistic submission to evil power... It is rather a courageous confrontation of evil by the power of love.'[3] After Crozer, King went on to Boston University, where he gained his doctorate for a Comparison of the Concept of God in the two very different theologians, Paul Tillich and Henry Nelson Weiman.

In 1953, aged twenty four, King became pastor of a Baptist church in Montgomery. His involvement in the struggle against racial discrimination began two years later when Rosa Parks, a black woman, was arrested because she refused to give up her seat to a white man, as required by what were known as the Jim Crow laws. In response, the black population of the town, led by King, boycotted the Montgomery Bus Company for over a year. During the campaign, King's house was bombed and he was arrested for a time, but the campaign was successful, as the Supreme Court ruled that segregation on all public transport was illegal.

Already influenced by Mahatma Gandhi's non-violent activism, King, with his wife, went to India in 1959, 'not as a tourist, but as a pilgrim,' to visit the Gandhi family. He met many people who had known Gandhi and placed a wreath at the shrine of the Raj Ghat, where Gandhi's body had been cremated. His time in India profoundly affected King by deepening his understanding of nonviolent resistance and his commitment to America's struggle for civil rights. In a radio address made during his final evening in India, King said,

'Since being in India, I am more convinced than ever before that the method of nonviolent resistance is the most potent weapon available to oppressed people in their struggle for justice and human dignity. In a real sense, Mahatma Gandhi embodied in his life certain universal principles that are inherent in the moral structure of the universe, and these principles are as inescapable as the law of gravitation.'

Martin and Coretta were deeply shocked by the plight of the untouchables and by seeing so many people sleeping on the streets. On his return, Martin determined to live as simply as possible. He even said to Coretta, 'You know, a man who dedicates himself to a cause doesn't need a family' - Gandhi's wife herself had a difficult life. Coretta says, amazingly, that she was not hurt by what he said, but felt that having a family 'gave him a kind of humanness which brought him closer to the mass of the people.'[4]

King soon realised that simplifying his life was not easy. He could not do his job without a telephone and as he had to travel a lot, he needed a car. When, sometime later, it was suggested that, on his release from prison, he should be collected in a Cadillac, he objected, telling Coretta, 'You just drive our car and I'll drive it back.'

On his return from India, King organised and led marches for black peoples' right to vote, for desegregation, and for labour and other basic civil rights. He was clear about the need for legislation. I still remember his words when I heard him speak in London, that 'you cannot make a man love me, but you can make laws to stop him lynching me.' As a result of his efforts, the Civil Rights (1964) and the Voting Rights (1965) Acts were passed. Wide publicity for King's campaigns helped to make the Civil Rights Movement the key issue in American domestic politics in the sixties. He was, however, stirring up opposition. The FBI started wiretapping King in 1961, fearing that Communists were infiltrating the Civil Rights Movement. No evidence of this was found. As someone observed 'there were no more Communists in the movement than Eskimos in Florida.' Later, the FBI tried to discredit King by suggesting that he engaged in extramarital affairs – a charge denied by Martin Luther and his family.

The biggest event was the March on Washington in 1963, in which over a quarter of a million people participated. Although there was criticism of King for agreeing to President John F Kennedy's wish to soften the march's message, King's address, delivered at the Lincoln Memorial, 'I have a Dream' electrified the crowd and is regarded as one of the finest speeches in the history of American oratory. It ended with this celebrated passage:

'I have a dream that one day this nation will rise up and live out the true meaning of its creed: "We hold these truths to be self-evident: that all men are created equal."

I have a dream that one day on the red hills of Georgia the sons of former slaves and the sons of former slave owners will be able to sit down together at the table of brotherhood.

I have a dream that one day even the state of Mississippi, a state sweltering with the heat of injustice, sweltering with the heat of oppression, will be transformed into an oasis of freedom and justice.

I have a dream that my four little children will one day live in a nation where they will not be judged by the color of their skin but by the content of their character.

I have a dream today.

I have a dream that one day, down in Alabama, with its vicious racists, with its governor having his lips dripping with the words of interposition and nullification; one day right there in Alabama, little black boys and black girls will be able to join hands with little white boys and white girls as sisters and brothers.

I have a dream today.

I have a dream that one day every valley shall be exalted, every hill and mountain shall be made low, the rough places will be made plain, and the crooked places will be made straight, and the glory of the Lord shall be revealed, and all flesh shall see it together...

And when this happens, when we allow freedom to ring, when we let it ring from every village and every hamlet, from every state and every city, we will be able to speed up that day when all of God's children, black men and white men, Jews and Gentiles, Protestants and Catholics, will be able to join hands and sing in the words of the old Negro spiritual, "Free at last! free at last! thank God Almighty, we are free at last!"'[5]

On several occasions, King said that black Americans should receive compensation for the injustices and disadvantages from which they suffered – demands which he developed in his book, *Why We Can't Wait*.

In 1965, King and others tried to organise a march from Selma to the state capital, Montgomery. The first attempt, however, was halted because of mob and police violence – but pictures of police brutality on what became known as 'Bloody Sunday' were shown extensively on American television. The march finally went ahead on March 25th, when King delivered his speech 'How Long, Not Long.'

In 1966, King and others tried to spread the movement to the North of the USA. King moved into Chicago's slums to experience at first hand the poverty of the people there. Their marches were met with hostility, but King persisted despite death-threats. It was at this time that Jesse Jackson, then a seminary student, became involved in the Civil Rights movement, of which he was to become a prominent leader.

Already, King was expressing doubts about the United States' role in the Vietnam War, calling the US government 'the greatest purveyor of violence in the world today.' He also recognised the unjust distribution of wealth in the world. 'A true revolution of values will soon look uneasily on the glaring contrast of poverty and wealth... across the seas.' 'True compassion' he said, 'is more than flinging a coin to a beggar; it comes to see that the edifice which produces beggars needs restructuring.' Such views, however, alienated the mainstream media.

In 1968, King organised the 'Poor People's Campaign' to address issues of economic injustice – but then tragedy struck. On a visit to Memphis, Tennessee, in support of black sanitary public works employees, King delivered his famous speech, 'I've been to the Mountaintop,' in which he said,

'And then I got to Memphis. And some began to talk about the threats that were out. What would happen to me from some of our sick white brothers?

Well, I don't know what will happen now. We've got some difficult days ahead. But it doesn't matter with me now. Because I've been to the mountaintop. And I don't mind. Like anybody, I would like to live a long life. Longevity has its place. But I'm not concerned about that now. I just want to do God's will. And He's allowed me to go up to the mountain. And I've looked over. And I've seen the promised land. I may not get there with you. But I want you to know tonight, that we, as a people, will get to the promised land. And I'm happy, tonight. I'm not worried about anything. I'm not fearing any man. Mine eyes have seen the glory of the coming of the Lord.'[6]

King had just returned to the hotel and was standing on a balcony when a shot rang out. King was pronounced dead at St. Joseph's Hospital at 7:05 p.m. The assassination led to a nationwide wave of riots in more than 60 cities.

Five days later, President Lyndon B. Johnson declared a national day of mourning for the lost civil rights leader. A crowd of 300,000 attended his funeral that same day. The Vice-President attended on behalf of Lyndon B. Johnson, who was holding a meeting on the Vietnam War. At his widow's request, King eulogized himself. His last sermon at Ebenezer Baptist Church, a recording of his famous 'Drum Major' sermon was played at the funeral. In that sermon King made a request that at his funeral no mention of his awards and honors be made, but that it be said that he tried to 'feed the hungry', 'clothe the naked', 'be right on the [Vietnam] war question', and 'love and serve humanity'. At King's request, his good friend Mahalia Jackson sang his favorite hymn, 'Take My hand, Precious Lord.'

Two months after King's death, James Earl Ray was arrested at Heathrow airport and quickly extradited to Tennessee and charged with King's murder. He confessed to the assassination, although he recanted this confession three days later. On the advice of his attorney, Ray took a guilty plea to avoid a trial conviction and thus the possibility of receiving the death penalty. Ray was sentenced to a 99-year prison term. He spent the remainder of his life attempting (unsuccessfully) to withdraw his guilty plea and secure the trial he never had.

King received numerous honours, including twenty honorary degrees. President Ronald Regan signed a bill creating a federal holiday to honour King, called Martin Luther King day, which was observed for the first time on January 20th, 1986. King is one of the ten 20th century martyrs from across the world who are depicted in statues above the Great West Door of Westminster Abbey in London. In the spring of 2006, a stage play about King, *Passages of Martin Luther King*, was produced in Beijing, China with King portrayed by Chinese actor, Cao Li.

King's influence extended beyond America to include the Black Consciousness Movement and Civil Rights Movements in South Africa. King's work was cited by and served as an inspiration for another black Nobel Peace prize winner who fought for racial justice in that country, Albert Lutuli (c.1898-July 21, 1967), who was Chief of his tribe and president-general of the African National Congress.

King's wife, Coretta Scott King, followed her husband's footsteps and was active in matters of social justice and civil rights until her death in 2006. Already in the same year Martin Luther King was assassinated, Mrs. King had established the King Center in Atlanta, Georgia, dedicated to preserving his legacy and the work of championing nonviolent conflict resolution and tolerance worldwide. I once had the privilege of meeting her and was impressed by her tranquility and continuing total commitment to non-violence.

King's workload was enormous. In the eleven years between 1957 and 1968 he is estimated to have travelled over six million miles and to have spoken some twenty-five hundred times. It is true that King's movement faltered in the latter stages, after the great legislative victories of 1965, but even the sharp attacks by more militant blacks and such prominent critics as Malcolm X, have not diminished his stature. Some critics advocated violence, others wanted segregation not integration

Clergy of many Christian denominations, as well as rabbis, marched with Luther King. Soon after the announcement that he had won the Nobel Peace Prize for 1964, Martin, who was in hospital, was visited by the Roman Catholic Archbishop of Atlanta. He congratulated Martin and asked him, 'May I give you my blessing?' 'Of course,' Martin replied. Then the Archbishop sank to his knees by the bedside and quietly asked, May I receive your blessing?' King said afterwards how beautiful it was that a Roman Catholic Archbishop should want a blessing from a Protestant called Martin Luther![7]

King was committed to integration and non-violence – both values deeply founded upon his Christian conviction. In his Washington address, he warned his supporters,

'But there is something that I must say to my people who stand on the warm threshold which leads into the palace of justice. In the process of gaining our rightful place we must not be guilty of wrongful deeds. Let us not seek to satisfy our thirst for freedom by drinking from the cup of bitterness and hatred.

We must forever conduct our struggle on the high plane of dignity and discipline. We must not allow our creative protest to degenerate into physical violence. Again and again we must rise to the majestic heights of meeting physical force with soul force. The marvelous new militancy which has engulfed the Negro community must not lead us to a distrust of all white people, for many of our white brothers, as evidenced by their presence here today, have come to realize that their destiny is tied up with our destiny. They have come to realize that their freedom is inextricably bound to our freedom. We cannot walk alone.'[8]

Martin Luther King, like Gandhi, was clear that non-violent resistance was not for cowards. Its aim was 'not to defeat or humiliate the opponent, but to win his friendship and understanding.'[9] At the end of a non-violent campaign, Martin Luther King hoped there would be greater understanding and even respect between those who opposed each other instead of the bitterness and resentment, which those who have been defeated usually feel. His campaign, he insisted was against the 'forces of evil rather than against persons who happen to be doing evil... We are out to defeat injustice and not white persons who may be unjust.'[10] Like Gandhi, Martin Luther King also accepted the possibility of suffering, believing as the New Testament taught, that suffering love could be redemptive. Moreover, he was convinced that 'the universe is on the side of justice.' The non-violent resister 'knows that in his struggle for justice he has cosmic companionship.[11]

CHAPTER NOTES

1. *The Autobiography of Martin Luther King, Jr,* Edited by Clayborne Carson, London, Little Brown and Company, 1999, IPM and Abacus edition, 2008, p. 2.
2. *Autobiography,* p. 15.
3. *Autobiography,* p. 26.
4. Coretta Scott King, *My Life With Martin Luther King, Jr,* Hodder and Stoughton, 1969, p. 192 pp. 192-3.
5. www.usconstitution.net/dream.html and *Autobiography,* pp. 223-7.
6. *Autobiography,* p. 365.
7. Coretta Scott King, *My Life With Martin Luther King, Jr,* p. 17.
8. www.usconstitution.net/dream.html.
9. Martin Luther King, *Stride Toward Freedom,* Gollancz, 1959, p. 96.
10. *Stride Toward Freedom,* p. 96.
11. *Stride Toward Freedom,* p. 100.

94

Haile Selassie I

Haile Selassie I was Emperor of Ethiopia and an important twentieth century African and international statesman, who gave firm support to the League of Nations and the United Nations. He was himself an Ethiopian Orthodox Christian, but he is regarded by Rastafarians as God Incarnate and hence has been seen as a symbol of black pride. Haile Selassie was named 'Man of the Year' by *Time Magazine* in 1935.

Haile Selassie was at birth known as Lij Tafari Makonnen. Lij or 'child' is a title given to those of noble birth. He was born on July 23rd, 1892. His father was a chief adviser to the Ethiopian emperor Menelik II. Tafari inherited imperial blood through his maternal grandmother. He was given the title of 'commander of the gate' at the age of thirteen and after his father's death in 1906, Tafari assumed the titular governorship of Selale. He soon became governor of two provinces, where he pursued progressive policies and increased the authority of the central government.

On the death of Emperor Menelik II in 1913, his son, who had a reputation for scandalous behaviour, was soon deposed. Menelik's daughter then became Empress and Tafari was named Regent and heir apparent. As Crown Prince, Tafari continued a moderate programme of modernization. He also gained Ethiopia's admission to the League of Nations in 1923, promising to eradicate slavery, which was still common in Ethiopia. He also toured Europe to learn about recent developments in education, manufacturing and medical care. He said, 'we need European progress only because we are surrounded by it. That is at once a benefit and a misfortune.'[1] His 'rich, picturesque court dress' attracted the attention of the media. His entourage included a pride of lions, which he used as gifts to the President of France and to King George V of Britain. It has been said that 'rarely can a tour have inspired so many anecdotes.'[2] The real importance of the tour, however, was that Ethiopia was the only independent African country and not a colony of a European power. Moreover, the Crown Prince was the only black leader on the world scene.

In 1928, popular support for Tafari persuaded the Empress to crown him King and, after her death in 1930, he became the 'King of the Kings of Ethiopia' and the Emperor Haile Selassie I. Already, however, Mussolini was plotting to avenge the defeat suffered by the Italians in the First Italo-Abyssinian War. The Italians, with a population of 42 million, who made extensive use of chemical weapons, were too strong for the Ethiopians, whose people numbered only 12 million. The council of state agreed that Haile Selassie with his family should leave the country to preserve the Imperial dynasty and to plead Ethiopia's case at the League of Nations. Haile Selassie emphasised that the principle of collective security was central to the role of the League of Nations. 'In a word', he said, 'it is international morality that is at stake. Have the signatures appended to a treaty value only in so far as the signatory Powers have a personal, direct and immediate interest involved?' Already, however, the disastrous policy of appeasement was in the ascendant. Token sanctions were agreed, but Ethiopia was left to its fate. 'God and history' he said, 'will remember your judgment.' His speech although it failed in its main purpose made Haile Selassie the hero of anti-Fascists around the world and won him the accolade of 'Man of the Year' from *Time Magazine*. Years later he demonstrated his continuing support for collective security by committing Ethiopian troops to join the UN defence of South Korea.

Haile Selassie spent his years of exile (1936-1941) at Bath in England, keeping the sufferings of the Ethiopian people before the eyes of the world. In a Christmas broadcast in America he called for 'all peace loving people to co-operate and stand firm in order to promote lawfulness and peace.'

In January 1941, Ethiopian troops and the British 'Gideon Force,' which was led by Colonel Charles Orde Wingate (1903-44), recaptured Addis Ababa, the capital of Ethiopia. After the Second World War, Ethiopia became a charter member of the United Nations. Haile Selassie was a staunch ally of the West but also a strong advocate of decolonisation – although Ethiopia itself was caught up in a prolonged war with neighbouring Eritrea. In 1954, Emperor Haile Selassie was the first head of state since the end of the Second World War to visit West Germany.

At home, Haile Selassie introduced moderate social and constitutional reforms. He also eventually gained independent or autocephalic status for the Ethiopian Orthodox Church from the Egyptian Coptic

Church. The Ethiopian Church is the largest of the Eastern Independent Churches. These are Syrian, Armenian, Coptic and Ethiopian churches, which do not recognise the authority either of the Pope or the Orthodox Patriarch in Istanbul, both of whom regard some of the Eastern Churches as heretical. They are characterised by the deep spirituality and asceticism of many monks. The Ethiopian Church is very ancient, although historical details are few. It has its own traditions, which in turn have influenced Rastafarians. The Ethiopian Bible contains a number of books, such as the Ascension of Isaiah and the Shepherd of Hermes, which are not found in the Western Bible. The Apostles Creed is not used. The year 2007 in the Gregorian calendar was the year 2,000 in the calendar of the Ethiopian Church. Other traditions, such as circumcision and ritual food laws, show Jewish influence.

The Ethiopian Church has had close links with the Coptic Church in Egypt, which prior to Haile Selassie's intervention had claimed the right to appoint the *abuna* or chief bishop. In 1959, the Coptic Pope Cyril VI recognised the Ethiopian *abuna* or bishop as Patriarch-Catholics, although retaining a primacy of jurisdiction. There are some Uniate Christians in Ethiopia, who recognise the Pope's authority, while keeping some local traditions.

Despite attempted coups, Haile Selassie retained power throughout the Nineteen-sixties and in 1963 presided over the establishment of the Organisation of African Unity. Outside Ethiopia he enjoyed great respect. As the longest serving Head of State he was given precedence over other leaders at the state funerals of John Kennedy and Charles de Gaulle. At home, however, Marxism was winning support from many of the Ethiopian intelligentsia. The situation deteriorated sharply after the devastating famine in North-Eastern Ethiopia. Riots broke out in 1974 and later in the year Haile Selassie was deposed and imprisoned in the Grand Palace, with some members of his own family.[3] He died a year later of - in the words of the state media - of 'respiratory failure.' Some Rastafarians question whether Haile Selassie actually died in 1975.

The Marxist regime fell in 1992. Subsequently, Eritrea broke away to become an independent country. Ethiopia is now a democracy, but the political situation remains troubled and unsettled.

Haile Selassie was a very significant ruler who played an important part in helping Africans' recover their dignity and regain control of their future. He also, not of his choice, became a central figure in the still growing Rastafarian movement, which regards him as the black Messiah. This is one reason why he deserves to be included in this book.

Rastafarians think of Haile Selassie as God incarnate, called *Jah*. This is partly because of his titles, which include *King of Kings, Lord of Lords* and *Conquering Lion of the Tribe of Judah*. These are titles also used of the Messiah in the Book of Revelation at the end of the Bible. According to Ethiopian tradition, these titles had already been given to the Ethiopian emperors as early as the tenth century BCE. The Solomonic Dynasty of Ethiopia was founded in 980 BCE by Menelik I. It is claimed that he was the son of the famous King Solomon of Judah – son of King David – and the Queen of Sheba. We know from the Bible that the Queen of Sheba visited King Solomon in Jerusalem and that King Solomon 'gave the Queen of Sheba all she desired and asked for, besides what he had given her out of his royal bounty.' Certainly they gave each other lavish gifts. Did Solomon also give her a son? The Bible is too discrete for us to know for sure. Rastafarians, on the basis of the Ethiopian national epic, *Kebra Negast*, believe he did and argue, therefore, that the African people are among the true children of Israel or therefore Jews. Certainly Beta Israel (or 'House of Israel') black Jews, also known as Falashas, have lived in Ethiopia for many centuries, practising circumcision and observing the Sabbath, Jewish festivals and some food laws. A number of Ethiopian black Jews have been resettled in Israel in recent times.

Rastafarianism – sometimes called Rasta – is a loose knit movement or 'way of life' which encourages black people to find and affirm their own identity. The movement began among the working and peasant classes of Jamaica in the early thirties and was linked to hopes of a return to Africa, from which their ancestors had been shipped across the Atlantic as slaves. Marcus Garvey (1887-1940) is regarded as the 'prophet' or 'John the Baptist' of the movement, although he never himself became a Rastafarian.

Garvey in his speeches in the nineteen twenties often said, 'Look to Africa, when a black king shall be crowned for the day of deliverance is at hand.' The coronation of Emperor Haile Selassie in 1928 seemed to confirm these predictions. Garvey was a publisher, journalist, Black Nationalist and orator. In August 1914, he founded the Universal Negro

Improvement Association (UNIA) as a way of joining all Africa and its Diaspora into 'one great body to establish a country and absolute government of their own.' Within six years the UNIA claimed four million members. In the early twenties, however, Garvey, at that time in the USA, was accused of fraud and found guilty. Two days later, he issued his famous 'First Message to the Negroes of the World from Atlanta Prison,' saying

'Look for me in the whirlwind or the storm, look for me all around you, for, with God's grace, I shall come and bring with me countless millions of black slaves who have died in America and the West Indies and the millions in Africa to aid you in the fight for Liberty, Freedom and Life.'

Following his early release Garvey was deported back to Jamaica, where he as welcomed by a huge crowd.

Garvey spent his last years in London, where he died in 1940. After the War, his remains were exhumed and taken back to Jamaica. In 1964, he was declared to be Jamaica's first national hero. Martin Luther King, who laid a wreath at his shrine in 1965, said of Garvey that he was 'the first man of colour to lead and develop a mass movement. He was the first man on a mass scale and level to give millions of Negroes a sense of dignity and destiny. And make the Negro feel he was somebody.'[4]

Rastafarian beliefs are not very clearly defined. Some Rastafarians see their faith as related to Ethiopian Christianity, others belong to the Protestant Churches and some emphasise the connection with Judaism. This in part depends on whether a person thinks of Rastafarianism as a religion or an ideology. The Bible is held in high esteem, although Rastafarians complain that the English translations incorporate changes dictated by white power. Their critics object to the Rastafarian reliance on the King James Authorised translation and their tendency to take Biblical quotations out of context. Some Rastafarians have taken an interest in the version in Amharic, which is the most widely used of the many languages spoken in Ethiopia.

Emperor Haile Selassie is regarded as worthy of worship by Rastafarians, some of whom speak of him as a reincarnation of Jesus. They admire the dignity that Haile Selassie showed in meeting world leaders and in speaking to the press. Some believe that one day Haile Selassie will come back and the righteous shall return to Africa, although when he met with Rastafarian leaders during his visit to Jamaica, he is reported to have told them to first liberate the people of Jamaica and then to emigrate to Ethiopia. So the policy has been 'liberation before repatriation.' Very few Rastafarians took up his offer to provide some land for them in Ethiopia.

Enormous crowds greeted Haile Selassie when he visited Jamaica on 21st April in 1966. The day is still celebrated as Grounation Day and is the second holiest day after the Emperor's Coronation, which is remembered on November 2nd. During his visit Haile Selassie did not rebuke Rastafarians for their exalted regard for him. Indeed, he presented the faithful elders – and them alone - with gold medallions.

Rastafarians are inspired by their vision of Zion. They reject modern society, which they call Babylon – 'the great whore' of the Book of Revelation. The movement developed among oppressed and suffering black people and has won support by giving African people and their descendants who live in exile self-confidence and pride in themselves and their values and culture. Living close to nature is seen as part of their African heritage and demonstrated in their dreadlocks and in the use of the *ganja* herb or cannabis, which is said to cleanse the body and mind and to exalt the soul. The identification with Africa is also shown in the use of the colours of the Ethiopian flag: red, gold and green, which with the addition of black are the colours of the Pan-African Unity movement.

In keeping with dietary laws of the Old Testament, most Rastafarians do not eat pork or shellfish and quite a number prefer natural foods and are vegetarian or vegan. Alcohol is regarded as unhealthy and a tool of Babylon – the modern world – to confuse people.

There are two types of ceremonies. One is a reasoning ceremony at which *ganja* is smoked and ethical, social and religious issues are discussed. The other is a holy day, called a grounation or a *bingi*, which is a word derived from *Nyabinghi*, which is believed to be an ancient and now extinct order of militant East African black people committed to ending oppression.

Rastafarians are known for their dreadlocks. The book of Leviticus in the Bible says, 'They will not make tonsures on their heads, shave the edges of their beards, or gash their bodies.'[5] The book of Numbers also says of anyone who takes a vow of a Nazirite, that 'during the entire period of his vow of separation no razor may be used on his head.'[6] Samson was a Nazirite.[7] In part, dreadlocks were adopted to contrast the hair of black men to the straight hair of most white men. The practice may also have been copied from the Mau Mau of Kenya, who grew their 'dreaded locks' while in hiding in the mountains during the insurrection.

If Rastafarians are quickly recognised by their dreadlocks, it is Reggae music that has done most to make Rastafarianism known throughout the world. Reggae was born among the poor black people of Trenchtown, a large ghetto area of Kingston, Jamaica. Jamaican musicians blended traditional Jamaican folk music and drumming with American jazz. Reggae became internationally popular in the seventies. Bob Marley and other musicians who were devout Rastafarians included Rastafarian chanting in their music. Soon Reggae became a vehicle by which many oppressed people, including Native Americans, Australian Aborigines and Africans, many of whom were still subject to colonial rule, could express pride in their culture and confidence in their future.

Rastafarianism has changed not only the consciousness of black people, but also the consciousness of people of every colour. It offers a distinctive spiritual path. Moreover, it has helped to bring about the profound political changes of the latter years of the twentieth century, which saw the end of European imperialism.

In a famous speech delivered at the United Nations in 1968, and popularized in the song 'War' by Bob Marley (1945-1981), Haile Selassie said:

'That until the philosophy which holds one race superior and another inferior is finally and permanently discredited and abandoned: That until there are no longer first-class and second class citizens of any nation; That until the color of a man's skin is of no more significance than the color of his eyes; That until the basic human rights are equally guaranteed to all without regard to race; That until that day, the dream of lasting peace and world citizenship and the rule of international morality will remain but a fleeting illusion...'

In his heart, Haile Selassie believed his vision was more than a dream because of his confidence that 'God's judgment will eventually visit the weak and the mighty alike.'[8]

CHAPTER NOTES

1. Joel Augustus Rogers, *The Real Facts about Ethiopia*, 1936, p. 27.
2. Anthony Mockler, *Haile Selassie's War*, 2003, pp. 3-4.
3. Haile Selassie had six children by Empress Menen Asfaw.
4. Quoted by Columbus Salley in *The Black 100: A Ranking of the Most Influential African-Americans, Past and Present*, Citadel Press, 1999, p. 82.
5. Leviticus 21,5. (Jerusalem Bible) The 'they' in the text are priests. A tonsure is the act of shaving the head or the crown of the head, often as a preliminary to becoming a priest or a monk.
6. Numbers 6, 5 (NIV).
7. Judges, 13, 5 (NIV).
8. Haile Selassie I.,*My Life and Ethiopia's Progress: The Autobiography of Emperor Haile Sellassie*, translated from Amharic by Edward Ullendorff, New York: Frontline Books, Vol 2, 1999, p. 25

95

Thich Nhat Hanh

Thich Nhat Hanh, who is a Vietnamese Buddhist monk, has devoted his life to working for peace and helping the suffering. The movement for 'Engaged Buddhism,' of which he was a pioneer, with its emphasis on reform of the unjust structures of society, marks a new development in the long history of Buddhism. From his Plum Village Monastery Thich Nhat Hanh, has helped to spread the Buddha's message of mindfulness in the West by his talks and writings.

Thich Nhat Hanh is often referred to just as '*Thay*' or 'Teacher. The word *Thich* itself, which means 'of the Buddha's clan,' is a title used of all monks and nuns in Vietnam. Thich Nhat Hanh was born in central Vietnam in 1926. He joined a Zen monastery when he was sixteen and was ordained as a monk in 1949. Soon afterwards, he founded the An Quang Buddhist Institute, which has become a leading centre of Buddhist studies in Vietnam. He also founded a new monastery, called Phuong Boi or 'Fragrant Palm Leaves,' which even now he remembers fondly.

In 1961, Thich Nhat Hanh went to the United States to study world religions at Columbia and Princeton Universities. To understand the subsequent course of Thich Nhat Hanh's life in the following years, it is necessary, first, to know something of Vietnam's troubled history in the twentieth century.

France was the colonial power until the Second World War, although there was already a growing movement for national liberation, led by Ho Chi Minh (1890-1969). During the Second World War Vietnam was conquered by Japan. After the war finished, there was an ever more bitter struggle between the French in the south and the Communists in the north. In 1954, following the Communist victory at Dien Bien Phu, the country was divided into North and South Vietnam.

In the South, the Catholic leader Ngo Dinh Diem (1901-1963) gained power, and with American financial support, survived until 1963, when he was killed in a coup. It was at this point, because of the worsening situation in the country that, at the urgent request of his fellow monks, Thich Nhat Hanh returned to Vietnam. After a period of chaos, the military took charge in the South and were given increasing support by the United States in an effort to halt the advance of the Viet Cong. In 1965, President Johnson ordered the bombing of North Korea and soon afterwards landed 3,500 marines in South Korea. By 1968, there were over half a million American combat troops in Vietnam, although there was bitter opposition to the war from many quarters. In 1973, a cease-fire was agreed and American troops were withdrawn. Within two years, with the fall of Saigon, the government in the South collapsed and the Socialist republic of the now unified Vietnam was established in 1976.

Thich Nhat Hanh returned to Vietnam in 1964. Soon, with the support of a group of university teachers, he founded the School of Youth for Social Service. This equipped young people to go into the countryside to set up schools and health clinics and later to help rebuild villages, which had been bombed. Thich Nhat Hanh was convinced that in a similar situation, the Buddha himself would not have withdrawn to a temple to meditate. Temples might house the Buddha' statues, but his living presence was to be found among those whose compassion impelled them to help the villagers. As he wrote in his journal,

'To isolate oneself in a temple is useless for those who wish to know the Buddha. Those who withdraw like this only demonstrate that they are not true disciples of the Buddha. The Buddha is to be found where there are beings who suffer.'[1]

Thich Nhat Hanh also canvassed support for his total opposition to the war. He made several visits to the United States. One of those whom he contacted was Martin Luther King, to whom he had written a letter entitled 'Searching for the Enemy of Man.' Martin Luther King, whom he persuaded to speak out against the conflict, nominated Thich Nhat Hanh for the Nobel Peace Prize. King said, that the ideas for peace of 'this gentle monk from Vietnam' would, if applied, 'build a monument to ecumenism, to world brotherhood, to humanity.'[2] Thich Nhat Hanh also established a close relationship with members of the Fellowship of Reconciliation, which was a leading Christian pacifist organisation, although it now also welcomes pacifists of other faiths.

In 1969, Thich Nhat Hanh was asked by the Unified Buddhist

Church of Vietnam to set up a Buddhist Peace Delegation to the Paris Peace Talks. When a Peace Accord was signed in 1973, however, he was not allowed to return to the country and was not able to go back until 2005. Nonetheless, Thich Nhat Hanh continued to do what he could for the suffering people of Vietnam, especially the so-called 'boat people' and the many children who had been orphaned. Many Vietnamese, especially those who feared reprisals from the Communists, had fled in boats hoping to find refuge elsewhere. The conditions in the boats were appalling. Many of them were attacked by pirates. Thich Nhat Hanh, as director of a project of the World Conference on Religion and Peace acquired three boats, which searched, with limited success, for the endangered boats and tried to ensure their safety. Even, when they did reach another country, the refugees were often forced back into the boats and towed out to sea. As Thich Nhat Hanh wrote later, 'We were hunted and chased like animals.'[3]

Thich Nhat Hanh also raised money to help the starving children. Instead of building orphanages, he decided to approach people in the West to sponsor the children. 'We had already found village families who were willing to take care of an orphan, if we could provide six dollars a month for the child's food and schooling. Whenever possible, we tried to place a child in the home of a relative... These orphans had the great advantage of growing up in a family environment, for life in an orphanage was almost like that in an army camp. This is an example of how we can improve things by searching for new ways to practice generosity.'[4]

Thich Nhat Hanh also had a concern for artists who had been thrown into prison. Perhaps more remarkable was his work with American war veterans, who had been responsible for so much of the suffering of his own people. He was aware that many of the veterans were tormented by nightmares of the atrocities. He helped them to see that even torturers and executioners, like the refugees, are victims of an inhuman system. As he said,

'Every side is our side. There is no evil side. These veterans, with their war experiences, are the burning flame of a candle, whose light reveals the roots of war, and the way to peace.'[5]

Exiled from his home country, Thich Nhat Hanh settled in France. At first, he established a small community of 'The Order of Inter-Being' at a place he named 'Sweet Potato', a hundred miles South-west of Paris. In 1982, he established Plum Village, which is a large retreat centre near Bordeaux. It is divided into three hamlets, which are a few miles apart. One is for men and the other two are for women. There is also accommodation for those who come for retreats. Like the Christian Taizé Community, founded by Brother Roger (1915-2005), Plum Village attracts large numbers of people who come for spiritual guidance. Besides guiding the community, Thich Nhat Hanh also travels widely to lecture and lead retreats. He is a prolific author and many of his talks have been published.

The emphasis of Thich Nhat Hanh's teaching is on mindfulness in everyday life. The intention is to live wholly in the present. This is based on the Buddha's teaching of contingent being, which Thich Nhat Hanh explains simply in this way:

'Though it is our habit to think that leaves are born in the spring, Gautama realised that this leaf had always existed, implicit in the sunlight, in the clouds, and in the tree itself. Hence this leaf had really never been born at all. Seeing this, he saw that his being too, had no origin. Like the leaf, he simply manifested through a temporary from, which had its origin in time. Yet neither he nor the leaf had ever been born, and hence they could never die... Then he saw how the existence of one phenomenon makes all other phenomena possible, through interdependence.'[6]

A person learns to recognise the key principles of interdependence and no-self by living a moral life of simplicity and by meditation. Thich Nhat Hanh emphasizes the importance of mindfulness or total awareness of the present moment:

'Breathing in, I calm the body.
Breathing out, I smile.
Dwelling in the present moment,
I know this is a wonderful moment.[7]

Thich Nhat Hanh emphasizes the importance of smiling. A smile, he says, can relax hundreds of muscles in the face. A smile is a sign that one is master of the self, but it benefits other people as well as the self.

Thich Nhat Hanh has suggested that the walking meditation is even more helpful than sitting meditation and breath control. In walking meditation a person should concentrate just on the physical act of walking and avoid talking or thinking. 'Everything in its own time. One thing at a time.' 'The miracle is not to walk on water,' he has said, 'the miracle is to walk on the green earth, in the present moment, to appreciate the peace and beauty that are available now.'[8] To reinforce this mindfulness of the present moment, members of Plum Village sign an agreement with the flight of stairs they most often use. They agree to practise meditation every time they go up or down and never to take them absent-mindedly.

Awareness of interdependence helps a person to identify with and feel part of others – both the so-called 'good' and the 'wicked.' This is vividly expressed in Thich Nhat Hanh's poem, 'Please call me by my True Names:'

I am the child in Uganda, all skin and bones,
My legs as thin as bamboo sticks,
And I am the arms merchant, selling deadly,
Weapons to Uganda.

I am the twelve year old girl, refugee
On a small boat
Who throws herself into the ocean
After being raped by a sea pirate,
And I am the pirate, my heart not yet capable
Of seeing and loving…[9]

This sense of interdependence extends to the natural world:

Peace is every step.
The shining red sun is my heart.
Each flower smiles with me.
How green, how fresh all that grows.[10]

Such an approach underlies Thich Nhat Hanh's deep personal and practical involvement in peace work and the relief of suffering. He has been one of the leaders of what is known as 'Engaged Buddhism.' Thich Nhat Hanh himself, credits the origination of this concept to a King Tran Nhan Tong (1258-1308), an enlightened ruler, philosopher and poet, who abdicated his throne to become a monk and who founded the Bamboo Forest tradition, is which is still strong in Vietnam. The concept could also be said to derive from the concept of the bodhisattva who dedicates himself to the relief of suffering. Withdrawal from the world, which in the past had been seen as the ideal way of life, was now seen as 'a preliminary moral, spiritual and intellectual training' which equipped a person 'to be strong enough to come out later and help others.'[11] Engaged Buddhists, many of whom now belong to an International Network founded by Sulak Sivaraksa (b.1933) of Thailand, recognise that this involves a struggle with the powerful and a reform of the structures of society, which create suffering, as well as offering help to the victim. Dr B R Ambedakar (1891-1956) who encouraged the Untouchables of India to become Buddhists, even questioned the Second Noble Truth, that suffering results from desires and ignorance. He felt this might stop people seeing that some people are victims of oppression and injustice and in no way responsible for their sufferings.

During the struggle against the Vietnam War, Thich Nhat Hanh came close to Christians, such as the American Jesuit priest Daniel Berrigan, who was imprisoned for his acts of resistance to the war. These contacts helped to change the unfavourable opinion of Christianity that he formed while Ngo Dinh Diem, who was a Roman Catholic, was President of Vietnam. Because of the Buddhist monks' opposition to the war, Ngo Dinh Diem forbade the celebration of Wesak, which is one of the most important Buddhist festivals.

As he learned about Christianity, Thich Nhat Hanh began to emphasise the example of Jesus in his talks. 'The life of Jesus', he said, 'is his most basic teaching, more important even that faith in the resurrection or faith in eternity.'[12] Stressing Jesus' commitment to the way of non-violence, especially in the Sermon on the Mount, he said, 'the teachings must be practiced as they were lived by Jesus.'[13]

Now, on the altar of his hermitage in France there are images of both Buddha and Jesus. 'Every time I light incense,' Thich Nhat Hanh has said, 'I touch both of them as my spiritual ancestors.'[14] 'The Living Christ', he says, 'is the Christ of Love, always generating love'. Thich Nhat Hanh has not tried to convert Christians to Buddhism. Instead he has urged Christians to keep Christ alive by their way of life, showing those around them that love, understanding and tolerance are possible. He observes that the *Anguttara Nikaya* says, 'There is a person whose appearance on earth is for the well-being and happiness of all.' It then asks, 'Who is that person?' Thich Nhat Hahn comments, 'For Buddhists, that person is the Buddha. For Christians, that person is Jesus Christ. Through your daily life, you can help that person continue. We need only to walk in mindfulness, making peaceful, happy steps on our planet. Breathe deeply and enjoy your breathing. Be aware that the sky is blue and the birds' songs are beautiful. Enjoy being alive and you will help the living Christ and the living Buddha continue for a long, long time.'[15]

CHAPTER NOTES

1. Quoted in Jean-Pierre and Rachel Cartier, *Thich Nhat Hanh: The Joy of Full Consciousness*, translated by Joseph Rowe, Berkeley, California, North Atlantic Books, 2002.

2. In fact, no award was made in 1967 and King was criticised for defying convention by making known his nomination of Thich Nhat Hanh.

3. *The Joy of Full Consciousness*, p. 9.

4. *The Joy of Full Consciousness*, p.10.

5. *The Joy of Full Consciousness*, p.11.

6. Quoted in *Joy of Full Consciousness*, p. 14.

7. Thich Nhat Hanh, *Peace is Every Step*, London, Rider, 1991, p. 10.

8. Thich Nhat Hanh, *Touching Peace*, Berkeley, Parallax Press, 1992, p. 1.

9. Thich Nhat Hanh, *Being Peace*, Berkeley, Parallax Press, 1987, pp. 63-64.

10. Thich Nhat Hanh, *Peace is Every Step*, p.ix.

11. Words of the Sri Lankan Buddhist monk Walpola Rahula in *The Path of Compassion*, ed Fred Eppsteiner, Berkeley, Parallax Press, 1988, pp. 103-104.

12. Thich Nhat Hanh, *Living Buddha, Living Christ*, New York,

Riverhead Books, 1995, p. 36.

13. Thich Nhat Hanh, *Living Buddha, Living Christ*, p. 70.
14. Thich Nhat Hanh, *Living Buddha, Living Christ*, p. 6.
15. Thich Nhat Hanh, *Living Buddha, Living Christ*, p. 59.

96

Patrick Dodson

Patrick Dodson, who was Australia's first ordained Catholic priest, has worked tirelessly for reconciliation between Australia's Aboriginal people and the rest of the population. He was a member of the Royal Commission into Aboriginal Deaths in Custody and first chairman of the Council for Aboriginal Reconciliation.

Patrick Dodson, who was born on 29th January 1948, was of mixed Aboriginal and Irish descent. Because Patrick, as he found out more about his family roots, was to become very aware of the terrible suffering such policies inflicted on many Aboriginal people, it is important to give the family history in some detail.

Patrick traces his Aboriginal roots through his mother Patricia and her father Paddy Djiagween to Paddy's father Jilwa and Wanan, who over one hundred and fifty years ago lived in the country that Patrick calls home. This is Yawuru country in Jirriginngan, which is now called Broome on the North West coast of Australia. Traces of human habitation found at a rock shelter at Koolan Island, O'Connor, are said to date back some 27,000 years. Like other Yawuru, Jilwa and Wanan hunted for fish and kangaroos and large lizards and at low tide they collected pearl shells.

Jilwa and Wanan knew the power of the country and followed the *Bugarigarra* or Dreaming Time. Dreaming has different meanings for different Aboriginal people. It is a complex network of knowledge, faith and practices that derive from stories of creation. It dominates all spiritual and physical aspects of Aboriginal life. The Dreaming sets out the structures of society, the rules of social behaviour and the ceremonies performed in order to maintain the life of the land. The Dreamtime stories tell of the creation of the earth and of animals and of humans. The journeys of the Spirit Ancestors across the land, which created the features of the landscape, are recorded in Dreaming tracks. 'The Dreaming' in the words of Merv Penrith an Elder of Wallaga Lake, 'means our identity as people. The cultural teaching and everything, that's part of our lives here, you know? ... it's the understanding of what we have around us.'[1]

This identity is intimately related to the Land. Patrick Dodson once asked Christian readers to imagine Aboriginal Australians before the 'white invasion:'

'As to your knowledge of the land, your country, you would know every tree, every rock, because through the Dreaming, the great ancestors came this way. And they are still here. They live. They must be revered, appeased, paid attention to. It is they who cause conception as a woman walks near. When the child is born he calls that part of the country "Father."'[2]

Well before the time of Patrick's great grandparents, the first white men had reached the area. In 1699, men from the ship of the buccaneer and explorer William Dampier had come ashore looking for water not far from where Patrick grew up. Dampier described the people of Western Australia as the 'miserablest people in the world.' 'I did not perceive that they did worship anything... These people speak somewhat thro' the throat, but we could not understand one word that they said.'[3]

Dampier spoke of the Aboriginals as almost 'sub-human', which was to be the opinion of many of the first white settlers. In Patrick Dodson's words,

'The Dampier view that Aboriginal people were somehow less human than their visitors and new masters carried on. Time and time again in the history of Kimberley there were punitive killings, kidnapped labour, sexual exploitation, and laws and policies that were brutal in their delivery while noble in their intentions. At its heart at there was no recognition of humanity. It was always viewed as entirely appropriate, even by those sympathetic to Aboriginal people, that decisions should be made for Aboriginal people, not by us, giving us no right of choice, no power over our own lives. There was little recognition of the rights of our people, of our families, to be ourselves, to be allowed the dignity of human choices.'[4]

In 1837 another exploratory boat, the *Beagle*, reached the shores of North West Australia and less that thirty years later an expedition headed by Police Inspector Panter arrived in the area. Western Australians then started to colonise the land, although at first they met resistance from the Yawuru. At the same time ships seeking pearl were arriving. One find in 1884 was the famous and priceless Southern Cross, with nine shells in the shape of a cross, for which the boy who found it was paid £10. It was eventually given to Pope Leo XIII and is now in the vaults of the Vatican. Among the settlers to arrive in the area in 1856 were Protestants from Northern Ireland John and Matilda Fagan and their young son Joseph, escaping the poverty of Ireland and hoping to make a new life on the other side of the world.

The young boy Joseph, who became a stockman, was in time to have a long-term relationship with an Aboriginal woman called Noala or Nawurla. Their daughter, Elizabeth Grace, Patrick's grandmother, was to marry Paddy Dijagween, who has already been mentioned. Their daughter was Patricia Mary Djiagween, who was to be Patrick's mother. Relationships between white stockmen and black women were common. Some were forced and others did not last long. Others were long-standing relationships of mutual regard and affection, as Joseph's relationship with Noala seems to have been. Certainly Joseph always acknowledged his daughter and tried to protect her interest. Before he died he made out a will leaving his entire estate to his 'presumed daughter' Elizabeth Djiagween. But because Elizabeth was an Aboriginal, control of the estate passed to the Chief Protector (so-called) of Aborigines, Auber Octavius Neville. For years, Elizabeth and her husband struggled to get access to at least some of the money that was rightfully theirs. Neville, however, influenced by pseudo-scientific theories of eugenics, was deeply committed to the policy that 'natives not of full blood should be absorbed into the people of the Commonwealth.'[5] Neville favoured 'miscegenation', which was the attempt to breed out the half-caste population. If half-castes were separated from 'full-bloods' and married with whites, their children would lose skin colour and become 'just like white people' in a few generations. As to children of full Aboriginal descent, they could be forcibly taken from their home and placed in a government institution.

Elizabeth Grace and Paddy Dijagween, as already mentioned had a daughter Patricia Mary Djiagween who was Patrick's mother. His father, whom Patricia met during the wartime and married in 1947, was Snowy Dodson.[6] After a time they separated and Patricia, who drank a lot, fell foul of the authorities. Patrick remembers with horror the day on which his mother was arrested. 'The coppers bundled Mum into the back of the Toyota, with a cage on it. They bunged her into the back of it. Then they were gone, just dust, and we were wondering what the hell was happening.'[7] After this, Patrick was looked after by relatives.

When Patrick finished primary school, he was selected, under a scheme to educate part-Aboriginal children in the south of Australia, to attend a boarding college run by Missionaries of the Sacred Heart (Catholic) near Hamilton in Western Victoria. On his first night, when he got into bed in his dormitory, 'there was a stampede of boys running up the stairs to have a look at me.'[8] Most of them had never seen a black boy. Patrick was helped to adjust to a strange new world by the family of Tony Gartlan – he and Tony had both been in trouble and punished on Patrick's first day. Patrick did well at the school. He passed his intermediate and leaving examinations; for two years running he was captain of the school football team, and he was elected captain of the school by popular vote.

It was at school that he began to hear a call to the priesthood and asked to join the Missionaries of the Sacred Heart. In March 1969, after a novitiate year and his first year of seminary studies in Canberra, Patrick recited his temporary vows of chastity, poverty and obedience. His studies took seven years: four years of philosophy and three of theology. He was ordained priest in 1975.

Although in 1972 the Queensland government of Joh Bjelke-Petersen had ruled that 'no aboriginal shall leave a reserve ... without permission of the protector,' the coming to power of Gough Whitlam's government marked a change in attitude. It was quick to set up a commission to report on 'traditional rights and interests in, and in relation, to land.'

In this atmosphere of social change Patrick was asked as part of a seven day Eucharistic Congress in Melbourne to organise a three day conference for over five hundred Aboriginal people to discuss the relationship between the Church and the Aboriginals. It was a controversial event and some walked out dismissing it as 'tokenism.' 'They called the mob who were going to dance in the liturgy, exhibition niggers. I was surprised by the vehemence.'[9]

Patrick himself was, however, to find holding together his

Aboriginality and his Catholic faith became ever more difficult. He hoped to find a way of adapting Catholic rituals and theology to fit the cultural side of Aboriginal life. In a meeting with his Bishop he described the need for an indigenous mass, which expressed the Catholic faith in a way meaningful for the community. The Bishop was totally opposed to the idea, saying:

'It is not possible for an initiated man to be a practising Catholic. I agree with an old man who once told me that once an Aboriginal is initiated into the old ways, you can wipe him off as a true Christian and a man who can survive successfully in the twentieth century.'[10]

The Bishop's attitude was typical of most churches until fairly recently. Similar conflicts have arisen in Africa and Asia about how far traditional practices could be integrated into Christian life and worship. Another Aboriginal leader Wadjularbinna Doomadgee deplored this failure of the Christian churches to listen to the Aboriginals, saying,

'The sad thing about it all was the missionaries didn't realise that we already had something tied in with what they'd brought us. They saw different as inferior and they didn't ask us what it was that we had... Our people, before the white man came were very spiritual people. They were... connected to the land and creation through the Great Spirit. There was a good great and a great evil spirit.'[11]

Despite the Bishop's rebukes, Patrick immersed himself more fully in the way of life of the Aboriginal people, including their ceremonial life. Fr Brian McCoy was surprised when he arrived in Wadeye, where Patrick was working, to be met by him wearing a *naga* or loincloth and painted ready for a ceremony. The Bishop increasingly disapproved also of Patrick's involvement in community politics. As a famous cartoon by P Nicholson put it 'Politics should be kept out of paternalism.'[12] Patrick's position as a priest also became even more difficult as he formed a relationship with Annunciata Dartinga, who in January 1980 gave birth to their daughter. Patrick was temporarily relieved of his priestly duties.

By this time, his brother Mick had become a lawyer, working with the Victorian Aboriginal Legal Service. Patrick decided that he should try the law and studied for a time at Monash University. The issue of Aboriginal Land Rights was, however, becoming an important political issue. The Australian Catholic Relief Agency called on Patrick to speak about the issue to many white audiences. He approached the subject from the context of 'Liberation theology', which was in the ascendant at that time. Patrick insisted that all the questions about the Aboriginals were 'caught up in our understanding of land rights.'[13]

Patrick was becoming a national figure and in 1981 he was asked to chair a National Aboriginal Conference in Canberra, which met in parallel to the World Council of Indigenous Peoples Conference. Patrick was then asked to resume his priestly activities and to work in Alice Springs in the centre of Australia. Besides his parish work, he soon became involved with local Aboriginal organisations. He was also asked to attend a conference on Indigenous Peoples and Multi-Nationals in the USA. When Patrick asked permission to attend the Conference, the Bishop replied, 'Yes, it certainly sounds important, but not for you. You can go if you want, but don't bother coming back.' 'That was one thing,' Patrick said, 'that made me roll my swag.'[14] Patrick now recognised that his main work must be with the Aboriginals. His disagreements with the bishop became national news. Patrick started working with the Central Land Council and became involved in struggles with the Hawke government.

In 1988, Australia celebrated the two hundredth anniversary of Captain James Cooke's arrival in Australia, which for the Aboriginals was a disaster. To try in some way to placate Aboriginal feeling, the Prime Minister Bob Hawke that year attended the annual Barunga Sports and Cultural Festival, near the town of Katherine, where Patrick had grown up. There, Hawke accepted the need for a treaty which recognised the Aboriginals' 'prior ownership and sovereignty' of the land.[15]

In 1989 Patrick returned to work in Yawuru country, which also meant he could be near his grandfather, who was to die in 1991 at the age, it was said, of one hundred and eleven. In 1989, also, Patrick married his partner Barbara Shaw, with whom he had had a son, Adrian. The marriage did not last long and the couple divorced in 1994.

Although back home, Patrick still had a national role and served on the Commission into Aboriginal Deaths in Custody, which was set up to investigate the deaths of twenty-nine Aboriginal men and three Aboriginal women who had died in custody during the period 1980-89. The Commission's report did not substantiate allegations of murder or foul play, although it said that many officials had failed in their 'duty of care.' The report was rejected by many Aboriginal groups. Patrick, however, had been clear that the Commission should not be the last word on those who had died, but mark the beginning of 'a new and better chapter' in the history of Western Australia. The report, as Patrick wished, highlighted the years in which Aboriginals had been dispossessed of their land, which was the root cause of why many Aboriginals were in custody.[16] The Commission made over three hundred recommendations and called for a process of reconciliation that would be 'an achievement of pride not only for all Australians but for all humankind.'[17]

Two weeks after the Report on Aboriginal Deaths was published, a bill was introduced to set up a Council for Aboriginal Reconciliation, which gained support from all parties. Patrick was asked to be the first chairman of the newly created Council for Aboriginal Affairs, but it took a phone call from the Prime Minister Bob Hawke to persuade him to accept. The Prime Minister accepted Patrick's one condition – that he could continue to live in Broome. Patrick did not know that Hawke's days as Prime Minister were numbered.

A Decade of Reconciliation began in September 1991. Attempts were made by the Council for Aboriginal Reconciliation to bring Aboriginal leaders together with senior executives of mining companies to help them develop mutual respect and to find common ground. The work of the Council was hampered by political compromise and legal decisions. The reluctance of the Howard government to fulfil the hopes with which the Decade began eventually led Patrick to resign in 1997. He also called in vain for an apology, which a new Australian Prime Minister Kevin Rudd has at last issued in February 2008.[18] There is also, as Patrick makes clear, a need for money to repair the damage done to the Aboriginal People during the last two hundred years. Many Aboriginals have been brutalised by the process of assimilation.

'Ultimately,' as Patrick says, reconciliation is about 'how best to recognise the right of indigenous people to be indigenous people within the complexity of our western democratic structure and to accommodate that rather than suppress it.'[19] This requires other Australians to recognise that the Aboriginals live by different values. Patrick Dodson has tried to help them recognise that the essence of Aboriginal people's identity is very much tied to their spirituality, which has its basis in land. As his grandfather said, 'The sun rises, wind blows, grass grows, the tide comes and goes. No one can ever take your land.'

The continued search for reconciliation is urgent not just in Australia, but in the many societies in which the land and the rights of indigenous people have been stolen. For, as Patrick has said, 'it is about the essence of our quality as human beings.'[20] Indeed it is a question for many societies of how to accommodate differences and about a new relationship with Nature.

Patrick has never given up hope that reconciliation is possible and has spent a lifetime working for it. He has even been called Australia's Nelson Mandela.[21]

This is the text of the Prime Minister's Apology:

Today we honour the Indigenous peoples of this land, the oldest continuing cultures in human history.

We reflect on their past mistreatment.

We reflect in particular on the mistreatment of those who were Stolen Generations – this blemished chapter in our nation's history.

The time has now come for the nation to turn a new page in Australia's history by righting the wrongs of the past and so moving forward with confidence to the future.

We apologise for the laws and policies of successive Parliaments and governments that have inflicted profound grief, suffering and loss on these our fellow Australians.

We apologise especially for the removal of Aboriginal and Torres Strait Islander children from their families, their communities and their country.

For the pain, suffering and hurt of these Stolen Generations, their descendants and for their families left behind, we say sorry.

To the mothers and the fathers, the brothers and the sisters, for the breaking up of families and communities, we say sorry.

And for the indignity and degradation thus inflicted on a proud people and a proud culture, we say sorry.

We the Parliament of Australia respectfully request that this apology be received in the spirit in which it is offered as part of the healing of the nation.

For the future we take heart; resolving that this new page in the history of our great continent can now be written.

We today take this first step by acknowledging the past and laying claim to a future that embraces all Australians.

A future where this Parliament resolves that the injustices of the past must never, never happen again.

A future where we harness the determination of all Australians, Indigenous and non-Indigenous, to close the gap that lies between us in life expectancy, educational achievement and economic opportunity.

A future where we embrace the possibility of new solutions to enduring problems where old approaches have failed.

A future based on mutual respect, mutual resolve and mutual responsibility.

A future where all Australians, whatever their origins, are truly equal partners, with equal opportunities and with an equal stake in shaping the next chapter in the history of this great country, Australia.

CHAPTER NOTES

1. www.dreamtime.net.au/indigenous/spirituality.
2. Quoted by Kevin Keeffe in *Paddy's Road*, Canberra, Aboriginal Studies Press, 2003, p. 25.
3. *Paddy's Road*, pp. 26-7.
4. *Paddy's Road*, p. 28.
5. *Paddy's Road*, pp. 106-7.
6. Snowy Dodson died of a gunshot wound in 1960.
7. *Paddy's Road*, p. 176.
8. *Paddy's Road*, p. 192.
9. *Paddy's Road*, p. 216.
10. *Paddy's Road*, p. 245 Kevin Keefe notes that many Missionary fathers regarded the bishop's statement as 'unsupportable,

unfounded and insensitive.'

11. www.dreamtime.net.au/indigenous/spirituality.

12. In *The Age*, 23.6.81, reproduced in *Paddy's Road*, p. 251.

13. *Paddy's Road*, p. 257.

14. *Paddy's Road*, p. 265.

15. *Paddy's Road*, p. 279.

16. *Paddy's Road*, pp. 294-6.

17. Australia. Royal Commission into Aboriginal Deaths in Custody and P.L Dodson, Canberra, AGPS, 1991, v 5, 38.32.

18. The text of the apology is printed at the end of the chapter. 19. *Paddy's Road*, p. 317.

20. *Paddy's Road*, p. 320.

21. Peter Botsman, www.workingpapers.com.au.

97

The Dalai Lama

His Holiness the 14th Dalai Lama Tenzin Gyatso, exiled head of state and spiritual leader of Tibet, has sustained the Tibetan people through their trials both in their homeland and in Diaspora. By his example, teaching and worldwide travel, he has made Tibetan Buddhism far more widely known. He embodies the spirit of non-violence and inter-faith fellowship.

The Dalai Lama was born in a small village in North Eastern Tibet on 6th July 1935. His birth name was Lhamo Dhondrub. At the age of two, he was recognised to be the reincarnation of his predecessor the 'Great Thirteenth' Dalai Lama Thubten Gyatson (1876-1933) and an incarnation of the Avalokitesvara, the Buddha of Compassion. His other titles include 'Ocean of Wisdom', 'Wish-fulfilling Gem' and 'The Presence.' His enthronement ceremony took place in Lhasa, the capital of Tibet, on 22nd February 1940.

Tenzin Gyatso was taken as a young child from his village to live in the Potala, a royal fortress of, it is said, one thousand rooms. In a three hour tour we only saw a few of the elaborately decorated rooms. Tenzin Gyatso's education started at the age of six and eventually he completed the Geshe Lharampa (Doctorate of Buddhist Philosophy degree) at the age of 25. Once he had learned to write, he embarked on the vast field of Tibetan learning. This included as minor subjects: drama, dance, music, astrology and poetry. The major subjects were; Sanskrit, dialectics, arts, crafts, metaphysics and the philosophy of religion. The method of education is reminiscent of nineteenth century schooling in the West: copy-book work, lectures and learning by heart, but also debate with the teacher. Mediation was a regular part of the curriculum. The young Dalai Lama had a great interest in mechanical objects and he also spent hours observing the life of ordinary people through a telescope.

Tibetan Buddhism or *Vajrayana* is a distinct form of Buddhism, although closely related to Mahayana Buddhism. The Dalai Lama is a monk, belonging to the 'Yellow Hats' or dominant *Gelukpa* school of Tibetan Buddhism, which was founded by Tsong Khapa Losang

Drakpa (1357 – 1419), whom we have already met.[1]

With a Chinese invasion looming, the Dalai Lama was invested with the power of his office at the early age of fifteen in 1950. Four years later he went on a journey to Beijing to seek a compromise with Chairman Mao, but this was in vain. Tibetan resistance to forced collectivization in East Tibet and acts of cruelty by the Chinese army continued to grow. By 1958, Lhasa, the capital city, was swollen with refugees. The situation became increasingly tense, especially after a massive anti-Chinese demonstration early in 1959. In March of that year, the Dalai Lama was invited by the Chinese to a theatrical show in an army camp, *without* his bodyguards. Fearing his arrest, the Dalai Lama left the city, disguised as an ordinary soldier. He and a few companions made the dangerous and arduous journey across the Himalayas to exile in India. 'We must have been a pitiful sight to the handful of Indian guards that met us at the border,' he writes in his autobiography, 'eighty travellers, physically exhausted and mentally wretched from our ordeal.'[2]

In retaliation, the Chinese, immediately and ruthlessly, crushed the Tibetan uprising and, according to their own figures, killed 84,000 people in military action. Many more died of suicide, torture or starvation. A year later the International Commission of Jurists pronounced China guilty of genocide and it is estimated that well over a million Tibetans have been killed during the Chinese occupation. More that 120,000 Tibetans are now in exile.

The Dalai Lama settled in the beautiful foothills of the Himalayas at Dharamsala - twelve hours by bus from Delhi – which has become the seat of the Tibetan government-in-exile. Appeals to the United Nations have been in vain and His Holiness is still in exile. Many Chinese are now settled in Tibet. The Tibetans have been harshly oppressed and except in remote areas, the Tibetan way of life has been largely destroyed. The Dalai Lama, soon after reaching India, saw that his immediate task was to save both the Tibetan exiles and their culture. Tibetan refugees were rehabilitated in agricultural settlements. There are now Tibetan communities spread across India and worldwide. A Tibetan educational system has been established and at Dharamsala itself there are many institutions to promote Tibetan culture and learning. Over two hundred monasteries-in-exile have been established. The Dalai Lama has also promulgated a democratic constitution for the governance of the exiled Tibetans. Almost at once he started to learn English, but says he is still embarrassed by the terrible mistakes which he makes.

Since 1967, the Dalai Lama has travelled extensively. He has met many heads of state, although some have been hesitant because they were aware that to do so was to risk offending the Chinese government. The Dalai Lama's travels have raised the profile of Tibet and kept the tragic situation there in the public eye.

The Dalai Lama is committed to non-violence. For this and his continuing efforts to reach a peaceful resolution with China he was awarded the Nobel Peace Prize in 1989. On one occasion, he was being pressed to support an economic boycott of Chinese goods, but, I remember him replying, 'I could never do anything that would hurt the Chinese people.' 'If we look at history', he has written, 'we find that, in time, humanity's love of peace, justice and truth always triumphs over cruelty and oppression. This is why I am such a fervent believer in non-violence. Violence begets violence.'[3]

The Dalai Lama, believing that violence begets violence and inevitably causes suffering, argues for a whole new mind-set that sees war for what it really is, that is a 'fire' that spreads and whose fuel is living people. Emphasising the need for everyone to create the external conditions for disarmament by inner purification and by countering their negative thoughts and emotions, he recognizes that 'military dis-establishment' cannot be achieved overnight. But he insists the world cannot hope to enjoy true peace as long as authoritarian regimes are propped up by armed force. As a first step, national armed forces could be disbanded leaving a global police force which would protect 'against the appropriation of power by violent means.'[4]

The Dalai Lama is also committed to interfaith co-operation. He has met many religious leaders, including the Pope. He has spoken at a great variety of interfaith occasions and was the main speaker at the closing public session of the 1993 Parliament of World Religions in Chicago, which was attended by over twenty thousand people. He has twice spoken at interfaith services, which I helped to arrange for the World Congress of Faiths in London. At one, he said, that we need a variety of religions, just as we like a variety of foods, because of the different mental dispositions of each human being. Each religion has certain unique ideas or techniques and learning about them can only enrich one's own faith.[5]

In his book *The Good Heart*, which is a reflection on Jesus' 'Sermon on the Mount', the Dalai Lama gives a clear statement of his approach to interfaith work. He affirms that 'harmony among different religious traditions is extremely important, extremely necessary.'[6] 'The purpose of all the major religions is not to construct big temples on the outside, but to create temples of goodness and compassion *inside* our hearts. Every major religion has the potential to create this.'

He suggests five ways of promoting religious harmony:

1. Meetings of scholars to promote empathy and to improve our knowledge of each other.
2. Meetings between people, genuine practitioners, of different religions who have had some deep spiritual experience.
3. Occasional meetings of religious leaders as they demonstrate to the public the importance of tolerance and understanding.
4. People of different religious traditions should go on pilgrimage together and visit each other's holy places. He mentions that he had himself done this, for example on a pilgrimage to Jerusalem. While praying in holy places associated with another religion, he had, he said, 'felt a genuine spiritual experience.'
5. He insists that prayer and meditation are essential for inner transformation. The best way to overcome feelings of exclusivity is 'to experience the value of one's own path through a meditative life, which will enable one to see the value and preciousness of other traditions.'

The Dalai Lama added that it was important to be aware of the differences between religions, because instead of a universal religion, we need different religions because people are different.[7]

In calling for a spiritual revolution, The Dalai Lama has reached out effectively, beyond those who practice a religion, to a wider audience. 'It does not much matter,' he has said, 'whether or not a person is a religious believer. Far more important is that they be a good human being.'[8] As a human being, therefore, the Dalai Lama feels he has a responsibility 'to serve all humanity without recourse to religious faith.'[9] He distinguishes between religion, which concentrates on articles of belief, and spirituality, which is concerned 'with those qualities of the human spirit – such as love and compassion... - which bring happiness both to the self and to others.'[10]

The spiritual revolution, of which he speaks, entails an ethical revolution. How we behave affects other people. Indeed, every act has a universal dimension. My call, he says, is 'for a radical re-orientation away from our habitual preoccupation with self towards concern for the wider community of beings with whom we are connected, and for conduct which recognizes others' interests alongside our own.' Although this is the teaching of most religions, it is also, he suggests, based on ordinary common sense.

'If you cannot for whatever reason be of help to others, at least don't harm them. Consider yourself a tourist. Think of our planet as it is seen from space, so small and insignificant and yet so beautiful. Could there really be anything gained from harming others during our stay here? Is it not preferable, and more reasonable to relax and enjoy ourselves quietly, just as if we were visiting a different neighbourhood? Therefore, if in the midst of your enjoyment of the world you have a moment, try to help in however small a way, those who are downtrodden and those who, for whatever reason, cannot help themselves. Try not to turn away from those whose appearance is disturbing, from the ragged and unwell. Try never to think of them as inferior to yourself. If you can, try not even to think of yourself as better than the humblest beggar. You will look the same in your grave.'[11]

The Dalai Lama has strongly supported the interfaith movement and participated in meetings of Parliament of Religions and other interfaith organizations. One of his first meetings was with the Trappist monk Thomas Merton, shortly before his tragic death in Thailand in November 1968.

In discussion with Christians the Dalai Lama has explained the difficulty for Buddhists of belief in a Creator God. 'Within [the Buddhist] philosophical world view it is almost impossible to have any room for a temporal, eternal, absolute truth. Nor is it possible to accommodate the conception of a divine Creation.'[12] Yet he goes on to say that although at the theoretical level the conceptions of God and Creation are a point of departure between Buddhists and Christians, he believes some aspects of the reasoning that leads to such a belief are common to both Buddhists and Christians. He mentions that everything in nature has a cause, so it may be helpful to posit a first cause or a Creator and it is plausible to credit the Creator with omnipotence. The Dalai Lama says that he thinks the value of a belief in a Divine Creator is to give urgency to a person's commitment to become a good ethical human being. Such a belief 'gives you a sense of purpose in your existence. It is very helpful in developing moral principles.'[13]

The Dalai Lama in his writings about Jesus has concentrated on the Sermon on the Mount. The Dalai Lama compares Jesus' saying 'Love your neighbour and hate your enemy' with Mahayana Buddhist text, 'If you do not practice compassion toward your enemy then towards whom can you practice it?'[14] The Dalai Lama teaches that genuine compassion springs from a clear recognition that the other also experiences suffering and that the other is worthy of compassion and affection. Buddhists sometimes suggest that we should be grateful to those who hurt and afflict us as they provide us with the opportunity to show our compassion. As an ancient Tibetan prayer puts it:

> 'Through people's hate we discover Dharma
> And find benefits and happiness. Thank you those who hate us.
> Through cruel adversity, we discover Dharma
> And find the unchanging way. Thank you, adversity.'[15]

The Dalai Lama describes himself as 'a simple Buddhist monk.' He spends at least five and a half hours a day in prayer, meditation and study. He also prays during odd moments, such as meals or when travelling. 'I try to live my life pursuing what I call the Bodhisattva ideal' of dedicating myself 'entirely to helping all other sentient beings towards release from suffering.'[16]

Certainly, the 14th Dalai Lama will long be remembered for his humour, his commitment to non-violence and his compassion for all suffering beings. It is too early to judge how lasting his influence will be. The future of Tibet remains uncertain and no one knows whether the world will heed his call for a spiritual revolution.

CHAPTER NOTES

1. See chapter 50.
2. Dalai Lama, *Freedom in Exile*, London, Hodder and Stoughton, 1990, Revised edtn, Abacus, 1998, p. 158.
3. Dalai Lama, *Ancient Wisdom, Modern World: Ethics for a New Millennium*, London, Little, Brown and Company, 1999, p. 187.
4. *Ancient Wisdom, Modern World*, p. 199.
5. Marcus Braybrooke, *A Wider Vision*, Oxford, Oneworld, 1996, p. 120.
6. Dalai Lama, *The Good Heart*, Ed. Robert Kiely, London, Rider, 1996, p. 39.
7. *The Good Heart*, pp. 39-42. See also, *Ancient Wisdom, Modern World*, chapter 15.
8. *Ancient Wisdom, Modern World*, pp. 19-20.
9. *Ancient Wisdom, Modern World*, p. 20.
10. *Ancient Wisdom, Modern World*, pp. 22-3.
11. *Ancient Wisdom: Modern World*, pp. 245-6.
12. *The Good Heart*, p. 82.
13. *The Good Heart*, pp. 55-6.
14. *The Good Heart*, p. 48.
15. *1,000 World Prayers*, p. 215.
16. *Freedom in Exile*, p. 224ff.

98

Desmond Tutu

Discrimination in all forms has been increasingly challenged by spiritual leaders in the twentieth century. Gandhi opposed caste barriers in India and Martin Luther King lead the civil disobedience campaign against blacks in America. Desmond Tutu, who became Archbishop of Cape Town, was the most vocal opponent of the apartheid regime in South Africa. After its collapse, Tutu headed the Truth and Reconciliation Commission, which paved the way for a new multi-racial nation. Tutu showed that the moral voice of a religious leader can have an impact on political life. He demonstrated that 'forgiveness' is relevant to inter-communal as well as inter-personal relationships.

Desmond Mpilo Tutu was born on October 7th, 1931. He was directly descended on both sides from the two largest language and cultural groups in the country. His mother, Matse - a powerful formative influence on his life - was a Motswana. Chiefdoms of this group had lived in the central and north-western interior of South Africa for at least eight hundred years. Desmond's father, Zachariah Zelilo Tutu, belonged to amaMfengu group of Xhosa speaking people. Their origins are debated, but they were among the best educated of the African peoples. Nelson Mandela described the amaMfengu as 'our clergymen, policemen, teachers, clerks and interpreters.'[1]

Zechariah Tutu was himself a primary school teacher in Klerksdorp, one of the first white settlements in Transvaal. It was there Desmond was born. He was the second son. The first child had died in infancy, so Desmond was a 'letlomela' - a child whose predecessor had not survived. Desmond himself as a young child became very ill with polo. 'My dad prepared for a funeral', Desmond's elder sister Sylvia recalled.[2]

When Desmond was four, the family moved to the smaller town of Tshing. The family lived in a simple rectangular flat-roofed building, in the compound of the Methodist Church, where there was a junior school, of which Zachariah was principal. The house had three rooms: the parents' bedroom, a kitchen and a living room, which was also the children's bedroom. There was no electricity, so study at night was by candlelight.

When Desmond was about ten, his mother returned to the Reef in search of work. The family, therefore, moved several times as Zachariah looked for work, which was near to his wife. Despite the changes of school, Desmond did well in class. By the time he was fourteen, he had settled at St Paul's Anglican school in Munsieville – now part of Mogale City, near Johannesburg. He lodged at a hostel linked to the Church of Christ the King in Sophiatown, which was run by members of the Community of the Resurrection, a high-church Anglican monastic order, which was to have a profound influence on Desmond Tutu.

In 1943, Fr Trevor Huddleston was appointed to head the Community's work in Sophiatown. 'He was so un-English in many ways,' Tutu said. He was 'very fond of hugging people, embracing them and in the way in which he laughed. He did not laugh like many white people, only with their teeth. He laughed with his whole body.'[3] Huddleston encouraged Tutu to read widely. Tutu, also, became a server at the church.

In May 1947, Tutu was taken ill with tuberculosis and sent to a sanatorium near Alexandra Township, on the opposite side of Johannesburg. It was there that Tutu first experienced a 'God-moment, almost an epiphany.' 'Once somebody started coughing up blood you knew it was curtains... I was haemorrhaging a lot one day... I remember that I went to the bathroom and I was vomiting blood and I said, "God, if it means I am going to die, OK; if I am going to live, OK..." Through having said that I experienced a strange sort of peace.'[4] Tutu remembers Huddleston's care for him during the long months of illness. It was difficult for his family to visit, but on one occasion, his father announced that he should now be recognized as a man, for which the essential requirement was circumcision - a practice that missionaries had tried in vain to stop. As Tutu was in hospital, he could not join an initiation school and the procedure was done surgically.

Tutu wanted to study to become a doctor, but the family could not afford the fees. Instead, in 1951, he went to a teacher's college and took his first teaching post in 1954 and in the following year moved to Krugersdorp High School. It was now that he and Leah entered into a serious relationship and were married in 1955. It was in the same year that, to implement the *apartheid* policy of racial segregation,

Sophiatown was cleared. The government also tried to control children's minds by their new education policies, which Oliver Tambo, who became the leader of the African National Congress in exile, described as 'the most evil act of all.'[5] Desmond, after discussion with Leah, decided he could not be 'a collaborator in this nefarious scheme.'[6] With Trevor Huddleston's encouragement, he was put forward for ordination.

In 1958, he started his theological training at St Peter's College in Rosettenville in Johannesburg, which was run by the Community of the Resurrection. Whilst he was at College, on March 21st, 1960, police in Sharpeville, south of Johannesburg, opened fire on a crowd peacefully demonstrating against the pass laws. With no warning, 1,000 rounds of ammunition were fired in les than a minute. 69 people died and nearly 200 were injured. Church leaders protested, the international media headlined the massacre, and the Government crackdown started. In December 1960, Tutu was ordained, but after a short time of parochial work, he left South Africa in the autumn of 1962, to study at King's College, London.

In 1966, he returned to South Africa to teach at St Peter's College, which had become part of the newly established Federal Theological Seminary. Tutu's career advanced rapidly. In 1972, he became African Director of the Theological Education Fund, which allowed him to travel widely in Africa, at a time when many African countries had recently gained independence. In 1974, Tutu just failed to be elected Bishop of Johannesburg, but the following year he became dean of the city's St Mary's Cathedral, although he was soon to move to become Bishop of Lesotho.

Tutu was now a public figure. Before his move, children from Soweto, protesting at educational changes imposed on them by the government, were fired on with tear gas and bullets. Tutu voiced his outrage, but was saddened by the silence of the white community. He left Johannesburg with a heavy heart. In September 1977, he was called back to preach at the funeral service of Steve Biko, who was killed in police custody. Tutu declared that

'Steve had started something that was quite unstoppable. The powers of injustice, of oppression, of exploitation have done their worst and they have lost...because the God of the Exodus ... is a God of justice and liberation and goodness.'[7]

Six months later in March 1978, Tutu was back in South Africa as head of the South African Council of Churches (SACC). Looking back, it can be seen that by then the tide was turning against apartheid. The first injury to government forces was inflicted in November 1976. In 1977, the United Nations Security Council instituted a mandatory arms embargo.

In 1984, Tutu was back once more in Johannesburg – now, as bishop. Two years later, Tutu was elected Archbishop of Cape Town and head of the Anglican Church in South Africa. His ten years in office, was to see the transition from the apartheid regime to a multi-racial South Africa. It was at the beginning of 1990 that Prime Minister de Klerk ended the ban on political parties, released Nelson Mandela (b. 1918) from his long years of imprisonment and prepared for negotiations. Almost immediately on his retirement, Tutu was chosen to head the Truth and Reconciliation Commission. Today his is a voice of conscience listened to with respect around the world.

Was Tutu a politician rather than a priest? The accusation is made against any church leader whose commitment to justice embarrasses those in power. Prime Minister P W Botha wrote to him, 'The question must be posed whether you are acting on behalf of the kingdom of God, or the kingdom promised by the ANC and the SACP. If it is the latter, say so, but do not then hide behind the structures and the cloth of the Christian church, because Christianity and Marxism are irreconcilable opposites.' Tutu responded that his position derived from the Bible. 'The Bible and the Church predate Marxism and the ANC by several centuries... Our marching orders come from Christ himself and not from any human being.' He gave many quotations from the Bible to support his position and concluded, 'I work for God's Kingdom. For whose Kingdom with your apartheid policy do you work? I pray for you, as I do for your ministerial colleagues, every day by name. God bless you.'[8] When Tutu started work at SACC, he introduced compulsory daily staff prayers and regular Bible studies. 'These things,' he said, 'are at the centre of our lives.'[9] Many Christians in the twentieth century, and not just liberation theologians, have emphasised that God is on the side of the poor and marginalised. Yet members of the Dutch Reformed Church drew other lessons from the Bible. The Vatican, too, has not always been supportive of those priests who championed the downtrodden.

What influence did Tutu have on the ending of apartheid? Bill Burnett, who was Archbishop of Cape Town when Tutu was first approached to become general secretary of SACC, asked him, 'Is liberation what the Churches can and should do, for in the final analysis it will be political pressures and/or guns that decide the issue, unless the whites change. Will a black SACC change whites?'[10]

Many factors contributed to the end of apartheid: the fear of a bloody civil war, international isolation, sanctions and an economic and sporting boycott and the outstanding leadership of Nelson Mandela. Yet the influence of the voice of conscience in political life should not be underestimated. At the start of the Second World War, the poet W H Auden wrote, 'All I have is a voice to undo the folded lie.'[11] The voice of millions raised in protest helped to topple the Communist regimes of Eastern Europe. As former American Vice-President Al Gore said,

'The leveraging of moral authority to persuade people of the rightness of a particular course of action is a very tangible power... Throughout history some of the most important changes of all have come because of the exercise of moral leadership on the part of individuals who may not have any formal political power at all.'[12]

Tutu, with the Anglican Church as his base, was that voice in South Africa and to the world. Throughout the apartheid era some Christians were vocal in their condemnation of it. Tutu affirmed both his faith in God's liberating power, and the eventual 'victory of light over the darkness of apartheid ... the victory of life over the death of apartheid.' 'We are the rainbow people of God! We are unstoppable. Nobody can stop us on our march to victory! Nothing will stop us, for we are moving to freedom! ... For God is on our side!'[13]

Tutu was committed to change by non-violent means, but as the government was deaf to the protests, he said, 'I can understand when ... people feel they have exhausted all non-violent avenues.'[14] Tutu favoured the use of sanctions and disinvestment. He also wrote private appeals to leading statesmen.

Despite difficulties in being allowed a passport, Tutu also alerted the world church – indeed the world - to the cruelty of apartheid. I remember at the 1983 Assembly of the World Council of Churches, held in Vancouver, how his arrival and his words electrified the gathering. In 1984, in accepting the Nobel Peace Prize, he said:

> This award is for mothers who sit at railway stations trying to eke out an existence, selling potatoes… This award is for you, fathers, sitting in a single-sex hostel, separated from your children for eleven months a year. This award is for you mothers in the KTC squatter camps of Cape Town, whose shelters are destroyed callously every day and who sit on soaking mattresses in the winter rain, holding whimpering babies… This award is for you, the 3.5 million of our people who have been uprooted and dumped as if you were rubbish.'[15]

Tutu helped to bring an end to the apartheid regime. Equally important, he was committed to healing the wounds of that struggle. The lead was given by Nelson Mandela, who became the first President of a multi-racial South Africa. Mandela had trained as a lawyer. He then became active in the leadership of the African National Congress, which became the main vehicle of opposition. He was arrested and served twenty-seven long years of cruel imprisonment on Robben Island. Yet, when he was released, Mandela 'did not emerge from prison spewing words of hatred and revenge. He amazed us all by his heroic embodiment of reconciliation and forgiveness.'[16] Tutu has acknowledged that 'Our miracle almost certainly would not have happened without the willingness of people to forgive, exemplified spectacularly in the magnanimity of Nelson Mandela.'[17]

When hostilities end, the wounds and the bitterness still fester. In some situations, the victors prosecute their opponents as 'war-criminals.' This may count as justice, but not as reconciliation. When Tutu visited Rwanda, where Hutu extremists had hacked to death over 800,000 members of the Tutsi group, he warned them against pressing for 'total justice' in response to the genocide. The two groups had struggled for years for superiority. If the Tutsi showed no mercy, Tutu warned, then one day the Hutus might regain power and perpetrate another atrocity. Only restorative justice could break the cycle of reprisal and counter-reprisal. In other situations, there may be a 'blanket' amnesty, as in Chile after the fall of Augusto Pinochet. This, however, denies justice to the victims and is a superficial reconciliation that is unlikely to last. In Guatemala, besides the Historical Clarification Commission, set up by the UN, to study the conflicts of the period 1962-1994 and to recommend measures to promote peace and reconciliation, the Catholic Church established a 'Recovery of Historical Memory Project.' Led by Bishop Gerardi, the process was based on the Biblical verse, 'the truth will set you free.'[18] Having someone to listen to their story certainly helped the victims and some of the perpetrators were freed from their guilt by admitting what they had done. As one witness said, 'the only way wounds will be healed' is by bringing them to the light.[19] The Project, however, lacked executive power so there was truth but not justice or compensation for the victims. The brutal murder of Bishop Gerardi two days after he had presented the findings of the Project showed that the government did not have the power to enforce justice.

In South Africa, the Truth and Reconciliation Commission, which Tutu headed, offered a conditional amnesty, if a person made a full and public confession of criminal activity. There were three committees: one to investigate violation of human rights; another to decide an amnesty, which was not granted unless the whole truth was told; and a third to recommend reparation to assist rehabilitation of the victims. Tutu concentrated on the investigation of human rights abuses.

The important achievements of the Commission are widely recognised. Even so, there are questions about its work. Perhaps the most persistent is whether the process allowed justice to be done. A person who made a full confession was freed from criminal or civil liability. Tutu has insisted that 'public exposure and humiliation' was a big price for the perpetrator to pay.[20] Amnesty was only granted to those who pleaded guilty. The police officers who killed Steve Biko were not granted amnesty because they claimed, falsely, that they only acted in self-defence. The restorative justice of the Commission, Tutu held, embodied the African spirit of *ubuntu*, which involves the healing of broken relationships. Moreover it was intended that victims should receive compensation, although the procedures for that were lengthy and unsatisfactory.

There were further questions. It was acknowledged that the focus was too much on high profile figures. Some members of ANC, who argued that they only acted as they did because they had been provoked by the apartheid regime, were resentful that the process equated the actions of the government and those of the ANC. Other people commented that the hearing was too religious.

These questions should in no way hide the remarkable achievements of the Truth and Reconciliation Committee. It gave South Africans one history not two. It ensured that the cruelty of apartheid could not be hidden. It encouraged members of all communities to share in creating a new nation.

Alex Boraine, Tutu's deputy in the Commission, said, 'I don't think the Commission could have survived without the presence and person and leadership of Desmond Tutu.'[21] John Allen, Tutu's biographer, ends his book in this way,

'By promoting a vision of reconciliation in which the principles of *ubuntu* were applied to repair the fractures in society, Desmond Tutu held out to the world as it entered the twenty-first century an African model for expressing the nature of human community. It is perhaps in this contribution that future generations will find his greatest legacy.'[22]

In Tutu's own words, 'Without forgiveness there really is no future.'[23] He has in recent years tried to promote this in situations of conflict in many parts of the world and is a champion of those who are oppressed in any part of the globe.

CHAPTER NOTES

1. Quoted by John Allen in *Rabble-Rouser for Peace, The Authorised Biography of Desmond Tutu*, London, Rider, 2006, p. 13.
2. *Rabble-Rouser*, p. 19.
3. *Rabble-Rouser*, p. 44.
4. *Rabble-rouser*, p. 46.
5. *Rabble-rouser*, p. 60.
6. *Rabble-rouser*, p. 61.
7. *Rabble-rouser*, p. 164.
8. *Rabble-rouser*, p. 292.

9. *Rabble-rouser*, p. 169.

10. *Rabble-rouser*, p. 165.

11. W.H Auden, 'September 1st, 1939' was published in 1940.

12. *Rabble-rouser*, p. 394.

13. *Rabble-rouser*, pp. 333-4.

14. *Rabble-rouser*, p. 172.

15. *Rabble-rouser*, p. 213.

16. Desmond Tutu, *No Future Without Forgiveness*, London, Rider, 1999, p. 39.

17. Desmond Tutu in *Exploring Forgiveness*, eds Robert D Enright and Joanna North, University of Wisconsin Press, 1998,p. xiii. See also Nelson Mandela, *Long Walk to Freedom*, Randbury, South Africa, Purnell, 1995.

18. John 8, 32.

19. Quoted by David Tombs in *Explorations in Reconciliation*, Ed David Tombs and Joseph Liechty, Aldershot, Ashgate, 2006, p. 91.

20. Desmond Tutu, *No Future Without Forgiveness*, p. 48.

21. *Rabble-Rouser*, p. 370.

22. *Rabble-rouser*, p. 396.

23. The title of chapter 11 of Tutu's book, *No Future Without Forgiveness*, p. 206.

99

Seyyed Hossein Nasr

Seyyed Hossein Nasr is one of the foremost contemporary scholars of Islamic and Religious studies. A prolific author he has written numerous books, which show the relevance of Islam to many contemporary issues. He is also an influential exponent of the 'Traditionalist School' also known as the 'perennial philosophy.'

Seyyed Hossein Nasr was born in 1933 in Teheran, Persia. His family were Shi'ite Muslims. His father and grandfather were physicians to the royal family. The title 'Nasr,' which means 'victory,' was conferred on his grandfather by the King of Persia. His father was also one of the founders of modern education in Iran. In his mother's family there were several notable scholars and spiritual leaders. One of his ancestors was a Sufi saint, whose tomb is still visited by pilgrims to this day.

Seyyed Hossein Nasr first went to school in Teheran, following the usual Persian curriculum and also learning French. At the age of thirteen, he was sent for further education to the USA to Peddie School in Highstown, New Jersey, where he became familiar with the English language, Western culture and Christianity. He then went to the Massachusettes Institute of Technology (MIT) where he studied physics. He was, however, soon disillusioned with the course, which concentrated on scientific matters and ignored metaphysical questions. The disillusionment led in his second year at MIT to an intellectual and spiritual crisis, although his belief in God was not shaken. Nasr's dissatisfaction with the physics course was confirmed by the British philosopher Bertrand Russell (1872-1970). On a visit to MIT, Russell said that physics dealt with mathematical structures and not the nature of physical reality. Seyyed Hossein Nasr persisted with the course at MIT, but devoted much of his time to reading widely about philosophy. He was also introduced to the writings of René Guénon, whose works are of central importance to the Traditionalist School. Nasr said of him, 'Guénon, as he is reflected in his writings, seemed to be more an intellectual function than a man.'[1]

To understand Nasr, therefore, it is helpful to know a little about the

Traditionalists and especially René Guénon and Frithjof Schuon.

René Jean Marie Joseph Guénon (November 15, 1886 – January 7, 1951) - also known as Sheikh 'Abd al-Wahid Yahya after his acceptance of Islam - was a French-born author. His field was metaphysics, applied to the study of cultural tradition. He was born in Blois, France, into a Catholic household. As a student Guénon became very critical of modern society and when he moved to Paris in 1907, he became deeply involved in a series of underground cultural movements, including theosophy, spiritualism, occultism, gnosticism, and a Shivaite branch of Hinduism. At the same time, he learned about Islam and Christianity, and later about Buddhism. Guénon became a Sufi Muslim sometime between 1911-1912 - although he did not reveal his conversion and was later married in a Catholic church. Despite his conversion, Guénon championed the validity of other religions as vehicles of the 'Universal Truth.'

Guénon's critique of the modern world, which was in the grip of the Dark Age (Kali Yuga), aimed at creating an intellectual elite able to retrieve a long forgotten spiritual knowledge that once formed the core of all traditional societies. Guénon's writings provided the Traditionalists with their theoretical foundation.

Guénon thought was developed by the German-Swiss philosopher Frithjof Schuon (1907-1998). Frithjof was born in Switzerland. His father, who was from Southern Germany, was a violinist, but after his father's early death his mother returned to France with her two sons. Frithjof Schuon, therefore, was fluent in French and German and later learned Arabic. In the nineteen thirties he travelled several times to North Africa and met Guénon and several Sufi teachers. After the war, he travelled to America and lived for some time with Native Americans.

Of his many books - written in French - his first and most important was *The Transcendent Unity of Religions,* of which the English translation appeared in 1953. The poet T S Eliot said of it, 'I have met with no more impressive work in the comparative study of Oriental and Occidental religion.' For Schuon, who was deeply influenced by Advaita or Non-Dual Hindu philosophy, the perennial religion is the underlying religion which is differently expressed in the world religions. Early in his life, Schuon met a black marabout or Muslim saint from Senegal. The old man drew a circle on the ground with various lines converging at the centre. He said to the young Frithjof, 'God is in the centre, all paths lead to him.' Schuon claimed to be *'universalist* because free of all denominational formalism' but also *'dogmatist,* because far from all subectivist relativism, we believe that knowledge exists.'

Schuon's writings and his emphais on a spiritual discipline influenced Nasr's own way of life. Other Traditionalists who influenced Nasr were the Ceylonese scholar and expert on art Ananda Coomaraswamy (1877-1947), the art historian Titus Burckhardt (1908-1984) and the Sufi scholar Martin Lings (1909-2005). The Traditionalist movement divided in 1948-50 after a split between Guénon and Schuon. The movement also influenced Ken Wilber and the 'Integral Thought' developed by followers of Sri Aurobindo.

The discovery of this traditional metaphysical approach, resolved Nasr's intellectual crisis. Seyyed Hossein Nasr became convinced that Truth is real and can be attained by intellectual knowledge guided and illuminated by divine revelation.

After graduating from MIT, Seyyed Hossein Nasr pursued his studies at Harvard and also travelled widely. His doctoral degree on 'Conceptions of Nature in Islamic Thought' was published in 1964.

Although he was offered a post in America, Nasr returned to Iran to teach at Teheran University. There, he helped to expand the University's philosophy curriculum and encouraged students to become versed in their own intellectual tradition as a basis on which then to approach and critique other traditions. He also took an interest in the University's teaching of Persian language and literature.

In 1972, Nasr was appointed by the Shah of Iran to be President of Aryamehr University, which was to be modelled on MIT, but firmly based in Iranian culture and Islamic thought. In the following year, the Queen of Iran established the Imperial Iranian Academy of Philosophy and appointed Seyyed Hossein Nasr to be its head. He attracted leading scholars to take part in its seminars and built up a remarkable library. Nasr continued to travel widely, lecturing at many universities, as well as writing a variety of important books.

All this was, for a time cut short, by the Iranian revolution. Nasr and his family had to flee to the United States. After teaching for a time at Temple University, he moved in 1984 to the George Washington University, which is now a leading centre for the study of religions and philosophical and interfaith dialogue. Nasr edited the two volumes on Islamic Spirituality in the *Encyclopaedia of World Spirituality*, of which the chief editor was Ewert Cousins. The books reflect Nasr's deep appreciation of the Sufi tradition. He has also taken an active interest in the Foundation for Traditional Studies. He has written over fifty books.

In the current context, the term 'Traditionalist' may be confusing. Hans Küng identifies three ways in which Muslims may approach the future and indeed have reacted to the impact of the military, economic and cultural dominance of Western powers.

The first way, which Küng calls 'Traditionalist Islam' is 'religious isolation (or) religious substance with no relation to the modern world. This approach is based on the unchanging teaching of the Qur'an and the *Sunnah* (or 'customary practice'). The state should be a theocracy, as in Saudi Arabia, with the laws based on *shariah* or Islamic law. This approach is typified by Ayotollah Khomeini, who was largely responsible for the revolution in Iran that overthrew the Shah and forced Nasr to flee from the country.

The second way is 'Radical Secularism', in which Islam is emptied of religious content and becomes an ideology, such as Pan-Arabism or nationalism or socialism. The practice of Islam as a private religion is allowed, but priority is given to science, technology and democracy. The obvious example is Turkey under Mustafa Kemal Attatürk, who abolished Shar'iah courts, closed Qur'anic schools, forbad Islamic forms of dress and replaced Arabic script with the Latin alphabet.

The third way Küng calls 'Postmodern Islam' This implies the religious emancipation of Islam, whereby the original Islamic religion based on the revelation of the Qur'an is related to the modern world. 'Islamic identity is renewed through belief in the one God and God's righteousness; an uncurtailed Islamic sense of history, but in the postmodern paradigm.' The consequence is 'postmodern emancipation and communication with today's world of nations and religions.'[2]

Any such schematic presentation over simplifies and people's choices are not entirely consistent. Nonetheless, Küng's summary highlights the very different ways in which Muslims may see the future and helps to explain the intensity of debate within the world of Islam and the very different ways in which Muslims want to relate to modernity and to other nations and religions. Even so, it is clear that

Nasr belongs to the third category and is not a 'traditionalist' in Küng's sense of the word.

The third approach is that of many scholars who are faithful to the teaching of Islam and are confident that it has an important contribution to make to the future of the world. This is the approach of which Nasr is one of the most articulate and influential advocates. Unlike some radical scholars who want to see changes in the traditional teaching of Islam, Nasr is committed to the unchanging revelation of God's word in the Qur'an and to the authority of Shar'iah. 'The central theophany of Islam, the Qur'an, is the source *par excellence* of all Islamic spirituality. It is the Word manifested in human language... Likewise the soul and inner Substance of the Prophet are the complementary source of Islamic spirituality.'[3]

Nasr also has confidence in the power of reason to interpret and apply God's revelation in a changing world. His position is similar to that of the Indian Muslim scholar Maulana Wahiduddin Kahn (b.1925) - popularly known as Islam's spiritual ambassador to the world - who called for 'an understanding of Islam that is both rooted in the original sources of Islam, while at the same time willing wholeheartedly, although critically, to engage with modernity, responding positively to serious concerns such as questions of peace, inter-religious dialogue and political activism.'[4]

Nasr's writings cover a wide range of subjects. This is because 'Islam embraces all of human life, both the outward and inward. Any comprehensive work on Islam,' he wrote, 'would have to consider both the socio-political and economic dimension as well as the inner dimension.'[5]

Nasr has given particular attention to Islam's relation to Nature and was one of the first religious leaders to recognise the importance of the environmental issues. 'Religion and Ecology' which is emerging now as a subfield in the academic discipline of religious studies, owes much to Seyyed Hossein Nasr. In his Rockefeller Lectures in 1966 in Chicago,[6] published as *Man and Nature*, Nasr had said that the environmental crisis is not simply the result of bad engineering or bad planning, but is in reality a spiritual and religious crisis.

'In order to have peace and harmony with nature one must be in harmony and equilibrium with Heaven, and ultimately with the Source and Origin of all things. He who is at peace with God is also at peace with His creation, both with nature and man.'[7]

Nasr chose to return to the topic of Religions and the Environment in a lecture he gave to the International Interfaith Centre in Oxford in 1994. Nasr began by stressing the urgency of the topic:

'Let me assert categorically that this is a challenge which no serious person can avoid simply by delaying to confront it with the hope of facing it later. There is no greater catastrophe than the lack of political will of nations, whether they be leftist or rightist, democracies or dictatorships, republics or monarchies, as well as individuals, to face this question. At any point within the spectrum of political institutions throughout the globe one sees the lack of will power to deal with issues which are absolutely crucial and which must be faced now. This is precisely the point where the role of religion must enter with its God-given intuitive grasp of truth, an intuitative power, which includes but is not limited to mere analysis of events.

Everyone is involved from Muslims to Hindus to Buddhists to followers of the primal religions in the Polynesian Islands or Africa, to Christians, Protestants, Catholics, to agnostics and atheists... We fight about everything else, but we are agreed upon how to go about destroying the globe.'[8]

Nasr, after surveying the attitude of many religions to Nature, observed that Western Christianity alone has 'surrendered the cosmos completely to the non-religious way of looking at it.' The vast majority of the people of the world, however, are still religious. Our relationship to Nature, especially in view of the deadly threat to the environment, should, therefore, be a central concern of interfaith dialogue, of which he has been a keen advocate and practitioner.

Like other Traditionalists Nasr affirms the universality of God's revelation as well as the particularity of each religion. 'The Spirit manifests itself in every religious universe where the echoes of the Divine Word are still audible, but the manner in which the manifestations of the Spirit take place differs from one religion to another. In Islam, the Spirit breathes through all that reveals the One and leads to the One, for Islam's ultimate purpose is to reveal the Unity of the Divine Principle and to integrate the world of multiplicity in the light of that Unity.'[9]

Acknowledging the Spirit's presence in other religious traditions besides his own, Nasr recognises the importance of interfaith dialogue, not just so that we understand each other, but that also by mutual sharing we may grow in understanding the truth. 'The destinies of Islam and Christianity are intertwined,' Nasr has written, 'God has willed both religions to exist and be the ways of salvation for millions of human beings.' In the face of intolerance and fanaticism, Nasr hopes that the voice of understanding and harmony will prevail, because 'it is based upon the truth and surely Christ whose second coming is accepted by both Christians and Muslims shall not come but by truth, that truth which he asserted himself to be according to the Gospel statement and which the Qur'an guarantees as being triumphant at the end, for there will finally arrive the moment when it can be asserted with finality that "Truth has come and falsehood has perished."'[10]

CHAPTER NOTES

1. Seyyed Hossein Nasr, *Knowledge and the Sacred.* (The Gifford Lectures for 1980), New York, State University of New York Press, 1981.
2. Hans Küng, *Islam, Past, Present and Future,* translated by John Bowden, Oxford, Oneworld, 2007, p. 467.
3. *Islamic Spirituality* I, edited by Seyyed Hossein Nasr, New York, Crossroad, 1985, London, SCM Press, 1989, p. xv.
4. Quoted by Marcus Braybrooke in *What Can We Learn from Islam,* Alresford, John Hunt, O books, 2002, pp. 131-2.
5. *Islamic Spirituality,* p.16.
6. Published as *Man and Nature: The Spiritual Crisis in Modern Man,* London, George Allen and Unwin, 1968, Unwin Paperbacks, 1990.
7. *Man and Nature,* p. 136.
8. Newsletter of the International Interfaith Centre, Oxford, No 1, 1994.
9. *Islamic Spirituality,* p. xv.
10. Seyyed Hossein Nasr, 'The Islamic View of Christianity', *Concilium* 183, 1986, pp.10ff. Küng quotes these words with approval, see Küng, *Islam,* p. 535. The quotation from the Qur'an is from Surah 17, 81.

100

Rosemary Ruether

Rosemary Ruether has been called 'one of the most influential and celebrated of feminist theologians.'[1] She has pioneered influential changes in twentieth century Christian thinking. As a champion of Christian feminism, she has challenged the patriarchal theology and structures of the Church. She has insisted that Christian theology must rid itself of anti-Judaism. As a champion of liberation theology she has called for justice for the downtrodden people of the earth and spoken up for the rights of Palestinians. She has stressed the urgent need for the Churches to relate seriously to the ecological crisis and share in Earth healing.

Rosemary Radford Ruether was born in 1936 in Georgetown in the USA. Her mother was a Catholic and her father an Episcopalian. Her extended family included Jews, Mexicans, Unitarians, Quakers and Russian Orthodox, so that a multiplicity of perspectives living together has always seemed normal to her. She has described her childhood as religiously ecumenical, humanistic and freethinking, as compared to the parochialism of many of her Catholic contemporaries. She was twelve when her father died. After this tragedy, her mother and she moved to California, where Rosemary's primary role models were women. She attended Scripps College as an undergraduate from 1954-58. She originally intended to study art, but soon switched to classics.

During her last year at college, she married Hermann Ruether, who was a political scientist. They shared the responsibility of bringing up their three children and maintaining a home. Ruether studied for her doctorate, which was on the Cappadocian church father Gregory of Nazianzus (329-89), at the School of Theology at Claremont.

In her mid-twenties, Ruether was caught up in the civil-rights movement and then the peace movement – on occasion spending time in jail. She taught for ten years at Howard University School of Religion, which was becoming a centre of Black Liberation theology. During the period after the Second Vatican Council, she was keen to push forward the reforms that the Council had initiated. Her first book, *The Church Against Itself* (1967) was a critique of the doctrine of the church. She

became at this time a friend of the Trappist monk Thomas Merton
(1915-68) and Gregory Baum (b. 1923), who was a theological advisor at
the Second Vatican Council.

Ruether was one of the pioneers of feminist theology and has
devoted much effort to exposing the sexism inherent in Christianity.
She is, however, convinced that the Christian tradition is essentially
egalitarian and has the potential to become more inclusive of women.
This is why, unlike some feminist theologians, she has remained a
member of the Church. Feminist theology began with criticism of the
way women's experience had been ignored and questioned the
theological assumptions that justified patterns of male dominance. Her
collection of essays *Religion and Sexism* (1974) was one of the first of its
kind. It documented the misogyny of the texts, beliefs and practices of
the Judaeo-Christian tradition.

The opening paragraph of her more recent *Sexism and God Talk*
(1983) gives a taste of her style:

> '"I am the Lord thy God. Thou shalt have no other gods before Me,"
> bellowed God the Father, as He seated Himself high upon His
> Cherubim throne and surveyed the ranks of angels doing obeisance
> to Him. Having expelled the quarrelsome Sons of Heaven... they
> left to rape the daughters of humankind...From this violence all
> sorts of monsters had been born.'[2]

In the Ancient Near East, she argued, the divine was pictured as the
Primal Matrix or Ground of Being or the womb within which all things
were generated. These traditions were suppressed by the monotheism
of the Hebrew people. Yet the Bible sees God as the liberating saviour.
The Bible's polemic against idolatry means that God is neither male nor
female, although male and female language may be used of God. To
indicate this, Ruether chose to speak of God/ess, signifying that as yet
we have no adequate name for the divine. 'Intimations of Her/His
name will appear as we emerge from false naming of God/ess modelled
on patriarchal alienation.'[3]

This is not just a question of language, but of how we picture God.
To speak of God as the 'Primal Matrix' is affirm the presence or
immanence of God in the world, whereas male languages suggests a

God 'up in the sky', over and above the world. 'God is not a "being" removed from creation, ruling it from outside in the manner of a patri-archal ruler' Ruether has written, 'God is the source of being that underlies creation.'[4] God supports us in the struggle for change in our way of life, but, respecting our freedom, God does not save us despite ourselves. Critics question whether Ruether gives enough weight to the transcendence or greatness of God/ess.

Ruether has made a feminine critique of many doctrines. For example, in her study of Marian doctrines, *Mary: The Feminine Face of the Church* (1977), the Magnificat[5] is seen as a song of liberation and Mary as a sign of hope to the oppressed. Like other feminist theologians, Ruether has been among the more radical critics of traditional Christology. They object to the argument that because Christ was a male, only men can represent Christ as priests. Moreover, the maleness of Jesus even seems to imply the maleness of God and that salvation is only for men. One chapter in *Sexism and God-talk* has the provocative title 'Can a Male Saviour Save Women?'[6] This was possible, Ruether argued elsewhere, if one started with the person of Jesus portrayed in the Gospels rather than with the Christ of the creeds. 'Once the mythology about Jesus as Messiah or divine Logos, with its traditional masculine imagery, is stripped off, the Jesus of the Synoptic Gospels can be recognised as a figure remarkably compatible with feminism.'[7] Not that Jesus was a feminist, but his criticism of the religious and social authorities was akin to that of feminists today. Jesus renewed the prophetic vision; he spoke of God as Abba or 'Father' and he was concerned for women from the marginalized strata of society. Jesus' ability 'to speak as liberator does not reside in his maleness but in the fact that he has renounced the system of domination and seeks to embody in his person the new humanity of service and mutual empow-erment.'[8]

Ruether's criticism of traditional beliefs about Christ reflects not only her feminist theology but grew out of her awareness that the Church's traditional anti-Jewish teaching has been used by anti-Semites and has contributed enormously to the suffering of the Jews through the centuries. In a challenging phrase, Ruether said that anti-Judaism was 'the left-hand of Christology.'[9] By this she meant that the claim that Jesus is the Messiah is at the same time a negative comment on the Jews for not recognising him as such.[10] Her book *Faith and Fratricide* (1974) provoked enormous discussion and at least one volume was devoted to scholarly responses to her arguments.[11]

Much of what she said would now be accepted by critical scholars and even, in moderated language, in official statements of the churches.[12] It is now recognised with shame that in the past the Jews were often blamed by the Church for 'deicide' or the murder of God and this was one reason why for so many centuries they were treated as second-class citizens in Christendom. The Nazi ideology was different and based on nineteenth century pseudo-scientific claims that the Aryans were a master race. But, as Ruether pointed out, most people did not recognise a distinction between the anti-Judaism of the Church and Nazi hatred of the Jews. 'They simply heard both the Church and the Nazis say that Jews were despicable and ... the basic Nazi message that the Jews were to be robbed, expelled and "done away with was" perfectly in accord with long held "Christian" assumptions.[13]

Ruether, while reading for her BA thesis, had become aware that what Judaism meant by the Messiah was very different to what Catholics understood by the term. It is now widely recognised that Jewish Messianic expectation in the first century CE was very varied. Christians, Ruether said, gave a new meaning of 'divine saviour' to the title Messiah. Jewish rejection of the Messiah – in the Christian sense - was then used by the Church against the Jews, who became Christianity's 'shadow side' that had to be repressed.

To rid the belief in Christ of anti-Jewish overtones, Ruether said that Christian claims should be understood as proleptic [or provisional] and anticipatory rather than final and fulfilled.

'The crucifixion of the Messiah by the unredeemed forces of history cannot be overcome by the proclamation of Easter and then transformed into a secret triumph. Easter gives no license to vilify those who "cannot see it." Indeed we must see that Easter does not cancel the crucifixion at all. There is no triumph in history. Easter is hope against what remains the continuing reality of the cross.'[14]

Ruether also suggested that although the cross and resurrection were central to the belief of the Christian community, other faith communities are based on different foundational events or 'paradigms.' This is in effect is to abandon the traditional universal claims of the Church and to recognise that God/ess relates to humanity in particular ways or 'paradigms' through different faith communities. It is now common for Christians to recognise that God's covenant with the Jewish people is still valid and has not been superseded by the new covenant in Christ. Ruether, however, goes further and suggests that there are different but complementary paradigms of hope in each of the great faiths.

Ruether, as we have seen, pictured Jesus as challenging the prevalent patriarchal structures of society, with its hierarchy and oppression. Here her theology is similar to that of Liberation theologians, who see Jesus as the champion of the poor who sets people free from economic and political injustice. Amongst the oppressed, women have in most societies been the most downtrodden and have suffered the most. Ruether, therefore, brought her feminists insights to bear on the structural violence of society, insisting in *God and the Nations* (1995) that redemption in Christ has a social dimension. She coined the phrase 'the inter-structuring of oppression,' arguing that all forms of oppression have common roots in patriarchal thinking.

Ruether's concern for the victims of oppression has also led her to champion the rights of the Palestinians and to be sharply critical of the policies of Israeli governments. In *The Wrath of Jonah: Religious Nationalism in the Arab-Israeli Conflict* (1989), which she wrote with her husband, she examined the historical roots of Zionism, the steps taken to establish a Jewish state and the development of the Israeli-Palestinian conflict. She also looks at Christian responses to these three topics. She has also co-edited two volumes about the *Intifada* or Palestinian revolt.[15]

Besides rejecting Christian Zionism, Ruether is critical of those Christians who - aware of the Churches' appalling record in relation to the Jews - wish to compensate by uncritical support for the state of Israel. Moreover, even if the Covenant, which included the promise of land, is still valid, the 'land has never been a land of one people... Many peoples continued to live side by side with Hebrews during the period of Hebrew hegemony.'[16] Ruether also insists that Christians, who believe that God is a God of all nations, 'cannot accept an ethnocentric notion of God and of God's election of one people at the expense of others.'[17] 'Only a vision of God', she insisted, 'that loves and commands justice for all peoples can create the framework for the just co-existence of the two people, Israelis and Palestinians, and the three religions, Judaism, Christianity and Islam, calling them to be equal partners, brothers and sisters, in sharing the land together in justice and peace.'[18]

Ruether has now become increasingly focussed on the ecological crisis and she is sometimes spoken of as an 'ecofeminist theologian.' This concern is deeply rooted in her theology. 'The working assumption of feminist theology,' she wrote in *Sexism and God-talk*, 'has been the dynamic unity of creation and redemption.' She has criticised the traditional Christian approach, which has set 'man' above the non-human in a way that allows the human infinite rights to manipulate, use up, or destroy the non-human. 'Indians, by contrast, have a sense of the human and the non-human as one family of life... The human is not outside, but within, the great web of life.'[19]

Ruether returned to these themes in *Gaia and God: An Ecofeminist Theology of Earth Healing* (1992). Ruether is clear that healing the earth requires more that 'technological "fixes"'[20] and depends upon healing other broken relationships. 'It demands a social reordering to bring about just and loving interrelationships between men and women, between races and nations, between groups presently stratified into social classes... It means that we must speak of eco-justice.'[21] It requires 'a new consciousness, a new symbolic culture and spirituality.'[22] It is not enough to replace the male monotheistic God of the Bible with *Gaia*, as a personified immanent divinity. 'We need a source of life that is "yet more" than what presently exists... To believe in divine being means to believe' that the qualities of consciousness and altruistic care in ourselves 'are rooted in and respond to the life power from which the universe itself arises.'[23]

Ruether has courageously addressed many of the most important challenges that need to be faced today. She has done so with a deep faith, which has never hidden from the failings of the Church, but which has retained the confidence that, with patient passion, revolutionary change is possible.

Many of those included in this book have also hoped for dramatic change and a new world based on spiritual and moral values. Their dreams have never been completely fulfilled for as Ruether warns, 'Life is not made whole "once and for all"... it is made whole again and again, in the renewed day born from the night and in the new spring that arises from each winter... Love for our real communities of life and for our common mother, Gaia, can teach us patient passion that is not burnt out in a season, but can be renewed season by season.'[24]

Yet the dreams of those about whom I have written and their self-sacrificing efforts to realise them can encourage us to hope and pray and work for that revolution which is needed to ensure a future 'not just for us, but for our children, for the generation of living beings to come.'[25]

In Rosemary Ruether's words:

'What we can do is to plant a seed, nurture a seed-bearing plant here and there, and hope for a harvest that goes beyond the limits of our powers and the span of our lives.'[26]

This is what those who are 'Beacons of the Light' achieved. We are still today harvesting the seeds that they planted.

CHAPTER NOTES

1. Linda Hogen in *The Oxford Companion to Christian Thought* p. 629.
2. Rosemary Ruether, *Sexism and God Talk: Toward a Feminist Theology*, Boston Beacon Press, London, SCM Press, 1983, p. 1.
3. *Sexism and God Talk: Toward a Feminist Theology*, p. 71.
4. R Ruether, *Women and Redemption, A Theological History*, Minneapolis, Fortress Press, 1998, p. 223.
5. The Magnificat is Mary's hymn of praise that she was to have a special baby. Luke 1, 46ff.
6. See John Bowden in *Christianity the Complete Guide*, Ed. John Bowden, London, Continuum, 2005, p. 225. Reuther also wrote an essay in *Reconstructing the Christ Symbol: Essays in Feminist Theology* Ed Maryanne Stevens, 1993 and Wipf and Stock pbk 2004.
7. *Sexism and God Talk*, p. 135. The Synoptic Gospels are Matthew, Mark and Luke.
8. *Sexism and God Talk*, p. 137.
9. Ruether, *To Change the World*, New York, Crossroad, 1981, p. 31.
10. See, for example, a verse in Charles Wesley's hymn 'Lo, he comes with clouds descending.' Speaking of the Second Coming of Christ,

Wesley wrote:

Those who set at nought and sold him,

Pierced and nailed him to the tree,

Deeply wailing,

Shall the true Messiah see.

11. *AntiSemitism and the Foundations of Christianity*, ed Alan T Davies, New York, Paulist Press, 1979.

12. See further, Marcus Braybrooke, *Time to Meet*, London, SCM Press, 1990, *passim*.

13. *AntiSemitism and the Foundations of Christianity*, p. 250.

14. *AntiSemitism and the Foundations of Christianity*, p. 251.

15. With Marc H Ellis, *Beyond Occupation: the American Jewish, Christian and Palestinian Voices for Peace*, Boston, Beacon Press 1990 and with Naim S Ateek and Marc H Ellis, *Faith and the Intifada: Palestinian Christian Voices*, Maryknoll, Orbis Books, 1992.

16. R Ruether, 'Christian Zionism and Main Line Western Churches' in *Challenging Christian Zionism*, London, Melisende, 2005, p. 157.

17. 'Christian Zionism and Main Line Western Churches', p. 157.

18. 'Christian Zionism and Main Line Western Churches', p. 162.

19. *Sexism and God Talk*, p. 250. Ruether refers to Vine Deloria's book *God is Red*. New York, Grosset and Dunlap, 1973.

20. R Ruether, *Gaia and God: an Ecofeminist Theology of Earth Healing*, HarperSan Francisco and London, SCM Press, 1993, p.9.

21. *Gaia and God*, p. 3.

22. *Gaia and God*, p. 4.

23. *Gaia and God*, p. 5.

24. *Gaia and God*, p. 273.

25. *Gaia and God*, pp. 273-4.

26. *Gaia and God*, p. 274.

Adam and Eve	Manikkavacacar	Elijah ben Solomon
Abraham	Saicho and Kukai	Mendelssohn
Zoroaster	Ramanuja	John and Charles Wesley
Vyasa	Al Ghazali	Seraphim of Sarov
Akhenaten	Abelard	William Wilberforce
Krishna	Maimonides	William Blake
Rama and Sita	Avicenna and Averroes	Sri Ramakrishna and
Moses	Hildegard of Bingen	Vivekananda
David	Honen, Shinran and	Sayyid Iqbal Khan and
Isaiah	Nichren	Muhammed Iqbal
Jeremiah	Eisai and Dogen	Nakayama Miki
Lao-tzu	Ibn 'Arabi	Baha' Allah
Confucius	Francis of Assisi and	Te Whiti-O-Rongomai
Mahavira	Clare	Rudolf Steiner
Buddha	Aquinas	Freud and Jung
Plato	Mother Julian of	Tagore
Aristotle	Norwich	Black Elk,
Asoka	Tsong Khapa Losang	Gandhi
Mary	Drakpa	Albert Schweitzer
Jesus	Kabir	Aurobindo
Peter	Eckhart	Teilhard De Chardin
John	Jalal-ad-Din ar-Rumi	Francis Younghusband
Paul	Sergius of Radonezh	Pope John XXIII
Johannan ben Zakkai and	Guru Nanak	Bede Griffiths
Rabban Gamaliel II	Akbar	Khalil Gibran
Origen	Martin Luther	Martin Buber
Constantine and Helen	Thomas Cranmer	Mother Teresa
Augustine of Hippo	Ignatius Lloyola	Yukitaka Yamamoto
John Climacus and	Mirabai and Tulsidas	Elie Wiesel
Gregory of Sinai	John Calvin	Martin Luther King
Benedict	Servetus	Haile Selassie I
Brigid	Teresa of Avila and	Thich Nhat Hahn
Nagarjuna	John of the Cross	Patrick Dodson
Muhammad	Guru Arjan Dev and	The Dalai Lama
A'isha	Guru Gobind Singh	Desmond Tutu
Sankara	George Fox	Seyyed Hossein Nasr
Rabia	Baal Shem Tov and	Rosemary Ruether

Which Beacon Shines Most Brightly?

So which Beacon shines most brightly?

You have been presented with the evidence, now it is time to judge. You may, of course, think other names should have been included. But one hundred names is a *short* list.

To remind you who they are, their names are on the opposite page in roughly historical order.

It may help to distinguish certain categories, although some people belong to more than one. This means that names are not necessarily mentioned in the ranking that I am bold enough to give them. I give priority to those whose influence extends beyond their own particular faith.

First there are the founders of religion. For me, Jesus Christ (1) comes first. Partly this is a personal confession. It is primarily through him that I have experienced God's love and forgiveness and I have tried throughout my life to be his follower. More objectively, Christianity is the largest religion. Moreover many people of other religions and of no religion have a high regard for the person of Jesus although they may not accept the claim of the Church that he was the only Son of God.

In terms of size, Islam, after Christianity has the most followers. It is said there are now more Muslims in the world than Roman Catholics. Islam too dominates the news today. Yet I believe the Buddha's message of non-violence will grow in influence and now has a world-wide appeal. So I put Gotama Buddha (2) second and the Prophet Muhammad (3) third. In any case, Muslims while deeply honouring Muhammad as the Messenger of God, insist that he was only a man. Divine claims are made for both Jesus and the Buddha. Similar claims are made for the Hindu Avatars Krishna (4) and Rama and Sita (5), whom I place fourth and fifth.

The founders of smaller religions also deserve to be honoured and their followers although fewer in number have been immensely influential. Moses (6), through whom God rescued the Israelites from Egypt and gave to them the Law or Torah, comes sixth. His monotheism and deep sense of God's moral concern has influenced not only Judaism, but also Christianity and Islam and through them world society and the whole idea of human rights. Jainism also has a comparatively small number of followers, but the importance of its teaching of non-violence is increasingly recognised, so Mahavira (7) is number seven. The founder of Sikhism, Guru Nanak (8), emphasised that God does not belong to one religion but is the God of all people. As Sikhs become more widely dispersed throughout the world this message will be heard more loudly – so Guru Nanak comes eighth. A similar universalism was proclaimed by Baha' Allah (9), so he comes ninth. Zoroastrians are few in number today, but Zoroaster (10) was perhaps the first monotheist and emphasised God's call for a moral life. Zoroaster comes tenth. Moses rather than Abraham is usually spoken of as 'the founder' of Judaism, but the Biblical story goes back to Abraham, who is now often spoken of as the father of three religions: Judaism, Christianity and Islam, so I place Abraham (11) eleventh.

Ancient Greece is remembered for its philosophers rather than for the Gods of Olympus. The writings of Plato (12), who comes twelfth, and Aristotle (13), who comes thirteenth, have permeated the thought of Western civilization and influenced Judaism, Christianity and Islam. Lao-Tzu (14), who is number fourteen and Confucius (15), who is number fifteen, have had a similar lasting influence on Chinese thought. They have to some extent been eclipsed by the rise of Communism in China, but they are reasserting their influence. As China becomes more powerful, perhaps they will overtake Plato and Aristotle.

Some people stand out for their radiant holiness, which still today continues to attract and inspire people from many backgrounds. Francis of Assisi (16) is perhaps the best loved of all these saints so he, with Clare is number sixteen. The Sufi mystic Jalal-ad-Din ar-Rumi (17) has a large and growing following and is number seventeen, followed by Ibn Arabi (18). Both insist that the religion of love transcends religious labels. Rabia (19), who made love central to Sufism is number nineteen and her Christian spiritual twin Mother Julian (20), who said 'love is my meaning' is number twenty. Both were noted for their humility and would be astonished even to have been included in the book. Sri Ramakrishna (21) followed several religious paths, which he said, all lead to the same mystical experience of the Divine. His disciple Swami Vivekananda saw this as evidence for his claim that all religions lead to

God. Eckhart (22) is perhaps the most significant Western mystic and his blending of the Personal and Absolutist experience of the Ultimate Reality provides a meeting point for Western and Eastern mysticism.

A number of people have had a formative influence on their religious tradition. In Christianity, I put Paul (23) first and Augustine (26) second. Mary (30) the Mother of Jesus has attracted the devotion of thousands of the faithful during the centuries and is remarkable for her humility and total acceptance of God's will. Peter (34) and John (33), two of the first disciples of Jesus, helped to shape the growth of Christianity. Which should I put first? The Papacy, with its enormous influence, claims to have inherited the authority given by Jesus to Peter to be the leader of the disciples, but perhaps even more to be treasured is John's Gospel, one of the most profound books ever written, which has had a lasting influence on the Christian Church and is appreciated by people of other faiths. Sankara (24) by his writings determined all subsequent philosophical reflection in Hinduism. His non-dual position was rejected by Ramanuja (29), the philosophical defender of Hindu theistic devotion. Nagarjuna (25) is the most influential Buddhist thinker and in part Sankara and Ramanuja responded to him. Al-Ghazali (27), after the Prophet himself, is said to have had the greatest influence on Muslim thought, followed by Avicenna and Averroes (28), who both made a vital contribution to the development of Islamic thought. Johannan ben Zakkai (35) ensured the survival of Judaism after the destruction of Jerusalem and its Temple by laying the foundations of Rabbinic Judaism, although Maimonides (31) has an even higher reputation. Guru Arjan Dev and Guru Gobind Singh (32) gave lasting shape to the Sikh faith and community. Isaiah (36) and Jeremiah (37) are highly esteemed both by Jews and Christians.

Others continue to inspire people today by their writings, which reflect their own spiritual experience. The poems of Kabir (40), who rejected religious labels, are increasingly being known and appreciated. The Catholic mystics Teresa of Avila (41) with St John of the Cross, and the Orthodox Christian teachers of the 'Prayer of the Heart' John Climacus and Gregory of Sinai (42) are now being appreciated by many spiritual seekers who do not belong to either church. Sergius of Radonezh (82) and Seraphim of Sarov (43), both of the Orthodox tradition, handed on teaching of the 'Jesus Prayer,' which Christians of many traditions now use. The poems and vision of William Blake (38) and of Rabindranath Tagore (39) are appreciated in the East and the West. Khalil Gibran (92) is widely read, although he admitted that his life did not match the ideals enshrined in his writings. Manikkavacakar (68), a South Indian devotional poet, deserves to be far better known. There has not been room to discuss the contribution of artists and musicians and architects, many of whom have enriched the spiritual life of humankind. Mirabai and Tulsidas (69) popularised their message by their songs and poetry.

Many of those mentioned in the book were very significant in the growth of their faith community, but do not have the universal appeal of those mentioned already. It is hard, therefore, to determine the order in which to place them. Their influence is partly determined by the size today of the religion to which they belonged. It is easier to speak of each religion in turn, so the names are not mentioned in the order in which I place them.

Two great eighteenth century Jewish figures Baal Shem Tov and Elijah ben Solomon rank together (45) and Mendelssohn (44) anticipated the various ways in which Judaism was to respond to the modern world.

In Christianity the two most original thinkers were Origen (46) and Abelard (48) Their ideas are attracting new interest today. The thinking of Aquinas (47) shaped Catholic theology for nearly nine hundred years and is till hugely influential as the Roman Catholic Church is still the largest Christian church. The founding figures of other churches have also had a continuing influence. Martin Luther (53) led the Protestant break away from the Catholic Church which has still not been healed. Lutheranism is a world body, but as many Christians belong to churches which look to Calvin (54) as their founder. Cranmer (57) had a pivotal role in the early development of the Church of England, from which the Anglican communion was to grow. Benedict (59) who shaped the pattern of western monasticism and Ignatius Loyola (56), a leader of the Catholic Reformation, have also had worldwide influence. Rather later, in the second half of the seventeenth century, George Fox (58) started the movement of Quakers or Friends, who although still a comparatively small number, have had an influence out of all proportion to their size. In the eighteenth century the evangelical revival led by John and Charles Wesley (55) resulted in the establishment of the Methodist Church, which now has a large world-wide following.

In Islam, A'isha (49) sometimes described as the favourite wife of the Prophet Muhammad, played a vital role in transmitting *hadith* or stories or about what the Prophet said and did, which have shaped Muslim practice and belief.

In Buddhism, Tsong Khapa Losang Drakpa (73) purified Tibetan Buddhism and gave a shape to it that has lasted through the centuries. Several people played a part in establishing various forms of Buddhism in Japan: Saiko and Kukai, (50) Honen, Shinran and Nichiren (51) and Eisai and Dogen (52)

It is harder to judge the lasting influence of more recent figures. It is easier perhaps to identify major new developments in the spiritual life of humankind and see the people named as representatives of these developments. It is significant that in recent years people of outstanding holiness have also been active in significant changes in the life of the world. Perhaps most notable is Mahatma Gandhi (60) best known for his advocacy of non-violence in the struggle for Indian independence. He insisted that non-violence was a spiritual discipline. He rejected caste divisions and encouraged fellowship among people of different religions. The Dalai Lama (61) is also committed to non-violence and has strongly advocated interfaith dialogue and co-operation. He has been tireless in reminding the world of the plight of the Tibetan people under Chinese rule. He has ensured the survival of Tibetan culture and religion among the exiled Tibetans.

Many people of faith have challenged the injustices in the world. Desmond Tutu (63) made known to the world the cruelties of *apartheid*, which condemned the majority of South Africans, who were black or coloured, to live as second or third class citizens. After the collapse of the *apartheid* regime, Tutu headed the Truth and Reconciliation Commission, which perhaps for the first time applied the principle of forgiveness, usually seen as a private virtue, to public life and political conflict. Martin Luther King (62) was also deeply committed to non-violence in the struggle to gain full civil rights for the black population in the USA. He and others have increased awareness of the evils of racism, which afflict so many societies. In so doing they have highlighted the importance of affirming basic human rights for all people.

Others have championed the cause of the suffering and oppressed. Some like Mother Teresa (66), who dedicated her life to caring for the destitute and the dying especially in Calcutta and Albert Schweitzer (65), who spent much of his life as a doctor in a remote part of Africa, devoted their lives to caring for the poor. Others challenged the causes of deprivation and marginalization. William Wilberforce (64) led the campaign against the slave trade. Others have given voice to the great injustices suffered by indigenous people in many parts of the world. Te Whiti-O-Rongomai (72) tried by non-violent means to protect the Maori way of life in New Zealand. Black Elk (70) witnessed the sufferings of Native Americans and affirmed their spiritual values and sense of being one with Nature. Patrick Dodson (74) increased awareness in Australia of the oppression of the Aboriginal people, whose way of life was destroyed by the seizure of their land. He has led the way in the search for reconciliation between white Australians and the Aboriginal people. Appreciation of the culture and spirituality of indigenous people and their sense of belonging to the Land has been an important factor in the growth of the Environmental movement.

As weapons of war have become more terrible the search for peace has become ever more significant. Yukitaka Yamamoto (75) experienced the devastation of the first Atomic bombs and devoted himself to work for peace. Thich Nhat Hahn (76) struggled for peace during the horrors of the Vietnam War. Peace requires justice. In many places, the destruction of indigenous people and their way of life amounted to genocide, but the most terrible example of genocide was the Nazi's attempt to exterminate all the Jews of Europe during the Holocaust or Shoah. Elie Wiesel (71), perhaps more than anyone has by his writings made the world aware of the hideous cruelties perpetrated in the concentration camps. Less well known are the sufferings of the Ethiopian people, who were invaded by the Italians in 1936. Emperor Haile Selassie (80) tried to alert the conscience of the world and pleaded in vain with the League of Nations to take action. Haile Selassie is also regarded as divine by the Rastafarians who have led the way in championing the rights of black people everywhere.

Many people have recognised, in Hans Küng's words that 'there will be no peace in the world without dialogue between the religions.' Kabir and the Sikh Gurus dismissed religious differences and Akhenaten and Akbar emphasised that there is One God. Servetus (81) who in his time was regarded as a heretic by the Church tried genuinely to appreciate the teachings of Judaism and Islam. Swami Vivekananda, the disciple of Sri Ramakrishna, and Baha' Allah, the founder of the Baha'i religion - both of whom have already been mentioned – were advocates of inter-faith understanding, as the Dalai Lama has also been. Pope John XXIII (77) recognised the importance of this and of building a new relationship between Christians and the Jewish people. Besides initiating vital changes in the life of the Roman Catholic Church, he helped to transform the attitude of its members towards other Christians and adherents of other religions and world views. Francis Younghusband (83), who founded the World Congress of Faiths, devoted much of his life to encouraging a fellowship of faiths and the recognition of the ethical values, which are shared by the religions. Bede Griffiths (85) was one of those who explored most deeply the spiritual and theological meeting of religions, especially of Christianity and Hinduism. Similarly, Thich Nhat Hahn and the Dalai Lama have increased Buddhist-Christian understanding and the Muslim scholar Seyyed Hossein Nasr (84) has advocated the 'Perennial Philosophy', which speaks of an underlying spiritual harmony which transcends the differences between religions. Seyyed Hossein Nasr has also called for religions to recognise the spiritual importance of harmony with Nature.

There has been in the last century, besides the growing recognition of the evils of racism, greater awareness of the oppression suffered by women through the centuries, often reinforced by the teachings and practices of world religions. Rosemary Ruether (86) has been one of the most articulate advocates of feminism and an acute critic of the patriarchal attitudes endemic in religion. She has also highlighted the anti-Judaism to be found in much Christian teaching, advocated the rights of the Palestinian people and emphasised the importance of concern for the environment.

Evidence of the dominant patriarchal attitudes of religion is the fact that too few women are included in this book and so often the language of religion and the pictures of God are masculine. Yet, of course, women have made an enormous contribution to the development of spirituality and goddesses are prominent in some traditions. The great mystics Rabia and Mother Julian have already been mentioned, but there have been many more women mystics who I have not included for lack of space. Some women were also leaders of religious revival. Teresa of Avila, already mentioned (41) was a reformer and also a very influential spiritual guide. Brigid (88) was and one of the patron saints of Ireland; Hildegard (89) was a powerful leader and her songs and poems have become popular in recent years. The poems of Mirabai, already mentioned, have inspired many people in India. Nakayama Miki (87) was the founder of one of the new Japanese religions and women have been leaders of other new religions and spiritual movements in Japan and elsewhere. Mary, A'isha and Sita, who was the consort of Rama, have been highly regarded in their respective religions.

Darwin's theory of evolution posed a serious challenge to some traditional religious beliefs, especially the Biblical account of the creation of the world in seven days. The 'survival of the fittest' seemed deterministic and to leave little room for a loving God. Two thinkers especially sought to apply the evolutionary principle to their religious understanding of life: Aurobindo (90) and Teilhard de Chardin (91). Religions have also had to come to terms with growing awareness of the importance of the unconscious thanks to the psychological insights of Freud and Jung (67) .

Other thinkers have concentrated on trying to integrate the insights of modern knowledge with the traditional beliefs of their religious tradition. Sayyid Iqbal Khan and Muhammad Iqbal (93) and Seyyed Hossein Nasr, already mentioned, have tried to do this for Islam as has Martin Buber (79) has for Judaism. Rosemary Ruether is one of many Christian theologians who have tried to do this. One of the most creative and seminal thinkers, who defies being labelled, was Rudolf Steiner (78).

Several rulers have had a decisive influence for the good on religious life. Perhaps I should have put them higher on the list, but perhaps too cynically, I wonder if their motivation was perhaps political as well as religious – hoping that the religion they favoured would in turn help to unify their subjects. Asoka (94) was a remarkably benevolent ruler who did much to promote the spread of Buddhism. David (95) is remembered as a model king of Israel. The Psalms attributed to him have played a central role in the devotional life of many Jews and Christians. Constantine (96), encouraged by his mother Helen, abandoned the traditional paganism and emperor worship of the Roman Empire, when he converted to Christianity. Akhenaten (98), an early ruler of Egypt and Akbar (97) a Mughal Emperor both instituted major religious reforms and emphasised the oneness of God. Their new religions, however, had little lasting impact.

I realise that I have omitted Adam and Eve (99), who according to the Bible were the first human beings and Vyasa (100), traditionally regarded as the author of the Hindu scriptures. They are, however, mythical figures and I hope will be content that their chapters came near the beginning of the book.

The above summary has unfairly categorised people who were multi-faceted in their gifts, inspiration and influence. More important than putting them in order is to appreciate the particularity of their contribution to the amazingly rich and varied spiritual creativity to which we are heirs. Each of the great spiritual traditions has enormous gifts to share with the world. Treasuring our own tradition, we are enriched by learning to appreciate the wisdom and holiness of other faith communities. In so doing, as in a beautiful garden we marvel at the variety of the flowers and plants, so in contemplating the flowers of the Spirit our hearts are uplifted and we become more aware of the precious gift of life, which is to be treasured and which we share with other people and with all living beings.

1. Jesus
2. Buddha
3. Muhammad
4. Krishna
5. Rama and Sita,
6. Moses
7. Mahavira
8. Guru Nanak
9. Baha' Allah,
10. Zoroaster
11. Abraham

12. Plato,
13. Aristotle,
14. Lao-tzu,
15. Confucius,
16. Francis of Assisi & Clare
17. Jalal-adDin ar-Rumi
18. Ibn' Arabi
19. Rabia,
20. Mother Julian of Norwich
21. Sri Ramakrishna and
    Vivekananda

22. Eckhart
23. Paul
24. Sankara
25. Nagarjuna
26. Augustine of Hippo
27. Al-Ghazali
28. Avicenna and Averroes
29. Ramanuja
30. Mary
31. Maimonides
32. Guru Arjan Dev and Guru Gobind Singh
33. John
34. Peter
35. Johannan ben Zakkai and Rabban Gamaliel II
36. Isaiah
37. Jeremiah
38. William Blake
39. Tagore
40. Kabir
41. Teresa of Avila and John of the Cross
42. John Climacus and Gregory of Sinai
43. Seraphim of Sarov
44. Mendelssohn
45. Baal Shem Tov and Elijah ben Solomon
46. Origen
47. Aquinas
48. Abelard
49. A'isha
50. Saicho and Kukai
51. Honen, Shinran and Nichiren
52. Eisai and Dogen
53. Martin Luther

54. John Calvin
55. John and Charles Wesley
56. Ignatius Loyola
57. Thomas Cranmer
58. George Fox
59. Benedict
60. Gandhi
61. The Dalai Lama
62. Martin Luther King
63. Desmond Tutu
64. William Wilberforce
65. Albert Schweitzer
66. Mother Teresa
67. Freud and Jung
68. Manikkavacakar
69. Mirabai and Tulsidas
70. Black Elk
71. Elie Wiesel
72. Te Whiti-O-Rongomai
73. Tsong Khapa Losang Drakpa
74. Patrick Dodson
75. Yukitaka Yamamoto
76. Thich Nhat Hahn
77. Pope John XXIII
78. Rudolf Steiner
79. Martin Buber
80. Haile Selassie
81. Servetus
82. Sergius of Radonezh
83. Francis Younghusband
84. Seyyed Hossein Nasr
85. Bede Griffiths
86. Rosemary Ruether
87. Nakayama Miki
88. Brigid
89. Hildegard of Bingen
90. Aurobindo

91. Teilhard de Chardin
92. Khalil Gibran
93. Sayyid Iqbal Khan and
    Muhammed Iqbal
94. Asoka
95. David

96. Constantine and Helen
97. Akbar
98. Akhenaten
99. Adam and Eve
100. Vyasa

Bibliography

Details of books of reference are given below.
Details of publication of other books cited are given in the Chapter Notes,where the books are first mentioned.

1,000 World Prayers, Ed Marcus Braybrooke, Alresford, John Hunt, 2003

Abraham's Children, Ed by Norman Solomon et al., London T and T Clark, 2005

Christianity the Complete Guide, Ed. John Bowden, London, Continuum, 2005

Dasgupta, Surendranath *A History of Indian Philosophy,* Delhi, Motilal Banarsidass, 1975

Encyclopaedia Britannica, 15th Edition, Chicago and London Encylopaedia Britannica, Inc, 1977

Encyclopaedia of Sikhism, Patiala, Punjabi University, 1996,

Fisher, Mary Pat, *An Anthology of Living Religions,* Upper Saddle River, N.J., Prentice Hall, 2000

Fisher, Mary Pat, *Living Religions,* Upper Saddle River, NJ, Prentice-Hall, (1991), 1999

From Primitives to Zen, Ed Mircea Eliade London, Collins, 1967

International Bible Commentary, Collegeville, Minnesota, The Liturgical Press, 1998

Johnson, Paul *A History of the Jews,* London, Weidenfeld and Nicolson, 1987

Lesser, Roger, *Saints and Sages of India,* New Delhi, Intercultural Publications, 1992

Lutterworth Dictionary of the Bible, Ed Watson Mills, Cambridge, The Lutterworth Press, 1990 and Mercer Press 1994

Mahadevan, T M P, *Outlines of Hinduism,* Bombay, Chetana, 1956

Moorman, J R H, *History of the Church of England,* London, A and C Black, 1953, Revd edtn 1958

New Peake Commentary on the Bible, Thomas Nelson and Sons, 1962

New SCM Dictionary of Christian Spirituality, Ed Philip Sheldrake, London, SCM Press, 2005

Oxford Bible Commentary, Ed John Barton and John Muddiman, Oxford, Oxford University Press, 2001

Oxford Companion to Christian Thought, Ed Adrian Hastings et.al. Oxford, Oxford University Press, 2000

Oxford Dictionary of World Religions, Ed John Bowker, Oxford, Oxford University Press, 1997

Panikkar, Raimundo, *The Vedic Experience*, London, Darton, Longman and Todd, 1977

Smith, Vincent A *The Oxford History of India*, (Edited by Percival Spear), Oxford, Clarendon Press, 1958, 1970 edtn

The Torah: a Modern Commentary, (ed) W. Gunther Plaut New York, Union of American Hebrew Congregations, 1981

Universal Wisdom, Ed Bede Griffiths, London, Fount, 1994

World Scriptures, Ed Andrew Wilson, St Paul, Minnesota, Paragon House, 1995

Index of Names

The index is of names of people mentioned in the text. References are to the chapter numbers. Numbers in Bold indicate that the person is the subject of the chapter. Numbers followed by 'n' indicate that the reference is to the relevant chapter notes.

à Kempis, Thomas 49, 68

Aisha Bint Abi Bakr 32, **33**

Abbott, Nabia 33

Abd al-Muttalib 32

Abdu'l-Baha 75

Abel 65

Abelard, Peter **40,** 48

Abhishiktananda, Swami, (Henri le Saux, Fr),

Abraham (Abram) **2,** 5, 65, 75, 8

Absalom 9

Abu Bakr 32, 33, 53

Abu Tali 32

Abu Ya 'qub Yus, Caliph 42

Abul Fazl 63, 64

Adam **1**

Eve **1**

Addison 43

Buber, Adele 89

Adler, Alfred 78

Agathia 69

Agrippa, King 23

Ahaz 10

Ahmad 39

Akbar, Emperor 59, **63,** 64, 73

Akhenaten

Akhenaten (Amenhotep IV) **5,** 8,78

Akiva (Akiba), Rabbi 1, 8

Al –Farabi 42

Al Ghazali

Ala' ad-Dawlah 42

Alan T Davies, 100

Albert Einstein 82

Albertus Magnus 17, 48

al-Bukari 32

Alexander the Great 3, 17, 24

Alexander, Tsar 69

Alexis, Metropolitan 54

al-Ghazali 32, 35, **39,** 41, 42 46

Al-Ghazali,

Ali 32, 33

Ali ben Yusuf 41

Al-Juzjani 42

Allen, John 98

al-Mansurr, Caliph 42

Alston, A J 59n

Alypius 27

Amaldas 87

Ambedakar, B R 95

Ambrose 9, 27

Amenhotep III 5

Ammonius Saccas 25

Amoz 10

Anagrika Dharmapala 15

Ananias 23

Anastasia, 26

Andrew, St 22, 21

Andrews, Charles Frere 79, 81

Angad Dev, Guru, 55

Angelo, Brother 47
Anne Boleyn, Queen, 57
Anne, Gabiel, Sister, 69
Anne, St 19, 56
Anselm, 40, 48
Antal 36
Anthony, St 29
Antiochus IV (also known as
Antiochus Epiphanes) 24
Antonio Monserrat, Father 63
Aquinas, Thomas, St 17, 39, 40, 42,
48
Arinori Hino 44
Ariston 16
Aristotle 16, 17, 42, 48
Arius 25, 26
Arjan Dev, Guru 64
Arjuna 6
Arminius, Jacobus 68
Armstrong, Regis 47n
Arnold, Edwin, Sir 81
Arnold, Thomas, Sir 73
Arsenios 28
Arthur, Prince, 57
Asaph 9
Asha 87
Asoka, Emperor 18, 31, 34
Astralabe 40
Ataturk 53
Ateek, Naim S 100n
Athanasios Paliouras, 26n
Athanasius 26
Atherton Mark 30
Atisa, 31, 50
Atmananda Swami 34n
Attwater, Donald 54n
Auden, W H 98

Augustine of Hippo, St 17, 26 27,
56
Augustine, St, Archbishop of
Canterbury, 27
Aurangzeb, Emperor, 64
Aurobindo, Akroyd Ghose, Sri 83,
87
Averroes (Ibn Rushd) 17, 42, 46,
48
Avery-Peck, Alan J 24
Avicenna (Ibn Sina) 17, 39, 42,
Azraqi 19

Ba'al Shem Tov (The Besht) 1, 66,
67, 69, 92
Bab (Mirza Husayn 'Ali) 75
Baba Virsa Singh 20
Bach, John Sebastian 82
Baha'ad-Din Walad, 53
Baha'Alla (Mirza Husayn 'ali
Nuri) 75
Bahira 32
Baillie D M 20
Bakes, Richard 45n
Balaram 6
Bamerjee, Victor 90n
Barabbas 88
Barker, Sir Ernest, 27
Bar-Kokhba 24
Barnabas 23
Barrows, John Henry 72n
Barry, Patrick OSB. 29
Barth, Karl 19
Barton John 9nt
Baruch 11, 24
Basho 45
Basil the Great, St 29

Basire, James 71
Bathsheba 9
Baum, Gregory 100
Beatrice 46
Beattie, Tina 19
Beckford, William 70
Beckwith, Francis J 75n
Bell, G, Bishop 85
Benedict Alapatt, Fr 87
Benedict XV, Pope 86
Benedict, St **29**
Benjamin 23
Benjamin of Tuleda 41
Berdyaev, Nicolas 25
Bergson, Henri 73, 84
Berkovits Eliezer 2
Bernard of Clairvaux 40, 43
Bernhard, Isaac 67
Bernini 62
Berrigan, Daniel 95
Berry, Father Thomas 84
Bertrand Russell 82
Besant, Annie 77
Best,Gary 68
Beza, Theodore 60
Bharatan Kumarappa 81n
Biko Steve 98
Bindusara 18
Bishop, Peter D 81n
Bjelke-Petersen, Joh 96
Black Elk **80**
Blake, William **71,** 88
Blavatsky H P Mrs 77
Bleuler, Eugen 78
Bloch, Johannan 89n
Blochmann, H 63n
Bly, Robert 59

Bobrinskoy, Boris 69
Bodhidharma 45Boehme, Jakob 89
Boethius 17, 43
Bogdan Chmielnicki 66
Bolle, Kees W 6nt
Bonaventure 48
Bonnet, Charles 67
Bonney Charles, 71
Boraine, Alex 98
Botha, P W 98
Botsman, Peter 96
Bovo 43
Bowden, Hugh 26
Bowden, John 19, 100n
Bowden, John
Bradlaugh, Charles 76
Braybrooke, Marcus 23n, 30n,
83n, 79n 90n 97n 99n, 100n
Brigid, St **30**
Broadwell, Liz 49nt
Brocca 30
Bronowski, J 71n,
Brown, Joseph Epes 80
Brown, Peter 27
Brown, Professor 75
Bryce, John 76
Buber Solomon 89
Buber, Carl 89
Buber, Martin (Mordechai) 20, **89,** 66
Buddha 3, **15,** 18, 45, 52, 72, 75, 87, 95
Budha, Bhai (Brother) 64
Buffalo Bill 80
Burckhardt, Titus, 99
Burke 70
Bushrui, Suheil 88

Butcher, Carmen Acevedo 43n

Caedmon 30
Caesar, Emperor 23.
Calvin John (Jean Chauvin) 58, **60**, 61
Camus 35
Candrakirti 31
Carlyle, Thomas 32, 56
Carpiceci Alberto Carlo 5
Carter, Sydney 49
Cartier, Jean-Pierre 95n
Cartier, Rachel 95n
Catherine Boucher 71
Catherine II of Russia 69
Catherine of Aragon, Queen, 57
Catherine of Siena, St, 49, 62
Celano 47
Celsus 25
Cement of Alexandria 25
Ch'in Shih Hua, Emperor13
Chadwick, Henry 27
Chadwick, Owe 56n
Chandragupta, Emperor 18
Charles I, King of England 65
Charles II, King of England, 65
Charles V, Emperor 56
Chaucer, Geoffrey 49
Chetanananda, Swami 72n
Che-yi 37
Chief Seattle (also Chief Sealth) 80n
Chitrabhanu Shri 14
Chittick, William C 46n
Christie Agatha 5
Christudas 87
Chrysostom, St John 3

Chuang-tzu 12
Cicero 27
Clanchy M T, 40n
Clare **47**
Clark, Susan J 84n
Clarkson, Thomas 70
Cleary Thomas 12n.
Clement of Alexandria 17
Clement of Rome 21
Clement XIV, Pope 58
Clément, Olivier, 25n
Cleon 16
Clissold, Stephen, 62
Clothair, King 30
Clucas, Joan Graff 90n
Coates, Harper Havelock 44n
Cobbett, William 70
Cohn-Sherbok, Dan 92
Coleridge, Samuel Taylor 56, 71
Columba, St 30
Columbanus, St 30
Confucius 12 **13**
Confucius 67
Constantine Emperor **26**, 28
Constantius, Flavius Valerius, 26
Cook, M
Cooke, James, Captain 76, 96
Coomaraswamy, Ananda, 99
Copernicus 78
Cornelius 21
Countess of Huntingdon 68
Cousins, Ewert 99
Coverdale, Myles 57
Cragg, Kenneth 33
Cranmer, Thomas 57
Crispus 26
Cromwell, Oliver 65

Cromwell, Thomas 57
Crow, Jim 93
Curzon, Lord 75, 83
Cyril VI, Coptic Pope 94
Cyrus the Great 3, 10, 11, 24

D S Sarma 72
Dalai Lama, Tenzin Gyatso 15, 50
   20, **97,**
Dampier, William 96
Dante 32, 39, 46,52, **71**
Dartinga, Annunciata 96
Darwin 78
Das Gupta Surendranath 38n, 85
David King **9,** 10, 11, 19 20, 61, 65,
   94
David, Brown 84
David, Fränkel 67
Day, Fred Holland 88
de Cuéllar, Javier Pérez 90
de Gaulle, Charles 94
de Klerk, 98
Decius,Emperor 25
Deguchi Nao 74
Demosthenes 70
Denaux Adelbert 19
Derrida, Jacques 52
Desiderius, 29
Devaki 6
Dhalla M.N 3nt
Diana, Princess 90
Dide, 61
Didron, A N 61n
Diocletian, Emperor 26, 27
Dion 16
Dionysius I 16
Dionysius II 16

Dionysius the Areopagite 17, 40
Djiagween, Elizabeth Grace 96.
Dmitri Donskoi, the Prince of
   Moscow, 54
Dodson, Snowy 96
Dodson, Adrian 96
Dodson, Michael (Mick) 96
X Dodson, Patrick **96**
Dogen 31, **45**
Dominic' St 48
Domitian, Emperor 22,
Donnelly, John Patrick 58n
Dostoevsky Fyodor 28
Dov Baer 66
Du Boulay, Shirley 87n
Dughdhova 3
Dunn, James D G 22, 23, 61

Eckhart, Meister 41, **52**
Edward VI, King of England, 57
Edward, Conze 31
Edwards, Mark 22
Einstein 14
Eisai (also known as Senko
Kokushi **) 45**
Eliade Mircea 5nt, 18, 78
Elijah ben Solomon (Gaon of
Vilna) **66,** 67
Eliot, T S 49, 99
Elizabeth 19
Elizabeth I, Queen of England
Elizabeth I, Queen of England, 63,
   65, 70
Ellis, Marc H 100n
Ellwood Robert S 74
Ellwood Thomas 65
Emmerich Catherine 19

Englebert, Omer 47n

Ephrem the Syrian 20

Epiphanius 25

Equiano, Olaudah 70

Erasmus 60

Eric Sharpe 79n

Erigena (see Scotus, John)

Esau 2

Estienne Robert 61

Euclid 16, 42

Eugenius III, Pope 43

Eusebius 25

Eve 19

Ezekiel 80

Ezra 24

Fagan, John 96

Fagan, Joseph 96

Fagan, Matilda 96

Faizi 63

Farel, William 60

Farid al-Din 'Attar 35

Fatima 33, 35

Fausta 26

Feldman Louis H 24

Fell Margaret 65

Ferdinand II, King of Spain 70

Festus, Governor 23

Filippa, Sister, 47n

Fisher, Mary Pat 55n, 64

Fox (Lago), Mary 65

Fox Christopher 65

Fox George **65**, 70

Fox, George

Francis of Assisi, St **47**

Franco, General 62

Frederick II of Germany 47

Frederick the Great, 67

Frederick, Prince of Saxony, 56

French, Patrick 85n

Freud, Martha (née Benays) 78

Freud, Sigmund 5,**78**, 89

Friedman, Jerome 61n

Friedman, M 89n

Fry, Elizabeth 70

Fulbert, Canon, 40

Galen **42**

Gamaliel Rabbi 23

Gamaliel the Elder 24

Gandhi Mahatma 6, 7, 20, 29, 76,
      79 **81**, 93, 98

Gartlan, Tony 96

Garvey, Marcus 94

Gaudapada 34

Gedaliah 11

Geiger, Abraham 20

Gengis Khan 63

Genshin Sozu 44

Geoffrey of Monmouth 26

George III, King of England 70

George Whitfield 68

Gerardi, Bishop 98

Gerhard Tersteegen 1nt

Gerhard von Rad 1nt

Germanus 20

Gideon 9

Gillet, Lev 54

Giotto 47

Gobind Singh,(Gobind Rai) Guru
      64, 55

Goethe, Johnann Wolfgang von
      73, 77

Go-Fushimi, Emperor of Japan 44

Goldstone, Lawrence and Nancy 61n
Goliath 9
Goodman, L E 42n
Gordon, Governor 76
Gore, Al 98
Govindapada 34
Gratian 60
Gregory IX, Pope 42
Gregory of Nazianzus St, 100
Gregory of Nyssa 8, 17, 25
Gregory of Sinai **28**
Gregory Palamas, St 28
Gregory the Great, Pope 27, 28, 29
Gregory X, Pope 48
Gregory X, Pope 49
Gregory XIII, Pope 62
Grey, George, Sir 76n
Grey, Lady Jane 57
Griffiths, Bede (Alan Richard) 6nt, 85n, **87**
Grousset, René 84
Guénon, René 99
Guibert of Gembloux 43
Gupta, K N 83
Gurbachan Singh Talib 64
Tegh Bahadur, Guru 64.

Habig, Marion 47n
Hackel, Alfred 61n
Hagar 2
Hague, William 70
Haile Selassie I **94**
Haldane, J S 85
Hale, G W, Mrs 72
Halliday Jon, 12n
Harbison, John 59

Harpur, James 23
Harries, Richard 61
Hartog, Jan de 65
Harvey, Peter 45n
Hasan 33
Haskell, Mary 88
Hawke, Bob 96
Hawkins, Captain John 70
Hayley, William 71
Hazrat Inyat Khan 35n
Helen
Hélène Schweitzer (née Bresslau) 82
Héloïse 40
Henry VIII, King
Henry VIII, King of England, 29, 57
Henry, Patrick 29
Heraclas, Bishop
Heracleaon 25
Herod the Great 3, 24, 57
Herod, King 22
Herpyllis 17
Herzl, Theodor 89
Herzog, Isaac, Rabbi 86
Hezekiah 10
Hilda 30
Hildegard **43**
Hillel, Rabbi 24
Hilton, Walter 49
Hippolytus St 10
Hisao 91
Hitler, Adolf 89
Ho Chi Minh 95
Hobson, William 76
Hogen Linda 100n
Holman Hunt 22

Honen **44**

Honorius III, Pope 47

Hooker, Morna D 23n

Hopkey, Sophia 68

Hopkins, J 31

Hosie Lady 13n

Hsieh Ho 12

Hsuan Chwang 34

Hsun Tzu 13

Huddleston, Trevor, Fr 98

Huei-kuo 37

Humayan 63

Hurtado, L W 23

Husain 33

Husain, S Abid 73n

Husam ad-Din Chelebi 53

Hutaosa, Queen. 3

Huxley, Aldous 52

Ibn 'Arabi 35, **46**

Ibn Arabi

Ibn Tufay 42

Ibrahim (Abraham) 32

Idelette de Bure 60

Ignatius Loyola **58**

Ignatius of Antioch 21

Ikeda Daisaku 74, 91

Imaoka, Shininchiro 91

Innocent III, Pope 47

Innocent IV, Pope 47

Ippen (also known as Yugyo
    Shonin) 44

Iqbal, Afzal 53n

Isa (the Qur'anic name for Jesus)
    19

Isaac 2, 8

Isaac ben Solomo n Luria 66

Isaiah **10**

Ishmael 2

Isidor 69

Jackson, A V Williams 3nt

Jackson, Jesse 93

Jacob 2, 8, 65

Jacob W 20

Jacobi, Friedrich Heinrich 67

Jahangir, Emperor, 64

Jalal-ad-Din ar-Rumi, 20,32 35, 53,
    73

James, St 19,22

James Dunn 61

James I, King of England 64

James II, King of England, 65

James, the brother of Jesus, 21

Janaka King 7

Jaras 6

Jefferson, Thomas 61, 71

Jehoiakim 11

Jehudi 11

Jeremiah **11**

Jerome 25, 27

Jesse 9

Jesus 8,19, **20**, 21, 22, 28, 39, 48, 56,
    65, 72, 75, 77, 79, 81, 82, 87, 88,
    89, 91, 92, 95, 100

Jethro 8

Jilwa 96

Joachim 19

Joad, C E M 85

Johanan ben Zakkai **24**

John (John surnamed Mark) 23

John St, 19, 20, 21 **22**, 25, 47, 54, 88

John Climacus, St **28,** 54

John Huss 68

John Locke 61
John Marenbon 40
John of Damascus, St 28
John of the Cross (Juan) 52, **62**, 90
John Paul II, Ppoe, 69,86n
John the Baptist, St 20, 21, 57
John XXIII, Pope **86**, 90
John, Abbot of Sarov, 69
Johnson, Lyndon B, President 93, 95
Johnson, Paul 41n, 67
Joinville 35
Jonathan, 9
Joseph 2, 19, 20
Joshua 8, 9
Josiah 11
Jotham 10
Jowett, Benjamin 36
Jü-ching (Rujing) 45
Judah Halevi 32
Julian of Norwich, Mother 29, **49**
Julius II, Pope, 57
Jung 25
Jung Chang 12
Jung, Carl 19,**78**
Justinian Emperor 28
Jutta, Mistress 43

K'ung 13
K'ung Li (Po Yü) 13
Kabir **51**
Kakunyo Shonin 44
Kalpana Chawla 84
Kamsa, 6
Kanchipurna 38
Kant Immanuel 2, 67, 89
Kasturbai 81

Kavi Vistaspa, king, 3
Keating, H R F 84n
Keating, Maurice 84n
Keeffe, Kevin 96
Kempe Margery 49
Kennedy, John, President 93, 94
Keshub Chander Sen 85
Keturah 8
Khadijah 32
Khalil Gibran, **88**
Kholsa, K 53n.
Kiely, Robert 97n
Kierkegaard, Sören 89
King George V of Britain, 94
King, Ursula, Professor 83n, 84
King, Alberta Williams. 93
King, Coretta Scott 93
King, Martin Luther
King, Martin Luther 76, **93**, 94, 95, 98
King, Martin Luther, Senior 93
Kiril 54
Klimenko, Michael 54n
Ko Hung 12
Kolodiejchuk, Brian 90n
Korah 9
Knitter, Paul 87n
Krishna **6**, 7, 34, 59, 72, 75, 81, 87
Krishnamurti, Jiddu 77
Kukai **37**, 44
Kumarajiva, 31
Küng, Hans 99
Kuresa 38

Lactantius 26
Lakshmana 7
Lamb, Charles 71

Lancel, Serge 27
Lao-tzu **12** 13
Latimer 57
Lavater 67
Lawrence, D H 71
Lazarus 22
Leah 2
Leaman, Oliver 41n, 42n
Lee, Levine I A 24
Leibniz 41 ht.
Lemaître, Solange 84n
Leo XIII, Pope 96
Leo, Brother 47
Lesser Roger, 7nt, 36, 51n 59n
Lessing, Gotthold Ephraim 67
Levens Jon D 16n
Levi-Strauss, Claude 78
Lewis, C S 87
Licinius, Emperor 26
Liechty, Joseph 98n
Lin Biao 13
Lin-chi I-hsüan 45
Lings, Martin 33, 99
Llewelyn, Robert 49nt
Lloyd, Gareth 68
Locke, John 67
Lombard Peter 60
Lombard Peter 61
Lorenz, Caroline and Rod 80n
Lot 2
Louis IX, King of France 35
Lovelock, James 85
Low, Mary 30
Loyola, Ignatius 60
Luibheid, Colm 28
Luke St, 19, 20, 21, 22, 23
Luther 23, 32 55, **56,** 57, 58, 60, 93

Lutuli, Albert 93

M.S Dasudi 88n
Maccabees 24
Maddocks, Fiona 43
Madhva 38
Madhva 87
Mahadev Desai 81
Mahadevan T M P. 4n, 83n
Mahapurna 38
Mahavira **14**
Mahinda 18
Mahmud of Ghazna 42
Maimonides, Moses 32, 39, **41,** 67
Makarios 28
Malcolm X 93
Malik b Anas 42
Mallinatha 14
Manasseh 10
Manavalan, K.A 38n
Mandana Misra 34
Mandela, Nelson 76, 96, 98
Mani 27
Manikkavacakar **36**
Mankeji Limji Hataria 3
Mann, Thomas 5
Mao Tse-tung 12, 13, 97
Mark (also John Mark) St 20, 21,
    22, 39, 82
Marley, Bob 94
Maro 88
Marsh, John 22
Marsh, Josiah 65
Martianus Lucanius 60
Mary Magdalene, 20
Mary, Queen of England, 57
Mary, the Virgin, **19,** 20, 22, 48, 86,

100n

Maryam 46

Masui, Jacque 83n

Matthew, St 8 19, 20, 21 35 40

Matthews, Gary L 75n

Mauriac, François 92

Maximinian, Emperor 26

McCoy, Brian 96

McCrickard, Janet E 30

McGuckin, John Anthony 28

Mead Richard 61

Mel St 30

Melanchthon 56

Mencius 13

Mendel Dessau 67

Mendelssohn Felix 67

Mendelssohn Moses **67**

Menelik II, Emperor of Ethiopia, 94

Menen Asfaw, Empress 94n

Merton, Thomas, 29, 97, 100

Mexican Joe 80

Mian Mir 64

Michal 9

Middleton, Charles, Sir 70

Milinda, King 15

Miller, Joseph 70

Milnes, Richard Monkton, (Lord Houghton) 35

Milton

Milton John 16, 65

Mirabai 51, **59**

Mircea Eliade 18

Miriam 8

Mirra Richard (b. Alfassa), the 'Mother' 83

Mitrofan 54

Mockler, Anthony 94n

Monica 27

Montefiore, Claude 20

Moon, Sun Myung, 74 Reverend,

Moore, L 28

Moorman, J R H 65

More, Thomas, Sir, 19, 57

Morris, William 71

Moses **8,** 5, 65, 75, 78

Moshe Rosman 66

Motovilov 69

Mrinalini Devi 79

Mubarak, Shaik 63

Mudd John 9nt

Muggeride, Malcolm 90

Muhammad 8, 9, **32,** 35, 39, 46, 72, 75, 81, 88

Muhammad b 'Ami 35

Muhammad Iqbal, Sir **73**

Muilenburg, J 61n

Muir, William 73

Mussolini 94

N A Vicam 18

Nagarjuna 18, **31,** 45, 52

Nagasena 15

Naimy Mikhail 88

Nakayama Miki, **74**

Nakayama Zembei 74

Nanada 6

Nanak, Guru **55**

Nan-yüan 45

Napoleon 28, 67

Narharidas 7, 59

Nasr, Seyyed Hossein 46, **99**

Nath 9

Nathamuni 38

Nawaz Sharif, 90
Neale J M 40n
Nebuchadnezzar 11
Nebu-sharrussu-ukin, (Nebo-Sarasekim) 11
Nefertiti Queen 5
Nehemiah 24
Nehru, Jawaharlal 34, 81
Neihardt, John G 80
Nero, Emperor 21, 23
Nestorius 19
Netanel ibn Fayyumi 32
Neusner, Jacob 24
Neville, Auber Octavius 96
Newman, Barbara 43n
Newton, Isaac, Sir, 61, 67
Ngo Dinh Diem 95
Nichiko 44
Nichiren **44**
Nicholas of Cusa 89
Nicholson P 96
Nicholson, R A 46n, 53n
Nicholson, Reynold A
Nicomachus 17
Nietzsch, Friedrich 20, 89, 73,77,88
Nikkyo Niwano 74
Niko 44
Nikodimos 28
Nimma 51
Niru 51
Nirvedananda, Swami 72n
Niwano, Nikkyo 91
Noah 65
Noala or Nawurla 96

O'Connor, Kathleen M 11
O'Callaghan, J F 58n

Oda Nobinaga 37, 91
Olcott, H S, Colonel 77
Omar Khayyam 39
Onesimus 23
Orde Wingate, Charles 94
Origen
Origen 11,17, **25,** 49
Osiander 57
Otto R, 1, 52

Paddy Djiagween, Paddy 96
Padmasambhava 50
Page, Christopher 43
Paine, Thomas 71
Paisii, St 28
Palmer Martin 12n
Pande, G.C 34n
Panter, Police Inspector 96
Paramarubyananda, Swami (Jules Monchanin, Fr), 87
Parks, Rosa 93
Parrinder Geoffrey 19, 20
Parsvanatha 14
Pasca, Sister 87n
Pascal Blaise 39
Patricia 96
Patrick, St 27, 30
Patwant Singh 55n, 64
Paul (also called Saul) St 1, 11, 17, **23,** 27, 40, 56, 62,68, 82
Paul III, Pope 58
Paul VI, Pope 29
Paulinus 27
Paulos Evergetinos 28
Peabody, Josephine 88
Pedro de Ribadeneira 58
Pelagius 27

Penn, William 65

Penrith, Merv 96

Pericles 16

Perictione 16

Perrin, David 49nt

Pestel, T 20

Peter

Peter (also Simon Peter) **21**, 22, 26,86

Peter (brother of Sergius) 54

Peter Hebblethwaite 86n

Peter I of Russia 54

Peter the Great of Russia 69

Peter the Venerable 40

Pfister, Oskar 78

Pharaoh 2

Philemon 23

Philip 10

Philip II, King of Spain 62

Philip King of Macedonia 17

Philo of Alexandria 17

Pilate, Pontius 20

Pilgrim, Richard 74

Pinochet, Augusto 98

Pir Vilayat Inayat Khan 35n

Pitt, William (Pitt the Younger) 70

Pius IV, Pope 62

Pius IX, Pope 75, 86

Pius X, Pope 86

Pius XII, Pope 86

Plato 3, **16**, 17, 25, 27

Plaut W. Gunther 1nt, 8nt

Pliny the Elder 3

Plotinus 17, 27, 39, 42

Polanco Juan 58

Pompey 24

Pope Innocent III 40

Pope John XXIII

Pope, G U 36

Porphyry 17, 25

Posidius, Bishop of Calama 27

Pound, Ezra 79

Pourusaspa 3

Prabhu R K 81n

Prabhupada Bhaktivedanta Swami 6

Priestley, Joseph 71

Ptolemy 21

Pye, Michael 74

Pythagoras 16, 25

Pythia 17

Rabban Gamaliel II **24**

Rabelais 60

Rabia **35**

Rachel 2

Radegund 30

Radha 6

Radha Kumud Mookerji 18

Radhakrishnan, Sarvepalli 34,72, 63 85

Raimundo Panikkar 4nt

Ram Das, Guru 64

Ram Mohan Roy 20 , 73,79, 67

Rama

Rama **7**, 34, 72, 51 59, 81

Ramakrishna

Ramakrishna

Ramakrishna, Sri (Gadadhar) 20, **29,72,** 85

Ramakrishnananda, Swami 38n

Ramana Maharshi 34

Ramananda 51

Ramanuja

Ramanuja 4, 29, 34, **38,** 51, 59,87
Rameses II 8
Ramkumar 72
Ramsay, James 70
Rana Kumbha 59
Rao, U R 81n
Raphael 17
Ratnavali 59
Ravana 7
Ray, James Earl 93
Rebecca, 2
Reimarus, Samuel 82
Rendawa 50
Renee Web 87n
Reynolds, Joshua, Sir 71
Reza, A 53n
Rhys Davids, Mr and Mrs 15
Richard Mckeon 18
Richeld, Lady 19
Ridley 57
Riemenschneider, Johannes 76
Rimpoche, L 31
Robert J Miller 20
Robinson Hayyim 2
Robinson, John, Bishop 89
Rodd C.S 9nt
Rodolfo Aquaviva, Father 63
Roger of Taizé, Brother 95
Rogers, Joel Augustus 94n
Roland H Bainton, 61n
Rolle, Richard 49
Roscelin of Compiègne 40
Rosemary, Sister SLG 51
Rosenzweig, Franz 89
Ross, Hugh McGregor 65
Ross, Nancy Wilson 45n
Roth Norman 41n

Rousseau, Jean-Jacques 70
Rowe, Joseph 95n
Rsabha (Adinatha) 14
Rudd, Kevin 96
Ruether, Hermann 100
Ruether, Rosemary Radford **100**
Rufinus 25
Rukmani T.S 34n
Rukmini 6
Runciman, Stephen
Ruskin, John 71,81
Russell, Bertrand 99
Russill 87
Russsell, Norman 2 8
Ryland, William, 71
Ryugaku Ishizuka 44n

Saadia Khawar Khan Chisti 33
Sagovsky, Nicholas, 19
Saicho **37, 44**
Saladin 41
Salah ad-Din Zarkub 53
Salley, Columbus 94n
Samson 9, 94
Samuel 9
Samuel ibn Tibbon 41
Sankara 4, 29, **34,** 52, 84, 87
Santirakshita 50
Sarad Devi 79
Sarah (Sarai) 2
Sarutahiko Okami 91
Saul (see Paul)
Saul, King 9, 23
Saul, King of Israel
Sawfan 33
Sayo Kitamura 74
Sayyid Iqbal Khan, Sir 67, **73**

Schiller, Freidrich 89

Schimmel, Annemarie 35

Schopenhauer, Arthur 52, 77

Schuman, Robert 86

Schuon, Frithjof 99

Schweitzer, Albert 20, **82**

Scot Michael 48

Scott, Dick 76n

Scotus, John 52

Seaver, George 85n

Seneca 60

Sennacherib 10

Septimius Severus, 25

Seraphim of Sarov, St 28 **69**

Sergius of Radonezh, St **54**

Servetus, Michael 60 **61**

Shah Jahan, Emperor 73

Sham ad-Din 53

Shammai, Rabbi 24

Shanks, Hershel 24

Shapur II, King of Persia, 26

Sharp, Granville 70

Shaw, Barbara 96

Sheba, Queen 94

Sher Shar Sur 63

Shesh Sanatana, Acharya 59

Shinran **44**

Shoghi Effendi Rabbani 75

Shotoku, Prince 37

Shrimad Rajach 14

Shunjo 44

Siger of Brabant 48

Sikandar Lodi,Emperor 51

Si-ma Qien 12

Simeon the Stylite, St 29

Simon, Maurice 66n

Sita **7**, 51

Sivananda Sri Swami 4

Smith, Adam 70

Smith, Margaret 35n, 39n

Smith, Peter 75n

Smith, Vincent A 63n, 73n

Smuts, General 81

Socrates 16, 67

Solomon 11

Solomon 24

Solomon, King 9, 94

Solomon, Norman 19n

Solon 16, 67

Songsten Gampo, King of Tibet 50

Soothill, William Edward 13n

Sorensen, Reg 81

Sours, Michael W 75n

Southern, Sir Richard 40

Spangenberg, 68

Spear, Percival 63n

Spiess, Karl von, 61n

Spink, Kathryn 90n

Spinoza, Baruch 41, 67

Stefan (brother of Sergius) 54

Steiner Rudolf **77**, 83

Steiner, Johann 77

Stephen Gardiner, Bishop, 57

Stephen, James 70

Stevens, Maryanne 100n

Subhadrangi 18

Sudah bint Zamm 33

Sulak Sivaraksa 95

Sulakni, 55

Sultan Walad 53

Sultana 88

Sun Bu-er 12

Suso, Henry 52

Suzuki D T 52, 85

Swedenborg, Emanuel 71
Symeon the New Theologian 28

Tagore, Debendranath 79
Tagore, Rabindranath 51, **79,** 85
Tambo, Oliver 98
Tamerlane (Timur) 63
Tarak 59
Tasman, Abel Janszoon 76
Tauler, Johann 52
Te Miringa Hohaia 76n
Te Wherowhero 76
Te Whiti-O-Rongomai **76**
Teasdale Wayne 29
Teilhard de Chardin, Pierre 83, **84**
Telford, John 56n
Temple William 3, 16
Tennyson, Alfred, Lord 53, 63
Terah 2
Teresa (or Thérèse) of Lisieux 62,
    90
Teresa of Avila **62**
Teresa, Mother (Agnes Gonxha
Bojaxhiu) **90**
Tertullian 21
Tetzel, Johann 56
Thecla 23
Theodore the Studite, St 54
Theodosius of the Caves, St 54
Theodosius, St 69
Thich Nhat Hanh 20, **95**
Thi-Song Detsan, King of Tibet 50
Thomas M M 20
Thomas, Hugh 70n
Thomas, St 20, 34
Thomson J A K 16n
Thoreau 81

Tiglath-pileser 10
Tilak 4
Tillich, Paul 61, 77
Timothy Beardsworth 1nt
Tiye 5
Tohu 76
Tolstoy 81
Tombs, David 98n
Torrell, Jean-Pierre
Totila, King 29
Townshend, George 75n
Tran Nhan Tong, King 95
Trapnell, Judson B 87n
Trimble, Robert, Colonel 76n
Tseng 13
Tsong Khapa Losang Drakpa 31,
    50, 97
Tulsi Acharya 14
Tulsidas 7, 51,**59,**
Tutankhaman 5
Tutu, Desmond Mpilo **98**
Tutu, Leah 98
Tutu, Matse 98
Tutu, Sylvia 98
Tutu, Zachariah Zelilo 98
Tyndale, William 57

Ullendorf, Edward 94n
Um Ruman 33
Underhill Evelyn 51, 52
Urban II, Pope 40
Uriah 9
Ursula, Sister, 62
Uzziah 10

Valentius 25
Valmiki 7,59

Van der Peet, 90

Vasudeva 6

Vaudeville, Charlotte 51n

Venantius Fortunatus 30

Vicam, N A 18

Victoria, Queen 73, 75,80

Vine Deloria 100n

Visvamitra 7

Vivekananda, Swami   29, 72, 85

Voltaire 61

Vyasa

Vyasa **4**

Wadjularbinna Doomadgee 96

Wahiduddin Kahn, Maulana 99

Walleser, Max 31

Walpola Rahula 95n

Walshe, Maurice O'Connell   52

Walter, Judy 87n

Wanan 96

Waraqa 32

Ware Kallistos, Bishop 20, 28

Warham William Archbishop 57

Waterfield Robin 88

Watson Mills 21

Watt, W.Montgomery 39n

Weller, Charles

Wesley, Charles **68,** 85, 100n

Wesley, John 60, **68,** 70

Wesley, John

Wesley, Samuel 68

Wesley, Susanna 68

Whirlwind Chaser 80

Whitehead A N 16

Whitlam, Gough 96

Widor, Charles Marie 82

Wiesel, Bea 92

Wiesel, Elie **92**

Wiesel, Hilda 92

Wiesel, Marion 92

Wiesel, Sarah 92

Wiesel, Shlomo, 92.

Wilberforce, William 68, **70,** 71

Wildiers, N M 84n

Wilken, Robert L 26

Wilkinson, Roy 77

William of Champeaux 40

William of Tocco 48

Williams, Paul 31

Williams, Rowan, Archbishop 62

Willmann, Carlo 77

Winckler, Paula 89

Winkworth, Catherine 56n

Winter, Tim 32

Wittgenstein, Ludwig 89

Wodicka, Tod 49

Woodford, J R, Bishop 48

Wordsworth William 1, 71

Wordsworth, William

Wrede, William 82

Wu, Emperor of China 45

Wulstan, Bishop 70

Wycliffe, John 57

Xavier, Francis, St 58

Xenophon 16

Yacob Yosef 66

Yajnasri, King 31

Yamamoto, Yukitaka **91**

Yamamoto, Yukitero 91

Yamatohime-no-Mikoto, Princess
   91

Yamuna 38

Yang Xiong 13

Yasodhara 15

Yates, William 79

Yazdegird III 3

Younghusband, Francis 63, **85**

Yu 13

Yusuf Ali 73, 85

Zaehner, R C 83

Zakir Hussain 73

Zander, Valentine 69

Zayd 32

Zebedee 22

Zechariah 19

Zechariah 67

Zedekiah 11

Zenran 44

Zoa, Émile 77

Zoroaster (Zarathustra) **3**, 75, 81

Zwingli, Ulrich 56

BOOKS

O is a symbol of the world, of oneness and unity. In different cultures it also means the "eye," symbolizing knowledge and insight. We aim to publish books that are accessible, constructive and that challenge accepted opinion, both that of academia and the "moral majority."

Our books are available in all good English language bookstores worldwide. If you don't see the book on the shelves ask the bookstore to order it for you, quoting the ISBN number and title. Alternatively you can order online (all major online retail sites carry our titles) or contact the distributor in the relevant country, listed on the copyright page.

See our website www.o-books.net for a full list of over 500 titles, growing by 100 a year.

And tune in to myspiritradio.com for our book review radio show, hosted by June-Elleni Laine, where you can listen to the authors discussing their books.

mySpiritRadio